Commercial exploitation of attributes of an individual's personality, such as name, voice and likeness, forms a mainstay of modern advertising and marketing. Such indicia also represent an important aspect of an individual's dignity which is often offended by unauthorised commercial appropriation.

This volume provides a framework for analysing the disparate aspects of the problem of commercial appropriation of personality and traces, in detail, the discrete patterns of development in the major common law systems. It also considers whether a coherent justification for a new remedy may be identified from a range of competing theories. The considerable variation in substantive legal protection reflects more fundamental differences in the law's responsiveness to new commercial practices and different attitudes towards the proper scope and limits of intangible property rights.

Including detailed critical analyses of leading cases in English, Canadian and Australian law, with detailed comparative references to the United States, this volume will be essential reading for academics and practitioners specialising in intellectual property law.

HUW BEVERLEY-SMITH is Visiting Research Fellow at the School of Law, King's College, London, and was formerly Lecturer in Law in the Department of Law, University of Wales, Aberystwyth, and Visiting Research Fellow at the Max-Planck Institute for Foreign and International Patent, Copyright and Competition Law in Munich.

Cambridge Studies in Intellectual Property Rights

As its economic potential has rapidly expanded, intellectual property has become a subject of front-rank legal importance. *Cambridge Studies in Intellectual Property Rights* is a series of monograph studies of major current issues in intellectual property. Each volume will contain a mix of international, European, comparative and national law, making this a highly significant series for practitioners, judges and academic researchers in many countries.

Series editor
Professor William R. Cornish, *University of Cambridge*

Advisory editors
Professor François Dessemontet, University of Lausanne
Professor Paul Goldstein, Stanford University
The Hon. Sir Justice Robin Jacob, The High Court, England and Wales

A list of books in the series can be found at the end of this volume.

The commercial appropriation
of personality

Huw Beverley-Smith

CAMBRIDGE UNIVERSITY PRESS
Cambridge, New York, Melbourne, Madrid, Cape Town, Singapore, São Paulo

Cambridge University Press
The Edinburgh Building, Cambridge CB2 2RU, UK

Published in the United States of America by Cambridge University Press, New York

www.cambridge.org
Information on this title: www.cambridge.org/9780521800143

© Huw Beverley-Smith 2002

This book is in copyright. Subject to statutory exception
and to the provisions of relevant collective licensing agreements,
no reproduction of any part may take place without
the written permission of Cambridge University Press.

First published 2002

A catalogue record for this publication is available from the British Library

ISBN-13 978-0-521-80014-3 hardback
ISBN-10 0-521-80014-5 hardback

Transferred to digital printing 2005

I fy Rhieni

Diolch, o galon, am bopeth
dros y blynyddoedd

Contents

Preface	*page* xi
Table of cases	xiii
Table of statutes	xxxiii

Part I A framework · 1

1 The problem of appropriation of personality · 3
Introduction · 3
Interests in personality · 5
Economic and dignitary interests · 8
Perspectives · 12

Part II Economic interests and the law of unfair competition · 25

2 Introduction · 27

3 Statutory and extra-legal remedies · 32
Copyright · 33
Performers' rights · 34
Registered trade marks · 36
Extra-legal remedies · 48

4 Goodwill in personality: the tort of passing off in English and Australian law · 59
Introduction · 59
The essential elements of passing off · 60
Goodwill · 61
Misrepresentation · 72
Damage · 97
Conclusions · 107

5 Unfair competition and the doctrine of misappropriation · 111
Introduction · 111
Misappropriation of intangibles · 112

vii

viii   Contents

The development of the common law tort of appropriation of personality	115
The scope and limits of the tort	122
Conclusions	136

Part III Dignitary interests — 139

6 Introduction — 141

7 Privacy and publicity in the United States — 145

Introduction	145
The development of the right of privacy in the United States	146
Conceptions of privacy	159
The development of the right of publicity in the United States	171
Accounting for the differences	189
Conclusions	198

8 Privacy interests in English law — 200

Introduction	200
Piecemeal recognition of privacy interests in English law	202
The privacy jurisprudence of the ECHR and commercial exploitation of personality	211
Towards a general right of privacy	214
Insights from Canada and Germany	224
Appropriation of personality and United Kingdom legislative initiatives	238
Interests in freedom from mental distress	241
Conclusions	248

9 Interests in reputation — 249

Introduction	249
The economic and dignitary aspects of reputation	250
The core injury to reputation cases	253
Defamation and invasion of privacy	258
Defamation, privacy and appropriation of personality	265
Conclusions	269

Part IV Pervasive problems — 271

10 Property in personality — 273

Introduction	273
Notions of property	274
Property in intangibles	276
Property in personality	281
Conclusions	286

11 Justifying a remedy for appropriation of personality — 287

Introduction	287
Natural rights of property	288

Contents ix

Utilitarian arguments	299
Economic efficiency	308
Preventing or reversing unjust enrichment	311
Protecting personal dignity	313
Conclusions	314

Part V Conclusions · 317

12	The autonomy of appropriation of personality	319
	Bibliography	330
	Index	349

Preface

Commercial appropriation of personality is not a new phenomenon, although debate concerning its status and mode of legal regulation is becoming increasingly topical. The practice of using celebrities and ordinary individuals with no obvious public profile to help sell a vast range of goods and services flourishes. Yet relatively little attention has been devoted to the legal basis on which some of these often lucrative arrangements are based. The roots of this study lie in English law which has been reluctant to provide substantive legal protection for the attributes of an individual's identity. The other major common law jurisdictions have, to varying degrees, been less reluctant to do so. The different patterns in several jurisdictions call for a detailed analysis of the leading cases and central concepts which illustrate quite different dynamics of legal development in the multifarious jurisdictions. Readers accustomed to dealing with intellectual property rights might be somewhat wary of digressions into the theories which lie behind the protection of personal dignity and human rights. However, commercial appropriation of personality is a curiously hybrid problem which demands that several lines of enquiry be pursued.

Inevitably, a compromise has had to be struck between breadth and depth of coverage. The main sources of comparison are the major common law jurisdictions. The Australian courts have been rather more progressive in adapting the traditional English causes of action, while the Canadian courts have gone further and in a distinctly different way. Coverage of the substantial United States jurisprudence concerning commercial appropriation of personality has had to be more selective. To American lawyers, the whole project may have a vaguely nineteenth-century feel, as the English courts continue to debate whether to recognise interests that the US courts have recognised and protected in various forms for over a century. While the American courts concern themselves with defining the scope and limits of intellectual property rights in personality which have developed largely through a mass of state case law, latterly supplemented by state statutes and codes, the English courts have

xi

xii   Preface

yet to address the question of whether intellectual property rights may be recognised in attributes of personality and what form any protection should take.

The Human Rights Act 1998 has a particular significance for the developing English law of privacy and this book is not unique in being written against an uncertain background. The full extent to which the values of the European Convention on Human Rights may influence the development of the English common law are not likely to become apparent for some time.

While some account of the approaches taken in civil law jurisdictions is given from time to time, readers should not expect a comprehensive treatment. The patterns of development in the major civil law jurisdictions and the complex issues which have been raised are sufficiently distinct to warrant a far more thorough treatment based on a substantially different comparative structure from that offered here. A subsequent volume, *Privacy, Property and Personality* (Cambridge University Press), written with two expert German and French scholars, Ansgar Ohly and Agnes Lucas-Schloetter, is planned to appear in 2003.

This book is based on my University of Wales doctoral thesis, although it has been substantially revised and updated. A particular debt of gratitude is owed to my doctoral supervisor, Allison Coleman, for her constant support and encouragement, and to Professor W. R. Cornish and Professor R. A. W. Kidner who examined the thesis. I would like to thank my former colleagues and students in the Department of Law at Aberystwyth, and the staff of the National Library of Wales and the Institute of Advanced Legal Studies. I am especially grateful to the Max-Planck Institute for Foreign and International Patent, Copyright and Competition Law, Munich, for providing the financial resources for me to be able to be there for most of 2000, when the bulk of the work for this book was completed.

I am indebted to several people for taking the time to read and comment on various chapters of the book and would like to take this opportunity to thank Robert Burrell, Bill Cornish, Ansgar Ohly, Richard Ireland and John Linarelli. Their comments and suggestions were extremely valuable, although, of course, I am entirely responsible for any errors. As Series Editor, Bill Cornish has been unfailingly helpful and supportive at every stage of this project, for which I am extremely grateful. Finally, I would like to thank Finola O'Sullivan, Jennie Rubio and all the staff at Cambridge University Press for their courtesy and efficiency at every stage in the production of this work which includes all materials available to me at the end of August 2001. Subsequent developments are outlined at http://www.commercialpersonality.com.

Table of cases

A *v.* B [2000] EMLR 1007	*page* 207
A. Bernardin et Cie *v.* Pavilion Properties Ltd [1967] RPC 581	61
Abdul-Jabbar *v.* General Motors Corp., 85 F 3d 407 (9th Cir. 1996)	182
Abernethy *v.* Hutchinson (1825) 3 LJ Ch 209	147
AD2000 Trade Mark [1997] RPC 168	39
Adu p/k/a Sade *v.* Quantum Computer Services Inc. WIPO Case No. D2000-0794	55
Al Hayat Publishing Co. Ltd *v.* Sokarno (1996) 36 IPR 214	62
Alcock *v.* Chief Constable of South Yorkshire Police [1992] 1 AC 310	15, 242
Allison *v.* Vintage Sports Plaques, 136 F 3d 1443 (11th Cir. 1998)	181
American Cyanamid Co. *v.* Ethicon Ltd [1975] AC 396	67, 77, 221
Anheuser Busch Inc. *v.* Budejovicky Budvar NP [1984] FSR 413	61, 62
Annabel's (Berkeley Square) Ltd *v.* Schock [1972] RPC 838	77, 100
ANNE FRANK Trade Mark [1998] RPC 379	43
Anthony *v.* University College of Cape Coast [1973] 1 GLR 299	257
Argyll *v.* Argyll [1967] Ch 302	207
Arsenal Football Club Plc *v.* Reed [2001] ETMR 860	45, 80, 81
Ashdown *v.* Telegraph Group Ltd [2001] 3 WLR 1368	221, 222
Associated Newspapers Group Plc *v.* Insert Media Ltd [1991] 1 WLR 571	83, 99
Athans *v.* Canadian Adventure Camps Ltd (1977) 80 DLR (3d) 583	14, *121–2*, 123, 128, 130, 131, 133, 135

xiii

xiv   Table of cases

Athlete's Foot Marketing Associates Inc. *v.* Cobra
   Sports Ltd [1980] RPC 343 — 61
Atkinson *v.* John E. Doherty & Co. 80 NW 285 (1899) — 151, 172
Attia *v.* British Gas Plc [1988] QB 304 — 12, 242
Attorney-General *v.* Guardian Newspapers (No. 2)
   [1990] 1 AC 109 — 202, 207, 208, 209, 220
Attorney-General *v.* Guardian Newspapers Ltd [1987]
   1 WLR 1248 — 224
Aubry *v.* Éditions Vice-Versa Inc. (1998) 78 CPR
   (3d) 289 — 135, *225–7*
AUDI-MED Trade Mark [1998] RPC 863 — 106
Authors Guild Inc. *v.* Old Barn Studios Ltd.,
   e-Resolution Case No. AF-0582 a–i — 57
B *v.* H Bauer Publishing Ltd [2002] EMLR 8 — 209, 223
BACH and BACH FLOWER REMEDIES Trade
   Marks [1999] RPC 1 — 44
BACH and BACH FLOWER REMEDIES Trade
   Marks [2000] RPC 513 — 36, 39
Barber *v.* Time Inc. 159 SW 2d 291 (1948) — 162
Barnes *v.* Old Barn Studios Ltd, WIPO Case
   No. D2001-0121 — 56–7
Baron Philippe de Rothschild, SA *v.* La Casa
   de Habana Inc. (1987) 19 CPR (3d) 114 — 123, 129, 134
BARRY ARTIST Trade Mark [1978] RPC 703 — 47
Barrymore *v.* News Group Newspapers Ltd [1997]
   FSR 600 — 207
Bassey *v.* Icon Entertainment Plc [1995] EMLR 596 — 35
BBC *v.* Celebrity Centre Productions Ltd (1988)
   15 IPR 333 — 78
BBC Worldwide Ltd *v.* Pally Screen Printing Ltd
   [1998] FSR 665 — 80
Beevor *v.* Old Barn Studios Ltd WIPO Case
   No. D2001-0123 — 57
Bentley Motors (1931) Ltd *v.* Lagonda Ltd and
   Bentley (1947) 64 RPC 33 — 47
Berkoff *v.* Burchill [1996] 4 All ER 1008 — 252, 260
Bernstein *v.* Skyviews & General Ltd [1978]
   QB 479 — 206
Bi-Rite Enterprises Inc. *v.* Button Master, 555
   F Supp. 1188 (1983) — 183, 185

Blair *v.* Associated Newspapers Plc (Queen's Bench Division, 13 November 2000)	207
Blennerhasset *v.* Novelty Sales Services Ltd (1933) 175 LT 392	264
BMW AG and BMW Nederland BV *v.* Deenik [1999] ETMR 339	37
Boardman *v.* Phipps [1966] 2 AC 46	281
Bollinger *v.* Costa Brava Wine Co. Ltd [1960] RPC 16	59, 112
Bonito Boats Inc. *v.* Thunder Craft Boats Inc., 489 US 141 (1989)	31
Bonnard *v.* Perryman [1891] 2 Ch 269	65, 67, 268
Bradley *v.* Hall 720 NE 2d 747	246
Bradley *v.* Wingnut Films [1993] 1 NZLR 415	244
Branham *v.* Celadon Trucking Services, Inc. 744 NE 2d 514	247
Branson *v.* Bower (No. 1) [2001] EMLR 800	221
Branson *v.* Bower (No. 1) (Queen's Bench Division, 21 November 2000)	221
Bravado Merchandising Services Ltd *v.* Mainstream Publishing (Edinburgh) Ltd [1996] FSR 205	45
British Diabetic Association *v.* Diabetic Society Ltd [1995] 4 All ER 812	63
British Legion *v.* British Legion Club (Street) Ltd (1931) 48 RPC 555	73, 102
British Medical Association *v.* Marsh (1931) 48 RPC 565	66
British Sugar Plc *v.* James Robertson & Sons Ltd [1996] RPC 283	36, 39, 45
British Telecommunications Plc and Others *v.* One in a Million Ltd and Others [1999] FSR 1	47, 53, 61
Britt Allcroft (Thomas) LLC *v.* Miller (2000) 49 IPR 7	83
Brown *v.* Julie Brown Club WIPO Case No. D2000-1628	56
Bulmer (H. P.) Ltd and Showerings Ltd *v.* Bollinger SA [1978] RPC 79	72
Burghartz *v.* Switzerland (1994) 18 EHRR 101	212
Burris *v.* Azadani [1995] 1 WLR 1372, 1377	244
Byron *v.* Johnston (1816) 2 Mer 29 (35 Eng Rep 851)	*63*, 65, 262
Cadbury Schweppes Inc. *v.* Fbi Foods Ltd [2000] FSR 491	280, 281
Cadbury-Schweppes Pty Ltd *v.* Pub Squash Co. Pty Ltd [1981] 1 WLR 193	112
Cain *v.* Hearst Corp., 878 SW 2d 577 (Tex. 1994)	263

xvi   Table of cases

Canessa v. J. I. Kislak Inc., 97 N.J. Super 327,
   235 A 2d 62 (1967)   185
Canon Kabushiki Kaisha v. M-G-M Inc. [1999]
   ETMR 1   36, 46
Cardtoons v. Major League Baseball Players,
   95 F 3d 959 (10th Cir. 1996)   296, 299, 302,
      306, 307, 311
Carson v. Here's Johnny Portable Toilets Inc.,
   698 F 2d 831 (6th Cir. 1983)   15, 182, 302
Central Hudson Gas & Elec. Corp. v. Public
   Service Commission of New York,
   447 US 557 (1980)   185
Chandler v. Thompson (1811) 3 Camp 80, 170 ER
   1312   206
Chappell v. United Kingdom (1990) 12 EHRR 1   212
Charleston v. News Group Newspapers Ltd
   [1995] 2 WLR 450   247, 257
Cheatham v. Paisano Publications, Inc., 891
   F Supp. 381 (WD Ky 1995)   181, 247
Cheney Bros. v. Doris Silk Corp., 35 F 2d 279
   (2nd Cir. 1929)   31
Cher v. Forum Intern Ltd, 692 F 2d 634
   (CA Cal. 1982)   185
Children's Television Workshop Inc. v.
   Woolworths (New South Wales) Ltd [1981]
   RPC 187   79, *87–8*, 93
Chocosuisse Union Des Fabricants Suisses
   de Chocolat v. Cadbury Ltd [1988]
   RPC 17 (ChD) [1999] RPC 826 (CA)   59
CIBA Trade Mark [1983] RPC 75   43
Clark v. Associated Newspapers Ltd [1998] 1 All
   ER 959   63
Clark v. Freeman (1848) 11 Beav 112
   (50 Eng Rep 759)   4, 9, 11,
      64–6, 70,
      101, 116–17,
      156, 266–7,
      268–9, 273,
      320, 326
Clock Ltd (The) v. Clock House Hotel Ltd
   (The) (1936) 53 RPC 269   59, 73, 85,
      92, 98

Coco *v.* A. N. Clark Engineers Ltd [1969] RPC 41	208
Cole *v.* Turner (1704) Holt KB 108, 90 ER, 958	242
Comedy III Productions, Inc. *v.* Gary Saderup, Inc., 106 Cal.Rptr.2d 126 (Cal. 2001)	186, 187
Compco Corp. *v.* Day-Brite Lighting Inc., 376 US 234 (1964)	31
Conagra Inc *v.* McCain Foods (Aust) Pty Ltd (1992) 23 IPR 193	61
Consorzio del Prosciutto di Parma *v.* Marks & Spencer Plc [1991] RPC 351	14, 60, 61
Corelli *v.* Wall (1906) 22 TLR 532	4, 193, 259, 265, 326
CORGI Trade Mark [1999] RPC 549	47, 106
Corliss *v.* Walker, 57 Fed Rep 434 (1893)	150, 172
Corliss *v.* Walker, 64 Fed Rep 280 (1894)	151
Cornelius *v.* De Taranto [2001] EMLR 329	243
Cossey *v.* United Kingdom (1990) 13 EHRR 622	212
Costanza *v.* Seinfeld, 719 NYS 2d 29 (NYAD 1 Dept 2001)	184
Costello-Roberts *v.* United Kingdom (1995) 19 EHRR 112	212
County Sound Plc *v.* Ocean Sound Ltd [1991] FSR 367	61
Cowley *v.* Cowley [1901] AC 450	163, 321
Crawford and Son *v.* Bernard and Co. (1894) 11 RPC 580	46
Creation Records Ltd *v.* News Group Newspapers Ltd [1997] EMLR 444	209
Croft *v.* Day (1843) 7 Beav 84 (49 ER 994)	65
Cruise and Kidman *v.* Southdown Press Pty Ltd (1992–3) 26 IPR 125	204
Current Audio Inc. *v.* RCA Corp., 337 NYS 2d 949 (Sup Ct 1972)	133, 226
Dagenais *v.* CBC [1994] 3 SCR 835	224
Daniels *v.* Thompson [1998] 3 NZLR 22	21
De Bernieres *v.* Old Barn Studios Ltd WIPO Case No. D2001-0122	57
Debenham *v.* Anckorn, *Times*, 5 March 1921	256
Derbyshire County Council *v.* Times Newspapers [1993] AC 534	219, 220
Deutsche Renault AG *v.* Audi AG [1995] 1 CMLR 461	36

xviii Table of cases

Dixon *v.* Holden (1869) 20 LT Rep 357	66
Dockrell *v.* Dougall (1897) 78 LT 840	11, 70
Dockrell *v.* Dougall (1899) 15 TLR 333	4, 9, 66, 100, 117, 156, 193, 257, 258, 267–8, 273, 320, 321, 325
Donaldson *v.* Beckett (1774) 2 Bro PC 129	147, 301
Donoghue *v.* Stevenson [1932] AC 562	204
Douglas *v.* Hello! Ltd [2001] 2 WLR 992	4, 49, 179, 202, 205, *210–11*, 214, 215, 217–18, 221, 222–3, 225, 323
Douglass *v.* Hustler Magazine Inc., 769 F 2d 1128	182, 262, 309
Dowell et al. *v.* Mengen Institute (1983) 72 CPR (2d) 238	123, 128
Du Plessis *v.* De Klerk 1996 (3) SA 850	215, 216, 217
DuBoulay *v.* DuBoulay (1869) LR 2 PC 430	163, 273, 321
Dubrulle *v.* Dubrulle French Culinary School Ltd (2001) 8 CPR (4th) 180	126
Dudgeon *v.* United Kingdom (1982) 4 EHRR 149	212
Dunlop Rubber Co. Ltd *v.* Dunlop [1920] 1 IR 280	254, 264
Eastman Photographic Co. Ltd *v.* Griffiths (John) Cycle Corp. Ltd (1898) 15 RPC 105	104
Edison *v.* Edison Polyform Mfg Co., 67 A 392 (1907)	9, 16, 156–7, 281
Elvis Presley Enterprises, Inc. *v.* Capece, 950 F Supp. 783, (S.D.Tex 1996)	182
ELVIS PRESLEY Trade Marks [1997] RPC 543	45, 321
ELVIS PRESLEY Trade Marks [1999] RPC 567	4, 39–41, 44, 55, 73, 80–1, 93, 179
Erven Warnink BV *v.* Townend & Sons (Hull) Ltd [1979] AC 731	59, 60, 72, 98, 112, 113
Estate of Presley *v.* Russen, 513 F Supp. 1339 (DNJ 1981)	133, 184, 226, 283, 302
Ewing *v.* Buttercup Margarine Ltd [1917] 2 Ch 1	73
Ex Parte Island Records [1978] Ch 122	280

Table of cases   xix

Executrices of the Estate of Diana, Princess of Wales'
  Application [2001] ETMR 254   41
Factors Etc. Inc. *v.* Pro Arts Inc. 579 F 2d 215
  (2nd Cir. 1978)   283
Fairfield *v.* American Photocopy Equipment Co.
  291 P 2d 194 (1955)   158
Feist Publications Inc. *v.* Rural Telephone
  Service Co. Inc. 499 US 340   304
Fido Dido Inc. *v.* Venture Stores (Retailers)
  Pty Ltd (1988) 16 IPR 365   79
Fielding *v.* Variety Inc. [1967] 2 QB 841   7, 242
First Victoria National Bank *v.* United States,
  620 F 2d 1096 (1980)   282
Flake *v.* Greensboro News Co. 195 SE 55 (1938)   16, 157–8
Florida Bar *v.* Went for It Inc., 515 US 618 (1995)   185
Fogg *v.* McKnight [1968] NZLR 330   242
Forbes *v.* Kemsley Newspapers Ltd (1951)
  68 RPC 183   63
44 Liquormart, Inc. *v.* Rhode Island, 517 US
  484 (1996)   186
Frazer *v.* Evans [1969] 1 QB 349   281
Garbett *v.* Hazell, Watson & Viney Ltd and Others
  [1943] 2 All ER 359   256, 264
Gautier *v.* Pro-Football Inc., 106 NYS 2d 553 (1951)   158, 173
Geisler *v.* Petrocelli, 616 F 2d 636 (2nd Cir. 1980)   264
General Electric Co. *v.* General Electric Co. Ltd
  [1972] 1 WLR 729   81
General Motors Corp. *v.* Yplon SA [1999] ETMR 122   47, 106
Glaxo Group and Others *v.* Dowelhurst Ltd (No. 2)
  [2000] FSR 529   36
Godbout *v.* Longueuil (City) (1997) 152 DLR (4th)
  577   226
Gould Estate *v.* Stoddart Publishing Co. (1997)
  30 OR (3d) 520   124–5, 132–4
Gould Estate *v.* Stoddart Publishing Co. (1998)
  80 CPR (3d) 161   33, 124–5
Graham *v.* John Deere Co., 383 US 1 (1985)   306
Grant *v.* Esquire Inc., 367 F Supp 876 (SDNY 1973)   181
Griffiths *v.* Bondor Hosiery Co. Ltd, *Times*, 10, 11 and
  12 December 1935   255
Griswold *v.* Connecticut, 381 US 479 (1965)   161

xx   Table of cases

Haelan Laboratories Inc. *v.* Topps Chewing Gum Inc., 202 F 2d 866 (2nd Cir. 1953)	16, 126, 174–6, 177, 183, 194, 282, 283, 327
Halliwell *v.* Panini (Unreported, High Court, Chancery Division, 6 June 1997)	4, 68, 69, 82
Handyside *v.* United Kingdom (1979–80) 1 EHRR 737	213, 219
Harris *v.* Harris [2001] 2 FLR 895	224
Harrison and Starkey *v.* Polydor Ltd. [1977] FSR 1	77
Harrods Ltd *v.* Harrodian School Ltd [1996] RPC 697	102, 106–7, 112
Harrods Ltd *v.* R. Harrod Ltd (1924) 41 RPC 74	73, 99–100
Harrods Ltd *v.* Schwartz-Sackin & Co. Ltd [1986] FSR 490	14, 29, 112, 324
Hayward & Co. *v.* Hayward & Sons (1887) 34 Ch D 198	251
Heath *v.* Weist-Barron School of Television Canada Ltd (1981) 62 CPR (2d) 92	123, 128, 134
Hellewell *v.* Chief Constable of Derbyshire [1995] 1 WLR 804	18, 207, 209, 214
Henderson *v.* Radio Corp. Pty Ltd [1969] RPC 218	14, 30, 69, *85*–7, 98, 101, 104–5, 109
Henley *v.* Dillard Dept Stores, 46 F Supp. 2d 587 (N.D.Tex 1999)	182
Herbage *v.* Pressdram Ltd [1984] 1 WLR 1160	67
Hertel *v.* Switzerland (1999) 28 EHRR 534	220
Hexagon Pty Ltd *v.* Australian Broadcasting Commission (1975) 7 ALR 233	29
HFC Bank Plc *v.* Midland Bank Plc [2000] RPC 176	81
Hickman *v.* Maisey [1900] 1 QB 752	206
Hill *v.* Church of Scientology of Toronto (1995) 126 DLR 129	215, 216, 224–5
Hines *v.* Winnick (1947) 64 RPC 113	63
Hirsch *v.* S. C. Johnson & Sons Inc., NW 2d 129 (1979)	182
Hodgkinson & Corby Ltd *v.* Wards Mobility Ltd [1994] 1 WLR 1564	14, 29, 112, 324

Table of cases

Hoffman *v.* Capital Cities/ABC, Inc., 255 F 3d 1180
  (9th Cir. 2001) — 186
Hogan *v.* A. S. Barnes & Co. Inc., 114 USPQ 314
  (Pa. Comm. Pl. 1957) — 176–7, 178
Hogan *v.* Koala Dundee Pty Ltd (1988) 83
  ALR 187 — 76, 82, *92–5*, 105, 108
Holdke *v.* Calgary Convention Centre Authority
  [2000] ACWS (3d) 1281 — 128, 136
Honey *v.* Australian Airlines Ltd and Another [1989]
  ATPR 40-961, affirmed (1990) 18 IPR 185 — 69, 91
Honeysett *v.* News Chronicle, *Times,*
  14 May 1935 — 254–5, 257, 261, 263–4
Hood *v.* W. H. Smith and Son Ltd, *Times,*
  5 November 1937 — 255, 257, 264
Hook *v.* Cunard Steamship Co. [1953] 1 WLR 682 — 242
Horton *v.* Tim Donut Ltd (1998) 75 CPR (3d) 451 — 123, 126, 135
Howell *v.* New York Post Co. 612 NE 2d 699
  (NY 1993) — 154
Hulton *v.* Jones [1910] AC 20 — 256
Hulton Press Ltd *v.* White Eagle Youth Holiday
  Camp Ltd (1951) 68 RPC 126 — 102, 104
Hunter *v.* Canary Wharf Ltd [1997] 2 WLR 684 — 245
Hustler Magazine Inc. *v.* Falwell, 485 US 46 (1988) — 247
Hutchence *v.* South Seas Bubble Co. Pty Ltd (1986)
  64 ALR 330 — 69, *88–9*
IHT Internationale Heiztechnik *v.* Ideal Standard
  [1994] 3 CMLR 857 — 36
Imperial Group PLC *v.* Philip Morris Ltd
  [1984] RPC 293 — 81
Imutran Ltd *v.* Uncaged Campaigns Ltd [2001]
  2 All ER 385 — 220, 221
International News Service *v.* Associated Press,
  248 US 215 (1918) — 28, 31, 113, 114, 177, 279
IRC *v.* Muller & Co.'s Margarine Ltd
  [1901] AC 217 — 61, 115, 278
Jacubowski *v.* Germany (1995) 19 EHRR 64 — 220
JANE AUSTEN Trade Mark [2000] RPC 879 — 41
Janvier *v.* Sweeney [1919] 2 KB 316 — 244
John *v.* MGN [1996] 3 WLR 593 — 7, 10, 242

xxii   Table of cases

John Walker & Sons Ltd *v.* Henry Ost & Co. Ltd [1970] RPC 489	112
Joseph *v.* Daniels (1986) 11 CPR (3d) 544	123, 136
Joyce *v.* Sengupta [1993] 1 All ER 897	256
Kaye *v.* Robertson [1991] FSR 62	15, 22, 67, 70–1, 162, 179, 195, 196, *202–4*, 218, 222, 248, 321, 324, 328
Kean *v.* McGivan [1982] FSR 119	63
Khashoggi *v.* IPC Magazines Ltd [1986] 1 WLR 1412	67
Khodaparast *v.* Shad [2000] EMLR 265	251, 256
Khorasandjian *v.* Bush [1993] QB 727	244
Kidson *v.* SA Associated Newspapers Ltd 1957 (3) 461 (W)	143
Kirk *v.* A. H. & A. W. Reed [1968] NZLR 801	260–1, 263
Krouse *v.* Chrysler Canada Ltd (1972) 25 DLR (3d) 49	*115–18*, 123, 127, 129, 130, 131, 284–5, 325–6
Krouse *v.* Chrysler Canada Ltd (1973) 40 DLR (3d) 15	14, 118–21, 123, 134
Lady Anne Tennant *v.* Associated Newspapers Group Ltd [1979] FSR 298	34
Lake *v.* Wal-Mart Stores Inc., 582 NW 2d 231 (Minn. 1998)	263
Landa *v.* Greenberg (1908) 24 TLR 441	63
Landham *v.* Lewis Galoob Toys Inc., 227 F 3d 619 (6th Cir. 2000)	181
Lego System Aktieselskab *v.* Lego M. Lemelstrich Ltd [1983] FSR 155	75, 77, 102–3
Lennon *v.* News Group Newspapers Ltd [1978] FSR 573	207
Lerman *v.* Chuckleberry Publishing Inc., 521 F Supp. 228 (SDNY 1981)	181
Ley *v.* Hamilton (1935) 153 LT 384	242
Lipiec *v.* Borsa (1997) 31 CCLT 294	116
Lloyd Schuhfabrik Meyer & Co. GmbH *v.* Klijsen Handel BV [2000] FSR 77(ECJ)	46
Loendersloot *v.* Ballantine & Son Ltd [1998] FSR 544	37

Table of cases	xxiii

Lonhro Ltd *v.* Shell Petroleum Co. Ltd (No. 2) [1982]
  AC 173 — 280
Lord *v.* McGregor (British Columbia Supreme Court,
  10 May 2000) — 116
Lugosi *v.* Universal Pictures Cal. 603 P2d 425 (1979) — 166, 284, 302
Lynch *v.* Knight (1861) 9 HL Cas. 577, 11 ER 854 — 15, 242
Lyngstad *v.* Anabas Products Ltd
  [1977] FSR 62 — 4, 13, 33, 68, 70, 75, 77, 79, 82, 84, 88, 94
Mackay *v.* Buelow (1995) 24 CCLT (2d) 184 — 116
Mad Hat Music Ltd *v.* Pulse 8 Records Ltd [1993]
  EMLR 172 — 35
Mail Newspapers *v.* Insert Media (No. 2) [1988]
  2 All ER 420 — 14, 29, 60, 112, 324
Malone *v.* Metropolitan Police Commissioner
  [1979] 1 Ch 344 — 15, 195
Malone *v.* United Kingdom (1985) 7 EHRR 14 — 212
Marca Mode CV *v.* Adidas AG [2000] All
  ER (EC) 694 — 46
Marion Manola *v.* Stevens & Myers, *NY Times,*
  15 June 1890 — 147
Marks *v.* Jaffa, 26 NYS 908 (Super Ct 1893) — 150
Markt Intern and Beermann *v.* Germany (1990)
  12 EHRR 161 — 220
Martin Luther King Jr Center for Social Change Inc.
  v. American Heritage Products,
  296 SE 2d 697 (Ga. 1982) — 184, 284, 285
Martin Luther King Jr Center for Social Change Inc.
  v. American Products Inc., 694 F 2d 674
  (11th Cir. 1983) — 125
Massam *v.* Thorley's Cattle Food Co., (1880)
  14 Ch D 748 — 66
Matthews *v.* Wozencraft, 15 F 3d 432 (5th Cir. 1994) — 186, 303, 309
Maxim's *v.* Dye [1977] FSR 364 — 61
Maxwell *v.* Hogg (1867) 16 LR 2 Ch App 307 — 66
Mazatti *v.* Acme Products [1930] 4 DLR 601 — 266
Mazer *v.* Stein, 347 US 201 (1954) — 299
McCarey *v.* Associated Newspapers Ltd [1965] 2
  QB 86 — 7

xxiv   Table of cases

McCartan Turkington Breen *v.* Times Newspapers Ltd
    [2000] 3 WLR 1670 — 220
McCulloch *v.* Lewis A. May (Produce Distributors) Ltd
    (1948) 65 RPC 58 — 4, 13, *73–5*,
    82, 100–2,
    110, 193
McLoughlin *v.* O'Brian [1983] 1 AC 410 — 242
Meering *v.* Grahame-White Aviation Co. Ltd
    (1920) LT 44 — 242
Melvin *v.* Read 297 P 91 (1931) — 162
Memphis Development Foundation *v.* Factors
    Etc. Inc., 616 F 2d 956 (1980) — 184, 284,
    296, 305–6
Merchandising Corporation of America Inc. *v.*
    Harpbond Ltd [1983] FSR 32 — 33, 321
Mercury Communications Ltd *v.* Mercury Interactive
    (UK) [1995] FSR 850 — 32
Messenger *v.* Gruner & Jahr Printing and Pub.,
    208 F 3d 122 (2nd Cir. 2000) — 153, 185
Mhlongo *v.* Bailey 1958 (1) SA 370 (W) — 143
Millar *v.* Taylor (1769) 4 Burr 2303 — 300
Mills *v.* News Group Newspapers Ltd [2001]
    EMLR 957 — 209, 217,
    221, 223
Minister of State for the Army *v.* Dalziel
    (1944) 68 CLR 261 — 276
Mirage Studios *v.* Counter-Feat Clothing Co. Ltd
    [1991] FSR 145 — 40, 75,
    78–80, 82, 83
Miss World (Jersey) Ltd *v.* James Street
    Productions Ltd [1981] FSR 309 — 100
Modern Fiction *v.* Fawcett (1949) 66 RPC 230 — 63
Mogul Steamship Co. *v.* McGregor Gow & Co.
    (1889) 23 QBD 598 — 114
Monson *v.* Tussauds Ltd [1894] 1 QB 671 — 258, 259
Monty and Pat Roberts, Inc. *v.* Keith, WIPO
    Case No. D2000-0299 — 56
Moorgate Tobacco Co. Ltd *v.* Philip Morris Ltd
    (No. 2) (1984) 56 CLR 414 — 13, 14, 23,
    29, 30, 112,
    113, 114,
    278, 312

Morgan *v.* Odhams Press [1971] 1WLR 1239	256
Morris *v.* Danna, 411 F Supp. 1300 (1976)	161
Motschenbacher *v.* R. J. Reynolds Tobacco Co.,	
498 F 2d 821 (9th Cir. 1974)	122, 178, 181, 182, 282
Muller *v.* Switzerland (1991) 13 EHRR 212	220
Munden *v.* Harris 134 SW 1076 (1911)	157, 281, 311
Murray *v.* Ministry of Defence [1988] 1 WLR 692	242
Murray *v.* United Kingdom (1995) 19 EHRR 193	213
Nash *v.* Sheen [1953] CLY 3726	242
National Provincial Bank *v.* Ainsworth [1965] AC 1175	276
Nestle UK Ltd *v.* Zeta Espacial SA [2000] ETMR 226	43
Neutrogena Corp. *v.* Golden Ltd [1996] RPC 473	81
New York Times Co. *v.* Sullivan, 376 US 254 (1964)	247
Newcombe *v.* Adolf Coors Co., 157 F 3d 686	
(9th Cir. 1998)	188, 249
Newsweek Inc. *v.* BBC [1979] RPC 441	104
Nice and Safe Attitude Ltd *v.* Piers Flook [1997]	
FSR 14	61, 82
Nicrotherm Electrical Co. Ltd *v.* Percy [1957] RPC	
207	281
Niemietz *v.* Germany (1993) 16 EHRR 97	212
Nilsen and Johnsen *v.* Norway (2000) 30 EHRR 878	219
Oasis Stores Ltd's Trade Mark Application	
[1998] RPC 631	106
O'Brien *v.* Pabst Sales Co., 124 F 2d 167	
(5th Cir. 1941)	173–4, 188
O'Keeffe *v.* Argus Printing and Publishing Co. Ltd	
1954 (3) SA 244 (C)	142, 143
O'Shea *v.* MGN Ltd and Free4internet.net Ltd [2001]	
EMLR 943	222, 256
Pacific Dunlop Ltd *v.* Hogan (1989) 87 ALR 14	69, 76, 81, 82, 95–7, 107, 296
Page *v.* Smith [1996] AC 155	242
Palmer *v.* National Sporting Club Ltd (1906)	
2 MacG CC 55	326
Palmer *v.* Schonhorn Enterprises Inc.,	
232 A 2d 458 (1967)	178, 181
Paracidal Pty Ltd *v.* Herctum Pty Ltd (1983) 4 IPR 201	69, 89
Paramount Pictures Inc *v.* Leader Press Inc.,	
24 F Supp. 1004 (1938)	173

xxvi   Table of cases

Parfums Christian Dior SA *v.* Evora BV [1998] RPC 166	37
Parker & Son (Reading) Ltd *v.* Parker [1965] RPC 323	70
Parker-Knoll Ltd *v.* Parker Knoll International Ltd [1962] RPC 265	81
Parmiter *v.* Coupland (1840) 6 M&W 108	252, 260
Pasley *v.* Freedman (1789) 100 ER 450	119
Paulsen *v.* Personality Posters, Inc., 299 NYS 2d 501 (1968)	186
Pavesich *v.* New England Life Insurance Co. 50 SE 68 (1905)	16, 154–6, 165–6, 169, 172, 191, 193, 195, 204, 327
Philips Electronics BV *v.* Remington Consumer Products [1998] RPC 283	36
Philips Electronics NV *v.* Remington Consumer Products Ltd [1999] RPC 809 (CA)	39, 45
Philips Electronics NV *v.* Remington Consumer Products Ltd [2001] RPC 745 (ECJ)	37, 39, 45
Pianotist Co.'s Application (1906) 23 RPC 774	40
Pinky's Pizza Ribs on the Run Pty Ltd *v.* Pinky's Seymour Pizza & Pasta Pty Ltd (1997) ATPR ¶41–600	99
Pirone *v.* MacMillan Inc., 894 F 2d 579 (2nd Cir. 1990)	184
Plumb *v.* Jeyes Sanitary Compounds Co. Ltd, *Times*, 15 April 1937	259–60, 263
Poiret *v.* Jules Poiret Ltd (1920) 37 RPC 177	70
Pollard *v.* Photographic Co. (1889) 40 ChD 345	18, 147, 322, 326
Powell *v.* Birmingham Vinegar Brewery Co. Ltd (1896) 13 RPC 235	36
Prince Albert *v.* Strange (1849) 2 DeG & Sm 652, 64 ER 293	148, 207
Prince Albert *v.* Strange (1849) 1 Mac & G 25, 41 ER 1171	147, 148, 207
Pursell *v.* Horn (1838) 8 AD & E, 602, 112 ER	242
R. *v.* Advertising Standards Authority, ex parte SmithKline Beecham Plc [2001] EMLR 598	51
R *v.* Advertising Standards Authority ex parte the Insurance Service Plc (1990) 2 Admin LR 77	51

Table of cases

R *v.* Broadcasting Complaints Commission, ex parte Barclay [1997] EMLR 62	206
R *v.* Broadcasting Standards Commission ex parte British Broadcasting Corp. [2000] 3 WLR 1327	206
R *v.* Chief Constable of the North Wales Police and others ex parte AB and Another [1997] 4 All ER 691	18
R *v.* Department of Health ex parte Source Informatics Ltd [2001] QB 424	207
R *v.* Home Secretary, ex parte Simms [2000] 2 AC 115	220
R *v.* Khan (Sultan) [1996] 3 All ER 289	202
R *v.* Press Complaints Commission, ex parte Stewart-Brady [1997] EMLR 185	49
Racine *v.* CJRC Radio Capitale Ltee (1977) 35 CPR (2d) 236	123, 128, 134
Rantzen *v.* Mirror Group Newspapers [1994] QB 670	10
Ratcliffe *v.* Evans [1892] 2 QB 524	251
Rattner *v.* BuyThisDomainName WIPO Case No. D2000-0402	58
Re Burford (H.G.) & Co. Ltd's Application [1919] 2 Ch 28	42
Re Coca-Cola's Application [1986] RPC 421	114
Re Fanfold Ltd's Application (1928) RPC 199	44
Re McDowell's Application (1926) 43 RPC 313	36
Re Mister Long Trade Mark [1999] ETMR 406	39
Re X [1975] 1 All ER 697	15
REACT Trade Mark [2000] RPC 285	46
Reckitt & Colman Ltd *v.* Borden Inc. [1990] 1 WLR 491	14, 60, 112, 114
Reddaway *v.* Banham (1896) 13 RPC 429	59, 72, 324
Registrar of Trade Marks *v.* Du Cros (W&G) Ltd [1913] AC 624	40
Renwick *v.* News and Observer Publishing Co., 312 SE 2d 405 (N.C. 1984)	263
Retail, Wholesale & Department Store Union, Local 580 *v.* Dolphin Delivery Ltd (1987) 33 DLR (4th) 174	216
Reynolds *v.* Times Newspapers Ltd [1999] 3 WLR 1010	220, 251
Rickless *v.* United Artists Corp. [1988] QB 40	28
River Wear Commissioners *v.* Adamson (1876) 1 QBD 551	171

xxviii   Table of cases

Roberson *v.* Rochester Folding Box Co., 171 NY 538 (1902)	16, *151–3*, 155–6, 172, 191, 192, 193, 228, 257, 327
The Robert Marley Foundation *v.* Dino Michelle Ltd (Unreported Suit No. C.L. R115-1992, High Court of Jamaica, 12 May 1994)	122, 125, 285–6
Roberts *v.* Boyd WIPO Case No. D2000-0210	55
Rodgers (Joseph) & Sons Ltd *v.* W. N. Rodgers & Co. (1924) 41 RPC 277	70
Roe *v.* Wade, 410 US 113 (1973)	161
Rogers *v.* Grimaldi, 875 F 2d 994 (2nd Cir. 1989)	15, 181, 186
Rookes *v.* Barnard [1964] AC 1129	251
Rosenberg *v.* Martin, 478 F 2d 520 (1973)	161
Roth *v.* Roth (1992) 9 CCLT (2d) 141	116
Routh *v.* Webster (1849) 10 Beav 561 (50 ER 698)	*63–5*, 101, 322
Rowland *v.* Mitchell [1897] 1 Ch 71	44
Ruffin-Steinback *v.* dePasse, 82 F Supp.2d 723 (E.D.Mich. 2000)	186
Rumcoast Holdings Pty Ltd *v.* Prospero Publishing Pty Ltd (1999) 48 IPR 75	62
Russell *v.* Marboro Books, 183 NYS 2d 8 (1959)	249
Rylands *v.* Fletcher (1866) LR 1 Ex 265	204, 325
S *v.* A 1971 (2) SA 293 (T)	143
S *v.* I 1976 (1) SA 781 (RAD)	143
SA CNL-Sucal NV *v.* HAG GF AG [1990] 3 CMLR 571	36
Sabel BV *v.* Puma AG, Rudolf Dassler Sport [1998] RPC 199	37, 46
Scandecor Development AB *v.* Scandecor Marketing AB [2001] ETMR 800	36
Schuyler *v.* Curtis, 15 NYS 787 (Sup Ct 1891)	150, 172
Schuyler *v.* Curtis, 42 NE 22 (1895)	150
Scott *v.* Sampson (1882) 8 QBD 491	252
Sears, Roebuck & Co. *v.* Stiffel Co., 376 US 225 (1964)	31
Shaw *v.* Berman (1997) 72 CPR (3d) 9	135
C. A. Sheimer (M) Sdn Bhd's Trade Mark Application [2000] RPC 484	47, 106
Shelley Films Ltd *v.* Rex Features Ltd [1994] EMLR 134	209, 214

Table of cases	xxix

Silber *v.* BCTV (1986) 69 BCLR 34 (SC) — 225

Sim *v.* H. J. Heinz & Co. Ltd [1959] 1 WLR 313 — 4, *67–8*, 70, 100, 193, 257, *268–9*, 273, 320, 325

Sim *v.* Stretch (1936) 52 TLR 669 — 252, 259

Smith, Hayden & Co.'s Application (1946) 63 RPC 97 — 40

Sony Music Productions Pty Ltd *v.* Tansing (1993) 27 IPR 649 — 83, 121, 179

Spalding (A. G.) & Bros. *v.* Gamage (A. W.) Ltd (1915) 32 RPC 273 — 59, 61, 67, 72, 98

Spencer (Earl and Countess) *v.* United Kingdom (1998) 25 EHRR CD 105 — 213

Sperry Rand Corp. *v.* Hill 356 F 2d 181 (1966) — 249

Sports & General Press Agency Ltd *v.* 'Our Dogs' Publishing Co. Ltd [1917] 2 KB 125 — 326

Springsteen *v.* Burgar WIPO Case No. D2000-0235 — 55–6

Stanley *v.* Georgia, 394 US 557 (1969) — 161

Star Industrial Co. Ltd *v.* Yap Kwee Kor [1976] FSR 256 — 61, 97, 104, 277

The State of Tennessee, Ex Rel. The Elvis Presley International Memorial Foundation *v.* Crowell, 733 SW 2d 89 (Ten. App 1987) — 125, 184, 285

Stephano *v.* News Group Publications, 485 NYS 2d 220 (Ct App. 1984) — 184

Stephens *v.* Avery [1988] 2 WLR 1280 — 207, 208

Stockwell *v.* Kellog Company of Great Britain, *Times*, 31 July 1973 — 256, 264

Strickler *v.* National Broadcasting Co., 167 F Supp. 68 (SD Cal. 1958) — 176

Stringfellow *v.* McCain Foods (GB) Ltd [1984] RPC 501 — 70, 78, 82, 99, 103–4

Sumner, p/k/a Sting *v.* Urvan WIPO Case No. D2000-0596 — 57

Sunday Times *v.* United Kingdom (1979–80) 2 EHRR 245 — 219

Sutcliffe *v.* Pressdram [1991] 1 QB 153 — 10

Taco Bell Pty Ltd *v.* Taco Co. of Australia Inc. (1981) 42 ALR 177 — 98

xxx   Table of cases

Taittinger SA *v.* Allbev Ltd [1993] FSR 641	106, 112
Talmax Pty Ltd *v.* Telstra Corp. Ltd (1996) ATPR ¶41–535, 42	97, 104
Tapling *v.* Jones (1865) 11 HLC 290, 11 ER 1344	206
TARZAN Trade Mark [1970] RPC 450	40
Tavener Rutledge Ltd *v.* Trexapalm Ltd [1977] RPC 275	75–6, 81, 82, 94
10th Cantanae Pty Ltd *v.* Shoshana Pty Ltd (1987) 79 ALR 299	69, *89–91*, 109, 121
Teofani & Co. Ltd *v.* Teofani [1913] 2 Ch 545	42
TGI Friday's Australia Pty Ltd *v.* TGI Friday's Inc. (1999) 45 IPR 43	98
Titan Sports, Inc. *v.* Comics World Corp., 870 F 2d 85 (2nd Cir. 1989)	186
Tolley *v.* J. S. Fry & Sons Ltd [1930] 1 KB 467	258
Tolley *v.* J. S. Fry & Sons Ltd [1931] AC 333	18, 173, 191, 193, *253–4*, 257, 266, 325, 326
Tony Alessandra D/B/A Alessandra & Associates *v.* Inss and Allesandra's, WIPO Case No. D2001-0619	58
Tot Toys Ltd *v.* Mitchell [1993] 1 NZLR 325	95, 105, 108
Tuck *v.* Priester (1887) 19 QBD 629	147
Tucker *v.* News Media Ownership Ltd [1986] 2 NZLR 716	244
Twentieth Century Fox Film Corp. *v.* South Australian Brewing Co. Ltd (1996) 34 IPJ 225	83, 97, 104
Uhlaender *v.* Henricksen, 316 F Supp. 1277 (1970)	178, 282, 294
University College of Cape Coast *v.* Anthony [1977] 2 GLR 21	257
Uren *v.* John Fairfax & Sons Pty Ltd (1965–6) 117 CLR 118	251
Valiquette *v.* The Gazette (1992) 8 CCLT (2d) 302	225
Venables *v.* News Group Newspapers Ltd [2001] WLR 1038	208, 213, 223
Victoria Park Racing and Recreation Grounds Co. Ltd *v.* Taylor (1937) 58 CLR 479	23, 29, 32, 112, 113, 206, 276, 278
Vieright Pty Ltd *v.* Myer Stores Ltd (1995) 31 IPR 361	98

Villers *v.* Monsley (1769) 2 Wils KB 403	260
Vine Products & Co. Ltd *v.* Mackenzie & Co. Ltd [1969] RPC 1	59–60, 112, 324
Wagamama Ltd *v.* City Centre Restaurants Plc [1995] FSR 713	36, 45, 46
Waits *v.* Frito-Lay Inc., 978 F 2d 1093 (9th Cir. 1992)	182, 185
Walker *v.* Brewster (1867) LR 5 Eq 2	206
Wallis *v.* London Mail Ltd, *Times*, 20 July 1917	255, 264
Walt Disney Productions Ltd *v.* Triple Five Corp. (1992) 93 DLR (4th) 739	98
Walter *v.* Alltools Ltd (1944) 61 TLR 39	242
Walter *v.* Ashton [1902] 2 Ch 282	64
Waring *v.* WDAS Broadcasting Station, 35 USPQ 272 (1937)	177
Watts *v.* Morrow [1991] 1 WLR 1421	12, 242
WCVB-TV *v.* Boston Athletic Association, 926 F 2d 42 (1st Cir. 1991)	279
Wheaton *v.* Peters, 26–33 US 1055 (1834)	147-8
White *v.* Chief Constable of South Yorkshire Police [1999] 2 AC 455	242
White *v.* Samsung Electronics America, Inc., 971 F 2d 1395 (9th Cir. 1992)	182, 185
White *v.* Jones [1995] 2 AC 207	196, 197
Whitney *v.* California (1927) 274 US 357	224
Wilkinson *v.* Downton [1897] 2 QB 57	19, 191, *243–5*, 247, 322, 325
Willard King Pty Ltd *v.* United Telecasters Ltd [1981] 2 NSWLR 547	29
William Coulson & Sons *v.* James Coulson & Co. [1887] 3 TLR 46	203
Williams *v.* Hodge (1887) 4 TLR 175	9, 11, *65–6*, 70, 320
Williams *v.* Settle [1960] 2 All ER 806	22, 34
Wilson *v.* Wilkins (1930) 25 SW 2d 428	246
Winer *v.* United Kingdom (1986) 48 DR 154	213
Winterson *v.* Hogarth WIPO Case No. D2000-0235	55
Wombles Ltd *v.* Wombles Skips Ltd [1975] FSR 488	75
Wood *v.* Sandow, *Times*, 30 June 1914	255, 264
X *v.* Iceland (1976) 5 DR 86	212
X *v.* United Kingdom, Application No. 5877/72	212
Youssoupoff *v.* Metro-Goldwyn-Mayer Pictures Ltd (1934) 50 TLR 581	252

xxxii　Table of cases

Zacchini *v.* Scripps-Howard Broadcasting Co.,
　433 US 562 (1977)　　*179–80*, 187, *301–2*, 312
Zana *v.* Turkey (1999) 27 EHRR 667　219
Zim *v.* Western Publishing Co., 572 F 2d 1318 (1978)
　(5th Cir. CA)　184, 185

Table of German cases

RG 28.12.1899, RGZ 45, 170 (1899) (*Bismarck*)　229
BGHZ 13, 334 (1954) (*Schacht*)　230–1
BGHZ 15, 249 (1954) (*Wagner*)　231
BGHZ 20, 345 (1956) (*Dahlke*)　231, 232
BGHZ 26, 349; BGH GRUR 1958, 408 (1958)
　(*Herrenreiter*)　22, 231
BGHZ 35, 363 (1961); BGH GRUR 1961, 105 (1961)
　(*Ginsengwurzel*)　233
BverfGE 30, 173 (1971) (*Mephisto*)　233
BverfGE 34, 269 (1973) (*Soraya*)　233
BGH 17.05.82 (Case No. I ZR 73/82) (1982)
　(*Fresh Cell Cosmetics*)　234
BGH 14.10.86 (Case No. VI ZR 10/86) (1986) (*Nena*)　235
OLG Hamburg 08.05.89 (Case No. 3 W 45/89) (1989)
　(*Heinz Erhardt*)　234
BGH, NJW 1996, 1128 (1995) (*Caroline*)　236–7
BGH 1.12.1999 (1999)(*Dietrich*)　234

Table of statutes

Statute of Anne 1710: An Act for the Encouragement of Learning by Vesting the Copies of Printed Books in Authors or Purchasers of Such Copies 8 Anne c. 19	*page* 30
Common Law Procedure Act 1854	64
Copyright Act 1911	
s. 31	147
Law Reform (Miscellaneous Provisions) Act 1934	
s. 1(1)	124
Trade Marks Act 1938	
s. 9	39
s. 10	39
Defamation Act 1952	
s. 3(1)	203
Copyright Act 1956	
s. 4	34
Patents Act 1977	
s. 25	278
s. 30(1)	277
s. 30(6)	277
s. 48	277
Data Protection Act 1984	239
Consumer Protection Act 1987	
s. 2(2)(b)	101
Copyright Designs and Patents Act 1988	33
s. 1	33
s. 1(1)	277
s. 4	33
s. 9	33
s. 9(2)(aa)	33
s. 9(2)(ab)	33
s. 11	33
s. 12(1)	278

xxxiii

xxxiv   Table of statutes

s. 17(3)	33
ss. 28–76	278
s. 84	63, 262
s. 85	33
s. 85(2)	33
s. 90	277
s. 180(2)	35
s. 181	35
s. 182	35
s. 184	35
ss. 180–212	302

Broadcasting Act 1990

s. 9	48

Courts and Legal Services Act 1990

s. 58	191

Trade Marks Act 1994

s. 1(1)	39
s. 3(1)(b)	39, 41
s. 3(6)	41, 43
s. 4	38
s. 5(3)	47, 106
s. 10(1)	45
s. 10(2)	46
s. 10(3)	47, 106
s. 11	40
s. 11(2)	45
s. 12	40
s. 22	277
s. 24(3)	277
ss. 24–6	277
ss. 28–31	277
s. 32(2)(c)	43
s. 32(3)	43
s. 42	277
s. 43	278
s. 46	277, 278
s. 46(1)	43
s. 47	43
s. 56	62

Broadcasting Act 1996

s. 107(1)	206
s. 119	206

Table of statutes	xxxv

Protection from Harassment Act 1997	247
Data Protection Act 1998	
s. 7	205
s. 11	205
s. 13(2)	205
s. 32(1)	205
Human Rights Act 1998	48, 202, 210, 211, 214, 225
s. 6(1)	214
s. 9(1)	215
s. 12	220, 222
s. 12(1)	221
s. 12(3)	221
s. 12(4)	221, 223
Access to Justice Act 1999	
Sched. 2, para. 1	190
s. 27(1)	191

Table of foreign legislation

Australia

Trade Practices Act 1974 (Cth)	88
s. 52	97

Canada

Canadian Trade Marks Act, RSC 1985, c. T-13	
s. 9(1)	39
Charter of Human Rights and Freedoms RSQ c. C-12 (Quebec)	17, 111, 225, 226

Germany

Kunsturhebergesetz (KUG) (Artistic Copyright Act) 1907	
s. 22	229, 231, 232
s. 22(3)	235
s. 23	229
s. 23 II	236

United States

Lanham Trademark Act 1946, 15 USC §1125	
s. 43(a)	15
s. 43(c)(1)	105

xxxvi   Table of statutes

Copyright Act 1976, 17 USC §301	148
Uruguay Round Agreements Act, 17 USC §1101	302
California Civil Code §3344 and §3344.1 (The Astaire Celebrity Image Protection Act)	184, 185
Tennessee Code §47-25-1104 (Personal Rights Protection Act 1984)	184
Indiana Code §32-13-1-8	184
New York Civil Rights Law §51	153, 185
New York Civil Rights Law §50	184, 153

Table of International Instruments

European Convention on the Protection of Human Rights and Fundamental Freedoms 1950	17, 144, 202
Article 6	224
Article 8	205, 211, 212–13, 217–18, 222, 223
Article 10	219–20, 222, 224
Universal Declaration of Human Rights	17
United Nations Charter	17
Paris Convention for the Protection of Industrial Property, 1968	
Article 10 *bis*	27, 56

Part I

A framework

1 The problem of appropriation of personality

Introduction

The essence of the problem of appropriation of personality may be put very simply: if one person (A) uses in advertising or merchandising the name, voice or likeness of another person (B) without his or her consent, to what extent will that person (B) have a remedy to prevent such an unauthorised exploitation? The practice of using valuable attributes of personality such as name, likeness and voice in advertising and merchandising is common. In many cases B might be a famous person, although this is not invariably the case, since the images of people with no obvious public profile have often been used in advertising. Ordinariness does not necessarily confer immunity from unauthorised commercial exploitation, although those most likely to seek legal redress are the famous and the well-to-do.

The practice of appropriating personality has a long history. As early as 1843 the *Edinburgh Review* noted that Mr Cockle's Antibilious Pills were recommended by, amongst others, ten dukes, five marquesses, seventeen earls, sixteen lords, an archbishop, fifteen bishops and the advocate general, before it went on to castigate advertisers for fabricating most of their product endorsements.[1] Ironically many of these figures were comparatively unknown until the advertisers conferred an enhanced measure of celebrity upon them, leading the public to identify with them solely in their capacity as endorsers of the advertisers' products.[2] With the advent of the Industrial Revolution and the proliferation of consumer products, manufacturers and advertisers sought new ways to market and differentiate their wares from those of their rivals. Queen Victoria seems to

---

The publisher has used its best endeavours to ensure that the URLs for external websites referred to in this book are correct and active at the time of going to press. However, the publisher has no responsibility for the websites and can make no guarantee that a site will remain live or that the content is or will remain appropriate.

[1] Cited by T. Richards, *The Commodity Culture of Victorian England* (London, 1990), 22 and 84. See, also, J. P. Wood, *The Story of Advertising* (New York, 1958), 123.

[2] *Ibid.*, 84.

4   The commercial appropriation of personality

have enjoyed the dubious distinction of being one of the first people whose image was commercially exploited on a grand scale in England. During her Jubilee celebrations of 1887 hundreds of advertisers flooded the market with one of several forms of the Queen's image in order to sell such items as perfumes, powders, pills, lotions, soap, jewellery and cocoa.[3] Since then the practice of using celebrity as a commodity has become an enduring feature of the business of advertising and merchandising.[4] Fame, celebrity, or what modern gurus of advertising and promotion refer to as 'high visibility' has developed into an asset which can be used to sell products, attract audiences, generate charity donations and promote political or social causes.[5]

Various jurisdictions have developed markedly different solutions to the problem and there has been comparatively little uniformity in approach. The roots of this study lie in the English common law which has been reluctant to provide a remedy for appropriation of personality, and over the years a broad range of plaintiffs have failed to secure redress for the unauthorised use of indicia of their identity.[6] Other jurisdictions have, to varying degrees, rejected the rigid English approach, employing a number of different legal concepts to provide redress for the multifarious aspects of appropriation of personality. At various points, in the several systems, causes of action based on misrepresentation, misappropriation, defamation and invasion of privacy have all been employed to protect underlying interests in property, reputation and privacy. The discrete patterns of development in the major common law and civil law jurisdictions[7] reflect quite different attitudes towards commercial exploitation of personality which, in turn, reflect the relative importance attached to underlying values such as personal dignity and property rights. Moreover, the separate developments in various jurisdictions reveal significant differences in the dynamics and methods of legal change.

---

[3] *Ibid.*, 86.
[4] See, e.g., W. Wernick, *Promotional Culture* (London, 1991), 106 et seq.; J. Marconi, *Image Marketing* (Chicago, 1997), Ch. 4.
[5] See I. J. Rein *et al.*, *High Visibility* (London, 1987), 7.
[6] See, e.g., *Clark* v. *Freeman* (1848) 11 Beav 112; *Williams* v. *Hodge* (1887) 4 TLR 175; *Dockrell* v. *Dougall* (1899) 15 TLR 333 (surgeons); *Corelli* v. *Wall* (1906) 22 TLR 532 (author); *McCulloch* v. *Lewis A. May (Produce Distributors) Ltd* (1948) 65 RPC 58 (broadcaster); *Sim* v. *H.J. Heinz & Co. Ltd* [1959] 1 WLR 313 (actor); *Lyngstad* v. *Anabas Products Ltd* [1977] FSR 62; *Halliwell* v. *Panini* (Unreported, High Court, Chancery Division, 6 June 1997) (pop groups); *ELVIS PRESLEY Trade Marks* [1999] RPC 567 (estate of deceased singer); *Douglas* v. *Hello! Ltd* [2001] 2 WLR 992 (actors).
[7] Although reference is made, where appropriate, to civil law jurisdictions, they are not the book's primary concern. See, generally, H. P. Götting, *Persönlichkeitsrechte als Vermögensrechte* (Tübingen, 1995); J. C. S. Pinckaers, *From Privacy Towards a New Intellectual Property Right in Persona* (The Hague, 1996); M. Isgour and B. Vinçotte, *Le Droit à l'image* (Brussels, 1998); H. Beverley-Smith, A. Ohly and A. Lucas-Schloetter, *Privacy, Property and Personality* (Cambridge, forthcoming, 2003).

Interests in personality

Appropriation of personality

The problem of appropriation of personality is commonly discussed as an aspect of 'character merchandising', with a distinction usually being drawn between real persons and fictitious characters, although the problem is also commonly referred to as 'personality merchandising', or endorsement.[8] Without dwelling too long on the semantics, it should be noted that each of these phrases is somewhat misleading.

First, a human being is not a 'character', other than in a colloquial sense. Second, the underlying basis for legal liability is substantially different in each case. Character merchandising is a compendious term covering a variety of activities[9] and underlying rights such as copyright, trade marks and business goodwill. In most systems, protection for a fictitious character can often be secured through copyright law which is based on some degree of original creative effort or investment on the part of the creator, or through unfair competition law in its various forms. A 'real' person's image does not usually result from such original mental or physical effort, and the underlying basis of, and justifications for, legal protection are not the same. A third and related point is that while the unauthorised exploitation of fictitious characters usually results in damage to the creator's purely economic interests, appropriation of personality can affect non-pecuniary or dignitary interests, in addition to any injury to economic interests. This is a crucial distinction, elaborated upon in the text below. Use of the terms 'character merchandising' or 'personality merchandising' reinforces the perception that a person's image is purely an asset, when, in truth, there is a complex interaction between economic and dignitary interests. The fourth point relates to the use of the term 'endorsement'. As will become apparent, the legal notion of an endorsement is rather nebulous and uncertain. Moreover, many unauthorised uses of a person's name or image are made in circumstances which do not imply that the plaintiff has endorsed a product or service, but merely suggests some loose connection or association.[10] Consequently, reliance on the term 'endorsement' is unhelpful and liable to be misleading. Finally, it is rare to describe a legal wrong in terms of a particular commercial practice. It is more common to describe a wrong by reference to the interest protected or the nature of a particular kind of conduct such as trespass, negligence, deceit or appropriation

---

[8] See, generally, J. Adams, *Character Merchandising*, 2nd edn (London, 1996).

[9] See H. E. Ruijsenaars, 'The WIPO Report on Character Merchandising' (1994) 25 IIC 532; 'Legal Aspects of Merchandising: The AIPPI Resolution' [1996] EIPR 330.

[10] See text accompanying note 23 below.

6 The commercial appropriation of personality

of personality. One does not, generally, speak of an infringement of a person's right to merchandise his character.[11]

Since appropriation of personality is better viewed as an autonomous problem and cause of action, it is important to draw a clear distinction between appropriation of personality and the business of character merchandising. Talk of 'character merchandising' does little to help one understand the problem of appropriation of personality and the phrase may as well be jettisoned at the outset.

The broader picture

The problem of appropriation of personality, and the underlying interests in personality that may be damaged by unauthorised commercial exploitation, cannot be understood without an appreciation of the wider context.[12] It is natural that any legal system should give priority to claims for physical injury and in earlier times these injuries were the law's primary concern. As society and modern living conditions change, however, plaintiffs inevitably claim redress for other kinds of harm. Although interests in physical well-being still probably rank highest in any hierarchy of claims, interests in reputation, personal privacy, and interests in freedom from mental distress become increasingly important.[13] Usually, violations of individual personality are of a non-pecuniary nature, not only because they cannot be assessed in money terms with any mathematical accuracy, but also because they are usually of inherently non-economic value.[14] Nevertheless, the increasing commodification of the human image demands that any modern classification of interests in personality[15]

[11] Cf. P. Jaffey, 'Merchandising and the Law of Trade Marks' [1998] IPQ 240, 263 et seq.

[12] See, e.g., R. Pound, 'Interests of Personality' (1914) 28 HarvLRev 343, 445, setting out the well-known taxonomy of interests in personality consisting of five main groups: (i) interests in the physical person; (ii) interests in freedom of will; (iii) interests in honour and reputation; (iv) interests in privacy and sensibilities; and (v) interests in belief and opinion. Cf. P. D. Ollier and J. P. Le Gall, 'Various Damages' in A. Tunc (ed.) *International Encyclopaedia of Comparative Law* (Tübingen, 1981), *Vol. XI: Torts*, Ch. 10, 63, defining interests in personality as 'the collection of values enjoyed by an individual within the society of which he is a member: injury to honour or reputation, deprivation of liberty, invasion of privacy, injury to feelings, convictions, beliefs'.

[13] Cf. the reluctance to recognise liability for nervous shock in the tort of negligence, where the courts' restrictive approach to claims for psychiatric illness tends to reflect the view that injury to the mind is less worthy of community and legal support than physical injury to the body. See, e.g., Law Commission Consultation Paper No. 137, 'Liability for Psychiatric Illness' (London, 1995), para. 4.11, citing N. J. Mullany and P. R. Handford, *Tort Liability for Psychiatric Damage* (Sydney, 1993), 309, and see 241–8 below.

[14] Ollier and Le Gall, 'Various Damages', 63.

[15] See, e.g., E. Veitch, 'Interests in Personality' (1972) 23 NILQ 423, suggesting that the English law may be rationalised according to a single general principle providing that:

The problem of appropriation of personality

should take account of the fact that a person's name or features are also valuable economic assets. These de facto values are often commercially exploited in advertising and merchandising, although the precise legal status of such arrangements differs from country to country and rests on very slender foundations in English law.

Although pecuniary loss and non-pecuniary harm are often inextricably intertwined, the two aspects need to be separated since in some jurisdictions compensation for material losses caused by an injury to interests in personality encounters no obstacles, whereas compensation for non-pecuniary harm is subject to restrictions.[16] For example, the French Civil Code does not draw a distinction between material and 'moral' harm, and protects both aspects under the general principle, contained in articles 1382 and 1383 of the Code Civil, that everyone must pay for the harm caused by his *faute*.[17] In English law, on the other hand, damage to interests in personality is generally not actionable unless it also affects some interests of substance. Although the law of defamation takes cognisance of the damage to a plaintiff's non-pecuniary interests,[18] the action is, theoretically at least, grounded on the economic or social damage done to the plaintiff as third parties withdraw from their relationships with him.[19] Despite the fact that American law shares the same heritage as English law, it has broken away from its historical roots, and one area where a marked difference can be seen between English and American law is in the greater protection in the United States for interests in personality, through torts of invasion of privacy and intentional infliction of mental distress.[20] Similarly, in Germany, although the general clause in §823 para. I BGB (the German Civil Code) limits protection to the physical aspects of a person – body, health, life or freedom – the general provision has been expanded through judicial development to embrace interests in personality.[21] These patterns of developments, and their relevance to the problem of appropriation of personality, are examined in detail in Part III.

'whosoever acts in such a manner as foreseeably to cause injury to another either in the tranquillity of his mind or in the assets of his personality may either be restrained or made to repair that damage'.

[16] *Ibid.* See, generally, K. Zweigert and H. Kötz, *An Introduction to Comparative Law*, 3rd edn (Oxford, 1998), 685 et seq.

[17] See 144 below.

[18] *John* v. *MGN* [1996] 3 WLR 593, 608 *per* Bingham MR; *McCarey* v. *Associated Newspapers Ltd* [1965] 2 QB 86, 104 *per* Pearson LJ; *Fielding* v. *Variety Inc.* [1967] 2 QB 841, 855 *per* Salmon LJ.

[19] See Chapter 9.

[20] See *Restatement, Second, Torts* (1977) §652A et seq., and §46 et seq., respectively.

[21] See 227–33 below.

8 The commercial appropriation of personality

Economic and dignitary interests

Markedly different solutions to the problem of appropriation of personality have been developed in various jurisdictions. With a number of doctrinal bases competing for pre-eminence, the nature of the problem itself often tends to become obscured. It is essential to gain a firm grasp of the concrete problem of appropriation of personality which an interest-based classification tends to promote. The following scheme, intended as an aid to a clearer understanding of the problem, rather than an end in itself, sets out the main interests that might be injured as a result of an unauthorised appropriation of personality. A broad division may be made between first, economic or pecuniary interests in personality, and second, non-pecuniary or dignitary interests.

(1) Economic interests:
    (i) existing trading or licensing interests
    (ii) other intangible recognition values
(2) Dignitary interests:
    (i) interests in reputation
    (ii) interests in personal privacy
    (iii) interests in freedom from mental distress

Economic interests

An economic interest, strictly defined, might have the following features:[22] (i) a finite sum of money can provide complete recompense for an invasion of such an interest and (ii) a plaintiff should feel no further sense of loss, having received a sum of money which accurately reflects the value of what has been lost; if the plaintiff does feel a sense of unsatisfied loss, then his interest is not purely economic or, rather, the plaintiff has some non-economic interest in addition to his economic interest. Furthermore, (iii) an economic interest is capable of objective valuation, and cannot be a purely economic interest if it has a subjective value for its owner, and (iv) it is an interest based on exchange; if there is no market in what a person has lost, that person has not suffered damage to an economic interest strictly defined. The fact that many people have valuable de facto economic interests in their personality is well known, although it is often difficult to reconcile such interests with the types of damage to economic interests which are actionable injuries.

Existing trading or licensing interests This first category covers the interests of those who might have a de facto economic interest in their

---

[22] See, e.g., P. Cane, *Tort Law and Economic Interests*, 2nd edn (Oxford, 1996), 5.

The problem of appropriation of personality

name, voice or likeness and who might be actively involved in exploiting their fame for money. Obvious examples are musicians, sportsmen or performers and it is quite usual to find the images of such people being used in advertising and merchandising. Sportsmen, for example, often endorse products which might be within their field of expertise such as sports equipment and clothing and an endorsement of this kind will often be an effective way of boosting sales of such goods. On the other hand, a sportsman's image might be used in connection with goods or services that are totally un-related to the sportsman's sporting activity, for example, jewellery, cars, restaurant and telecommunications services. Companies frequently wish to associate their products or services with the image of a famous person in a way which falls short of endorsement of any particular product. Indeed, in the advertising business, a distinction is often drawn between (i) 'tools of the trade' endorsements, a term which is largely self-explanatory; (ii) 'non-tools' endorsements, involving products on which celebrities do not depend in their primary field of activity, and (iii) 'attention grabbing devices' which involve using the names or images of celebrities on, or in connection with, goods or services without suggesting any endorsement.[23]

Other intangible recognition values Fame is a rather peculiar commodity and it seems to be a fact of advertising practice that manufacturers of goods and suppliers of services can find the use of the images of a vast range of people beneficial to them in some way. The benefit might result from a suggestion of endorsement or merely by a more vague association. Apart from the more common cases such as pop-stars and sportsmen, people of high professional standing,[24] holders of public office and politicians are often desirable people with whom to associate products or services. Although such people would not normally be actively trading in their image by granting licences or entering into endorsement deals,[25] they may still have what might be referred to as 'recognition value'. Their names or images are familiar to the public, but their potential for endorsing or being associated with products remains latent and unrealised, until an ingenious advertiser, with or without seeking prior permission, finds a suitable use for them. Often the link between the subject and the product is extremely tenuous and might only occur to those working in

---

[23] See Rein *et al.*, *High Visibility*, 59.

[24] Some of the earliest (English) authorities concerned with unauthorised commercial exploitation of personality involved the use of the names of leading members of the medical profession, e.g., *Clark* v. *Freeman* (1848) 11 Beav 112; *Williams* v. *Hodge* (1887) 4 TLR 175; *Dockrell* v. *Dougall* (1899) 15 TLR 333. Cf. *Edison* v. *Edison Polyform Mfg Co.* 67 A. 392 (1907) (inventor).

[25] Cf. Rein *et al.*, *High Visibility*, 49.

10   The commercial appropriation of personality

advertising circles. The significance of the distinction between these two categories will become apparent in examining the role played by unfair competition law in its various forms.[26] While English law has adhered to a fairly orthodox approach, insisting on the existence of some business goodwill or trading activity which might be the subject of a misrepresentation, other jurisdictions, most notably the United States[27] and Canada,[28] have been willing to protect intangible recognition value un-related to any conventional business or trading activity.

Dignitary interests

No ready definition of the term 'dignitary interests' can be found in the legal literature, reflecting the fact that there is no coherent notion of human dignity as a legal value.[29] In one sense, dignitary interests might be regarded as coterminous with 'interests in personality' in the broadest sense identified above, although this is obviously tautologous, and useless for the present purposes of identifying a blanket term for non-pecuniary or non-economic interests in name, voice and likeness. Consequently, it must suffice to define dignitary interests negatively in relation to economic interests. Accordingly, (i) a finite sum of money might not provide complete recompense for the invasion of a dignitary interest, and (ii) a plaintiff might remain unsatisfied after an award of damages. Moreover, (iii) dignitary interests cannot be objectively valued but, rather, are inherently subjectively valued interests, since (iv) there is no market by which to value such interests since they are not normally exchanged. Taking an injury to reputation as an obvious example, it is clear that a sum of money might not provide complete recompense, and even an award of damages that would seem very generous, if not excessive, to an objective observer might not give a plaintiff complete satisfaction. The difficulty in placing any objective value on a dignitary interest such as reputation is reflected in the widely divergent awards of damages for defamation,[30] which have caused some concern, although this has more to do with the fact that assessment lies in the hands of the jury.[31] This, in turn, reflects the fact that there is

---

[26] See Chapter 2 and text accompanying note 43 below.
[27] See Chapters 2 and 7.   [28] See Chapter 5.
[29] See, generally, D. Feldman, 'Human Dignity as a Legal Value' [1999] PL 682 and [2000] PL 61.
[30] See, e.g., *Sutcliffe* v. *Pressdram* [1991] 1 QB 153; *Rantzen* v. *Mirror Group Newspapers* [1994] QB 670, and see, generally, H. McGregor, *McGregor on Damages*, 17th edn (London, 1997), paras. 1889–92.
[31] Since *John* v. *MGN* [1996] 3 WLR 593, it is permissible to draw the attention of libel juries to levels of awards in personal injury cases, although there is, in turn, no precise correlation between personal injury and a specific sum of money (*ibid.*, 614 *per* Bingham MR).

The problem of appropriation of personality

no market in which a person may trade his reputation for money; the notion that a person might sell the right to defame him to another is plainly absurd. Although a market exists for the use of the images of celebrities in advertising, this market relates to those celebrities' 'recognition value'. Their reputation, privacy or dignity are not, as such, traded.

Interests in reputation Everyone has an interest in their personal reputation, be they famous celebrities or ordinary people. Interests in reputation are troublesome in that they defy the broad division between economic and dignitary interests.[32] For present purposes, it must suffice to note that an injury to a person's reputation can cause financial harm, and can also cause harm which cannot be expressed in money terms. For example, assume that a well-known surgeon's name or image is used without his consent in an advertisement for a dubious and possibly harmful medicinal product.[33] This might well injure his reputation and disclose a cause of action for defamation. The damage to his interests might take a number of forms. He might, for example, suffer financial loss as a result of being lowered in the estimation of right-thinking members of society, as potential patients, clients and other third parties withdraw from their business and social relationships with him. Equally, he might suffer from the hurt feelings, distress, humiliation and injured dignity that might result from the association with a quack medicine.

Interests in personal privacy The notion of privacy is difficult to define and, for the purposes of outlining the various de facto interests, a simple dictionary definition such as 'freedom from intrusion or public attention' or 'avoidance of publicity' will suffice.[34] A central problem is that of reconciling a person's claim to privacy with the person's status as a public figure. There is nothing incongruous about an unknown person claiming that his privacy has been invaded by unauthorised commercial exploitation. Nevertheless, it is difficult to reconcile a celebrity's claim that his privacy has been invaded as a result of unauthorised commercial exploitation of personality with that celebrity's exploitation of his image either personally, or vicariously through licensed merchandisers and advertisers. On the other hand, some people do not actively seek celebrity but find that it is thrust upon them, without having done anything to

---

[32] See, further, Chapter 9.

[33] Cf. *Clark* v. *Freeman* (1848) 11 Beav 112; *Williams* v. *Hodge* (1887) 4 TLR 175; *Dockrell* v. *Dougall* (1899) 15 TLR 333.

[34] *Concise Oxford Dictionary*, 8th edn (Oxford, 1990). See, further, 160 below.

12   The commercial appropriation of personality

encourage it,[35] while others might find that their position in professional or public life has effectively stripped them of their privacy. The development of the right of privacy in the United States, and the subsequent development of the right of publicity, partly as a result of the celebrity/privacy paradox, is particularly instructive and is examined in detail in Part III.

Interests in freedom from mental distress Here the concern lies with the interests that a person might have in protecting his sensibilities or feelings. Several different terms are used to describe an injury to such interests, for example, mental distress, frustration, anxiety, displeasure, vexation, tension or aggravation.[36] What needs to be emphasised is that we are not concerned with nervous shock, or psychiatric damage, to use the phrase that is currently preferred by the courts, that is, a state of physical or mental illness, or neurosis and personality change which the law recognises in certain circumstances.[37] For the sake of convenience these interests are labelled under the rather cumbersome phrase of interests in freedom from mental distress.[38] In some circumstances unauthorised commercial exploitation of personality might result in injured feelings or mental distress. The extent to which such interests are protected in various legal systems and the relationship between such interests and interests in personal privacy also demand a brief examination.[39]

Perspectives

Such is the nature of the problem of appropriation of personality. Although the interests that are capable of being damaged are heterogeneous, two dominant perspectives may be identified. First, what may be generically labelled the unfair competition perspective, concerned with the economic torts dealing with unfair competition. Second, the privacy, or, rather more broadly, the dignitary torts perspective concerned with the various causes of action which protect dignitary interests. These perspectives, in turn, reflect two pervasive themes: first, the use of personality as

[35] See, e.g., Samuel Beckett's determined rejection of his sudden fame following the award of the 1969 Nobel Prize, recounted by J. Knowlson, *Damned to Fame: The Life of Samuel Beckett* (London, 1996), 570–3.

[36] *Watts v. Morrow* [1991] 1 WLR 1421, 1445 *per* Bingham LJ (damages for distress and inconvenience caused by the physical consequences of a breach of contract).

[37] *Attia v. British Gas Plc* [1988] QB 304, 317 *per* Bingham LJ. See, generally, A. M. Dugdale (ed.), *Clerk and Lindsell on Torts*, 18th edn (London, 2000), 319–35.

[38] The American Law Institute categorises such interests under the almost identical term 'interests in freedom from emotional distress': see *Restatement, Second, Torts* (1977) §46.

[39] See 241–8 below.

The problem of appropriation of personality

trading symbol, a result of the increasing attractiveness, if not commercial imperative, of using celebrity recognition values to generate sales; second, the idea of personality as an aspect of personal dignity which represents the increasing value placed on the protection of personal dignity in mature legal systems. Although it is often difficult to separate these de facto economic and dignitary interests,[40] it will be more convenient to examine them separately before drawing the strands together in Part V. Since this book benefits from comparisons with a number of different jurisdictions, it will be useful to summarise the various approaches taken in each jurisdiction at the outset. A certain degree of selectivity is required and the different jurisdictions have been chosen mainly with a view to analysing the discrete approaches to the problem of appropriation of personality in the major common law systems, rather than providing an exhaustive survey.[41]

The unfair competition perspective

The phrase 'unfair competition' is commonly used in three distinct ways:[42] first, as a synonym for the tort of passing off; second, as a generic term to cover the broad range of legal and equitable causes of action available to protect a trader against unlawful trading activities of a competitor; and third, as a label for a general cause of action for the misappropriation of valuable intangibles, a cause of action which has so far been rejected in Commonwealth jurisdictions. Use of the term in the first two senses is liable to mislead in that they might wrongly imply that the relevant actions are confined to proceedings against a competitor, while use of the phrase in the second sense is also liable to mislead since it wrongly implies that there is a unity of underlying principle between the causes of action, when in fact this is not the case.[43] Although the discussion is concerned, at different points, with unfair competition in all three of these senses, the term 'unfair competition' itself is only used in the generic sense.

Misrepresentation and the tort of passing off in England and Australia
In England, plaintiffs have been unsuccessful in attempting to persuade the courts that unauthorised commercial exploitation of personality can amount to passing off.[44] In Australia, however, the courts have been

---

[40] See text above.
[41] Reference should be made to separate works for each jurisdiction, cited where appropriate.
[42] *Moorgate Tobacco Co. Ltd* v. *Philip Morris Ltd (No. 2)* (1984) 56 ALR 414, 439–40 *per* Deane J.
[43] *Ibid.*
[44] See, e.g., *McCulloch* v. *Lewis A. May (Produce Distributors) Ltd* (1948) 65 RPC 58; *Lyngstad* v. *Anabas Products Ltd* [1977] FSR 62, and see, further, Chapter 4.

14   The commercial appropriation of personality

willing to take a far more expansive approach to the tort, and several actions for unauthorised commercial exploitation of personality have succeeded on this basis.[45] Passing off involves three key elements:[46] first, the interest protected is the plaintiff's property right in the goodwill or reputation attaching to his goods, name or mark; second, the conduct of the defendant must involve some form of misrepresentation leading to confusion or deception among consumers; and third, the misrepresentation must damage the plaintiff's goodwill. Bringing appropriation of personality within the scope of the tort of passing off involves considerable stretching of these three elements.[47] The practical and conceptual difficulties in extending the tort to cover cases of appropriation of personality, and the wider impact that such an extension might have on the tort of passing off as a whole, are considered in detail in Chapter 4.

The misappropriation doctrine and the Ontario tort of appropriation of personality So far, both the English and the Australian courts have resisted developing the tort of passing off into a wider tort of unfair competition involving the misappropriation of valuable intangibles,[48] for reasons which need not be pursued for the moment.[49] Similarly, the Canadian courts have not accepted such a general tort.[50] However, the Ontario courts have recognised that the misappropriation of a person's name or likeness for advertising purposes constitutes an independent tort, separate and distinct from the tort of passing off.[51] These developments beyond the tort of passing off, concerning both the wider misappropriation doctrine and the much narrower Ontario tort of appropriation of personality, are discussed in Chapter 5.

The right of publicity in the United States In the United States a right of publicity exists which allows a person, usually (though not necessarily) a celebrity, to control the commercial exploitation of his name, voice, likeness or other indicia of personality. Liability is based not on

[45] See *Henderson* v. *Radio Corp. Pty Ltd* [1969] RPC 218 and the subsequent line of authorities (84–92 below).

[46] See *Reckitt & Colman Ltd* v. *Borden Inc.* [1990] 1 WLR 491, 499; *Consorzio del Prosciutto di Parma* v. *Marks & Spencer Plc* [1991] RPC 351, 368.

[47] See Chapter 4.

[48] *Moorgate Tobacco Co. Ltd* v. *Philip Morris Ltd (No. 2)* (1984) 56 ALR 414, 445; *Harrods Ltd* v. *Schwartz-Sackin & Co. Ltd* [1986] FSR 490, 494; *Mail Newspapers* v. *Insert Media (No. 2)* [1988] 2 All ER 420, 424; *Hodgkinson & Corby Ltd* v. *Wards Mobility Ltd* [1994] 1 WLR 1564, 1569.

[49] See 112–15 below.   [50] See 115–37 below.

[51] *Krouse* v. *Chrysler Canada Ltd* (1973) 40 DLR (3d) 15; *Athans* v. *Canadian Adventure Camps Ltd* (1977) 80 DLR (3d) 583; and see 115 below.

The problem of appropriation of personality

15

misrepresentation leading to consumer confusion or deception,[52] but on the *misappropriation* of the commercial value of a person's identity.[53] The protection which most states provide is the most extensive in any common law jurisdiction, though there are considerable differences between individual states in the degree of protection afforded.[54] Although the right of publicity is often regarded as an aspect of unfair competition law,[55] it has its roots elsewhere and, surprisingly perhaps, neither the law of passing off nor the misappropriation doctrine played much part in its development. Rather, the right of publicity evolved from the right of privacy and, since its development cannot be understood without tracing the history of its progenitor, it is reserved for discussion in Part III.

The dignitary torts perspective

Like the generic use of the phrase 'unfair competition', the phrase 'dignitary torts' is merely intended as a common label for a number of torts which protect a person's dignity in some way or other. The phrase is rather more common in the United States[56] than in English law,[57] partly because of the latter's traditional reluctance to recognise such 'dignitary' torts as torts of invasion of privacy[58] or intentional infliction of mental distress,[59] although any grouping of 'dignitary' torts is likely to be highly subjective. In addition to the most obvious candidate, defamation, one might also include the torts of false imprisonment or battery, although these might more usually be regarded as protecting interests in the physical person. Similarly, several civil law jurisdictions have a more advanced notion of the protection of personal dignity, through codified

---

[52] Liability for misrepresentation is based on section 43(a) of the Lanham Trademark Act (1946), 15 USC §1125 (a), although this has played a relatively limited role, given the existence of the right of publicity. See 180–7 below.

[53] *Rogers* v. *Grimaldi*, 875 F 2d 994 (2nd Cir. 1989), 1003–4; *Carson* v. *Here's Johnny Portable Toilets Inc.*, 698 F 2d 831 (6th Cir. 1983), 834–5.

[54] See, generally, J. T. McCarthy, *The Rights of Publicity and Privacy*, 2nd edn (New York, 2001).

[55] Witness its recent inclusion in the *Restatement, Third, Unfair Competition* (1995) §46 et seq.

[56] See, e.g., C. O. Gregory and K. Kalven, *Cases and Materials on Torts*, 2nd edn (Boston, 1969), part II and esp. 1186.

[57] Cf. P. Cane, 'The Basis of Tortious Liability' in P. Cane and J. Stapleton (eds.) *Essays for Patrick Atiyah* (Oxford, 1991), 372, including 'dignitary interests' as one of the seven basic types of interest that tort law protects.

[58] *Kaye* v. *Robertson* [1991] FSR 62, 66 *per* Glidewell LJ; *Malone* v. *Metropolitan Police Commissioner* [1979] Ch 344, 374 *per* Megarry VC; *Re X* [1975] 1 All ER 697, 704 *per* Denning MR.

[59] *Lynch* v. *Knight* (1861) 9 HL Cas. 577, 598 *per* Lord Wensleydale; *Alcock* v. *Chief Constable of South Yorkshire Police* [1992] 1 AC 310, 401 *per* Lord Ackner. See, further, Chapter 7.

16   The commercial appropriation of personality

provisions and judicial development.[60] Here we are concerned with torts which protect primarily mental interests in emotional tranquillity, privacy or freedom from mental distress. This perspective obviously differs from the unfair competition perspective in that it focuses on the harm done to a person's dignitary interests, rather than damage to the commercial value. However, this distinction is not always clear and reflects the difficulty in fully separating economic and dignitary interests.[61]

The right of privacy in the United States In the early years of the twentieth century in the United States the right of privacy established itself as the primary vehicle for protecting interests in personality from unauthorised commercial exploitation. Indeed, such cases featured prominently in the early development of the tort.[62] As originally conceived, the right of privacy gave legal expression to the rather nebulous principle of 'inviolate personality' and secured a person's right 'to be let alone'.[63] This provided legal protection for dignitary interests which had previously fallen outside other legal and equitable causes of action such as defamation, trespass and breach of confidence.[64] However, from a relatively early period in its development it became clear that the right of privacy could be used to secure what were essentially economic rather than dignitary interests in preventing the unauthorised commercial exploitation of a person's valuable attributes in name and likeness.[65] Although the right of privacy eventually begat the right of publicity,[66] which many now regard as better placed among the unfair competition torts,[67] this was not before a great deal of conceptual controversy came to surround the proper rationale, scope and limits of the right of privacy. Indeed, its conceptual uncertainty was such that it was seized upon by a broad range of plaintiffs concerned with securing protection for a highly disparate range of interests. It is against this uncertain conceptual background that the development of an essentially dignitary interest in privacy into an essentially economic interest in publicity is traced.

---

[60] See, generally, C. Von Bar, *The Common European Law of Torts Vol. I* (Oxford, 1998), 591–610, and see 144 below.

[61] See text above.

[62] See *Roberson* v. *Rochester Folding Box Co.*, 171 NY 538 (1902); *Pavesich* v. *New England Life Insurance Co.*, 50 SE 68 (1905).

[63] S. Warren and L. Brandeis, 'The Right to Privacy' (1890) 4 HarvLRev 193, 205; *Pavesich* v. *New England Life Insurance Co.*, 50 SE 68 (1905).

[64] See 146–50 below.

[65] See, e.g., *Edison* v. *Edison Polyform Mfg Co.*, 67 A 392 (1907); *Flake* v. *Greensboro News Co.*, 195 SE 55 (1938).

[66] *Haelan Laboratories Inc.* v. *Topps Chewing Gum Inc.*, 202 F 2d 866 (2nd Cir. 1953).

[67] See note 56 above.

The problem of appropriation of personality

Several parallel developments may be seen in the Canadian provinces, in the form of statutory torts of invasion of privacy in Manitoba, British Columbia, Newfoundland and Saskatchewan; developments in Quebec, based on *The Quebec Charter of Human Rights and Freedoms* and the *Civil Code*; the Ontario common law tort of appropriation of personality; and the embryonic common law tort of invasion of privacy.[68] Although reference is made to these developments at various points, the Canadian law of privacy does not require separate treatment since most of the conceptual and practical issues are adequately highlighted in tracing the developments in the United States. Similarly, an examination of Australian law in this context adds nothing to the discussion since there is no tort of invasion of privacy in Australia[69] and no significant divergence from English law in this respect.

Human dignity in international conventions and constitutional provisions On an international level, the notion of human dignity is alluded to and given effect in various instruments. Thus, the Preamble to the Charter of the United Nations (1945) states a desire to 'reaffirm faith in fundamental human rights, in the dignity and worth of the human person'.[70] Similarly, the European Convention on Human Rights draws on the notion of human dignity citing, in its preamble, the Universal Declaration of Human Rights, adopted by the General Assembly of the United Nations, which refers to the dignity and worth of the human person.[71] In some civil law jurisdictions the notion of human dignity is enshrined in constitutional provisions. For example, Art. 1 of the German Basic Law (*Grundgesetz*) or Constitution of Bonn (1949) provides that 'the dignity of man shall be inviolable. To respect it shall be the duty of all state authority' while Art. 2(1) provides that '[e]veryone has the right to the free development of his personality, in so far as he does not violate the rights of others or offend against the constitutional order or the moral code'. Although constitutional provisions do not apply directly in disputes between private individuals, by virtue of the doctrine of 'Drittwirkung' or 'indirect effect' the German courts have been able to interpret the civil law in accordance with the values embodied in the Constitution in creating a general right of personality. It remains to be seen, following the Human

---

[68] See Chapter 5.
[69] See, generally, J. G. Fleming, *The Law of Torts*, 8th edn (Sydney, 1992), Ch. 26; M. Henry (ed.), *International Privacy, Publicity and Personality Laws* (London, 2001), Ch. 3.
[70] See, generally, H. J. Steiner and P. Alston, *International Human Rights in Context*, 2nd edn (Oxford, 2000), Ch. 3, and 1365.
[71] Universal Declaration of Human Rights, Preamble and Art. 1, and see, generally, Feldman, 'Human Dignity', Part I, 688.

18   The commercial appropriation of personality

Rights Act 1998, how the values of the European Convention on Human Rights will influence the English common law in developing new causes of action which protect, whether directly, or indirectly, an individual's dignity.[72]

The tort of defamation in English law So far, English law has declined to adopt the approach taken in the United States, either through judicial development of a right of privacy or through legislation. Of all the de facto dignitary interests outlined above, the only interests that are protected by the substantive causes of action in English law are interests in reputation. In English law, relief for unauthorised appropriation of personality has only been available insofar as the particular facts disclosed a cause of action in defamation,[73] apart from exceptional cases in which breach of contract or an obligation of confidence could be established.[74] However, it is arguable that in some defamation cases the courts have interpreted the requirements of the tort of defamation benevolently, and have, in effect, been giving limited recognition to interests in privacy.[75] Such an argument can only be properly evaluated after an examination of the development and competing conceptions of the right of privacy in the United States.

Due to the importance of the cause of action for invasion of privacy in the United States, the law of defamation has played a relatively limited role in dealing with the problem of appropriation of personality. Indeed, most of the defamation authorities examined in Chapter 9 are English, and there is no significant divergence in approach either in Canada or Australia which merits attention.

Intentional infliction of mental distress in the United States and England The final member of the dignitary torts genus which falls to be considered is the American tort of intentional infliction of mental distress. While the cause of action is fairly well established in the United States,[76] it is still in an embryonic form in English law and deserves to be considered for two reasons. First, in the context of appropriation of personality, the case law in the United States shows that the tort of intentional infliction of mental distress is sometimes used as a supplementary cause of action to invasion of privacy, particularly where the defendant's

---

[72] See 214–24 below.

[73] See, e.g., *Tolley* v. *Fry & Sons Ltd* [1931] AC 333, and see, generally, Chapter 9.

[74] See, e.g., *Pollard* v. *Photographic Co.* (1889) 40 ChD 345. Cf. *Hellewell* v. *Chief Constable of Derbyshire* [1995] 4 All ER 473, 476; *R* v. *Chief Constable of the North Wales Police and others ex parte AB and Another* [1997] 4 All ER 691 (disclosure of information concerning paedophiles to caravan site owner necessary in public interest). See, further, 207–11 below.

[75] See 258–61 below.   [76] See *Restatement, Second, Torts* (1977) §46 et seq.

The problem of appropriation of personality   19

conduct is outrageous and might foreseeably cause mental anguish or distress, though it should be noted that such cases are comparatively rare.[77] Second, it has sometimes been suggested that the rule in *Wilkinson* v. *Downton*[78] could be extended to give recognition to some interests in privacy in English law. Although interests in freedom from mental distress might be regarded as a subset of interests in personal privacy, the relationship between the two interests and their legal protection is not altogether clear and thus merits a brief discussion.[79]

The divergent approaches

The seemingly simple problem of appropriation of personality can affect a multifarious range of interests which may be broadly classified as either economic or dignitary interests; these will be considered in detail respectively in Part II and Part III. The problem has generally been approached from the two main perspectives outlined above: the unfair competition and dignitary tort perspectives. First, lawyers concerned with intellectual property naturally tend to see appropriation of personality (or personality merchandising, or endorsement)[80] as a matter which falls within their field, albeit somewhat on the periphery. It is commonplace that once commercial value attaches to a thing or intangible, human nature and commercial factors will demand that greater protection be secured against exploitation by others. Thus, demands for protection of the valuable attributes of a person's name, voice or likeness form part of the 'unending miscellany'[81] of claims which lie at the margins of intellectual property. Intellectual property lawyers are primarily interested in rights of an essentially economic nature, the paradigm example being the patent system, while copyright, at least in the common law tradition, is also an essentially economic right.[82] Although trade marks fit rather uneasily with the notion of an intellectual creation, since they derive their value as indicia of the business goodwill of a trader, they are also rights of an essentially economic nature and are universally treated as aspects of intellectual property. Hence the focus is on protecting the economic aspects of personality through an extension of the existing causes of action for unfair competition.[83] To this end the English and Australian courts

---

[77] See 246–7 below.   [78] [1897] 2 QB 57.   [79] See 241–8 below.
[80] Cf. text accompanying note 8 above.
[81] W. R. Cornish, *Intellectual Property*, 4th edn (London, 1999), 11.
[82] See J. A. L. Sterling, *World Copyright Law* (London, 1998), 15 et seq.; G. Davies, *Copyright and the Public Interest* (Weinheim, 1994), Ch. 6; A. Strowel, '*Droit d'auteur* and Copyright: Between History and Nature' in B. Sherman and A. Strowel (eds.), *Of Authors and Origins* (Oxford, 1994), 239 and 248.
[83] Most of the English law literature approaches the problem from this perspective. For a sample, see, e.g., Adams, *Character Merchandising*, Ch. 4; H. Carty, 'Character

20 The commercial appropriation of personality

have, to varying degrees, been concerned with extending the scope of the passing off action, while their American and Canadian counterparts have gone much further in developing new categories of unfair competition. Secondly, the problem has been approached from a dignitary torts perspective, focusing on the injury to personal dignity. Again, the English and Australian courts have generally been much slower to develop new remedies for invasion of personal privacy than the courts in the United States.[84] Even where a remedy for invasion of privacy is contemplated, appropriation of personality is frequently seen as a 'cuckoo in the nest' which might better be addressed by an extension of other causes of action such as passing off.[85]

The fact that the problem is generally approached from one of these divergent perspectives[86] can often obscure the essentially hybrid nature of the problem of appropriation of personality. Moreover, the primary purposes of these different branches of the law are very different. By aligning the problem with intellectual property, the predominant preoccupation tends to be with protecting economic interests, and securing compensation for damage to those interests. On the other hand, in approaching the problem from a dignitary interests perspective, although gaining compensation for damage to reputation or loss of privacy might be a primary concern, the bare fact of violation of such interests might in itself be important, and a plaintiff might be equally concerned with gaining vindication or satisfaction for the affront to personal dignity which results from such violation. The fact that these aims are rather different is often overlooked when approaching the problem from one perspective or the other.

Merchandising and the Limits of Passing Off' (1993) 13 LS 289; A. Coleman, 'The Unauthorised Commercial Exploitation of the Names and Likenesses of Real Persons' [1982] EIPR 189; J. Holyoak, 'United Kingdom Character Rights and Merchandising Rights Today' [1993] JBL 444; G. Hobbs, 'Passing Off and the Licensing of Merchandising Rights' [1980] EIPR 47 and 79. Similarly, for Australian literature, see: S. K. Murumba, *Commercial Exploitation of Personality* (Sydney, 1986), Chs. 4 and 5; C. Pannam, 'The Unauthorised Use of Names or Photographs in Advertisements' (1966) 40 ALJ 4; D. R. Shanahan, 'Image Filching in Australia: The Legal Provenance and Aftermath of the Crocodile Dundee Decisions' (1991) 81 TMR 351; A. Terry, 'The Unauthorised Use of Celebrity Photographs in Advertising' (1991) 65 ALJ 587.

[84] P. H. Winfield, 'Privacy' (1931) 47 LQR 23, was the first attempt to look at the problem from this perspective and remains one of the most detailed. In marked contrast, much of the American literature dealing with appropriation of personality has approached it as an aspect of the law of privacy (see Chapter 7).

[85] R. Bagshaw, 'Obstacles on the Path to Privacy Torts' in P. Birks (ed.) *Privacy and Loyalty* (Oxford, 1997), 133, 140.

[86] T. Frazer, 'Appropriation of Personality – A New Tort?' (1983) 99 LQR 281, is a notable exception.

The problem of appropriation of personality

The converging aims of tort law

It is commonplace that the law of tort serves a number of different aims[87] such as compensation, disgorgement, corrective justice or punishment, deterrence, and a residual group of aims which may be described as vindication, satisfaction or appeasement. When the harm to an individual's personality interests is non-pecuniary there tends to be a convergence of the different purposes of tort law and, in particular, conceptions of compensation, appeasement and punishment tend to coincide.[88] In such cases the law seems to be as much concerned with the bare fact of violation of a particular interest in personality as it is with the effect that it has on the plaintiff. Freedom from harm is not the primary or sole concern, and the infringement of the interest is in itself objectionable.[89] For example, as mentioned above, a plaintiff bringing an action for injury to reputation, which has both economic and dignitary aspects, might have two primary purposes: first, to clear his name, and second to be compensated. Thus he might first want a retraction or an apology, and second an award of damages as compensation for his loss.

In most common law systems, the second purpose of bringing a legal action, securing compensation, generally overshadows the plaintiff's first aim, gaining satisfaction or vindication, and it is arguable that in some cases the plaintiff's aims might be in inverse priority to what the law actually recognises.[90] Indeed, if it is accepted that the law of civil wrongs has two main aspects – the first encapsulated in the notion of compensation for loss aligning it with social security, the second and more powerfully normative aspect emphasising its exhortatory and retributive functions – it must be conceded that the first aspect has been predominant while the second has been forced into an incidental or subsidiary role.[91] The modern emphasis on compensation obscures what might be described as the 'inner nature' of the tort action, where damages for non-pecuniary losses do not compensate the plaintiff, but rather 'put the plaintiff in possession of a sum of money which in the court's judgment ought to be

---

[87] See *Daniels v. Thompson* [1998] 3 NZLR 22, 68, and see, generally, G. L. Williams, 'The Aims of the Law of Tort' [1951] 4 CLP 137; D. Harris, 'Can the Law of Torts Fulfil its Aims' (1990–1) 14 NZULR 113; Cane, *Tort Law and Economic Interests*, 465–92; L. M. Linden, *Canadian Tort Law*, 4th edn (Toronto, 1988), 1–20; W. P. Keeton, *Prosser and Keeton on the Law of Torts*, 5th edn (St Paul, 1984), 5 et seq.

[88] Law Commission, Consultation Paper No. 132, 'Aggravated, Exemplary and Restitutionary Damages' (London, 1993), 23, and the references cited.

[89] *Ibid.*, 24.

[90] Ollier and Le Gall, 'Various Damages', 98–9.

[91] P. Birks (ed.), *Wrongs and Remedies in the Twenty-First Century* (Oxford, 1996), vi, and see, further, A. M. Linden, 'Torts Tomorrow – Empowering the Injured' in N. J. Mullany and A. M. Linden (eds.) *Torts Tomorrow: A Tribute to John Fleming* (Sydney, 1998), 321.

22   The commercial appropriation of personality

enough to satisfy his vindictive feelings against the wrongdoer'.[92] Other systems recognise more openly the fact that an award of damages is a reflection of the satisfaction due to the plaintiff for the disparagement of his personality, rather than for tangible economic loss as conventionally understood. Thus, for example, in Germany, a plaintiff whose image appeared without his consent to advertise a sexual tonic, subjecting him to ridicule and humiliation, was entitled to damages as a satisfaction for the affront to his dignity, rather than as a reflection of any actual pecuniary loss suffered, or any unjust enrichment gained by the defendant.[93]

In the case of the common law torts that are actionable *per se*, that is, without proof of special damage, the interest protected by a particular tort is considered important enough for its infringement to be actionable without proof of loss. Although the compensatory principle, which presupposes loss, has attained prominence today, the historical significance of the torts actionable *per se* suggests that tort law was and still is equally concerned with the protection of particular interests as it is with compensating loss. The torts actionable *per se*, such as libel, false imprisonment, and trespass to the person, are all wrongs which directly protect interests in personality and by their very nature involve elements of intangible loss such as diminution of reputation, insult, outrage, distress or loss of dignity, which are, to varying degrees, reflected in awards of damages.[94] In some cases, damage to a plaintiff's personal dignity is reflected in an award of exemplary damages,[95] and, in the absence of specific substantive remedies, such dignitary interests only receive incidental protection through a casuistic application of the traditional causes of action.[96] More progressive common law jurisdictions, most notably the United States and certain Canadian provinces, have gone further in protecting interests in personality by developing new substantive causes of action for invasion of privacy and intentional infliction of mental distress. Similarly, German law has developed enhanced protection for an individual's personality which, although cast in rights-based terminology which at first glance seems alien to common law systems, has much in

---

[92] J. M. Kelly, 'The Inner Nature of the Tort Action' (1967) 2 IrJur (NS) 279, 287. This has been more recently labelled as the 'psychological empowerment' of the victim of tortious conduct (Linden, 'Torts Tomorrow', 327).

[93] BGHZ 26, 349; BGH GRUR 1958, 408 (*Herrenreiter*), and see 230–3 below.

[94] See McGregor, *Damages*, paras. 1844, 1850 and 1894–5; Law Commission, 'Aggravated, Exemplary and Restitutionary Damages', para. 2.25.

[95] See, e.g., *Williams* v. *Settle* [1960] 2 All ER 806 (substantial exemplary damages following breach by defendant newspaper of plaintiff's copyright in wedding photographs of plaintiff's deceased relative). For background to the case see W. F. Pratt, *Privacy in Britain* (London, 1979), 136. See also G. Dworkin, 'Privacy and the Press' (1961) 24 MLR 185.

[96] See, e.g., *Kaye* v. *Robertson* [1991] FSR 62.

The problem of appropriation of personality 23

common, in terms of the process of development, with the common law systems.

Synopsis

The unfair competition and the dignitary torts perspectives provide the two main approaches to the problem of appropriation of personality. The multifarious interests that unauthorised commercial exploitation of personality can affect call for a variety of legal responses, and demand an examination of several different causes of action. However, there are significant drawbacks with both these perspectives, and, arguably, neither can encompass the whole of the problem in a realistic and conceptually coherent manner. A central argument presented in this book runs as follows: if it is considered that interests in personality should be protected from unauthorised commercial exploitation (without prejudging the issue before considering some underlying justifications),[97] then the best way to proceed is for the courts or legislature to formulate a new and suitably narrow rule of liability. Such an approach avoids several pitfalls. In relation to economic interests and the unfair competition perspective, there are two main advantages. First, it avoids stretching the tort of passing off and resorting to highly artificial reasoning; even at its most flexible, the tort of passing off is a somewhat awkward and unsatisfactory response to the problem of appropriation of personality. Second, it avoids introducing a wider doctrine of misappropriation of valuable intangibles, with the attendant difficulties of placing appropriate limits on such a doctrine and its possibly harmful effects on free competition. English law, in particular, has been traditionally suspicious of causes of action cast in the form of such wide generalisations.[98] In relation to dignitary interests, such an approach avoids the need for artificial interpretations of the requirements of the tort of defamation. Moreover, difficulties in reconciling a remedy for appropriation of personality with the notion of a right of privacy (in itself a protean and much contested concept)[99] may be circumvented. Finally, although conceptual tidiness should not necessarily be regarded as a paramount consideration, such an approach provides the best means of protecting both economic and dignitary interests in a coherent and unified manner.

---

[97] See Chapter 11.

[98] See *Victoria Park Racing and Recreation Grounds Co. Ltd* v. *Taylor* (1937) 58 CLR 479, 509 *per* Dixon J, noting the Anglo-Australian rejection of a cause of action for misappropriation based on a wide generalisation; *Moorgate Tobacco Co. Ltd (No. 2)* v. *Philip Morris Ltd (No. 2)* (1984) 56 CLR 414, 445 *per* Deane J.

[99] See Chapter 7.

24   The commercial appropriation of personality

The hybrid nature of the problem of appropriation of personality and the fact that it can affect both economic and dignitary interests demands that it be approached from two separate perspectives. Nevertheless, in pursuing the two primary perspectives, it is worthwhile bearing in mind that it is possible to find an essential unity in appropriation of personality. The disparate nature of the problem and the divergent solutions which have developed in the several common law and civil law jurisdictions are perfectly capable of being rationalised in the form of a modest addition to the existing catalogue[100] of common law torts.

[100] See B. Rudden, 'Torticles' (1991–2) 6/7 *Tulane Civil Law Forum* 105, identifying at least seventy separate torts in the common law jurisdictions.

Part II

Economic interests and the law
of unfair competition

2 Introduction

Part II considers the extent to which economic interest in personality may be protected from the first main perspective: unfair competition. The major common law and civil law jurisdictions adopt rather different approaches to unfair competition in general, and appropriation of personality in particular. These approaches, and the relative importance of statutory and common law causes of action in protecting economic interests in intangibles, need to be grasped at the outset.

Article 10 *bis* of the Paris Convention for the Protection of Industrial Property obliges signatories to provide effective protection against unfair competition which is contrary to honest practices in industrial or commercial matters. Three particular aspects are expressly included: (i) creating confusion with or discrediting the establishment, the goods or the commercial activities of a competitor; (ii) making false allegations which discredit the establishment, goods, or the industrial or commercial activities of a competitor; and (iii) giving indications liable to mislead the public as to the nature, manufacturing process, characteristics, suitability for purpose or quantity of goods.[1] Beyond these acts, case law and legislation in various jurisdictions have provided protection, to varying degrees and in various forms, against such activities as the violation of trade secrets, comparative advertising and misappropriation or free riding (such as the dilution of the value of a trade mark in the absence of confusion). The major common law and civil law jurisdictions give effect to these obligations in different ways,[2] either by means of specific legislation,[3] or

---

[1] Paris Convention for the Protection of Industrial Property, Art. 10 *bis* (3). Cf. World Intellectual Property Organisation, *Model Provisions on Protection Against Unfair Competition* (Geneva, 1996), containing an expansive approach to Art. 10 *bis*, and see W. R. Cornish, 'Genevan Bootstraps' [1997] EIPR 336.

[2] See, e.g., F. K. Beier, 'The Law of Unfair Competition in the European Community – Its Development and Present Status' [1985] EIPR 284; World Intellectual Property Organisation, *Protection Against Unfair Competition* (Geneva, 1994); A. Kamperman Sanders, *Unfair Competition Law* (Oxford, 1997), 24–77.

[3] See, e.g., in Germany, *Gesetz gegen den unlauteren Wettbewerb*, 7 June 1909; Kamperman Sanders, *Unfair Competition*, 56.

28   The commercial appropriation of personality

by means of general codified[4] or common law actions which may be supplemented, in turn, by piecemeal statutory provisions. Within the common law systems, the phrase 'unfair competition' is often used in three distinct ways: in the broadest sense, as used above, as a generic term to cover a wide range of legal and equitable causes of action dealing with unfair trading; as a synonym for the tort of passing off; and, finally, as a label for a general cause of action based on the misappropriation of valuable intangibles.[5] While the latter form of unfair competition has emerged in the United States, it has been rejected in English and Australian law.

The origins of the common law misappropriation doctrine

The origins of the misappropriation doctrine, which Anglo-Australian courts have so far resisted, lie in the well-known decision of the United States Supreme Court in *International News Service* v. *Associated Press.*[6] According to the majority, the defendant's conduct in taking and transmitting news from the early editions of the plaintiff's east-coast newspapers and publishing it in its own west-coast papers as early or even earlier than the plaintiff's own papers (taking advantage of the time differential) amounted to unfair competition. Without being burdened with the expense of gathering the news itself, it had interfered with the plaintiff's business, diverting profits from those who had earned it through expenditure of labour, skill and money, to those who had not. In short, the defendant sought to reap where it had not sown.[7] For the majority, unfair competition was not to be limited to cases of *misrepresentation*, where the defendant attempted to pass off its goods as those of the plaintiff; rather, liability could be based on the defendant's *misappropriation* of the plaintiff's 'quasi property' in the news matter, which was merely the material from which the parties were seeking to make money.[8]

While Holmes J, partially dissenting, limited the complaint to the implied misrepresentation that the news was the defendant's own news, which should not be published without an acknowledgement of source,[9] Brandeis J went further, arguing that the fact that a product of the mind had cost its producer money and labour to produce, and had a value for which others were willing to pay, was not sufficient to provide it with the legal attribute of property. The attribute of property was only conferred on incorporeal productions in certain classes of cases where public policy had seemed to demand it, and was confined to productions which, in

---

[4] See, e.g., in France, Art. 1382 French Civil Code.
[5] See 13 above.   [6] 248 US 215 (1918).
[7] *Ibid.*, 239–40.   [8] *Ibid.*, 241–2.   [9] *Ibid.*, 246–8.

Economic interests: introduction

some degree, involved creation, invention or discovery. Otherwise, intangible property was only protected in a limited sense because of a special relationship such as contract or trust between the plaintiff and the defendant, or because of the nature of the defendant's act such as conduct amounting to unfair competition.[10] The consequence of the majority's decision, according to Brandeis J, would be a considerable extension of property rights, and a corresponding curtailment of free use and knowledge of ideas;[11] in his view, the courts were ill equipped to decide the limits which should be set on any new property right in news.[12]

Misappropriation in Anglo-Australian courts

Brandeis J's dissenting judgment has formed the basis of the rejection of a general cause of action based on misappropriation of valuable intangibles in Anglo-Australian jurisdictions which have refused to protect 'all the intangible elements of value ... which may flow from the exercise by an individual of his powers or resources whether in the organization of a business or undertaking or the use of ingenuity, knowledge, skill or labour'.[13] Intellectual property rights are dealt with 'as special heads of protected interests and not under a wide generalization'[14] and the crucial factor will be whether an intangible falls within one of the discrete recognised categories rather than the fact that the intangible creation has some form of value. Nevertheless, Deane J, sitting in the High Court of Australia, noted in *Moorgate Tobacco Co. Ltd (No. 2)* v. *Philip Morris Ltd* that '[t]he rejection of a general action for "unfair competition" or "unfair trading" does not involve a denial of the desirability of adopting a flexible approach to traditional forms of action when such an approach is necessary to adapt them to meet new situations and circumstances'.[15] Such an approach is deemed to be more consistent with the limits of the traditional common law and statutory causes of action, and better reflects the balance between competing claims and policies that the legislature deems appropriate. The boundaries between what is and what is not actionable should not be obliterated 'by the importation of a cause

---

[10] *Ibid.*, 250–1.   [11] *Ibid.*, 263.   [12] *Ibid.*, 267.

[13] *Victoria Park Racing and Recreation Grounds Co. Ltd* v. *Taylor* (1937) 58 CLR 479; *Moorgate Tobacco Co. Ltd* v. *Philip Morris Ltd (No. 2)* (1984) 56 CLR 414, 445; *Hodgkinson & Corby Ltd* v. *Wards Mobility Ltd* [1994] 1 WLR 1564, 1569; *Mail Newspapers* v. *Insert Media (No. 2)* [1988] 2 All ER 420, 424; *Harrods Ltd* v. *Schwartz-Sackin & Co. Ltd* [1986] FSR 490, 494; *Chocosuisse Union Des Fabricants Suisses de Chocolat* v. *Cadbury Ltd* [1998] RPC 117, 127. Cf. *Willard King Pty Ltd* v. *United Telecasters Ltd* [1981] 2 NSWLR 547, 552; *Hexagon Pty Ltd* v. *Australian Broadcasting Commission* (1975) 7 ALR 233, 251.

[14] *Victoria Park Racing and Recreation Grounds Co. Ltd* v. *Taylor* (1937) 58 CLR 479, 509.

[15] *Moorgate Tobacco Co. Ltd* v. *Philip Morris Ltd (No. 2)* (1984) 56 CLR 414, 445.

30   The commercial appropriation of personality

of action whose main characteristic is the scope it allows, under high-sounding generalizations, for judicial indulgence of idiosyncratic notions of what is fair in the market place'.[16]

Passing off, misappropriation and appropriation of personality

One example of the flexible approach to the traditional causes of action given by Deane J in the *Moorgate Tobacco* case was the expansive approach adopted with regard to the tort of passing off, in particular its extension to cover the deceptive or confusing use of names or other indicia to suggest some commercial association or endorsement.[17] Nevertheless, while the Australian courts have proved to be highly adept at developing the tort of passing off to provide a remedy in cases of appropriation of personality, the English courts have refused to follow their lead. The next two chapters consider the role that the tort of passing off plays in protecting interests in personality, tracing different patterns in three separate jurisdictions. The conservative approach of the English courts contrasts with the more liberal approach in Australia, and the entirely different approach adopted in the Canadian province of Ontario. Indeed, the development in Ontario of a separate tort of appropriation of personality requires extended discussion in Chapter 5.

A clear distinction therefore needs to be drawn between four separate notions: first, the modern English tort of passing off which does not, on present authorities, encompass damage to interests in personality as such; second, the extended Australian form of passing off which does embrace damage to interests in personality; third, a general tort of misappropriation of intangibles; and, fourth, a *sui generis* tort of appropriation of personality. As between the first two, it would be an over-generalisation simply to describe the English tort of passing off as orthodox or conservative, compared to the more flexible approach in Australia. However, in the specific area of endorsement and merchandising, the Australian courts have shown a great deal more flexibility in adapting the tort of passing off to meet new circumstances. The differences between the positions in England and Australia are analysed in examining the essential elements of the tort of passing off and, as will become clear, there are considerable difficulties in reconciling the problem of appropriation of personality with a tort based on misrepresentation.[18] These difficulties have surfaced in some Canadian authorities and Chapter 5 looks beyond

---

[16] *Ibid.*

[17] *Ibid.*, citing the decision of the High Court of New South Wales in *Henderson v. Radio Corp. Pty Ltd* [1969] RPC 218.

[18] See 72–97 below.

the tort of passing off and considers the third and fourth notions noted above. The Ontario courts have shown that it is possible to develop a *sui generis* tort of appropriation of personality without developing a wider general tort of misappropriation of intangibles.

The legacy of the American misappropriation doctrine

Returning briefly to the misappropriation doctrine engendered in *International News Service* v. *Associated Press*,[19] despite being frequently cited the decision has been sparingly applied.[20] While early cases sought to limit the decision to its facts,[21] the biggest fetter on the cause of action for misappropriation has been the constitutional doctrine that federal statutory intellectual property rights such as copyright and patents are supreme and, in any conflict, pre-empt the application of state laws.[22] More recently, the American Law Institute has effectively disowned the misappropriation doctrine, arguing that liability should only arise for the misappropriation of intangible trade values under the rules provided by federal or state intellectual property statutes, under the rules relating to trade secrets, or under the rules governing the right of publicity.[23] Most jurisdictions in the United States recognise a right of publicity which allows a person to control the commercial exploitation of his name, voice or likeness, and this right is often treated as an aspect of unfair competition law.[24] However, neither the misappropriation doctrine nor the more traditional tort of passing off played an important part in its development. Rather, its origins lie in the entirely separate right of privacy and, as previously noted, its development cannot properly be understood without an understanding of the development of its progenitor.[25] These issues are addressed in Part III.

---

[19] 248 US 215 (1918). See, generally, D. G. Baird, 'Common Law Intellectual Property and the Legacy of *International News Service* v. *Associated Press*' (1983) 50 U Chi L Rev 411.

[20] *Restatement, Third, Unfair Competition* (1995) § 38 comment *c*.

[21] See, e.g., *Cheney Bros.* v. *Doris Silk Corp.*, 35 F 2d 279 (2nd Cir. 1929), 280. As Deane J noted in *Moorgate* (note 15 above at 443), this has been the general, though by no means universal, trend.

[22] See, e.g., *Sears, Roebuck & Co.* v. *Stiffel Co.*, 376 US 225 (1964); *Compco Corp.* v. *Day-Brite Lighting Inc.*, 376 US 234 (1964); *Bonito Boats Inc.* v. *Thunder Craft Boats Inc.*, 489 US 141 (1989).

[23] *Restatement, Third, Unfair Competition* (1995) § 38.

[24] Witness its inclusion in *ibid.*, §§ 46–9, and see 187–9 below. Cf. WIPO, *Model Provisions on Protection Against Unfair Competition*, Art. 2(2)(vi).

[25] See Chapter 7.

3 Statutory and extra-legal remedies

Anglo-Australian courts have not protected intangible elements of value under any wide generalisation, but under specific heads of protected interests.[1] The common law tort of passing off has proved to be the most useful vehicle in protecting economic interests in personality, though to a much greater extent in Australia than in England. The protection afforded by the statutory intellectual property regimes is patchy and incomplete, and, in the case of trade marks, depends on proactive steps being taken to register a mark.[2] In view of the costs involved, this is only worthwhile if there is a significant existing or future merchandising business. Nevertheless, some protection is better than none and the usefulness of trade mark registrations and copyright protection should not be underestimated from a practical standpoint, not least for the reason that they provide something reasonably concrete which may be licensed or assigned to third parties. In the absence of a valid action in passing off, copyright and registered trade marks, however limited in scope, might be the only licensable subject matter.[3] Thus, the relatively limited role that statutory intellectual property rights play in protecting interests of personality is outlined, before considering the common law causes of action. The following sections focus on English law, since space precludes a detailed comparative survey.[4]

---

[1] *Victoria Park Racing and Recreation Grounds Co. Ltd* v. *Taylor* (1937) 58 CLR 479 *per* Dixon J.

[2] See, e.g., *Mercury Communications Ltd* v. *Mercury Interactive (UK)* [1995] FSR 850 at 863–4 *per* Laddie J on the advantages of trade mark registration.

[3] See also 72–97 below (nature of the licensing connection for passing off).

[4] See, generally, M. Henry (ed.), *International Privacy, Publicity and Personality Laws* (London, 2001); J. Adams, *Character Merchandising* (London, 1996), 245–6, 237–45, 272–6; H. G. Richard, *Canadian Trade Marks Act Annotated* (Toronto, 1991–2000), 12–4; R. T. Hughes, *Hughes on Trade Marks* (Toronto, 1999), §24; J. Olsen and S. Maniatis (eds.), *Trade Marks: World Law and Practice* (London, 1998); J. Lahore, *Patents, Trade Marks and Related Rights, Vol. I* (Sydney, 1996), 54, 155; J. T. McCarthy, *McCarthy on Trade Marks and Unfair Competition*, 4th edn (St Paul, Minn., 1999), Ch. 13.

Copyright

Copyright protection extends to the categories of works set out in the Copyright Designs and Patents Act 1988.[5] Thus, copyright may subsist in a photograph or drawing of a person where the photograph or drawing is an original artistic work.[6] However, the first ownership of the copyright vests in the author of the work, the artist or the photographer, or, where the photograph is taken or drawing is made in the course of employment, the employer.[7] The subject of a drawing or photograph will not enjoy copyright.[8] Infringement of an artistic work will extend to making a three-dimensional copy of a two-dimensional work and vice versa,[9] although proving infringement of a drawing might be difficult and is a matter of fact in each case.[10] Ownership of copyright in a sound recording will vest in the producer[11] and copyright in a film will vest in the producer and the principal director.[12] Therefore copyright will provide limited scope for an action to prevent the unauthorised use of a person's voice by that person himself, for example where an actor's voice from a film is exploited.[13]

The Copyright Designs and Patents Act 1988 allows a limited right of privacy to a person who, for private and domestic purposes, commissions the taking of a photograph or the making of a film. By virtue of section 85, the commissioner is entitled to prevent copies of the photograph being issued to the public, the work from being exhibited or shown in public, or broadcast or included in a cable programme service, subject to some exceptions, such as the incidental inclusion of the photographs or films in another copyright work, and acts done under statutory authority.[14] This provision is not so much a matter of principle but a

---

[5] See, generally, K. Garnett, J. Rayner James and G. Davies, *Copinger and Skone James on Copyright*, 14th edn (London, 1999), 54 et seq.

[6] Copyright Designs and Patents Act (CDPA) 1988, s. 1 and s. 4.

[7] *Ibid.*, ss. 9–11.

[8] See, e.g., *Lyngstad* v. *Anabas Products Ltd* [1977] FSR 62, 65 (unauthorised merchandisers had legitimately obtained copyright in the photographs of the plaintiff pop group Abba from an independent studio). See also *Gould Estate* v. *Stoddart Publishing Co.* (1998) 80 CPR (3d) 161, 168–70 (Ontario Court of Appeal) (subject of photographs and literary material in magazine article had no proprietary interests in the absence of an agreement to the contrary).

[9] CDPA 1988, s. 17(3).

[10] See, e.g., *Merchandising Corporation of America Inc.* v. *Harpbond Ltd* [1983] FSR 32 (portrait of plaintiff not infringement of a sketch and facial make-up could not constitute an artistic work in the form of a painting).

[11] CDPA 1988, s. 9(2)(aa).

[12] CDPA 1988, s. 9(2)(ab). See, generally, Garnett, Rayner James and Davies, *Copinger*, 240–4.

[13] It may be protected by performers' rights: see text below.

[14] CDPA 1988, s. 85(2).

34   The commercial appropriation of personality

consequence of the change in first ownership of copyright in the 1988 Act. Under the Copyright Act 1956, section 4, the commissioner of the photograph was the first owner, and was consequently able to control any unauthorised exploitation of the copyright work. The shifting of first ownership from the commissioner to the author made it necessary to provide the commissioner with a limited right of privacy to maintain the same position as under the 1956 Act.[15] In practice, the circumstances where a person commissions a photograph are limited, typical examples being wedding photographs and videos, or formal portraits.[16] Indeed, the state of photographic art has evolved considerably since the time when a person had to sit formally to have his photograph taken, which would usually have involved commissioning the services of a professional photographer.[17]

New artists and performers will seek the maximum publicity for the minimum expense and are often unwilling or unable to insist on control of the manner in which their images are exploited. Ownership of copyright in such cases is to some extent subject to private contractual arrangement and although it is practically impossible to prevent having one's photograph taken without one's consent, some protection may be grounded on copyright.

Performers' rights

A degree of protection may also be secured by means of performers' rights,[18] particularly where the performer does not own copyright in the material being performed (the work might be in the public domain or

[15] An unsuccessful attempt was made to expand these limited provisions: see Photographs and Films (Unauthorised Use) Bill 1994. For the Lords debates see *Hansard, Fifth Series*, HL, vol. 552, cols. 919–30, 28 February 1994; *Hansard, Fifth Series*, HL, vol. 553, cols. 74–84, 18 March 1994; *Hansard, Fifth Series*, HL, vol. 554, cols. 1625–36, 11 May 1994.

[16] See, e.g., *Williams* v. *Settle* [1960] 2 All ER 806. Cf. *Lady Anne Tennant* v. *Associated Newspapers Group Ltd* [1979] FSR 298 (plaintiff, Lady in Waiting to Princess Margaret, able to obtain damages for copyright infringement following defendants' publication of a picture of the Princess dressed as Mae West at private party; copyright vested in the plaintiff who had taken the pictures, which had subsequently been taken from her possession by her son and sold by a third party to the *Daily Mail*).

[17] See S. Warren and L. Brandeis, 'The Right to Privacy' (1890) 4 HarvLRev 193, 211, arguing that whereas, previously, the law of contract could provide a person with sufficient means of controlling the commercial exploitation of his photograph, changing technological and social conditions entailed resort to the law of tort. See 146–50 below.

[18] See, generally, R. Arnold, *Performers' Rights*, 2nd edn (London, 1997). For comparative references see, e.g., H. G. Richard and L. Carrière, *Canadian Copyright Act Annotated* (Scarborough, Ont., 1993) (looseleaf), 14.01–1; J. Lahore, *Copyright and Designs* (Sydney, 1996), 54,041 et seq.

the copyright is owned by another person).[19] Rights in performances subsist in qualifying[20] live performances given by one or more individuals, which extend to: dramatic performances (which include dance and mime); musical performances; readings or recitations of literary works; and performances of variety acts or similar presentations.[21] Thus, the dramatic performance of an actor, dancer or mime artist may be protected regardless of whether the individual concerned enjoys rights in any underlying work; indeed, it does not seem that a dramatic performance needs to be a performance of any specific work and an improvised dramatic performance may qualify for protection.[22] Musical performances, not necessarily limited to performances of a particular work, and thus including improvised performances, may also be protected. Given that the link between the subject matter of an advertisement and the product or service being advertised is often extremely tenuous, it is not difficult to imagine an advertisement featuring performances by street artists or buskers which may thus be protected. Similarly, a recitation of a literary work by an actor or celebrity may be protected, even though the person reciting the work does not own copyright in the literary work or sound recording. Performances of variety acts may also be a relevant category, although many variety acts will come within the scope of dramatic performances.[23] Sporting performances generally fall outside the categories set out in section 180(2) of the 1988 Act, although some sports such as ballroom dancing and ice skating might be categorised as forms of dance for the purposes of s. 180(2)(a). It is arguable that since improvised performances may be protected, protection should logically extend to sportsmen who might be regarded as performers who improvise within the constraints imposed by the rules of a particular sport and, on one view, only snobbery prevents a sportsman from being treated in the same way as an opera singer.[24]

Performers' rights extend to the fixation and live broadcasting or cable transmission of live performances; the public performance and broadcasting or cable transmission by means of a recording made without consent; dealings in illicit recordings; and to equitable remuneration for exploitation of a sound recording.[25] Furthermore, rights to reproduction,

---

[19] See, e.g., *Mad Hat Music Ltd* v. *Pulse 8 Records Ltd* [1993] EMLR 172; *Bassey* v. *Icon Entertainment Plc* [1995] EMLR 596.

[20] CDPA 1988, s. 181.   [21] CDPA 1988, s. 180(2).

[22] See R. Arnold, *Performers' Rights*, 42.   [23] *Ibid.*, 45.

[24] *Ibid.*, 46 and 39. See also V. Pasek, 'Performers' Rights in Sport: Where Does Copyright Stand?' (1990) 8 CW 13, esp. 15; 'Performers' Rights in Sport: The Experts Comment' (1990) 9 CW 12.

[25] CDPA 1988, ss. 182–4.

36   The commercial appropriation of personality

distribution, rental and lending in the form of assignable property rights also subsist, which are actionable in the same way as copyright.[26]

Registered trade marks

Nature and functions

It will be helpful to set out some of the functions of trade marks and the way they relate to commercial exploitation of personality, for the purposes of both the present discussion and the discussion in the ensuing chapters. From a very early time traders recognised the potential which lay in using the names and images of famous persons to distinguish their wares from those of their rivals and the practice of using personalities as trading symbols flourishes today. How does this commercial practice square with the underlying functions of modern trade marks, both registered and unregistered?

Traditionally, trade marks were seen as serving to indicate the source, albeit anonymous,[27] of goods, and the English courts have historically accorded the greatest weight to this function.[28] It is also frequently contended that trade marks further serve to provide an indication or guarantee of quality on which consumers can, in practice, rely; although consumers may be indifferent as to the product's precise origin, they may well seek an assurance that a product is of a certain quality.[29] Such a guarantee is not an absolute legal guarantee since the manufacturer is at liberty to vary the quality, although this is usually against his own economic interests.[30] Thus, the origin function, broadly construed, encompasses

---

[26] CDPA 1988, s. 191I. See, generally, R. Arnold, *Performers' Rights*, Ch. 4.

[27] See, e.g., *Powell* v. *Birmingham Vinegar Brewery Co. Ltd* (1896) 13 RPC 235, 250; *Re McDowell's Application* (1926) 43 RPC 313, 337.

[28] See *Wagamama Ltd* v. *City Centre Restaurants Plc* [1995] FSR 713, 730; *Scandecor Development AB* v. *Scandecor Marketing AB* [2001] ETMR 800, 808; *Philips Electronics BV* v. *Remington Consumer Products* [1998] RPC 283, 300; *BACH and BACH FLOWER REMEDIES Trade Marks* [2000] RPC 513, 533. See also *British Sugar Plc* v. *James Robertson and Sons* [1996] RPC 283, 298 *per* Jacob J, going so far as to suggest that indication of origin is the sole purpose which permeates the Directive and the Trade Marks Act 1994.

[29] See, e.g., *SA CNL-Sucal NV* v. *HAG GF AG* [1990] 3 CMLR 571, 583; *IHT Internationale Heiztechnik* v. *Ideal Standard* [1994] 3 CMLR 857, 877; *Deutsche Renault AG* v. *Audi AG* [1995] 1 CMLR 461, 475; *Canon Kabushiki Kaisha* v. *MGM Inc.* [1999] ETMR 1, 8.

[30] *SA CNL-Sucal NV* v. *HAG GF AG* [1990] 3 CMLR 571, 583; *Scandecor Development AB* v. *Scandecor Marketing AB* [2001] ETMR 800, 809; *Glaxo Group and Others* v. *Dowelhurst Ltd (No. 2)* [2000] FSR 529, 540. Cf. Parks, '"Naked" Is Not a Four-Letter Word: Debunking the Myth of the "Quality Control Requirement" in Trade Mark Licensing' (1992) 82 TMR 531, esp. 535–45. See also E. Hanak, 'The Quality Assurance Function of Trademarks' (1975) 65 TMR 318; L. Akazaki, 'Source Theory and Guarantee Theory in Anglo-American Trade Mark Policy: A Critical Legal Study' (1990) 72 JSPTO 255.

Statutory and extra-legal remedies

both the source of the product and its key qualities which allow it to be differentiated from rival products.[31] More important, for present purposes, is the protection which is increasingly claimed for the value of a trade mark as an advertising or merchandising symbol.[32] Rather than being seen as an indication of origin, either in its strict sense, or in a broader sense encompassing quality guarantee or product differentiation functions, the mark is regarded as a 'silent salesman',[33] triggering an association between the consumer and the goods or services and seeking to sell such goods or services, or, more controversially, seeking to sell itself. Such an approach does not rely on the notion of consumer confusion relating to a product's source or quality but seeks to protect the mark's marketing power.[34] Rather than rewarding the manufacturer with protection for consistently producing goods of a certain quality,[35] it sanctions legal protection for the investment in the promotion of a product,[36] and, as such, borders on protection against misappropriation.[37]

Consider a practical example where a pre-prepared packaged meal, for retail, bears the name and picture of a well-known chef. Only the very naive would assume that the meal has been prepared by the celebrity chef himself and has originated from his kitchen, or is somehow manufactured by that chef himself. On the other hand, his name and image clearly serve to differentiate that particular product from those of rival manufacturers,

---

[31] See, e.g., *Parfums Christian Dior SA* v. *Evora BV* [1998] RPC 166, 180 *per* Jacobs AG, citing W. R. Cornish, *Intellectual Property*, 3rd edn (London, 1996), 529. See also *Loendersloot* v. *Ballantine & Son Ltd* [1998] FSR 544, 552–3; *Sabel BV* v. *Puma AG, Rudolf Dassler Sport* [1998] RPC 199, 209.

[32] See F. Schechter, 'The Rational Basis of Trademark Protection' (1927) 40 Harv L Rev 813, and see also T. Martino, *Trademark Dilution* (Oxford, 1996), esp. 72–8; M. Strasser, 'The Rational Basis of Trademark Protection Revisited: Putting the Dilution Doctrine into Context' 10 Fordham Intell Prop Media & Ent LJ 375, 389–90 (2000).

[33] Schechter, 'Rational Basis', 818.

[34] Cf. *Philips Electronics NV* v. *Remington Consumer Products Ltd* [2001] RPC 745, 753 (ECJ) *per* Colomer AJ, drawing a distinction between, on the one hand, a trade mark, which seeks to protect the identity of the origin of goods, thereby indirectly protecting the goodwill which the goods attract, and, on the other hand, designs and patents which seek to protect the economic value in the goods themselves which derives from a particular design or technical performance.

[35] See note 29 above.

[36] See *Parfums Christian Dior SA* v. *Evora BV* [1998] RPC 166, 180. Jacobs AG (*ibid.*, 180–1) seems to adopt a rather narrow and somewhat sceptical view of the advertising or investment functions, stating that 'those functions seem to me to be merely derivatives of the origin function: there would be little purpose in advertising a mark if it were not for the function of that mark as an indicator of origin, distinguishing the trade mark owner's goods from those of his competitors. In my view, therefore, even if other facets of trade marks might require protection in certain circumstances, the court's emphasis on the origin function of trade marks was, and remains, an appropriate starting point for the interpretation of Community law relating to trade marks.' Cf. *BMW AG and BMW Nederland BV* v. *Deenik* [1999] ETMR 339, 354.

[37] See A. Kamperman Sanders, *Unfair Competition Law* (Oxford, 1997), 107–8.

and might attract a purchaser's attention in a way in which a particular brand name, or particular style of packaging, might fail to do. Some consumers may regard the appearance of the name and image of the celebrity chef as an indication or guarantee that the food is of a certain quality. Alternatively, the appearance of the name and image of the celebrity chef may simply function as an advertising device with consumers placing no reliance on its appearance, as either an indication of origin or a guarantee of the product's quality. Take another common example, where the name and image of a famous pop star appears on a T-shirt, or other item of merchandise. Here the use of the name and image serves a slightly different purpose; it does not necessarily serve to indicate the precise source of manufacture or precise identity of the manufacturer, indeed the purchaser may be indifferent to these matters. Some purchasers may take the appearance of the celebrity's name and image as an indication that he has authorised the use of his image. Some might also assume that such authorisation is an effective guarantee of the quality of the merchandise. Others might be indifferent as to whether or not the T-shirt has been authorised, and would not take such authorisation as a guarantee of quality; they simply wish to purchase a T-shirt bearing the name or image of their favourite celebrity, and might be indifferent as to its source or quality. Whatever reliance is placed on these different factors by different consumers, what is clear is that the name and image of the celebrity can serve a de facto merchandising function, selling itself rather than any particular goods, a function that is slightly different from the advertising function. Such a merchandising function is quite considerably removed from the orthodox functions of trade marks.

The registrability of names

Such are the underlying bases for trade mark protection. To what extent can indicia of personality, particularly personal names, be registered as trade marks? Personal names are not a special category of trade mark, as such. The Trade Marks Act 1994 prohibits the registration of a sign which consists of or contains various Royal arms and flags, a representation of any member of the Royal Family, or any words, letters or devices likely to suggest Royal patronage or authorisation.[38] However, no particular privilege extends to others and an applicant need not seek a person's express permission before seeking to register his or her name as a trade mark, although, according to registry practice, an objection will be made on the grounds of bad faith, unless the applicant can show

[38] Trade Marks Act (TMA) 1994, s. 4.

Statutory and extra-legal remedies 39

that the application is made with the consent of the person concerned, or his legal representatives.[39] Section 1 of the Trade Marks Act 1994 defines a trade mark as 'any sign capable of being represented graphically which is capable of distinguishing goods or services of one undertaking from those of other undertakings' and expressly includes personal names within this definition. Any mark is prima facie registrable as long as it is capable of being represented graphically, and is capable of distinguishing goods or services of one undertaking from those of another,[40] provided, inter alia, that it is not devoid of distinctive character, one of the absolute grounds for refusal of registration.[41] When assessing whether a surname possesses that capacity at the date of application, it is necessary to bear in mind that surnames 'are naturally adapted to identify all individuals so named', although, in relation to ordinary or commonplace surnames, evidence of acquired distinctiveness often takes time to develop.[42]

The English courts' reluctance to allow broad rights in indicia of identity through trade marks legislation can be seen in *ELVIS PRESLEY Trade Marks*,[43] one of the last cases to be decided under the Trade Marks Act 1938. The central issue was whether the names 'Elvis', 'Elvis Presley' and a signature mark 'Elvis A. Presley' were capable of distinguishing the goods of the applicants, Elvis Presley Enterprises Inc., the successors in title to Elvis Presley's merchandising business. The applications were opposed by Mr Sid Shaw, who had been trading in Elvis Presley memorabilia through a company using the trade mark 'Elvisly Yours', registered in respect of a wide range of goods relating to Elvis.

Under sections 9 and 10 of the Trade Marks Act 1938, the applicant had to satisfy positive requirements of distinctiveness and show that the mark was either 'adapted to distinguish' or 'capable of distinguishing' its goods or services for registration in Part A or Part B of the register respectively. A more descriptive mark will have lower inherent distinctiveness and will be less likely to distinguish the applicant's goods from those

---

[39] Trade Marks Registry Work Manual (1998; see http://www.patent.gov.uk), Ch. 6, para 9.11.2. Cf. the Canadian Trade Marks Act, RSC 1985, c. T-13, s. 9(1)(k)–(l), prohibiting the registration of 'any matter that may falsely suggest a connection with any living individual' and 'the portrait or signature of any individual who is living or has died within the preceding thirty years'.

[40] See *Philips Electronics NV* v. *Remington Consumer Products Ltd* [2001] RPC 745, 754 (ECJ); cf. *Philips Electronics NV* v. *Remington Consumer Products Ltd* [1999] RPC 809, 818 (CA). See also *BACH and BACH FLOWER REMEDIES Trade Marks* [2000] RPC 513, 524; *AD2000 Trade Mark* [1997] RPC 168, 171, and see, generally, D. Kitchin *et al.*, *Kerly's Law of Trade Marks and Trade Names*, 13th edn (London, 2001), Ch. 2.

[41] TMA 1994, s. 3(1)(b). See *Philips Electronics NV* v. *Remington Products Ltd* [1999] RPC 809, 818; *AD2000 Trade Mark* [1997] RPC 168, 173; *British Sugar Plc* v. *James Robertson & Sons Ltd* [1996] RPC 281, 305.

[42] *Re Mister Long Trade Mark* [1999] ETMR 406, 410.

[43] [1999] RPC 567.

40   The commercial appropriation of personality

of other traders. Relying on the decision in the *TARZAN Trade Mark* case,[44] where the name 'Tarzan' was denied registration on the basis that it referred directly to the subject matter of the goods, it was held that the marks 'Elvis' and 'Elvis Presley' described goods relating to Elvis Presley, and were not distinctive of the connection between the goods and the applicants' business.[45] Robert Walker LJ applied the well-known test set out by Lord Parker in *Registrar of Trade Marks* v. *Du Cros (W&G) Ltd*: whether the mark itself is likely to become distinctive of the applicant's goods, which depends, in large part, on the question whether 'other traders are likely, in the ordinary course of their business and without any improper motive, to desire to use the same mark, or some mark nearly resembling it, upon or in connection with their own goods'.[46] Although the signature mark was held to be distinctive under section 9(1)(b), it could not be said that there was no reasonable likelihood of deception or confusion being caused to a substantial number of members of the public, between the applicants' mark, and the opponent's earlier mark 'Elvisly Yours', written in a similar cursive script.[47] Accordingly, registration was refused.

The arguments that the *TARZAN* decision should be limited to its facts (a fictitious character whose name had once been an invented word) and that rival traders could not legitimately wish to use the names 'Elvis' and 'Elvis Presley' according to the *Du Cros (W&G)* test[48] were rejected.[49] Similarly, the Court of Appeal rejected an argument that a general rule had evolved[50] preventing a trader from making unauthorised use of a celebrity's name in order to sell his own goods on the basis that use of a celebrity's name implied a licence or endorsement and that, as a corollary, the applicants' marks could not result in deception or confusion for the purposes of sections 11 and 12 since they were regarded as successors in title to the deceased celebrity's merchandising rights.[51] It was held that there was no universal public assumption that the use of a name in such circumstances would be regarded as having been licensed or franchised. Such a view represented an over-simplification of the authorities and was inconsistent with the principle that each case must be decided on its own

---

[44] [1970] RPC 450.   [45] [1999] RPC 567, 578.   [46] *Ibid.*, 579.

[47] *Ibid.*, 567, 586, applying the test set out in *Pianotist Co.'s Application* (1906) 23 RPC 774 and *Smith, Hayden & Co.'s Application* (1946) 63 RPC 97. Morritt LJ dismissed the appeal in respect of the signature mark on the basis that there was no evidence as to its genuineness: [1999] RPC 567, 592.

[48] *Registrar of Trade Marks* v. *Du Cros (W&G) Ltd* [1913] AC 624.

[49] [1999] RPC 567, 583.

[50] From a line of cases culminating in the decision in *Mirage Studios* v. *Counter-Feat Clothing Co. Ltd* [1991] FSR 145. See 73–84 below.

[51] *Ibid.*, 583–4.

facts.[52] The applicants had failed to educate the public that the names 'Elvis' and 'Elvis Presley' were being used by them and their licensees in a trade mark sense.[53]

This approach has been followed in Registry cases decided under the Trade Marks Act 1994. Thus, in *Executrices of the Estate of Diana, Princess of Wales' Application*,[54] an application to register the mark 'Diana, Princess of Wales' for a wide range of goods and services was rejected. In the absence of any right of personality, Diana, Princess of Wales did not own any rights in her name, as such. While personal names might readily be taken to denote a particular trade source, this was not necessarily the case where a famous name was concerned, where use of the name might merely identify the subject matter of the goods. The evidence did not show that consumers would expect all commemorative articles bearing the Princess's name to have been produced and sold under the control of a single undertaking responsible for their quality. In this respect, the claim of the Estate was weakened by the fact that other signs such as an official logo and hallmark had been used on goods to indicate their authorisation, which suggested that the name alone was not capable of indicating the relevant trade connection.[55] Similarly, in *JANE AUSTEN Trade Mark*,[56] an application to register the name 'Jane Austen' in respect of toiletries and similar goods was rejected, following opposition proceedings by the trustees to the Jane Austen Memorial Trust, which were purportedly brought to protect the dignity and reputation of Jane Austen as a literary figure rather than to protect the Trust's own economic interests.[57] It was successfully argued that the mark was devoid of distinctive character under section 3(1)(b) of the Trade Marks Act 1994. Given the extent of Jane Austen's fame, the name could only be seen by the public as indicating the subject matter of the goods, rather than their source. A further objection that the application had been made in bad faith, based on section 3(6) TMA 1994, was rejected; there was no general presumption that it was inappropriate to register the name of a historical literary figure as a trade mark and the goods with which the registration was concerned would not damage Jane Austen's standing as an author or her literary heritage.[58]

---

[52] *Ibid.*, 597, *per* Simon Brown LJ.   [53] *Ibid.*, 584 *per* Robert Walker LJ.
[54] [2001] ETMR 254.
[55] *Ibid.*, 271, and see B. Isaac, 'Merchandising or Fundraising?: Trade Marks and the Diana, Princess of Wales Memorial Fund' [1998] EIPR 441. See, also, C. Waelde, 'Commercialising the Personality of the Late Diana, Princess of Wales – Censorship by the Back Door?' in N. Dawson and A. Firth (eds.) *Perspectives on Intellectual Property, Vol. VII: Trade Marks Retrospective* (London, 2000), 211.
[56] [2000] RPC 879.   [57] *Ibid.*, 891.   [58] *Ibid.*, 890–1.

42   The commercial appropriation of personality

The approach adopted under the English courts and UK Registry reflects a fairly orthodox view of the underlying nature and functions of registered trade marks. Where a mark is sufficiently distinctive and serves to distinguish the applicant's goods from those of rival traders, registration will be available. What is clear is the reluctance of the court to widen the scope of trade mark registrability to provide protection for the merchandising value of a mark or symbol.

In approaching the issue of distinctiveness, the UK Trade Marks Registry starts from the premise that words which are surnames will not be registrable prima facie unless it is likely that they will be taken as signs identifying goods from a single source, having regard to: the commonness of the surname; the size of the market; and the nature of the goods.[59] Beyond that, a (somewhat arbitrary) general guiding rule of convenience provides that if there is a frequency greater than 100 entries in the London telephone directory, the mark will be regarded as common. However, more common surnames may be capable of distinguishing goods or services where the goods or services originate from a limited number of traders (for example, airline services) since the fewer the sources of origin, the greater the likelihood that a surname will, if used recurrently, distinguish the goods or services of a particular undertaking.[60] A surname with initials is regarded as having a slightly higher capacity to distinguish and may be accepted even if the surname is more common, with regard to the general (100 entry) rule.[61] Full names, and combinations of two or more surnames or two or more forenames may be accepted prima facie on the basis that they have a greater capacity to distinguish goods from a single source, since it is unlikely that rival traders would legitimately wish to use such a combination.[62] While a single forename may be accepted prima facie for goods, Registry practice provides for an objection to single forenames as trade marks for certain services (Class 42: food and drink, hygienic and beauty care, etc.) in the absence of evidence of distinctiveness, on the basis that such names are frequently used for businesses such as hairdressers and restaurants and it would be inappropriate to grant nationwide rights in respect of such services, without evidence of distinctiveness.[63] Beyond these guideline figures, evidence that a name has acquired distinctiveness through use will be required and the more common the name, the greater the evidence required.[64] These criteria

[59] Trade Marks Registry Work Manual (1998), Ch. 6, para 3.12.1, as amended by Practice Amendment Circular 6/00 (reprinted in (2000) 29 *CIPA Journal*, 278).
[60] *Ibid.*   [61] *Ibid.*, 3.12.5.   [62] *Ibid.*, 3.12.8.   [63] *Ibid.*, 3.12.6.
[64] For examples of cases decided under previous legislation, see, e.g., *Teofani & Co. Ltd* v. *Teofani* [1913] 2 Ch 545 and *Re Burford (H.G.) & Co. Ltd's Application* [1919] 2 Ch 28, and see, generally, T. A. Blanco White and R. Jacob, *Kerly's Law of Trade Marks and Trade Names*, 12th edn (London, 1986), 8-53–8-54.

Statutory and extra-legal remedies 43

are considerably more relaxed than the relevant figures which applied under the previous Act.[65]

Clearly, it will be easier to register an unusual name since a common name such as Smith or Jones will be devoid of distinctive character. Consequently, those blessed with an unusual and distinctive name will have no difficulty in securing registration. Although the late guitarist Frank Zappa did not have a problem in establishing distinctiveness,[66] fellow musicians Brian Jones (or his estate) or Robert Smith might have greater problems. Similarly, footballer Mark Jones would have greater problems in establishing distinctiveness than fellow footballer Jurgen Klinsmann.[67] Although it may be possible for a celebrity with a more common name to establish that the name has acquired distinctiveness through use, in many cases use in the course of trade will be limited, particularly in the early stages of setting up a merchandising programme. In this respect, trade mark registration will clearly not be a means of securing monopoly rights in a name *in vacuo*. Each trade mark application must include a statement of the goods or services in relation to which registration is sought,[68] and a statement that the trade mark is being used in relation to those goods or services by the applicant himself, or with his consent, or that he has a bona fide intention that the trade marks should be so used.[69] Failure to fulfil this requirement might result in a refusal to register on the grounds that the application was made in bad faith.[70] Moreover, the trade mark is liable to be revoked if it has not been used within a period of five years by or with the consent of the owner of the trade mark, or if any use has been suspended for a period of five years without proper reason.[71]

Signatures, portraits and other indicia

In some cases, indicia other than names, such as an individual's signature, may be registered as a trade mark, although registration only secures rights in the form that the signature is represented, and not the name itself.[72] Signature marks are relatively common in the fields of sports and fashion, particularly on sporting equipment and clothing, although they

[65] See *CIBA Trade Mark* [1983] RPC 75, 86.   [66] See, e.g., UK Registration 1123495.
[67] See, e.g., UK Registration 1586827.
[68] TMA 1994 s. 32(2)(c). The classes of goods for which registration may be sought are set out in the Trade Marks Rules 1994, schedule 4. See generally, Adams, *Character Merchandising*, 77.
[69] TMA 1994 s. 32(3).   [70] *Ibid.*, s. 3(6).
[71] *Ibid.*, s. 46(1). See, generally, *Nestle UK Ltd* v. *Zeta Espacial SA* [2000] ETMR 226.
[72] It is doubtful whether copyright may subsist in a person's signature: see *ANNE FRANK Trade Mark* [1998] RPC 379 (Trade Marks Registry) (no copyright in signature for purposes of invalidity proceedings based on earlier right under s. 47 Trade Marks Act 1994).

44 The commercial appropriation of personality

are usually used in conjunction with a name or device mark, since the signature alone, in the absence of considerable education of the public, will rarely identify the goods as being those of a particular manufacturer. Thus, from a practical standpoint, a signature trade mark may, by itself, be of limited value. Although it may be said that a signature is prima facie distinctive of the person who signs it,[73] this is not inevitably so. At one extreme, and probably most common, are signatures which consist of a unique and highly distorted way of representing the author's name, while at the other extreme a person may adopt a signature which might be indistinguishable from the printed form of the name. While Laddie J at first instance in *ELVIS PRESLEY Trade Marks* held that the signature mark in question fell into the latter category, the majority of the Court of Appeal held that it was sufficiently distinctive, although registration was refused on the basis that it conflicted with the opponent's previously registered mark.[74]

A portrait of a person may also be a distinctive sign which is capable of distinguishing the goods or services of one undertaking from those of another.[75] Registration will be of a particular image which constitutes a distinctive sign,[76] rather than an image as such and the value of such a trade mark registration may be severely limited by the narrow scope for infringement of such a mark, even within the fairly generous infringement provisions under the 1994 Act. According to the practice of the UK Registry, as with personal names, an objection will be made on the grounds of bad faith where the mark consists of or includes the portrait of a living or recently deceased person (but only where that person is 'well-known') in the absence of the written consent of that person or his representatives.[77]

Scope of infringement of registered marks

The Trade Marks Act 1994 contains considerably broader infringement provisions than its predecessor, which, in part, explains the courts'

---

[73] *Re Fanfold Ltd's Application* (1928) RPC 199, 203.

[74] [1999] RPC 567, 586–7 *per* Robert Walker LJ and 596 *per* Simon Brown LJ. Morritt LJ (590–2) decided against the applicant on the basis that the authenticity of the signature had not been established and that it did not serve to distinguish the applicant's goods in a trade mark sense. Cf. *BACH and BACH FLOWER REMEDIES Trade Marks* [1999] RPC 1, 43–5 (stylised representation of signature allowed registration subject to disclaimer of the word 'Bach').

[75] See, e.g., *Rowland* v. *Mitchell* [1897] 1 Ch 71, for an example under previous legislation, and see, generally, Blanco White and Jacob, *Kerly on Trade Marks*, 12th edn, 8–58.

[76] See, e.g., UK Registration 2036489 (close-up portrait of racing driver Damon Hill in racing helmet).

[77] See Trade Marks Registry Work Manual (1998), Ch. 6, para. 9.11.3. Cf. note 39 above.

Statutory and extra-legal remedies 45

cautious approach to the question of what may be registered.[78] According to the balance of authorities, it is not necessary that the defendant's use of a sign in the course of trade be use as a trade mark in order to infringe.[79] Thus, a defendant must look to the express exceptions to the scope of an infringement action, such as 'the use of indications concerning the kind, quality, quantity, intended purpose, value, geographical origin, the time of production of goods or of rendering of services, or other characteristics of goods or services'.[80] The alternative view that there must be use as a trade mark in a way which indicates trade origin would take many uses in merchandising outside the ambit of trade mark infringement. Thus, where a particular sign used on a product is not perceived to be an indication of origin, but is seen merely as a decoration for the product or as a 'badge of support, loyalty or affiliation',[81] there would be no infringement. The authorities on this point are somewhat unsettled and await a definitive ruling from the European Court of Justice,[82] which has not, thus far, addressed the issue.[83]

Limited guidance can be found on the scope of infringement of registered trade marks specifically concerning signatures, personal names or portraits, and the question of infringement generally is 'more a matter of feel than science'.[84] To take the simplest example, where there is identity in terms of the mark and goods,[85] then there will be no problem in establishing infringement. Thus where an identical name, signature or portrait mark is used on identical goods, infringement will be made out. Minor differences, such as a slightly different script or portrait, will arguably make the mark fall outside these provisions. In respect of a word mark, an application for registration is treated as being limited to the graphical form shown in the application, unless the applicant includes a statement that the application is for registration of the word without regard to its graphical form,[86] and a similarly narrow approach might be expected in relation to the infringement provisions under the Act.[87]

---

[78] See *ELVIS PRESLEY Trade Marks* [1997] RPC 543 at 559 *per* Laddie J, and see, generally, Kitchin *et al.*, *Kerly's Law of Trade Marks*, Ch. 13.

[79] *British Sugar Plc* v. *James Robertson & Sons Ltd* [1996] RPC 281, 290; *Philips Electronics NV* v. *Remington Consumer Products Ltd* [1999] RPC 809, 823.

[80] TMA 1994, s. 11(2). See, e.g., *Bravado Merchandising Services Ltd* v. *Mainstream Publishing (Edinburgh) Ltd* [1996] FSR 205.

[81] *Arsenal Football Club Plc* v. *Reed* [2001] ETMR 860, 880.   [82] *Ibid.*

[83] See *Philips Electronics NV* v. *Remington Consumer Products Ltd* [2001] RPC 745 (ECJ).

[84] *Wagamama Ltd* v. *City Centre Restaurants Plc* [1995] FSR 713, 732 *per* Laddie J.

[85] TMA 1994, s. 10(1).

[86] Trade Marks (Amendment) Rules 1998, r. 5, para. 4 (SI 1998/925).

[87] Cf. *Bravado Merchandising Services Ltd* v. *Mainstream Publishing (Edinburgh) Ltd* [1996] FSR 205, 209 (marks held to be identical despite differences in typeface from registered mark).

46   The commercial appropriation of personality

In practice, most cases will fall under section 10(2), which provides for infringement where the marks are identical and the goods or services are similar, or where the marks are similar and the goods or services are identical, and there exists a likelihood of confusion, assessed globally, which includes within such notion the likelihood of association.[88] In assessing the similarity of marks, the court must determine the degree of visual, aural or conceptual similarity and, where appropriate, evaluate the importance to be attached to those different elements, taking account of the category of goods or services in question and the circumstances in which they are marketed and having regard to imperfect recollection or picture of the mark.[89] This is when the limited value of trade mark registrations for portrait and signature marks, in particular, becomes evident. A signature, by definition, is a unique form of representing one's personal name. Dissimilarity of a fairly minor nature will arguably render the later mark incapable of being regarded as confusingly similar to the registered mark. Thus, the same name, written in a sufficiently different style would not infringe the registered signature mark.[90] Similarly with portrait marks the registration only extends to a particular representation of an image, rather than an image as such. Lack of similarity will again be a problem and it will be difficult to establish confusion. To take an earlier example, if a celebrity chef's portrait is represented in a different manner, or a slightly different portrait is used, there will obviously be no identity of marks and establishing confusing similarity may well be difficult. Use of a name which is similar, rather than identical, to a registered mark is unlikely to arise, since in most cases of appropriation of personality the aim is to take advantage of the commercially beneficial associations of a (celebrity) name, although some forms of advertising proceed by more subtle allusion to a name, or nickname, of a celebrity. In such cases, the similarity of the marks will fall to be assessed generally. Beyond these two situations, infringement may also be established where the mark is identical or similar and is used on goods or services dissimilar to those for which it is registered, where the mark has a reputation in the United Kingdom and use of the mark without cause takes unfair

---

[88] *Marca Mode CV* v. *Adidas AG* [2000] All ER (EC) 694; *Canon Kabushiki Kaisha* v. *MGM Inc.* [1999] ETMR 1; *Sabel BV* v. *Puma AG, Rudolf Dassler Sport* [1998] RPC 199.

[89] *Lloyd Schuhfabrik Meyer & Co. GmbH* v. *Klijsen Handel BV* [2000] FSR 77, 84 (ECJ); *REACT Trade Mark* [2000] RPC 285, 288 (Appointed Person). See also *Wagamama Ltd* v. *City Centre Restaurants Plc* [1995] FSR 713, 720, and see, generally, C. Morcom, A. Roughton and J. Graham, *The Modern Law of Trade Marks* (London, 1999), 115–8.

[90] Cf. *Crawford and Son* v. *Bernard and Co.* (1894) 11 RPC 580 (Court of Session) (no infringement of signature mark 'Daniel Crawford' by respondent's own signature 'Robert Crawford' for Scotch whisky).

Statutory and extra-legal remedies 47

advantage of, or is detrimental to, the distinctive character or the repute of the mark.[91] Again, the main problem will lie in establishing identity or similarity of the marks before the issues of reputation and unfair advantage or detriment to the distinctive character or repute of the mark can be considered.[92]

In some cases, the registration of a personal name may become so distinctive of a particular business that its subsequent use by the individual concerned might be restrained. For example, under previous legislation, the owners of the trade mark 'Bentley' for motor cars were able to restrain their former designer W. O. Bentley and rival car maker Lagonda from using the name 'Bentley' in a confusingly similar manner which, on the facts, did not amount to the bona fide use of his own name as a designer, where the words 'Lagonda' and 'Bentley' were given much greater prominence than the rest of the advertisement text.[93] Clearly, this is a factor to be borne in mind when considering any dealings with the registered marks.

Economic interests in personality comprise of existing trading interests and latent recognition values.[94] Trade mark registration will only be relevant to the former category, comprising of a relatively small number of people who are actually trading in their image by exploiting it themselves or by granting licences to others. The fact that registration must be sought in the first instance, and that such a process of registration is relatively time-consuming and expensive obviously limits the scope of trade mark law in addressing cases of appropriation of personality. The reluctance of the English courts to allow trade mark registration to be used as a vehicle for protecting economic interests in personality compounds the inherent limitations of what may be registered as trade marks, and the relatively narrow scope for infringement of those rights.

---

[91] TMA 1994, s. 10(3).

[92] See *General Motors Corp.* v. *Yplon SA* [1999] ETMR 122, 129–33; *British Telecommunications Plc and Others* v. *One in a Million Ltd* [1999] FSR 1, 25; *C. A. Sheimer (M) Sdn Bhd's Trade Mark Application* [2000] RPC 484, 503 (Appointed Person); *CORGI Trade Mark* [1999] RPC 549, 557–9 (Appointed Person); and see also A. Michaels, 'Confusion in and About Sections 5(3) and 10(3) of the Trade Marks Act 1994' [2000] EIPR 335.

[93] *Bentley Motors (1931) Ltd* v. *Lagonda Ltd and Bentley* (1947) 64 RPC 33. See, also, *BARRY ARTIST Trade Mark* [1978] RPC 703 (Registry) (fashion designer's application to register his signature in respect of clothing was refused on the basis that it would be confusingly similar to a prior registration of the same mark by a company from which the applicant had subsequently departed, although that did not prevent him from using his signature in his capacity as a designer as opposed to its use on actual finished goods).

[94] See 8–10 above.

48 The commercial appropriation of personality

Extra-legal remedies

Introduction

While English law has denied a substantive remedy for commercial appropriation of personality as such, various codes of practice in the advertising industry provide norms which operate as a form of 'soft law'.[95] These norms have not been reflected in the substantive law, although they will become increasingly important, since the courts are expressly obliged to have regard, inter alia, to any relevant privacy code in exercising the balance between freedom of expression and other rights under the Human Rights Act 1998.[96] A new set of international norms is being established in respect of internet domain names, considered briefly below.

The Independent Television Commission Code

Television advertising in the United Kingdom is regulated by the Independent Television Commission (ITC), a statutory body set up under the Broadcasting Act 1990, section 9.[97] Television advertisements are subject to formal pre-transmission approval and clearance by the Broadcast Advertising Clearance Centre (BACC), an organisation set up and funded by the broadcasters themselves. Thus, any potentially infringing advertisements are dealt with at an earlier stage than is the case with press advertisements.[98] The ITC has a power under the Act to compel licensed television providers (terrestrial and satellite commercial broadcasters) to exclude certain advertisements which breach the various ITC codes. The relevant provisions, for present purposes, are contained in the Code of Advertising Standards and Practice. Under the heading 'Protection of privacy and exploitation of the individual', it is provided that there should be no portrayal of, or reference to, individual living persons without their permission excepting non-offensive or non-defamatory advertisements for books, films, magazines, etc., which feature the person referred to in the advertisement. The BACC guidelines provide that unauthorised reference to individuals is construed widely and extends to impersonations and caricatures of well-known persons, regardless of whether there is any likelihood of viewers or listeners being confused as to the identity of the person featured; wherever the parody

---

[95] I. Ramsay, *Advertising, Culture and the Law* (London, 1996), 152.
[96] Section 12(4). See, generally, 218–24 below.
[97] See http://www.itc.org.uk. The content of television programmes is subject to a separate statutory scheme, which forms one of the piecemeal statutory recognitions of privacy, examined in Chapter 8.
[98] See text below.

clearly identifies an individual, permission must be sought.[99] It is also provided that testimonials (expressions of view or statements of experience of a real person) should be genuine and supported by documentary evidence before being accepted by the broadcasters, and should not be used in a manner which is likely to mislead. This is aimed at protecting viewers' interests, rather than the privacy or economic interests of those featured.[100]

The Press Complaints Commission

The Press Complaints Commission[101] is an independent body set up to consider and adjudicate complaints relating to the editorial content of newspapers and magazines.[102] It protects both the rights of individuals and the public's right to know.[103] The Code of Practice[104] covers sixteen discrete topics, although most complaints relate to the accuracy of newspaper content (around two-thirds annually) followed by infringements of privacy (around one complaint in six).[105] Clause 3 of the Code provides that '(i) everyone is entitled to respect for his or her private and family life, home, health and correspondence. A publication will be expected to justify intrusions into any individual's private life without consent.' Further, cl. 3 specifically states that 'the use of long lens photography to take pictures of people in private places without their consent is unacceptable', with 'private places' being defined as places 'where there is a reasonable expectation of privacy'. According to the Commission, there are areas open to the public where people may be considered to have a reasonable expectation of privacy and, equally, places which are privately owned where an individual would not have such an expectation. Thus, there was a reasonable expectation of privacy where a celebrity was photographed inside a cathedral,[106] but not where an actor was photographed outside a hotel, although the public or private status of the property was a matter of dispute.[107]

---

[99] Independent Television Commission, *Code of Advertising Standards and Practice*, December 1998, r. 15.

[100] *Ibid.*, r. 29.

[101] See http://www.pcc.org.uk, and see, generally, L. Blom-Cooper and L. R. Pruitt, 'Privacy Jurisprudence of the Press Complaints Commission' (1994) 23 Anglo. AmLR 133; R. Pinker, 'Human Rights and Self Regulation of the Press' (1999) 4 Comms L 51; C. Munro, 'Self-Regulation in the Media' [1997] PL 6.

[102] On the availability of judicial review, see *R* v. *Press Complaints Commission, ex parte Stewart-Brady* [1997] EMLR 185, 189.

[103] See *Douglas* v. *Hello! Ltd* [2001] 2 WLR 992, 1018 *per* Brooke LJ.

[104] Press Complaints Commission, *Code of Practice* (London, 1999).

[105] See the annual reports, reproduced at http://www.pcc.org.uk.

[106] Complaint by Sir Paul McCartney, Report 43, 30 May 1998.

[107] Complaint on behalf of Sean Connery, Report 47, 25 April 1999.

50   The commercial appropriation of personality

These provisions are subject to exceptions which may be in the public interest which include '[d]etecting or exposing crime or a serious misdemeanour; protecting public health and safety and preventing the public from being misled by some statement or action of an individual or organisation'.[108] Freedom of expression is explicitly mentioned as being in the public interest, and the Commission states that it will have regard to the 'extent to which material has, or is about to, become available to the public'. In any case where the public interest is invoked a full explanation is required of the editor concerned, demonstrating how the public interest was served, with a higher burden imposed in cases involving children. Thus, for example, the publication of a photograph of a prisoner in an article commenting on an operational decision by prison authorities was held to be of legitimate public interest,[109] unlike the publication of details of an actress's sex life.[110] Many of the complaints relating to privacy come from individuals with no obvious public profile rather than celebrities, which partly reflects the speed and low cost of the complaints process,[111] and the fact that the (mainly tabloid) press often intrudes into the lives of quite ordinary people.

The Advertising Standards Authority Code

Press advertisements are regulated by the British Code of Advertising Practice,[112] administered by the Advertising Standards Authority,[113] a private body set up by the advertising industry to regulate its own affairs,[114] and the workings of the Code provide an insight into the kind of conduct which is dealt with outside or on the margins of English law. The Code does not define an advertisement but lists the communications and material to which it applies: most non-broadcast media such as newspapers, magazines, posters, cinema and video commercials and mailing lists. The most important exceptions include broadcast media, covered by the ITC Code (see text above), the contents of books, and packages and wrappers, the latter being a potentially fruitful medium for unauthorised merchandisers.[115]

---

[108] See, e.g., complaint by Stephen Billington, Report 43, 23 August 1998.
[109] Complaint by Beverley Fielden, Report 53, 29 August 2000.
[110] Complaint by Granada Television on behalf of Ms Georgia Taylor, Report 51, 18 June 2000.
[111] See Pinker, 'Human Rights and Self Regulation', 52.
[112] *British Code of Advertising Practice*, 10th edn (London, 1999).
[113] See http://www.asa.org.uk.
[114] See, generally, G. Crown, *Advertising Law and Regulation* (London, 1998), 474–578; G. Robertson and A. G. L. Nicol, *Media Law*, 3rd edn (London, 1992), 559–61.
[115] *Code of Advertising Practice*, paras. 1.1–1.2.

Statutory and extra-legal remedies

The British Code of Advertising Practice expressly states that it does not have the force of law[116] and an advertiser contravening the Code will be asked to withdraw or amend the advertisement,[117] although a voluntary undertaking is often given and honoured. In the case of non-compliance, advertisers will usually be denied advertising space by duly notified media organisations and may be subject to adverse publicity following a finding of a breach of the Code.[118] The Code also emphasises the publishers' prerogative to refuse to accept an advertisement for publication regardless of whether it might conform to the provisions of the Code, although this depends on the views of individual publishers.[119] If a misleading advertisement or promotion continues to appear after the Advertising Standards Authority has ruled against it, the matter can be referred to the Director General of Fair Trading, who can seek an undertaking from anyone responsible for commissioning, preparing or disseminating it that it will be discontinued. Failing that, an injunction can be sought to prevent further publication.[120] The decisions of the ASA are subject to judicial review,[121] although this is rarely exercised.[122]

Under the heading 'protection of privacy', the current Code provides that 'advertisers should not unfairly portray or refer to people in an adverse or offensive way'. The Code urges advertisers to obtain written permission before (i) referring to or portraying members of the public or their identifiable possessions, excepting incidental inclusions such as crowd scenes; (ii) referring to people with a public profile although references that accurately reflect the contents of books, articles or films may be acceptable without prior permission;[123] and (iii) 'implying personal approval of the advertised product'. The Code goes on to state that prior permission may not be needed when the advertisement contains nothing that is inconsistent with the positions or views of the person featured.[124] This is somewhat perplexing and can only be taken to refer to some objective standard in determining what might be inconsistent with the positions or views of the subject. Clearly the provision would cover a straightforward case such as where a well-known temperance campaigner's image

---

[116] *Ibid.*, para. 1.3. [117] *Ibid.*, para. 68.6.
[118] *Ibid.*, para. 68.39. [119] *Ibid.*, para. 68.28.
[120] Control of Misleading Advertisements Regulations 1988, SI 1988, No. 915 as amended (SI 1995, No. 1537).
[121] *R* v. *Advertising Standards Authority ex parte the Insurance Service Plc* (1990) 2 Admin LR 77.
[122] See, generally, Crown, *Advertising Law*, 476, and see, e.g., *R.* v. *Advertising Standards Authority, ex parte SmithKline Beecham Plc* [2001] EMLR 598.
[123] *Code of Advertising Practice*, para. 13.1. [124] *Ibid.*, para. 13.2.

52 The commercial appropriation of personality

is used in connection with alcoholic products. However, a person might object to the unauthorised exploitation of his image for highly subjective reasons, due to an aversion to a particular kind of product or business, or stemming from a simple desire not to be associated with any kind of commercial advertising; beliefs or opinions which might not be generally well known. References to the deceased are required to be made with particular care to avoid offence or distress under the Code,[125] while 'members of the Royal Family should not normally be shown or mentioned in advertisements without their prior permission' excluding incidental references unconnected with the advertised product or references to biographical materials such as books, articles or films.[126] Use of the Royal arms and emblems should only be made with prior permission.[127] Apart from the privacy provisions, the Code provides that testimonials and endorsements should be genuine and should only be used with the express written permission of those giving them.[128]

Previous editions of the Code placed rather more emphasis on protecting economic interests, although complaints from those occupying positions in trades or professions which necessarily entail a high degree of public exposure could only be entertained when the effect of the advertisement was 'to substantially diminish or to abrogate their right to control the circumstances or terms upon which their name, likeness, or reputation was used on a commercial basis'.[129] This might, arguably, have applied to any unauthorised use, given that exclusivity is often an important factor in contracts concerning merchandising or endorsement and an exclusive licence will generally be much more valuable. It is not clear why the provisions on economic interests were omitted from the current edition, although they were rarely invoked. For example, in the period between 1989 and 1995, under the 8th edition of the Code, only one complaint, brought by footballer Paul Gascoigne in respect of an advertisement for insurance services, concerned the protection of essentially economic interests. Although it was held that the advertisement did not imply any endorsement of the advertisers' service, it was capable of diminishing or abrogating his right to control the circumstances or terms on which he might exploit his name, likeness or reputation on a commercial basis.[130] The other complaints related to what were essentially privacy interests. Thus, for example, a Member of Parliament's complaint regarding an advertising leaflet which falsely attributed a testimonial for a company providing roofing services (which had in fact

---

[125] *Ibid.*, para. 13.3.   [126] *Ibid.*, para. 13.4.
[127] *Ibid.*, para. 13.5.   [128] *Ibid.*, para. 14.
[129] *British Code of Advertising Practice*, 8th edn (London, 1988), para. 17.3.
[130] ASA Monthly Report 10, March 1992.

Statutory and extra-legal remedies 53

been unsatisfactory) was upheld.[131] Similarly, a complaint regarding a national press advertisement for anti-perspirant, featuring a photograph of the President of the National Union of Mineworkers, accompanied by the caption 'for when you're really sweating', was held to be grossly offensive in view of the impending outcome of an investigation into handling of Union funds. Such gratuitous use for an unrelated advertising purpose was held to be highly distasteful, even though public figures could not expect the same degree of privacy as private individuals.[132]

The relatively small number of complaints concerning invasion of privacy brought under the Code each year suggests that there is little danger of a flood of litigation engulfing the courts, should a tort of appropriation of personality be recognised. There are obvious limits to the scope of such a code of practice, given the limited range of media to which it applies and the increasingly slender foundations of voluntary self-regulation on which any such scheme rests.[133] Nevertheless, from a practical standpoint, there is something desirable in a self-regulatory system which provides some degree of protection for privacy while also providing a means of alternative dispute resolution which avoids the costs and delay of the courts.[134]

The Uniform Domain Name Dispute Resolution Policy

The unauthorised use of internet domain names is a widespread phenomenon which is not confined to the names of businesses and extends to the names of individuals. While an action may be available in the tort of passing off,[135] most disputes concerning personal names have been resolved through extra-legal dispute resolution procedures. Domain name registrations are administered by a number of organisations, which usually allocate registrations on a first-come, first-served basis, and do not confer any intellectual property rights in the name; the arrangement between the authority and the registrant is contractual.[136] For example, in the United Kingdom, the domain name registrar Nominet UK Ltd

---

[131] ASA Case Report 185, September 1990. Cf. ASA Case Report 192, April 1991 (use of football manager's photograph in connection with airline services held not to suggest any endorsement and was not inconsistent with his status as a public figure).

[132] ASA Case Report 187, November 1990.

[133] See, e.g., R. Rijkens and G. E. Miracle, *European Regulation of Advertising* (Oxford, 1986), 41–3, summarising arguments for and against a system of self-regulation in advertising. The self-regulatory role of the press in relation to privacy and related issues is constantly challenged as inadequate: see Ch. 8 below at 238–41.

[134] See M. Arden, 'The Future of the Law of Privacy' (1998–9) 9 KCLJ 1, 18.

[135] See *British Telecommunications Plc & Others* v. *One in a Million Ltd* [1999] FSR 1.

[136] See, generally, Kitchin *et al.*, *Kerly's Law of Trade Marks*, Ch. 21.

54   The commercial appropriation of personality

(a company limited by guarantee) operates its own dispute resolution policy. This has replaced an earlier and more limited policy and has been modelled, in part, on the Uniform Domain Name Dispute Resolution Policy, although there are significant differences.[137]

The Uniform Domain Name Resolution Policy (UDRP; 24 October 1999)[138] has been adopted by the Internet Corporation for Assigned Names and Numbers (ICANN) (a non-profit corporation). The policy is incorporated by reference in registration agreements used by all accredited domain name registrars for generic top-level domain names (initially those ending in .com, .net, .org, and now the new additions: .aero, .biz, .coop, .info, .museum, .name, .pro).[139] It has also been adopted by certain managers of country-code top-level domains. The procedures are intended to provide a cheap and speedy resolution for bad faith and abusive registrations of domain names. Disputes are referred to an independent administrative panel, composed of between 1 and 3 arbitrators, appointed from a list of over 120 drawn from 30 countries, to administer the dispute in accordance with the ICANN policy and rules. The most popular dispute resolution mechanisms are administered by the World Intellectual Property Organisation[140] and the Disputes.org/eResolution.ca Consortium.[141] Panel decisions are not subject to any system of binding precedent. There is no choice of law provision and, under the rules, a panel must decide a complaint on the basis of, inter alia, 'any rules and principles of law that it deems applicable',[142] and tends to apply the law of the parties' country of origin. While such authority is influential, it is not, however, binding. The remedies available to successful complainants are limited to an order that the disputed domain name(s) be transferred to the complainant or cancelled. There is no power to make a monetary award or an order for costs.

The administrative procedures are mandatory where a third party claims that the registered domain name is: (i) identical or confusingly similar to a trademark or service mark in which the complainant has rights;

---

[137] See http://www.nominet.org.uk. See D. Osborne and T. Willoughby, 'Nominet's New Dispute Resolution Procedure – They CANN Too!' (2001) 6 Comms L 95. For an analysis of the previous policy see D. Osborne, 'Domain Names, Registration and Dispute Resolution and Recent UK Cases' [1997] EIPR 644.
[138] See http://www.icann.org.
[139] See, generally, J. M. Gitchel, 'Domain Name Dispute Policy Provides Hope to Parties Confronting Cybersquatters' (2000) JPTOS 611; R. Chandrani, 'ICANN Now Others Can' [2000] Ent LR 39; S. Jones, 'A Child's First Steps: The First Six Months of Operation – The ICANN Dispute Resolution Procedure for Bad Faith Registration of Domain Names' [2001] EIPR 66; D. Curley, 'Cybersquatters Evicted: Protecting Names Under the UDRP' [2001] Ent LR 91.
[140] See http://www.wipo.org.   [141] See http://www.disputes.org.
[142] Rules for Uniform Domain Name Dispute Resolution Policy, r. 15(a).

Statutory and extra-legal remedies

and (ii) the registrant has no rights or legitimate interests in respect of the domain name; and (iii) the domain name has been registered and is being used in bad faith. The complainant must prove that each of these three elements are present.[143] The UDRP provides a non-exhaustive definition of bad faith, where it can be established that registration was (i) primarily for the purpose of 'selling, renting, or otherwise transferring the domain name registration' to the complainant or a competitor, for consideration in excess of actual costs directly related to the domain name; (ii) to prevent the owner of the trade mark or service mark from using the mark in a corresponding domain name, provided a pattern of such conduct can be established; (iii) primarily for the purpose of disrupting the business of a competitor; (iv) to attract, for commercial gain, internet users by creating a likelihood of confusion with the complainant's mark as to source, sponsorship, affiliation or endorsement.[144]

The procedure has allowed a number of well-known individuals to secure a transfer of domain names consisting of their personal names. In *Winterson* v. *Hogarth*[145] a well-known author, Jeanette Winterson, was able to secure a transfer of the top-level domain names (ending in .com, .org and .net) which the respondent had registered with a view to selling them by auction. Since both parties were resident in the United Kingdom the Panel considered the relevant decisions of the English courts,[146] holding that the rules did not require that the trade mark be registered.[147] While the decision of the English Court of Appeal in *ELVIS PRESLEY Trade Marks*[148] was noted, it was not regarded as determining the question whether common law rights could subsist in an individual name under English law.[149] In applying English law, the Panel took the view that the complainant would have a valid cause of action in passing off to prevent the use of her name and was satisfied that the respondent had not used the domain names in good faith. A transfer of the relevant domain names to the complainant was ordered.

However, in *Springsteen* v. *Burgar*[150] the majority of the Panel questioned whether the previous decisions[151] established the principle that the names of very well-known celebrities could acquire the necessary distinctive secondary meaning which would give rise to rights equating to

---

[143] Uniform Dispute Resolution Policy, para. 4(a).

[144] *Ibid.*, para. 4(b).   [145] WIPO Case No. D2000-0235.   [146] See note 142 above.

[147] See, also, *Roberts* v. *Boyd*, WIPO Case No. D2000-0210; *Adu p/k/a Sade* v. *Quantum Computer Services Inc.*, WIPO Case No. D2000-0794.

[148] See note 43 above.

[149] *Winterson* v. *Hogarth*, WIPO Case No. D2000-0235, para. 6.8.

[150] WIPO Case No. D2000-1532.

[151] *Winterson* v. *Hogarth*, WIPO Case No. D2000-0235; *Roberts* v. *Boyd*, WIPO Case No. D2000-0210; *Adu p/k/a Sade* v. *Quantum Computer Services Inc.*, WIPO Case No. D2000-0794.

56 The commercial appropriation of personality

unregistered trade marks. The majority also took the view that previous Panels had concluded too readily that the mere registration of the name as a domain name, and other names of a similar nature, constituted an attempt to prevent the legitimate owner of registered or common law trade mark rights from obtaining a 'corresponding domain name'. This, according to the majority, effectively placed the burden of proof on the registrant in establishing good faith, rather than on the complainant in establishing bad faith. Although the registered domain name ('brucespringsteen.com') was identical to the complainant's unregistered mark, the majority held that the registrant had demonstrated that he had some rights or legitimate interests in respect of the domain name, and that the complainant had failed to establish that it was registered, and had been used, in bad faith. The registration did not prevent the complainant from using the mark in a corresponding domain name, for the purpose of para. 4(b)(ii) of the UDRP, since he had already registered the domain name 'brucespringsteen.net' for his official website. Neither could it be said, on the facts, that the registrant had registered the name 'primarily for the purpose of disrupting the business of a competitor' (UDRP para. 4(b)(iii)), nor had he 'intentionally attempted to attract other users to his website by creating a likelihood of confusion as to source, sponsorship, affiliation or endorsement' (UDRP para. 4(b)(iv)). It was 'relatively unlikely that any user would seek to go straight to the internet and open the site "brucespringsteen.com" in the optimistic hope of reaching the official Bruce Springsteen website'; internet users would 'not expect all sites bearing the names of celebrities or famous historical figures or politicians, to be authorised or in some way connected with the figures themselves'. Any attempt to curtail the internet's use as 'an instrument for purveying information, comment, and opinion on a wide range of issues and topics' should, according to the majority, be resisted.

Subsequent decisions have treated the criticisms in the *Springsteen*[152] decision as obiter and have affirmed that complainants may succeed on the basis of common law rights. As noted in *Brown* v. *Julie Brown Club* authors and performers can establish common law rights in the tort of passing off to protect their names as indicators of source, a form of unfair competition of the kind defined in the Paris Convention.[153] A defendant should not be allowed to supply goods or put on performances which the consuming public are led to believe consist of the author's work when they consist of a substitute.[154] Similarly, in *Barnes* v. *Old Barn Studios Ltd*

---

[152] Cf. *Monty and Pat Roberts, Inc.* v. *Keith*, WIPO Case No. D2000-0299.

[153] Paris Convention for the Protection of Industrial Property, Article 10 *bis* (see, generally, 27 above).

[154] *Brown* v. *Julie Brown Club*, WIPO Case No. D2000-1628.

Statutory and extra-legal remedies 57

it was noted both that the fact that a name may be difficult to register as a trade mark does not prevent it being a common law trade mark which may be protected by the tort of passing off and that the overwhelming preponderance of panel decisions regard common law marks as coming within the remit of the policy.[155] Thus, in a series of joined cases, a number of well-known authors were able to secure the transfer of domain names incorporating their personal names.[156]

The situation is rather more difficult where a registrant is not actually using the contested domain name to point to a web site. In such a case a complainant will find it more difficult to establish that mere registration of a name, without use on an active web site, amounts to bad faith since registration *and* use in bad faith are required.[157] However, panels have held, on the facts, that bad faith does not require a positive act on the part of the registrant and inactivity may, in certain circumstances, amount to bad faith,[158] although this might be seen as effectively placing the burden of proof on the registrant rather than the complainant.

Although an individual's personal name is usually distinctive, in some cases a *nom de plume* or stage name may be regarded as a non-distinctive common word in which trade mark rights cannot subsist, although such cases will be relatively rare. For example, in *Sumner, p/k/a Sting* v. *Urvan* the complainant failed to establish any trade mark rights in the name 'Sting', even though it was accepted that he was world-famous as a musician performing under that name.[159] Unlike the previous cases, the personal name concerned was also a common word in the English language, with a number of different meanings. Neither was there any evidence of bad faith which would have been necessary to establish a claim. Significantly, the Panel questioned whether the procedure should extend beyond trade marks and service marks to cover geographical indications or personality rights,[160] although subsequent panels have not expressed similar doubts.

The procedure has been invoked mainly by celebrities, who might be expected to have common law trade mark rights in their names. It has also been applied quite liberally in a small number of cases where complainants with a high public profile have been held to enjoy common law

---

[155] *Julian Barnes* v. *Old Barn Studios Ltd*, WIPO Case No. D2001-0121.
[156] See *ibid.*, and *De Bernieres* v. *Old Barn Studios Ltd*, WIPO Case No. D2001-0122; *Beevor* v. *Old Barn Studios Ltd*, WIPO Case No. D2001-0123; and see also *The Authors Guild Inc.* v. *Old Barn Studios Ltd*, e-Resolution Case No. AF-0582 a–i.
[157] Uniform Dispute Resolution Policy, para. 4(a).
[158] See *Authors Guild Inc.* v. *Old Barn Studios Ltd*, e-Resolution Case No. AF-0582 a–i and the decisions cited.
[159] WIPO Case No. D2000-0596.
[160] *Ibid.*, citing *Report of the WIPO Internet Domain Name Process*, 30 April 1999.

58 The commercial appropriation of personality

rights on limited evidence that the name has been used as a mark in commerce. Thus, for example, a high-profile investment banker, financial adviser and political fundraiser was able to secure a transfer of a domain name using his name.[161] It is unclear to what extent a remedy will be open to private individuals with no registered trade mark rights and nothing akin to goodwill in respect of some business, trade or profession which might form the subject matter of common law trade mark rights.[162] Ultimately, the question whether a name has a sufficiently distinctive character and whether there has been bad faith use are questions of fact.[163] This reflects the position in determining whether goodwill may subsist in a name at common law for the purposes of the tort of passing off, an area where the English and Australian authorities, at least, are somewhat unsettled. This is considered in the next chapter.[164] As the UDRP expands to cover new top-level domains, it remains to be seen to what extent the system will extend to cover new claims based on infringement of a personality right, rather than trade mark rights, against unauthorised commercial exploitation.[165]

---

[161] *Rattner* v. *BuyThisDomainName*, WIPO Case No. D2000-0402. Cf. *Tony Alessandra D/B/A Alessandra & Associates* v. *Inss and Allesandra's*, WIPO Case No. D2001-0619 (marketing consultant), and see World Intellectual Property Organisation, 'The Recognition of Rights and the Use of Names in the Internet Domain Name System: Interim Report of the Second WIPO Internet Domain Name Process' (Geneva, 12 April 2001), para. 177.

[162] See B. Isaac, 'Personal Names and the UDRP: A Warning to Authors and Celebrities' [2001] Ent LR 43, 52; D. Osborne, 'Don't Take My Name in Vain! ICANN Dispute Resolution Policy and Names of Individuals' (2000) 5 Comms L 127, 128. Cf. R. Chandrani, 'Cybersquatting – A New Right to Protect Individual Names in Cyberspace' [2000] Ent LR 171, 173.

[163] See, e.g., *Rattner* v. *BuyThisDomainName*, WIPO Case No. D2000-0402.

[164] See 61–71 below.

[165] See 'Interim Report of Second WIPO Domain Process', para. 185 et seq. Cf. G. E. Evans, 'Comment on the Terms of Reference and Procedure for the Second WIPO International Name Process' [2001] EIPR 61.

4   Goodwill in personality: the tort of passing off in English and Australian law

Introduction

At first glance, cases of appropriation of personality fit rather uneasily with the traditional notion of passing off. In its original, or classic, form the tort of passing off prevented a defendant from passing off his own goods as the plaintiff's goods,[1] although the basic formulation was gradually extended to cover misrepresentations that the plaintiff's goods were of a different class or of a different quality from what they actually were.[2] It also came to embrace cases 'where although the plaintiff and defendant were not competing traders in the same line of business, a false suggestion by the defendant that their businesses were connected with one another would damage the reputation, and thus the goodwill of the plaintiff's business'.[3] Thus a defendant was not entitled to carry on business in such a way as to lead the public to believe that he was carrying on the business of the plaintiff or that the defendant's business was connected with the plaintiff's business.[4] In more modern times the tort has been extended further to cover cases involving the misdescription of goods, or the misuse of a descriptive term, if a trader can show that he is a member of a class and that a particular word or name has become so distinctive of that class's products as to make their right to use the word or name, truthfully in describing their product, a valuable part of the goodwill of each trader in that class.[5]

These gradual extensions have, at various times, prompted speculation that a new and wider tort of unfair competition might be developing. For example, in *Vine Products & Co. Ltd* v. *Mackenzie & Co. Ltd*, Cross J stated that the decision in a previous case[6] had gone 'beyond the

---

[1] See, e.g., *Reddaway* v. *Banham* (1896) 13 RPC 429.
[2] *Spalding (A. G.) & Bros.* v. *Gamage (A. W.) Ltd* (1915) 32 RPC 273, 283–4.
[3] *Erven Warnink BV* v. *Townend & Sons (Hull) Ltd* [1979] AC 731, 741–2 *per* Lord Diplock.
[4] *The Clock Ltd* v. *The Clock House Hotel Ltd* (1936) 53 RPC 269, 275.
[5] *Erven Warnink BV* v. *Townend & Sons (Hull) Ltd* [1979] AC 731; *Chocosuisse Union Des Fabricants Suisses de Chocolat* v. *Cadbury Ltd* [1999] RPC 826 (CA).
[6] *Bollinger* v. *Costa Brava Wine Co. Ltd* [1960] RPC 16.

60   The commercial appropriation of personality

well-trodden paths of passing off and into the unmapped area of "unfair trading" or "unlawful competition"',[7] before going on to explain the decision as an example of the extended tort of passing off, rather than a new tort of unlawful competition.[8] The decision in *Erven Warnink* v. *Townend* prompted similar speculation,[9] although subsequent dicta have denied the existence of any all-embracing action, while acknowledging a more dynamic approach to legal protection against unfair trading. Characterising an act as unfair is not sufficient to make it actionable: the conduct must be brought within the parameters of the tort of passing off as set out by the House of Lords in *Erven Warnink*.[10] Even the most protean of torts[11] has fixed elements which limit its adaptability. The English courts have generally adhered to a fairly orthodox notion of passing off in cases of appropriation of personality, while their Australian counterparts have been far more willing to adapt the tort's central requirements to remedy cases of appropriation of personality. An analysis of the two approaches reveals considerable problems in stretching the tort to achieve these ends.

The essential elements of passing off

The starting point of any discussion of the modern tort of passing off is usually Lord Diplock's speech in *Erven Warnink* v. *Townend*, which set out five necessary (but not sufficient) elements which need to be present to create a valid cause of action: (i) a misrepresentation (ii) made by a trader in the course of trade, (iii) to prospective customers of his or ultimate consumers of goods or services supplied by him, (iv) which is calculated to injure the business or goodwill of another trader (in the sense that this is a reasonably foreseeable consequence) and (v) which causes actual damage to a business or goodwill of the trader by whom the action is brought or (in a *quia timet* action) will probably do so.[12] However, it is often preferable to analyse the key elements of the tort in terms of the 'classical trinity' of: '(i) a reputation (or goodwill) acquired by the plaintiff in his goods, name, mark etc. (ii) a misrepresentation by the defendant leading to confusion (or deception) causing (iii) damage to the plaintiff'.[13] In analysing the particular facts of a passing off action

---

[7] [1969] RPC 1, 23.   [8] *Ibid.*, 29.

[9] *Erven Warnink BV* v. *Townend & Sons (Hull) Ltd* [1979] AC 731. See, e.g., G. Dworkin, 'Unfair Competition: Is the Common Law Developing a New Tort?' [1979] EIPR 241.

[10] See *Mail Newspapers* v. *Insert Media (No. 2)* [1988] 2 All ER 420, 424 *per* Hoffmann J.

[11] *Erven Warnink BV* v. *Townend & Sons (Hull) Ltd* [1979] AC 731, 740 *per* Lord Diplock.

[12] *Ibid.*, 731, 742.

[13] *Consorzio del Prosciutto di Parma* v. *Marks & Spencer Plc* [1991] RPC 351, 368, following the remarks of Lord Oliver in *Reckitt & Colman Ltd* v. *Borden Inc.* [1990] 1 WLR 491, 499.

Goodwill in personality

it is usually advantageous to examine the three elements individually, even though they are often interactive and difficult to separate.[14] The contrasting approaches adopted by the English and Australian courts in interpreting the three key elements are analysed before considering the way in which the three elements interrelate.

Goodwill

Goodwill and reputation

Passing off protects the property in the business or goodwill likely to be injured by the defendant's misrepresentation.[15] The protected interest is a right of property in the plaintiff's business goodwill rather than in a particular mark or get-up in itself.[16] According to Lord Macnaghten's classic dictum in *IRC* v. *Muller & Co.'s Margarine Ltd*,[17] goodwill is 'the benefit and advantage of the good name, reputation and connection of a business. It is the attractive force which brings in custom.'[18] Indeed, goodwill seems to be inextricably linked to some form of business as Lord Macnaghten further stressed: '[g]oodwill has no independent existence. It cannot subsist by itself. It must be attached to a business. Destroy the business and the goodwill perishes with it, though elements remain which may perhaps be gathered up and revived again.'[19] Matters are complicated by the concurrent and seemingly alternative use of the term 'reputation' where some authorities state the need to show 'goodwill or reputation'.[20] The notion of 'reputation' is much wider than goodwill and, consequently, one that is easier to satisfy. The better view is that it is goodwill rather than a broader notion of reputation which the tort of passing off protects[21] and, as noted above, this goodwill is inevitably and

---

[14] *County Sound Plc* v. *Ocean Sound Ltd* [1991] FSR 367, 372.

[15] *Spalding (A. G.) & Bros.* v. *Gamage (A. W.) Ltd* (1915) 32 RPC 273 *per* Parker LJ cited with approval in *Reckitt & Colman Ltd* v. *Borden Inc.* [1990] 1 WLR 491, 510 *per* Lord Jauncey. See also *British Telecommunications Plc and Others* v. *One in a Million Ltd and Others* [1999] FSR 1, 10 *per* Aldous LJ.

[16] *Star Industrial Co. Ltd* v. *Yap Kwee Kor* [1976] FSR 256, 269 *per* Lord Diplock.

[17] [1901] AC 217.   [18] *Ibid.*, 223.   [19] *Ibid.*, 224.

[20] See, e.g., Nourse LJ in *Consorzio del Prosciutto di Parma* v. *Marks & Spencer Plc* [1991] RPC 351, 368. See, also, J. Drysdale and M. Silverleaf, *Passing Off Law and Practice*, 2nd edn (London, 1994), Ch. 3.

[21] *Anheuser Busch Inc.* v. *Budejovicky Budvar NP* [1984] FSR 413; *Nice and Safe Attitude Ltd* v. *Piers Flook* [1997] FSR 14, 20. See also *Athlete's Foot Marketing Associates Inc.* v. *Cobra Sports Ltd* [1980] RPC 343, 349 *per* Walton J, comparing the restrictive and expansive approaches to goodwill in, respectively, *A. Bernardin et Cie* v. *Pavilion Properties Ltd* [1967] RPC 581 and *Maxim's* v. *Dye* [1977] FSR 364. The Australian courts have gone further in recognising reputation, without actual trading goodwill in a particular jurisdiction, as sufficient: see, e.g., *Conagra Inc.* v. *McCain Foods (Aust) Pty Ltd* (1992) 23 IPR 193;

62   The commercial appropriation of personality

perhaps inextricably linked to a particular business. In *Anheuser Busch Inc.* v. *Budejovicky Budvar NP*,[22] Lord Oliver warned of the dangers of confusing 'goodwill which cannot exist in a vacuum, with mere reputation which may, no doubt, and frequently does, exist without any supporting local business, but which does not by itself constitute a property which the law protects'.[23]

A distinction also needs to be drawn between goodwill and reputation in the different sense of personal reputation, rather than commercial or trading reputation, although such a distinction is very difficult to draw, particularly when dealing with professional reputation, which is both an economic asset and an aspect of a person's dignity.[24] The protection given by the law to these interests differs markedly. Cases of libel, and some cases of slander, are actionable *per se*, without the need to show special damage.[25] On the other hand, while goodwill is universally regarded as a property right, passing off is not actionable in the absence of damage, or, in a *quia timet* action, the likelihood of damage. In cases involving statements which are damaging to personal or professional reputation the law will presume that some damage flows from the bare fact of infringement of a person's interests in reputation, whereas no such presumption is made in the case of misrepresentations; the plaintiff must show that damage to goodwill results, or is likely to result. The distinction between reputation and goodwill in this context will become clearer from an examination of the authorities in the text below.

Goodwill in professional, artistic or literary occupations

What will a plaintiff need to show in order to establish that he has goodwill, and to what extent does the plaintiff have to be engaged in a 'business' before he can be said to have goodwill? Put slightly differently, to what extent does the plaintiff have to be a trader? The courts have certainly held that a wide variety of people have standing to sue in passing off, and have allowed actions by plaintiffs who would not perhaps be 'traders'

Al Hayat Publishing Co. Ltd v. *Sokarno* (1996) 36 IPR 214; *Rumcoast Holdings Pty Ltd* v. *Prospero Publishing Pty Ltd* (1999) 48 IPR 75. By virtue of s. 56 of the Trade Marks Act 1994, in the absence of a business or goodwill in the United Kingdom a degree of protection may be provided where the mark is 'well-known', and an identical or similar mark is used in relation to identical or similar goods or services, where such use is likely to cause confusion. See, generally, C. Morcom, A. Roughton and J. Graham, *The Modern Law of Trade Marks* (London, 1999), 225–7.

[22] *Anheuser Busch Inc.* v. *Budejovicky Budvar NP* [1984] FSR 413.

[23] *Ibid.*, 470.

[24] Cf. the distinction between economic and dignitary interests, 8–12 above, and see, further, 250–2 below.

[25] See 251 below.

Goodwill in personality 63

in the ordinary or popular sense of the word. The notion of 'trade' has been widely interpreted and includes persons engaged in a professional, artistic or literary occupation.[26] In cases involving performers and writers the courts have accepted that a person might have goodwill in respect of his name for the purposes of bringing an action in passing off.[27] Thus, a children's writer's *nom de plume* could constitute part of the plaintiff's stock-in-trade as a writer where it had become identified with the plaintiff. While such protection might not extend to the misuse of a plaintiff's name as a private individual,[28] it would not seem to be limited to the misuse of a fancy name or *nom de plume*. Thus, a plaintiff should be able to bring an action in passing off to restrain an unauthorised use of his name, provided that he can show goodwill in respect of some business, trade or profession which might be damaged by the defendant's misrepresentation.[29] The early English authorities in this area are somewhat unclear and demand to be considered in some detail.

The early English authorities

In the earliest case, *Byron* v. *Johnston*,[30] the representatives of the poet Lord Byron (who was abroad at the time of the application) were granted an injunction to prevent the defendant from publishing a work in Lord Byron's name when it was not in fact his work. The report does not state on what grounds the injunction was granted, although the decision fits the pattern of the later passing off cases discussed above, where authors have been held to be entitled to injunctions provided they can show that they have goodwill and can satisfy the other elements of the tort. Subsequently, in *Routh* v. *Webster*,[31] an injunction was granted to prevent the unauthorised use of the plaintiff's name, where the defendants, the provisional directors of a joint stock company, had published prospectuses in which the plaintiff's name was used as that of a trustee of the

---

[26] *Kean* v. *McGivan* [1982] FSR 119. See also *British Diabetic Association* v. *Diabetic Society Ltd* [1995] 4 All ER 812, 819.

[27] *Landa* v. *Greenberg* (1908) 24 TLR 441. See also *Hines* v. *Winnick* (1947) 64 RPC 113 (plaintiff band conductor entitled to restrain from performing under his fancy name 'Dr Crock and his Crackpots'); *Modern Fiction* v. *Fawcett* (1949) 66 RPC 230 (author granted an injunction restraining the defendants from publishing under the pen name 'Ben Sarto'); *Forbes* v. *Kemsley Newspapers Ltd* (1951) 68 RPC 183 (plaintiff entitled to pen name 'Mary Delaney' in the absence of express or implied agreement that the name should belong to her employer).

[28] See *Landa* v. *Greenberg* (1908) 24 TLR 441 *per* Eve J.

[29] See, e.g., *Clark* v. *Associated Newspapers Ltd* [1998] 1 All ER 959 (false attribution of authorship of plaintiff author under the tort of passing off and s. 84 Copyright Designs and Patents Act 1988). As to the nature of the damage, see 97–107 below.

[30] (1816) 2 Mer 29 (35 Eng Rep 851).   [31] (1849) 10 Beav 561 (50 Eng Rep 698).

64   The commercial appropriation of personality

company. The plaintiff had not consented to be a trustee and feared that the defendants' use of his name might expose him to liability. In granting the injunction, Lord Langdale MR stated that the case should serve as a warning that the defendants could not make use of the names of other persons without their authority: 'What! Are they to be allowed to use the name of any person they please, representing him as responsible in their speculations and to involve him in all sorts of liabilities, and are they then to be allowed to escape the consequences by saying they have done it inadvertently? Certainly not.'[32] It has been persuasively argued that the decision in *Routh* v. *Webster* might well have been a result of the partnership and company law of that time.[33] The case preceded limited liability of the members of a company and the plaintiff would have been in the same position as a partner in terms of exposure to liability. Consequently, it is difficult to argue that it stands as authority for a general principle that the unauthorised use of a name will be restrained. It is equally difficult to determine whether the rule in *Routh* v. *Webster* is distinct from the tort of passing off. Where the plaintiff is a trader and has goodwill, the question is redundant since exposure to liability or the risk of such exposure is a recognised head of damage in passing off.[34] However, the limited rule in *Routh* v. *Webster* might remain relevant in the case of a private individual, who is not a trader, even in the widest sense of the word, which embraces those in professional, artistic and literary occupations,[35] when that individual is subjected to the risk of exposure to liability.

In a series of early cases involving professional surgeons the courts denied any legal remedy for the unauthorised use of a real person's name, illustrating both the restrictive early approach and the way in which the notion of goodwill merges with the notion of personal and professional reputation. An early and problematic authority is the decision in *Clark* v. *Freeman*[36] where the plaintiff, Sir James Clark, the Queen's physician, sought to prevent the defendants from selling their medicine as 'Sir J. Clarke's Consumption Pills' (*sic*). The plaintiff was well known to the medical profession and the public in general as a specialist in the treatment of consumptive diseases. The action was for libel. However, before the Common Law Procedure Act 1854 neither the courts of law nor the courts of equity could issue injunctions in cases of libel, since courts of equity could not hear cases of libel and since, prior to 1854, the courts

---

[32] *Ibid.* Followed in *Walter* v. *Ashton* [1902] 2 Ch 282.

[33] R. G. Howell, 'Is There an Historical Basis for the Appropriation of Personality Tort?' (1988) 4 IPJ 265.

[34] See C. Wadlow, *The Law of Passing Off*, 2nd edn (London, 1995), 144, and see, further, 101–2 below.

[35] See note 26 above.   [36] (1848) 11 Beav 112 (50 Eng Rep 759).

Goodwill in personality 65

of law could not issue injunctions at all.[37] At the time, the jurisdiction to grant an injunction could only be exercised by the Court of Chancery, which would only grant an injunction once the case had been put to a jury at common law.

In a somewhat confused and poorly reported judgment Lord Langdale MR stated that, although the publication might have been a serious injury to the plaintiff in libel, the correct proceeding was at common law, and it was not a matter which the Court of Chancery could decide.[38] The facts could not be likened to those of *Croft* v. *Day*,[39] an early passing off case, where the defendant attempted to pass off his own goods as those of another. Similarly, *Byron* v. *Johnston* (possibly an early passing off case, although the report is not entirely clear) and *Routh* v. *Webster* (better explained as an independent and very limited cause of action) were held not to apply. Nevertheless, Lord Langdale noted that '[i]f Sir James Clark had been in the habit of manufacturing and selling pills it would be very like the other cases in which the Court has interfered for the protection of property'.[40] This reasoning is somewhat inconsistent. The passage cited seems to indicate that the tort of passing off might be applicable, despite the fact that Lord Langdale had expressly rejected this proposition in an earlier passage. The passage cited is clearly inapplicable to the notion of a property right in personal or professional reputation, for the purposes of the law of defamation, since a cause of action in libel to protect such reputation does not depend on the plaintiff being able to show an injury to a trading or manufacturing interest. It is difficult to determine why Lord Langdale should speculate as to what the plaintiff's position might have been had he been trading or manufacturing medicines himself unless he contemplated the possibility of an action in the nature of passing off.

Later cases saw the courts reluctantly following *Clark* v. *Freeman*. In *Williams* v. *Hodge*[41] the plaintiff, another well-known surgeon, sought an interlocutory injunction to restrain the defendants from using his name in their trade catalogue for surgical instruments in such a way as to give the public the impression that one of the instruments was of the plaintiff's invention. The plaintiff had argued that it was contrary to the etiquette of the medical profession for a practitioner to hold himself out to the public as an inventor and that the defendant's action in putting his name to the surgical instrument in question would injure him and make him an

[37] See *Bonnard* v. *Perryman* [1891] 2 Ch 269, 283 *per* Coleridge CJ.
[38] (1848) 11 Beav 112, 117.
[39] (1843) 7 Beav 84 (49 ER 994). (The citation is missing from the report in *Clark* v. *Freeman*.)
[40] (1848) 11 Beav 112, 119.   [41] (1887) 4 TLR 175.

66   The commercial appropriation of personality

object of ridicule in his profession. It is not entirely clear on what basis the plaintiff sought the injunction. Counsel for the plaintiff argued that the defendant's untrue representations were calculated to injure the plaintiff in his business and came within *Massam* v. *Thorley's Cattle Food Co.*,[42] an early passing off case brought by the successors in title of Joseph Thorley, the inventor of the cattle food which bore his name, against a rival trader who traded under that name. The court dismissed the application for an interlocutory injunction, since it was bound by the authority of *Clark* v. *Freeman*, although Kay J stated that there had been a most unwarrantable use of the name of a man of great eminence in the medical profession, and that in his own view the defendants had no more right to use his name than to take his purse.[43] Had the matter been *res nova*, an injunction would have been allowed but in the event, the court felt bound by, and unable to depart from, *Clark* v. *Freeman*.

Prior to *Williams* v. *Hodge* the decision in *Clark* v. *Freeman* had been subject to criticism, although these critical dicta were not considered by the court in *Williams* v. *Hodge* itself. For example, in *Maxwell* v. *Hogg*[44] (concerning the right to the magazine title *Belgravia* rather than appropriation of personality), Lord Cairns stated that '[i]t always seemed to me that *Clark* v. *Freeman* might have been decided in favour of the Plaintiff, on the ground that he had a property in his own name'.[45] These decisions were cited in argument in the Court of Appeal in *Dockrell* v. *Dougall*,[46] where yet another well-known doctor, Morgan Dockrell, sought an injunction to restrain the use of his name in the defendant's advertisement for a remedy for gout. The plaintiff's claim for libel failed at first instance since the jury found on the facts that the defendant's statement was not libellous, and the appeal proceeded on the question whether the plaintiff had a property right in his name, an argument which was dismissed for want of authority. However, Vaughan Williams LJ went on to state, obiter, that the plaintiff might have had a cause of action if the plaintiff could have shown that he had suffered an injury to his 'property, business or profession',[47] although the jury had not found such damage. Thus, although the plaintiff failed on the facts, this dictum suggests that the Court might have contemplated an action in passing off, provided that the plaintiff could show an injury to his rights of property in his business or profession.

---

[42] (1880) 14 Ch D 748.   [43] *Ibid.*   [44] (1867) 16 LR 2 Ch App 307.
[45] *Ibid.*, 310. See also *Dixon* v. *Holden* (1869) 20 LT Rep 357, 358 *per* Malins VC. For a later disapproving dictum see *British Medical Association* v. *Marsh* (1931) 48 RPC 565, 574 *per* Maugham J.
[46] (1899) 15 TLR 333.   [47] *Ibid.*, 334.

Goodwill in personality

The modern English authorities

By the turn of the twentieth century the tort of passing off had developed a firmer theoretical foundation, expanding beyond misrepresentations that the goods of the defendant were those of the plaintiff, while the protected interest came to be identified as property in the goodwill of the plaintiff's business rather than the business as such.[48] Nevertheless, the notions of injury to personal reputation and injury to commercial goodwill continued to coincide in *Sim* v. *H. J. Heinz & Co. Ltd*,[49] where the well-known actor, Alastair Sim, sought an interlocutory injunction, based on libel and passing off, to restrain the defendants from simulating his distinctive voice in an advertisement. It was argued that a professional person such as an actor had a business or trade in his performances of dramatic or musical works in which goodwill subsisted. Such goodwill was a right of property akin to a right of property in the appearance and get-up of goods, which could be damaged by a misrepresentation leading to confusion amongst the public concerning his performances. The issues of fact to be determined in both the passing off and the libel actions were identical: identification and injury to reputation. Consequently, since an interlocutory injunction could not be granted in respect of the cause of action for libel, on the basis that the jurisdiction to grant an interlocutory injunction should only be exercised in the clearest of cases,[50] neither could an injunction be granted in respect of the claim for passing off. In the event McNair J did not need to decide the question of whether the plaintiff might have goodwill in respect of his voice for the purposes of bringing a passing off action, although he considered that it would be 'a grave defect in the law if it were possible for a party, for the purposes of commercial gain, to make use of the voice of another party without his consent'.[51] The decision was affirmed in the Court of Appeal, where Hodson LJ went slightly further and accepted that the plaintiff had an arguable case, although he questioned whether a person's voice, might, in truth, be regarded as his property, and whether there was anything in the nature of unfair competition in a common field.[52] While the first

[48] See *Spalding (A. G.) & Bros.* v. *Gamage (A. W.) Ltd* (1915) 32 RPC 273, and Wadlow, *Passing Off*, 27.

[49] [1959] 1 WLR 313.

[50] *Ibid.*, 316, citing *Bonnard* v. *Perryman* [1891] 2 Ch 269. The decision in *American Cyanamid Co.* v. *Ethicon Ltd* [1975] AC 396 does not seem to have affected this rule: see *Herbage* v. *Pressdram Ltd* [1984] 1 WLR 1160, 1162 *per* Griffiths LJ; *Khashoggi* v. *IPC Magazines Ltd* [1986] 1 WLR 1412, 1418 *per* Donaldson MR; *Kaye* v. *Robertson* [1991] FSR 62; and see, generally, A. M. Dugdale (ed.), *Clerk and Lindsell on Torts*, 18th edn (London, 2000), 1649.

[51] [1959] 1 WLR 313, 317.   [52] *Ibid.*, 319.

68   The commercial appropriation of personality

question invites rather abstract speculation as to whether such a new interest can be regarded as 'property',[53] the second question goes to the heart of the notion of misrepresentation, considered below. What is important for present purposes is that the notion that a person might have goodwill in respect of attributes of his personality, such as his voice, was not dismissed outright.

Nevertheless, an argument based on a similar notion was rejected in *Lyngstad* v. *Anabas Products*,[54] where the members of the Swedish pop group Abba sought to restrain the use of their names and pictures on unauthorised merchandise. The essence of the claim was that the plaintiffs, as entertainers, had built up a reputation which was associated in the public mind with their name and image, and that the defendants were exploiting that reputation for their own commercial purposes.[55] In dismissing the plaintiffs' claim Oliver J placed great significance on the absence of evidence that the plaintiffs carried on a business in the United Kingdom which might be confused with the business and goods of the defendant. The plaintiffs had not carried on any merchandising business in the country themselves, the only connection with a business in the United Kingdom being in respect of a licence for the use of their names and images on a jigsaw puzzle, granted to a third party by the group's record company rather than the group themselves, and which, in any event, had yet to come into effect at the time of the hearing.[56] Similarly, the notion that there was some proprietary right in the plaintiffs' names was dismissed as contrary to English authority. Moreover, the only possible inference from the evidence which the court was prepared to accept was that some members of the public might have thought that the plaintiffs had granted some form of licence for the use of their names, although Oliver J doubted whether there was any basis for such an inference, since, in his view, there was no general custom for such licences to be granted by pop singers and the evidence available suggested that this was not, indeed, the case.[57]

Failure on the part of a plaintiff to show significant existing business or trading activities can be problematic, particularly in interlocutory proceedings, which form the bulk of the reported English authorities in this area. The balance of convenience, according to the *American Cyanamid*[58] principles, will often be in the defendant's favour where the defendant

---

[53] See D. Lloyd, 'The Recognition of New Rights' [1961] CLP 39, and see, further, Chapter 10.
[54] [1977] FSR 62.   [55] *Ibid.*, 65.   [56] *Ibid.*, 64.
[57] *Ibid.*, 68. Cf. *Halliwell* v. *Panini* (Unreported, High Court, Chancery Division, 6 June 1997) where the plaintiff pop group had a significant merchandising business.
[58] *American Cyanamid Co.* v. *Ethicon Ltd* [1975] AC 396.

Goodwill in personality 69

has significant trading goodwill which may be damaged by the grant of an injunction. Moreover, if the plaintiff's interest is in a subsidiary licensing business, that is, a purely economic interest, a further factor against the plaintiff is the fact that damages would be an adequate remedy at trial.[59] Like most actions in this area, much will depend on the facts of each case.

Goodwill in personality in Australia

The restrictive approach adopted by the English courts may be contrasted with the more expansive course taken by the Australian courts, initiated in *Henderson* v. *Radio Corporation Pty Ltd*,[60] where the plaintiffs, a pair of professional ballroom dancers, were able to restrain the unauthorised use of their likenesses on the cover of a record. Evatt CJ stated that, although the remedy in passing off was necessarily only available where the parties were engaged in business, that expression would be used 'in its widest sense to include professions and callings'.[61] Manning J elaborated, stating that the development in advertising practices had 'opened up a new field of gainful employment for many persons, who, by reason not only of their sporting, but of their social, artistic, and other activities, which have attracted notoriety, have found themselves in a position to earn substantial sums of money by lending their recommendation or sponsorship to an almost infinite variety of commodities'.[62] Subsequently, plaintiffs who have been able to demonstrate goodwill for the purposes of passing off actions have included an actor,[63] a professional horse rider,[64] a pop group[65] and a television presenter.[66]

Summary

Economic interests in personality fall into two broad categories: existing trading interests and latent recognition values.[67] Some celebrities actively trade in their image, by exploiting it themselves or granting licences to

---

[59] See, e.g., *Halliwell* v. *Panini* (Unreported, High Court, Chancery Division, 6 June 1997).
[60] [1969] RPC 218. [61] *Ibid.*, 234. [62] *Ibid.*, 243.
[63] *Pacific Dunlop Ltd* v. *Hogan* (1989) 87 ALR 14.
[64] *Paracidal Pty Ltd* v. *Herctum Pty Ltd* (1983) 4 IPR 201.
[65] *Hutchence* v. *South Seas Bubble Co. Pty Ltd* (1986) 64 ALR 330.
[66] *10th Cantanae Pty Ltd* v. *Shoshana Pty Ltd* (1987) 79 ALR 279 (claim failed on facts). Cf. *Honey* v. *Australian Airlines Ltd* [1989] ATPR 40-961, affirmed (1990) 18 IPR 185 (Federal Court of Australia, Full Court) (plaintiff's status as amateur sportsman effectively precluded any business goodwill in respect of his image and there could be no misrepresentation that the plaintiff endorsed the defendants' business or their activities).
[67] See 8–10 above.

70 The commercial appropriation of personality

third parties, while the valuable attributes of other celebrities remain latent and unrealised.[68] Most, if not all of the plaintiffs in the cases discussed above, fall into the latter category.[69] In the early cases the unauthorised exploitation of the plaintiffs' names was inextricably linked with the notion of an injury to personal and professional reputation. Indeed, it was only in *Lyngstad* that the plaintiffs' image served as an economic asset akin to goodwill, rather than an aspect of their personal reputations and, correspondingly, the only case in which a claim for passing off was made in isolation, unaccompanied by a claim for libel, although the claim was ultimately unsuccessful. These observations reflect two different conceptions of goodwill in personality.[70] The early English authorities rejected the notion that a person might have had a property right in his name *per se*, although they came close to accepting the proposition that a person might have a cause of action if he could show that he had suffered damage to his business or profession.[71] According to the approach in *Lyngstad*, however, the relevant business or goodwill of the plaintiffs lay, not in their profession as singers or musicians, but in a kind of subsidiary business of exploiting their images for commercial purposes, which might be conducted by the plaintiffs themselves, or, more realistically, through granting licences to others, although Oliver J did not believe that it was common commercial practice to do so. In essence, the court was concerned with the extent of the group's existing trading interests, rather than their recognition value which had been generated by their activities in their business or profession as musicians.[72]

---

[68] Unauthorised exploitation might inform the plaintiff of this latent value which lies in his name or other attributes: see *Stringfellow* v. *McCain Foods Ltd* [1984] RPC 501, 545.

[69] *Clark* v. *Freeman* (1848) 11 Beav 112; *Dockrell* v. *Dougall* (1899) 15 TLR 333; *Williams* v. *Hodge* (1887) 4 TLR 175; *Sim* v. *Heinz* [1959] 1 WLR 313. Cf. *Lyngstad* v. *Anabas Products Ltd* [1977] FSR 62.

[70] We may leave aside cases where a business trades under the name of its owner or founder. In such cases the relevant goodwill which might be damaged by the defendant's misrepresentation does not relate to the personality of the owner or founder, but to the particular business carried on by the eponymous owner or his successors. See, e.g., *Rodgers (Joseph) & Sons Ltd* v. *W. N. Rodgers & Co.* (1924) 41 RPC 277 (cutlery manufacturers); *Poiret* v. *Jules Poiret Ltd* (1920) 37 RPC 177 (theatrical costumiers); *Parker & Son (Reading) Ltd* v. *Parker* [1965] RPC 323 (estate agency).

[71] See note 47 above. Similarly, in *Sim* v. *Heinz* (note 49 above), although the Court of Appeal was prepared to contemplate such an approach, the interlocutory nature of the proceedings and the fact that the claim was linked to the claim of libel in terms of the relevant questions of fact, did not allow the matter to be considered further.

[72] Cf. *Kaye* v. *Robertson* [1991] FSR 62, where the plaintiff actor was not found to be 'in the position of a *trader in relation to his interest in his story about the accident and recovery*' (*ibid.*, 69 *per* Glidewell LJ (italics supplied)) and thus failed to establish a cause of action in passing off to prevent the defendant newspaper from publishing a picture of him recovering in hospital following a serious accident. This was despite the Court's recognition that the plaintiff had 'a potentially valuable right to sell the story

Goodwill in personality 71

Although seemingly too narrow, the notion of the relevant business and goodwill limited to existing trading interests in respect of a person's image has its attractions. The elements of the tort of passing off are interactive and difficult to separate.[73] While the requirement of damage is considered in greater detail below, one preliminary point needs to be noted. If it is accepted that appropriation of personality damages economic interests which are entirely separate from that individual's personal reputation, then what, precisely, does that person lose? Ordinarily, a famous surgeon does not manufacture medicines. Neither do famous pop stars usually manufacture T-shirts. Consequently, there can be no direct diversion of trade from the plaintiff to the defendant as in the classic case of passing off goods. Thus, broadly speaking, an individual whose image is appropriated either suffers from being associated with the business of the defendant, or loses the licence fee which he might have charged had the defendants not exploited his personality without his consent.[74] This raises two points. First, and most immediately relevant, if a professional person finds that his image has been exploited without his consent, does that injure him in his profession? In the cases noted above the association of prominent surgeons with quack medicines could conceivably damage the plaintiffs in their professional capacity. The actions were for libel, although the possibility of an action in passing off was at least admitted. Modern commercial practices tend to suggest that a professional person's business might include commercial exploitation of the individual's personality and, in this respect, the approach in *Lyngstad* seems to be too narrow. However, it is a moot point as to how broadly the notion of a business or profession may be construed. For example, would a politician or a trade union leader be included within the notion of a person engaged in professional or business activities? Private individuals would almost certainly be excluded, since they lack goodwill in respect of their image, and rarely have goodwill in respect of their trade or profession which might be damaged by unauthorised appropriation of personality. The second point raises the question whether an allegedly injurious association or the loss of a notional licence fee can furnish the appropriate element of damage. This is considered in detail in the text below.

---

of his accident and recovery when . . . fit enough to tell it'. The Court was not concerned with the plaintiff's goodwill in his general capacity as an actor, but with his goodwill in respect of the sale of the story of his recovery, a much narrower notion indeed.

[73] See note 14 above.

[74] In the rather unusual case of *Kaye* v. *Robertson* (see note 72 above), the opportunity to sell his story exclusively to the highest bidder (claim failed on facts).

72   The commercial appropriation of personality

Misrepresentation

Introduction

The nature of the misrepresentation in the tort of passing off may take many different forms which are neither possible nor desirable to define.[75] In its original form the defendant would misrepresent that his goods were the goods of the plaintiff, or were of the same kind or quality as the plaintiff's.[76] Cases of appropriation of personality are generally concerned with misrepresentations relating to a connection between the defendant and the plaintiff, possibly in the form of a licensing or endorsement agreement, leading to confusion on the part of the public, resulting in damage or a real possibility of damage to the plaintiff. For present purposes the rather vague notion of a 'connection misrepresentation' may be refined into the following three separate categories: (i) a misrepresentation that the plaintiff's business and the defendant's business are connected (business connection misrepresentation); (ii)(a) a misrepresentation that the defendant's goods are licensed by the plaintiff and are of a certain kind, origin or quality, on which the public rely (strong licensing connection misrepresentation); (ii)(b) a misrepresentation that there is a licensing connection of some (vague) kind between the plaintiff and defendant (weak licensing connection misrepresentation); (iii) a misrepresentation that the defendant's goods or services are endorsed by the plaintiff (endorsement misrepresentation). Although category (ii) covers 'licensing connection' misrepresentations generally, it is advantageous, as will be seen below, to draw a distinction between the two variants (a) and (b). References to category (ii) misrepresentations may be taken to encompass both variants unless the context indicates otherwise.

The first type of misrepresentation is well established, and need not detain us long. By the beginning of the twentieth century, the tort of passing off had been extended from misrepresentations that the defendant's goods were the goods of the plaintiff to cover cases 'where although the plaintiff and defendant were not competing traders in the same line of business, a false suggestion by the defendant that their businesses were connected with one another would damage the reputation, and thus the goodwill, of the plaintiff's business'.[77] Thus, according to the classic principle, 'no man is entitled to carry on his business in such a way, or by

---

[75] *Bulmer (H. P.) Ltd and Showerings Ltd* v. *Bollinger SA* [1978] RPC 79, 99; *Spalding (A. G.) & Bros.* v. *Gamage (A. W.) Ltd* (1915) 32 RPC 273, 284.

[76] *Reddaway* v. *Banham* [1896] AC 199; *Spalding (A. G.) & Bros.* v. *Gamage (A. W.) Ltd* (1915) 32 RPC 273.

[77] *Erven Warnink BV* v. *Townend & Sons (Hull) Ltd* [1979] AC 731, 741–2 *per* Lord Diplock.

Goodwill in personality

such a name, as to lead to the belief that he is carrying on the business of another man, or to lead to the belief that the business which he is carrying on has any connexion with the business carried on by another man'.[78] The principle covers cases of misrepresentation leading to confusion that the defendant's business is the plaintiff's business itself, or is a branch of the plaintiff's business or is connected with the plaintiff's business.[79] The problem addressed at this point is the manner and extent to which the courts have expanded the scope of actionable misrepresentations from this classic principle to encompass misrepresentations of types (ii) and (iii) above. Although it is generally unhelpful to discuss appropriation of personality in terms of 'character merchandising',[80] as far as the current Anglo-Australian authorities are concerned, the two notions are inextricably intertwined. Despite the fact that our primary concern is with a misrepresentation of type (iii) above (endorsement), we will need to consider the move from (i) to (ii), which is as far as the current English authorities have developed. The central issue to be addressed is whether the move from (i) to (iii) is a logical development of categories of actionable misrepresentation or, alternatively, whether such a move goes beyond the bounds of passing off and effectively involves a new form of liability independent of the tort of passing off.

The nature of the misrepresentation in English law

In the first significant English case, *McCulloch* v. *Lewis A. May (Produce Distributors) Ltd*,[81] the plaintiff, a well-known children's radio broadcaster who went under the name of 'Uncle Mac', had a very wide reputation amongst listeners to his radio programme, and those who read his books, or came across him in his capacity as a children's lecturer and a personality well-known to children.[82] The defendant food manufacturer made and sold puffed wheat under the name of 'Uncle Mac's Puffed Wheat'. The plaintiff claimed that, by doing so, the defendant was trading on his reputation in a way which amounted to passing off. It was held that there was no right to a fancy name *in vacuo*, a proposition supported by the early English cases from *Clark* v. *Freeman* onwards. The plaintiff needed to establish that he had a reputation in that name, in respect of some profession, business or goods, and that the conduct of the defendant interfered with, or was calculated to interfere with, the conduct of

---

[78] *The Clock Ltd* v. *The Clock House Hotel Ltd* (1936) 53 RPC 269, 275 *per* Romer LJ.

[79] *Ewing* v. *Buttercup Margarine Ltd* [1917] 2 Ch 1, 11 *per* Cozens-Hardy MR. See also *Harrods Ltd* v. *R Harrod Ltd* (1924) 41 RPC 74; *British Legion* v. *British Legion Club (Street) Ltd* (1931) 48 RPC 555.

[80] See 5–6 above. Cf. *ELVIS PRESLEY Trade Marks* [1999] RPC 567, 580.

[81] (1948) 65 RPC 58.   [82] *Ibid.*, 61.

74   The commercial appropriation of personality

such profession or business in that it led, or was calculated to lead, the public to confuse the profession, business or goods of the plaintiff with the profession, business or goods of the defendant.[83] This much is unremarkable and perfectly consistent with the first type of misrepresentation noted above. Wynn-Parry J proceeded to state that 'the element of confusion is essential, but the element of confusion necessitates comparison', another uncontroversial proposition. However, His Honour introduced a novel and rather blunt instrument for assessing confusion, deducing that in all the previous cases where the court had intervened to restrain passing off there had been 'a common field of activity in which, however remotely, both the Plaintiff and Defendant were engaged and that it was the presence of that factor that accounted for the jurisdiction of the Court'.[84] On the facts, since the plaintiff was not engaged in any degree in producing or marketing puffed wheat, the defendant could not be said to be passing off the goods or business of the plaintiff, in using the fancy name used by the plaintiff.

The introduction of a common field of activity test was strictly unnecessary since the action could have been dismissed on the basis that there was little evidence of confusion amongst the public.[85] Alternatively, it could have been held that the plaintiff had not suffered any damage, a proposition that is altogether more attractive. Although the requirement of damage is dealt with in detail in the text below, a few points relating to the different notions of goodwill discussed above need to be noted immediately. Despite being technically obiter, the dicta on damage in *McCulloch* are illuminating. The first head of damage claimed, the risk of being exposed to litigation, was found to be 'wholly visionary and illusory', while the second head, the risk of damage to the plaintiff's professional reputation as a broadcaster and author and of injury to his means of subsistence and gaining a livelihood, was not regarded as a real or tangible risk. Goodwill in personality may be narrowly conceived as the goodwill subsisting in an actual business devoted to exploiting attributes of personality or, more broadly, as the goodwill subsisting in a person's business in the broader sense of his professional, artistic or literary occupation.[86] The difficulty with this latter approach is that, in the absence of some risk of exposure to liability, it might be difficult to persuade the court that the misrepresentation is likely to damage the plaintiff's goodwill in respect of his profession or business. Could the defendant's conduct in *McCulloch* have damaged the plaintiff's goodwill qua radio broadcaster, and would

[83] *Ibid.*, 64.   [84] *Ibid.*, 67.
[85] *Ibid.* See also J. Phillips and A. Coleman, 'Passing Off and the Common Field of Activity' (1985) 101 LQR 242.
[86] See 69–71 above.

Goodwill in personality 75

it have any effect on his business or profession? Obviously, the question is purely speculative, given the outcome, but the disparate nature of the respective businesses of the plaintiff and defendant suggest that the plaintiff would face a heavy burden in proving damage.[87]

The way in which the common field of activity was formulated[88] was hardly a model of inductive reasoning, and has subsequently been abandoned, at least as an absolute requirement.[89] However, this was not before the doctrine caused problems in cases where the plaintiff sought to expand the categories of actionable misrepresentation from category (i) (business connection misrepresentation) to category (ii) (licensing connection misrepresentation) above. For example, in *Wombles Ltd* v. *Wombles Skips Ltd*[90] the plaintiff assignees of the copyright in the fictitious Wombles characters were in the business of exploiting the Womble characters and had granted exploitation licences to third parties in respect of a wide range of goods. They sought an interlocutory injunction to restrain the defendants from using the word 'Wombles' in connection with their rubbish skips. Since there was no question of there being copyright in the name 'Wombles' alone,[91] the action lay solely in passing off, the essence of the misrepresentation being that the defendants were passing off their business as the business of the plaintiff. The action was dismissed by Walton J through a rather mechanical application of the common field of activity test: since the plaintiffs and defendants were not in common fields of activity (licensing copyright material and providing rubbish skips respectively), there could be no danger of confusion regarding any possible connection between the two businesses.[92]

Subsequently, in *Tavener Rutledge Ltd* v. *Trexapalm Ltd*[93] the issue arose as to whether a licensing connection between the plaintiff and defendant would be sufficient to amount to a misrepresentation that the two businesses were connected, a clearer move from notion (i) to notion (ii) above than in the *McCulloch* and *Wombles* cases. The plaintiffs, unlicensed manufacturers of 'Kojak' lollipops, sought an injunction against a lollipop manufacturer licensed by Universal Studios, the originators of the *Kojak* television series. The plaintiffs' apparent effrontery concealed the fact that they had been trading in the lollipops for over six months and had built up considerable goodwill in their 'Kojakpops'. Although the defendants had been conscientious in securing a licence for their lollipops, their late entry

---

[87] See, further, 100–1 below.
[88] Few cases were discussed in Wynn-Parry J's judgment, which drew largely on Maugham J's review of the authorities in *British Medical Association* v. *Marsh* (1931) 48 RPC 565.
[89] See *Lyngstad* v. *Anabas Products Ltd* [1977] FSR 62, 67; *Lego System Aktieselskab* v. *Lego M. Lemelstrich Ltd* [1983] FSR 155, 186; *Mirage Studios* v. *Counter-Feat Clothing Co. Ltd* [1991] FSR 145, 157.
[90] [1975] FSR 488.   [91] *Ibid.*, 491.   [92] *Ibid.*   [93] [1977] RPC 275.

76   The commercial appropriation of personality

into the market proved detrimental. The defendants' argument that the licence from Universal Studios afforded them a defence was rejected by Walton J on the basis that there was no common field of activity, either actual or existing in the minds of the public, between the owners of the name (whose business lay in the production of television serials) and the plaintiffs (whose business lay in the production of lollipops). The defendants argued that the practice of character merchandising was sufficiently well-known for the public to assume that the use of the name 'Kojak' had been licensed by the originators of the television series and that a certain level of quality control was exercised by the licensors.[94] Accordingly the public would be misled as to a connection between the business of the unauthorised merchandisers and the business of the licensors. Walton J was unimpressed by this argument and held that there was no evidence to suggest that the practice of character merchandising was well-known and that the public would infer the existence of a licence between merchandisers and the originators of original copyright material. This, in any case, would be insufficient. What would need to be shown was that the licensors' practice of exercising quality control over products bearing their name was sufficiently well-known that the public would not only infer the existence of a licence, but also infer that the licence was a guarantee of the product's quality. There was no evidence to suggest that this was the case.[95]

Thus, although there was no evidence to support the existence of a misrepresentation type (ii)(a), namely a misrepresentation relating to a licensing agreement which suggested quality control on which the public would rely, the prospect that such a misrepresentation might be actionable was at least admitted. What is interesting to note is that in his discussion of character merchandising, Walton J drew a distinction between the use of fictional characters and real people, observing that 'when one deals with a real person, one has a real person with real qualities and, therefore, his endorsement or the use of his name undoubtedly suggests, or may suggest in proper circumstances, an endorsement which may or may not exist'. With a fictional character such as Kojak on the other hand, 'nobody would imagine that the lollipops put out by the plaintiff company have actually been endorsed by Kojak, still less by the actor who plays the fictional character'. Thus, the possibility that it might be easier to infer the relevant misrepresentation in the case of a real person was admitted, although Walton J somehow did not think that this might apply in the case of the actor who played a fictional character.[96]

[94] *Ibid.*, 280.   [95] *Ibid.*, 280–1.
[96] *Ibid.*, 280. Cf. *Hogan* v. *Koala Dundee Pty Ltd* (1988) 83 ALR 187; *Pacific Dunlop Ltd* v. *Hogan* (1989) 87 ALR 14; and see discussion in text below.

Nevertheless, in *Lyngstad* v. *Anabas Products Ltd*,[97] members of the pop group Abba were unsuccessful in establishing a connection misrepresentation relating to a licensing or endorsement arrangement. The absence of a common field of activity between the parties' businesses was not fatal, since Oliver J preferred to interpret it as a shorthand term for the need to show a real possibility of confusion, rather than an absolute requirement.[98] The alleged confusion did not relate to the defendants' business in selling the merchandise and the plaintiffs' activities as singers. Rather, they argued that their activities as singers had generated a public interest and that the defendants were exploiting the band members' names and photographs for their own profit in a way which gave the public the impression that the goods sold by the defendants were associated with the plaintiffs in some way, in that the plaintiffs had either licensed the goods or had endorsed or approved the goods as proper goods for distribution. As such, the defendants should be enjoined on the basis that it might prejudice the band's opportunities for engaging in such business themselves, by granting licences for the use of their name and photographs to others.[99] Oliver J was prepared to accept that the association between the plaintiffs and defendants, at least to the extent that it implied some sort of approval on the part of the plaintiffs, was something that might be said to cause damage to the plaintiffs, if, for example, the goods were defective in quality.[100] On the facts, however, there was insufficient evidence of a real possibility of confusion in the minds of the public as to a connection between the plaintiffs and the defendants. In Oliver J's view the defendants were doing no more 'than catering for a popular demand among teenagers for effigies of their idols'.[101] The facts of the case were indeed rather weak since, as noted above, the plaintiffs had a very limited business in exploiting their image in this country, which was a crucial factor in view of the Court's very narrow notion of the relevant business goodwill.[102] There was nothing in the *American Cyanamid*[103] principles which compelled the granting of interlocutory relief merely on the basis of a persuasive authority in another jurisdiction[104] and, in any case, the balance of convenience was in the defendants' favour.[105]

---

[97] [1977] FSR 62, 67. See text accompanying note 56 for the facts.
[98] *Ibid.*, 67. See also *Annabel's (Berkeley Square) Ltd* v. *Schock* [1972] RPC 838, 844; *Lego System Aktieselskab* v. *Lego M. Lemelstrich Ltd* [1983] FSR 155, 186 *per* Falconer J.
[99] *Ibid.*, 66–7.   [100] *Ibid.*, 67.   [101] *Ibid.*, 68.
[102] See text accompanying note 55 above.
[103] *American Cyanamid Co.* v. *Ethicon Ltd* [1975] AC 396.
[104] See text below, 84–9.
[105] [1977] FSR 62, 68. See also *Harrison and Starkey* v. *Polydor Ltd* [1977] FSR 1 (claim that the defendants had misrepresented that a record of taped interviews between members of the Beatles and a journalist was made, recommended, approved, sponsored or licensed by the plaintiffs held to be 'quite ridiculous' (*ibid.*, 4), given the minimal likelihood of confusion on the facts).

78   The commercial appropriation of personality

Stringfellow v. *McCain Foods (GB) Ltd*[106] is closer to the classic type of misrepresentation in category (i) and conveniently illustrates some of the points made in relation to goodwill and misrepresentation. It was held in the Court of Appeal that the defendants' use of the name 'Stringfellows' in packaging and marketing frozen oven-ready chips did not, in itself, amount to a misrepresentation which would lead the public to believe that there was a connection between the defendants' business and the plaintiff's fashionable nightclub business.[107] Nevertheless, it was reluctantly held that the defendants' advertisement did, unwittingly, amount to a misrepresentation, due to its nightclub-related theme,[108] although it was ultimately held that the misrepresentation did not result in damage to the plaintiff.[109] On one view this was not a case of appropriation of personality as such: if the defendants were to derive any benefit from association with the name 'Stringfellow', it would be with the nightclub business rather than Mr Stringfellow himself. These two notions are easy to separate in law, although, in fact, the reputations of the two might be inextricably intertwined.[110] It is tempting to speculate what the position would have been if the plaintiff had been a well-known actor or entertainer with no nightclub business in which the goodwill might subsist, a point which brings us back to the different notions of goodwill and business discussed above. It is a moot point whether a misrepresentation in such a hypothetical scenario would lead to confusion amongst the public that 'Stringfellows' chips were connected with the business or profession of the plaintiff qua actor or entertainer. Again, the most relevant question is whether the plaintiff in such a case would suffer damage to his business or profession or, if not, whether some other element of damage might be found. This question must be reserved for fuller discussion below.

English law remains wary of expanding the categories of connection misrepresentation, outlined above, to include category (ii)(a) and (ii)(b) misrepresentations,[111] despite the decision in *Mirage Studios* v. *Counter-Feat Clothing Co. Ltd.*[112] The plaintiffs were the originators of the commercially successful cartoon characters the 'Teenage Mutant Ninja Turtles'. Crucially, in the Court's view, a substantial part of their business

---

[106] [1984] RPC 501.   [107] *Ibid.*, 538.   [108] *Ibid.*, 540.   [109] See 103–4 below.
[110] Cf. note 70 above.   [111] See text accompanying note 75 above.
[112] [1991] FSR 145. Cf. the earlier case of *BBC* v. *Celebrity Centre Productions Ltd* (1988) 15 IPR 333, an interlocutory application to restrain the defendants from publishing a magazine entitled *A to Z of Eastenders*. The defendants conceded that the plaintiffs had an arguable case in passing off, on the basis that the defendants' publication might be taken to be licensed or authorised by the plaintiffs. Accordingly, Falconer J (*ibid.*, 337) did not need to discuss the merits of the plaintiffs' case (an interlocutory injunction was granted on the facts), and the decision is of limited value on the relevant point of law.

Goodwill in personality 79

consisted of granting licences to third parties to use the 'Turtles' images on a very broad range of goods; at the time of the action over 150 licences, which included quality control provisions, had been granted in the United Kingdom alone.[113] The importance of the dual nature of the plaintiffs' business activity[114] (creation and exploitation through licensing of the rights in the characters) was stressed, since the unauthorised merchandise could cause serious damage to the plaintiff through lost licensing revenues and depreciation of the value of the licensing right through association with inferior goods.[115] Since the plaintiffs did not manufacture or sell goods themselves there could be no confusion between their business and the defendants' business as such. The only connection between the plaintiffs and the goods lay in the fact that they had licensed the 'Turtles' image to be used on those goods. The evidence showed that members of the public were aware that the 'Turtles' image would not normally be found on goods unless they were licensed by the plaintiff; in other words, the public connected the 'Turtles' characters with the plaintiffs. According to the Vice Chancellor that link between the goods sold and the plaintiffs' business was sufficient to found a cause of action in passing off.[116]

In this respect the approach taken in Australia in *Children's Television Workshop Inc.* v. *Woolworths (New South Wales) Ltd*[117] (the *Muppets* case) and *Fido Dido Inc.* v. *Venture Stores (Retailers) Pty Ltd*[118] was approved and followed. In the *Muppets* case the court accepted that there was a relevant misrepresentation by the defendants' use of the Muppet characters in their own merchandise, since there was evidence that the public, when seeing Muppets merchandise, would assume that a licence had been granted by the creators of the Muppets for the use of the characters. Similarly, in the *Fido Dido* case it was accepted that a misrepresentation as to a licensing connection indicating 'sponsorship, affiliation or approval' between the originators of the character 'Fido Dido' and the defendants could constitute the necessary misrepresentation for the purposes of a passing off action, although an injunction was refused on the balance of convenience.[119]

What is most significant about the *Mirage Studios* decision is that it was unnecessary for the plaintiffs to show affirmative evidence that the public would rely on the misrepresentation that the merchandise was licensed by the plaintiffs; if the misrepresentation was made there was

---

[113] [1991] FSR 145, 156. Cf. the limited nature of the plaintiffs' business in *Lyngstad*, text accompanying note 56 above.
[114] *Ibid.*   [115] *Ibid.*, 156.   [116] *Ibid.*   [117] [1981] RPC 187.
[118] (1988) 16 IPR 365.   [119] Cf. Wadlow, *Passing Off*, 314–15.

80   The commercial appropriation of personality

no need for further evidence to show that the misrepresentation was the cause of the public buying the goods in question. According to the Vice Chancellor the public 'expect to buy what they think they are getting, namely the genuine article'.[120] Accordingly, in the absence of evidence, a court must infer that, if the customer was aware that the product was not genuine, he would not buy it, but would seek the real object.[121] These passages must be read in the light of dicta in the Court of Appeal in *ELVIS PRESLEY Trade Marks*, where Robert Walker LJ noted that although the decision in *Mirage Studios* was 'clear and convincing' it did not give 'a green light to extravagant claims based on any unauthorised use of a celebrity's image, but makes clear... the relatively limited scope of the principle on which it proceeds'.[122] Similarly, Simon Brown LJ described the proposition that character merchandising is generally 'established and accepted in the public mind as properly the exclusive preserve of the character himself' as 'an altogether too simplistic view of the effect of the many authorities in this field and discounts utterly the well-established principle that all these cases ultimately must turn upon their own facts'.[123]

Indeed, there must not only be a misrepresentation but, on the facts of each case, the misrepresentation must be a material one. The name or representation of the character must have trade mark significance in respect of the goods about which the complaint is made and '[i]t is not sufficient that the public should believe that there is some sort of connection between the defendant and the licensor: the public must select the defendant's goods in reliance upon the assumed connection'.[124] What 'counts is whether there is confusion amongst that part of the public which cares'.[125] Although, in some cases, a plaintiff might establish that the public would wish to buy genuine goods, this is not universally true and consumers might well be indifferent as to whether a product was licensed or came from a particular source.[126] If the aim of attaching a character to merchandise is to add fun or glamour to that merchandise, then the representation is not material; an unauthorised product can have the same attraction and glamour as an authorised product.[127] As Laddie J put it at first instance in *ELVIS PRESLEY Trade Marks*, '[w]hen a fan buys a poster or a cup bearing an image of his star, he is buying a likeness, not a product from a particular source... He is likely to be indifferent as

---

[120] [1991] FSR 145, 159.   [121] *Ibid.*   [122] [1999] RPC 567, 582.
[123] *Ibid.*, 597.   [124] Wadlow, *Passing Off*, 313.
[125] *Arsenal Football Club Plc* v. *Reed* [2001] ETMR 860, 869 *per* Laddie J.
[126] See *BBC Worldwide Ltd* v. *Pally Screen Printing Ltd* [1998] FSR 665, 674.
[127] H. Carty, 'Character Merchandising and the Limits of Passing Off' (1993) 13 LS 289, 298.

Goodwill in personality

81

to the source.'[128] Evidence as to quality control exercised by the licensor may contribute to the plaintiff's task in establishing his case but is not conclusive; again, the supposed existence of quality control is only relevant if the public actually rely on such control supposedly exercised by the licensor.[129] Thus, although as a matter of law a relevant misrepresentation may be established, this may well be a rather difficult task in practice.

Public knowledge of practices such as merchandising or endorsement, belief in the existence of quality control or approval, and reliance on that belief are three separate matters.[130] Although actions for passing off are tried by a judge, sitting alone, the question whether there has been confusion as a result of the misrepresentation is essentially a 'jury question' in the sense that the likely effect of the misrepresentation on the members of the public must be considered, and the judge must put himself in the position of a potential buyer of the goods.[131] Where an action is brought at or before the defendant starts trading, the court 'must assess as best it can what is going to happen in the real world of the marketplace' although when the defendant has been trading for some time, the court 'can expect to be relieved of the need to speculate as to the likelihood of confusion and damage', since, in most cases, it will be able to see what has actually happened in the marketplace.[132]

Instances of actual deception will be useful evidence, although ultimately the Court's decision will not depend solely or even primarily on the evaluation of such evidence and '[t]he court must in the end trust to its own perception into the mind of the reasonable man'.[133] While a plaintiff might wish to rely on survey evidence in order to establish that a misrepresentation is a material one, on which the public rely, one of the main difficulties lies in formulating questions that are not leading,[134] and do not make the respondent enter 'into a field of speculation upon which that person would never have embarked had the question not been put'.[135]

---

[128] [1997] RPC 543, 554. See also *Arsenal Football Club Plc* v. *Reed* [2001] ETMR 860, 870 (name and nickname of a football club on merchandise regarded by purchasers as signs of allegiance or support, rather than indicating the source of the goods).

[129] Cf. *Tavener Rutledge* v. *Trexapalm*, text accompanying note 93 above.

[130] Wadlow, *Passing Off*, 316.

[131] *General Electric Co.* v. *General Electric Co. Ltd* [1972] 1 WLR 729, 738 *per* Lord Diplock, cited with approval in *Pacific Dunlop Ltd* v. *Hogan* (1989) 87 ALR 14, 28 *per* Sheppard J.

[132] *Arsenal Football Club Plc* v. *Reed* [2001] ETMR 860, 869 *per* Laddie J.

[133] *Parker-Knoll Ltd* v. *Parker Knoll International Ltd* [1962] RPC 265, 291–2 *per* Devlin LJ. See also *Neutrogena Corp.* v. *Golden Ltd* [1996] RPC 473, 495; *HFC Bank Plc* v. *Midland Bank Plc* [2000] RPC 176, 198.

[134] See Drysdale and Silverleaf, *Passing Off*, 181.

[135] *Imperial Group Plc* v. *Philip Morris Ltd* [1984] RPC 293, 302.

82   The commercial appropriation of personality

Experience in cases involving connection misrepresentations suggests that the answers given in any surveys will often be vague and inconclusive.[136]

The instances in which the English courts have been required to consider whether a misrepresentation relating to an endorsement or connection might be actionable have been limited. The issue was precluded from discussion by the application of the common field of activity test in *McCulloch* v. *May*[137] and, although the possibility was admitted, obiter, in *Tavener Rutledge* v. *Trexapalm*,[138] there was insufficient evidence to support such a claim when it came to be considered directly in *Lyngstad* v. *Anabas*.[139] In *Nice and Safe Attitude Ltd* v. *Piers Flook*[140] Robert Walker J declined to follow *Mirage Studios* and allowed a claim in passing off by a clothing manufacturer who had built up substantial goodwill (albeit somewhat parasitically) in his clothing business using the logo 'NASA', against a rival manufacturer who was licensed by the United States National Aeronautics Space Administration (which did not have any conventional trading activities in the United Kingdom). The Court refused to accept that the *Mirage Studios* case established that the defendant would be deemed to have been licensed by NASA (US), which would afford the defendant a defence. Subsequently, in *Halliwell* v. *Panini*,[141] the only case where the issue was considered directly, the absence of a disclaimer on the defendants' sticker collection bearing images of the plaintiff members of the Spice Girls pop group did not amount to a misrepresentation that would lead members of the public to buy the defendants' goods on the basis or mistaken belief that they were authorised by the plaintiffs. Some of the plaintiffs' own merchandise stated that the products were 'official', whereas others did not, and there could be no general inference that such goods would be officially licensed products. As such, it could not be said that the question of whether the goods were authorised was a material factor in any purchaser's decision. According to Lightman J, the defendants were merely 'catering for the popular demand for effigies and quotes of today's idols'.[142] Indeed, the evidence showed that other merchandise, against which no objection was made by the plaintiffs, only contained rather small and ineffective

---

[136] See *Hogan* v. *Koala Dundee Pty Ltd* (1988) 83 ALR 187, 192–5, and text accompanying note 199 below. See also *Pacific Dunlop Ltd* v. *Hogan* (1989) 87 ALR 14, 22 *per* Sheppard J, and, in English law, see *Stringfellow* v. *McCain Foods* [1984] RPC 510, 531–2 (minimal number of people believed in the existence of a business connection between the plaintiffs and defendants).

[137] See text accompanying note 81 above.   [138] See text accompanying note 96 above.

[139] See text accompanying note 101 above.   [140] [1997] FSR 14.

[141] Unreported, High Court, Chancery Division, 6 June 1997.

[142] Cf. *Lyngstad* v. *Anabas Products Ltd*, note 101 above.

disclaimers regarding the pop group's approval. The absence of a disclaimer in the instant case constituted a rather weak basis on which to proceed.[143]

A more restrictive approach to character merchandising and endorsement might be criticised as being inconsistent with commercial reality or, more particularly, the demands of the 'character merchandising industry'. However, attempts to widen (monopolistic) property rights beyond the scope conferred by copyright and trade mark law should arguably be resisted, particularly when such arguments are built on what is effectively a fiction of consumer confusion. It could be argued that it is this failure to distinguish that which serves as an indication of trade source, or guarantee of quality, from that which adds to the value of a product in its own right which undermines the approach adopted in *Mirage Studios*. While the former is the proper concern of the law of passing off, the latter is arguably the concern of copyright law, rather than passing off and trade mark law.[144] The introduction of a character right to supplement the law of copyright in literary, artistic and dramatic works, was expressly considered and rejected in the United Kingdom[145] and the obvious danger which lies in such an extension of the tort of passing off is that it confers much wider rights, and hence market power, to producers of characters than are conferred and properly delimited by copyright law. There is much force in the view that 'monopolies should not be so readily created'.[146]

One further point needs to be noted. Having followed the Australian authorities, the Vice Chancellor in *Mirage Studios* was faced with the problem of reconciling these authorities with the English authorities discussed above. The Vice Chancellor contrasted the situation where there was no copyright in a name, and therefore no licensable subject matter, as in the *Wombles* case, with the situation in *Mirage Studios* where the plaintiffs were engaged in licensing the copyright in the Ninja Turtles drawings. According to the Vice Chancellor the *Wombles*, *Tavener Rutledge* and *Lyngstad* decisions might still be good law on the basis that the defendants

---

[143] The courts will generally be reluctant to hold that a disclaimer negates any suggestion of a commercial connection. See, e.g., *Associated Newspapers Group Plc* v. *Insert Media Ltd* [1991] FSR 380, 387. Cf. *Sony Music Productions Pty Ltd* v. *Tansing* (1993) 27 IPR 649, 653; *Twentieth Century Fox Film Corp.* v. *South Australian Brewing Co. Ltd* (1996) 34 IPJ 225, 251; *Britt Allcroft (Thomas) LLC* v. *Miller* (2000) 49 IPR 7, 18, and see, generally, Wadlow, *Passing Off*, 195.

[144] Wadlow, *Passing Off*, 315.

[145] Whitford Committee, Report of the Committee to Consider the Law on Copyright and Designs, Cmnd 6732 (London, 1977), para. 909. The Committee took the view that any further protection should be left to the law of passing off or unfair competition law, although it did not make any recommendations on this matter.

[146] [1999] RPC 567, 598 *per* Simon Brown LJ.

84   The commercial appropriation of personality

had only used names in which no rights of property subsisted.[147] On a strict interpretation it is arguable that a misrepresentation concerning a commercial connection between the plaintiff and the defendant will only be actionable if it is a misrepresentation relating to the licensing of specific intellectual property rights such as trade marks or copyright. Such a strict interpretation would not support the broader view that a misrepresentation will be actionable if a defendant makes a misrepresentation that there is some form of licensing connection in general between the defendant and the plaintiff. However, such a fine distinction need not stand in the way of a broader application of the decision. Bearing in mind that one of the bases of the tort of passing off is the protection of consumers against confusion in the marketplace, it would be reasonable to take consumer perceptions into account. Indeed, it is doubtful whether the average consumer can be expected to distinguish between a situation where underlying intellectual property rights are licensed and a situation where no underlying intellectual property rights subsist. As the Vice Chancellor noted, given the changes in trading habits, cases where no underlying intellectual property rights subsist, such as those involving the licensing of a name, might require reconsideration on future occasions when the evidence before the court is different. The better view seems to be that such a distinction will be immaterial.[148] Two crucial questions will need to be addressed in future cases. First, whether a misrepresentation of type (iii) above[149] (endorsement connection) will be sufficient to amount to a misrepresentation that the goods or business of the defendant and the business of the plaintiff (broadly defined) are connected; second, to what extent the issue of public reliance on the misrepresentation will be a matter of inference, without the courts insisting on affirmative evidence. The English courts have maintained a rather restrictive approach and it is instructive to look to the Australian authorities, where the issue has been more fully addressed.

The nature of the misrepresentation in Australian law

The Australian courts have taken a more expansive approach to all the forms of connection misrepresentations noted above,[150] an approach

---

[147] *Ibid.*, 158. In *Lyngstad*, photographs of the plaintiffs were also used, although the plaintiffs did not enjoy copyright in those specific photographs, which might have formed the subject matter of a licence.

[148] See, e.g., Carty, 'Character Merchandising', 300; Drysdale and Silverleaf, *Passing Off*, 71; M. Elmslie and M. Lewis, 'Passing Off and Image Marketing in the UK' [1992] EIPR 270.

[149] See text accompanying note 75 above.   [150] *Ibid.*

Goodwill in personality 85

which, again, originated from the decision in *Henderson* v. *Radio Corporation Pty Ltd*.[151] The plaintiffs were a pair of well-known professional ballroom dancers whose picture had been included, without their permission, on the sleeve of a record of strict tempo dance music, primarily intended for instruction in such dance, but also meant to be bought by the public. The design of the record cover was such as to give prominence to the picture of the Hendersons dancing as, when viewed from a distance, would be the case in a shop display, a fact which, according to Evatt CJ, could easily lead to deception of possible purchasers.[152] Although the back of the record cover contained an express recommendation by another ballroom dancer, there was no suggestion of an express endorsement by the plaintiffs other than by virtue of the fact that their picture appeared on the cover. It seems that, in any case, the appearance of the plaintiffs was largely fortuitous since the record was designed and manufactured in England and was reproduced under licence in Australia; until the plaintiffs complained, the defendant was unaware of the plaintiffs' identity. Nevertheless, the defendant refused to discontinue using the cover and the plaintiffs brought an action in passing off.

It was found, on the evidence, that the class of persons for whom the record was primarily intended (strict tempo dance students and instructors) would probably believe that the picture of the respondents on the cover indicated their recommendation or approval of the record.[153] Subsequently, it was held that the conduct of the defendant amounted to a misrepresentation that the business of the plaintiffs was connected with the business of the defendant, with the notion of a business, as noted above, being interpreted in its widest sense as including professions and callings.[154] The fact that the plaintiffs were not themselves in the business of making and selling records was regarded as irrelevant, and it was not necessary to show that the defendant was competing in a common field of activity.[155] According to Evatt CJ, to establish a cause of action in passing off it was sufficient for the plaintiffs to prove that the defendant was falsely representing either his goods as those of the plaintiff or that his business was the same as, or connected with, the business of the plaintiff.[156] In this respect there was nothing revolutionary about such an extension of the tort of passing off.

Significantly, the defendant conceded that it was falsely representing that the plaintiffs recommended, favoured or supported its record, presumably relying on the lack of competition in a common field as the

---

[151] [1969] RPC 218.   [152] *Ibid.*, 231.   [153] *Ibid.*, 232.
[154] *Ibid.*, 234.   [155] *Ibid.*, 233–4.
[156] *Ibid.*, 231, citing the dictum of Romer LJ in *The Clock Ltd* v. *The Clock House Hotel Ltd* (see note 78 above and accompanying text).

86 The commercial appropriation of personality

exculpatory factor which would allow it to continue to appropriate the plaintiffs' image for its own commercial advantage. It seems that both this concession, and the hope that the court would apply the common field of activity test strictly, was misguided. It is doubtful whether, as a matter of principle, the mere fact that a professional person's name or picture appears on a product is sufficient to constitute an endorsement or recommendation in that person's professional capacity, which, in turn, amounts to a misrepresentation that the professional's business is connected to the defendant's business. This is where the proximity of the nature of the businesses of the defendants should become relevant; where the businesses are closely connected it would be easier to infer that a misrepresentation might lead to confusion amongst the public between the businesses of the plaintiff and defendant. It is interesting to speculate what the position might have been if the plaintiffs' picture had been used on an entirely unconnected item such as a box of soap powder. In such a case, the inference that the plaintiffs' business as professional dancers was connected with the business of a soap manufacturer would be more difficult to make out. As such, the application of the tort of passing off would seem to be limited to 'tools of the trade' endorsements, which might result in some connection between the goods or services of the defendant and the business or profession of the plaintiff.

There are a number of ambiguities in some of the passages in Evatt CJ's judgment. Having noted that the defendants had appropriated the plaintiffs' professional reputation for their own commercial ends, Evatt CJ went on to reject the proposition that 'a court of equity has no power to restrain the [defendant] from falsely representing that the [plaintiffs] recommend its products, unless the [plaintiffs] can prove that their professional reputation has thereby been injured, or that, in some other way, their capacity to earn money by the practice of their profession has thereby been impaired'.[157] His Honour then went on to state that:

It is true that the coercive power of the court cannot be invoked without proof of damage, but the wrongful appropriation of another's professional or business reputation is an injury in itself, no less, in our opinion, than the appropriation of his goods or money. The professional recommendation of the [plaintiffs] was and still is theirs, to withhold or bestow at will, but the [defendant has] wrongfully deprived them of their right to do so and of the payment or reward on which, if they had been minded to give their approval to the [defendant's] record, they could have insisted.[158]

These passages raise a number of issues. First, and most obvious, is the question-begging nature of the final part of the passage cited immediately

[157] [1969] RPC 218, 236.   [158] *Ibid.*

Goodwill in personality

above. The plaintiffs could only have insisted on a fee if they had a valid cause of action, which was precisely the issue under discussion. The existence of such a cause of action in passing off would depend on the ability to show damage, a requirement considered in detail in the text below. Furthermore, it is unclear from the passages whether the remedy in passing off would be limited to misrepresentations which might damage the plaintiffs in their business or profession, or whether it would extend a remedy in cases where there was no injury to the plaintiffs in such a capacity.

The narrow interpretation would effectively limit the plaintiffs' remedy to cases where 'tools of the trade' endorsements were concerned; the relevant misrepresentation would relate to the fact that the plaintiffs' business qua dance instructors was connected with the business of the defendant and would be damaged by the defendant's misrepresentation. The broader interpretation tends towards viewing a plaintiff's capacity to endorse products unconnected with their business or profession either as a business in itself (that is, a licensing or trading business) or as a property right in itself. The former might be said to be the proper concern of the tort of passing off, where the protected interest would be the goodwill in the business or profession of the plaintiff. The latter lies outside the tort of passing off, and amounts to a property right in the attributes of an individual's personality, such as a right of publicity, a notion which will be considered in due course.[159] Indeed, the reference to a 'wrongful appropriation' was ambiguous. Did this mean that liability could be based on misappropriation of such a property right *simpliciter*, or was there still a need to show a misrepresentation, leading to consumer confusion or deception? Read as a whole, Evatt CJ's judgment indicated the need for a misrepresentation, rather than misappropriation of an independent property right, a view that was confirmed by Manning J's judgment although, like Evatt CJ, Manning J's treatment of the requirement of damage was ambiguous.[160]

The decisions which immediately followed *Henderson* did not resolve these difficulties since they were concerned with misrepresentations in categories (i) and (ii) above,[161] rather than being concerned with the troublesome notion of endorsement, association or approval. In *Children's Television Workshop Inc.* v. *Woolworths (NSW) Ltd* [162] the plaintiffs, the producers of the television show *Sesame Street*, which featured the 'Muppets' characters, were held to be able to restrain the defendants from selling unlicensed 'Muppets' merchandise. It was held that the defendants'

---

[159] See below, 171–89.   [160] *Ibid.*, 243. See, further, below at 104–5.
[161] See text accompanying note 75 above.   [162] [1981] RPC 187.

88   The commercial appropriation of personality

conduct would deceive the public into believing that the defendants' goods were licensed by, or associated with, the plaintiffs, which was sufficient to amount to a connection between the businesses of the plaintiffs and defendants, thus bringing the case within the classic principle of passing off.[163] According to Helsham CJ, once the relevant business nexus between the plaintiffs and defendants had been established, in the sense that consumers would believe that the business of the defendants was connected with the business of the plaintiffs, then it would follow that the legitimate business interests of the plaintiffs were being jeopardised. The loss of licensing opportunities was sufficient damage, without the need to show an adverse effect on the plaintiffs' reputation and consequent damage to business resulting from the fact that the defendants' goods were of an inferior quality.[164]

Again, despite the fact that *Hutchence* v. *South Seas Bubble Co. Pty Ltd*[165] involved the commercial exploitation of the images of a pop group, the troublesome notion of endorsement did not need to be considered. The facts were essentially similar to those of the earlier English decision in *Lyngstad* v. *Anabas*[166] to the extent that the members of a pop group (INXS) sought to restrain unauthorised merchandisers. The facts of *Hutchence* were much stronger, however, since the defendants were exploiting what was undoubtedly copyright material,[167] and, more important, the plaintiffs had a considerable and well-established business in licensing merchandise. The likelihood of confusion was considerable in this case, since the plaintiffs and defendants were in direct competition in the same market.[168] The interesting point relates to the nature of the misrepresentation. Wilcox J noted the scale and method of modern merchandise licensing arrangements and held that it was probable that consumers would assume that the merchandise being sold was approved by the plaintiffs, in return for a royalty or other fee. Despite the fact that there were signs and labels indicating that the goods were 'bootleg' merchandise which was not authorised by the plaintiffs, the defendants were held liable, under the Trade Practices Act and the tort of passing off, for misrepresenting that their T-shirts had 'a sponsorship or approval' of the plaintiffs, which did not in fact exist.[169] It seems that the plaintiffs' authorised merchandise was of a high quality, in contrast to the defendants' goods, which were deficient in terms of styling, choice of fabric and other matters. The balance of convenience on the interlocutory application favoured the plaintiffs, and it was not necessary for them to

---

[163] See note 78 above.   [164] [1981] RPC 187, 194–5.   [165] (1986) 64 ALR 330.
[166] See note 97 above.   [167] Cf. text accompanying note 147 above.
[168] (1986) 64 ALR 330, 340.   [169] *Ibid.*, 336–9.

Goodwill in personality

show affirmative evidence that consumers would rely on the guarantee of quality which was implicit in the fact that the goods were authorised by the plaintiffs.[170]

Neither was the notion of endorsement considered in any detail in *Paracidal Pty Ltd* v. *Herctum Pty Ltd*,[171] where the plaintiff, a Spanish horse master, rider and trainer, secured an injunction restraining the defendants from using a substantial reproduction of a photograph of the plaintiff and his horse in an advertisement for their riding display. There was no question that the plaintiff, who was well-known as a horseman in Australia, had the relevant goodwill, and the facts of the case seemed stronger than those in *Henderson*. The business of the plaintiff (training and performing in an equine troupe) and the business of the defendants (running a wildlife sanctuary where spectacles of an equine and equestrian kind were presented) were in a similar field,[172] and the likelihood of confusion between the two businesses was considerable.[173] Moreover, in this case, the association between the businesses, or the suggestion of endorsement by the plaintiff, was likely to injure the plaintiff in his profession and business as a horse master. In this respect, the case was a classic 'tools of the trade' type appropriation, where there was a real danger of confusion regarding a connection between two *businesses*. In this sense, *Paracidal* is arguably more consistent with the classic notion of passing off, and the first category of connection misrepresentation,[174] than *Henderson*.

Commercial connection and endorsement

Subsequently, in *10th Cantanae Pty Ltd* v. *Shoshana Pty Ltd*,[175] the relevant misrepresentation related to an endorsement or association – that is, a category (iii) misrepresentation. The plaintiff was a well-known television presenter named Sue Smith who had, in the past, appeared in advertisements to endorse various products. The defendants published an advertisement for Blaupunkt video recorders featuring a woman (who bore no physical resemblance to the plaintiff) watching a television set, accompanied by the caption 'Sue Smith just took total control of her video recorder'. It was held that the plaintiff was a person engaged in business in the widest sense of the term and, as such, had protectable goodwill. What needed to be shown, according to Wilcox J, was a misrepresentation that the plaintiff endorsed, or was otherwise associated with, the defendants' video recorder in such a way that would be likely

---

[170] *Ibid.*, 344.   [171] (1983) 4 IPR 201.   [172] *Ibid.*, 202.   [173] *Ibid.*, 206.
[174] See paragraph accompanying note 75 above.   [175] (1987) 79 ALR 299.

90 The commercial appropriation of personality

to result in members of the public being misled.[176] In this respect, the plaintiff's case was weak on its facts. The advertisement contained nothing more than the fairly common name, 'Sue Smith', and did not contain any information pointing unequivocally to the plaintiff, since the person depicted in the advertisement did not look like the plaintiff. Moreover, the plaintiff did not call any evidence to establish that any person had in fact been misled into thinking that the advertisement referred to the plaintiff, and Wilcox J held that it was appropriate to infer that there was no such evidence.[177] To find for the plaintiff on the identification issue was tantamount to allowing the plaintiff an effective monopoly on the common name 'Sue Smith', at least in circumstances where there was no express disclaimer that an advertisement did not refer to the plaintiff.[178]

The vague nature of the notion of connection, endorsement or association remained troublesome, and the subject of differing interpretations. Although Wilcox J held that the plaintiff had not been sufficiently clearly identified in the advertisement, he noted, obiter, that, had the facts been stronger in this respect, he would have held that the defendant had misrepresented that the plaintiff had associated herself with the advertised product, and that '[r]eaders might infer that she endorsed the product – at least in a vague way – as being suitable for purchase'. In Wilcox J's opinion, no matter how debased the currency of endorsement may have become, it could not be said that readers of advertisements remained unaffected by the introduction into an advertisement of a respected name. Pincus J took a stricter view, arguing that 'it should not be too readily accepted that the mere mention of a name in an advertisement necessarily connotes that the goods advertised have any characteristic – for example, that they have been approved, or even examined, by the person named'. Passing off was not necessarily constituted by the mere unauthorised use of a person's name or picture in an advertisement[179] and Pincus J also rejected the notion of 'sponsorship', which is sometimes, though erroneously, assumed to be coterminous with the terms 'endorsement' or 'approval'. As Pincus J noted, the term 'sponsorship', in a commercial context, indicates the fact that a commercial or other organisation or person stands behind, and partly finances, some activity such as a sporting event or a television show.[180] Sponsorship and endorsement are separate but complementary practices. While every inch of a racing car might be covered with brand names, and logos of various commercial organisations, and while the driver himself might be similarly covered from head to toe, the display does not indicate endorsement, but

---

[176] *Ibid.*, 302.   [177] *Ibid.*, 303.   [178] *Ibid.*, 302 *per* Wilcox J.
[179] *Ibid.*, 306.   [180] *Ibid.*, 307.

Goodwill in personality

indicates the sponsorship provided by the businesses in return for publicity. Although the driver may be said to endorse certain products, he does not sponsor them. Similarly, in *10th Cantanae*, the person depicted in the advertisement could not be said to have 'sponsored' Blaupunkt videos.[181]

Subsequently, the lack of an endorsement in any real sense was held to be significant in *Honey* v. *Australian Airlines and Another*.[182] Although the first defendant's advertisement featured the plaintiff prominently, the prominence given to the defendants' logo was minimal, since the advertisement was primarily intended to promote sport in schools, rather than the airline's business itself. Similarly, the second defendant, a religious group, had not sought to make use of the identity of the plaintiff, and had not named him, but had merely intended to use the picture to illustrate an activity, or type of life, in one of their publications. Thus, according to Northrop J, the facts of the case were different from the facts of *10th Cantanae* in the sense that the present case did not involve a typical advertisement relating to the sale of goods. In *Honey* it could not be established that a reasonably significant number of people would infer that the plaintiff was giving his endorsement to the defendants' businesses,[183] and, as noted above, the fact that the plaintiff was an amateur athlete led the Court to the conclusion that the plaintiff did not have the relevant goodwill in a business or professional capacity.[184] In advertising parlance, the advertisement did not involve a 'tools of the trade' type of endorsement, or even a 'non tools' endorsement, but involved the use of what could at most be described as an 'attention grabbing device', involving the use of the name or image of a celebrity in connection with goods or services without implying any endorsement.[185]

Thus, in the few cases which concerned a category (iii) endorsement misrepresentation, the notion of endorsement, association or connection remained rather vague and ill defined. The basic assumption common to misrepresentations in both categories (ii) (unspecified licensing connection) and (iii) (endorsement connection) seemed to be that the unauthorised use of a person's image in an advertisement or in merchandising would suggest that the plaintiff had declared his approval of the defendant's goods or services, and that their businesses were thereby associated or connected with each other. Such a misrepresentation would presumably lead to public confusion and, in turn, would presumably

---

[181] *Ibid.*
[182] [1989] ATPR 40–961, affirmed (1990) 18 IPR 185 (Federal Court of Australia, Full Court).
[183] [1989] ATPR 40–961, 50, 499.   [184] See text accompanying note 175 above.
[185] See Chapter 1.

92 The commercial appropriation of personality

lead to damage, or the risk of damage, to the plaintiff's business. Thus, through these presumptions, the unauthorised commercial exploitation of personality could come within the classic notion of passing off which encompasses misrepresentations that two businesses are connected with each other.

Character misappropriation

However, in *Hogan* v. *Koala Dundee Pty Ltd*,[186] Pincus J preferred a more radical approach. The defendants had made unauthorised use of images deriving from the plaintiffs' film, 'Crocodile Dundee', and, in particular, had used the name 'Dundee' and a composite image on signs inside and outside their shops and on their merchandise. The composite image consisted of a koala, wearing a bush hat with teeth in its band, a sleeveless vest, and carrying a knife, an image which was strongly reminiscent of the plaintiff Paul Hogan's role in the film. As Pincus J put it, the defendants had made use of these images 'in the hope of having their customers make a mental connection with Paul Hogan or the film or both – or to put it more simply, of cashing in on "Crocodile Dundee"'.[187] As such, the claim was not a typical case of appropriation of personality, in the sense that the defendants were not simply trading on the image of a single individual, but were trading on the associations with the film and its principal character, although it was practically impossible to draw a distinction between the actor in his personal capacity and the actor in his film role; the two were inextricably intertwined.

The plaintiffs claimed that the conduct of the defendants amounted to a misrepresentation which had misled the public as to: (i) whether the defendants' business was owned by, or conducted under a franchise or licence from, the plaintiffs; (ii) whether the defendants or their goods had the endorsement of or were affiliated or associated with the plaintiffs; and (iii) whether the defendants' goods or business had the sponsorship or approval of the plaintiffs.[188] As such, there was nothing revolutionary in the claims. The first claim came squarely within the first type of connection misrepresentation noted above,[189] and safely within the classic principle set out by Romer LJ in *The Clock Ltd* v. *The Clock House Hotel Ltd*, which encompasses situations where the business of the defendant is connected with the business of the plaintiff.[190] The second and third claims also came safely within the extended notion of passing off, represented by misrepresentations of type (ii), or, more precisely, (ii)(b), above – that

---

[186] (1988) 83 ALR 187.   [187] *Ibid.*, 189.   [188] *Ibid.*, 190.
[189] See text accompanying note 75 above.   [190] See note 78 above.

Goodwill in personality

is, misrepresentations relating to the existence of a licensing connection between the plaintiff and defendant, a category which has long been accepted in Australia.[191] The plaintiffs were Hogan himself and the film's makers, Rimfire Films, which had received an assignment of the merchandising rights from the production company which owned the script, a company which was, in turn, owned by Hogan himself. There was no doubt that the second plaintiff had a business both in making the film and in granting merchandising licences, which could be damaged by a misrepresentation that the goods of the defendant were licensed by the second plaintiff.

Pincus J preferred not to analyse the problems in terms of a category (ii) misrepresentation, that the defendant's goods were licensed by the plaintiff, and proceeded to set out a novel and startlingly wide proposition. According to Pincus J it was 'possible to bring a passing off action in respect of an image, including a name, unconnected with any business at all'. He went on to state that

> I think the law now is, at least in Australia, that the inventor of a sufficiently famous fictional character having certain visual or other traits, may prevent others from using his character to sell their goods and may assign the right so to use the character. Furthermore, the inventor may do these things even where he has never carried on any business at all, other than the writing or making of the work in which the character appears . . . The characteristics of such a suit are not necessarily precisely the same as the older type. In particular, an assignment of a right in a character need not assign any business.[192]

This proposition is very wide, and totally at odds with the orthodox English position and the extended Australian approach which holds that a passing off action does not confer any rights in respect of a name (or image) in itself, but in the goodwill of a business; such goodwill has no independent existence and consequently cannot be assigned in gross. In effect, it is tantamount to the judicial recognition of a *sui generis* character right, a proposition that has been explicitly rejected in English law.[193] A wide-ranging tort of character misappropriation could well have the effect of tipping the balance in favour of the creator (whose skill, effort and investment is supposed to be adequately encouraged and rewarded by the law of copyright), to the detriment of a competitor's freedom to market his goods in the most attractive way possible. Creators of works of fiction should arguably be subjected to the rigours of the market, and in the absence of copyright protection their characters should not

---

[191] *Children's Television Workshop Inc.* v. *Woolworths (NSW) Ltd* [1981] RPC 187.
[192] (1988) 83 ALR 187, 196.
[193] See note 145 above. See also White Paper, *Reform of Trade Marks Law*, Cm 1203 (1990), paras. 4.42–3; *ELVIS PRESLEY Trade Marks* [1999] RPC 567, 580 and 597.

94 The commercial appropriation of personality

be protected. An action in passing off will be available where there is a *material* misrepresentation relating to a licensing connection, resulting in real damage to an existing business goodwill,[194] whether in the form of an injurious association between the plaintiff's business and the defendant's shoddy goods or business, or where the plaintiff has goodwill in respect of an *existing* business in licensing copyright material in the form of a loss of licence fees. It is arguable that the economic interests of the creators of characters should not be protected any further.

What is most relevant for the purposes of the immediate discussion is the nature of the defendant's conduct, and the fact that Pincus J rejected the notion that liability should be based on a *misrepresentation* relating to a licensing connection in favour of liability based upon *misappropriation per se*. Contrary to the previous Australian authorities, Pincus J preferred the second and more ambiguous approach in the *Henderson* case, which suggested that liability need not be based on misrepresentation, but that misappropriation of commercial reputation was in itself sufficient,[195] although Pincus J widened the proposition even further to include the 'wrongful association of goods with an image properly belonging to the [plaintiff]'.[196] In Pincus J's view, there was 'a degree of artificiality in deciding image-filching cases . . . on the basis that the vice attacked is misleading the public about licensing arrangements'.[197] It could not be said that the public had been led to think that there was a precisely known kind of connection between the plaintiff and the defendant, and, moreover, an enquiry as to whether the public would believe that a licence had been granted by the plaintiff would involve ascertaining the public's views on the state of the law relating to character advertising, rather than any factual matter. The members of the public who would think that a licence must have been granted for the use of the name would be guessing as to the law's requirements, and guessing on a matter which was not at all clear in law.

These findings reflected the inconclusive nature of the survey evidence presented by both parties in *Hogan*,[198] and illustrated the incongruity of basing such an action on the issue of whether the public had been misled about the existence of licensing arrangements. Such issues were very much in the back of the minds of members of the public, and were

---

[194] Hence the natural reluctance of the English courts to grant interlocutory injunctions against businesses with existing goodwill, at the suit of plaintiffs who have yet to enter the market and who claim novel forms of misrepresentation without being able to show clear damage to goodwill. See *Lyngstad* v. *Anabas Products Ltd* [1977] FSR 62, 70; *Tavener Rutledge Ltd* v. *Trexapalm Ltd* [1977] RPC 275, 281–2.

[195] See text accompanying note 160 above.   [196] (1988) 83 ALR 187, 198.

[197] *Ibid.*   [198] *Ibid.*, 192–5.

Goodwill in personality

necessarily vague and inaccurate. As Pincus J observed, '[u]nlike a representation as to the origin or quality of goods, use of mere images in advertising, although presumably effective to generate sales, does not necessarily do so by creating, or relying on, any conclusions in the minds of the buying public'.[199] In the absence of such inconclusive evidence, Pincus J would have thought that a substantial number of people would associate the images with the plaintiffs' film, but that a lesser number would be inclined to think that the shop had some commercial connection with the film. Thus there would have been difficulties in establishing that there was a misrepresentation, and that it was a misrepresentation on which the public relied.[200] Nevertheless, this did not prevent Pincus J from holding, on the facts, that there had indeed been 'a clear representation of association with the film's images', and damage in the form of a lost licence fee,[201] and the injunction which was issued restrained the defendants from using the images in a way which was 'calculated to induce the public to believe that the [defendant] or goods sold by it is or are associated with the film'.[202] As has subsequently been observed by the High Court of New Zealand, such an approach results 'not so much from a finding of actual deception or independent damage as the tacit assumption that there should be a right of property in names, reputations and artificial images for character merchandising purposes'.[203] If this is the case, it is doubtful whether passing off is the best vehicle for securing such an aim.

Pincus J's novel approach has not been followed in subsequent Australian cases. In *Pacific Dunlop Ltd* v. *Hogan*[204] the Full Court of the Federal Court of Australia maintained the need to show a misrepresentation and damage to goodwill, rather than the broader notion of misappropriation set out in *Hogan* v. *Koala Dundee*. In *Pacific Dunlop* the complaint concerned an advertisement featuring a parody of a scene from the film *Crocodile Dundee*, in which Hogan's character managed to repel an attack by a mugger by producing a knife superior to the knife brandished by his assailant. In the defendants' advertisement the main character managed to fend off the attacker due to his superior 'Grosby Leatherz' shoes. The issue of identification was decided in favour of the plaintiffs (again, Paul Hogan and the film makers), and, at first instance, it was held that a substantial number of the public would assume that there was 'some association of a commercial nature' between the plaintiffs and the

---

[199] *Ibid.*, 195.   [200] Cf. text accompanying note 120 above.
[201] (1988) 83 ALR 187, 200 (despite having noted the circularity of such reasoning (*ibid.*, 198)).
[202] *Ibid.*, 202.   [203] *Tot Toys Ltd* v. *Mitchell* [1993] 1 NZLR 325, 363.
[204] (1989) 87 ALR 14.

96 The commercial appropriation of personality

producers of the advertisement and the product being advertised.[205] In common with the *Koala Dundee* case, the defendants were associating their product with images from the film, although it was again difficult to draw a distinction between the exploitation of the fictitious 'Crocodile Dundee' character and Hogan's own personality. The first plaintiff had previously exploited his image in several advertisements, and the character 'Crocodile Dundee' was strongly identified not only with the actor playing it but with the already well-recognised personality of the actor.[206]

The majority found the defendants liable in passing off. The relevant issue on appeal, according to Beaumont J, was 'whether a significant section of the public would be misled into believing, contrary to the fact, that a commercial arrangement had been concluded between the plaintiff and the defendant under which the plaintiff agreed to the advertising', a question which was to be answered in the affirmative.[207] Burchett J preferred to express the matter differently. In his view, the relevant question to be addressed was whether the advertisement conveyed a false endorsement of the shoes themselves by the plaintiff. Character merchandising, in Burchett J's view, 'should not be seen as setting off a logical train of thought' in the minds of the public, and its importance lies in the creation of an association of the product with the character, not in making precise misrepresentation. Accordingly, to ask whether the consumer reasoned that the plaintiff had authorised the advertisement was to ask a question which was 'a mere side issue'. What mattered, according to Burchett J, was the fact that the consumer wished to identify with the character or personality and was moved 'by a desire to wear something belonging in some sense to Crocodile Dundee (who is perceived as a persona, almost an avatar, of Mr Hogan)'. According to His Honour, the arousal of such a feeling by Hogan himself could not be regarded as misleading, since 'the value he promises the product will have is not in its leather, but in its association with himself'. An unauthorised advertisement, on the other hand, would be misleading since it would lack that valuable association between the product and the celebrity.[208] While this approach is arguably less artificial than an approach which presumes that the consumer is aware of, or concerned with, the existence of a commercial relationship between the plaintiff and the defendant, it sanctions, in effect, the protection of a celebrity's power of endorsement or product association *per se*. The reasoning is some way removed from the logical analysis which brings appropriation of personality, or character merchandising, within the orthodox notion of passing off: a misrepresentation (on which consumers rely)

---

[205] *Ibid.*, 38.   [206] *Ibid.*, 35.
[207] *Ibid.*, 42. Sheppard J dissented on the facts.   [208] *Ibid.*, 44–5.

Goodwill in personality   97

which leads consumers to believe that the business of the defendant is connected (by licence, association or endorsement) with the business of the plaintiff, resulting in damage, or its likelihood, to the plaintiff's business.

The requirement of misrepresentation was subsequently maintained in *Talmax Pty Ltd* v. *Telstra Corp. Ltd*,[209] where it was held that the defendant's advertisement featuring a photograph of the plaintiff swimmer misrepresented, for the purposes of an action under section 52 of the Trade Practices Act and the tort of passing off, that the plaintiff was 'sponsored' by the defendant and had consented to the 'use of his name, image and reputation' in its advertising and supported the defendant's telecommunications services.[210] Similarly, in an artificial character merchandising case, *Twentieth Century Fox Film Corp.* v. *South Australian Brewing Co. Ltd*, it was held that the defendants' use of the term 'Duff Beer', deriving from *The Simpsons* television cartoon series, amounted to a misrepresentation suggesting an association between the defendants' beer and the plaintiffs' business in producing cartoons and its extensive associated merchandising business, which might damage the plaintiffs' licensing business.[211] What is most significant for present purposes is that liability was based on misrepresentation rather than the broader notion of character misappropriation along the lines of *Koala Dundee*.

The inevitable impression conveyed is that while the Australian courts are paying lip service to the requirement of a misrepresentation relating to a connection between two businesses, in reality, in cases of appropriation of personality, they have been protecting a celebrity's power of endorsement *in vacuo*.[212] These conclusions are supported by the nature of the damage that the courts have been prepared to accept.

Damage

Passing off does not protect a property right in a name or other indicium, but protects property in the underlying goodwill of a business.[213] Although the basis of the tort is interference with a property right, the

---

[209] (1996) ATPR ¶41–535 (Supreme Court of Queensland – Court of Appeal).
[210] *Ibid.*, 42, 828. The Court (*ibid.*, 42, 828–9) took a very broad view as to the relevant damage.
[211] (1996) 34 IPJ 225, 246 (Federal Court of Australia – General Division).
[212] See R. G. Howell, 'Personality Rights: A Canadian Perspective: Some Comparisons with Australia' (1990) 1 IPJ (Australia) 212, 219; J. McMullan, 'Personality Rights in Australia' (1997) 8 AIPJ 86, 91. Cf. D. R. Shanahan, ' "Image Filching" in Australia: The Legal Provenance and Aftermath of the "Crocodile Dundee" Decisions' (1991) 81 TMR 351, 365.
[213] *Star Industrial Co. Ltd* v. *Yap Kwee Kor*, note 16 above.

98   The commercial appropriation of personality

tortious nature of the cause of action is reflected in the fact that the cause of action is incomplete unless the plaintiff can show damage, or the likelihood of damage, to his goodwill.[214] Thus, to succeed in a passing off action, the plaintiff must satisfy the fifth of Lord Diplock's criteria in *Erven Warnink*[215] (or the third element in the classical trinity)[216] and show that the defendant's misrepresentation causes actual damage to his business or goodwill, or, in a *quia timet* action, the probability of damage. Again this is an area where there is considerable divergence between the English authorities and the Australian authorities, particularly in the line of cases that have followed the *Henderson* decision.

Two distinct approaches may be found, which reflect the manner in which the tort has expanded from its early origins.[217] In the classic action for passing off, where the defendant misrepresented that his goods or his business were the plaintiff's goods or business,[218] there would almost automatically have been a diversion of trade from the plaintiff to the defendant, which invited little discussion of the issue of damage.[219] However, with the widening of the categories of actionable misrepresentations, and the move away from the classic factual situation, the requirement of damage became increasingly important to distinguish between misrepresentations which were actionable in passing off and those which were not. Indeed, in *Erven Warnink*, which broadened the category of actionable misrepresentations, moving away from the classic action, the need to show damage was clearly stated.[220] However, an alternative approach seems to presume that the plaintiff has suffered damage if the other essential elements can be shown. This seems to be the approach taken by the Full Court of the High Court of New South Wales in *Henderson*,[221] although it is difficult to accept as a general rule, and this aspect of the decision in *Henderson* is not only inconsistent with the English authorities but also with subsequent decisions of the Federal Court of Australia which insist on the need to prove damage.[222]

---

[214] P. Cane, *Tort Law and Economic Interests*, 2nd edn (Oxford, 1996), 78.
[215] See text accompanying note 12 above.   [216] See text accompanying note 13 above.
[217] See, generally, Wadlow, *Passing Off*, Ch. 3.
[218] *Spalding (A. G.) & Bros.* v. *Gamage (A. W.) Ltd* (1915) 32 RPC 273; *The Clock Ltd* v. *The Clock House Hotel Ltd* (1936) 53 RPC 269.
[219] See Wadlow, *Passing Off*, 155, and D. Young, *Passing Off*, 3rd edn (London, 1994), 62.
[220] See text accompanying note 12 above.
[221] *Henderson* v. *Radio Corp. Pty Ltd* [1969] RPC 218, 236. See also *Walt Disney Productions Ltd* v. *Triple Five Corp.* (1992) 93 DLR (4th) 739, 747 (Alberta Court of Queen's Bench).
[222] See, e.g., *Taco Bell Pty Ltd* v. *Taco Co. of Australia Inc.* (1981) 42 ALR 177 (Full Court); *Vieright Pty Ltd* v. *Myer Stores Ltd* (1995) 31 IPR 361, 369 (Full Court); *TGI Friday's Australia Pty Ltd* v. *TGI Friday's Inc.* (1999) 45 IPR 43, 50 (Full Court); and see Wadlow, *Passing Off*, 155.

Goodwill in personality 99

The overwhelming bulk of the authorities suggest that damage is an essential element which the plaintiff needs to prove in order to succeed in an action for passing off, although the strictness of the requirement to show damage might well vary from case to case. Where both parties are clearly appealing to the same group of customers, and there is a clear intention to exploit the plaintiff's goodwill, it might be easier to establish actual or likely damage[223] than in cases where the parties' respective fields of activity are different, and where the court might require fuller proof of damage.[224] In cases of appropriation of personality the plaintiff and the defendant will not be competing in the same field of business, and a plaintiff will, on an orthodox analysis, find it difficult to establish damage. For example, a celebrity television presenter does not ordinarily manufacture and sell video recorders, a celebrity athlete does not usually run an airline business, and celebrity dance instructors do not normally manufacture and sell records. Thus there can be no diversion of trade in the sense of the classic passing off action where the plaintiff loses sales as his customers go to the defendant as a result of the defendant's misrepresentation. Nevertheless, even the classic notion of passing off is not so narrow, and encompasses misrepresentations that a defendant's goods or services are connected with the plaintiff. Consequently there are a number of different possible heads of damage which fall to be considered. Some are well established, while others are more uncertain. The following five heads of damage are considered in turn: (i) injurious association; (ii) exposure to liability; (iii) loss of control; (iv) loss of a licensing opportunity; (v) dilution.

Damage through an injurious association

Arguments for extending the tort of passing off to encompass appropriation of personality rely on the notion of a licensing or endorsement agreement to bring such conduct within the classic principle that a defendant should not represent that his business is the business of the plaintiff, or is connected with the business of the plaintiff.[225] If such a misrepresentation can be proven, then a well-established head of damage will be damage in the form of an injurious association between the plaintiff and the defendant. For example, in *Harrods Ltd* v. *R. Harrod Ltd*[226] the plaintiffs,

---

[223] *Associated Newspapers Group Plc* v. *Insert Media Ltd* [1991] 1 WLR 571, 579–80 *per* Browne-Wilkinson VC.
[224] *Stringfellow* v. *McCain Foods (GB) Ltd* [1984] RPC 501. See also *Pinky's Pizza Ribs on the Run Pty Ltd* v. *Pinky's Seymour Pizza & Pasta Pty Ltd* (Supreme Court of Victoria Court of Appeal) (1997) ATPR ¶41–600, 44, 283 *per* Tadgell JA.
[225] See note 78 above.   [226] (1924) 41 RPC 74.

100   The commercial appropriation of personality

owners of the famous department store, were granted an injunction to prevent the defendant, a money lending company, from trading under a confusingly similar name on the basis that they might be damaged by being associated with the defendants in the minds of the public. Similarly, in *Annabel's (Berkeley Square) Ltd* v. *Schock*[227] the plaintiff owners of a high-class night club were granted an interlocutory injunction to restrain the defendants from using the name 'Annabel's' for an escort agency. The association between the reputable club and an escort agency which had 'but an indifferent public image'[228] was held to be likely to damage the plaintiff's goodwill to an unquantifiable extent.

Two different conceptions of goodwill in relation to cases of appropriation of personality may be identified.[229] The first relates to a person's goodwill in respect of his profession or artistic or literary occupation, while the second and much narrower conception relates to the plaintiff's goodwill in respect of his actual business of exploiting his image, or in granting licences for exploitation. A question already broached is whether unauthorised commercial exploitation of an individual's personality can damage that person in relation to his business or profession. In the early professional cases several well-known surgeons were unable to prevent the unauthorised commercial exploitation of their names. Although the actions were for libel, the possibility was at least admitted in *Dockrell* v. *Dougall* that a person might have a remedy if the plaintiff could show that he had suffered injury to his property, business or profession.[230] Similarly, in *Sim* v. *Heinz* the possibility was admitted that an actor might have goodwill in respect of his performances which might be damaged by the unauthorised imitation of that actor's voice, although Hodson LJ doubted whether there was anything in the nature of competition in a common field.[231] In this respect it is instructive to note the dicta of Wynn-Parry J on the issue of damage in *McCulloch* v. *May*.[232] Although the common field of activity doctrine has now been discredited, at least as an absolute requirement,[233] it might still be relevant in assessing damage or the likelihood of damage. In *McCulloch* Wynn-Parry J dismissed the claim of a risk of damage to the plaintiff's professional reputation as an author and broadcaster, and to his means of gaining a livelihood, as not being a real or tangible risk. Indeed, this finding may have been sufficient to

---

[227] [1972] RPC 838.
[228] On which, see *Miss World (Jersey) Ltd* v. *James Street Productions Ltd* [1981] FSR, 309, 311 *per* Denning MR.
[229] See text accompanying note 70 above.
[230] (1899) 15 TLR 333 (see text accompanying note 47 above).
[231] [1959] 1 WLR 313 (see text accompanying note 49 above).
[232] (1948) 65 RPC 58 (see text accompanying note 81 above).
[233] See note 89 above.

Goodwill in personality 101

dismiss the claim without introducing the troublesome common field of activity doctrine. Such an approach would effectively dismiss many cases of appropriation of personality. If goodwill subsists in a person's business or profession (including artistic and literary occupations), then it might often be difficult to show damage to goodwill in that business or profession. Of course, it would largely be a matter of fact in each case, and some unauthorised exploitation, such as the unauthorised use of a surgeon's name, might be more likely to damage the plaintiff's goodwill than others, for example the unauthorised use of a radio broadcaster's name.

In Australia, in *Henderson* v. *Radio Corp. Pty Ltd*, at first instance, the plaintiff ballroom dancers had claimed that they might suffer damage as a result of being associated with the music of Art Gregory, whose orchestra played the music featured on the record, although it was not shown that Art Gregory's music was in any way inferior.[234] Similarly, damage through association with an orchestra other than the one with which the plaintiffs were usually associated was rejected as being too speculative to amount to a real and tangible risk of damage.[235]

Damage through exposure to liability / risk of litigation

A plaintiff might allege that he has been exposed to liability or the risk of litigation if a defendant makes a misrepresentation that his business is in some way associated with the plaintiff. This head of damage overlaps with the previous head, and there is also a considerable overlap between this head of damage and the rule in *Routh* v. *Webster*.[236] Much will depend on the facts of the individual case and it will probably be comparatively rare for an unauthorised appropriation of personality to lead to the danger of exposing the plaintiff to liability, although section 2(2)(b) of the Consumer Protection Act 1987 holds that liability extends to any person who has held himself out as producer of the product by putting his name or trade mark on the product, when damage is caused by a defect in the product.[237] It is not altogether impossible to think of circumstances where this might happen, for example a variation on the facts of *Clark* v. *Freeman*[238] and some of the other professional cases, where the names of well-known surgeons were used on quack medicines. Nevertheless, in the case of more benign products or services, appropriation of personality will not ordinarily expose the plaintiff to liability; indeed, such a claim

---

[234] [1969] RPC 218, 226.   [235] *Ibid.*
[236] (1849) 10 Beav 561 (50 ER 698). See text accompanying note 31 above.
[237] See Wadlow, *Passing Off*, 165; J. Adams, *Character Merchandising*, 2nd edn (London, 1996), Ch. 7.
[238] (1848) 11 Beav 112. See text accompanying note 36 above.

102 The commercial appropriation of personality

was dismissed as being wholly visionary or illusory in *McCulloch* v. *May*, where the product in question was breakfast cereal.[239]

Loss of control

This head of damage is more uncertain. In some cases the plaintiff might claim that the defendant's misrepresentation that their businesses are connected might be damaging in that it involves a loss of the plaintiff's control over his own reputation, even though there is no risk of an injurious association, or risk of exposure to liability. Indeed, the defendant's business might be completely innocuous, unlike a situation involving the previous two heads of damage. In a few limited cases the courts have accepted loss of control as a relevant head of damage. For example, in *British Legion* v. *British Legion Club (Street) Ltd*[240] the defendants' club was carried on in a proper manner, and there was nothing to suggest that the plaintiffs might be damaged by an injurious association on account of the way in which the club was being run, or that the defendants might be exposed to litigation. Nevertheless, Farwell J held that there was a possibility of damage if the defendant encountered trouble in the form of financial problems or trouble with licensing laws, while conceding that there was little likelihood that such problems would in fact arise. A rather more fanciful scenario was given in *Hulton Press* v. *White Eagle Youth Holiday Camp*[241] where it was held that the publishers of *Eagle* magazine might be damaged in respect of a misrepresentation that they were connected with the defendants' holiday camp, if there were a disaster, a bad accident or an epidemic at such a holiday camp.

More recently, in *Lego System Aktieselskab* v. *Lego M. Lemelstrich Ltd* it was accepted that the plaintiffs' inability to control their reputation amounted to a risk of damage to their goodwill,[242] although there were also other relevant heads of damage which have also, in turn, been questioned.[243] It may be that some of the decided cases were right on their facts, and showed a real risk of damage as a result of loss of control. However, where there is no real likelihood of such damage resulting from loss of control, the proposition that loss of control is a sufficient head of damage in itself is obviously difficult to reconcile with the requirement of damage as an essential element of the tort of passing off. If this were

---

[239] (1948) 65 RPC 58, 67 *per* Wynn-Parry J.
[240] (1931) 48 RPC 555.   [241] (1951) 68 RPC 126.
[242] [1983] FSR 155, 195. See also the obiter dicta of Millet LJ in *Harrods Ltd* v. *Harrodian School Ltd* [1996] RPC 697, 715.
[243] See Wadlow, *Passing Off*, 173; H. Carty, 'Heads of Damage in Passing Off' [1996] EIPR 487, 490.

Goodwill in personality

the case, then almost any connection misrepresentation would amount to a loss of the plaintiff's ability to control his reputation to some extent, making the requirement of damage largely superfluous. The better view seems to be that loss of control is insufficient as a head of damage, and a plaintiff in an appropriation of personality case is unlikely to succeed by merely claiming that unauthorised exploitation has resulted in a loss of control of the manner in which the attributes of his personality are to be exploited. Although injurious association or risk of liability can be more easily squared with the requirement that damage must result from the defendant's misrepresentation, loss of control arguably lies beyond the bounds of passing off and is tantamount to a claim for misappropriation.

Loss of a licensing opportunity

The notion of goodwill in personality may be approached in two ways.[244] On the one hand, the relevant goodwill might relate to a person's business in the broad sense, embracing professional, artistic or literary occupations. Thus, unauthorised commercial exploitation of personality might damage that person's goodwill, in respect of his profession, such as medicine, acting, broadcasting and such like. The first two heads of damage examined above are primarily concerned with such a conception of goodwill. On the other hand, the relevant goodwill might lie in a person's subsidiary business of exploiting his image, through advertising or merchandising, or through granting licences to third parties. This is a much narrower conception of goodwill in personality though not an unattractive notion, since it helps to focus on the precise nature of the damage that the plaintiff might suffer. Thus, if a plaintiff can establish the first two elements of the tort, then he might argue that his business in licensing his image might be damaged through the loss of the opportunity to charge the defendant a fee for the use of his image. Alternatively, where the plaintiff does not trade in his image for the moment, he might argue that the defendant had damaged his potential for licensing the use of his image in the future. Both of these propositions are highly dubious.

Although the English courts have not addressed this issue directly, similar arguments have been given short shrift by the Court of Appeal. In *Stringfellow* v. *McCain Foods (GB) Ltd* the plaintiffs claimed that the use of the word 'Stringfellows' in association with frozen chips would damage their reputation and prejudice their future chances of exploiting the benefit of the goodwill associated with the name through merchandising

---

[244] See text accompanying note 68 above.

104   The commercial appropriation of personality

activities.[245] In rejecting this argument, Slade LJ did not find it necessary to consider in detail the law relating to the granting of merchandising rights and was prepared to assume that a person carrying on business under a particular name with a valuable goodwill might be able in practice to exploit that name for profit.[246] However, the evidence did not establish that, but for the showing of the defendants' advertisement, the plaintiffs would have been able to exploit merchandising rights in the name 'Stringfellows' or that the defendants' advertisement had prejudiced or would be likely to prejudice the plaintiffs' chances of profitable exploitation of the name. In Slade LJ's view, 'in regard to this head of alleged potential damage, one is in the field of pure speculation and this is not enough to ground an action for passing off, particularly against an innocent defendant'.[247]

In Australia, in *Henderson* v. *Radio Corp. Pty Ltd*, the findings of damage at first instance, in the form of a restriction on the plaintiffs' ability to expand into a related field,[248] were rejected on appeal. However, Evatt CJ went on to state that the wrongful appropriation of another's business or professional reputation was an injury in itself. The defendant had wrongfully deprived the plaintiffs of their right to bestow or withhold their professional recommendation, and had thereby deprived them of the fee on which they could have insisted.[249] Similarly, Manning J stated that the effect of the defendant's conduct had been to 'deprive the plaintiffs of the fee or remuneration they would have earned if they had been asked for their authority to do what was done'.[250] This aspect of the decision in *Henderson* and subsequent cases[251] is the most troubling, and the circularity of the reasoning has not gone un-noticed. The problems were

[245] [1984] RPC 501, 544.

[246] *Ibid.*, 544. Counsel for the appellants had showed that the plaintiffs had not registered the name 'Stringfellows' under the Trade Marks Act 1938, and also showed that the plaintiffs could not have granted a legally valid licence for the use of the name and referred the Court to the decision of the Privy Council in *Star Industrial Co. Ltd* v. *Yap Kwee Kor* [1976] FSR 256.

[247] [1984] RPC 501, 545.

[248] [1969] RPC 218, 228, following *Eastman Photographic Co. Ltd* v. *Griffiths (John) Cycle Corp. Ltd* (1898) 15 RPC 105 and *Hulton Press Ltd* v. *White Eagle Youth Holiday Camp Ltd* (1951) 68 RPC 126, where the respective fields of expansion were in turn rather implausible. Cf. *Newsweek Inc.* v. *BBC* [1979] RPC 441, 448 *per* Denning MR, and see, generally, Wadlow, *Passing Off*, 171–2.

[249] See passage cited in text accompanying note 158 above.

[250] [1969] RPC 218, 243.

[251] See *Talmax Pty Ltd* v. *Telstra Corp. Ltd* (1996) ATPR ¶41–535, 42, 828 (Supreme Court of Queensland – Court of Appeal); *Twentieth Century Fox Film Corp.* v. *South Australian Brewing Co. Ltd* (1996) 34 IPJ 225 (this head of damage was rather more convincing since it involved an element of injurious association (although the Court did not characterise it as such) in that the plaintiffs had refused to license their artificial characters for use on alcohol and tobacco products).

Goodwill in personality

succinctly summarised by Fisher J in the High Court of New Zealand, in *Tot Toys Ltd* v. *Mitchell*:[252]

It is axiomatic that damage must be proved or presumed as one of the ingredients of passing off. It has never been sufficient for the plaintiffs to fill this gap by arguing that their loss is loss of the right to charge the defendant a fee for continuing conduct the lawfulness of which is the subject currently under inquiry. To accept that proposition would be to deny that damage is an essential and independent element of the tort. And if the defendant's conduct is otherwise lawful, it cannot be rendered unlawful upon the ground that it might induce others to act in the same way without the plaintiff's permission. Yet in *Crocodile Dundee*[253] and similar decisions, the damage relied upon has been prejudice to the opportunity to license the merchandising 'right' to the defendant and to others. The plaintiff has a right to exact a fee for character merchandising only if he has an enforceable right to prevent others from using his image without his permission. In the present context he has the right to prevent others only if he can sue them in passing off. He can sue them in passing off only if he can show a loss. The only loss he can show is the loss of the right to insist upon a fee for the character merchandising. So the argument is circular. Unless there is some damage other than loss of potential character merchandising rights, one might think that the action would fail on that ground.[254]

It is difficult to come to any conclusion other than that the Australian courts have been resorting to a legal fiction.[255]

Dilution

Although the status of this head of damage is uncertain[256] it deserves to be considered briefly. As the underlying bases for trade mark protection have arguably shifted to embrace supposedly new economic functions, there have been corresponding demands to recognise new heads of damage. The dilution doctrine, as developed in the United States, protects a trade mark against the 'gradual whittling away' of the identity of a mark in the public's mind, through its use by rival traders on non-competing goods.[257] Such damage does not depend on confusion as to the origin or

---

[252] [1993] 1 NZLR 325.
[253] *Hogan* v. *Koala Dundee Pty Ltd* (1988) 83 ALR 187.
[254] [1993] 1 NZLR 325, 362.   [255] Wadlow, *Passing Off*, 151.
[256] *Ibid.*, 174–7. See also H. Carty, 'Dilution and Passing Off: Cause for Concern' (1996) 112 LQR 632.
[257] See F. Schechter, 'The Rational Basis of Trademark Protection' (1927) 40 HarvLRev 813, 825. Section 43(c)(1) Lanham Trademarks Act 1946 (15 USC §1125(c)(1)) now provides a federal anti-dilution law. See, generally, J. T. McCarthy, *McCarthy on Trade Marks and Unfair Competition*, 4th edn (St Paul, Minn., 1999), §24; T. Martino, *Trade-mark Dilution* (Oxford, 1996); M. Strasser, 'The Rational Basis of Trademark Protection Revisited: Putting the Dilution Doctrine into Context' (2000) 10 Fordham Intell Prop Media & Ent LJ 375, 404–16.

106   The commercial appropriation of personality

quality of the goods, but protects the advertising power and commercial attraction of the mark. This notion has been introduced into the statutory trade marks scheme by sections 5(3) and 10(3) of the Trade Marks Act 1994,[258] giving effect to Arts. 4(3) and 5(2) of the Trade Marks Directive,[259] although the Act does not affect the tort of passing off.[260] The closest that the courts have come to recognising dilution as a head of damage at common law has been in *Taittinger SA* v. *Allbev Ltd*[261] where the defendants sold a non-alcoholic soft drink as 'Elderflower Champagne'. The Court of Appeal held that there was a danger of confusion between the plaintiffs' champagne and the defendants' elderflower champagne, and also that there was a danger that the defendants' conduct would 'erode the singularity and distinctiveness of the description "Champagne" and so cause the first plaintiffs damage of an insidious but serious kind'.[262] It is unclear whether dilution can be a head of damage in its own right. In *Taittinger* the dicta on dilution were obiter, since there was evidence that damage would result from confusion, and consequent loss of sales or injurious association.

Subsequently, in *Harrods Ltd* v. *Harrodian School Ltd*[263] the plaintiffs, the owners of the well-known department store, sought to prevent the defendants from carrying on a private preparatory school under the name of 'The Harrodian School' on the old site of the Harrods' staff club (The Harrodian Club) in Barnes. The plaintiffs contended that the defendant had deliberately set out to exploit their reputation by suggesting a connection between the school and the department store, in the sense that the public would believe that the defendants sponsored or backed the school. There was no evidence of confusion relating to the fact that the businesses of the plaintiff and defendant were connected. As to damage, there was no likelihood of damage to the plaintiffs' business through an injurious association and, although there had been a minor sex scandal at the school, it was regarded as insufficient to constitute such damage. The interesting point for present purposes is that the validity of dilution as a head of damage was questioned. Millet LJ noted that the law does not protect the value of a brand or name as such, but only the value of the goodwill that it generates, and that the law insists on proof of confusion

---

[258] See *Oasis Stores Ltd's Trade Mark Application* [1998] RPC 631; *AUDI-MED Trade Mark* [1998] RPC 863; *CORGI Trade Mark* [1999] RPC 549; cf. *C. A. Sheimer (M) Sdn Bhd's Trade Mark Application* [2000] RPC 484, 506.

[259] Council Directive 89/104 on Trade Marks, OJ L40/1. See *General Motors Corp.* v. *Yplon SA* [1999] ETMR 122.

[260] Trade Marks Act 1994, s. 2(2).   [261] [1993] FSR 641.

[262] *Ibid.*, 678 *per* Bingham MR, and see *ibid.*, 670 *per* Peter Gibson LJ.

[263] [1996] RPC 697. See also H. Carty, 'Passing Off at the Crossroads: *Harrods Ltd* v. *Harrodian School Ltd*' [1996] EIPR 629.

Goodwill in personality

to justify its intervention. The erosion of the distinctiveness of a brand name by its degeneration into common use does not depend on confusion at all. Millet LJ stated that he had 'an intellectual difficulty in accepting the concept that the law insists upon the presence of both confusion and damage and yet recognises as sufficient a head of damage which does not depend on confusion'.[264]

Again, this goes to the root question of whether unauthorised commercial exploitation of personality is conducted in a way which leads to confusion amongst the public concerning a connection between the business of the plaintiff and the business of the defendant. This is, of course, a matter of fact to be decided in each particular case and cannot be conclusively affirmed or denied either way. Although the gravamen of a celebrity's complaint might lie in the fact that use of his image by others is diminishing the commercial power of his attributes of personality, and reducing the value which lies for him in his own exploitation,[265] a cause of action in passing off is dependent on establishing confusion and damage. It would seem that damage in the form of dilution of the marketing power of a celebrity's attributes of personality would not be sufficient in itself to support an action for passing off. Some other head of damage would need to be shown, although, given the foregoing discussion, other heads of damage might, in turn, be equally difficult to establish.

Conclusions

Two models

The expansive approach taken in Australia and the restrictive approach taken in England in relation to appropriation of personality may be summarised as follows. The first, restrictive, model in fact encompasses two variants, reflecting the different conceptions of goodwill as either goodwill in a business or profession, or goodwill in a subsidiary licensing business, the latter appearing in parentheses. Under a restrictive model, the following elements would need to be shown:

(i) that the plaintiff has goodwill in relation to his business or profession (or a business in licensing attributes of his personality); (ii)(a) that the defendant misrepresents that his business is connected with the business or profession of the plaintiff, possibly through a licensing or endorsement agreement; (ii)(b) that the public relies on the misrepresentation, believing the representation to be an implicit guarantee of the nature or quality of the goods or services; (iii) the plaintiff suffers damage, or the likelihood of damage, to his goodwill in his business or

---

[264] [1996] RPC 697, 716.
[265] See *Pacific Dunlop Ltd* v. *Hogan* (1989) 87 ALR 14, 25 *per* Sheppard J.

108   The commercial appropriation of personality

profession through (a) loss of sales, (b) an injurious association, (c) exposure to liability or litigation (or (d) the loss of a licence fee).

Under the more liberal Australian approach, it must be shown that:

(i) the plaintiff has goodwill in relation to his business or profession; (ii) that the defendant misrepresents that the plaintiff has endorsed the goods or services of the defendant in the sense that the public will form the erroneous belief that the goods or services are authorised or licensed; (iii) that the plaintiff has suffered damage in the form of the lost licence fee that he could have charged had the defendant not exploited his name without his consent.

Three fictions?

At its most flexible the application of the tort of passing off to the problem of appropriation of personality involves a misrepresentation which no one believes, causing damage either to goodwill in a vague notion of a business or profession, or the loss of a licence fee, the enforceability of which is itself based on the existence of a valid cause of action for passing off. A three-legged stool cannot stand up with one leg missing, let alone two. Nevertheless, the Australian courts have managed to prop up the tort of passing off through a liberal use of fictions. The only case which has sought to depart from the current Australian line of reasoning, in favour of a more direct approach, is the decision of Pincus J in *Hogan* v. *Koala Dundee*,[266] basing liability on *misappropriation* rather than misrepresentation.[267] As far as the present discussion is concerned, this was the right reasoning in the wrong case. It is submitted that *Koala Dundee* is best understood as a character merchandising case, where the defendants drew on the elements of the main character's fictional attributes (sleeveless vest, bush hat, knife) and other elements of the script (the name 'Dundee', and the similar style of print), rather than a case of appropriation of personality, involving the image of Paul Hogan himself.[268] While this might set up a potentially alarmingly wide tort of character appropriation,[269] cases of appropriation of personality involve different considerations, and a new form of liability based on misappropriation is arguably easier to justify[270] since, as has been stressed throughout, appropriation of personality can only be properly understood by considering both economic and dignitary interests. Moreover, a suitably narrow tort of appropriation of personality need not set a wider precedent for artificial character merchandising, nor amount to a general tort of misappropriation of intangibles.[271]

---

[266] See text accompanying note 186 above.   [267] (1988) 83 ALR 197, 196.
[268] See text accompanying note 192 above.   [269] See text accompanying note 193 above.
[270] As Fisher J noted in *Tot Toys Ltd* v. *Mitchell* [1993] 1 NZLR 325, 363.
[271] See 112–15 below.

Goodwill in personality

If the effective fictions inherent in adapting the tort of passing off to protect character merchandising and attributes of personality were applied generally, the shape of the tort would be radically altered. Although the categories of actionable misrepresentation have expanded quite some way from cases where one trader passed off his goods as the goods of another trader, the tort has been kept within reasonable bounds by the need to show confusion, resulting in damage or a real likelihood of damage. Indeed, in view of the open-ended nature of the potentially actionable misrepresentations, the requirement of damage assumes a central importance as an 'acid test' for distinguishing between those misrepresentations which are actionable in passing off, and those which are not.[272] If the damage requirement were to be relaxed, or completely abandoned, then the tort of passing off could potentially become a very wide and powerful monopoly right, which might have to be attenuated by, for example, requiring an element of intention.[273] In Australia passing off has not, as yet, developed into such a wide monopoly right and decisions subsequent to *Henderson* v. *Radio Corp. Pty Ltd* have maintained the requirement of damage in the same manner as the English authorities. However, cases involving appropriation of personality and character merchandising have been treated as a special category to which the normal rules of passing off do not apply. This immediately begs the obvious question of why such cases deserve to be treated separately, when such an approach is logically indefensible.

Anglo-Australian law is not 'susceptible to the facile generation of new torts',[274] in contrast with the United States, where the courts are more willing to develop new forms of common law liability to meet new social conditions and trading practices.[275] Thus, either a plaintiff's claim is denied in a way which might offend common notions of social justice,[276] or the claim is admitted by manipulating existing torts, and by making liberal use of fictions. The former approach has prevailed in the limited English case law in this area, where embracing cases of appropriation of

---

[272] Wadlow, *Passing Off*, 149–50.

[273] J. D. Heydon, *Economic Torts*, 2nd edn (London, 1978), 137–8.

[274] W. L. Morison, 'Unfair Competition and Passing Off – The Flexibility of a Formula' (1956) 2 Sydney L Rev 50, 60.

[275] Most notably separate rights of privacy and publicity: see Chapter 7 below. Cf. *Henderson* v. *Radio Corp. Pty Ltd* [1969] RPC 218, 237 *per* Manning J, noting that calls for the introduction of a new tort of invasion of privacy were entirely different from the issue of what causes of action actually existed at common law. See also *10th Cantanae Pty Ltd* v. *Shoshana Pty Ltd* (1987) 79 ALR 299, 300 *per* Wilcox J: 'Anglo-Australian law does not, of course, recognise privacy interests, as such, although the expansion of the protection given by the law of passing off which was effected in *Henderson* v. *Radio Corp.* goes some distance towards covering the appropriation cases'.

[276] Cf. the extra-legal norms discussed in Chapter 1.

110   The commercial appropriation of personality

personality has been regarded not only as an unjustifiable extension of the tort of passing off but as the effective judicial creation of a new remedy, which the courts have not been prepared to countenance.[277] The latter approach has been adopted in Australia, an approach which is not objectionable in itself, as long as the fictions do not pervade to the extent that the whole underlying basis of a tort is altered. The Australian experience in relation to character merchandising and appropriation of personality reveals such fears to be somewhat illusory, and the more relaxed requirements as to the materiality of the misrepresentation, and the form of damage to goodwill, seem to have been largely confined to a limited class of cases.

Judicial conservatism or deference to the legislature should not become absolute bars to limited, interstitial law-making by the courts. In the hands of the Australian courts the classical trinity of goodwill, misrepresentation and damage have proved to be fairly pliable notions, rather than rigid requirements. One may legitimately wonder whether the courts would be exercising a much wider discretion in developing a new tort of appropriation of personality from existing precedents and principles than they are currently exercising in manipulating the requirements of goodwill, misrepresentation and damage, and nebulous notions such as sponsorship, association and endorsement. In this respect, the approach taken by the Canadian courts in developing a new tort of appropriation of personality, examined in the next chapter, represents a more direct and intellectually honest approach.

[277] See *McCulloch* v. *May* (1948) 65 RPC 58, 67 *per* Wynn-Parry J.

5 Unfair competition and the doctrine of misappropriation

Introduction

This chapter considers two separate notions which lie beyond the tort of passing off: a broad-based action for misappropriation of intangibles, and a much narrower *sui generis* tort of appropriation of personality. As regards the latter, the common law jurisdictions in Canada, most notably Ontario, have preferred not to follow the Australian example, and have recognised that the misappropriation of another person's name or likeness may, in certain circumstances, be an actionable wrong in itself. It should be noted that several parallel developments may be seen in the Canadian provinces: first, the statutory torts of invasion of privacy in Manitoba, British Columbia, Newfoundland and Saskatchewan;[1] second, developments in Quebec, based on *The Quebec Charter of Human Rights and Freedoms*[2] and the *Civil Code*;[3] third, the Ontario common law tort of appropriation of personality; fourth, the embryonic common law tort of invasion of privacy. This chapter is only concerned with the common law tort of appropriation of personality which has been largely, although not exclusively, the work of the Ontario courts. Although the common law tort is still very much in its infancy, its development and scope are outlined below. Before doing so, the much wider, and more uncertain, notion of a tort of misappropriation of intangibles is considered briefly.

---

[1] Privacy Act, RSM 1987, c. P125; Privacy Act, RSBC 1996, c. 373; Privacy Act, RSN 1990, c. P-22; Privacy Act, RSS 1978, c. P-24. See, generally, D. Vaver, 'What's Mine Is Not Yours: Commercial Appropriation of Personality Under the Privacy Acts of British Columbia, Manitoba and Saskatchewan' (1981) 15 UBCL Rev 241; M. Chromecek and S. C. McCormack, *World Intellectual Property Guidebook Canada* (New York, 1991), Ch. 7; L. Potvin, 'Protection Against the Use of One's Own Likeness' (1997) 11 IPJ 203, 212–17; M. Henry (ed.), *International Privacy, Publicity and Personality Laws* (London, 2001), Ch. 7.

[2] RSQ c. C-12. See 225–7 below.

[3] SQ 1991, c. 64.

112   The commercial appropriation of personality

Misappropriation of intangibles

At various times it has been suggested that the Commonwealth courts have been going beyond the bounds of the tort of passing off and entering the realms of a new tort of unfair competition or misappropriation as the categories of actionable misrepresentation have been expanded[4] and the requirement of damage accepted as being more readily satisfied.[5] Nevertheless, the modern restatements clearly emphasise the need for a *misrepresentation* leading to damage to the plaintiff's goodwill.[6] Although the dicta in which the courts have denied the existence of a cause of action offer little guidance,[7] there has been considerable academic debate concerning the prospects for such a tort and its merits.[8] These issues have been discussed in detail elsewhere and, for present purposes, only a few salient points need be noted.

The breadth of the new cause of action envisaged varies. One view holds that the Anglo-Australian system 'is now ready for the adoption of a general principle of liability that will cover all situations of "reaping without sowing" on the part of a competitor'.[9] Such a broad principle would dispense with the need for any of the established intellectual

---

[4] *Vine Products & Co. Ltd* v. *Mackenzie & Co. Ltd* [1969] RPC 1, 23 and 29 *per* Cross J. The categories of misrepresentation were enlarged in particular in the sixties and seventies by cases such as *Bollinger* v. *Costa Brava Wine Co. Ltd* [1960] RPC 16 and *John Walker & Sons Ltd* v. *Henry Ost & Co. Ltd* [1970] RPC 489, which took passing off beyond misrepresentations relating to some distinguishing name or mark or get-up to embrace cases involving the misuse of a descriptive name, culminating in the modern restatement in *Erven Warnink BV* v. *Townend & Sons (Hull) Ltd* [1979] AC 731.

[5] See *Taittinger SA* v. *Allbev Ltd* [1993] FSR 641. Cf. *Harrods Ltd* v. *Harrodian School Ltd* [1996] RPC 697, 715 *per* Millet LJ. See H. Carty, 'Dilution and Passing Off: Cause For Concern' (1996) 112 LQR 632, 656 and 664.

[6] *Erven Warnink BV* v. *Townend & Sons (Hull) Ltd* [1979] AC 731, 742; *Reckitt & Colman Ltd* v. *Borden Inc.* [1990] 1 WLR 491, 499.

[7] See, e.g., *Hodgkinson & Corby Ltd* v. *Wards Mobility Ltd* [1994] 1 WLR 1564, 1569; *Mail Newspapers* v. *Insert Media (No. 2)* [1988] 2 All ER 420, 424; *Harrods Ltd* v. *Schwartz-Sackin & Co. Ltd* [1986] FSR 490, 494; *Cadbury-Schweppes Pty Ltd* v. *Pub Squash Co. Pty Ltd* [1981] 1 WLR 193, 200 *per* Scarman LJ (Privy Council). In Australia, see *Victoria Park Racing and Recreation Grounds Co. Ltd* v. *Taylor* (1937) 58 CLR 479, 509 *per* Dixon J; *Moorgate Tobacco Co. Ltd* v. *Philip Morris Ltd (No. 2)* (1984) 56 CLR 414, 445 *per* Deane J.

[8] See W. R. Cornish, 'Unfair Competition? A Progress Report' (1972) 12 JSPTL 126; G. Dworkin, 'Unfair Competition: Is the Common Law Developing a New Tort?' [1979] EIPR 241; H. Brett, 'Unfair Competition – Not Merely an Academic Issue' [1979] EIPR 295; P. Burns, 'Unfair Competition: A Compelling Need Unmet' [1981] EIPR 311; S. Ricketson, 'Reaping Without Sowing: Unfair Competition and Intellectual Property Rights in Anglo-Australian Law' (1984) UNSWLJ (special issue) 1; J. Adams, 'Is There a Tort of Unfair Competition?' [1985] JBL 26; A. Terry, 'Unfair Competition and the Misappropriation of a Competitor's Trade Values' (1988) 51 MLR 296; A. Kamperman Sanders, *Unfair Competition: A New Approach* (London, 1996).

[9] Ricketson, 'Reaping Without Sowing', 30.

Unfair competition and doctrine of misappropriation   113

property regimes, both statutory and common law, since the subject matter currently protected thereunder would be subsumed within a new, generalised action.[10] Such an approach is clearly at odds with the orthodox position in Anglo-Australian law, whereby intangibles are protected under special heads of protected interests rather than under a wide generalisation. A person's labour or efforts in creating a valuable intangible does not in itself give rise to a property right; protection will only be afforded if such an intangible falls within a recognised category which law or equity protects.[11] General overarching theories of liability have not, as a rule, found favour in the English common law tradition, where tortious liability is limited to a number of discrete rules prohibiting certain specific kinds of harmful activity and development is largely a matter of incremental extension by analogy with the established heads of liability.[12]

On a more modest level are proposals for a narrow tort of misappropriation of business values which would supplement the existing statutory and common law intellectual property regimes,[13] although plaintiffs would still have to overcome the judicial antipathy to such a tort, which can be explained by a number of factors. In common with other new developments a dynamic and proactive approach is deemed to be inconsistent with the proper balance between the courts and legislature, where the courts should follow the trends in legislation which reflect the views of successive parliaments.[14] As Brandeis J argued in his dissenting judgment in *International News Service* v. *Associated Press*,[15] which formed the basis of the subsequent rejection of an action for unfair competition in Anglo-Australian law,[16] the courts are ill equipped to make the investigations which should precede a determination of the limitations which should be set upon any new property right.[17] Nevertheless, such an approach, if taken to its logical conclusion, would preclude the courts from developing or recognising any new form of property right. Moreover, it is arguable that the courts are in no worse a position than the legislature to develop such new intellectual property rights. Indeed, many of

---

[10] *Ibid.*, 31.
[11] *Victoria Park Racing and Recreation Grounds Co. Ltd* v. *Taylor* (1937) 58 CLR 479, 509 *per* Dixon J.
[12] See, generally, Chapter 2.
[13] See, e.g., Terry, 'Unfair Competition and Misappropriation'.
[14] *Erven Warnink BV* v. *Townend & Sons (Hull) Ltd* [1979] AC 731, 740.
[15] 248 US 215 (1918).
[16] *Victoria Park Racing and Recreation Grounds Co. Ltd* v. *Taylor* (1937) 58 CLR 479, 509 *per* Dixon J; *Moorgate Tobacco Co. Ltd* v. *Philip Morris Ltd (No. 2)* (1984) 156 CLR 414, 444–5 *per* Deane J.
[17] 248 US 215 (1918), 267.

114   The commercial appropriation of personality

the statutory intellectual property regimes are codifications of rules and principles developed over time by the courts.[18]

Even if these general objections to judicial law-making may be overcome, it could still be argued that the notion of unfair competition or misappropriation is too vague, and is 'a cause of action whose main characteristic is the scope it allows, under high-sounding generalizations [*sic*], for judicial indulgence of idiosyncratic notions of what is fair in the market place'.[19] Indeed, the long-held view that 'to draw a line between fair and unfair competition, between what is reasonable and unreasonable, passes the power of the Courts'[20] has a continuing influence in English law.[21] In recent years differing opinions as to the proper balance to be struck between the promotion of free competition and the suppression of unfair competition have been expressed, and different conclusions reached at the highest judicial level.[22] Obviously, the courts have a considerable leeway in interpreting the individual requirements of the tort of passing off, seen clearly in the particular context of appropriation of personality and character merchandising cases.[23] Nevertheless, the difficulties in striking a balance between fair and unfair competition under a new and arguably vague principle have understandably dissuaded the courts from encouraging the development of such a new tort. Fears of such uncertainty have loomed large in the Anglo-Australian rejection of such a tort. As Deane J noted in *Moorgate*, commenting on the misappropriation doctrine engendered in the *International News Service* decision, 'one searches in vain in the majority judgment for any identification of the ingredients of that general wrong'.[24]

Problems of definition also abound,[25] and the proponents of a new tort of misappropriation have, for the most part, avoided offering any definition beyond 'misappropriation of a competitor's trade values',[26] or 'the creation of some intangible business value, for example, a new name, or mark, manufacturing process, design, marketing format, or literary or

---

[18] Terry, 'Unfair Competition and Misappropriation', 315, citing D. G. Baird, 'Common Law Intellectual Property and the Legacy of *International News Service* v. *Associated Press*' (1983) 50 U Chi L Rev 411, 417.

[19] *Moorgate Tobacco Co. Ltd* v. *Philip Morris Ltd (No. 2)* (1984) 156 CLR 414, 416 *per* Deane J.

[20] *Mogul Steamship Co.* v. *McGregor Gow & Co.* (1889) 23 QBD 598, 625–6 *per* Fry LJ.

[21] Cornish, 'Unfair Competition? A Progress Report', 126.

[22] See *Re Coca-Cola's Application* [1986] RPC 421. Cf. *Reckitt & Colman Ltd* v. *Borden Inc.* [1990] 1 WLR 491, and see J. Drysdale and M. Silverleaf, *Passing Off Law and Practice*, 2nd edn (London, 1995), 4–6.

[23] See Chapter 4.

[24] *Moorgate Tobacco Co. Ltd* v. *Philip Morris Ltd (No. 2)* (1984) 156 CLR 414, 441.

[25] See M. Spence, 'Passing Off and the Misappropriation of Valuable Intangibles' (1996) 112 LQR 472, 475–8.

[26] Terry, 'Unfair Competition and Misappropriation'.

Unfair competition and doctrine of misappropriation 115

artistic creation'.[27] Although some see the difficulties in precisely defining the subject matter of any right as a major, if not irresolvable, flaw,[28] it should be borne in mind that goodwill, the protected interest in the tort of passing off, 'is a thing very easy to describe, [but] very difficult to define',[29] and remains a rather flexible notion.[30] Calls for the recognition of new causes of action usually prompt objections based on difficulties of definition, and such objections have loomed large in the English debate on the merits of introducing a general tort of invasion of privacy.[31] The broader a proposed new right, the more indefinite it is likely to be. There is much to commend the view that the two broad notions of actions for unfair competition or misappropriation, and a general remedy for invasion of privacy, should be rejected in favour of a narrowly circumscribed *sui generis* tort of appropriation of personality. Such a tort is already in its infancy in Canada and it is to its development that we now turn.

The development of the common law tort of appropriation of personality

The genesis of the common law tort of appropriation of personality in Ontario[32]

In *Krouse* v. *Chrysler Canada Ltd*[33] the Canadian courts embarked on a new approach, going beyond the tort of passing off and engendering a new tort of appropriation of personality. Unfortunately, although displaying boldness of approach, neither the judgments at first instance nor those on appeal are models of conceptual clarity. The plaintiff professional football player had previously exploited his image in advertising and merchandising on a fairly modest level, although it was not in doubt that he did 'possess a saleable advertising power'.[34] The defendants, manufacturers of motor cars, distributed a 'spotter', essentially an elaborate poster which helped identify the various teams playing in the Canadian Football League, while simultaneously advertising Chrysler cars. In the centre of the poster was a picture of the plaintiff in action, wearing his usual number 14 jersey. By looking for number 14 in the Hamilton team

---

[27] Ricketson, 'Reaping Without Sowing', 31.
[28] Spence, 'Passing Off and Misappropriation', 475.
[29] *IRC* v. *Muller & Co.'s Margarine Ltd* [1901] AC 217, 223–4 *per* Macnaghten LJ.
[30] See, generally, Chapter 4.   [31] See Chapter 8.
[32] The fullest treatment in the Canadian literature can be found in J. Irvine, 'The Appropriation of Personality Tort' in D. Gibson (ed.), *Aspects of Privacy Law* (Toronto, 1980), 163, and R. G. Howell, 'The Common Law Appropriation of Personality Tort' (1986) 2 IPJ 149. See also E. M. Singer, 'The Development of the Common Law Tort of Appropriation of Personality in Canada' (1998) 15 CIPR 65.
[33] (1972) 25 DLR (3d) 49.   [34] *Ibid.*, 60.

116   The commercial appropriation of personality

window in the poster, a person would be able to identify the subject of the photograph as Krouse.

Unlike the English and Australian cases discussed in the previous chapter, the plaintiff's claim was not based on passing off. Indeed, it is difficult to determine from the report precisely on what basis the case was argued. The claim, although presented under the rubric of 'invasion of privacy', appeared to have distinct and severable elements: (i) invasion of privacy *per se*; (ii) appropriation of the plaintiff's identity for commercial purposes; (iii) breach of confidence; (iv) breach of contract; and (v) unjust enrichment. The first claim, that the wrongful publication of the picture constituted a completed wrong which was actionable *per se*, was held to be novel in principle, and Haines J declined to rule on the issue of whether there was a common law right to privacy.[35] Having dismissed the claims based on breach of contract and confidence (strangely included despite an express agreement between counsel excluding claims of breach of contract, confidence, copyright or defamation),[36] Haines J proceeded to what he regarded as the 'guts' of the case: the claim that 'the plaintiff [had] become identified with the products of the defendants and . . . had . . . his chances of advertising for other automobile manufacturers seriously affected'.[37] Such a claim raised three key issues of fact and law: whether the plaintiff had a 'saleable product advertising ability'; whether such an ability was a property right protected by law; and whether the defendant's poster was an appropriation of such a right.

The first question was answered in the affirmative, and it was found that the second question could also be answered affirmatively, based on two 'separate but closely related lines of cases': passing off, and the right of an individual to the elements of his identity.[38] Following an examination of the early English professional cases, and the early authorities on passing off,[39] Haines J concluded that '[o]nce it is established that Krouse is in the business of being used in advertisements, it becomes apparent that either line of cases will support an award'.[40] *Clark v. Freeman*[41] was distinguished on the basis that unlike Sir James Clark, who was not 'in the habit of manufacturing and selling pills', Krouse was '"in the

---

[35] *Ibid.*, 56. The Ontario courts have since recognised the existence of a common law tort of invasion of privacy: see *Roth v. Roth* (1992) 9 CCLT (2d) 141; *Mackay v. Buelow* (1995) 24 CCLT (2d) 184, 186–8; *Lipiec v. Borsa* (1997) 31 CCLT 294, 300. Cf. *Lord v. McGregor* (British Columbia Supreme Court, 10 May 2000) (no common law right of privacy in British Columbia, despite 'some academic interest and case authority to support the notion that the common law tort of privacy is an emerging field' (*ibid.*, para. 13)). See also J. D. R. Craig, 'Invasion of Privacy and Charter Values: The Common Law Tort Awakens' (1997) 42 McGill LJ 355, 367–9.

[36] *Krouse v. Chrysler Canada Ltd* (1972) 25 DLR (3d) 49, 54.

[37] (1972) 25 DLR (3d) 49, 58.   [38] *Ibid.*, 62.   [39] See, generally, Chapter 4.

[40] (1972) 25 DLR (3d) 49, 68.   [41] (1848) 11 Beav 112, see 64–5 above.

Unfair competition and doctrine of misappropriation

habit of manufacturing and selling" his image for advertising purposes'.[42] Similarly, *Dockrell* v. *Dougall* [43] was distinguished on the basis that Krouse was not claiming a property right in his name *per se*, but was claiming '"injury to him in his property", his valuable commercial property right of being used in an advertisement'.[44] Regardless of whether such attempts at distinguishing the early English precedents are deemed to be convincing, what is clear is that Haines J was prepared to recognise a new property right in the commercial saleability of an individual's personality. What is also clear is that such a property right was independent of any notion of goodwill in a business or profession, unlike the orthodox approach to passing off in Anglo-Australian law, which requires goodwill, in respect of a business or profession, which is damaged by the defendant's misrepresentation.

In this respect, the Court's treatment of passing off was erroneous. According to Haines J the passing off strand was even more clearly on point, since 'what could be a more precise example of an "improper appropriation of the plaintiff's reputation" than appropriating that reputation in the commercial exploitation of one's goods'.[45] If, Haines J reasoned, it were accepted that there was a general business of giving endorsements, and that the plaintiff was involved in such a business, then passing off would be established. This is an alarmingly lax interpretation, based on the unwarranted assumption that passing off is constituted simply by a *misappropriation*. The Court did not consider whether the three essential elements had been established: a misrepresentation leading to damage to the plaintiff's business in licensing his image, or, more contentiously, his business or profession as a footballer.[46] Passing off was dealt with cursorily, and might only have been considered to provide an additional, and more orthodox, basis for the decision, in case the first ground, based on appropriation of personality, was rejected on appeal.

In effect, the decision in *Krouse* was initiating an entirely new approach. What seemed to dictate the issue were the facts that the plaintiff had a (modestly) valuable economic asset in his name and image, and that the defendants had made unauthorised use of these attributes of the plaintiff's personality in their advertising. Although, in turn, an attempt was made at distinguishing the early professional cases which denied the notion of a property right in a name, while at the same time relying on the authorities in passing off, the ultimate decision was, strictly speaking, inconsistent with both strands of authority. There is scope for disagreement as to whether a valid distinction may be drawn between a property right in a name *per se*, and a 'valuable property right of being used in an

---

[42] (1972) 25 DLR (3d) 49, 68.   [43] (1899) 15 TLR 333, see 66 above.
[44] (1972) 25 DLR (3d) 49, 68.   [45] *Ibid.*   [46] Cf. 107–10 above.

118   The commercial appropriation of personality

advertisement'.[47] Equally, it is difficult to reconcile a property right in a plaintiff's commercial saleability with the notions of goodwill subsisting in a business or profession which is damaged by the defendant's misrepresentation, elements which are necessary for a valid cause of action in passing off. As Haines J noted in an earlier passage, although a nominative approach to the existing causes of action might fail to produce an appropriate remedy, it did not mean that the plaintiff would be without a remedy and in His Honour's view, '[a] person's rights should not turn on "falling between the stools"'.[48]

The defendants appealed, arguing that there was no valid cause of action, since the use of the plaintiff's image was not libellous, and since there was an absence of a common field of activity on which to found an action in passing off. The Ontario Court of Appeal found for the defendants on the passing off claim, by maintaining the need to show a common field of activity.[49] In Estey JA's view, 'the buying public would not buy the products of the [defendants] on the assumption that they had been designed or manufactured by the [plaintiff], nor would the public be understood to have accepted the spotter as being something designed and produced by the [defendants]'.[50] This application of the common field of activity test precluded a more sophisticated assessment of whether there might be a material misrepresentation leading to confusion and damage to the plaintiff when the case might have been relatively strong on its facts, since the plaintiff clearly had goodwill in respect of a subsidiary business which might have been damaged by a misrepresentation. In England and Australia the common field of activity test is no longer seen as an absolute requirement, but merely a factor in determining whether there has been confusion and damage.[51] This aspect of the *Krouse* decision is clearly inconsistent with the subsequent authorities, and requires no further discussion.

Nevertheless, Estey JA went on to hold that 'the common law does contemplate a concept in the law of torts which may be broadly classified as an appropriation of one's personality'.[52] Unfortunately, it is difficult to identify any clear pattern of inductive reasoning. The authorities in 'the several fields of tort' which His Honour examined[53] consisted largely of defamation cases where plaintiffs met with varying degrees of success, cases based on implied contract, some 'very isolated cases which can be explained on other grounds'[54] and passing off cases, although these were

---

[47] (1972) 25 DLR (3d) 49, 68.   [48] *Ibid.*, 55.   [49] See 74–6 above.
[50] *Krouse* v. *Chrysler Canada Ltd* (1973) 40 DLR (3d) 15, 25–6.
[51] See 75 and 85 above.
[52] *Krouse* v. *Chrysler Canada Ltd* (1973) 40 DLR (3d) 28.
[53] *Ibid.*, 22–5.   [54] *Ibid.*, 22.

Unfair competition and doctrine of misappropriation 119

clearly unhelpful in the light of the Court's prior finding on the issue of the common field of activity. No attempt was made to analyse these disparate authorities in detail, and the synthesis of the new rule amounted to little more than a bare assertion that the authorities supported the existence of a cause of action for appropriation of personality. Early in his judgment Estey JA noted that where a case was only new in the instance, rather than new in principle, a court would be perfectly competent to apply existing principles to new fact situations,[55] although he did not identify what the relevant principles might be, beyond noting that, in the past, actions had sometimes 'succeeded in contract, sometimes in tort, and sometimes on some vague theory of property law'.[56]

What seemed to have dictated the outcome in *Krouse* was not the formal authorities, but the underlying reasons of substance,[57] particularly the apparent commercial reality that a professional athlete had earning power, not only in his role as an athlete, 'but also in his ability to attach his endorsement to commercial products or undertakings or to participate otherwise in commercial advertising'.[58] The plaintiff's real grievance lay in the interference with this de facto economic interest, and, like Haines J at first instance, the Ontario Court of Appeal was unwilling to let the existing causes of action lead to a denial of the plaintiff's ability to protect such interests from unauthorised exploitation. There is room for genuine disagreement as to whether this is legitimate interstitial law-making, or a usurpation of the legislature's function in an area where the courts are ill equipped to make the necessary policy choices and to strike the necessary balance between competing interests. Such arguments are obviously not unique to this area. Experience from the United States shows an equally active approach being adopted by the courts in respect of the development of the rights of privacy and publicity, although there are a number of factors which explain the greater degree of judicial activism displayed in the American courts.[59]

Although the existence of a tort of appropriation of personality was affirmed on appeal in *Krouse*, the claim was dismissed on its facts in a manner which was potentially very limiting to the tort's future development. It was held that the defendants' poster did not associate the plaintiff with the defendants' products but, rather, the defendants had

---

[55] *Ibid.* citing *Pasley* v. *Freedman* (1789) 100 ER 450.
[56] *Krouse* v. *Chrysler Canada Ltd* (1973) 40 DLR (3d) 15, 22.
[57] For a distinction between substantive and formal reasoning see P. S. Atiyah and R. S. Summers, *Form and Substance in Anglo-American Law* (Oxford, 1987), Ch. 1, and see, further, 192–4 below.
[58] (1973) 40 DLR (3d) 15, 19.   [59] See 189–98 below.

120   The commercial appropriation of personality

'sought to gain a trade advantage by associating themselves with the popular game of football and not any particular team or participant'. Indeed, according to Estey JA, the 'usage of a press-type action photograph by the [defendants] [was] not unlike the implicitly authorized use of sporting news and sporting features to promote the appeal of television stations, which carry sport reports as a regular service to their readers'.[60] Viewed in the context of the poster as a whole, the plaintiff's claim was rather weak on its facts, since the evidence showed that the photograph had been selected for its artistic effect in depicting a dynamic action scene from a football game not because it depicted Krouse in particular,[61] although the plaintiff might have understandably been annoyed at having been singled out, particularly since the spotter device allowed him to be identified from the number on his shirt. However, the general effect of the defendants' advertisement could not be said to have diminished the plaintiff's ability to exploit his name or image in advertising or merchandising.

In dismissing the plaintiff's claim on its facts, Estey JA went on to contrast the facts with a situation where a hockey player's signature might appear on a hockey stick, or where a professional athlete was depicted driving a car manufactured by the advertisers. Also, several passages of the judgment refer to the notion of an endorsement, although it is easy to exaggerate the significance of this factor. On the one hand, it is arguable that the element of endorsement could take the tort back from the notion of *appropriation* to the notion of a *misrepresentation*; as such, the tort of appropriation of personality would be little different from the tort of passing off. On the other hand, the element of endorsement could be viewed as 'a threshold issue establishing a sufficient degree of nexus before the defendant can be said to have *culpably usurped* the plaintiff's personality'.[62] This seems to be the better view. Indeed, there is no necessary correlation between misrepresentation and endorsement, and the confusion possibly stems from the erroneous assumption that it might be actionable in passing off to misrepresent that a plaintiff has endorsed a defendant's goods or services. This is not sufficient and, for a case of appropriation of personality to be actionable in passing off, it must be shown that the defendant has made a misrepresentation that the goods or business of the defendant are connected with the business or profession of the plaintiff in a way which damages (or is likely to damage) the business or profession of the plaintiff.[63] An 'endorsement' is simply a declaration of one's approval of something or someone. While the notion of an endorsement by the plaintiff (or the plaintiff's licence, or approval) might be

[60] (1973) 40 DLR (3d) 15, 30.   [61] *Ibid.*
[62] Howell, 'The Common Law Appropriation of Personality Tort', 170 (italics in original).
[63] See 72–84 above.

Unfair competition and doctrine of misappropriation 121

a factor which causes the public to make a connection between the business of the defendant and the business or profession of the plaintiff, the misrepresentation relates to the public's belief that there is a connection between the *businesses* of the plaintiff and defendant; a misrepresentation relating to an endorsement in itself is insufficient. Moreover, the damage which may be actionable in passing off is the damage (or in a *quia timet* action, the real likelihood of damage) to the goodwill of the plaintiff's business. A loss of an endorsement opportunity in itself is not a form of legal damage which is actionable in passing off.[64] Nevertheless, the lax approach adopted by the Australian courts effectively allows recovery for such damage, and the line of cases which follow this approach might be better understood as involving a right of publicity, although the Australian courts have refused to acknowledge openly the existence of such a right.[65]

The new approach initiated in *Krouse* was followed by the Ontario High Court in *Athans* v. *Canadian Adventure Camps Ltd.*[66] The plaintiff, an eminently successful water-skier, had previously exploited his image using, in particular, a photograph of himself skiing in a distinctive pose and setting. This photograph was regarded as the plaintiff's 'trademark' (in a purely colloquial sense, since it was not a registered trade mark) and had become particularly associated with the plaintiff amongst the water-skiing *cognoscenti*. The defendants, who ran a boys' summer camp in which water-skiing was a major feature, published an advertisement, featuring a stylised line drawing of the 'trademark' photograph. Although the drawing was not intended to represent a particular person, the evidence showed a striking similarity between the drawing and the plaintiff's photograph.[67] The plaintiff's action in passing off was dismissed on a more reasoned and orthodox analysis than in *Krouse*. Henry J held that there was insufficient evidence that the defendants' advertisement was likely to lead to confusion between the business of the plaintiff and the business of the defendants. In large part this resulted from the fact that there was no evidence that a significant segment of the public would be sufficiently acquainted with the sport of water-skiing to identify the drawings with the plaintiff, and it was insufficient that a small number of people with an intimate knowledge of the sport would identify the plaintiff.[68]

Nevertheless, the Court proceeded to find for the plaintiff on the basis that the plaintiff had 'a proprietary right in the exclusive marketing for gain of his personality, image and name'.[69] According to Henry J,

---

[64] See 103–5 above.
[65] *Sony Music Australia Ltd and Michael Jackson* v. *Tansing* (1994) 27 IPR 649, 653–4 *per* Lockhart J, and 656 *per* French J. Cf. *10th Cantanae Pty Ltd* v. *Shoshana Pty Ltd* (1987) 79 ALR 299, 300 *per* Wilcox J.
[66] (1977) 80 DLR (3d) 583.   [67] *Ibid.*, 588   [68] *Ibid.*, 591.   [69] *Ibid.*, 592.

122   The commercial appropriation of personality

the advertisement did not imply that the plaintiff was connected in any way with the camp, and there was no suggestion that he was endorsing, sponsoring or participating in the camp's activities in any way. Moreover, there was no evidence that even those with intimate knowledge of the sport of water-skiing would form such an impression, and, on the evidence as a whole, according to Henry J the actions of the defendants did 'not amount to a wrongful appropriation of Mr Athans's personality as such'.[70] Nevertheless, this did not conclude the matter since it was held that '[t]he commercial use of [the plaintiff's] representational image by the defendants without his consent constituted an invasion and *pro tanto* an impairment of his exclusive right to market his personality'.[71] This constituted an aspect of the tort of appropriation of personality, which entitled the plaintiff to damages in the 'amount he ought reasonably to have received in the market for permission to publish the drawings'.[72] Thus, *Athans* seemed to go further than *Krouse* in making pure misappropriation, regardless of any association or endorsement, actionable in tort. Furthermore, the decision adopted a very relaxed approach as to the need for the plaintiff to be identified. Although Athans's personality as such had not been appropriated, Henry J held that his 'representational image' had been appropriated. In this respect, the decision in *Athans* goes much further than the American right of publicity, in that the unauthorised use of the plaintiff's representational image was found to be actionable even though only a *de minimis* number of people would have been able to identify the plaintiff from the defendants' drawing.[73]

The scope and limits of the tort

Although the decisions in *Krouse* v. *Chrysler Canada Ltd* and *Athans* v. *Canadian Adventure Camps Ltd* remain the leading authorities, the tort of appropriation of personality has been considered, and its existence confirmed, in several subsequent Canadian cases, while the reasoning has also been followed by the Jamaican High Court.[74] Most of the Canadian cases have been interlocutory proceedings, with little or no elucidation of

---

[70] *Ibid.*, 594.   [71] *Ibid.*, 595.   [72] *Ibid.*, 596.

[73] See J. T. McCarthy, *The Rights of Publicity and Privacy*, 2nd edn (New York, 2001), §6.149. To be an actionable infringement of the right of publicity, the unauthorised appropriation must sufficiently identify the plaintiff, otherwise it cannot be said that his identity has been misappropriated nor his interests violated: see *Motschenbacher* v. *R. J. Reynolds Tobacco Co.*, 498 F 2d 821 (9th Cir. 1974), 824, and see, further, 182 below.

[74] *The Robert Marley Foundation* v. *Dino Michelle Ltd* (Unreported Suit No. C.L. R115/1992, High Court of Jamaica, 12 May 1994). This case goes somewhat further than the Canadian cases (see 125 below).

Unfair competition and doctrine of misappropriation 123

the relevant points of law. The Canadian tort of appropriation of personality therefore remains a rather amorphous cause of action, which has most often been interpreted as an aspect of the law of privacy, although most writers recognise that the *Krouse* line of cases involve something related to, although different from, privacy, and its inclusion in discussions of privacy is probably no more than a matter of expository convenience.[75] In the absence of an authoritative appellate decision, it is difficult to determine the conceptual basis, scope and limits of the tort and any analysis involves a degree of extrapolation from the existing authorities. Nevertheless, it is convenient to explore the nature of the tort, and its relationship with the tort of passing off, in terms of: (a) the protected interest, (b) the nature of the damage and (c) the nature of the defendant's conduct.

The protected interest

While the tort of passing off protects a property right in the underlying goodwill of a business, the tort of appropriation of personality protects 'a proprietary right in the exclusive marketing for gain of [a plaintiff's] personality, image and name'.[76] Although the stated basis of the property right is a 'commercially saleable product advertising ability',[77] it does not seem that prior commercial exploitation of personality is a necessary prerequisite for recovery. Despite the fact that plaintiffs have included several professional sportsmen,[78] and a professional actor who had appeared extensively in television advertising,[79] other plaintiffs such as an amateur body-builder,[80] participants in a conference on unemployment[81] and a family whose name was 'synonymous with wealth and luxury'[82] have not been denied standing to sue on account of the fact that they had not previously exploited their names or images in advertising or commerce. Thus, a cause of action for appropriation of personality is not limited

---

[75] See, e.g., L. M. Linden, *Canadian Tort Law*, 4th edn (Toronto, 1988), 52–3; L. N. Klar, *Tort Law* (Toronto, 1991), 56; P. Burns, 'The Law of Privacy: The Canadian Experience' (1976) 54 Can B Rev 1, 13 and 21–13; and see, also, G. H. L. Fridman, *Fridman on Torts* (London, 1990), 521–2. Cf. D. Gibson, 'Common Law Protection of Privacy: What to Do Until the Legislators Arrive' in L. N. Klar (ed.), *Studies in Canadian Tort Law* (Toronto, 1977), 343.

[76] *Athans* v. *Canadian Adventure Camps Ltd* (1977) 80 DLR (3d) 583, 592.

[77] *Krouse* v. *Chrysler Canada Ltd* (1972) 25 DLR (3d) 49, 58 *per* Haines J.

[78] *Krouse* v. *Chrysler Canada Ltd* (1973) 40 DLR (3d) 15; *Athans* v. *Canadian Adventure Camps Ltd* (1977) 80 DLR (3d) 583; *Racine* v. *CJRC Radio Capitale Ltee* (1977) 35 CPR (2d) 236. See also *Horton* v. *Tim Donut Ltd* (1998) 75 CPR (3d) 451 (estate of deceased hockey player).

[79] *Heath* v. *Weist-Barron School of Television Canada Ltd* (1981) 62 CPR (2d) 92.

[80] *Joseph* v. *Daniels* (1986) 11 CPR (3d) 544 (claim failed on facts).

[81] *Dowell et al.* v. *Mengen Institute* (1983) 72 CPR (2d) 238 (claim failed on facts).

[82] *Baron Philippe de Rothschild, SA* v. *La Casa de Habana Inc.* (1987) 19 CPR (3d) 114.

124   The commercial appropriation of personality

to those with existing trading interests, and is potentially broad enough to cover those with latent recognition value in respect of their personality. However, although the tort clearly embraces *economic* interests in personality, it is unclear whether the tort is broad enough to encompass *dignitary* interests such as privacy, or freedom from mental distress.[83] This point is pursued in greater detail below in examining the nature of the damage.

While goodwill cannot have an existence independent of a particular business, and subsists only to the extent that the underlying business continues,[84] the proprietary right in the exclusive marketing of a personality protected by the tort of appropriation of personality is not so limited. Although the tort protects what is described as a 'proprietary' right, its duration is uncertain. Again, this raises broader questions relating to the underlying basis of liability and the dual perspective of the economic and dignitary aspects of appropriation of personality. By aligning the problem of appropriation of personality with the intellectual property torts, the primary concern lies with securing the economic interests of the plaintiff.[85] On the other hand, by aligning the problem of appropriation of personality with dignitary torts, such as defamation and invasion of privacy, the focus shifts to protecting and vindicating personal dignity. In English law an action for defamation, the only significant English dignitary tort, is a purely personal tort action which, unlike most other causes of action, dies with the person;[86] reputation and injured dignity are generally of no concern to a deceased person. Similarly, in the United States, where the issue has received the most detailed consideration, an action for invasion of privacy generally dies with the person.[87]

The question of the nature of the Canadian tort of appropriation of personality, and whether it survives the owner of the proprietary right in the exclusive marketing of personality, image and name for commercial gain, has not received full consideration. In *Gould Estate* v. *Stoddart Publishing Co.*[88] the estate of the late concert pianist Glenn Gould brought an action for damages for infringement of copyright and appropriation of personality, in respect of a biography of Gould, published by the defendants, which the estate had not authorised. Copyright in the photographs vested in the defendants, while Gould's oral statements in the interview did not attract copyright which might have given the estate standing to sue.[89] The Ontario Court of Appeal preferred to decide the issue solely on the basis of copyright and did not consider the issue of appropriation of personality. In the absence of a commission for valuable consideration

---

[83] See, generally, Chapter 1.   [84] See 61–2 above.   [85] See 19–20 above.
[86] Law Reform (Miscellaneous Provisions) Act 1934, s. 1(1).
[87] See 183–4 below.   [88] (1997) 30 OR (3d) 520.   [89] *Ibid.*, 529.

by the plaintiff, ownership of copyright in the photographs vested in the defendants as owners of the original negative or photograph. So did copyright in the literary material: the plaintiff's casual and unstructured oral utterances were insufficient to attract copyright.[90]

On the question whether a cause of action for appropriation of personality survived the death of the individual, at first instance Lederman J stated, obiter, that most American jurisdictions which recognised a right of publicity had held that such a right was devisable and descendible. His Honour went on to distinguish the situation under the provincial Privacy Acts[91] in Canada, where the cause of action for privacy or appropriation of personality is extinguished by the death of the individual, preferring the view that the constraints which applied to the statutory cause of action did not apply to the common law action for appropriation of personality. His Honour also drew a distinction between the right of privacy and right of publicity in the United States,[92] noting that the former is a personal tort, intended to protect an individual's interests in dignity and peace of mind, while the latter 'protects the commercial value of a person's celebrity status'.[93]

Lederman J regarded the common law tort of appropriation of personality as more closely analogous with the American right of publicity than with the tort of invasion of privacy. Indeed, His Honour referred explicitly to the appropriation tort as a 'right of publicity', noting that

[t]he right of publicity, being a form of intangible property under Ontario law akin to copyright, should descend to the celebrity's heirs. Reputation and fame can be a capital asset that one nurtures and may choose to exploit and it may have a value much greater than tangible property. There is no reason why such an asset should not be devisable to heirs.[94]

This approach has been adopted in Jamaica in *The Robert Marley Foundation* v. *Dino Michelle Ltd*,[95] where the successors in title of the late musician were successful in obtaining damages and an injunction for the unauthorised use of Bob Marley's image on T-shirts and other merchandise. The Court adopted the reasoning in two American right of publicity cases,[96] and held that the right to the exclusive exploitation of Marley's name and image survived his death, even though there was no evidence that Marley had licensed the use of his image during his lifetime.

---

[90] *Gould Estate* v. *Stoddart Publishing Co.* (1998) 80 CPR (3d) 161, 168–70.
[91] See note 1 above.   [92] See Chapter 7.
[93] (1997) 30 OR (3d) 520, 528.   [94] *Ibid.*
[95] Unreported Suit No. C.L. R115/1992, High Court of Jamaica, 12 May 1994.
[96] *Martin Luther King Jr Center for Social Change Inc.* v. *American Products Inc.*, 694 F 2d 674 (11th Cir. 1983); *The State of Tennessee, Ex Rel. The Elvis Presley International Memorial Foundation* v. *Crowell*, 733 SW 2d 89 (1987). See, further, Chapter 7.

126   The commercial appropriation of personality

Subsequently, in *Horton* v. *Tim Donut Ltd* the personality rights of deceased hockey player Tim Horton (taking the form of trade mark licences and consents to use his likeness)[97] were treated as having been assigned by Horton during his lifetime to a company of which he was a 50 per cent partner. The issue of whether his widow had a right to the commercial exploitation of his personality as against the company was left open, since it was decided, on the facts, that there had been no unauthorised appropriation.[98] Relying on the *Athans* and *Krouse* line of authority, Lax J identified the gravamen of the tort as 'the usurpation of the plaintiff's right to control and market his own image'. Accordingly, there could be 'no interference where the celebrity gives over the right'.[99] This seems to treat the nature of the interest as an assignable proprietary interest rather than a personal tortious cause of action, although there is nothing in *Krouse* or *Athans* to support such a conclusion. Again, what seemed to dictate the conclusion were the underlying reasons of substance, notably the practice of licensing or assigning (rather nebulous) personality rights.

A number of issues arise, some of which may only be noted as pointers for later discussion. First, it is clear that Lederman J in *Gould Estate* regards the tort of appropriation of personality essentially as a right of publicity, distinct from the statutory causes of action for infringement of privacy. This approach aligns the tort of appropriation of personality with the intellectual property torts protecting economic interests, rather than the dignitary torts protecting personal dignity; indeed, the law of copyright was Lederman J's preferred analogy. Naturally, the claim in *Gould Estate* itself involved the economic interests of the estate rather than the dignitary interests of the deceased pianist, although Lederman J's dictum, being purely obiter, was clearly directed towards the tort of appropriation of personality as a whole rather than the particular facts of the case. Similarly, in *Horton* the claim concerned the economic interests of the defendant assignees. Nevertheless there are other analogies, particularly with the dignitary torts, that are considered in Part III and it is difficult to draw a sharp distinction between economic and dignitary interests, and the causes of action which protect them. Furthermore, there are considerable difficulties in justifying a remedy for appropriation of personality, either as a dignitary right of privacy, an economic right

---

[97] *Quaere* whether the latter constitutes any assignable subject matter. Cf. *Haelan Laboratories Inc.* v. *Topps Chewing Gum Inc.*, 202 F 2d 866 (2nd Cir. 1953), 868, and see 175 and 183 below.

[98] (1998) 75 CPR (3d) 451, 460.

[99] *Ibid.*, 451, 459. Cf. *Dubrulle* v. *Dubrulle French Culinary School Ltd* (2001) 8 CPR (4th) 180 (plaintiff's consent defeated claim of appropriation of personality against the defendant culinary school bearing his name and the defendant had developed its own distinct name and personality separate from that of the plaintiff).

Unfair competition and doctrine of misappropriation 127

of publicity or a *sui generis* cause of action embracing both aspects.[100] Although reputation[101] and fame are often valuable economic assets, the question whether, on balance, they should be protected by the law is an entirely different matter. Property rights do not inhere in everything that has an economic value, and a certain degree of policy choice and balancing of competing interests is necessary in determining whether and to what extent an intangible should be protected as a property right.

Damage to the plaintiff

A valid cause of action in passing off depends on the plaintiff being able to show damage (or, in *quia timet* proceedings, a real likelihood of damage) to his goodwill in his business or profession, as a result of the defendant's misrepresentation. The forms of damage are various, although the English courts, unlike their Australian counterparts, have not accepted that the loss of a licence fee can furnish the appropriate element of damage for a passing off action. Under such an approach damage is effectively a matter of fiction, and the reasoning is circular, since the ability to insist on a licence fee depends on establishing a valid action in passing off.[102] Under the Canadian tort of appropriation of personality, the damage takes the form of an appropriation of a plaintiff's property right in the exclusive marketing of his own image. An important question to address is the extent to which the plaintiff must show actual damage to his property right, or whether damage will be presumed, and appropriation of personality will be actionable *per se*.

It will be recalled that in *Krouse* v. *Chrysler Canada Ltd*, at first instance, Haines J held that the claim that the unauthorised commercial exploitation of the plaintiff's personality constituted an invasion of privacy *per se*, without the need to show damage (by analogy with libel *per se*), was novel in principle and had to be rejected.[103] On appeal, the existence of a separate cause of action, based on appropriation of a property right in the exclusive marketing of the plaintiff's personality was affirmed, and it is interesting to note the basis on which the Ontario Court of Appeal recognised the new cause of action. Estey JA noted that the plaintiff 'founded his claim on the existing principles of trespass' and sought to apply those principles to a new field. However, His Honour went on to state that

---

[100] See, further, Chapter 11.
[101] 'Recognition value' might be a more appropriate term, since protection of 'reputation', as such, is long established and reasonably well delineated in the tort of defamation: see 250–3 below.
[102] See 103–5 above.   [103] (1972) 25 DLR (3d) 49, 54–6.

128   The commercial appropriation of personality

[t]respass would not in any case appear to be the appropriate basis for any such alleged wrongful appropriation since such a wrong would fall within the classification of an action on the case, or in more recent legal history in an action for trover or conversion in its modern form. Thus, the plaintiff must prove both injury and damages if he is to succeed in the action.[104]

Subsequently, in *Athans* v. *Canadian Adventure Camps Ltd*, the plaintiff was held to have suffered damage to the exclusive right to market his personality,[105] while in *Heath* v. *Weist-Barron School of Television Canada Ltd*,[106] it was held that the plaintiff six-year-old actor's claim for general and special damages disclosed a valid cause of action. More recently, in *Holdke* v. *Calgary Convention Centre Authority* the Alberta Provincial Court rejected a claim brought by a trick roper for unauthorised use of footage of him performing his act at Canada's Cowboy Festival, in an advertisement for the festival. To succeed, the plaintiff would have to show 'the commercial value of the asset he owns and which has been misappropriated' and there was no evidence that the plaintiff would have been able to negotiate a fee for the advertisement.[107]

However, some dicta have suggested that the tort of appropriation of personality might be actionable *per se*. In *Racine* v. *CJRC Radio Capitale Ltee*[108] the plaintiff succeeded in an action for unfair dismissal and appropriation of personality after having his contract with a radio station for football commentary prematurely terminated. Marin J stated that a 'transgression by a [defendant] is actionable *per se*; and, if there has been such a transgression then relief can be given', before going on to draw an analogy with libel, where an action may be sustained even though the plaintiff's economic interests do not suffer any actual damage.[109] The decision in *Racine* was, however, a lower County Court decision, given orally, and one which should be treated cautiously. Nevertheless, some subsequent cases lend some support for the proposition that the tort might be actionable *per se*. In *Dowell et al.* v. *Mengen Institute*,[110] the plaintiffs sought an interlocutory injunction to restrain the showing of a film taken at a conference for unemployed workers at which the plaintiffs had participated. During the conference the plaintiffs were portrayed as being emotional, and in one case seditious, and the essence of the plaintiffs' complaint was that what they regarded as a normal conference, involving a conventional exchange of views, had been turned into a psychological encounter group 'designed to disinter and expose their innermost feelings about the subject of being unemployed'.[111] The existence of a cause

[104] (1973) 40 DLR (3d) 15, 27.   [105] (1977) 80 DLR (3d) 583, 596.
[106] (1981) 62 CPR (2d) 92.   [107] [2000] ACWS (3d) 1281.
[108] (1977) 35 CPR (2d) 236.   [109] *Ibid.*, 240.
[110] (1983) 72 CPR (2d) 238.   [111] *Ibid.*, 240.

Unfair competition and doctrine of misappropriation 129

of action for appropriation of personality was confirmed, although the plaintiffs' claim failed on the facts, since they had signed documents authorising the defendants to use their names, likenesses and words in the documentary. What is interesting to note is that the Court did not seek to limit the potential application of the tort to cases where the plaintiff had suffered actual damage to economic interests in commercial exploitation. As such, the possibility that the tort might protect dignitary interests, such as interests in personal privacy, was left open. In a later case, *Baron Philippe de Rothschild, SA* v. *La Casa de Habana Inc.*,[112] the Ontario High Court of Justice restrained a cigar merchant from using the name of the Rothschild family as his business name. The part of the judgment dealing with the claim for appropriation of personality contains nothing more than the bare assertion that '[o]ne cannot commercially exploit another's name or likeness without his permission'[113] and the decision was not based on any evidence that the plaintiffs had suffered any damage, or evidence that they had exploited their name commercially. This suggests that the Court was prepared to protect what was essentially a privacy interest.

Thus, although it is tolerably clear that, in Canada, the common law recognises a property right in personality, the position remains uncertain as to whether infringement of that right is actionable *per se*, or whether proof of damage must be shown. To hold that the relevant damage can take the form of a lost licence fee which a plaintiff would otherwise have received is to resort to a circular argument. More broadly, to base the very existence of such a property right on its supposed economic value, when that economic value is in itself dependent on the extent of legal protection, is equally circular.[114] While the High Court and Court of Appeal of Ontario in *Krouse* purportedly based the new proprietary right on the de facto values of a professional athlete's image,[115] their findings were essentially based on certain rudimentary and un-challenged assumptions. Indeed, Haines J's dictum at first instance, that '[o]ne would think that the wrongful appropriation of that which in the business world has commercial value and is traded daily must *ipso facto* involve a property right which the Courts protect',[116] betrays an alarmingly casual approach to an issue which is essentially question-begging. If it were generally accepted that commercial value compels legal protection as property, then the public domain would be much poorer indeed.

---

[112] (1987) 19 CPR (3d) 114.   [113] *Ibid.*, 115.

[114] F. S. Cohen, 'Transcendental Nonsense and the Functional Approach' (1935) 35 Colum L Rev 809, 815–17.

[115] *Krouse* v. *Chrysler Canada Ltd* (1972) 25 DLR (3d) 49, 59–62; (1973) 40 DLR (3d) 15, 19–20.

[116] *Krouse* v. *Chrysler Canada Ltd* (1972) 25 DLR (3d) 49, 61–2.

130   The commercial appropriation of personality

These issues are considered more fully in Part IV. As to the importance of damage as an essential element in the tort of appropriation of personality, the difficult question is whether plaintiffs in cases such as *Krouse* (had he eventually been successful) and *Athans* had suffered any real loss. Were they in any worse a position than they had previously been, before their images had been used without their consent? There are several difficulties in this area, particularly in ascertaining a market value of the property right that has been appropriated, assuming that there is a relevant market in the first place. For example, in *Athans* the plaintiff's previous activities had consisted of competing professionally for prizes and endorsing products related to water-skiing. Henry J found difficulty in the fact that Athans had not previously endorsed holiday camps such as the defendants' and rejected the plaintiff's claim that he would have asked for a fee of $5,000, in addition to a percentage of the camps' profits, on the basis that there was no evidence that he would have received such remuneration in the market or after negotiation with the defendant. In the event damages were assessed at what Henry J acknowledged to be an arbitrary amount of $500.[117] In *Krouse* at first instance, Haines J made the following telling comments on the difficulty of assessing damages: '[t]he plaintiff has been unable to prove the general negative that his ability to get rival endorsements has been diminished, and there is expert evidence that it has not. Damages are therefore reduced to the level of unjust enrichment. The plaintiff must be compensated for the wrongful appropriation of his property right in using his picture for advertising purposes.'[118]

Such dicta point to the difficulties in insisting that damage is an essential element of the tort when, in many cases, plaintiffs will face considerable difficulties in establishing damage. In this respect it might be more realistic, despite the courts' insistence to the contrary,[119] to accept that the tort is indeed actionable *per se*.

Thus the position may be approached from three broad standpoints. First, the tort of appropriation might be actionable *per se*, and the plaintiff would not need to show that he had suffered any material damage as a result of the unauthorised commercial exploitation of his personality. As such, the tort would have the potential to cover interests in personal privacy, or injuries in freedom from mental distress, feelings or sensibilities, which is possibly why the notion of actionability *per se* was expressly

---

[117] *Athans* v. *Canadian Adventure Camps Ltd* (1977) 80 DLR (3d) 583, 596.

[118] *Krouse* v. *Chrysler Canada Ltd* (1972) 25 DLR (3d) 49, 68. Compensating the plaintiff, rather than disgorging the defendant's ill-gotten gains, seemed to be the Court's primary concern.

[119] See text accompanying note 104 above.

rejected in *Krouse*.[120] Second, the approach which the Court of Appeal purported to set out in *Krouse* requires that the plaintiff be able to show material damage to his economic interests, and mere injured feelings or loss of privacy will not give rise to a cause of action. As such, the tort of appropriation of personality would be a very narrow and limited addition to the economic torts. The third approach is essentially a fudge of the first two approaches, where the need to show damage is stated although the need to show affirmative evidence of actual material loss is interpreted loosely.[121] Viewed as a whole the authorities to date resemble such a fudge, which awaits an authoritative ruling, or a body of case law which takes the tort in one direction or the other. Ultimately, the issue turns on the value that is placed on the underlying interests and the question of whether either economic or dignitary interests in personality deserve to be protected. On the one hand, there is much to be said, not least in the interests of certainty, for the view that only injuries to material interests which are capable of real proof can be actionable where a person's name, voice or likeness is used without his consent; unless a plaintiff can show damage to such material interests, or show that his reputation has been injured in a defamatory way, no action will lie.[122] On the other hand, such an approach precludes recovery for harm to dignitary interests other than interests in reputation, such as interests in privacy and freedom from mental distress. It is difficult to draw any conclusions without examining the problem from a dignitary interests perspective[123] and without addressing the difficult task of justifying a new remedy.[124]

The defendant's conduct

While a valid cause of action in passing off is dependent on the plaintiff being able to show that the defendant has made a misrepresentation that his goods or business are connected to the business or profession of the plaintiff, under the Canadian tort it is sufficient to show a *misappropriation* by the defendant of the plaintiff's proprietary right in the exclusive marketing of his personality. Although the Ontario Court of Appeal in *Krouse* decided that misappropriation was sufficient without misrepresentation, the notion of endorsement was maintained. However, there is no necessary correlation between misrepresentation and endorsement,

---

[120] *Krouse* v. *Chrysler Canada Ltd* (1972) 25 DLR (3d) 49, 68.
[121] *Krouse* v. *Chrysler Canada Ltd* (1972) 25 DLR (3d) 49, 69 (Ontario High Court); *Athans* v. *Canadian Adventure Camps Ltd* (1977) 80 DLR (3d) 583, 594 and 596.
[122] Irvine, 'The Appropriation of Personality Tort', advocates such a conservative approach.
[123] See Part III.   [124] See Part IV.

132   The commercial appropriation of personality

and the requirement of endorsement is better understood as a general threshold test to help establish liability.[125] More recently, in *Gould Estate v. Stoddart Publishing Co.*,[126] after reviewing the authorities Lederman J noted that 'it would seem open to the court to conclude, on a contextual basis, that the tort of appropriation of personality is restricted to endorsement-type situations'.[127] It will be recalled that the case involved a claim by the estate of the deceased musician, Glenn Gould, to restrain the defendants from publishing photographs of Gould and interviews with him in a biography. There is clearly a grave danger to freedom of expression and dissemination of news and information if the tort of appropriation of personality could be used to prevent the publication of biographical material, or material with a legitimate news value. The plaintiffs' claim posed such a danger, and it was natural that the courts should be wary of such a claim. The Ontario Court of Appeal decided the issue solely on the basis of copyright.[128] The approach adopted by Lederman J in dismissing the claim at first instance, although technically obiter, has somewhat unfortunate consequences for the possible future development of the tort.

The claim could simply have been dismissed on the grounds that the estate of a deceased person had no standing to sue. Such an approach would have been perfectly consistent with authority, since each of the plaintiffs in the previous cases had been living individuals and, indeed, there is nothing in the cases prior to *Gould Estate* to suggest that the proprietary right in the exclusive marketing of a person's image survives that person's death. Indeed, the authorities suggested that the right was a purely personal right.[129] However, such a simple approach was not adopted, probably because Lederman J, as noted above, preferred the view that the tort of appropriation of personality was effectively a right of publicity in the American mould and, as such, should descend to a deceased person's heirs.[130] This left the Court with the need to find another way of disposing of the plaintiffs' claim, which Lederman J succeeded in doing on two separate bases.

Having noted that the appropriation of personality tort was limited to endorsement type situations,[131] His Honour went on to note the limits which have been placed on the right of publicity by the American courts, where the scope of the right of publicity has been balanced against the

---

[125] See text accompanying note 62 above.   [126] (1997) 30 OR (3d) 520.
[127] *Ibid.*, 525.   [128] See text accompanying note 88 above.
[129] Cf. the subsequent decision in *Horton v. Tim Donut Ltd* (1998) 75 CPR (3d) 451 and text accompanying note 98 above.
[130] See text accompanying note 88 above.   [131] See text accompanying note 127 above.

Unfair competition and doctrine of misappropriation   133

societal interests in free expression guaranteed by the First Amendment.[132] Accordingly, the right of publicity has not been successfully invoked in cases involving the dissemination of thoughts, ideas, newsworthy events or matters of public interest, and the notions of 'newsworthiness' and 'public interest' extend far beyond the dissemination of news in the sense of current events, and embrace all types of factual, educational and historical data, or even entertainment and amusement.[133] In Lederman J's view, similar considerations of freedom of expression should animate the Canadian courts in placing limits on the tort of appropriation of personality. Thus, His Honour concluded that

[i]n the end then, and perhaps at the risk of oversimplifying, it seems that the courts have drawn a 'sales vs. subject' distinction. Sales constitute commercial exploitation and invoke the tort of appropriation of personality. The identity of the celebrity is merely being used in some fashion. The activity cannot be said to be about the celebrity. This is in contrast to situations in which the celebrity is the actual subject of the work or enterprise, with biographies perhaps being the clearest example. These activities would not be within the ambit of the tort. To take a more concrete example, in endorsement situations, posters and board games, the essence of the activity is not the celebrity. It is the use of some attributes of the celebrity for another purpose. Biographies, other books, plays and satirical skits are by their nature different. The subject of the activity is the celebrity and the work is an attempt to provide some insights about that celebrity.[134]

Accordingly, the biography in question fell into the 'subject' category and could not be said to give rise to a cause of action for appropriation of personality.

It is not entirely clear whether this was based on the Canadian cases or the American case law.[135] On balance it was probably the American authorities, since the limited Canadian case law on appropriation of personality does not provide much support for such a distinction. Indeed, the Canadian cases do not, in reality, support the proposition that the tort of appropriation of personality only applies in 'endorsement' situations. For example, in *Athans* v. *Canadian Adventure Camps Ltd* Henry J expressly held that the plaintiff had not endorsed the camp and neither did 'the use of his image in the form of the drawings constitute an endorsement or other association with the camp'.[136] The unauthorised

---

[132] (1997) 30 OR (3d) 520, 526.
[133] *Ibid. per* Lederman J citing *Current Audio Inc.* v. *RCA Corp.*, 337 NYS 2d 949 (Sup Ct 1972).
[134] (1997) 30 OR (3d) 520, 527 *per* Lederman J.
[135] *Current Audio Inc.* v. *RCA Corp.*, 337 NYS 2d 949 (Sup Ct 1972), and *Estate of Presley* v. *Russen*, 513 F Supp. 1339 (1981) were the only two American cases cited.
[136] (1977) 80 DLR (3d) 583, 596.

134   The commercial appropriation of personality

use of the plaintiff's 'representational image' in itself was held to constitute an impairment of his exclusive right to market his personality, and thus came within the ambit of the tort of appropriation of personality.[137] Nevertheless, in *Gould Estate*, Lederman J interpreted *Athans* as being consistent with the endorsement context, on the basis that the representational image had been used by the defendants in their camp's promotional brochure.[138] In other cases, which were not cited by Lederman J, the Canadian courts do not seem to have confined the tort to endorsement situations. For example, in *Racine* v. *CJRC Radio Capitale Ltee*,[139] there was no suggestion that the plaintiff football player had endorsed the defendant's radio station, neither was there any suggestion that the plaintiff aristocrat had endorsed the defendant's cigar business in *Baron Philippe de Rothschild, SA* v. *La Casa de Habana Inc.*,[140] nor any suggestion that the plaintiff child actor in *Heath* v. *Weist-Barron School of Television Canada Ltd* had endorsed the defendant's television school.[141] Unauthorised use was deemed to be sufficient in these cases, with no suggestion of endorsement.

The only support for the endorsement criterion can be found in pure obiter dicta in the decision of the Ontario Court of Appeal in *Krouse*, where Estey JA contrasted the facts of the case, where the defendants had essentially associated their products with the game of football in general, with the hypothetical situation where a hockey player's signature was used on a hockey stick, or where a professional athlete was photographed driving one of the advertisers' cars.[142] Thus, in the first significant case, the Court was keenly aware of the danger 'of extending the law of torts to cover every such exposure in public not expressly authorized'. Indeed, it was observed that '[p]rogress in the law is not served by the recognition of a right which, while helpful to some persons or classes of persons, turns out to be unreasonable disruption to the community at large and to the conduct of its commerce'.[143]

Naturally, the recognition and subsequent development of any new right involves a balancing of competing interests, and the delineation of a new tortious cause of action inevitably entails entering into uncharted waters. Logical development is not, however, served by drawing specious distinctions based on the inherently nebulous concept of an endorsement. Where a balance must be struck between competing interests, it is surely better that the balance should be achieved by an open consideration

---

[137] *Ibid.*, 595.   [138] (1997) 30 OR (3d) 520, 525.
[139] (1977) 35 CPR (2d) 236.   [140] (1987) 19 CPR (3d) 114.
[141] (1981) 62 CPR (2d) 92.
[142] *Krouse* v. *Chrysler Canada Ltd* (1973) 40 DLR (3d) 15, 30 and 27.
[143] *Ibid.*, 30.

of the relevant principles and policies, rather than by extracting largely unsupportable distinctions from the limited case law. Ultimately, in *Gould Estate*, the broad principles of freedom of expression imported from the American case law provided a sounder basis for the decision, and while Lederman J was naturally concerned with delivering a judgment that was consistent with the Canadian authorities, the reasoning which was employed, based on the supposed endorsement requirement, was somewhat unconvincing. Nevertheless, the passage from Lederman J's judgment reproduced above was cited, and the reasoning adopted with approval in *Shaw* v. *Berman*,[144] where the musician Artie Shaw brought an action, based on appropriation of personality, for a share of the profits from a biographical film based on his life and work. The film in question fell into the 'subject' category, and no action for appropriation of personality could be maintained. Pitt J did not elaborate on Lederman J's reasoning in *Gould Estate*. Subsequently, in *Horton* v. *Tim Donut Ltd*,[145] the approach in *Gould* was interpreted as providing a more explicitly policy-based distinction between, on the one hand, works falling within the public interest where private interests gave way to broader social interests in freedom of expression and, on the other hand, activities predominantly of a commercial nature where such broader interest did not conflict. The distinction based on endorsement was not adopted and it is submitted that a more open policy-based approach is to be preferred. The Supreme Court of Canada, in an appeal from the Quebec Court of Appeal concerning the Quebec *Charter of Human Rights and Freedoms*, has rejected a distinction based on categories of information (socially useful information and commercial information), preferring a more open balancing of the rights at issue.[146] This is discussed further below after considering the broader impact of constitutional and charter values.

Finally, the defendant's unauthorised use of the plaintiff's image must be in a way which identifies the plaintiff. This is unproblematic where an individual's name or likeness is used, although several of the Canadian cases have been on the borderline of identifiability. For example, in *Krouse* the plaintiff could be identified by the number on his shirt, through the use of the 'spotter' device, although, taken in its general context, it was held that the defendants were associating themselves with the game of football in general rather than with Krouse in particular. Had a simple portrait of the plaintiff standing alone been used the outcome might well have been different. In *Athans* v. *Canadian Adventure Camps Ltd*, as noted above, the Court took a very liberal view on the identification issue, it

---

[144] (1997) 72 CPR (3d) 9, 18.
[145] (1998) 75 CPR (3d) 451, 458. See text accompanying note 98 above.
[146] *Aubry* v. *Éditions Vice-Versa Inc.* (1998) 78 CPR (3d) 289, 309.

136   The commercial appropriation of personality

being sufficient to show that the defendants had appropriated the plaintiff's 'representational image', regardless of the fact that very few people would identify the representational image with the plaintiff.[147] However, in *Joseph* v. *Daniels*,[148] the British Columbia Supreme Court rejected an amateur bodybuilder's claim for unauthorised appropriation of personality on the grounds that he had not been sufficiently identified. The photograph in question featured the plaintiff holding a kitten, although only his torso was depicted. According to Wallace J 'for the defendant to be found liable he must be taking advantage of the name, reputation, likeness, or some other components of the plaintiff's individuality or personality which the viewer associates with the plaintiff'.[149] By depicting only the plaintiff's torso, the defendant had avoided any reference to the plaintiff and had not used 'any proprietary interest associated by the public with the plaintiff's individuality'.[150] Again, in *Holdke* v. *Calgary Convention Centre Authority*[151] the Alberta Provincial Court took a stricter approach to the question of identifiability. The video footage of the plaintiff trick roper performing an impromptu roping act at a cowboy festival, used without his consent in an advertisement for the festival, did not identify the plaintiff (or his stage persona as 'Frank Holt') by name. Moreover, the plaintiff was not dressed in the usual manner of his cowboy alter ego. There was no evidence that the plaintiff, or his alter ego, were so well-known that his persona would be recognisable in the advertisement, and thus nothing to establish that the commercial value of his image had been misappropriated. In common with the other elements of the tort of appropriation of personality, it is difficult to identify any clear rule. This awaits an authoritative appellate judgment, although the case law on the right of publicity in the United States may provide some assistance in considering the competing arguments.[152]

Conclusions

While the Canadian courts have taken a very different and arguably much less artificial approach to cases of appropriation of personality than their English and Australian counterparts, the tort is very much in its infancy, particularly when compared to the much more mature and developed right of publicity in the United States. Relatively limited reference has been made to the US jurisprudence. This is somewhat surprising (despite the constraints of precedent) given that the US courts have had to address the same issues in reconciling a cause of action for appropriation

[147] See text accompanying note 73 above.   [148] (1986) 11 CPR (3d) 544.
[149] *Ibid.*, 549.   [150] *Ibid.*   [151] [2000] ACWS (3d) 1281.
[152] See 180–7 below.

with the general notion of privacy, and in determining the 'proprietary' nature of the protected interest, particularly the issue of descendibility.[153] The detailed requirements and scope of the Canadian tort remain to be fully delineated, particularly the question of the precise nature of the damage which might be actionable. Indeed, the tensions inherent in limiting the tort to cases involving actual material damage are apparent, and the tort has the potential to develop into a truly *sui generis* cause of action embracing both economic interests and dignitary interests such as privacy and freedom from mental distress. As it stands, however, the Canadian common law tort of appropriation of personality remains a rather limited addition to the economic torts.

[153] See, below, 183–4.

Part III

Dignitary interests

6 Introduction

Systems rooted in English common law have traditionally given limited recognition to 'dignitary interests', used here as a generic term for the essentially non-pecuniary interests that a person might have in his own personality: reputation, personal privacy and freedom from mental distress. English law knows no concept similar to the Roman law *injuria*, which, in English, would mean insult or outrage, though neither word suggests the true nature of the Roman idea which 'embraced any contumelious disregard of another's rights or personality'.[1] The essence of the delict lay in the insult rather than the loss to the plaintiff, and the money compensation represented solace for injured feelings or affronted dignity rather than compensation in the ordinary sense;[2] thus the primary purpose of the action was to punish the defendant by the infliction of a pecuniary penalty.[3]

Although by the early twelfth century wrongs were widely identified in England by reference to two separate components, economic loss (*damnum*) and affront to personal honour (*dedecus*), the notion of *injuria*, or affront to honour, disappeared as an operative element in English tortious liability and was completely eclipsed by the element of economic loss.[4] By the time that the common law permitted actions on the case for defamatory words in the sixteenth century, due in part to the deficiencies of the remedies available in the Church courts,[5] the notion of *injuria* had been lost from the English common law. It is possible that if the king's courts had shown an earlier interest in defamation, around the early thirteenth century, the common law of defamation might have developed along Roman lines, and might have embraced the notion of insult

[1] B. N. Nicholas, *An Introduction to Roman Law* (Oxford, 1962), 216.
[2] *Ibid.*, 217.
[3] R. G. McKerron, *The Law of Delict*, 7th edn (Cape Town, 1971), 9.
[4] See J. S. Beckerman, 'Adding Insult to *Iniuria*: Affronts to Honor and the Origins of Trespass' in M. S. Arnold *et al.* (eds.) *On the Laws and Customs of England* (Chapel Hill, 1981), 178–9, for some possible reasons.
[5] See J. H. Baker, *An Introduction to English Legal History*, 3rd edn (London, 1990), 495–7.

142   The commercial appropriation of personality

as well as economic loss as the foundation of tortious liability.[6] Indeed, in Pollock's view, 'the law went wrong from the beginning in making the damage and not the insult as the cause of action'.[7]

The disappearance of the notion of *injuria* from English common law had quite profound implications. Despite the fact that the notion of a legal injury derived its vocabulary from the Roman law concept of *injuria*, the element of affront or injury to the plaintiff's feelings disappeared. In the absence of a general remedy such as the *actio injuriarum*, systems rooted in English common law have been slow to grant remedies for affronts to dignity, and redress depends on the expansive judicial interpretation of existing torts[8] and statutory provisions. Recovery for invasion of other interests, such as privacy and freedom from mental distress, has only been achieved parasitically, where other substantive interests such as reputation, property, or interests in the physical person have been affected.[9] Protection against appropriation of personality has largely been secured, in English law, through the tort of defamation, which protects an individual's reputation in the eyes of others.[10] An attack on an individual's honour, interfering with dignity, integrity and privacy, often lies beyond what can be encompassed within the notion of injury to reputation.[11]

The juncture of civil and common law

Significantly, in South Africa, which has something of a hybrid legal system displaying characteristics of both civil Roman–Dutch law and English common law,[12] protection against unauthorised commercial exploitation of personality has been secured through the *actio injuriarum*. The South African law of delict rests on the twin foundations of *damnum injuria datum* and the *actio injuriarum*. While the former has become the general remedy for wrongs to interests of substance, the latter affords a general remedy for wrongs to interests of personality.[13] In the *actio injuriarum*, two essential elements of liability must be established: first, an act constituting an impairment of the plaintiff's personality; and secondly, *animus injuriandi*, or wrongful intent[14] (although the defendant's motive is irrelevant, and it is not necessary to prove any ill-will or spite, it being

[6] Beckerman, 'Adding Insult to *Iniuria*', 181.
[7] F. Pollock, *The Law of Torts*, 12th edn (London, 1923), 243.
[8] See *O'Keeffe* v. *Argus Printing and Publishing Co. Ltd* 1954 (3) SA 244 (C), 245; J. Burchell, *Principles of Delict* (Cape Town, 1993), 149.
[9] See 249–50 below.   [10] See 250–2 below.
[11] See D. Feldman, 'Secrecy, Dignity, or Autonomy? Views of Privacy as a Civil Liberty' (1994) 47 CLP 41, 56–7.
[12] K. Zweigert and H. Kötz, *An Introduction to Comparative Law*, 3rd edn (Oxford, 1998), 235.
[13] McKerron, *The Law of Delict*, 10.   [14] *Ibid.*, 53.

Dignitary interests: introduction

sufficient to show that the injuries suffered by the plaintiffs were inflicted with deliberate intention, rather than accidentally or negligently).[15] The *actio injuriarum* protects a triad of interests comprising of *fama*, *corpus* and *dignitas*.[16] While the first concerns the law of defamation, and the second deals with infringement of a person's physical integrity and personal liberty, the third provides an essentially residual category of personality rights which do not fall under the first two categories.[17]

Thus, the unauthorised publication of a person's photograph and name for advertising purposes could be 'capable of constituting an aggression upon that person's *dignitas*', amounting to an *injuria*, for example where a picture of a plaintiff was used in an advertisement for rifles, pistols and ammunition.[18] Although the plaintiff had consented to having her photograph taken whilst in the act of aiming a pistol, such consent only extended to its use in a newspaper article; the essence of the complaint related to use of the plaintiff's name and photograph for advertising purposes.[19] There was no question of an aggression on the plaintiff's person (*corpus*) or reputation (*fama*), and the action was based purely on the violation of the plaintiff's dignity.[20] Thus, the notion of *dignitas*, which is protected as part of the *actio injuriarum*, has been held to be broad enough to include a right to privacy,[21] and although it has been argued that a right of privacy should develop as a *sui generis* action, the better view seems to be that it should be regarded as an aspect of *dignitas*, protected by the *actio injuriarum*.[22]

Overcoming the common law's legacy

Other common law jurisdictions, most notably the United States, have been more willing to overcome the legacy in developing new causes of action to protect such dignitary interests in personality. The development

---

[15] *Ibid.*, 56.

[16] R. Zimmermann, *The Law of Obligations* (Oxford, 1996), 1083; *Roman Law, Contemporary Law, European Law* (Oxford, 2001), 150–1.

[17] Zimmermann, *The Law of Obligations*, 1084. Cf. R. Pound, 'Interests of Personality' (1914) 28 HarvLRev 343.

[18] *O'Keeffe* v. *Argus Printing and Publishing Co. Ltd* 1954 (3) SA 244 (C). Cf. *Kidson* v. *SA Associated Newspapers Ltd* 1957 (3) 461 (W). See also *Mhlongo* v. *Bailey* 1958 (1) SA 370 (W).

[19] *O'Keeffe* v. *Argus Printing and Publishing Co. Ltd* 1954 (3) SA 244 (C) 247.

[20] *Ibid.*

[21] *S* v. *A* 1971 (2) SA 293 (T), 297 'I have no doubt that the right to privacy is included in the concept of *dignitas*, and that there is no dearth of authority for this proposition'; *S* v. *I* 1976 (1) SA 781 (RAD) 784 '[plaintiff's] *dignitas* was invaded by the invasion of her privacy', cited in Zimmermann, *The Law of Obligations*, 1084.

[22] See, generally, D. J. McQuoid-Mason, *The Law of Privacy in South Africa* (Cape Town, 1978), 125 et seq.

of the right of privacy in the United States, and its evolution into a multi-faceted cause of action, protecting both economic and dignitary interests, is traced in Chapter 7. The right of privacy eventually begat the separate and distinct right of publicity, which, although perhaps better described as an aspect of unfair competition law, can only be understood in the historical context of its creation in the dignitary tort of invasion of privacy. For English and Australian lawyers, this provides an important insight into the means by which a hybrid problem such as appropriation of personality may be addressed.

Some international instruments, most notably the European Convention on Human Rights, provide for a broad-based right to private life, although this falls some way short of a general right to personal dignity. Similarly, other systems provide more principled protection of individual dignity, guaranteeing personal dignity (in various forms) as a basic right, often given effect by general codified provisions.[23] For example, Art. 9 of the French Civil Code states that '[e]veryone has the right to respect for his privacy', although privacy was protected casuistically before it was incorporated as a general principle in the Civil Code.[24] In Germany, on the other hand, although the *actio injuriarum* was rejected and excluded from the Civil Code (BGB),[25] it has, to a certain extent, managed to infiltrate the law in the form of the general right to personality,[26] which was largely the creation of the courts, drawing, in support, on constitutional principles.[27]

English law has only recently begun to contemplate a move from the traditional casuistic approach to protecting personal dignity towards a more principled approach – in particular, through the recognition of a general right of privacy. The Human Rights Act 1998 and the jurisprudence of the European Convention on Human Rights have provided the pretext, if not the substantive basis, for the new developments.[28] A clear direction has yet to emerge and both the experience in Germany in developing a right of personality based on constitutional principles[29] and the common law patterns of development which have emerged from almost a century of judicial initiative in the United States will be instructive for some time to come.[30]

---

[23] See 211–14 below.
[24] See, generally, E. Picard, 'The Right to Privacy in French Law' in B. S. Markesinis (ed.) *Protecting Privacy* (Oxford, 1999), 49.
[25] See Zimmerman, *The Law of Obligations*, 1085–94.
[26] *Ibid.*, 1092.   [27] See 230–3 below.   [28] See 214–24 below.
[29] See 227–37 below.   [30] See Chapter 7 below.

7 Privacy and publicity in the United States

Introduction

The development of the right of privacy in the United States has been profoundly influenced and shaped by academic commentators, perhaps more than any other comparable body of law. It is difficult to determine the place that the problem of appropriation of personality occupies in relation to a general right of privacy without an awareness of the dominant competing conceptions, discussed below. The central problem which emerges lies in reconciling economic and dignitary aspects of personality within a cause of action that developed primarily to protect dignitary rather than economic interests. This conflict can be seen in the subsequent development of the right of publicity in the United States. This emerged as a separate and distinct right from the right of privacy due to the difficulties in reconciling the notion of a right to privacy with the need to protect the essentially economic interests that a (usually famous) person might have in his own image.

Although there are interesting developments in the law of privacy elsewhere, particularly in Canada, a detailed analysis of the Canadian authorities contributes relatively little to an understanding of the relationship between the concept of privacy and the problem of appropriation of personality. By the same token, there is no significant divergence between the law of privacy in England and that in Australia[1] which merits attention and, thus, no important points of contrast between the two systems require elucidation. This chapter therefore focuses on the United States. It should be borne in mind that there are often substantial differences between different states with respect to the law regarding the rights of privacy and publicity. The following discussion can only provide a general sketch and concentrates on the key stages of evolution and the dominant

---

[1] See, generally, M. Henry (ed.) *International Privacy, Publicity and Personality Laws* (London, 2001), Ch. 3; J. G. Fleming, *The Law of Torts*, 9th edn (Sydney, 1998), Ch. 26; S. Theedar, 'Privacy in Photographic Images' [1999] PLPR 59.

145

146   The commercial appropriation of personality

principles in the law of privacy in the United States so far as they are relevant to the problem of appropriation of personality.

The development of the right of privacy in the United States

The Warren and Brandeis thesis

The development of the right to privacy did not result from a bold act of judicial synthesis of pre-existing heads of liability into a new general rule, but resulted largely from an influential article by Samuel Warren and Louis Brandeis in the *Harvard Law Review*.[2] Indeed, the development of the right of privacy in the United States provides a rare example of the influence of academic writing on the development of the common law and, according to Larremore's often-cited observation, the article is possibly unique in that it initiated and outlined a new field of jurisprudence.[3] It spawned a great wealth of academic literature, and a large body of case law, and demands a careful analysis since the authorities which the authors invoked in support of their argument for a right of privacy were primarily English cases from the nineteenth century. Thus, at the outset, it is worth noting that the profound differences between the laws in the two jurisdictions are not organic.[4]

Although a certain degree of myth surrounded the circumstances which gave Warren and Brandeis the impetus to write their article,[5] it is clear that the authors were concerned with the activities of the press, which they felt was 'overstepping in every direction the obvious bounds of propriety and decency'.[6] In particular, they mentioned the effects of 'recent inventions and business methods' and the fact that '[i]nstantaneous photographs and newspaper enterprise' had 'invaded the sacred precincts of private and domestic life'.[7] Another particular concern was the 'unauthorised

---

[2] 'The Right to Privacy' (1890) 4 HarvLRev 193.

[3] W. Larremore, 'The Law of Privacy' (1912) 12 Colum L Rev 693. See also K. Zweigert and H. Kötz, *Introduction to Comparative Law*, 3rd edn (Oxford, 1998), 702: 'perhaps the most famous and certainly the most influential law review article ever written'.

[4] See, further, 189–98 below.

[5] W. L. Prosser ('Privacy' (1960) 48 CalifLRev 383, 383) suggested that what spurred the authors into action was the unwanted publicity given to the wedding of Warren's daughter, though this view has now been effectively discredited: see J. H. Barron, 'Warren and Brandeis, The Right to Privacy, 4 HarvLRev 193 (1890): Demystifying a Landmark Citation' (1979) 13 Suffolk UL Rev 875, 891–4, cited by D. W. Leebron, 'The Right to Privacy's Place in the Intellectual History of Tort Law' (1991) 41 Case West Res L Rev 769.

[6] (1890) 4 HarvLRev 193, 196.

[7] *Ibid.*, 195. See, also, A. Westin, *Privacy and Freedom* (London, 1967), 338.

Privacy and publicity in the United States

circulation of portraits of private persons',[8] citing a contemporaneous case brought in New York,[9] where an actress sought to prevent the manager of the theatre in which she was appearing from making use of a photograph of her on stage, which had been taken surreptitiously without her consent. Indeed, it has been suggested that surreptitious photography and the unauthorised use of photographs were matters of widespread concern at the time.[10]

Despite a superficial similarity between invasion of privacy and the law of libel and slander, in that both seemed to be concerned with injury to wounded feelings, defamation rested on damage to reputation, concerning a person's external relations with the community, an injury of an essentially material rather than spiritual nature. Neither did the law recognise a principle by which compensation could be granted for mere injury to feelings, though injury to feelings could be taken into account in assessing damages where a substantive legal injury could be established,[11] albeit only parasitically.[12] Having noted the limits of causes of action for breach of contract[13] and confidence,[14] and the absence of any common law concept of insult to honour, akin to Roman law, Warren and Brandeis looked elsewhere for support for a right to privacy.[15] In essence they argued that the protection afforded by common law copyright in particular circumstances[16] was merely the application of a more general right

---

[8] (1890) 4 HarvLRev 193, 195.

[9] *Marion Manola* v. *Stevens & Myers, NY Times*, 15 June 1890. A preliminary injunction was issued ex parte, and a time was set for argument of the motion for a permanent injunction, but the defendants did not appear to oppose the motion. See Warren and Brandeis, 'The Right to Privacy', 195, note 7.

[10] See Leebron, 'Privacy in Tort Law', 774.

[11] Warren and Brandeis, 'The Right to Privacy', 197.

[12] T. A. Street, *The Foundations of Legal Liability* (Northport, N.Y., 1906), Vol. I, 461.

[13] *Prince Albert* v. *Strange* (1849) 1 Mac & G 25, 41 ER 1171; *Tuck* v. *Priester* (1887) 19 QBD 629; *Pollard* v. *Photographic Co.* (1889) 40 ChD 345.

[14] *Abernethy* v. *Hutchinson* (1825) 3 LJ Ch 209; *Prince Albert* v. *Strange* (1849) 1 Mac & G 25, 41 ER 1171; *Pollard* v. *Photographic Co.* (1889) 40 ChD 345. In earlier times, the state of photographic art was such that a person's photograph could not be taken without his consciously 'sitting' for his portrait and the law of contract or trust could provide a prudent man with sufficient means of preventing the unauthorised circulation of his portrait. Since new technology allowed a person to be photographed surreptitiously, the authors argued that the doctrines of contract and trust were inadequate, necessitating resort to the law of tort: Warren and Brandeis, 'The Right to Privacy', 211.

[15] Ibid., 198. See the discussion of the Roman law concept of *injuria*, 141–2 above.

[16] In England, since the decision in *Donaldson* v. *Beckett* (1774) 2 Bro PC 129, copyright in published works derives entirely from statute. However, common law copyright continued to subsist in unpublished works for a period after the decision in *Donaldson*, until it was finally abolished by the Copyright Act 1911, s. 31. This gave the author rights of control over his work up to and until it was published, at which point, statutory copyright would govern. Similarly, in the United States, it was held in *Wheaton* v. *Peters*, 26–33 US 1055 (1834), that copyright was derived entirely from statute. However, copyright

148   The commercial appropriation of personality

to privacy.[17] The common law allowed every individual the right to determine the extent and manner in which his thoughts might be communicated, a right which existed irrespective of the method of expression adopted, the nature or value of the thought or emotion, or the quality of the means of expression.[18] In each case, the argument ran, an individual was entitled to decide whether what was inherently his own should be given to the public. This right was not lost when the author himself communicated his production to the public and was entirely independent of the statutory copyright laws, since these were aimed at securing the profits of publication for their author. The common law right served a different purpose and allowed the author absolute control over the act of publication and, indeed, the more fundamental decision of whether there should be any publication at all.

While conceding that the basis for the right to prevent publication of manuscripts and works of art was a right of property, cases beyond those involving the reproduction of literary and artistic compositions called for an alternative, non-proprietary, basis, since the value of the subject matter did not lie in the profits of publication, but in the peace of mind or relief afforded by the ability to prevent any publication at all.[19] Although they acknowledged that the courts had based their decisions on the narrow grounds of protection of property, the authors argued that the cases were 'recognitions of a more liberal doctrine'.[20] For example, in the celebrated English case principally relied on, *Prince Albert* v. *Strange*, the plaintiff sought to restrain the defendant from publishing a catalogue of impressions, taken by a workman, of etchings made by the plaintiff, which were of a private and domestic nature. The judgments both at first instance[21] and on appeal[22] were based on the conventional grounds of breach of common law copyright and breach of confidence. However, Warren and Brandeis laid great emphasis on a number of passages in the judgment of Knight-Bruce VC at first instance[23] which stressed that the plaintiff was

---

continued to exist in the common law of individual states in unpublished works, and it is with this common law right, which subsisted until publication, that Warren and Brandeis were concerned. Since the Copyright Act 1976, 17 USC §301, the dual system of state common law copyright for unpublished works and statutory copyright for published works has been replaced by a single federal statutory copyright. Copyright now vests at the moment a work is created, that is the point at which the work is fixed in a tangible form for the first time, rather than the time of publication. Consequently, common law copyright is now of limited importance: see, e.g., P. Goldstein, *Copyright* (Boston, 1989), 504 et seq., and see, generally, S. M. Stewart, *International Copyright and Neighbouring Rights*, 2nd edn (London, 1989).

[17] Warren and Brandeis, 'The Right to Privacy', 198.
[18] *Ibid.*, 199.   [19] *Ibid.*, 200.   [20] *Ibid.*, 204.   [21] (1849) 2 DeG & Sm 652.
[22] (1849) 1 Mac & G 25.   [23] (1849) 2 DeG & Sm 652, 670 and 696–7.

Privacy and publicity in the United States

entitled to privacy in respect of his private etchings. Principally from these passages, and dicta in the judgment of Lord Cottenham LC on appeal,[24] Warren and Brandeis discerned a broader principle, concluding that:

> the protection afforded to thoughts, sentiments, and emotions, expressed through the medium of writing or of the arts, so far as it consists in preventing publication, is merely an instance of the enforcement of the more general right of the individual to be let alone. It is like the right not to be assaulted or beaten, the right not to be imprisoned, the right not to be maliciously prosecuted, the right not to be defamed ... The principle which protects personal writings and all other personal productions, not against theft and physical appropriation, but against publication in any form, is in reality not the principle of private property, but that of inviolate personality.[25]

Thus, the law afforded a principle which could be invoked to protect the privacy of the individual from invasion by the over-intrusive press, by photographers or by the use of modern devices for recording and reproducing scenes or sounds. Such protection should not be limited to conscious products of labour, based on a need to encourage effort, since the right to privacy was part of the more general right to the immunity of the person and the right to one's personality.[26] The emphasis lay on the dignitary nature of invasion of privacy; the basis of the law's intervention was the protection of personal dignity rather than the protection of property rights. The principle which they claimed had been applied to protect personal writings and any other productions of the intellect or of the emotions was not a principle of private property but the right of privacy. By arguing for the extension of what was claimed to be a pre-existing right to cover personal appearance, sayings, acts or personal relations, the charge of advocating judicial legislation could be avoided; what was envisaged was the mere application of an existing principle to a new set of facts rather than the introduction of a novel principle.[27]

What is clear from this summary is that Warren and Brandeis were able to marshal some authorities in support of their argument that a right to privacy already existed in law. Any possible defects in inductive reasoning are of minor importance for present purposes,[28] since what ultimately mattered was the fact that their argument was later accepted by the courts in most jurisdictions in the United States. It is also clear that the problem of appropriation of personality, if not central, was certainly

---

[24] (1849) 1 Mac & G 25, 42 and 47.   [25] 'The Right to Privacy', 205.
[26] *Ibid.*, 206–7.   [27] *Ibid.*, 213.
[28] R. Dworkin has argued that the Warren and Brandeis thesis is sometimes taken to be a kind of brilliant fraud, though sound in its ambition: *Taking Rights Seriously* (London, 1977), 119. Cf. R. Wacks who doubts whether such a view can be found in the privacy literature: *Personal Information* (Oxford, 1989), 31.

150   The commercial appropriation of personality

prominent in the Warren and Brandeis conception of a right to privacy, and was clearly one of the particular evils that they sought to address. Moreover, many of the earliest cases which sought to test the new right of privacy theory involved the unauthorised use of a person's name for advertising purposes.

The early case law

In the ensuing decade plaintiffs tested the new privacy theory in a number of cases.[29] In *Schuyler* v. *Curtis*[30] the relatives of a deceased philanthropist sought to prevent the building of a statue in her memory, which was to be placed next to a statue of a well-known agitator. The Supreme Court of New York County determined that a right of privacy did exist, citing the Warren and Brandeis article. Despite the fact that the plaintiff was a well-known philanthropist, she remained a private person and had not surrendered her right of privacy. However, the decision was reversed by the Court of Appeals[31] which, without denying that a right of privacy might exist, held that whatever right of privacy the plaintiff might have enjoyed did not survive her death. Between these two judgments, in *Marks* v. *Jaffa*,[32] the Superior Court of New York City granted an injunction restraining the use of an actor's name and picture in a popularity contest in a newspaper, relying on the decision of the Supreme Court of New York County in *Schuyler* and the Warren and Brandeis article.

Similarly, in *Corliss* v. *Walker*[33] the widow of a deceased inventor sought an injunction, on the basis of invasion of privacy, to restrain the publication of a biographical sketch and picture of her late husband, arguing that he had been a private character during his lifetime. Colt J rejected this argument, taking the view that, since Mr Corliss had held himself out as an inventor and had enjoyed world-wide repute, he had ceased to be a private character. Consequently, the free speech interests and the liberty of the press outweighed the plaintiff's interests, and the first instance decision in *Schuyler* v. *Curtis* was cursorily distinguished as a case involving the erecting of a statue rather than a case where a right of publication was at issue. However, the facts allowed an injunction to be granted to restrain the use of the photographs, but not the biographical material, on the conventional grounds of breach of an implied contractual term.[34]

---

[29] Although Prosser stated that the article had little immediate effect on the law ('Privacy' (1960) 48 Calif L Rev 383, 384), Leebron, 'Privacy in Tort Law', 792–4, has persuasively shown that the article's impact in academic circles, and in the courts, was immediate and significant.
[30] 15 NYS 787 (Sup Ct 1891).   [31] *Schuyler* v. *Curtis*, 42 NE 22, 25 (1895).
[32] 26 NYS 908 (Super Ct 1893).   [33] 57 Fed Rep 434 (1893).   [34] *Ibid.*, 436.

Privacy and publicity in the United States

Subsequently, an action was brought to dissolve the injunction granted at first instance[35] when it transpired that one of the photographs was procured independently of any contractual relationship with the plaintiff. It was held that although a private individual might enjoin the publication of his photograph, different considerations applied to a public character and it was stated that '[a] statesman, author, artist or inventor, who asks for and desires public recognition, may be said to have surrendered this right [of privacy] to the public'.[36] However, outside New York, the Supreme Court of Michigan rejected the whole idea of a right of privacy in *Atkinson* v. *John E. Doherty & Co.*,[37] where the widow of the late Col. John Atkinson, a well-known lawyer and politician, sought to restrain the use of his name and likeness on a brand of cigars.

Although these lower court decisions are not particularly significant in themselves, they illustrate two central points. First, the fact that the embryonic right of privacy was quickly seized upon as a means to prevent unauthorised commercial exploitation of personality. Second, cases such as *Schuyler*, *Corliss* and *Atkinson* presaged the problem of reconciling a person's status as a public figure with that person's claim to a right of privacy, while *Corliss* also gave a foretaste of the problems in balancing a right of privacy with free speech interests and the liberty of the press. The first problem would later result in the development of the right of publicity, traced in the text below, while the second continues to tax the courts.[38]

Privacy on appeal

In 1902 the privacy issue came before the New York Court of Appeals in *Roberson* v. *Rochester Folding Box Co.*[39] Without the knowledge or consent of the plaintiff, a young girl suing through her guardian, the defendants had obtained a likeness of the plaintiff for use in their flour advertisement, accompanied by the caption 'flour of the family'. The plaintiff claimed that, as a result of the defendants' act of circulating 25,000 copies of the advertisement, she had been 'greatly humiliated by scoffs and jeers' of persons who had recognised her picture in the advertisement, and claimed that her good name had been attacked, 'causing her great distress and suffering both in body and in mind'.[40] Moreover, she claimed that 'she was made sick and suffered severe nervous shock, was confined

---

[35] *Corliss* v. *Walker*, 64 Fed Rep 280 (1894).   [36] *Ibid.*, 282.   [37] 80 NW 285 (1899).
[38] See, e.g., the works collected in R. Wacks (ed.) *Privacy* (Aldershot, 1993), Vol. II, pt III. See also B. S. Markesinis, 'The Right to Be Let Alone Versus Freedom of Speech' [1986] PL 67, arguing that the American courts have generally been over-protective of freedom of speech to the detriment of interests in personal privacy.
[39] 171 NY 538 (1902).   [40] *Ibid.*, 542.

152   The commercial appropriation of personality

to her bed and compelled to employ a physician'.[41] The plaintiff did not base her claim for an injunction and $15,000 damages on libel; indeed, she acknowledged that the likeness was a good one. Neither did she base her claim on the rule in *Wilkinson* v. *Downton*,[42] decided in England five years previously, which is somewhat surprising in view of the fact that she claimed to have suffered severe nervous shock as a result of the advertisement, and of the reliance of both parties on early English authorities.[43]

The gravamen of the plaintiff's complaint was that her portrait had been used without her consent to advertise the defendants' product, and that, as a result of the defendants' impertinence, she had been subjected to publicity which she found to be disagreeable. Although there was no direct guiding precedent, the Appellate Division of the Supreme Court of New York based its decision on an invasion of the plaintiff's right of privacy, a decision which the New York Court of Appeal overturned by a bare majority of four to three. The majority did not take the view that privacy was a pre-existing principle, emphasising the danger of a flood of (possibly spurious) claims.[44] Moreover, acceptance of such a claim would allow redress for injured feelings, which the majority was reluctant to embrace, in the absence of a clear common law principle.[45] In an exhaustive review of the authorities, Parker CJ interpreted the early English cases relied on by Warren and Brandeis narrowly, on the conventional grounds of either breach of trust or equity's jurisdiction to intervene to protect the plaintiff's property, and the obiter dicta in the American cases which supported the existence of a right of privacy were dismissed. Denying any wider principle protecting a plaintiff's feelings, the majority concluded that the right of privacy had not found an abiding place in New York law, and could not be incorporated 'without doing violence to settled principles of law'.[46] In emphasising the formal basis of equity's jurisdiction, the majority effectively ignored the efforts made by Warren and Brandeis to separate privacy from property interests, and the pains they took to base their right to privacy on the principle of inviolate personality.[47] Indeed,

---

[41] *Ibid.*, 543.   [42] [1897] 2 QB 57.

[43] The scope of the rule might have been uncertain or it could simply have been overlooked. The development of the tort of intentional infliction of mental distress in the United States belongs to a separate and slightly later chapter in American tort law: see 245–7 below.

[44] 171 NY 538 (1902), 545.

[45] *Ibid.*, 546–7, citing H. S. Hadley, 'The Right to Privacy' (1894) 3 Northwestern U L Rev 1, challenging the Warren and Brandeis thesis on the basis that equity had no concern with the feelings of an individual or with considerations of moral fitness, except in cases where the inconvenience or discomfort which an individual might have suffered was connected with the possession or enjoyment of property.

[46] 171 NY 538 (1902), 556.

[47] See Warren and Brandeis, 'The Right to Privacy', 205.

Privacy and publicity in the United States

the majority opinion arguably reflected the formalist approach for which late nineteenth-century jurisprudence has been heavily criticised.[48]

The dissenting minority took a more dynamic and flexible view of the Court's powers, stressing the need to extend the principles of the common law to remedy a wrong made possible by changing social conditions and commercial practices and rejecting the majority's insistence on basing the issue of liability on the invasion of a property interest. The right of privacy was regarded as a complement to the right to the immunity of one's person since the common law had always regarded one's person and property as inviolate.[49] Relying on the Warren and Brandeis analogy with private writings and other products of the mind, Gray J took the view that a writer had been protected in his right to a literary property in a letter against unauthorised publication, because it was property to which the right of privacy attached.[50] Consequently, according to the minority view, the plaintiff had the same property in the right to be protected against the use of her face for commercial purposes as she would have had if the defendants were publishing her literary compositions. If her face or her portraiture had value, then the value was exclusively hers until she granted the use to the public.

While Parker CJ for the majority felt that the Court could not grant a new remedy, thereby creating a new right of privacy, he did note that the legislature could intervene to create legislation prohibiting the unauthorised use of another's name or picture in advertising.[51] Accordingly, 'no embarrassment would result to the general body of the law' since the rule would only be applicable to the specific cases provided for by statute.[52] In the event, the decision in *Roberson* received widespread and immediate criticism both in academic circles[53] and amongst the general public, leading one of the majority judges to take the unusual step of writing an article in defence of the decision.[54] As a result, in the following year the New York legislature intervened and enacted a statute making the unconsented use of a person's name, portrait or picture for advertising, or for the purposes of trade, both a tort and a misdemeanour.[55]

---

[48] See Leebron, 'Privacy in Tort Law', 796.   [49] 171 NY 538 (1902), 564.

[50] *Ibid.*   [51] *Ibid.*, 545.   [52] *Ibid.*

[53] See Note, 'An Actionable Right of Privacy? *Roberson* v. *Rochester Folding Box Co.*' (1902) 12 Yale LJ 35.

[54] See D. O'Brien, 'The Right of Privacy' (1902) 2 Colum L Rev 437, which sought to address the criticisms made by 'such a well informed and conservative' journal as the *New York Times* on 23 August 1902 (*ibid.*, 438).

[55] NY Sess. Laws 1903 Ch. 132 ss. 1–2. The section exists in the same form in the New York Civil Rights Law §§50–1. It is the only type of invasion of privacy that New York recognises, and has been narrowly construed (see *Messenger* v. *Gruner & Jahr Printing and Pub.*, 208 F 3d 122 (2nd Cir. 2000), 125). The courts have refused to accept that other categories of invasion of privacy are actionable at common law, insisting that the

154   The commercial appropriation of personality

In stark contrast to the decision in *Roberson*, three years later, in *Pavesich v. New England Life Insurance Co.*,[56] the Supreme Court of Georgia recognised the existence of a right of privacy at common law. The plaintiff, an artist by profession, brought an action based on defamation and invasion of privacy against the defendants for publishing his picture, accompanied by a false testimonial, in their advertisements for life insurance. Giving the judgment of the Court, Cobb J conceded that the complete absence of a precedent for an asserted right should make the courts tread with caution, but noted that such an absence did not amount to a conclusive denial of the existence of a right.[57] With its emphasis on underlying principles, Cobb J's judgment has a distinct natural rights tone, starting from the proposition that, although an individual surrenders to society many rights and privileges which he would be free to exercise in the state of nature in exchange for the benefits which he receives as a member of society, he is not presumed to have surrendered all of his rights.[58]

In the Court's view, the foundation of the right of privacy lay in the instincts of nature. Privacy should be regarded as an absolute right which would belong to a person in a state of nature, which every person would be entitled to enjoy within or without society. It would thus take its place alongside other absolute rights such as the right of personal security and the right of personal liberty.[59] Consequently, one who wished to live a life of total or partial seclusion could choose the time, place and manner in which he would submit himself to the public gaze, and a right to withdraw from the public gaze was 'embraced within the right of personal liberty'.[60] Thus the Court viewed the right of privacy as a right derived from natural law, recognised by the principles of municipal law and guaranteed by the Constitutions of the United States and the State of Georgia in their provisions declaring that no person should be deprived of liberty except by due process of law.

Cobb J acknowledged that the main stumbling block in the way of the recognition of a right of privacy was the fact that its recognition would inevitably tend to curtail freedom of speech and of the press, though he regarded both as natural rights which should be enforced with due respect for each other.[61] Having concluded that a right of privacy existed, derived from a natural law liberty and enforceable in tort without special damage, Cobb J proceeded to consider the authorities, conceding that all the early English authorities relied on by Warren and Brandeis were based

balancing of the competing policy considerations underlying recovery for other kinds of invasions of privacy is a matter for the legislature: see, e.g., *Howell* v. *New York Post Co.*, 612 NE 2d 699 (N.Y. 1993), 703.
[56] 50 SE 68 (1905).   [57] *Ibid.*, 69.   [58] *Ibid.*
[59] *Ibid.*, 70.   [60] *Ibid.*   [61] *Ibid.*, 73.

Privacy and publicity in the United States

on conventional grounds such as interference with property, breach of trust, or breach of contract.[62] To this extent, he agreed with the decision of the majority in *Roberson*, but went on to criticise the conservatism of the New York Court of Appeals in denying a right which 'the instincts of nature' had proved to exist, and which was not disproved by judicial decision, legal history and legal writings.[63] The dissenting judgment of Gray J in *Roberson* was adopted in its entirety as an *ex post facto* justification of the conclusion which the majority of the Supreme Court of Georgia had already reached through its natural rights reasoning.[64]

Turning to the facts of the case, Cobb J saw no countervailing considerations concerning freedom of expression and concluded with a passage which deserves to be repeated in full.

> The knowledge that one's features and form are being used for such a purpose, and displayed in such places as such advertisements are often liable to be found, brings not only the person of an extremely sensitive nature, but even the individual of ordinary sensibility, to a realization that his liberty has been taken away from him; and, as long as the advertiser used him for these purposes, he cannot be otherwise than conscious of the fact that he is for the time being under the control of another, that he is no longer free, and that he is in reality a slave, without hope of freedom, held to service by a merciless master; and if a man of true instincts, or even ordinary sensibilities, no one can be more conscious of his enthralment than he is.

Needless to say, the defendant's appeal was dismissed, on the grounds of both invasion of privacy and libel, since it was also held that the publication of the advertisement was libellous in that the publication of the fictitious testimonials falsely suggested that the plaintiff had told a wilful falsehood either gratuitously or for consideration, when in fact he did not hold a policy with the defendant life assurance company.[65]

The contrasts between *Pavesich* and *Roberson* are deeper than the opposite results reached in each case. The decision in *Roberson* emphasised the limits of the courts' powers in creating new law and the practical dangers that would result from the assumption of such a power. The court called for legislative intervention, before its detailed and highly formal analysis of the case law denying a remedy for lack of formal authority. In stark contrast, the unanimous decision of the Supreme Court of Georgia in *Pavesich* laid emphasis on broad principles rather than a strict and formal analysis of the relevant precedents, which were invoked *ex post facto* to justify a conclusion which had already been reached. The general structure of the decision in *Roberson* resembles, in broad terms, the traditional English style of reasoning more closely than the decision in *Pavesich*. This reflects some fundamental differences in the patterns of legal reasoning

---

[62] *Ibid.*, 75.   [63] *Ibid.*, 78.   [64] *Ibid.*, 79.   [65] *Ibid.*, 81.

156   The commercial appropriation of personality

and legal theory which continue to account for the divergences between English and American law, and are explored below.[66]

As Prosser later noted,[67] *Pavesich* became the leading case and the courts in most states decided to follow the lead taken by the Supreme Court of Georgia in *Pavesich* rather than adopt the conservative stance taken by the New York Court of Appeals in *Roberson*. The details of the subsequent developments in each jurisdiction need not be traced here. What is important to note, for present purposes, is that the problem of the unauthorised use of a person's name or likeness was one of the particular problems which Warren and Brandeis sought to redress with their proposal for a right to privacy. It featured in some of the early cases where the existence of a right of privacy was mooted, and was obviously the gravamen of the complaint in *Roberson* and *Pavesich*. Conscious of the limitations of the pre-existing causes of action based on damage to reputation, property interests or breach of confidence, Warren and Brandeis sought greater protection for interests of personality through the right they identified as the right to inviolate personality.

Inviolate personality and the accretion of proprietary attributes

It is important to note that although the right of privacy was originally conceived as a right of inviolate personality, it quickly began to develop distinctly proprietary attributes. The process of designating a particular right as a 'property' right often involves no more than placing a descriptive label on that right; the term 'property' is used in a metaphorical sense, and the categorisation does not have any inherent significance.[68] However, looking behind the label or terminology used by the courts, and examining the substance of the interests, it is clear that in the earliest right of privacy cases, the courts were protecting interests of an essentially economic or proprietary nature rather than dignitary interests in inviolate personality.

For example, in an early right of privacy case, *Edison* v. *Edison Polyform Mfg Co.*,[69] the celebrated inventor Thomas A. Edison brought an action to restrain a company from using (i) his name as their corporate name, and (ii) his name and picture in advertisements for a medicinal preparation, Polyform, which he had invented several years previously and had sold to the defendants.[70] The assignment did not give the defendants permission

---

[66] See, further, 189–98 below.   [67] Prosser, 'Privacy', 386.
[68] See 276–86 below.   [69] 67 A 392 (1907).
[70] *Ibid*. In this respect, the case differs markedly from two early English cases involving the unauthorised use of the names of eminent surgeons (*Dockrell* v. *Dougall* (1899) 15 TLR 333 and *Clark* v. *Freeman* (1848) 11 Beav 112) in that the English cases involved what were essentially quack medicines. Consequently, the essence of the complaint in each case was injury to reputation, although, in the event, both claims for libel were unsuccessful. See, futher, 266–8 below.

Privacy and publicity in the United States

to use Edison's name and picture in connection with the medicine. The Court of Chancery of New Jersey held that the cases on the law of unfair trade had no application since the defendants did not pass off their goods as being goods of Edison's manufacture, but, rather, held out that he was connected with the enterprise and was supervising its work by certifying that the preparation was made according to the Edison formula.[71] The action for invasion of privacy succeeded, and Stevens VC noted that: '[i]f a man's name be his own property . . . it is difficult to understand why the peculiar cast of one's features is not also one's property, and why its pecuniary value, if it has one, does not belong to its owner, rather than to the person seeking to make unauthorized use of it'.[72] Thus *Edison* differed from the two leading privacy cases, *Roberson* and *Pavesich*, in that the plaintiff was well known, and, significantly, the right of privacy was seen as being capable of remedying injuries to interests of an economic nature in addition to injuries to inviolate personality.

In another early case, *Munden* v. *Harris*,[73] the plaintiff, a young boy suing through his next friend, brought an action for an injunction and damages for the unauthorised use of his picture in an advertisement for jewellery, on its face a claim for injured feelings or dignity. However, in giving judgment for the plaintiff, Ellison J, sitting in the Kansas City Court of Appeals, noted that a person might have a peculiarity of appearance from which he might benefit if it was used in advertising or merchandising. In such a case, '[i]t is a right which he may wish to exercise for his own profit, and why may he not restrain another who is using it for gain? If there is value in it, sufficient to excite the cupidity of another, why is it not the property of him who gives it the value and from whom the value springs?'[74] The Court concluded that a person had 'an exclusive right to his picture on the score of its being a property right of material profit', [75] and that general damages could be recovered without proving specific loss.[76] Although the use of the property label might not have been inherently significant, looking behind the label what was clear was the Court's acknowledgement of the economic or proprietary interest that any person might have in his own image.[77]

Again the economic aspect was stressed in *Flake* v. *Greensboro News Co.*,[78] where the Supreme Court of North Carolina allowed a claim for invasion of privacy by a radio announcer and dancer blessed with a

---

[71] 67 A 392 (1907). Cf. the discussion of classical passing off and 'connection misrepresentation' in English law, 72–84 above.

[72] 67 A 392 (1907).   [73] 134 SW 1076 (1911).

[74] *Ibid.*, 1078.   [75] *Ibid.*, 1079.   [76] *Ibid.*

[77] In referring to the value which excited the cupidity of another, Ellison J was essentially giving expression to the unjust enrichment rationale for a remedy for appropriation of personality. See, further, 311–13 below.

[78] 195 SE 55 (1938).

158   The commercial appropriation of personality

sylph-like figure, after her photograph had been used without her consent in an advertisement for bread. The Court stated that if it were conceded that a person's name or features could be a valuable asset for the purposes of advertising, then it followed that such features could not be used for advertising purposes without the consent of the owner,[79] although the damages awarded were nominal in view of the fact that the plaintiff's photograph was used mistakenly and of the defendants' offer of an apology.

However, it should be noted that in other cases involving appropriation of name or likeness in advertising the courts disregarded any economic interests and focused purely on the injury to feelings or dignity. For example, in *Fairfield* v. *American Photocopy Equipment Co.*,[80] where a lawyer's name was used without his consent in an advertisement for a photocopying machine, the California Court of Appeals stated that the gist of the cause of action for invasion of privacy was a wrong of a personal character resulting in injury to the plaintiff's feelings, without regard to any effect which the publication might have on a person's property, business, pecuniary interests, or standing in the community.[81] In other cases, the courts stressed that, although the right of privacy was intended primarily for the protection of an individual's personality against unlawful invasion, damages might include 'recovery for a so-called "property" interest inherent and inextricably interwoven in the individual's personality', although it was injury to the person not to property which established the cause of action.[82]

Thus, in addition to protecting essentially dignitary interests in cases such as *Pavesich*, a broad range of both economic and dignitary interests were being protected under the rubric of privacy. Economic interests need not necessarily be limited to existing trading interests, and might include some other valuable but latent recognition value.[83] It is not clear from the report in *Edison* whether the plaintiff was involved in the business of exploiting his own name. However, any unrealised potential was quickly seized upon by the defendants who were clearly aware of the benefits of using Edison's name on their products and as part of their trading name. Similarly, it is not clear whether the plaintiff in *Flake* had exploited the commercial value of her sylph-like figure, although the advertisers benefited from its association with their bread. The plaintiffs both in *Edison* and in *Flake* were well known, but in *Fairfield* v. *American Photocopy Co.* and in *Munden* v. *Harris* the plaintiffs were unknown, and their images had no obvious commercial value. While the court in *Fairfield*

---

[79] *Ibid.*, 64.   [80] 291 P 2d 194 (1955).   [81] *Ibid.*, 197.

[82] *Gautier* v. *Pro-Football Inc.*, 106 NYS 2d 553 (1951), 560 aff'd 107 NE 2d 485 (1952), 560 (claim for invasion of privacy under the New York Civil Rights Law).

[83] See 8–10 above.

Privacy and publicity in the United States 159

stressed that the injury suffered by the plaintiff lawyer was purely an injury to his dignitary interests, in *Munden* the court took the view that commercial value could lie in the image of an unknown person and essentially that what was worth taking was worth protecting.

It is difficult to draw any neat division between the multifarious de facto interests that different people might enjoy in their image. What the development of the law of privacy in the United States shows is that the new right could be used to protect a whole spectrum of economic and dignitary interests ranging from existing trading interests through to interests in feelings or sensibilities. Yet, even such a broad and expansive legal category as the right of privacy has boundaries, however ill defined. It soon became clear that the right of privacy was being used to secure protection for an extraordinarily disparate range of interests, resulting in considerable conceptual confusion regarding the proper scope and doctrinal basis for the right of privacy, with various competing conceptions of the right, considered below, being offered. Moreover, the difficulty in reconciling a right to privacy with a right to prevent the unauthorised commercial exploitation of essentially *economic* attributes in personality proved to be considerable, and led to the development of a separate right of publicity, outlined in the succeeding section.

It is necessary to draw clear distinctions between the two alternative bases of liability: the right of privacy and the right of publicity, and the underlying economic and dignitary interests that these causes of action protect. While the historical link between the development of the right of privacy and the problem of appropriation of personality in the United States is strong, the conceptual link is less certain. Despite the fact that appropriation of personality and the right of privacy might seem to be inextricably intertwined, there is no necessary conceptual link between a *general right* to privacy and the problem of appropriation of personality. Indeed, this point is particularly relevant when considering legal systems, particularly the Anglo-Australian system, where the problem of a remedy for appropriation of personality is often tied to the question of the desirability of introducing a general right to privacy. It is perfectly possible to develop a specific common law remedy for appropriation of personality while a separate debate concerning the desirability of a general right of privacy proceeds.[84]

Conceptions of privacy

In the United States the new legal category, cast in the broad terms of a right 'to be let alone', had obvious attractions for litigants seeking redress

---

[84] See, generally, 238–41 below.

160　　The commercial appropriation of personality

for increasingly disparate forms of damage to a number of different interests. In this respect, in its early years privacy was merely a residual category of tort law, covering cases where the harm was emotionally based.[85] Indeed, Prosser believed that when the tort of intentional infliction of mental suffering became fully developed and received general recognition, the great majority of privacy cases would possibly be absorbed into it.[86] However, this did not happen, and, partly due to the efforts of Prosser himself,[87] privacy remains an important, though rather ill-defined, legal category in American law. This indeterminacy is reflected in the traditional fear of recognising a right of privacy in English law: that it is an over-broad and hopelessly vague concept with uncertain limits and possibly harmful consequences for freedom of expression.[88] Undoubtedly, the concept of privacy has 'a protean capacity to be all things to all lawyers'[89] and its very vagueness lends itself well to manipulation. Thus, with varying levels of generality, the essence of the right of privacy has involved: the right to be 'let alone';[90] the protection of human dignity or inviolate personality;[91] a person's control over access to information about himself;[92] a person's limited accessibility to others;[93] and autonomy or control over the intimacies of personal identity.[94]

It is clear that these conceptions are influenced by the disparate range of activities that both laymen and lawyers commonly regard as involving damage to interests in personal privacy. These range from what many would regard as the core concerns of privacy, for example, the unauthorised use of personal data, the activities of peeping toms, long-lens surveillance, the taping of personal conversations, etc., to activities that might be regarded as being at the periphery of any notion of privacy, such as harassment, insulting behaviour or the depiction of a person in a false and unfavourable light. The most important competing conceptions of privacy demand to be examined in order to determine the place that appropriation of personality occupies in these rival schemes, and whether it is a core or peripheral concern of privacy law.

It should be noted at the outset that we are solely concerned with the common law tort of invasion of privacy rather than the constitutional right

---

[85] See G. E. White, *Tort Law in America – An Intellectual History* (Oxford, 1980), 174.
[86] *Ibid.*, citing Prosser's 1955 edition of *The Law of Torts*.
[87] See text below.　　[88] See 200–2 below.
[89] T. Gerety, 'Redefining Privacy' (1977) 12 Harv CR-CL Law Rev 233, 234.
[90] Warren and Brandeis, 'The Right to Privacy', 205.
[91] E. J. Bloustein, 'Privacy as an Aspect of Human Dignity: An Answer to Dean Prosser' (1964) NYULRev. 962, 1001.
[92] C. Fried, 'Privacy' (1968) 77 Yale LJ 475, 493.
[93] R. Gavison, 'Privacy and the Limits of Law' (1980) 89 Yale LJ 421, 423.
[94] Gerety, 'Redefining Privacy', 236.

Privacy and publicity in the United States 161

of privacy. The constitutional right developed later,[95] applying primarily as a control on government rather than as a control on the conduct of private individuals, and affording protection against, for example, unreasonable search and seizure[96] or interference with personal decisions relating to marriage and family relationships such as the use of contraceptives[97] or decisions concerning abortion.[98] As such, the constitutional right is very different in scope and much narrower than the common law tort,[99] since it reflects different notions of the appropriate behaviour of government officials as compared to private individuals.[100]

The reductionist paradigm

From an examination of the 300 or so cases that had been reported by 1960, Prosser concluded that the right of privacy was not one tort, but encompassed 'four distinct kinds of invasion of four different interests of the plaintiff... tied together by the common name, but otherwise have almost nothing in common except that each represents an interference with the right of the plaintiff, in the phrase coined by Judge Cooley, "to be let alone" '.[101] Prosser identified the following four torts, which he argued were subject to their own discrete rules: '(i) intrusion upon the plaintiff's seclusion or solitude; (ii) public disclosure of embarrassing private facts about the plaintiff; (iii) publicity which places the plaintiff in a false light in the public eye; and (iv) appropriation, for the defendant's advantage, of the plaintiff's name or likeness'.[102] However, despite his

[95] See, generally, R. F. Hixson, *Privacy in a Public Society* (New York, 1987), Ch. 4.
[96] See, e.g., *Stanley* v. *Georgia*, 394 US 557 (1969).
[97] See *Griswold* v. *Connecticut*, 381 US 479 (1965).
[98] See, e.g., *Roe* v. *Wade*, 410 US 113 (1973).
[99] See, e.g., *Morris* v. *Danna*, 411 F Supp. 1300 (1976), 1303, citing Prosser's quadripartite classification (see text below); *Rosenberg* v. *Martin*, 478 F 2d 520 (1973) (constitutional right to privacy could not be equated with the statutory right under New York law). The constitutional right is arguably more concerned with personal autonomy than with personal privacy: see, e.g., L. Henkin, 'Privacy and Autonomy' (1974) 74 Colum L Rev 1410, 1425.
[100] See P. L. Felcher and E. L. Rubin, 'Privacy, Publicity, and the Portrayal of Real People by the Media' (1979) 88 Yale LJ 1577, 1584. See, generally, J. Rubenfeld, 'The Right of Privacy' (1989) 102 HarvLRev 737.
[101] 'Privacy', 389.
[102] *Ibid.* Cf. G. Dickler, 'The Right of Privacy' (1936) 70 USLRev 435, 435–6, providing an earlier (and less influential) grouping under three labels: (i) intrusions on the personal life and affairs of others; (ii) disclosures of personal thoughts, habits, manners and affairs, etc.; and (iii) appropriations, involving elements of unfair trade practices and appropriation of potential profits. This latter class, Dickler argued, was different in that although the element of mental anguish was often present, it was not essential for recovery and was primarily concerned with preventing the defendant's unwarranted advancement of his own commercial interests.

162   The commercial appropriation of personality

assertion to the contrary, Prosser only identified three interests that were protected by his four torts scheme.[103] First, the intrusion tort protected a primarily mental interest which had been useful in filling out the gaps left by trespass, nuisance and the intentional infliction of mental distress.[104] Second, both the disclosure tort[105] and the false light tort[106] protected an interest in reputation, with the same overtones of mental distress that are present in defamation. Third, the appropriation tort protected 'not so much a mental as a proprietary [interest] in the exclusive use of the plaintiff's name and likeness as an aspect of his identity'.[107]

The categories are largely self-explanatory. The first tort, intrusion, deals with what is close to the popular notion of invasion of privacy, where a person's seclusion or solitude is invaded.[108] The tort was soon extended beyond purely physical intrusion to cover activities such as eavesdropping on a person's private conversation by means of wire-tapping or through the use of microphones,[109] the main limitations being the requirements that the intrusion must be offensive to a reasonable man, and that the subject matter of the intrusion was something which the plaintiff would be entitled to regard as private.[110] While the intrusion tort protects what Prosser referred to as primarily a mental interest, the second tort, disclosure, protects an interest in reputation. This is apparent from the fact that the tort is concerned with a *public* disclosure of private facts which would be offensive and objectionable to a reasonable man of ordinary sensibilities.[111] Prosser's third tort, publicity placing a person in a false light, also protects an interest in reputation and is very closely related to the tort of defamation, although it goes beyond the bounds of the tort of defamation in protecting sensibilities or feelings rather than reputation *stricto sensu*.[112]

---

[103] A fact noted by Bloustein, 'Privacy as Human Dignity', 965, and H. Gross, 'The Concept of Privacy' (1967) 42 NYULRev 34, 46.

[104] Prosser, 'Privacy', 392.   [105] *Ibid.*, 398.   [106] *Ibid.*, 400.   [107] *Ibid.*, 406.

[108] Cf. *Kaye* v. *Robertson* [1991] FSR 62 and see 202–11 below. Cf. *Barber* v. *Time Inc.* 159 SW 2d 291 (1948).

[109] See Prosser, 'Privacy', 390. In the United Kingdom, the Younger Committee took the view that no further legal protection beyond the established legal categories was necessary to prevent intrusions on home life by prying neighbours, landlords and others: see *Report of the Committee on Privacy*, Cmnd 5012 (London, 1972), paras. 119–20.

[110] See Prosser, 'Privacy', 391.

[111] See, e.g., *Melvin* v. *Read* 297 P 91 (1931) (actionable invasion of privacy where the defendant made and exhibited a film enacting the plaintiff's life-story revealing her past as a prostitute and defendant in a murder trial, thereby ruining her new life by exposing her past to the world and her friends). English law affords piecemeal protection primarily through the tort of defamation and the action for breach of confidence: see 207–11 and Chapter 9 below.

[112] See, further, Chapter 9.

Privacy and publicity in the United States 163

The category of primary interest for present purposes is the fourth: appropriation.[113] Prosser recognised that appropriation was a different matter from the other three categories and argued that the interest protected was 'not so much a mental as a proprietary one, in the exclusive use of the plaintiff's name and likeness as an aspect of his identity'.[114] The ambit of the appropriation category was governed by two main rules. First, the law would only protect a person's name as a symbol of his identity and would not protect the name in itself from being adopted by others; the existence of several thousand John Smiths showed that there was no right to the exclusive use of a name.[115] Secondly, as a consequence of the first rule, liability would only arise when a defendant pirated the plaintiff's identity for his own advantage. Although some statutes required that the plaintiff could show that the defendant had derived some pecuniary advantage, Prosser noted that the common law was not so limited and a defendant could be liable where, for example, he had used the plaintiff's name in a petition, or a telegram, or as the name of the father on a birth certificate.[116] Although it might have been argued that the use of a person's name in a defendant's newspaper or magazine was a use for the defendant's advantage, the courts had given greater weight to free speech considerations and had held that incidental inclusion of a person's name or likeness in a newspaper, book or magazine was not actionable.[117]

Prosser saw little point in discussing, as some courts had done, whether the right should be classified as a property right, since, even if it was not a property right, once it was protected by law it was a right of value which the plaintiff could exploit by selling licences. Indeed, in his view, evidence of its proprietary nature could be seen from the fact that an exclusive licensee had a 'right of publicity' which entitled him to prevent the use of the name or likeness by a third person.[118] The phrase 'right of publicity' was only mentioned in passing and was merely used as a label for the right of a licensee in the privacy cases that were concerned with commercial

---

[113] Prosser, 'Privacy', 401, made the rather strange assertion that there was little indication that Warren and Brandeis intended to direct their article at what was, in his scheme, the fourth branch of the tort, the exploitation of attributes of the plaintiff's identity, although, as noted above, Warren and Brandeis expressed particular concern at the 'unauthorised circulation of portraits of private persons' ('The Right to Privacy', 195); see text accompanying notes 7 to 10 above. It is difficult to imagine that the cases cited by Warren and Brandeis could come more clearly within Prosser's fourth category, and equally difficult to see how they could fall within any other of his categories.

[114] Prosser, 'Privacy', 406.

[115] Amongst the authorities Prosser cited in support of this proposition were two English cases, *DuBoulay* v. *DuBoulay* (1869) LR 2 PC 430 and *Cowley* v. *Cowley* [1901] AC 450.

[116] See Prosser, 'Privacy', 405, note 180, and the references cited.

[117] *Ibid.*, 405.   [118] *Ibid.*, 407.

164   The commercial appropriation of personality

appropriation, possibly because he did not want to disrupt his 'four torts' conceptual scheme by dividing the fourth tort into two, with an 'appropriation privacy' tort dealing with the mental distress aspect and a 'right of publicity' dealing with the economic aspect.[119] Other leading contemporary American tort scholars such as Harper and James were more aware of this distinction, and recognised that the two unrelated ideas of emotional distress (which most ordinary people would suffer) and purely financial loss (suffered by public figures) produced a legal schizophrenia which was not conducive to clarity of thought. In their view, a public figure would suffer from an invasion of an interest in publicity rather than an interest in privacy, and the law should draw an appropriately sharp distinction between cases involving financial considerations and cases involving purely emotional disturbances such as grief, humiliation and loss of personal dignity.[120] Ultimately, it became impossible to reconcile the notion of a purely commercial exploitation of personality with a right of privacy, as was seen by the development of the right of publicity, traced in the text below.

Despite these shortcomings, Prosser's re-interpretation of the law of privacy proved to be hugely influential, and was adopted by the American Law Institute in the second Restatement.[121] The fact that it was so influential, and so readily accepted, was not particularly surprising, given the need for an organising framework for such a diverse body of case law and Prosser's status as the leading contemporary tort scholar.[122] However, his views did not reign unchallenged.

A holistic conception

Four years later Bloustein proposed a general theory of individual privacy which attempted to reconcile the divergent strands of legal development and to re-establish privacy as a single, unified, legal concept.[123] Following a detailed critique of Prosser's analysis, Bloustein argued that

---

[119] See J. T. McCarthy, *The Rights of Publicity and Privacy*, 2nd edn (New York, 2001), §1.23.

[120] *The Law of Torts* (Boston, 1956), 689–90.

[121] See *Restatement, Second, Torts* (1977) §652. The order of the categories was changed slightly, the new order being: (1) intrusion upon solitude or seclusion; (2) appropriation of name or likeness; (3) disclosure of private facts; and (4) publicity placing the plaintiff in a false light.

[122] For an account of Prosser's contribution to tort law in America in general and the tort of invasion of privacy in particular, see G. E. White, *Tort Law in America*, Ch. 5, esp. 173–6. Prosser's framework has also provided the basis for studies of the developing law of privacy in other jurisdictions. See, e.g., D. J. McQuoid-Mason, *The Law of Privacy in South Africa* (Cape Town, 1978), which also provides an account of the law of privacy in several common law and civil law jurisdictions.

[123] Bloustein, 'Privacy as Human Dignity', 962.

Privacy and publicity in the United States

a common thread of principle running through all the cases could be discerned: the principle which Warren and Brandeis had identified as 'inviolate personality'.[124] The interest served in the privacy cases was in some sense a spiritual interest rather than an interest in property or reputation and the nature of the injury in a case of invasion of privacy, like the torts of assault, battery and false imprisonment, was an injury to a person's individuality and dignity. Accordingly, the legal remedy represented a social vindication of the human spirit rather than compensation for loss suffered.[125] Bloustein acknowledged that 'the words that we use to identify and describe basic human values are necessarily vague and ill defined',[126] yet he was rather more successful in outlining why the interest was important enough to merit legal protection than in delineating the right.[127] In terms of definition, his conception of privacy was hopelessly vague.[128]

In order to fit in with his general thesis, Bloustein was forced to treat the appropriation cases as being concerned with the protection of purely dignitary interests. According to his interpretation, cases such as *Pavesich* involved the plaintiff's interests in preserving his own personal dignity, rather than injuries to the plaintiff's proprietary interests as in Prosser's scheme.[129] He argued that the use of a person's photograph for advertising purposes had tendencies to degrade and humiliate, and only differed from other aspects of invasion of privacy, such as disclosure of private facts, in that the sense of personal affront and indignity would be provoked by the association of a person's name or likeness with a commercial product, *simpliciter*.[130] What was 'demeaning and humiliating' was the 'commercialization of an aspect of personality',[131] and in a passage redolent of Cobb J's dictum in *Pavesich* v. *New England Life Insurance Co.*,[132] Bloustein argued that:

[n]o man wants to be 'used' by another against his will, and it is for this reason that commercial use of a personal photograph is obnoxious. Use of a photograph for trade purposes turns a man into a commodity and makes him serve the economic needs and interests of others. In a community at all sensitive to the commercialization of human values, it is degrading to thus make a man part of commerce against his will.[133]

---

[124] *Ibid.*, 1001.   [125] *Ibid.*, 1002–3. Cf. 21–3 above.

[126] *Ibid.*, 1001.   [127] Gross, 'The Concept of Privacy', 53.

[128] See G. Dworkin, 'The Common Law Protection of Privacy' (1967) 2 U Tas LR 418, 433.

[129] Bloustein, 'Privacy as Human Dignity', 986.

[130] *Ibid.*, 986–7.   [131] *Ibid.*, 987.

[132] See note 57 above and accompanying text.

[133] Bloustein, 'Privacy as Human Dignity', 988.

166   The commercial appropriation of personality

In Bloustein's view, in most cases the name or likeness which was used had no intrinsic commercial value, or at best a purely nominal value which would not justify the costs of a legal action.[134] This involved playing down 'some few of the cases'[135] where the plaintiffs' images had a de facto commercial value, cases which, Bloustein suggested, had led Prosser and others such as Nimmer to the mistaken conclusion that the interest involved was a proprietary one. This purely dignitary analysis was distinctly at odds with the existence of the right of publicity, protecting predominantly commercial interests in personality, which had been developing in the eleven years prior to his article.[136] According to Bloustein, the very existence of a right of publicity depended on the fact that a name and likeness could only command a commercial price in a society which recognised a right to privacy allowing a person to control the conditions under which his name or likeness were used: there was no right of publicity, but 'only a right, under some circumstances, to command a commercial price for abandoning privacy'.[137] Every man had the right to prevent the commercial exploitation of his personality 'not because of its commercial worth, but because it would be demeaning to human dignity to fail to enforce such a right'.[138] Clearly, this analysis was the result of viewing appropriation of personality purely from the dignitary interests perspective, thus making it an aspect of an affront to human dignity which constituted the essence of invasion of privacy in Bloustein's scheme. This overlooked the fact that, in reality, advertisers would not pay famous people such as sports and entertainment personalities for giving up their privacy, but would pay because such persons' images already had a 'recognition value'.[139]

While Bloustein sought to challenge Prosser's reductionist approach by arguing that Prosser's four torts could be encompassed within a single concept of privacy, underpinned by a single unifying principle, the resulting alternative holistic conception of privacy and its underlying principle was hopelessly vague. In short, Bloustein was trying to do too much and other challenges to Prosser's account have been more successful.

Reductionism reappraised: a core conception of privacy

Perhaps the strongest and most thoughtful attack on the reductionist approach can be seen in the argument, propounded by Gavison, which

---

[134] *Ibid.*, 987.   [135] *Ibid.*, 988.   [136] See 171–9 below.
[137] Bloustein, 'Privacy as Human Dignity', 989.   [138] *Ibid.*
[139] See A. D'Amato, 'Comment on Professor Posner's Lecture on Privacy' (1978) 12 GaLRev 497, 499. See also *Lugosi v. Universal Pictures* Cal. 603 P2d 425 (1979), 438.

Privacy and publicity in the United States

restores privacy as a unitary legal concept, reflecting our extra-legal notions of privacy rather than breaking it down into component interests.[140] Although the appeal of the reductionist approach lies in underlining the fact that privacy is seldom protected in the absence of some other interest, the danger in this approach is that it might lead to the conclusion that privacy is not an important value and that its loss should not elicit legal protection.[141] If the concept is viewed as being largely parasitic and entails that protection may be secured by protecting separate primary interests such as property or reputation, its conceptual distinctiveness becomes uncertain.[142] Gavison argues that everyday speech reveals that the concept of privacy is coherent and useful in three different, but related, contexts: (i) as a neutral concept, which allows us to identify when a loss of privacy has occurred; (ii) as a distinctive value, since claims for legal protection of privacy are compelling only if losses of privacy are undesirable for similar reasons; and (iii) as a legal concept, that enables us to identify those occasions calling for legal protection. Accordingly, (i) losses of privacy, (ii) invasions of privacy and (iii) actionable violations of privacy are related in that each is a subset of the previous category. While reductionist analyses of privacy deny the utility of privacy as a separate concept and sever these conceptual links, Gavison argues that the use of the word 'privacy' in all three contexts reinforces the belief that they are linked and suggests that privacy is a distinct and coherent concept in all of these contexts.[143] The proposed neutral concept of privacy starts from the premise that an individual enjoys perfect privacy when he is completely inaccessible to others (obviously impossible in any society). This has three components: (i) the amount of information known about an individual; (ii) the attention paid to an individual; and (iii) the degree of physical access to an individual. These three elements of secrecy, anonymity and solitude are arguably distinct but interrelated, providing a richer definition than any centred around only one element, and better explain common intuitions as to when privacy is lost.[144]

However, any formulation of a core concept of privacy involves rejecting some claims which lie at the periphery. While the core encompasses typical invasions of privacy, such as the collection and dissemination of personal data, peeping toms, watching and photographing individuals, intruding into private places, eavesdropping and wiretapping, it does not include such activities as insulting, harassing or persecuting behaviour,

---

[140] R. Gavison, 'Privacy and the Limits of Law' (1980) 89 Yale LJ 421, 424.
[141] *Ibid.*   [142] R. Wacks, *Personal Information* (Oxford, 1989), 18.
[143] Gavison, 'Privacy and the Limits of Law', 423.   [144] *Ibid.*, 428–9.

168   The commercial appropriation of personality

presenting individuals in a false light, unsolicited mail and unwanted phone calls; neither does it include commercial exploitation. Although such invasions of privacy might all be included in an all-embracing and rhetorically forceful notion such as the 'right to be let alone',[145] such an approach covers almost any conceivable claim that might be made and denies any distinctiveness and meaning which invasion of privacy might have.[146] Similarly, although the coherence of privacy might lie in its relationship with human dignity, this does not always hold true. There are ways to offend human dignity and personality that have nothing to do with privacy; having to beg or sell one's body in order to survive is an affront to dignity, but does not involve a loss of privacy. Gavison expressly rejects commercial exploitation of personality as an aspect of privacy, noting that privacy 'can be invaded in ways that have nothing to do with such exploitation',[147] citing governmental wiretapping as an obvious example of an invasion of privacy with no hint of commercial exploitation.[148] Similarly, 'there are many forms of exploitation that do not involve privacy under the broadest conception'; individuals may be commercially exploited if they are compensated for their services at rates below the market price, although this does not seem to involve loss of privacy.[149]

Such an approach falls some way short of the somewhat extreme position that commercial exploitation *never* involves invasion of privacy. This involves reasoning along the lines that: (i) commercial appropriation is concerned with the exploitation of the images of celebrities, (ii) a person's position as a celebrity is inconsistent with a claim for a right to privacy, therefore (iii) commercial appropriation has nothing to do with privacy. The first premise is impossible to defend. Commercial practice in advertising suggests that this is simply not the case, a fact confirmed by the non-celebrity status of the plaintiffs in many of the American privacy cases. The second premise poses greater difficulties. Although there are certainly problems in reconciling a person's status as a celebrity with a claim for privacy, it is rather crude to argue that celebrity will automatically disentitle a person to a right of privacy.[150] A somewhat less extreme view holds that if, for example, a famous athlete finds that his name is used without his consent to promote sports equipment, then the essence of the complaint is the unauthorised commercial exploitation of a commercial asset; the concern is with the athlete's public reputation, rather than his

---

[145] *Ibid.*, 437.   [146] *Ibid.*, 437–8.   [147] *Ibid.*, 440.
[148] *Ibid.*, note 61.   [149] *Ibid.*
[150] Compare the divergent conclusions reached on this point in *Roberson* and *Pavesich* above, and see text accompanying note 165 below.

Privacy and publicity in the United States

private life.[151] Consider a case where an ordinary person finds his image being widely used without his consent in an advertisement for life insurance, on similar facts to those in *Pavesich* v. *New England Life Insurance Co.*[152] In such a case, the plaintiff might become subject to unwanted attention, which would thus affect the plaintiff's anonymity which, in Gavison's scheme, is one of the three core irreducible elements of privacy, which form the conception of privacy as limited accessibility. Thus the notion of privacy is relevant, although perhaps not central, in some cases of appropriation of personality which result in damage to a person's dignitary interests. Admittedly, cases where the plaintiffs are celebrities are more difficult to reconcile with the notion of a right to privacy, as we shall see in our account of the development of the right of publicity.

Attempts to banish commercial appropriation from privacy altogether are unrealistic, and involve taking a very broad view of what constitutes commercial appropriation, ultimately ascribing a commercial value to practically every image. For example, in *Pavesich*, the plaintiff's image had no intrinsic commercial value, and the advertisers could have used the image of 1,000 other similar persons at little extra cost or inconvenience. Rather, the essence of the plaintiff's complaint was the damage to his dignitary interests, which might be protected at law either as part of a general right of privacy or by a tort of appropriation of personality which might provide protection for either economic or dignitary interests, or, in appropriate circumstances, for both aspects. Again this highlights the basic point that looking at the problem purely from a commercial appropriation perspective, or from an exclusively dignitary right of privacy perspective,[153] distorts the true picture. Both economic and dignitary interests have to be taken into account.

Privacy as principle

Alternatively, the choice need not be limited to a simple adoption or rejection of the concept of privacy.[154] If the notion of privacy is sufficiently coherent as a social or psychological concept, then the question arises of

---

[151] See D. Gibson, 'Common Law Protection of Privacy: What to Do Until the Legislators Arrive' in L. Klar (ed.) *Studies in Canadian Tort Law* (Toronto, 1977), 343, 345, arguing that commercial appropriation 'has no place in a study of privacy law'; cited by D. Vaver, 'What's Mine Is Not Yours: Commercial Appropriation of Personality Under the Privacy Acts of British Columbia, Manitoba and Saskatchewan' (1981) 15 UBCL Rev 241, arguing (255) that '[i]t is sterile to argue that appropriation is not a facet of privacy'.

[152] See note 56 above and accompanying text.

[153] As in Bloustein's scheme: see text accompanying note 137 above.

[154] See P. A. Freund, 'Privacy: One Concept or Many?' in J. R. Pennock and J. W. Chapman (eds.) *Nomos XIII Privacy* (New York, 1971), 182.

170   The commercial appropriation of personality

whether it can be embodied within a legal system, having due regard to various competing interests. If we define an interest as a claim, demand, need or concern, and a right as a legally protected interest, then should privacy be accorded the status of an interest and then a right?[155] While rules are particularisations that describe the state of the law in a defined context, being prescriptive, with a relatively high degree of immediacy and precision, principles may be regarded as more plastic and more useful for predicting and shaping the course of legal development.[156] Thus, principles occupy the middle ground between abstract philosophical definitions and concrete legal applications. While never claiming to provide an abstract general definition, nor being so determinate in its effects as simple rules of precedent, the middle ground of principles can possibly encompass both.[157] Freund argues that the right of privacy is of cardinal worth as a principle, and that even if it would be seen as misleading to incorporate a right of privacy into a legal rule, it would be undesirable to exclude it as the term of a legal principle.[158] Indeed, it is worth noting that Warren and Brandeis sought to avoid the charge of advocating judicial legislation by arguing that what they envisaged was the mere application of a pre-existing principle to changing social conditions, rather than the introduction of a new principle.

Leaving aside the controversial role of rules and principles in general jurisprudence,[159] it is perfectly possible to refer to a master rule by which principles as well as rules of law may be identified. Accordingly, a court must apply statutory provisions, rules of precedent and the *rationes decidendi* of cases, but in a case to which no statutory provision or *ratio decidendi* applies, in coming to its decision the court must take into account principles derived from legislation, *rationes decidendi* of relevant cases and from relevant dicta.[160] Although legislation and binding precedent are the only ultimate sources of law, principles, which embody the persuasive sources, should not be excluded if only for the reason that principles play a considerable part in the solution of legal problems to which no rule is directly applicable.[161] Nevertheless, it should not be forgotten that it is possible to find dicta in support of more or less any principle if

---

[155] *Ibid.*, 194.   [156] *Ibid.*, 197.   [157] Gerety, 'Redefining Privacy', 239.
[158] Freund, 'Privacy: One Concept or Many?', 198. Warren and Brandeis, 'The Right to Privacy', 213, sought to avoid the charge of advocating judicial legislation by arguing that what they envisaged was the mere application of a pre-existing principle to changing social conditions, rather than the introduction of a new principle. See, also, E. M. Barendt, 'Privacy as a Constitutional Right and Value' in P. Birks (ed.) *Privacy and Loyalty* (Oxford, 1997), 12 (arguing that privacy should be seen primarily as a constitutional value rather than as a set of constitutional and statutory rights).
[159] See, e.g., R. Dworkin, *Taking Rights Seriously*, Chs. 2 and 3. Cf. H. L. A. Hart, *The Concept of Law*, 2nd edn (Oxford, 1994), 259–63.
[160] R. Cross and J. W. Harris, *Precedent in English Law*, 4th edn (Oxford, 1991), 215.
[161] *Ibid.*, 216.

Privacy and publicity in the United States 171

one takes the view that there are certain principles of law, which, though not expressed in judgments or statutory provisions, 'nevertheless must be held to qualify all that falls from judges in expounding the common law, and all that is to be found throughout the Statute Book in the various acts of Parliament'.[162] The interesting question from an English law perspective, in the wake of the Human Rights Act 1998, is the extent to which the fundamental values of the European Convention on Human Rights will influence the development of the common law. This point is pursued in the next chapter.

Summary

It is not surprising that such a vague and expansive category as privacy has received so much attention from academic commentators. The views outlined above, although broadly representative, are but a small sample of the voluminous literature that the right of privacy has generated. The distrust of broad general concepts in systems based on the English common law tends to militate against the acceptance of a general right underpinned by a highly abstract principle of inviolate personality such as that advocated by Bloustein. The advantage of Prosser's reductionist account lies in the fact that it manages to reduce a potentially vague concept into a number of autonomous torts, held together under a common umbrella title. Discussion can then proceed as to whether each or any of these individual torts can be justified, and whether they are strictly necessary to protect the interests which lie under the blanket term of 'privacy'. However, those such as Gavison, who believe in the coherence of the concept of privacy, in both its legal and extra-legal senses, reject such a pragmatic account of privacy, and seek to develop a core concept, which, although covering less ground, is arguably on a sounder conceptual footing. If, on the other hand, the principle of privacy is accepted, as it is in most legal systems, then it is perfectly possible to formulate rules which give effect to such a principle, without necessarily creating a new and indeterminate general right of privacy. The experience of the United States illustrates the problems with such a right, which can easily be avoided through the formulation of more narrow and specific rules.

The development of the right of publicity in the United States

Ultimately the right of privacy proved to be an unsatisfactory vehicle for protecting a person's economic interests in his name, likeness or voice and it was not long before the courts and academic commentators were

---

[162] *Ibid.*, citing Kelly CB in *River Wear Commissioners* v. *Adamson* (1876) 1 QBD 551.

172   The commercial appropriation of personality

formulating an alternative basis of liability. This became known as the right of publicity, which was in its embryonic stage in the period when Prosser and Bloustein proposed their rival conceptions of the right of privacy. Both effectively ignored this development. Prosser viewed the appropriation type of privacy as encompassing both economic and dignitary interests, while Bloustein refused to acknowledge the existence of economic interests in personality which might be the subject matter of a separate claim, since he preferred to view appropriation of personality exclusively as an injury to human dignity. In different ways, both underestimated the difficulties in reconciling a right of personal privacy with the notion of a predominantly commercial exploitation of personality, and the increasing momentum towards recognising the right of publicity as an entirely separate legal category.[163]

The problem in reconciling privacy and commercial exploitation

Even in the earliest right of privacy cases,[164] the difficulties in reconciling a person's status as a public figure with that person's claim for a right of privacy became apparent. This was one of the reasons why the New York Court of Appeals felt unable to recognise a right of privacy at common law in *Roberson* v. *Rochester Folding Box Co.*,[165] since the majority took the view that it was beyond the powers of the court to draw arbitrary distinctions which were best left to the legislature. However, in *Pavesich* v. *New England Life Insurance Co.*,[166] which became the leading case, the Supreme Court of Georgia was not prepared to allow such a difficulty to stand in the way of the recognition of a right of privacy. Like any other right, the right of privacy could be waived in certain circumstances, such as when a person put himself forward as a candidate for public office, or became prominent in a profession. This would not, however, amount to a total waiver, and such a person would be entitled to a right of privacy in respect of the aspects of his life which had no bearing on his fitness for public office or professional ability. In the Court's view, determining borderline cases of waiver of the right of privacy posed no greater difficulties than those

---

[163] Since the right of publicity protects predominantly economic interests in personality, it should, ideally, have been discussed in Part II. However, it is impossible to understand the development of the right of publicity without first having gained an understanding of the law of privacy and its limitations. Only a brief account can be given here. For a fuller discussion see McCarthy, *Rights of Publicity and Privacy*, §§1.6–1.11. See also O. R. Goodenough, 'The Price of Fame: The Development of the Right of Publicity in the United States' [1992] EIPR 55.

[164] See *Schuyler* v. *Curtis*, 15 NYS 787 (Sup Ct 1891); *Corliss* v. *Walker*, 57 Fed Rep 434 (1893); *Atkinson* v. *John E. Doherty & Co.* 80 NW 285 (1899).

[165] 171 NY 538 (1902) 554–5.   [166] 50 SE 68 (1905) 72.

Privacy and publicity in the United States 173

encountered in determining the borderline between what was actionable or not actionable in other areas of law, and could be left to the 'wisdom and integrity of the judiciary'.[167]

In the event, the difficulties were greater than the Supreme Court of Georgia in *Pavesich* had envisaged and in many jurisdictions, when celebrity plaintiffs claimed that their privacy had been invaded by the unauthorised use of their images, the courts refused to accept that they had suffered any indignity which could form the basis of an award of damages for mental distress, particularly where the celebrities were willingly licensing others to use their images to advertise or endorse products. The privacy label was taken at face value and the courts were unwilling to accept that the unpermitted commercial use of the identity of a public figure had invaded a right to be left alone.[168] By virtue of their status as public figures, some plaintiffs were deemed to have waived their right to privacy.

The decision of the Fifth Circuit Court of Appeals in *O'Brien* v. *Pabst Sales Co.* conveniently illustrates some of these difficulties.[169] The plaintiff, a well-known footballer, sued the Pabst beer company for using his photograph on its advertising calendar, claiming that the defendants had invaded his right of privacy. The plaintiff was particularly aggrieved since he was active in a temperance organisation and had refused offers to endorse beer and other alcoholic drinks. The Court held, by a majority, that since the plaintiff was one of the best-known and most publicised football players he was not a private person and had effectively surrendered his right to privacy; the publicity he received was only that which he was constantly seeking and receiving.[170] The publicity which O'Brien had involuntarily received from the use of his picture in the defendant's advertisement was treated in the same way as the publicity which he had voluntarily received as a result of his sporting fame, and in the Court's view, he could not validly object to either. It was also held that the publication of the calendar had not damaged the plaintiff by falsely representing that he was a beer drinker or that he endorsed or recommended drinking Pabst beer, on the basis that the business of making and selling beer was eminently respectable and that people of all persuasions drank beer. Consequently, the association of O'Brien's picture with a glass of beer could not possibly disgrace him or cause him damage.[171] Defamation was not specifically pleaded by the plaintiff, and these comments were made in the context of the claim of invasion of privacy.[172] It was noted,

---

[167] *Ibid.*   [168] See McCarthy, *Rights of Publicity and Privacy*, §1.6.

[169] 124 F 2d 167 (5th Cir. 1941). See also *Paramount Pictures Inc.* v. *Leader Press Inc.*, 24 F Supp. 1004 (1938); *Gautier* v. *Pro-Football Inc.*, 107 NE 2d 485 (1952).

[170] 124 F 2d 167 (5th Cir. 1941), 170.   [171] *Ibid.*, 169.

[172] Cf. *Tolley* v. *J. S. Fry & Sons Ltd* [1931] AC 333, and see 253–4 below, particularly the discussion of 'false light' privacy at 261–5.

174   The commercial appropriation of personality

obiter, that the only claim that might have been open to O'Brien would have been a *quantum meruit* claim for a reasonable sum for endorsing the defendant's beer, although the Court did not wish to express any opinion on the validity of such a claim. In the event, the plaintiff did not attempt to show that he had suffered any pecuniary damage, since he did not want to suggest, by making such a claim, that he impliedly endorsed the beer.

However, Holmes J, dissenting, argued that the plaintiff was entitled to precisely such a claim, distinct from the right of privacy, for the defendant's infringement of his property right to use his name and picture for commercial products,[173] a view based on an awareness and acknowledgement of the fact that commercial advertisers customarily paid for the right to use the name and likeness of a famous person. This was true in the plaintiff's case, since he had rejected an offer of $400 made by a New York beer company to endorse its beer.[174] Holmes J argued that the decision of the majority left the plaintiff and others like him without a remedy in a case where a non-libellous use was made of his image, which was contrary to usage and custom among advertisers who were 'undoubtedly in the habit of buying the right to use one's name or picture to create demand and goodwill for their merchandise'.[175] Accordingly, in the absence of an action for invasion of privacy, Holmes J was of the opinion that the defendant had committed a tort of misappropriating the plaintiff's valuable property right, entitling the plaintiff to damages or restitution.[176]

Thus it was becoming clear that the right of privacy was an unsuitable vehicle for protecting a person's predominantly economic interests in name or image and there were indications that the courts might be willing to formulate an alternative basis of liability. As the facts of *O'Brien* illustrate, it is difficult to speak in terms of *purely* economic or *purely* dignitary interests.[177] In O'Brien's case, the fact that his status as a celebrity had, in the majority's view, effectively deprived him of his right of privacy did not mean that he had no legitimate dignitary interests in his image. Indeed, an important interest in a person's name, voice or likeness is his interest in *controlling* the use of his image, which has both economic and dignitary aspects.

The birth of the right of publicity

In the first significant case, the decision of the Second Circuit Court of Appeals in *Haelan Laboratories Inc.* v. *Topps Chewing Gum Inc.*,[178] the parties were rival manufacturers of chewing gum. The plaintiff company had entered into contracts with famous baseball stars for the exclusive right

---

[173] 124 F 2d 167 (5th Cir. 1941).   [174] *Ibid.*   [175] *Ibid.*, 171.   [176] *Ibid.*
[177] See 19–23 above.   [178] 202 F 2d 866 (2nd Cir. 1953).

Privacy and publicity in the United States 175

to use their photographs in connection with its chewing gum products. With knowledge of the plaintiff's contracts with particular baseball players, the defendant deliberately induced the players to enter into contracts authorising the defendant to use their photographs in connection with the defendant's chewing gum. The defendant argued that even if such facts were proved, they disclosed no actionable wrong since the contracts with the baseball players were no more than waivers of the players' right to sue in tort for invasion of privacy. The right of privacy, in this case deriving from the New York statute, was a personal and non-assignable right. Consequently the contracts did not give the plaintiff any property right or other legal interest which would give title to sue. The situation was complicated by the fact that the defendant had not contracted with all of the players through its agent; some contracts were obtained by a third party, who then assigned the rights to the defendant. An action for deliberately inducing breach of contract was not available on the facts, since the breach of contract in question had been induced by the third party, and not by the defendant acting through its agent.

While impliedly accepting the defendant's arguments on the right of privacy point, the Court rejected the defendant's contention that the contracts created no more than a release of liability and that a plaintiff would have no other legal interest in the publication of his picture. Independently of the right of privacy, a person had 'a right in the publicity value of his photograph i.e., the right to grant the exclusive privilege of publishing his picture',[179] and such a grant could be validly made 'in gross', without an accompanying transfer of a business. Frank J acknowledged the fact that many prominent people did not suffer any injury to feelings from having their name or likeness exploited without their consent, but, rather, felt sorely deprived from not receiving any money for such exploitation. Thus the right of publicity was born, a right of property allowing a person to prevent the unauthorised commercial use of his identity and, furthermore, providing the corresponding right to grant exclusive rights of exploitation, which could potentially be enforced directly by a licensee. However, Judge Frank did not place much significance on the question of whether such a right should be regarded as a property right, taking the view that 'here as often elsewhere, the tag "property" simply symbolizes the fact that the courts enforce a claim which has a pecuniary worth'.[180]

Thus in *Haelan*, the Court was unwilling to work within the restrictive confines of the right of privacy, realising that it was an inadequate vehicle to deal with the problem of commercial appropriation, and preferring to

[179] *Ibid.*, 868.   [180] *Ibid.*

176   The commercial appropriation of personality

develop a new head of liability to allow the law to respond to changing commercial circumstances. In the short judgment, only two cases were cited in support of the new proposition, neither of which were considered in any detail, while two others were cursorily distinguished.[181] What dictated the outcome in the case were the reasons of substance underlying the dispute between the parties and the commercial reality that the images of famous people such as well-known baseball stars were, in effect, used as tradeable commodities.

As noted above, both Prosser and Bloustein gave this new and developing right short shrift in their rival conceptions of the right of privacy. While Bloustein denied the validity of any claim that was not based on an injury to human dignity, Prosser[182] felt that this new right could be accommodated within his appropriation privacy category. As McCarthy notes,[183] Prosser preferred to interpret *Haelan* narrowly as a case involving the right of an exclusive licensee against a third party rather than as a recognition of an entirely new and separate right. However, some of his contemporaries, such as Grodin, appreciated the importance of the decision, recognising that the courts had previously confused commercial interests with privacy interests, and urged the courts to follow the lead taken in *Haelan* and protect the two different interests under two separate doctrines.[184]

The growth of the right of publicity

Despite the efforts of those such as Nimmer,[185] who highlighted the deficiencies of the right of privacy and advocated increased recognition of the right of publicity, the courts were reluctant to accept the existence of the new right immediately.[186] Indeed, some courts preferred to base their decisions on more traditional bases of liability as is well illustrated by the decision of the Pennsylvania Court of Common Pleas in *Hogan* v. *A. S. Barnes & Co. Inc.*[187] The plaintiff was a well-known and highly successful professional golfer who had appeared on radio, television and in motion pictures, and was the author of a best-selling book of golf instructions. The defendants published a book entitled *Golf with the Masters* in

[181] *Ibid.*, 868.   [182] Prosser, 'Privacy', 406.
[183] McCarthy, *Rights of Publicity and Privacy*, §1.7.
[184] J. R. Grodin, 'The Right of Publicity: A Doctrinal Innovation' (1953) 62 Yale LJ 1123.
[185] M. B. Nimmer, 'The Right of Publicity' (1954) 19 Law ContProbl 203.
[186] See, e.g., *Strickler* v. *National Broadcasting Co.*, 167 F Supp. 68 (SD Cal. 1958), 70, where the court stated that it did not wish to 'blaze the trail' to establish a right of publicity as a cause of action in California, and see, generally, McCarthy, *Rights of Publicity and Privacy*, §1.9, and H. I. Berkman, 'The Right of Publicity – Protection for Public Figures and Celebrities' (1976) 42 Brook L Rev 527, 534 et seq.
[187] 114 USPQ 314 (Pa. Comm. Pl. 1957).

Privacy and publicity in the United States

which the names and photographs of several famous golfers, including the plaintiff, were prominently displayed on the jacket and in the text. The plaintiff had expressly refused his consent for the use of his name and photograph and brought an action for damages based on five separate causes of action: (i) invasion of privacy; (ii) unfair competition; (iii) infringement of right of publicity; (iv) libel; and (v) breach of a publisher's duty of fidelity to its author. The last two causes of action need not be considered here and, in any case, were dismissed by the Court.[188] As to the first claim for invasion of privacy, the Court distinguished a true case of invasion of privacy, where the plaintiff was an unknown person and had been unwillingly exposed to the glare of publicity, from a case involving a public figure such as an actor or athlete. In the latter case, the Court reasoned, the real nature of the complaint was that the commercial value which attached to the name or image had been exploited without payment.[189]

The second claim, based on the *International News Service* v. *Associated Press*[190] misappropriation doctrine, succeeded.[191] The Court held that while, generally speaking, the doctrine of unfair competition rested on the existence of fraud or deception, it did not regard 'palming off' (passing off) as a necessary requisite of unfair competition. In some circumstances, under the *INS* misappropriation doctrine, equity would protect against the unfair appropriation of another's labour or talent.[192] The plaintiff had 'an enforceable property right in the good will and commercial value of his name and photograph in connection with the game of golf' (*sic*),[193] the use of which had not been authorised. Thus, the defendants' conduct amounted to a misappropriation of the plaintiff's property right in the commercial value of his name and photograph. As to the plaintiff's third claim, infringement of the right of publicity, the Court took the view that the right of publicity, which had been recognised in *Haelan Laboratories*, was only another way of applying the doctrine of unfair competition and was simply unfair competition under another label rather than a separate cause of action: the 'right of publicity' was as apt a label as any.[194] It was further suggested that some of the cases based on an invasion of a right of privacy might have been more appropriately decided on the basis of what it saw as the right of publicity genus of unfair competition, although the

---

[188] *Ibid.*, 320–1.

[189] *Ibid.*, 314, 316, citing *Haelan Laboratories Inc.* v. *Topps Chewing Gum Inc.*, 202 F 2d 866 (2nd Cir. 1953), 868.

[190] 248 US 215 (1918). See, generally, Chapter 2 at 28–31.

[191] 114 USPQ 314, 317. The Court relied on a decision of the Pennsylvania Supreme Court in *Waring* v. *WDAS Broadcasting Station* 35 USPQ 272 (1937), which, in turn, had relied on the decision in *International News Service*.

[192] 114 USPQ 314, 319.   [193] *Ibid.*, 317.   [194] *Ibid.*, 320.

178　　The commercial appropriation of personality

Court did not consider that the decisions reached in the previous cases were wrong.[195]

Thus, the right of publicity was not instantly accepted as a new basis of liability and the courts in some jurisdictions preferred to work within the framework of the existing causes of action. However, the courts in most jurisdictions gradually acknowledged both that the right of privacy and the right of publicity were separate claims[196] and that the right of publicity was a distinctly independent tort and not an application of the misappropriation doctrine.[197] In *Uhlaender* v. *Henricksen*[198] it was recognised that the plaintiff baseball player's claim to prevent the unauthorised use of his name, and statistics concerning his athletic achievements, in the defendant's table baseball game was not a claim for invasion of privacy but a claim for the misappropriation of the commercial value of the plaintiff's name, stressing the pecuniary loss through interference with property rather than the injury to feelings.[199] On the other hand, in *Motschenbacher* v. *R. J. Reynolds Tobacco Co.*[200] the Ninth Circuit Court of Appeals held that the plaintiff had a proprietary interest in his identity, but declined to specify whether the right should be characterised as a right of privacy or a right of publicity.

It is interesting to note that although some courts such as the Pennsylvania court in *Hogan* v. *A. S. Barnes & Co. Inc.* preferred to treat the new right of publicity as an aspect of the misappropriation doctrine, generally the law of unfair competition did not play a great part in the development of the right of publicity in the United States. The courts relied on the *International News Service* misappropriation doctrine only until new rights such as the right of publicity had acquired their own separate identity.[201] McCarthy argues that although misappropriation may have provided a basis for the right of publicity in early cases, the right of publicity should not be viewed merely as an application of the misappropriation doctrine since it 'has developed and matured over time

---

[195] *Ibid.*

[196] It should be noted, nevertheless, that some courts and plaintiffs continued to base claims for invasion of essentially economic interests on invasion of privacy rather than right of publicity or misappropriation as in *Palmer* v. *Schonhorn Enterprises Inc.* 232 A 2d 458 (1967), involving the unauthorised commercial exploitation of the images of famous golfers Arnold Palmer, Gary Player and Jack Nicklaus: see, generally, Berkman, 'The Right of Publicity', 537.

[197] See, generally, McCarthy, *Rights of Publicity and Privacy*, §1.10; Berkman, 'The Right of Publicity', 534–41.

[198] 316 F Supp. 1277 (1970).　　[199] *Ibid.*, 1279–80.

[200] 498 F 2d 821 (9th Cir. 1974), 826.

[201] See D. G. Baird, 'Common Law Intellectual Property and the Legacy of *International News Service* v. *Associated Press*' (1983) 50 U Chi L Rev 411, arguing that, contrary to common fears, the misappropriation doctrine has not been used by the courts as 'a license to cut rough justice wherever they find competitive practices that they do not like'.

Privacy and publicity in the United States   179

into a distinct intellectual property right much more defined and precise than the amorphous misappropriation doctrine'.[202] Indeed, he argues that the right of publicity has grown out of its early partial reliance on both the tort of invasion of privacy and the misappropriation doctrine and can stand independently of its legal origins. This analysis certainly supports the view that appropriation of personality should be regarded as an autonomous cause of action, encompassing both economic and dignitary interests and, although sharing some common characteristics, is largely independent of other bases of liability. As a practical matter, unfair competition (used in the generic sense) and particularly the tort of passing off will remain important to the problem of appropriation of personality, particularly in the Anglo-Australian systems which are not susceptible to the facile generation of new torts.[203] The underlying differences between systems modelled on the English common law and the legal system of the United States and their bearing on the present problem are pursued in greater detail in the text below.

The recognition of the right of publicity

In 1977 the right of publicity was canonised, so to speak, by the Supreme Court in *Zacchini* v. *Scripps-Howard Broadcasting Co.*[204] The facts of the case were rather unusual and did not involve a typical situation such as the unauthorised commercial exploitation of a person's name or likeness in advertising. The plaintiff sued the defendants for damages for televising his human cannonball act, which he had performed at a county fair. The Ohio State Court had held that although the defendants' act

---

[202] McCarthy, *Rights of Publicity and Privacy*, §5.6[B][1].

[203] W. L. Morison, 'Unfair Competition and Passing Off – The Flexibility of a Formula' (1956) 2 Sydney L Rev 50, 60, and see 108–10 above. The prospects of a right of publicity in Australia have only been contemplated in tentative dicta. See *Sony Music Australia Ltd and Michael Jackson* v. *Tansing* (1993) 27 IPR 649 (Federal Court of Australia) where the right of publicity was not 'held to be part of the law of Australia at this stage of this country's development' (653 *per* Lockhart J) and its existence was described as 'little more than a glint in the eye of counsel' (656 *per* French J). The possibility for future development was left open (654 and 656) and it is possible that a right of publicity might evolve from the tort of passing off in Australia, although it is unclear whether the development will require an intermediate stage where liability is based on a general notion of misappropriation rather than misrepresentation. The bulk of the Australian authorities are against the notion of a broad-based action for unfair competition (see 112–15 above), and it is possible that the misappropriation stage may be by-passed, with the law evolving directly from liability based on misrepresentation to liability based on a right of publicity. Similarly, in the United Kingdom, the notion that a trader may not make unauthorised use of the name of a celebrity to sell his own goods has been rejected: *ELVIS PRESLEY Trade Marks* [1999] RPC 567, 583 and 597. Cf. *Kaye* v. *Robertson* [1991] FSR 62 and *Douglas* v. *Hello! Ltd* [2001] 2 WLR 992.

[204] 433 US 562 (1977).

180   The commercial appropriation of personality

was an actionable infringement of the plaintiff's right of publicity, the broadcast was privileged as a news report of a matter of legitimate public interest. The Supreme Court reversed the decision, holding that the reporting of the entire fifteen-second performance was not protected under the First Amendment. Crucially, the Supreme Court drew a clear distinction between invasions of privacy and infringement of a right of publicity:[205] while the interest protected through a cause of action for a false light invasion of privacy was an interest in reputation, with overtones of mental distress, the rationale underlying the right of publicity lay in 'protecting the proprietary interest of the individual in his act in part to encourage such entertainment'.[206] The aims of the law were considered to be analogous to the goals of patent and copyright law, focusing on the right of the individual to reap the reward for his endeavours, and had little to do with protecting feelings or reputation.[207] The Court approved the rationale which Kalven had identified for the appropriation branch of privacy:[208] preventing unjust enrichment by the theft of goodwill; no social value would be served by allowing the defendant to get for free something that had a market value and for which he would usually have to pay.[209] Furthermore, the free speech implications differed between false light privacy cases and right of publicity cases. While in false light privacy cases, the only way to protect a plaintiff's interests would be to attempt to minimise publication of the damaging matter, in right of publicity cases the only question, according to the Court, would be the question of who should be allowed to do the publishing. Ordinarily, a plaintiff such as the human cannonball in *Zacchini* would have no objection to the widespread dissemination of his act as long as he received the commercial benefit from such dissemination. Thus the free speech implications were less acute where a plaintiff merely wished to be compensated for an unauthorised exploitation without wishing to prevent any form of publication.[210]

The scope and limits of the right of publicity

Although space does not permit a detailed discussion of the scope of the right of publicity[211] and its infringement, its contours may be sketched, bearing in mind that there are considerable differences between the

---

[205] *Ibid.*, 572.   [206] *Ibid.*, 573.   [207] *Ibid.*
[208] H. Kalven, 'Privacy in Tort Law: Were Warren and Brandeis Wrong?' (1966) 31 Law ContProbl 326, 331.
[209] 433 US 562 (1977), 576.   [210] *Ibid.*, 575.
[211] See, generally, McCarthy, *Rights of Publicity and Privacy*, Chs. 3 and 4.

Privacy and publicity in the United States

statutory and common law provisions in different states.[212] It should also be noted that the right of publicity is not, as yet, quite as autonomous as some might suggest. Precedents from privacy cases continue to be used by the courts in determining the scope and limits of the right of publicity and the links between the two rights have yet to be fully severed, particularly in states where the right of publicity is in a relatively early stage of development.[213]

Liability arises where the defendant 'appropriates the commercial value of a person's identity by using, without consent, the person's name, likeness or other indicia of identity for the purposes of trade'.[214] Liability is based on misappropriation rather than misrepresentation, thus proof of deception or consumer confusion is not required.[215] The interest that is protected is the intangible value of the person's identity rather than trading or promotional goodwill. Despite some dicta to the contrary,[216] prior commercial exploitation by the plaintiff does not seem to be a necessary prerequisite.[217] Thus a plaintiff who does not exploit his image for the moment,[218] or a plaintiff who does not contemplate exploiting his image at all,[219] will not be precluded from claiming an infringement of his right of publicity. Furthermore, it has been stated that the 'appropriation of the identity of a relatively unknown person may result in economic injury or may itself create economic value in what was previously valueless'.[220]

---

[212] Suggestions have been made for a federal law: see, e.g., M. A. Hamilton *et al.*, 'Rights of Publicity: An In-Depth Analysis of the New Legislative Proposals to Congress' (1998) 16 Cardozo Arts & Ent LJ 209; E. J. Goodman, 'A National Identity Crisis: The Need For a Federal Right of Publicity Statute' (1999) 9 DePaul-LCA J Art & Ent L 227; R. S. Robinson, 'Preemption, The Right of Publicity, and a New Federal Statute' (1998) 16 Cardozo Arts & Ent LJ 183.

[213] See, e.g., *Allison v. Vintage Sports Plaques*, 136 F 3d 1443 (11th Cir. 1998), 1147: 'Alabama's commercial appropriation privacy right . . . represent[s] the same interests and address[es] the same harms as does the right of publicity as customarily defined'.

[214] *Restatement, Third, Unfair Competition* (1995) §46 and see text accompanying note 262 below.

[215] *Rogers* v. *Grimaldi*, 875 F 2d 994 (2nd Cir. 1989), 1003–4.

[216] See, e.g., *Lerman* v. *Chuckleberry Publishing Inc.*, 521 F Supp. 228 (SDNY 1981), 232.

[217] McCarthy, *Rights of Publicity and Privacy*, §4.7.

[218] See, e.g., *Palmer* v. *Schonhorn Enterprises Inc.*, A 2d 458, 462 (N.J. Super 1967).

[219] See, e.g., *Grant* v. *Esquire Inc.*, 367 F Supp 876 (SDNY 1973): '[i]f the owner of Blackacre decides for reasons of his own not to use his land but to keep it in reserve, he is not precluded from prosecuting trespassers' *per* Knapp J, 878.

[220] *Motschenbacher* v. *R. J. Reynolds Tobacco Co.*, 498 F 2d 821 (9th Cir. 1974), 824, n.11, and see *Restatement, Third, Unfair Competition* §46 comment *d*. Cf. *Landham* v. *Lewis Galoob Toys Inc.*, 227 F 3d 619 (6th Cir. 2000), 624 ('a plaintiff must demonstrate that there is value in associating an item of commerce with his identity'); *Cheatham* v. *Paisano Publications, Inc.*, 891 F Supp. 381 (WD Ky 1995), 385 (remedy available to those whose identity has commercial value, established by proof of (i) the distinctiveness of the identity and of (ii) the degree of recognition of the person among those receiving the publicity).

182   The commercial appropriation of personality

The unauthorised appropriation must be sufficient to identify the plaintiff, otherwise it cannot be said in any real sense that the plaintiff's identity has been misappropriated, nor his interest violated.[221] In this respect, the right of publicity differs from the law of registered and un-registered trade marks in that there may be liability despite there being no likelihood of confusion as to source or connection by way of endorsement or sponsorship.[222] The Restatement states that in relation to names, 'the name as used by the defendant must be understood by the audience as referring to the plaintiff', while in relation to visual likenesses, 'the plaintiff must be reasonably identifiable from the photograph or other depiction'.[223] McCarthy proposes a variation of the test applied in defamation and privacy cases:[224] that the statement was published 'of and concerning' the plaintiff and that the plaintiff is identifiable by the defendant's use to more than a *de minimis* number of persons.[225]

A person's identity may be appropriated in various ways[226] and although a plaintiff is most commonly identified by personal name (including former name),[227] nickname[228] or likeness, use of other indicia of identity such as a plaintiff's voice,[229] distinctive catch-phrase[230] or distinctively marked car[231] may give rise to liability. Protection has also been extended to cover more amorphous indicia of identity which might severally combine to identify the plaintiff, such as the plaintiff's distinctive style of dress, hairstyle and pose.[232] Intent to infringe another's right of publicity is not a necessary element of liability at common law and a mistake relating to the plaintiff's consent will not be a defence.[233]

---

[221] *Motschenbacher* v. *R. J. Reynolds Tobacco Co.*, 498 F 2d 821 (9th Cir. 1974), 826–7; *Waits* v. *Frito-Lay Inc.*, 978 F 2d 1093 (9th Cir. 1992), 1102.
[222] *Elvis Presley Enterprises, Inc.* v. *Capece*, 950 F Supp. 783 (S.D.Tex., 1996), 801; *Henley* v. *Dillard Dept Stores*, 46 F Supp. 2d 587 (N.D.Tex., 1999), 590.
[223] *Restatement, Third, Unfair Competition* §46 comment *d*.
[224] See *Restatement, Second, Torts* (1977) §564.
[225] McCarthy, *Rights of Publicity and Privacy*, §3.7, cited with approval in *Henley* v. *Dillard Dept Stores*, 46 F Supp. 2d 587 (N.D.Tex., 1999), 595.
[226] *Carson* v. *Here's Johnny Portable Toilets Inc.*, 698 F 2d 831 (6th Cir. 1983), 835–6.
[227] *Abdul-Jabbar* v. *General Motors Corp.*, 85 F 3d 407 (9th Cir. 1996).
[228] *Hirsch* v. *S. C. Johnson & Sons Inc.*, NW 2d 129 (1979), 137 (nickname 'Crazylegs' for well-known footballer used on shaving gel).
[229] *Waits* v. *Frito-Lay Inc.*, 978 F 2d 1093 (9th Cir. 1992).
[230] *Carson* v. *Here's Johnny Portable Toilets Inc.*, 698 F 2d 831 (6th Cir. 1983).
[231] *Motschenbacher* v. *R. J. Reynolds Tobacco Co.*, 498 F 2d 821 (9th Cir. 1974), 824.
[232] *White* v. *Samsung Inc.*, 971 F 2d 1395 (9th Cir. 1992), rehearing denied 989 F 2d 1512 (9th Cir. 1993). See also W. Borchard, 'The Common Law Right of Publicity is Going Wrong in the US' [1992] Ent LR 208; D. S. Welkowitz, 'Catching Smoke, Nailing Jell-O To a Wall: The Vanna White Case and the Limits of Celebrity Rights' (1995) 3 J. Intell Prop L 67.
[233] See *Douglass* v. *Hustler Magazine Inc.*, 769 F 2d 1128 (7th Cir. 1985), 1140, and *Restatement, Third, Unfair Competition* §46 comment *e*. McCarthy, *Rights of Publicity*

Privacy and publicity in the United States 183

From the earliest cases, it became clear that the right of publicity differed from the right of privacy in that it was a right of property which was freely assignable, rather than a personal right.[234] Thus where the right of publicity is assigned, the assignee has a direct cause of action against a third party infringer, rather than a mere release of liability for invasion of the subject's privacy. However, an assignment or licence of the right of publicity only transfers the right to exploit the commercial value of the assignor's image, and does not transfer any rights of privacy.[235] An exclusive (though not a non-exclusive) licensee will have a right to sue third party infringers, to the extent that their rights are infringed.[236]

One of the issues that caused greatest trouble for the courts and commentators was defining the duration of the right of publicity and, in particular, determining whether it was descendible.[237] While the right of privacy is a personal right which dies with the plaintiff, the right of publicity, as noted above, is usually described as a property right. Consequently, some argued that it follows that such a property right should be descendible and that the heirs of deceased figures should be allowed to profit from the valuable right that had been enjoyed by their famous ancestors. However, describing the right of publicity as a 'property' right is often only an acknowledgement of 'the fact that the courts enforce a claim which has a pecuniary worth'.[238] It does not automatically follow that because a right is labelled a 'property' right, that right should have all the attributes of property. Since the present concern is the relationship of the right of publicity with the right of privacy, this interesting issue need not detain us here.[239] There are considerable variations

and Privacy, §3.41 argues that the law of trade marks and unfair competition provides the most appropriate analogies where lack of intention to infringe is irrelevant for establishing liability. The position is similar in the English tort of passing off, where the mental element is irrelevant for establishing a misrepresentation: see C. Wadlow, *The Law of Passing Off*, 2nd edn (London, 1995), 200 et seq.

[234] *Haelan Laboratories Inc. v. Topps Chewing Gum Inc.*, 202 F 2d 866 (2nd Cir. 1953).

[235] *Bi-Rite Enterprises Inc. v. Button Master*, 555 F Supp. 1188 (1983), 1199; *Restatement, Third, Unfair Competition* §46 comment *g*.

[236] *Bi-Rite Enterprises Inc. v. Button Master*, 555 F Supp. 1188 (1983), 1200. See, generally, McCarthy, *Rights of Publicity and Privacy*, Ch. 10.

[237] The issue has generated a great deal of periodical literature which cannot be cited in full here. For a small sample, see, e.g., T. P. Terrell and J. S. Smith, 'Publicity, Liberty and Intellectual Property: A Conceptual and Economic Analysis of the Inheritability Issue' (1985) 34 Emory LJ 1; P. L. Felcher and E. L. Rubin, 'The Descendibility of the Right of Publicity: Is There Commercial Life After Death?' (1980) 89 Yale LJ 1125; Goodenough, 'The Price of Fame', and see, generally, McCarthy, *Rights of Publicity and Privacy*, Ch. 9.

[238] *Haelan Laboratories Inc. v. Topps Chewing Gum Inc.*, 202 F 2d 866 (2nd Cir. 1953), 868.

[239] See, further, Chapter 10.

184   The commercial appropriation of personality

between the statutory and common law provisions in different states.[240] For example, at common law, the descendibility of the right of publicity has been recognised in Georgia,[241] New Jersey[242] and (despite its initial denial)[243] in Tennessee.[244] Under statute, the right of publicity is descendible in California,[245] but in New York whatever rights of publicity exist are found in the privacy framework of section 50 of the Civil Rights Law[246] and any rights terminate at death.[247] Although many jurisdictions have not yet considered the descendibility issue, most of the jurisdictions which have done so have recognised that the right is descendible[248] and has a limited post mortem duration of between 10[249] and 100 years.[250]

Where the unauthorised commercial use of a person's identity is established, the defendant will be liable for the plaintiff's pecuniary loss, or, alternatively, for the defendant's own pecuniary gain. As in other areas of unfair competition, the plaintiff may establish either or both measures of relief, but may only recover the greater of the two amounts.[251] Although proof of monetary loss is not a prerequisite to recovery of damages, and although the plaintiff may be compensated purely for the deprivation of his right to control the use of the commercially valuable asset in his name or likeness, in the absence of specific loss such damages are likely to be nominal.[252] Because of the difficulty in proving loss to the plaintiff, or gain to the defendant that results from the unauthorised appropriation, the courts sometimes apply a measure of damages by reference to a lost licence fee, based on the fair market value of the unauthorised

---

[240]   See, McCarthy, *Rights of Publicity and Privacy*, Ch. 6, esp. §6.8, for an overview.
[241]   *Martin Luther King Jr Center for Social Change Inc.* v. *American Heritage Products*, 296 SE 2d 697 (Ga. 1982) esp. 704–6 for a review of the early case law.
[242]   *Estate of Presley* v. *Russen*, 513 F Supp. 1339 (1981).
[243]   *Memphis Development Foundation* v. *Factors etc. Inc.*, 616 F 2d 956 (1980).
[244]   *The State of Tennessee, Ex. Rel. The Elvis Presley International Memorial Foundation* v. *Crowell*, 733 SW 2d 89 (Ten. App 1987). For the complicated history of the descendibility of the right of publicity in Tennessee, see McCarthy, *Rights of Publicity and Privacy*, §9.5[B][10].
[245]   California Civil Code §3344 and §3344.1 (The Astaire Celebrity Image Protection Act).
[246]   *Costanza* v. *Seinfeld*, 719 NYS 2d 29 (NYAD 1 Dept 2001), 30; *Stephano* v. *News Group Publications*, 485 NYS 2d 220 (Ct. App. 1984), 224.
[247]   *Pirone* v. *MacMillan Inc.*, 894 F 2d 579 (2nd Cir. 1990). See S. A. McEvoy, '*Pirone* v. *Macmillan Inc.*: Trying to Protect the Name and Likeness of a Deceased Celebrity Under Trade Mark Law and the Right of Publicity' (1997) 19 Comm & L 51.
[248]   *Restatement, Third, Unfair Competition* §§46 comment *h*.
[249]   Tennessee Code §47-25-1104 (Personal Rights Protection Act 1984).
[250]   See, e.g., Indiana Code §32-13-1-8.
[251]   *Restatement, Third, Unfair Competition* §49 comment *d*.
[252]   *Zim* v. *Western Publishing Co.*, 573 F 2d 1318 (1978) (5th Cir. CA), 1327 note 19.

Privacy and publicity in the United States 185

use,[253] although such a calculation is rarely mathematically exact.[254] This applies not only to famous people, but also to private persons who may recover damages measured by the fee that the defendant would have been required to pay in order to secure similar services from other private persons or from professional models.[255] Such damages might not deprive the defendant of the full extent of his gain from the appropriation, though the courts sometimes give the plaintiff the benefit of the doubt in determining a fair market value, in order to prevent unjust enrichment and to ensure adequate deterrence.[256] In any case, full restitutionary relief in the form of an account of the defendant's profits is also available in appropriate circumstances.[257] Punitive damages may also be awarded, where appropriate.[258]

From the earliest cases, the courts recognised the tensions between controlling unauthorised appropriation (initially through a right of privacy)[259] and freedom of expression.[260] Liability will generally only arise where an individual's likeness or other indicium is used for the purposes of trade, such as in advertising or merchandising.[261] The seller's interests in attracting attention to his wares do not outweigh the personal and economic interests protected by the right of publicity.[262] Commercial appropriations of personality often falsely and misleadingly suggest that a celebrity is endorsing a product (although this is not a prerequisite for liability).[263] Since the First Amendment does not protect false and misleading commercial speech[264] (even commercial speech which does

---

[253] *Restatement, Third, Unfair Competition* §49 comment *d*, and see, e.g., *Cher* v. *Forum Intern Ltd*, 692 F 2d 634 (CA Cal. 1982).

[254] *Zim* v. *Western Publishing Co.*, 573 F 2d 1318 (1978) (5th Cir. CA), 1327 note 19.

[255] *Restatement, Third, Unfair Competition* §49 comment *d*, and see, e.g., *Canessa* v. *J. I. Kislak Inc.*, 97 N.J. Super 327, 235 A 2d 62 (1967).

[256] *Restatement, Third, Unfair Competition* §49 comment *d*.

[257] *Ibid.*, and see, e.g., *Bi-Rite Enterprises Inc.* v. *Button Master*, 555 F Supp. 1188 (1983).

[258] See, e.g., *Waits* v. *Frito-Lay Inc.*, 978 F 2d 1093 (9th Cir. 1992).

[259] See text accompanying note 39 above.

[260] See, generally, McCarthy, *Rights of Publicity and Privacy*, Chs. 7 and 8. Cf. S. R. Barnett, 'The Right of Publicity Versus Free Speech in Advertising: Some Counter-Points to Professor McCarthy' (1996) 18 Hastings Comm & Ent LJ 593.

[261] See, e.g., California Civil Code §3344 (use of indicia of identity 'on or in products, merchandise, or goods, or for purposes of advertising or selling, or soliciting purchases of, products, merchandise, goods or services') and, e.g., *White* v. *Samsung Electronics America, Inc.*, 971 F 2d 1395, 1401 (9th Cir. 1992); New York Civil Rights Law §51 ('any person whose name, portrait, picture or voice is used within this state for advertising purposes or for the purposes of trade') and, e.g., *Messenger* v. *Gruner & Jahr Printing and Pub.*, 208 F 3d 122 (2nd Cir. 2000).

[262] *Restatement, Third, Unfair Competition* §47 comment *a*.

[263] See note 215 above.

[264] See *Central Hudson Gas & Elec. Corp.* v. *Public Service Commission of New York*, 447 US 557 (1980), 563; *Florida Bar* v. *Went for It Inc.*, 515 US 618 (1995).

186   The commercial appropriation of personality

not mislead is generally subject to somewhat lesser protection),[265] the right of publicity may often trump the right of advertisers to make use of celebrity figures.[266]

Nevertheless, liability will not extend to circumstances where a person's identity is used primarily for the purpose of communicating information or expressing ideas.[267] This usually excludes use in news reporting, which would cover, for example, photographs of a celebrity's public appearances or public performances.[268] Although a public figure or someone who is presently newsworthy 'may be the proper subject of news or informative presentation', this does not extend to unrelated commercialisation of his identity or surrender of a right to privacy; although his privacy is necessarily limited by the newsworthiness of his activities, he retains the 'independent right to have [his] personality, even if newsworthy, free from commercial exploitation at the hands of another'.[269] Similarly, use of an individual's identity in works of fiction or in biographies will usually be allowed, regardless of whether the defendant gains a commercial advantage, since the notion of name, voice or likeness does not extend to a person's life story,[270] and any remedy would be limited to those available for defamation or false light invasion of privacy. Expressive works (including non-verbal visual representations) do not lose their constitutional protections when they are for purposes of entertaining rather than informing, although depictions of celebrities amounting to little more than the appropriation of the celebrity's economic value are not protected.[271] The right of publicity does not allow a right to control the celebrity's image by censoring disagreeable portrayals; once the celebrity thrusts himself or herself forward into the limelight, the First Amendment dictates that the right to comment on, parody, lampoon and

---

[265] See, generally, *44 Liquormart, Inc.* v. *Rhode Island*, 517 US 484 (1996).

[266] *Comedy III Productions, Inc.* v. *Gary Saderup, Inc.*, 106 Cal.Rptr.2d 126 (Cal. 2001), 133.

[267] See, generally, *Restatement, Third, Unfair Competition* §47.

[268] See, e.g., *Titan Sports, Inc.* v. *Comics World Corp.*, 870 F 2d 85 (2nd Cir. 1989); *Paulsen v. Personality Posters, Inc.*, 299 NYS 2d 501 (1968) (television comedian, who conducted mock campaign for presidency could not prevent marketing of a poster embodying his photograph since it constituted news or information of public interest).

[269] See *Titan Sports, Inc.* v. *Comics World Corp.*, 870 F 2d 85 (2nd Cir. 1989), 88, and the authorities cited.

[270] See, e.g., *Ruffin-Steinback* v. *dePasse*, 82 F Supp.2d 723 (E.D.Mich., 2000); *Matthews v. Wozencraft*, 15 F 3d 432 (5th Cir. 1994); *Rogers* v. *Grimaldi*, 875 F 2d 994 (2nd Cir. 1989).

[271] *Comedy III Productions, Inc.* v. *Gary Saderup, Inc.*, 106 Cal.Rptr.2d 126 (Cal. 2001) (drawings of images of deceased members of comedy act, reproduced on T-shirts sold for commercial gain, contained no significant transformative or creative contribution so as to be entitled to First Amendment protection). Cf. *Hoffman* v. *Capital Cities/ABC, Inc.*, 255 F 3d 1180 (9th Cir. 2001).

make other expressive uses of the celebrity image must be given broad scope.[272]

Summary

It is somewhat ironic that the Supreme Court should stress a utilitarian basis for the right of publicity, based in part on the need to encourage labour and investment.[273] It will be recalled that although Warren and Brandeis partly based their argument for a right of privacy on common law copyright, they emphasised that the right of privacy should be based on the principle of inviolate personality and did not wish that it should be limited to conscious products of labour based on a need to encourage effort.[274] With the decision in *Zacchini*, the wheel had turned full circle. The right of publicity had evolved considerably from its early origins in the right of privacy, based on the alleged principle of inviolate personality. From an early point in its history, the appropriation branch of privacy had developed distinctly proprietary attributes, before developing into a completely autonomous right of publicity, taking the form of a property right seemingly more akin to intellectual property rights such as copyright, patents and trade marks, than a right of personality. However, there are difficulties in aligning the right of publicity with the well-established core areas of intellectual property, and the justifications which underpin the latter apply uneasily to the right of publicity or a *sui generis* tort of appropriation of personality.[275]

Ultimately, we return to the fact that appropriation of personality is a hybrid problem encompassing a disparate range of interests, and the fact that it is not always possible to draw a clear distinction between economic and dignitary interests.[276] Although the development of a right of publicity provided greater protection for predominantly economic interests in personality which were difficult to accommodate within the doctrinal framework of privacy law, that did not mean that such interests could be categorised as exclusively economic interests. While the early law of appropriation privacy in the United States was rightly criticised for failing to draw an adequate distinction between, on the one hand, the dignitary aspects such as mental distress, humiliation and damage to personal dignity, and, on the other hand, the financial interests of celebrities,[277] it is possible for the distinction to become too sharp.

---

[272] *Comedy III Productions, Inc.* v. *Gary Saderup, Inc.*, 106 Cal.Rptr.2d 126 (Cal. 2001), 139.

[273] See text accompanying note 206 above.   [274] See text accompanying note 26 above.

[275] See Chapter 9.

[276] Cf. the strict definition of an economic interest at 8–10 above.

[277] See text accompanying note 120 above.

188   The commercial appropriation of personality

Consider a factual scenario similar to *O'Brien* v. *Pabst Sales Co.*,[278] where the plaintiff, a famous footballer and active temperance campaigner, failed to prevent the defendants from using his name and likeness in advertisements for beer. Although a market clearly existed for the use of the names and images of the famous footballers, the value of the use of the plaintiff's image could not be subject to purely objective measure. A specific sum of money could not overcome the plaintiff's fundamental objections to seeing his name and image being used to sell a product of which he disapproved: his dignitary interests took precedence over any economic gain that he might have made by allowing the use of his name. Although the court denied his claim for invasion of privacy, it would be artificial to regard his interest as a *purely* economic interest which might be protected by a right of publicity.

Consider this further example: F is a famous sportsman while O is an ordinary person. Either F or O's image is used in: (a) an advertisement for a leading brand of aftershave; (b) an advertisement for an inferior brand of aftershave; (c) an advertisement for car spare parts; (d) an advertisement for beer; (e) an advertisement for a pornographic magazine. O might object to any use of his image and claim that his privacy has been invaded in all of these examples. Although F might not be able to claim that his privacy has been invaded, by virtue of his status as a celebrity, he might object strongly to uses (d) and (e), and would never allow his image to be used in any such circumstances. F might also object to use (c) and perhaps use (b), while not objecting to use (a), for purely subjective reasons, even if, for example, the fees for each use were exactly the same: he might not wish to be associated with inferior aftershave or car spare parts. While example (e) and possibly example (d) (say the sportsman was a vigorous anti-alcohol campaigner) might involve an injury to reputation, which might be actionable in defamation, the others probably would not. What might the sportsman have suffered in seeing his image used in these circumstances? Clearly, it would be difficult to argue that his privacy has been invaded. Alternatively, could it be said that he has suffered mental distress, an indignity, economic loss, or the loss of an economic opportunity, or possibly a mixture of all of these? Some of these examples might be the concern of a right of publicity, while some might be regarded as involving damage to essentially dignitary rather than economic interests.

The basic point to note is that it is rather simplistic to attempt to draw a sharp distinction between damage to *purely economic* interests suffered

---

[278] See text accompanying note 170 above and see, e.g., *Newcombe* v. *Adolf Coors Co.*, 157 F 3d 686 (9th Cir. 1998).

Privacy and publicity in the United States

by celebrities and *purely dignitary* interests suffered by others. Although the development of the right of publicity put an end to the incongruity of a celebrity claiming invasion of a right of privacy, it does not mean that dignitary and economic interests will fall neatly under separate causes of action for invasion of privacy and infringement of the right of publicity. Indeed, as McCarthy notes, the law in the United States would be more coherent if the courts had recognised a *sui generis* legal right with damages measured by both mental distress and commercial loss. If the law had such a separately entitled category, things would be considerably easier to sort out compared to our present world of 'separate' rights of privacy by appropriation and a right of publicity.[279] The successful formulation of such a *sui generis* action in legal systems which do not follow the American model depends on a number of factors. First, the problem of appropriation of personality must be severed from the discussion of the desirability of introducing a general right of privacy, a problem discussed in the next chapter. Secondly, it needs to be considered whether there are any convincing underlying justifications for such a new remedy for appropriation of personality. Thirdly, and most important from an English law perspective, such a new remedy must be based on existing authorities, or logical extension of the authorities. These issues are addressed in the ensuing chapters.[280]

Accounting for the differences

Explaining the differences between English law and that of the United States is a formidable task which requires a full-length work of its own.[281] Nevertheless, a number of factors may be outlined, although some suggestions may only be made tentatively due to the impossibility of exposing them to objective proof or due to their inherently high level of generality. Taken together, these factors should help to explain how two superficially similar jurisdictions could have responded so differently to the same basic problem. The numerous reasons for the differences may be conveniently discussed under the following four broad subheadings, which inevitably overlap to a certain extent: (i) sociological factors; (ii) precedent and legal theory; (iii) political and institutional factors; and (iv) academic influences and differences in legal culture.

---

[279] McCarthy, *Rights of Publicity and Privacy*, §1.39.
[280] Chapters 11 and 12 respectively.
[281] The following discussion draws significantly on the comparative study of legal reasoning and legal theory in P. S. Atiyah and R. S. Summers, *Form and Substance in Anglo-American Law* (Oxford, 1987), and J. G. Fleming, *The American Tort Process* (Oxford, 1988).

190 The commercial appropriation of personality

Sociological factors

First, we might consider whether instances of invasion of privacy in general and unauthorised appropriation of personality in particular are more common in the United States and, more pertinently, were more common at the time when the law of privacy took shape. Amongst the concerns expressed by Warren and Brandeis were press intrusion and the unauthorised circulation of portraits, and it seems that they reflected a wider concern over these matters in contemporary American society.[282] Winfield suggested that one of the reasons which lay behind the difference between the law in England and that in the United States was the fact that 'questionable methods of advertisement are commoner in [the United States] than elsewhere'.[283] Extra-legal regulation through voluntary codes of practice in the advertising industry might also play a part in underpinning natural standards of fair dealing in the United Kingdom, although the grosser activities of the press frequently strain their system of self-regulation and often elicit calls for a statutory right of privacy to deal with the intrusion and disclosure aspects of privacy.[284]

A second possible reason is the view that the citizens of the United States are inherently more litigious than the British. Though the cultural roots of American litigiousness are difficult to identify, it has been suggested that it is a reflection of American individualism, competitiveness and moralism.[285] Americans, it seems, are inherently '"rights minded", possessed of an insatiable appetite for vindication' and ready to take any dispute to litigation.[286] Third, access to the courts is obviously an important factor, without which any litigious desire will remain unsatisfied. It is trite wisdom that access to English courts is only available in practice to those rich enough to pay the costs of litigation or those poor enough to qualify for state funding, although this is not available for actions in defamation or malicious falsehood.[287] The practical reality is that only those who are wealthy and have a valuable de facto asset in their image, or place a very high premium on their sense of personal dignity, will be able

---

[282] See text accompanying notes 7 to 10 above.

[283] 'Privacy' (1931) 47 LQR 23, 38, cited by L. Brittan, 'The Right of Privacy in England and the United States' (1963) Tulane L Rev 235, 240. See also J. D. R. Craig and N. Nolte, 'Privacy and Free Speech in Germany and Canada: Lessons for an English Privacy Tort' [1998] EHRLR 162, 167, noting the fact that Canada has traditionally not experienced an intrusive tabloid press and paparazzi, unlike the United States and many European countries.

[284] See 48–50 above.

[285] See Atiyah and Summers, *Form and Substance*, 189, and the references cited.

[286] Fleming, *American Tort Process*, 2. Cf. B. S. Markesinis, 'Litigation Mania in England, Germany and the USA: Are We So Very Different?' [1990] CLJ 233.

[287] Access to Justice Act 1999, Sched. 2, para. 1.

Privacy and publicity in the United States 191

to afford and justify the costs of litigation. In this respect, it is somewhat surprising that the plaintiffs in the leading early privacy cases, *Roberson* v. *Rochester Folding Box Co.*[288] and *Pavesich* v. *New England Life Assurance Co.*[289] were ordinary citizens with no obvious de facto economic interests in their likenesses. It is a matter of pure speculation whether contingency fee arrangements played a part in the litigation in these cases, although Fleming notes that, as early as 1881, the contingent fee was an all but universal custom of the legal profession.[290] This factor might be one of the most important which accounts for the development of the right of privacy, other dignitary torts, such as the intentional infliction of mental distress, and, more generally, the judicial activism which characterises much of American tort law. Speculative litigation becomes feasible, and, over time, helps transform judicial perceptions of the courts' role in bringing about legal change.[291]

Precedent and legal theory

It is generally accepted that a much looser doctrine of *stare decisis* operates in the United States than in England.[292] Lower courts have greater leeway to disregard precedents which might otherwise be binding, while higher courts, particularly state supreme courts and the United States Supreme Court, have greater power to overrule prior precedents. Furthermore, American courts are much more willing to evade inconvenient and otherwise binding precedents through distinguishing or interpreting their *rationes decidendi* flexibly. Obviously, differences result, in large part, from

---

[288] See note 39 above.   [289] See note 56 above.

[290] Fleming, *American Tort Process*, 196. It should be noted that the damages claimed in *Roberson* and *Pavesich* ($15,000 and $25,000 respectively, though only *Pavesich* was successful) were extremely high, bearing in mind the nature of the injury. These figures may be compared with the £100 damages awarded for nervous shock in England in *Wilkinson* v. *Downton* [1897] 2 QB 57 less than ten years previously, and the fact that the House of Lords ordered a new trial in respect of the award of £1,000 damages for a libellous use of a caricature of a golfer in *Tolley* v. *J. S. Fry and Sons Ltd* [1931] AC 333, an award which was found to be excessive. These figures reveal vast disparities, even allowing for inflation and differences in exchange rates. It is clear that the prospects of such high awards for invasion of privacy might outweigh any reluctance on the part of plaintiff or counsel to sue. Awards of such size would seemingly be more than adequate to compensate for mental distress, or provide vindication or satisfaction, while leaving sufficient change for the attorney's fees.

[291] Fleming, *American Tort Process*, 233. Although English law has moved closer to the American model, through the introduction of conditional fee arrangements (Courts and Legal Services Act 1990, s. 58, as amended by Access to Justice Act 1999, s. 27(1)), the practical impact of the new regime on litigation in general, and the development of new causes of action in particular, remain to be seen.

[292] See, generally, Atiyah and Summers, *Form and Substance*, Ch. 5; Cross and Harris, *Precedent*, 19–20.

192   The commercial appropriation of personality

the sheer volume of case law generated in the multiple jurisdictions. Although, in many cases, a relatively small number of state authorities will be binding, in other cases there will be a choice from an array of case law which can provide support for almost any legal proposition whatsoever. Ultimately, the courts have considerable leeway in applying a mass of precedents and many acknowledge that they may choose between conflicting precedents on substantive policy or value grounds, rather than adhering to their formal authority. Additionally, dissenting opinions are more frequently given in American courts which inevitably weaken the precedential value of decisions as clear and dependable rules. These form invitations, which are frequently accepted, for future courts to depart from a decision.[293] More conservative courts come under increasing pressure to follow the approach of the more dynamic and forward-looking jurisdictions and often succumb to such pressure in the name of national conformity.[294]

These factors are reflected in the theory propounded by Atiyah and Summers that, for all their superficial similarities, the English and American legal systems differ profoundly: the English legal system being highly formal and the American legal system being highly substantive. American courts, they argue, are much more inclined to adopt substantive reasoning, involving moral, economic, political or institutional considerations, while English courts adhere to formal reasoning, which is more rigidly rule-based, and which excludes, overrides, or at least diminishes the weight of, countervailing substantive reasons. These differences arguably contribute to fundamentally different visions of law in the two countries, the English being more formal, and the American more substantive.[295]

Bearing in mind the high level of generality inherent in such arguments, it is not difficult to see some of these factors at work in the development of the law of privacy in the United States. It will be recalled that some of the authorities that Warren and Brandeis marshalled in support of their right of privacy were early English cases. In the first significant case, *Roberson* v. *Rochester Folding Box Co.*,[296] the Supreme Court of New York refused to accept the plaintiff's claim for invasion of privacy, stressing the fact that there was no authority on which to base such a claim and that no mention of such a right was made by early legal commentators. Unlike Warren and Brandeis, the majority did not feel that privacy was a preexisting principle and interpreted the authorities relied on in the article

---

[293] See Atiyah and Summers, *Form and Substance*, 129–30.
[294] Fleming, *American Tort Process*, 36.
[295] Atiyah and Summers, *Form and Substance*, Ch. 1.
[296] See note 39 above and accompanying text.

Privacy and publicity in the United States

narrowly; equity did not have any concern with the feelings of individuals, except where the conduct complained of interfered with the use or enjoyment of property. As noted above, the majority opinion reflected the formalist approach for which late nineteenth-century jurisprudence has been heavily criticised. Reform of the law was deemed to be the province of the legislature, which duly intervened.[297] However, in what became the leading case, *Pavesich* v. *New England Life Assurance Co.*, the Supreme Court of Georgia acknowledged that the lack of precedent should make the courts tread with caution, but, nevertheless, held that it did not amount to a conclusive denial of such a right. What formed the basis of the decision were the reasons of substance; the right of privacy was regarded as a natural corollary of the fundamental right to personal liberty which the state and federal constitutions guaranteed. Although the Court conceded that all the early English authorities relied on by Warren and Brandeis were based on conventional grounds such as interference with property, breach of trust or breach of contract, they were not used as formal reasons for denying the existence of a right of privacy. The dissenting judgment of Gray J in *Roberson*, which drew largely on the Warren and Brandeis model of synthesis, was adopted in its entirety as an *ex post facto* justification of the conclusion which the majority of the Supreme Court of Georgia had already reached through its substantive natural rights reasoning.

The general approach of English courts is much closer to that of the New York Court of Appeals with its emphasis on the need for formal authority and high degree of deference to the legislature. The fact that it was *Pavesich* and not *Roberson* which became the leading case indicates that American courts have not allowed formal reasons to hamper the judicial development of the law of privacy. In English law, however, such formal reasons have been deployed to deny the possibility of a new remedy.[298]

Such an approach to precedent is also partly a reflection of prevalent legal theories and notions of what the courts can and cannot, or should and should not, do, which can be taken as a backdrop, though admittedly no more, against which the developments in the substantive law have taken place.[299] Formalism held sway in the United States at the end of the nineteenth century. Among its central tenets was the belief that the legal system was essentially complete and comprehensive and contained

---

[297] See note 55 above.

[298] *Dockrell* v. *Dougall* (1899) 15 TLR 333; *Corelli* v. *Wall* (1906) 22 TLR 532, 533; *Tolley* v. *J. S. Fry and Sons Ltd* [1930] 1 KB 467, 478 (CA); *McCulloch* v. *Lewis A. May (Produce Distributors) Ltd* (1948) 65 RPC 58, 67; *Sim* v. *H. J. Heinz & Co. Ltd* [1959] 1 WLR 313, 317.

[299] See, generally, Atiyah and Summers, *Form and Substance*, Ch. 9.

194   The commercial appropriation of personality

answers to virtually all questions that could arise; belief in the strict separation of powers and that only legislatures and not the courts should make law; belief in the inner logic of legal concepts as a primary tool of legal reasoning; and a belief in certainty and predictability as paramount legal ideals. However, during the early part of the twentieth century, the instrumentalists, and later the realists,[300] reacted against such views, stressing the social ends that the law must serve and advocating a much more active judicial role. This was highly congenial to a strongly substantive vision of law, involving the use of reasons of substance lying behind the decisions in applying a precedent rather than the application of formal syllogistic reasoning, and was congenial to judicial law-making in general.[301] In England, on the other hand, the predominant positivism tended and indeed still tends towards a dominant legislature with a relatively inert judiciary concerned only with following the law.[302] Indeed, only in relatively recent times have the English judiciary acknowledged that they do in fact have a limited power of interstitial law-making, although this power is sparingly exercised.[303]

Underlying political and institutional structure

The very different contributions that the courts have made to the development of the law in England and in the United States can also be explained by political and constitutional factors. In the English positivist tradition, law is seen as a body of rules laid down as a command of the sovereign; all rights derive from positive law and the judges are not to make or reform the law. This may be contrasted with the position in America, where sovereignty rests with the people, and the Constitution reflects the natural law idea that people have pre-existing moral rights such as

---

[300] It is perhaps no coincidence that the judgment of the Second Circuit Court of Appeals in *Haelen Laboratories Inc.* v. *Topps Chewing Gum Inc.* (see text accompanying note 178 above), the first important right of publicity case, was delivered by one of the more extreme members of the realist movement, Judge Jerome Frank. The emphasis on substantive reasons (the de facto commercial value of baseball players' identities, and the fact that these values were routinely traded) in preference to the application of strict rules, the cavalier approach to the rules of precedent, and the dynamic view of the judicial function seen in *Haelan* are just some of the hallmarks of the realist school. See J. Frank, *Law and the Modern Mind* (London, 1949), esp. Ch. 4, and see, generally, M. D. A. Freeman, *Lloyd's Introduction to Jurisprudence*, 6th edn (London, 1994), Ch. 8.
[301] Atiyah and Summers, *Form and Substance*, 255. For a full account of the impact of realism on tort law in America see G. E. White, *Tort Law in America*, Ch. 3.
[302] Atiyah and Summers, *Form and Substance*, 257.
[303] J. Steyn, 'Does Legal Formalism Hold Sway in England?' [1996] CLP 43, 48, citing Lord Reid's article, 'The Judge as Lawmaker' (1972) 12 JSPTL 22, as a critical breakthrough, whereas previously it had been considered impolitic for judges to acknowledge their creative role.

Privacy and publicity in the United States

the right to life and liberty.[304] As Brittan notes, one of the reasons for the growth of the right of privacy in the United States was the fact that its very existence was supported by the provisions of written constitutions guaranteeing civil rights and, as previously noted, in *Pavesich* the Supreme Court of Georgia regarded the right to privacy as a corollary of the right to personal liberty guaranteed by the Federal and State Constitutions.[305] However, as Brittan argues, although the existence of such constitutional provisions provided useful pegs on which to hang new causes of action, the vagueness of the provisions makes it clear that they were no more than pegs. The right to liberty and similar rights could justify a number of innovations in the law of tort.[306] It remains to be seen to what extent the values of the European Convention on Human Rights will impact on the development of the English common law. This is considered in the next chapter.

The institutional relationship between the legislature and the courts in both countries is a further crucial explaining factor. Unlike American courts, English courts can often assume that reform will be forthcoming from the legislature, if necessary, and the courts are often unwilling to make the changes themselves, reflecting the belief that legislative methods of law reform are superior.[307] Although this is sometimes no more than an excuse for judicial conservatism and passivity, it explains the dicta which express judicial disapproval of the defendants' conduct while denying any power to formulate a remedy in the limited English case law on privacy and appropriation of personality.[308] Legal change and law reform in English law 'is typically conceptualised in terms of sharp breaks with the past', with a clear distinction being drawn between what the law is and what it ought to be, a matter often decided after lengthy consideration and consultation by statutory reform agencies such as the Law Commission.[309] Thus, while it would be misleading to argue that the English common law is immune to reform, it is probably true that the methodology of legal change is different, and that legislative reform of the common law is much more frequent in England than in most American

---

[304] See, generally, Atiyah and Summers, *Form and Substance*, Ch. 8. See also R. A. Epstein, *'International News Service* v. *Associated Press*: Custom and Law as Sources of Property Rights in News' (1992) 78 Virg L Rev 85, making a similar point in the context of the emergence of new property rights, contrasting 'top down' positivism with 'bottom up' notions of rights deriving from the traditions and common practices of a community.

[305] See text accompanying note 56 above.

[306] Brittan, 'Privacy in England and the United States', 242–3.

[307] See Atiyah and Summers, *Form and Substance*, Ch. 5 esp. 141 et seq. For an expression of this view in the context of privacy in English law see *Malone* v. *Metropolitan Police Commissioner* [1979] 1 Ch 344, 372 *per* Megarry VC; *Kaye* v. *Robertson* [1991] FSR 62, 66 and 71.

[308] See 202–4 below.   [309] Atiyah and Summers, *Form and Substance*, 148–9.

196   The commercial appropriation of personality

states.[310] Indeed, state legislatures are arguably relatively inert in the tort field in the United States and, as Fleming argues, their indifference to proposals for tort law reform strengthens the case for judicial activity and weakens the arguments that the courts should not usurp the role of the legislatures.[311] As noted above, legislative reform of the fragmented English law of privacy, in the form of a new statutory tort, has not been forthcoming. At the same time, any deficiencies or lack of impetus on the part of the legislature have not been compensated by an active judiciary, and the English courts have remained (some might argue quite properly) wary of usurping the role of Parliament.[312] It remains to be seen whether legislation will be introduced or whether the English law of privacy will develop incrementally at common law. The early indications in the wake of the Human Rights Act 1998 are considered below.[313]

Academic influences and legal culture

The influence of academic writing has been profound in this area. Although neither Samuel Warren nor Louis Brandeis was an academic, their article was a scholarly attempt, in a leading scholarly journal, to highlight the deficiencies of the law as it stood and advocate the recognition of a new right. The effect of Prosser's reshaping of the privacy tort has been equally profound, and is seen by many as the modern conceptual source of the privacy tort.[314] Indeed, White argues that Prosser was at least partly responsible for the dramatic growth of the tort from its status as a residual category to an expansive quadripartite tort. In successive works, a classification seemingly made for convenience was expanded and refined until it hardened and solidified and was finally adopted as being synonymous with 'the law' in the *Second Restatement of Torts*.[315] Such a process can only result from lengthy reflection, and the nature of the judicial process rarely allows for such systematisation, especially when judges are faced with such a large bulk of authorities and 'a remorseless treadmill of cases that cannot wait'.[316] Perhaps the most telling difference between England and the United States is not the fact that there are academic writers who are able to formulate alternative bases of liability or impose order and structure on large and disparate bodies of case law;

---

[310] *Ibid.*, 140–1.
[311] Fleming, *American Tort Process*, 38 et seq. See also Markesinis, 'Litigation Mania', 242.
[312] See, e.g., *Kaye* v. *Robertson* [1991] FSR 62, 66 and 71.
[313] See 214–18 below.   [314] See Leebron, 'Privacy in Tort Law', 808.
[315] G. E. White, *Tort Law in America*, 177–8.
[316] *White* v. *Jones* [1995] 2 AC 207, 235 *per* Lord Steyn.

they are abundant in both jurisdictions, although English academics are arguably more reticent in criticising judicial decisions.[317] Rather, the difference lies in the fact that the courts in the United States actually pay heed to their efforts and the fact that they are cited by counsel and are thus considered by the courts in the first place.[318] There has been a long tradition of judicial unwillingness to treat academic writings as authoritative, or even persuasive, in English law although they are increasingly cited in some areas, particularly in the House of Lords. The interaction between the judiciary, practitioners and academia in the United States is rather stronger than in England and Wales,[319] where the channel of communication is a problem which is yet to be solved.[320]

Finally, the number of jurisdictions contributes to a markedly less homogeneous approach. While English judges and practitioners are part of the relatively small and intimate culture centred largely around the Inns of Court in London, American practitioners are much more widely spread. Partly as a result, American practitioners tend to be less conservative in outlook and are often more willing to start legal proceedings on new and unprecedented grounds,[321] helped in no small part by the contingency fee system mentioned above. That said, it should be borne in mind that the courts in some states are markedly more conservative than in some more 'liberal' states, possessing little reforming zeal and showing greater respect for a more rigid doctrine of *stare decisis*.[322] Ultimately, however, in both systems much depends on the nature and quality of the arguments presented by counsel. Writing extra-judicially, Lord Steyn has suggested that, in some civil cases in the House of Lords, counsel tend to concentrate too much on precedent and narrow conceptual arguments at the expense of the wider implications. While the balance of substantive arguments, and the evaluation of what would be the best legal solution, will often be decisive, Lord Steyn notes that '[c]ounsel do not always engage in argument on this higher ground'.[323]

These factors obviously cannot individually account for the development of the rights of privacy and publicity in the United States. Taken

---

[317] B. S. Markesinis and S. F. Deakin, *Tort Law*, 4th edn (Oxford, 1999), 58, citing A. Paterson, *The Law Lords* (London, 1982), 14–20.

[318] See, e.g., the comments of Lord Steyn in *White* v. *Jones* [1995] 2 AC 207, 235, and see B. S. Markesinis and N. Nolte, 'Some Comparative Reflections on the Right of Privacy of Public Figures in Public Places' in P. Birks (ed.) *Privacy and Loyalty* (Oxford, 1997), 113, 114, criticising the tendency amongst counsel to talk at excessive length in court at the expense of introducing comparative law materials in legal arguments.

[319] See, generally, Atiyah and Summers, *Form and Substance*, Ch. 14, esp. 398 et seq.

[320] See P. Birks, 'The Academic and the Practitioner' (1998) 18 LS 397, 401.

[321] See, generally, Atiyah and Summers, *Form and Substance*, Ch. 13.

[322] See Fleming, *American Tort Process*, 35.   [323] Steyn, 'Legal Formalism', 54.

198   The commercial appropriation of personality

together, however, they go some way towards explaining the sharp divergence between English and American law in this area. They also suggest that it is not a simple matter for the English courts to follow the lead of the American courts;[324] the differences between the two systems are too profound to allow simple replication.

Conclusions

Interests in privacy are part of the range of de facto interests that can be damaged by unauthorised commercial exploitation of personality. Due to its superficial attractions, a general right of privacy is often seen as a panacea for a number of different forms of damage to a number of different interests. Unauthorised disclosures of personal information, physical intrusions, harassment and unauthorised exploitation of personality all elicit calls for a general right of privacy. As experience from the United States shows, the inherently vague notion of privacy allows it to protect a disparate range of interests, although such flexibility inevitably results in a good degree of conceptual uncertainty. More important, such flexibility has potentially high costs for competing interests such as freedom of expression, particularly in a country such as the United Kingdom, where this has traditionally been seen as a residual liberty rather than a constitutionally guaranteed right.

However, the central problems of conceptual indeterminacy, the difficulty in balancing competing interests and, though perhaps to a lesser extent, the definitional problem can all be effectively circumvented by rejecting a general right of privacy in favour of more specific and narrowly circumscribed torts. A *sui generis* tort of appropriation of personality can avoid, or certainly reduce, such problems. That is not to say that a tort of appropriation of personality would be easy to delimit or that such a tort would not occasionally require a difficult balance to be struck between an individual's freedom from unauthorised commercial exploitation of his personal attributes, and the wider public interest in permitting the use of such attributes to communicate information and express ideas. Nevertheless, such problems would be less acute if such a large and unwieldy notion of a general right of privacy were rejected in favour of a narrower and more specific tort. Moreover, the development of the rights of privacy and publicity in the United States illustrates the difficulties in

---

[324] This suggestion has frequently been made. See, e.g., Justice, *Privacy and the Law* (London, 1970), para. 120, arguing that similar developments could take place in theory, though practical factors militated against such a view.

encompassing essentially economic interests in commercial exploitation within a tort remedy which is primarily concerned with protecting dignitary interests in personality. The unwieldy position of separate rights of privacy and publicity can be avoided by accommodating both within a *sui generis* tort.

8 Privacy interests in English law

Introduction

The courts in the United States were able to develop a common law tort of invasion of privacy, cast rather unusually in rights-based terms, through a synthesis of pre-existing authorities. The obvious irony for English lawyers was that the authorities principally relied on, at least in the original Warren and Brandeis thesis, were English cases from the nineteenth century. Over the century following the genesis of the law of privacy in the United States, English law stubbornly refused to follow a similar pattern.

There are four predominant approaches to problems of invasions of privacy.[1] First, the adjustment of existing causes of action to cover invasions of privacy. Second, the piecemeal addition of new causes of action, either by reference to the circumstances in which liability is imposed (e.g., harassment or appropriation of personality) or by explicitly labelling them as invasions of privacy. Third, a general remedy declaring that, in principle, every invasion of privacy is actionable, subject to necessary qualifications limiting recovery: this might be non-exhaustive, leaving the terms and scope open-ended or conversely might be exhaustive, defining the terms and circumstances for recovery comprehensively. Fourth, the declaration that every person has a right to privacy in a general and open-ended way, without specifying the circumstances in which privacy can be invaded. The first part of the chapter considers the limitations of the first two methods, while subsequent parts consider the possibilities for adopting the third and fourth approaches within the English common law tradition. In the wake of the Human Rights Act 1998, the law in this area is in a considerable state of uncertainty and it will be some time before a distinct new pattern of development emerges.

Such a course of development has to overcome the four basic objections to a general right of privacy which have traditionally been put forward and

---

[1] R. Gavison, 'Privacy and Its Legal Protection', D.Phil Thesis, University of Oxford (1975), 243. See also Justice, *Privacy and the Law* (London, 1970), para. 127.

Privacy interests in English law 201

may be usefully recalled. First, the problem of definition, which featured prominently in committee reports,[2] although the enactment of a new right is a different procedure and process from the elucidation of a concept. There is a fundamental difference between defining x and defining a right to x, whatever x might be, and the difficulty of choosing among competing alternative definitions should not be seen as a conclusive objection.[3] Indeed, privacy is arguably no less capable of bearing definite legal meanings than other overworked legal concepts such as 'property' or 'reputation'.[4] This reflects the second, and deeper, underlying problem of conceptual uncertainty. It is somewhat doubtful whether privacy is a sufficiently distinctive and coherent value to form the basis of a correspondingly coherent substantive legal right. Indeed, the attraction of the dominant reductionist approach in the United States lay in the fact that it overcame the inherent vagueness of privacy and reduced the notion to a number of separate rules which protected more readily identifiable interests.[5]

Furthermore, there are difficulties in balancing a right of personal privacy with the wider public interest values in freedom of information, which, in the abstract, might appear to be of equal weight and have been regarded as an extension of the judicial role 'too far into the determination of controversial questions of a social and political character'.[6] Finally,

[2] Younger Committee, Report on Privacy, Cmnd 5012 (1972), paras. 57–73 and para. 665 (the Committee's terms of reference were whether legislation was needed to provide further protection to individual citizens and commercial and industrial interests against intrusion into privacy by private persons and organisations, or by companies). Cf. Calcutt Committee, Report on Privacy and Related Matters, Cm 1102 (1990), paras. 12.13–12.18, where the Committee was satisfied that a statutory tort of infringement of privacy could be adequately defined and could specifically relate to the publication of personal information, including photographs, although this reflected a narrower conception of privacy, which in turn reflected the Calcutt Committee's narrower terms of reference than earlier reports (measures needed 'to give further protection to individual privacy from the activities of the press and improve recourse against the press for the individual citizen, taking account of existing remedies') (para. 1.1).
[3] N. MacCormick, 'Privacy: A Problem of Definition?' (1974) 1 JLS 75, 77.
[4] See D. Seipp, 'English Judicial Recognition of a Right to Privacy' (1983) 3 OJLS 325, 331; Calcutt Committee, Report on Privacy and Related Matters, para. 12.12. See, further, 273 and 249 below.
[5] See 161–4 above. R. Wacks, 'The Poverty of Privacy' (1980) 96 LQR 73, 81–6, draws heavily on the American experience in urging that the concept of privacy should not be admitted to English law, arguing that privacy has been confused with other issues, both as a tort law right (for example, with confidentiality, defamation and a proprietary interest in name or likeness) and in the constitutional sphere (for example, with liberties such as freedom from unreasonable search, freedom of association and freedom of expression) (*ibid.*, 78–81). Wacks argues that privacy is arguably an irredeemably nebulous concept and, whatever its merits as a general abstraction of an underlying value, it should not be used as a means to describe a legal right or cause of action (88), and see, further, R. Wacks, *Personal Information* (Oxford, 1989).
[6] Younger Committee, Report on Privacy, paras 652–3. Cf. Calcutt Committee, Report on Privacy and Related Matters, paras. 12.24–12.29.

202   The commercial appropriation of personality

and most fundamentally, it has been argued that a general right to privacy does not fit easily within English law, which is generally cast in terms of breaches of duties rather than positive declarations of rights,[7] the underlying guiding principle holding that what is not prohibited is permitted.[8] The last two objections cannot be sustained following the incorporation (a term used loosely) of the European Convention on Human Rights in the Human Rights Act 1998 which heralds a move towards a more explicit rights-based approach which inevitably involves a judicial balancing of competing rights.[9]

Piecemeal recognition of privacy interests in English law

In the absence of a general tort of invasion of privacy, English law has protected interests in privacy in piecemeal fashion in several disparate areas.[10] Thus, for some time, it has arguably been misleading to state that there is no law of privacy, the relevant questions being the extent of the piecemeal protection and the capability of the law to develop.[11] Protection has largely been achieved through casuistic applications of existing causes of action, not always under an explicit 'privacy' rubric. Although the Younger Committee stated in 1972 that 'the principle . . . is not in dispute, only the nature of the domestic legislation which is needed to implement it',[12] reform by Parliament has not been forthcoming. Similarly, the courts have traditionally been reluctant to develop the piecemeal protection into a more comprehensive general right or principle.[13]

There are clear limits to the traditional pragmatic approach, as the much-cited decision of the Court of Appeal in *Kaye* v. *Robertson* illustrates.[14] The plaintiff actor, Gorden Kaye, suing through his next friend, sought to prevent the publication of photographs and an article purporting to be the plaintiff's own exclusive story of his recovery from a

---

[7] See Calcutt Committee, Report on Privacy and Related Matters, para. 12.15; P. H. Winfield, 'Privacy', (1931) 47 LQR 23, 24.

[8] See, e.g., *Attorney-General* v. *Guardian Newspapers Ltd (No. 2)* [1990] 1 AC 109, 178 *per* Donaldson MR; *Douglas* v. *Hello! Ltd* [2001] 2 WLR 992, 1009 *per* Brooke LJ; Younger Committee, Report on Privacy, para. 35; and see, generally, A. Lester and D. Oliver (eds.), *Constitutional Law and Human Rights* (London, 1997), 102. Cf. N. MacCormick, 'A Note Upon Privacy' (1973) 89 LQR 23; N. S. Marsh, 'Hohfeld and Privacy' (1973) 89 LQR 183.

[9] See 218–24 below.

[10] See, generally, Seipp, 'Right to Privacy'; Justice, *Privacy and the Law*, Ch. 4.

[11] J. Steyn, 'Does Legal Formalism Hold Sway in England?' [1996] CLP 43, 54. Cf. R. Wacks, *The Protection of Privacy* (London, 1980), 5.

[12] Younger Committee, Report on Privacy, para. 662.

[13] *R* v. *Khan (Sultan)* [1996] 3 All ER 289, 301 *per* Lord Nicholls.

[14] [1991] FSR 62.

Privacy interests in English law 203

serious accident. The defendants had gained access to the plaintiff's hospital room, taking flashlight photographs and interviewing him at length when he was not in a fit state to consent to such an interview. Four separate causes of action were argued. The claim based on libel did not satisfy the rule that an interlocutory injunction should only be granted in the clearest cases, where any jury would come to the conclusion that the matter was libellous.[15] Passing off was cursorily dismissed since the plaintiff was not deemed to be in the position of a trader in relation to his story about his accident and recovery. Arguably, it deserved a little more attention, particularly since the Court recognised that Kaye had a potentially valuable right to sell his story to the highest bidder.[16] Trespass to the person, based on the grounds that the taking of flashlight photographs might have caused distress to the plaintiff, was dismissed due to the lack of evidence of any damage.[17] Moreover, the injunction sought was not intended to prevent another anticipated battery, but to prevent the defendants from profiting from their trespass in taking the photographs.[18]

The claim in malicious falsehood was eventually successful in that the defendant had maliciously published words which were false (the element of malice was satisfied by the fact that the reporters were perfectly aware that the plaintiff was in no fit state to give his consent to being interviewed), causing special damage to the potentially valuable right to sell the story of his recovery.[19] Significantly, the injunctions were framed to prevent the defendants from publishing the story as Kaye's *own* story, a right which only extended to his own personal story of his recovery, since anyone would be entitled to publish a story of the accident and its background, and general details of Kaye's recovery, so far as the information available to the public and to reporters allowed. On the surface, what was protected was the plaintiff's capacity to sell his own story as an exclusive story, probably to the highest bidder: in essence an economic interest. This would only have a value over and above any other objective report

---

[15] *Ibid.*, 66, applying *William Coulson & Sons* v. *James Coulson & Co.* [1887] 3 TLR 46.

[16] [1991] FSR 62, 68. See also C. Wadlow, *The Law of Passing Off*, 2nd edn (London, 1995), 305, and see Chapter 4 above. Cf. T. Bingham, 'Should There Be a Law to Protect Rights of Personal Privacy?' [1996] EHRLR 450, 457.

[17] [1991] FSR 62, 68. Cf. W. V. H. Rogers, *Winfield and Jolowicz on Tort*, 14th edn (London, 1994), 59, noting that, although commendably practicable, such an approach is difficult to reconcile with the fact that trespass is actionable *per se*.

[18] [1991] FSR 62, 69. See also P. Prescott, '*Kaye* v. *Robertson*: A Reply' (1991) 54 MLR 451, suggesting that the hospital might have been joined as a co-plaintiff, thus giving the plaintiff a cause of action for trespass to land. Cf. Bingham, 'Should There Be a Law to Protect Rights of Personal Privacy?', 457.

[19] [1991] FSR 67–8. The Defamation Act 1952, s. 3(1) provides that it is sufficient damage if the words published in writing are calculated to cause pecuniary damage to the plaintiff.

204　The commercial appropriation of personality

of the accident to the extent that it would include Kaye's own private thoughts and sentiments. Thus, it is arguable that what the Court was protecting, in effect, was the plaintiff's private thoughts and emotions: essentially, his privacy[20] or, alternatively formulated, the plaintiff's right to seclusion and solitude free from intrusion, which the Court refused to protect explicitly.[21] As Cane notes, '[i]t is surely an indictment of English law and society that judges feel the need to impute a desire to make a profit to someone in order to protect them from unwanted attention by the press'.[22]

While the Court of Appeal acknowledged that the facts of the case highlighted the failure of English law to protect personal privacy, any remedy was deemed to be a matter for the legislature rather than the courts,[23] an approach which has been criticised as too narrow a view of the judicial function in developing common law principles in accordance with contemporary ethical values and social needs.[24] Limited reference (understandable in interlocutory proceedings) was made to solutions in other jurisdictions, particularly the United States and Germany,[25] although, somewhat ironically, developments in both countries were largely the result of judicial initiatives rather than legislative intervention.[26] The Court of Appeal was clearly reluctant to follow a similar path.[27] It remains to be seen whether English law will maintain the tradition of flexible application of existing causes of actions[28] or whether such a casuistic approach will be abandoned in favour of a more principled approach.[29]

[20] As Bingham LJ candidly acknowledged: [1991] FSR 70.
[21] See note 18 above.
[22] P. Cane, *Tort Law and Economic Interests*, 2nd edn (Oxford, 1996), 80.
[23] [1991] FSR 62, 66 *per* Glidewell LJ, 70 *per* Bingham LJ, and 71 *per* Leggatt LJ. See also *Cruise and Kidman* v. *Southdown Press Pty Ltd* (1992–3) 26 IPR 125 where the Federal Court of Australia, although expressing sympathy with the plaintiff actors' desire to maintain their family privacy in attempting to prevent the defendant's magazine from publishing pictures of their child, stated that the right of privacy was not recognised in Australia and rejected causes of action based on breach of confidence, defamation and breach of copyright.
[24] A. Lester, 'English Judges as Lawmakers' [1993] PL 269, 285. English law in this area has lacked the bold judicial synthesis of Blackburn J in *Rylands* v. *Fletcher* (1866) LR 1 Ex 264 and Lord Atkin in *Donoghue* v. *Stevenson* [1932] AC 562. Cf. *Pavesich* v. *New England Life Insurance Co.* 50 SE 68 (1905), and see 324–9 below.
[25] [1991] FSR 62, 70 *per* Bingham LJ, citing B. S. Markesinis, *The German Law of Torts*, 2nd edn (Oxford, 1990), 316: 'English law . . . compares unfavourably with German law'. See also [1991] FSR 62, 71 *per* Leggatt LJ (noting the development of the rights of publicity and privacy as separate rights in the United States). Cf. D. Beddingfield, 'Privacy or Publicity? The Enduring Confusion Surrounding the American Tort of Invasion of Privacy' (1992) 55 MLR 111.
[26] See Chapter 7 above and 230–3 below.　[27] Cf. 324–9 below.
[28] See, e.g., P. Prescott, '*Kaye* v. *Robertson*: A Reply' (1991) 54 MLR 451.
[29] See, e.g., B. S. Markesinis, 'Our Patchy Law of Privacy – Time to do Something About It' (1990) 53 MLR 802.

Privacy interests in English law 205

There follows a brief sketch of the principal causes of action which provide indirect protection for interests in privacy.

Piecemeal statutory provisions

Pragmatic solutions and piecemeal recognitions have, of course, resulted from the rejection of either a general right to privacy or a general remedy for invasion of privacy. Section 85 of the Copyright Designs and Patents Act 1988, as already noted, provides a limited right to privacy for a person who commissions a photograph for private or domestic purposes, allowing him to prevent copies of the photograph from being, inter alia, issued to the public.[30] The most important statutory provision in practice is the Data Protection Act 1998, which regulates many activities involved in the holding and processing of personal data.[31] Although not ostensibly concerned with personal privacy, the Act implements EU Council Directive 95/46 which makes explicit reference to the underlying object of national laws on the processing of personal data: the protection of the right of privacy, as recognised by Article 8 of the European Convention on Human Rights, and 'the general principles of Community law'.[32] It has been suggested, obiter, that liability may arise under the Data Protection Act 1998 where a photograph is stored in digital form.[33] The Act provides that personal data should be processed fairly and lawfully and should not be processed unless the data subject has given his consent to the processing. This is subject to a possible exception for special purposes such as the publication of journalistic, literary or artistic material, where the data controller reasonably believes that, having regard, in particular, to freedom of expression, publication would be in the public interest.[34] The Act provides a right of access to personal data,[35] a right to prevent processing likely to cause damage or distress,[36] and a right to compensation. This right to compensation includes compensation for distress, regardless of damage, where the contravention relates to special purposes,[37] as defined in section 3, that is, journalistic, artistic or literary purposes.

Under the Broadcasting Act 1996 the Broadcasting Standards Commission (BSC)[38] has a duty to draw up and review a code setting

---

[30] See 33–4 above.
[31] See generally S. Chalton *et al.* (eds.) *Encyclopaedia of Data Protection* (London, 1988–2000), Part I. For a detailed discussion of the relationship between privacy and personal information, see Wacks, *Personal Information.*
[32] Preamble, para. 10 (see also paras. 2 and 11) and Art. 9.
[33] *Douglas* v. *Hello! Ltd* [2001] 2 WLR 992, 1007 *per* Brooke LJ.
[34] Section 32(1).   [35] Section 7.   [36] Section 11.   [37] Section 13(2).
[38] See, generally, V. Nelson, *The Law of Entertainment and Broadcasting*, 2nd edn (London, 2000), Ch. 33.

206   The commercial appropriation of personality

out principles and governing practices and to consider and adjudicate on complaints relating to the avoidance, inter alia, of 'unwarranted infringement of privacy in, or in connection with the obtaining of material included in, such programmes'.[39] The BSC is not concerned with establishing substantive legal rights. Its function is limited to providing a mechanism for making a complaint which, if upheld, can be subject to the publicity which the BSC considers appropriate.[40] Thus, the Court of Appeal refused to interfere with the BSC's decision that a limited company could make a fairness complaint regarding the secret filming of its employees in one of its shops for the purposes of a television programme, a claim made by the company itself rather than on behalf of its employees for the loss of privacy or distress that they might have suffered.[41] Although it was noted that the concept of a company's privacy is somewhat hard to grasp and difficult to apply where there are no 'sensitivities to wound, and no selfhood to protect',[42] the decision rested very much on the language and particular purpose of the Broadcasting Act 1996, concerned with broadcasting standards rather than legal rights, which justified 'a wider view of the ambit of privacy than might be appropriate in some other contexts'.[43]

Privacy and interests in property: trespass and nuisance

Early authorities denied the existence of a right of privacy relating to property.[44] For example, in *Chandler* v. *Thompson*[45] Le Blanc J stated that, although an action for opening a window to disturb the plaintiff's privacy was to be found in the books, he had never known such an action to be maintained, and later, in *Tapling* v. *Jones*, Baron Bramwell unequivocally stated that privacy was not a right, and that intrusion on it was no wrong or cause of action.[46] However, interests in privacy were seemingly, though not always explicitly, protected when a substantive cause of action such as trespass[47] or nuisance[48] could be established.

[39] Broadcasting Act 1996, s. 107(1).
[40] *Ibid.*, s. 119. See *R* v. *Broadcasting Standards Commission ex parte British Broadcasting Corp.* [2000] 3 WLR 1327, 1332 *per* Woolf MR, and 1339 *per* Mustill LJ.
[41] *Ibid.*   [42] *Ibid.*, 1340 *per* Mustill LJ.   [43] *Ibid.*, 1339 *per* Hale LJ.
[44] See, generally, Winfield, 'Privacy', 23, 24–30, and Seipp, 'Right to Privacy', 334–7.
[45] (1811) 3 Camp 80, 82, 170 ER 1312, 1313.
[46] (1865) 11 HLC 290, 305, 11 ER 1344, 1350.
[47] See, e.g., *Hickman* v. *Maisey* [1900] 1 QB 752; cf. *Bernstein* v. *Skyviews & General Ltd* [1978] QB 479, and see, also, *R* v. *Broadcasting Complaints Commission, ex parte Barclay* [1997] EMLR 62.
[48] See, e.g., *Walker* v. *Brewster* (1867) LR 5 Eq 2, 26; cf. *Victoria Park Racing and Recreation Grounds Co. Ltd* v. *Taylor* (1937) 58 CLR 479, 495–6 and 517.

Privacy interests in English law

Personal privacy and defamation

There is some support for the argument that the courts have been giving limited recognition to interests in personal privacy through benevolent interpretations of the tort of defamation. The inherent flexibility of the notion of an injury to reputation lends itself well to such an approach, although most authorities can be interpreted conventionally as injuries to reputation rather than invasions of privacy. Some interests in personal privacy closely resemble interests in reputation, particularly in cases involving what has been labelled 'false light' invasion of privacy, and the overlap between defamation and invasion of privacy is considerable. These issues are considered in detail in the next chapter.

Personal privacy and breach of confidence

The role that the action for breach of confidence plays in protecting interests in privacy has been openly acknowledged,[49] and in its comprehensive review in 1972, the Younger Committee took the view that it offered the most effective protection for privacy interests.[50] In an early case, *Prince Albert* v. *Strange*, an injunction was secured to prevent publication of a catalogue describing the plaintiff's private etchings on the grounds of an injury to property, even though the judgments at first instance[51] and on appeal[52] suggested that privacy was the right that was invaded. In the United States the decision was used as the principal basis for a general right of privacy. The English courts, on the other hand, extended protection to what may be regarded as privacy interests, typically in cases involving sensitive information relating to private domestic relationships.[53] While stopping some way short of developing a general principle the courts have become more explicit in acknowledging the role that it plays.[54]

---

[49] *Attorney-General* v. *Guardian Newspapers (No. 2)* [1990] 1 AC 109, 255 *per* Lord Keith. As G. W. Paton observed some time ago, 'at the first hint of breach of contract, trust or confidence, the courts seem to be willing to give protection to what is, in reality, privacy': 'Broadcasting and Privacy' (1938) 16 Can B Rev 425, 433.

[50] Younger Committee, Report on Privacy, para. 87; cf. Wacks, 'The Poverty of Privacy', 81–2.

[51] (1849) 2 DeG & Sm 652, 670 and 696–7, 64 ER 293, 301.

[52] (1849) 1 Mac & G 25, 47, 41 ER 1171, 1179.

[53] See, e.g., *Argyll* v. *Argyll* [1967] Ch 302 (marital confidences); *Stephens* v. *Avery* [1988] Ch 449 (lesbian relationship); *Barrymore* v. *News Group Newspapers Ltd* [1997] FSR 600 (homosexual relationship); *Blair* v. *Associated Newspapers Plc* (Queen's Bench Division, 13 November 2000) (family life); *A* v. *B* [2000] EMLR 1007 (private diary). Cf. *Lennon* v. *News Group Newspapers Ltd* [1978] FSR 573 (marital confidences).

[54] See, e.g., *Hellewell* v. *Chief Constable of Derbyshire* [1995] 1 WLR 804, 807 *per* Laws J (obiter); *R* v. *Department of Health ex parte Source Informatics Ltd* [2001] QB 424,

208   The commercial appropriation of personality

The availability of such incidental protection relies on establishing a valid cause of action for breach of confidence.[55] Three key elements are required. The information concerned must have: (i) the necessary quality of confidence about it; (ii) been imparted in circumstances importing an obligation of confidence; and (iii) been used without authorisation, possibly to the detriment of the party communicating it.[56] The second requirement poses the main obstacle in developing breach of confidence into a broader remedy for invasion of privacy. While a recipient of information will be bound by an obligation of confidence where he realises, on an objective basis, that the information is imparted in confidence,[57] it is not clear how broadly this requirement can be construed. On one view, 'the relationship between the parties is not the determining factor', rather it is 'the acceptance of the information on the basis that it will be kept secret that affects the conscience of the recipient of the information'.[58] While the traditional approach would require some voluntary communication or at least acquisition of the confidential information, which was the basis of an implied agreement, the broader interpretation would impose an obligation of confidence where a reasonable man, standing in the shoes of the defendant, would have assumed such an obligation. It has been held that a duty of confidence could arise independently of a transaction or relationship between parties. Thus, an obligation was imposed on the media not to disclose the identities of two young men convicted of murder, where the media had notice and there was a real danger of serious physical injury to, or the death of those seeking the confidentiality.[59] Such a jurisdiction only applies in exceptional circumstances.[60] It has not been extended to an interim injunction preventing the publication, in a newspaper, of details of a celebrity model's new address. There was very little evidence of risk to the plaintiff's personal safety and the defendant newspaper had an interest in freedom of expression, even if the information was of a trivial nature, having regard to the extent to which it had or was about to become public, through

---

440 per Simon Brown LJ. For a full discussion of the relationship between privacy and breach of confidence in this context see Wacks, *Personal Information*, Ch. 3. See also H. Fenwick and G. Phillipson, 'Confidence and Privacy: A Re-Examination' (1996) 55 CLJ 447; N. L. Wee Loon, 'Emergence of a Right to Privacy from Within the Law of Confidence?' [1996] EIPR 307. Cf. H. W. Wilson, 'Privacy, Confidence and Press Freedom: A Study in Judicial Activism' (1990) 53 MLR 43.

[55] See *Attorney-General* v. *Guardian Newspapers (No. 2)* [1990] 1 AC 109, 176.
[56] *Coco* v. *A. N. Clark Engineers Ltd* [1969] RPC 41, 47.   [57] *Ibid.*, 48.
[58] *Stephens* v. *Avery* [1988] 2 WLR 1280, 1286 per Browne-Wilkinson VC (obiter).
[59] *Venables* v. *News Group Newspapers Ltd* [2001] WLR 1038, 1065 per Butler-Sloss P.
[60] *Ibid.*

Privacy interests in English law

previous publicity and the fact that the plaintiff lived in a busy and populous town.[61]

While the duty of confidence can cover situations where information is unwittingly disclosed, whether by accident or mistake,[62] there is arguably no reason, in principle, why it should not cover surreptitiously obtained information.[63] Thus, the publication of surreptitiously obtained photographs of a film set[64] and a photographic shoot[65] have been restrained on the basis of breach of confidence although, on the facts, the photographers might be said to have been subject to an implied obligation of confidence. Both occasions were to be regarded as private in that photography was restricted, to varying degrees; although the photographers were not trespassing and their presence was tolerated, the signs on the film set[66] and the security measures in place once the photographic shoot had started[67] would make it clear that photography was not permitted. The gravamen of the complaints in these cases would seem to be the loss of commercial exclusivity relating to the marketing of publicity photographs for a film and album, respectively: damage to essentially economic interests. It has also been remarked, obiter, that telephoto photography, and subsequent disclosure, of a person engaged in a private act would be as much a breach of confidence as if a private letter or diary had been found or stolen and subsequently published. In such a case, it has been suggested, obiter, that although the cause of action would be breach of confidence, 'the law would protect what might reasonably be called a right of privacy'.[68]

Doubts have been expressed as to whether such an approach is, in general, valid, on the basis that it involves the use of a cause of action 'to purposes quite alien to [its] original object'.[69] Nonetheless, it reflects the incremental way in which the law has developed in other fields.[70] This is

---

[61] *Mills* v. *News Group Newspapers Ltd* [2001] EMLR 957, 969. See also *B* v. *H Bauer Publishing Ltd* [2002] EMLR 145 (information that plaintiff had been charged with and acquitted of rape not inherently confidential or of a personal or private nature).

[62] See *Attorney-General* v. *Guardian Newspapers (No. 2)* [1990] 1 AC 109, 281 *per* Lord Goff (obiter).

[63] See R. G. Toulson and C. M. Phipps, *Confidentiality* (London, 1996), 103. Cf. Law Commission, Report No. 110, 'Breach of Confidence', Cmnd 8388 (1981).

[64] *Shelley Films Ltd* v. *Rex Features Ltd* [1994] EMLR 134, 144–50.

[65] *Creation Records Ltd* v. *News Group Newspapers Ltd* [1997] EMLR 444, 451–5.

[66] *Shelley Films Ltd* v. *Rex Features Ltd* [1994] EMLR 134, 148–50.

[67] *Creation Records Ltd* v. *News Group Newspapers Ltd* [1997] EMLR 444, 455.

[68] *Hellewell* v. *Chief Constable of Derbyshire* [1995] 1 WLR 804, 807 *per* Laws J.

[69] B. Neill, 'Privacy: A Challenge for the Next Century' in B. S. Markesinis (ed.) *Protecting Privacy* (Oxford, 1999), 1, 10.

[70] Bingham, 'Should There Be a Law to Protect Rights of Personal Privacy?', 461. See, also, D. Eady, 'Opinion: A Statutory Right to Privacy?' [1996] EHRLR 243, 246.

210 The commercial appropriation of personality

perhaps why such an approach has found increasing judicial support as the English courts have begun to contemplate a new right of privacy in the wake of the Human Rights Act 1998.[71] This is likely to be an intermediate step, where breach of confidence is used as an aid to the development of a new cause of action. It is likely that the question of the validity of a free-standing cause of action for invasion of privacy will exercise the courts for some time before the conflicts between the different interests that may be protected within such a cause of action become apparent. In cases of appropriation of personality, the central problem will lie, as the experience in the United States illustrates, in reconciling the economic and dignitary aspects within a claim for invasion of privacy.

Some early indicators can be seen in the decision of the Court of Appeal in *Douglas* v. *Hello! Ltd.*[72] The plaintiff actors sought an injunction to restrain the defendants from publishing, in their magazine, photographs of their wedding. The plaintiffs had sold exclusive rights to the publication of the photographs to a rival magazine for a substantial sum of money. A number of causes of action were argued. The claim in malicious falsehood was dismissed on the basis that the defendants' statement that the photographs were 'exclusive' photographs was not one which a jury might regard as being false, either expressly or by implication, given the frequency with which newspapers and magazines claimed exclusivity in respect of their articles. Interference with contractual relations was not made out since there was no evidence that the defendants had instigated or had been involved in the taking of the illicit photographs and there was insufficient evidence that the defendants had used unlawful means to interfere with the existing contractual relations.[73]

The main focus was on the action for breach of confidence. Considerable efforts had been made to inform the guests and staff present at the reception that the occasion had characteristics of confidentiality: 'people were being trusted to participate in this private occasion, in whatever role, on the strict understanding that they might not take photographic images of what they saw'. As such, the Court held, it would certainly be arguable, if the appropriate facts could be established at trial, that the unauthorised photographs could constitute confidential information.[74] According to Brooke LJ it was 'well settled . . . that equity may intervene to prevent the publication of photographic images taken in breach of an obligation of confidence' if 'on some private occasion the prospective claimants make it clear, expressly or impliedly, that no photographic images are to be taken of them'. In such circumstances, all persons present would be bound by the obligation of confidence created by their knowledge (or imputed

---

[71] *Douglas* v. *Hello! Ltd* [2001] 2 WLR 992, 1036 *per* Keene, 1025 *per* Sedley LJ.
[72] [2001] 2 WLR 992.   [73] *Ibid.*,1033.   [74] *Ibid.*, 1008.

Privacy interests in English law   211

knowledge) of this restriction. However, it was possible that the photographs had been taken by an intruder, with whom no relationship of trust or confidence had been established. Therefore, the court went on to consider the possibility of a claim for invasion of privacy, even though, for other reasons, the balance of convenience, on the interlocutory application, favoured the defendants.[75] The discussion of privacy was influenced by the provisions of the Human Rights Act 1998, and the extent to which English law's traditional casuistic approach will be abandoned in favour of a more principled approach remains to be seen. The early authorities are discussed in the text below following a more general consideration of the impact of the European Convention on Human Rights (ECHR).

The privacy jurisprudence of the ECHR and commercial exploitation of personality

The impetus for the European Convention on Human Rights, as is well known, lay in the desire to ensure peace in Europe and secure fundamental human rights beyond the domestic jurisdiction of States, and applicable as against individual States, following the atrocities committed during the Second World War.[76] The jurisprudence of Art. 8 of the European Convention,[77] which protects a somewhat disparate range of rights,[78] has been mainly concerned with state intrusion into an individual's private and family life (construed disjunctively).[79] While the notion of 'private life' has not been defined exhaustively, it has not been restricted to an 'inner circle' where an individual may live his life as he chooses to the exclusion of the outside world. The notion has been interpreted broadly as

---

[75] *Ibid.*

[76] See, generally, H. J. Steiner and P. Alston, *International Human Rights in Context*, 2nd edn (Oxford, 2000), 786 et seq.; F. G. Jacobs and R. C. A. White, *The European Convention on Human Rights*, 2nd edn (Oxford, 1996), Ch. 1.

[77] Article 8 provides that:
(1) Everyone has the right to respect for his private and family life, his home and his correspondence.
(2) There shall be no interference by a public authority with the exercise of this right except such as is in accordance with the law and is necessary in a democratic society in the interests of national security, public safety or the economic well-being of the country, for the prevention of disorder or crime, for the protection of health or morals, or for the protection of the rights and freedoms of others.

[78] See, generally, Jacobs and White, *European Convention*, Ch. 10; C. Warbrick, 'The Structure of Article 8' [1998] EHRLR 32; D. Feldman, 'The Developing Scope of Article 8 of the European Convention on Human Rights' [1997] EHRLR 265; L. G. Loucaides, 'Personality and Privacy Under the European Convention on Human Rights' (1990) 61 BYBIL 175; J. Liddy, 'Article 8: The Pace of Change' (2000) 51 NILQ 397.

[79] See J. E. S. Fawcett, *The Application of the European Convention on Human Rights* (Oxford, 1987), 211.

212   The commercial appropriation of personality

embracing an individual's right to establish and develop relationships with others 'for the development and fulfilment of one's own personality',[80] and also as potentially covering activities of a professional or business nature, since they provide a significant opportunity to develop relationships with the outside world.[81] Thus, 'private life' has been held to include an individual's physical and moral integrity,[82] aspects of personal sexuality[83] and personal or private space.[84] It also embraces an individual's personal identity, such as the right to choose his own name,[85] and protection from activities such as surveillance and the holding of personal information by government authorities.[86]

Cases involving the unauthorised use of individuals' photographs have usually involved the taking and use of photographs by public authorities such as the police.[87] The Commission generally applies a two-stage test, examining, first, whether the photographs were obtained in a manner which involved an invasion of privacy and whether they related to a public or private incident and, second, the purpose for which the photographs were taken and subsequently used.[88] Thus, for example, there was no infringement of privacy where an applicant was photographed against her will while under arrest and during detention following a demonstration, due to the lack of intrusion and the public nature of the events. Moreover, the Commission considered it relevant that the photographs had been taken to allow future identification.[89] Thus, under Article 8(1), 'in determining whether a positive obligation exists, a fair balance must be struck between the general interest of the community and the interests of the individual'.[90] Even if an invasion of privacy is established, such an interference may be justified by the exceptions in Art 8., para 2.[91] For

[80] *X* v. *Iceland* (1976) 5 DR 86 (keeping of a dog not within the sphere of private life).
[81] *Niemietz* v. *Germany* (1993) 16 EHRR 97, 111 (search of business premises).
[82] *Costello-Roberts* v. *United Kingdom* (1995) 19 EHRR 112, 134.
[83] See, e.g., *Dudgeon* v. *United Kingdom* (1982) 4 EHRR 149 (regulation of homosexual relationships).
[84] See, e.g., *Chappell* v. *United Kingdom* (1990) 12 EHRR 1 (search order).
[85] See, e.g., *Burghartz* v. *Switzerland* (1994) 18 EHRR 101 (assumption of wife's family name by husband).
[86] See, e.g., *Malone* v. *United Kingdom* (1985) 7 EHRR 14.
[87] Cf. L. Potvin, 'Protection Against the Use of One's Likeness in Quebec Civil Law, Canadian Common Law and Constitutional Law (Part II)' (1997) 11 IPJ 295, examining the protection against, for example, photographing and surveillance of police suspects under the Canadian Charter of Rights and Freedoms.
[88] See S. H. Naismith, 'Photographs, Privacy and Freedom of Expression' [1996] EHRLR 150, 151.
[89] *X* v. *United Kingdom*, Application No. 5877/72, and see Naismith, 'Photographs and Privacy', 152.
[90] *Cossey* v. *United Kingdom* (1990) 13 EHRR 622, 639, and see, generally, R. Clayton and H. Tomlinson, *The Law of Human Rights* (Oxford, 2000), 821.
[91] See note 77 above.

Privacy interests in English law

example, photographs taken by the police may readily be justified on the basis of prevention of disorder or crime.[92]

Although the primary object of Art. 8 is to protect the individual against arbitrary interference by public authorities, it is well established that, beyond the primarily negative obligation, States have positive obligations under Art. 8 to protect private and family life, even in the sphere of private relations between individuals. State bodies are by no means the only infringers of privacy and a significant amount of such infringing action is undertaken by private bodies such as the press. Nevertheless, it remains unclear to what extent they can be brought within the scope of the Convention.[93] The margin of appreciation doctrine leaves the task of securing Convention rights and liberties to the legislature and courts of each Contracting State and demands that all domestic remedies should be exhausted.[94] Where doubt exists as to the effectiveness of the remedy, it must be tried.[95] In a case in which an applicant seeks to establish a positive obligation on the part of the state to provide a remedy where the actions of a non-state private party are concerned and where there is a potential conflict with other Convention rights, the European Court of Human Rights will usually allow a wide margin of appreciation.[96]

In *Winer* v. *United Kingdom* the applicant complained that there was no remedy in respect of true statements which, infringing his right of privacy, fell outside the scope of defamation. The Commission held that while the state could have positive obligations, the existing remedies, particularly the tort of defamation, provided sufficient protection against invasions of privacy and noted the Younger Committee's conclusions that a system of specific remedies for specific wrongs constituted adequate protection.[97] Such an approach is arguably unsatisfactory in that it fails to draw an appropriate distinction between interests in privacy and personal reputation.[98] In *Spencer (Earl and Countess)* v. *United Kingdom* the Commission dismissed the applicants' claim that the United Kingdom had failed to fulfil its obligations under Art. 8, where newspapers had published photographs (taken with a telephoto lens) of the second applicant recovering in a private clinic, accompanied by personal information

[92] See, e.g., *Murray* v. *United Kingdom* (1995) 19 EHRR 193 (taking and retention of photographs following arrest not a violation of Art. 8).
[93] See, generally, Jacobs and White, *European Convention*, 174.
[94] See *Handyside* v. *United Kingdom* (1979–80) 1 EHRR 737, and see, generally, Clayton and Tomlinson, *Human Rights*, 273.
[95] Jacobs and White, *European Convention*, 357.
[96] G. Phillipson and H. Fenwick, 'Breach of Confidence as a Privacy Remedy in the Human Rights Act Era' (2000) 63 MLR 665.
[97] (1986) 48 DR 154, 159 and 170.
[98] Phillipson and Fenwick, 'Breach of Confidence as a Privacy Remedy', 665, and see, further, Chapter 9 below.

214   The commercial appropriation of personality

concerning her illness and marriage and details of the personal affairs of the first applicant.[99] It was held that the applicants had not exhausted their domestic remedies, particularly a breach of confidence action against the newspapers.[100] The interpretation of the law of confidence was somewhat broad. While the notion of breach of confidence could conceivably apply, on the facts, to the disclosure of confidential information regarding the applicants by their former friends, it would be more difficult to apply to the second applicant's complaint regarding the taking and publication of photographs. It is not altogether clear that the English authorities which were relied on justified such a proposition,[101] although subsequent decisions have adopted a flexible approach.[102]

Towards a general right of privacy

The 'horizontal' effect of the Human Rights Act 1998

A distinction is commonly drawn between the vertical and horizontal effect of the Human Rights Act 1998 (HRA), with various refinements and intermediate possibilities. The wording of the HRA[103] and parliamentary statements[104] suggest that it is only intended to bind public authorities. Nevertheless, it is tolerably clear that the HRA is not limited to a vertical effect, concerning disputes between individual citizens and public authorities. This view is supported by the express inclusion of courts and tribunals within the definition of public authorities: as such, they are bound to take Convention standards into account in deciding a dispute between private individuals.[105] It is particularly noteworthy that

---

[99] Successful complaints were made to the Press Complaints Commission in relation to the articles in various newspapers: (1998) 25 EHRR CD 105, 107.

[100] *Ibid.*, 112.

[101] *Ibid.*, 115–17, relying on obiter dicta in *Hellewell* v. *Chief Constable of Derbyshire* [1995] 1 WLR 804 and the decision in *Shelley Films Ltd* v. *Rex Features Ltd* [1994] EMLR 134.

[102] See *Douglas* v. *Hello! Ltd*, note 71 above.   [103] Human Rights Act 1998, s. 6(1).

[104] *Hansard, Sixth Series*, HC, vol. 582, cols. 1231–2, 3 November 1997: '[w]e decided first of all that a provision of this kind should apply only to public authorities . . . and not to private individuals. The Convention has its origins in a desire to protect people from the misuse of power by the state, rather than from the actions of private individuals' (Lord Irvine LC); *Hansard, Sixth Series*, HC, vol. 314, col. 406, 17 June 1998: 'we decided that Convention rights should be available in proceedings involving what might be very broadly described as "the state", but that they would not be directly justiciable in actions between private individuals' (Mr Jack Straw).

[105] See also *Hansard, Sixth Series*, HL, vol. 583, col. 783, 24 November 1997: 'it is right as a matter of principle for the courts to have the duty of acting compatibly with the Convention, not only in cases involving public authorities, but also in developing the common law in deciding cases between individuals' (Lord Irvine LC). Cf. R. Buxton, 'The Human Rights Act and Private Law' (2000) 116 LQR 48, 58–9, cautioning against over-reliance on such parliamentary statements.

Privacy interests in English law   215

an amendment seeking to exclude the courts from the definition of a public authority, where the parties to a dispute did not include a public authority, was rejected. This was put forward expressly to forestall the development of a common law right of privacy.[106] The precise extent of the horizontal effect is subject to a range of intermediate possibilities, discussed at length elsewhere and only summarised here. Full, or direct, horizontal effect would require a court to give judgment in a way which is compatible with Convention rights in any case, whether it be a claim against a public authority or a claim between private individuals, subject to the limitation that a clear statute must prevail.[107] The balance of authority is against such a view.[108] The HRA does not directly incorporate the Convention rights by declaring expressly that they can be enjoyed by any person. Thus there is no cause of action for breach of Convention rights.[109] Moreover, a right cannot be based on the right of appeal against the decision of a court:[110] there must be something on which to ground an appeal.[111]

Experience from other jurisdictions facing a similar problem is illuminating,[112] although 'there is no universal answer to the problem of vertical or horizontal application of a bill of rights',[113] and caution should be exercised in drawing parallels with other jurisdictions with very different rights-based charters.[114] The Canadian Charter of Rights and Freedoms does not apply in a dispute between two private litigants relying on the common law, where no act of government is involved, since private parties do not owe each other constitutional duties,[115] although the courts 'ought to apply and develop the principles of the common

---

[106] *Hansard, Sixth Series*, HL, vol. 583, col. 771, 24 November 1997, Amendment no. 32 (Lord Wakeham). See, generally, R. Singh, 'Privacy and the Media: The Impact of the Human Rights Bill' in Markesinis (ed.) *Protecting Privacy*, 184.

[107] W. Wade, 'Human Rights and the Judiciary' [1998] EHRLR 520, 523–6; 'Horizons of Horizontality' (2000) 116 LQR 217, 218.

[108] See S. Grosz, J. Beatson and P. Duffy, *Human Rights: The 1998 Act and the European Convention* (London, 2000), 89; I. Leigh, 'Horizontal Rights, the Human Rights Act and Privacy: Lessons From the Commonwealth' (1999) 48 ICLQ 57, 83–5; Buxton, 'Human Rights Act and Private Law', 55; S. Kendtridge, 'Lessons from South Africa' in B. S. Markesinis (ed.) *The Impact of the Human Rights Bill on English Law* (Oxford, 1998), 25, 28.

[109] G. Phillipson, 'The Human Rights Act, "Horizontal Effect" and the Common Law: A Bang or a Whimper?' (1999) 62 MLR 824, 835, citing the parliamentary debates.

[110] HRA 1998, s. 9(1).

[111] Buxton, 'Human Rights Act and Private Law', 57.

[112] See, generally, Leigh, 'Horizontal Rights', 62–71; M. Hunt, 'The "Horizontal Effect" of the Human Rights Act' [1998] PL 423.

[113] *Du Plessis* v. *De Klerk* 1996 (3) SA 850, 871 *per* Kentridge AJ.

[114] *Douglas* v. *Hello! Ltd* [2001] 2 WLR 992, 1013 *per* Brooke LJ.

[115] *Hill* v. *Church of Scientology of Toronto* (1995) 126 DLR 129, 157 *per* Cory J.

216   The commercial appropriation of personality

law in a manner consistent with the fundamental values enshrined in the Constitution'.[116] The importance of the distinction between Charter *rights* and Charter *values* has been stressed: 'the Charter will "apply" to the common law only to the extent that the common law is found to be inconsistent with Charter values'.[117] Moreover, while the courts have traditionally been cautious regarding the extent to which they will amend the common law, a similar caution should apply in taking Charter values into account, leaving far-reaching changes of the common law to the legislature.[118] Similarly, in South Africa it has been held that the Bill of Rights contained in Chapter 3 of the Interim Constitution does not have a 'general direct horizontal application, but that it may and should have an influence on the development of the common law as it governs relationships between individuals'.[119] The South African approach drew, in part, on the German experience, where the rights of individuals entrenched in the Basic Law (constitution) are directly enforceable against the state.[120] In disputes between private individuals, such rights are not directly enforceable, but apply indirectly, by influencing rather than governing or overriding private law norms.[121]

Thus, although the HRA will not have direct horizontal effect, it is arguable that it will have indirect horizontal effect in claims between individuals in that existing law has to be interpreted, applied and, if necessary, developed to achieve compatibility with the Convention. While some measure of horizontal effect might be achieved through the interpretation of statutes applicable between private individuals, where there is no cause of action, the HRA does not provide a private individual with a cause of action against another private individual for a breach of his Convention rights.[122] However, the HRA does arguably impose a duty on the courts to develop the common law in a way which ensures compatibility with the Convention. Thus, an effective remedy in a particular case

---

[116] *Retail, Wholesale & Department Store Union, Local 580* v. *Dolphin Delivery Ltd* (1987) 33 DLR (4th) 174, 198 *per* McIntyre J.

[117] *Hill* v. *Church of Scientology of Toronto* (1995) 126 DLR 129, 157 *per* Cory J.

[118] *Ibid.*

[119] *Du Plessis* v. *De Klerk* 1996 (3) SA 850, 887 *per* Kentridge AJ. Cf. Kriegler J (*ibid.*, 915), dissenting, arguing that the Bill of Rights did govern 'all law, including that applicable to private relationships'. Thus, 'the whole gamut of private relationships is left undisturbed. But the State, as the maker of the laws, the administrator of laws and the interpreter and applier of the law, is bound to stay within the four corners of chapter 3.' See, generally, Hunt, 'Horizontal Effect', 432–4; Leigh, 'Horizontal Rights', 66–8.

[120] *Du Plessis* v. *De Klerk* 1996 (3) SA 850, 874–5.

[121] See, generally, B. S. Markesinis, 'Privacy, Freedom of Expression, and the Horizontal Effect of the Human Rights Bill: Lessons From Germany' (1999) 115 LQR 47, 50–1; P. E. Quint, 'Free Speech and Private Law in German Constitutional Theory' (1989) 48 Mary L Rev 247, 258–65. See, further, 230–3 below.

[122] See Hunt, 'Horizontal Effect', 438; Leigh, 'Horizontal Rights', 84–5.

Privacy interests in English law 217

might be secured 'through English law rather than round English law'.[123] The stronger version of this form of horizontal effect[124] envisages that the courts must interpret, apply and, if necessary, develop the law to achieve compatibility with the Convention.[125] A weaker form, on the other hand, denies any general duty to ensure compatibility of all private law with the Convention; rather, Convention rights will figure only as principles to which the courts must have regard.[126] Alternatively, the Act might be interpreted as prohibiting a court from acting in a way which is inconsistent with Convention rights rather than imposing a positive obligation that compels development consistent with Convention rights.[127]

A clear direction has yet to emerge, and predicting the course of development is somewhat difficult. It has been held that, while a court must have regard to the European Convention in litigation between private parties, that does not 'encompass the creation of free-standing causes of action based directly upon the articles of the Convention'.[128] In *Douglas* v. *Hello!* Sedley LJ was ready to contemplate some measure of indirect horizontal effect, holding that the claimants had a powerfully arguable case for a right of privacy which covered intrusions into the private lives of individuals. The law did not need to 'construct an artificial relationship of confidentiality between intruder and victim': it could 'recognise privacy itself as a legal principle drawn from the fundamental value of personal autonomy'.[129] According to Sedley LJ, it could be said 'with confidence that the law recognises and will appropriately protect a right of personal privacy'. This was based both on the need for equity and the common law 'to respond to an increasingly invasive social environment by affirming that everybody has a right to some private space' and on the need to give 'appropriate effect to the right to respect for private and family life' set out in Art. 8 ECHR.[130] This was not so much a legal innovation, merely a recognition, through the attaching of the privacy label, of what the courts had already protected over the years, although not in explicit privacy terms. If the move from confidentiality to privacy might

---

[123] A. Lester and D. Pannick, 'The Impact of the Human Rights Act on Private Law: The Knight's Move' (2000) 116 LQR 380, 383.

[124] Drawing on Kriegler J's dissent in *Du Plessis* v. *De Klerk* (see note 119 above).

[125] Hunt, 'Horizontal Effect', 434; Lester and Pannick, 'The Impact of the Human Rights Act on Private Law'; J. Beatson and S. Grosz, 'Horizontality: A Footnote' (2000) 116 LQR 385. Cf. Buxton, 'Human Rights Act and Private Law', 50–1; cf. Wade, 'Horizons of Horizontality', 218.

[126] Phillipson, 'Human Rights Act', 843. Cf. Buxton, 'Human Rights Act and Private Law', 59.

[127] Clayton and Tomlinson, *Human Rights*, 235.

[128] *Venables* v. *News Group Newspapers Ltd* [2001] WLR 1038, 1049 and 1075 *per* Butler-Sloss P; *Mills* v. *News Group Newspapers Ltd* [2001] EMLR 957, 967 *per* Collins J.

[129] [2001] 2 WLR 992, 1025.   [130] *Ibid.*, 1021.

218   The commercial appropriation of personality

be regarded as going beyond a modern restatement of a traditional form of protection, such a development could be seen as being consistent with the incremental change envisaged by the HRA.[131] It remains to be seen whether such an approach will find widespread judicial support, and the other members of the Court of Appeal in *Douglas* were somewhat more cautious. Keene LJ recognised that a court, as a public authority, could not act in a way which is incompatible with a Convention right, which arguably included developing the common law even where no public authority was party to the litigation. However, he regarded the question of whether this extended to creating new causes of action between private persons as more controversial.[132] Similarly, Brooke LJ refused to speculate whether recognition could be given to Convention rights by extending existing causes of action or recognising the existence of new relationships giving rise to enforceable legal rights.[133]

Of course, in any case the rights under Article 8 are not absolute. Article 8 requires private and family life to be respected by the state, as represented by the court, having regard to the full circumstances of the intrusion. On the facts in *Douglas* the intrusion 'was by uncontrolled photography for profit of a wedding which was to be the subject of controlled photography for profit': an invasion of an essentially economic interest. Consequently, the infringement of such an interest could be adequately compensated by money, through an award of damages or an account of profits, so an injunction was refused. The element of privacy which had been retained by the claimants, in the form of editorial control over the photographs, was regarded as being 'as much a commercial as a personal reservation', which could readily be translated into general damages. Sedley LJ did, however, acknowledge that there was no 'bright line between the personal and the commercial'. Commercial interests could not always be dealt with solely by an award of damages. Neither 'should it be thought that either Article 8 or our domestic law [would] never protect privacy which is being turned to commercial ends'.[134] Each case would turn on its own facts.

The balancing exercise

One of the principal objections to the development of a right of privacy has been its potentially harmful effect on freedom of expression, particularly the freedom of the press, which tended to obscure some of the

---

[131] *Ibid.*, 1026, citing Hunt, 'Horizontal Effect'.
[132] *Ibid.*, 1035 *per* Keene LJ.   [133] *Ibid.*, 1016. Cf. 1017.
[134] *Ibid.*, 1030. Cf. *Kaye* v. *Robertson* [1991] FSR 62 and note 22 above, where, somewhat ironically, a desire to make a profit was imputed to protect the plaintiff's privacy through the tort of malicious falsehood.

Privacy interests in English law 219

broader issues. The difficulty in balancing competing interests provided an enduring objection to the development of a general right of privacy,[135] although this can no longer be sustained in the era following the Human Rights Act.

The Strasbourg jurisprudence has tended to hold freedom of expression, guaranteed by Art. 10,[136] in high regard as 'one of the essential foundations of a democratic society and one of the basic conditions for its progress and for each individual's self-fulfilment'.[137] The restrictions on freedom of expression which are 'necessary in a democratic society' require the existence of a 'pressing social need'[138] and should be no greater 'than is proportionate to the legitimate aim pursued'.[139] Freedom of expression extends not only to information or ideas which are favourably received or regarded as inoffensive or as a matter of indifference, but also to those that offend, shock or disturb.[140] Although some early cases sought to give freedom of expression a preferred status over other competing interests,[141] there is no formal hierarchy of rights. When rights collide, the competing claims must be balanced in the particular circumstances of the case,[142] although the balancing exercise tends to start with a presumption in favour of freedom of expression with the exceptions being construed narrowly.[143] While great importance is attached to political expression, the principles are applied rather less vigorously in cases involving artistic and commercial expression.[144] Information of a commercial nature can be protected by Art. 10, although states enjoy a

---

[135] See note 6 above.

[136] 1. Everyone has the right to freedom of expression. This right shall include freedom to hold opinions and to receive and impart information and ideas without interference by public authority and regardless of frontiers. This Article shall not prevent States from requiring the licensing of broadcasting, television or cinema enterprises.

2. The exercise of these freedoms, since it carries with it duties and responsibilities, may be subject to such formalities, conditions, restrictions or penalties as are prescribed by law and are necessary in a democratic society, in the interests of national security, territorial integrity or public safety, for the prevention of disorder or crime, for the protection of health or morals, for the protection of the reputation or rights of others, for preventing the disclosure of information received in confidence, or for maintaining the authority and impartiality of the judiciary.

[137] See, e.g., *Nilsen and Johnsen* v. *Norway* (2000) 30 EHRR 878, 908.

[138] *Sunday Times* v. *United Kingdom* (1979–80) 2 EHRR 245, 275.

[139] See, e.g., *Derbyshire County Council* v. *Times Newspapers* [1993] AC 534, 550 *per* Lord Keith.

[140] *Handyside* v. *United Kingdom* (1979–80) 1 EHRR 737, 754; *Zana* v. *Turkey* (1999) 27 EHRR 667, 689.

[141] See, e.g., *Handyside* v. *The United Kingdom* (1979–80) 1 EHRR 737, 753, and see, generally, Clayton and Tomlinson, *Human Rights*, 1077 and the references cited.

[142] Phillipson and Fenwick, 'Breach of Confidence as a Privacy Remedy', 686.

[143] E. M. Barendt, *Freedom of Speech* (Oxford, 1985), 35.

[144] Clayton and Tomlinson, *Human Rights*, 1067.

220   The commercial appropriation of personality

wide margin of appreciation in cases involving statements made in the field of commercial competition which have been held to fall outside the 'basic nucleus protected by freedom of expression' and receive a lower level of protection than other ideas or information.[145] Thus, even the publication of truthful information may be prohibited in certain circumstances where, for example, there is an obligation to respect the privacy of others or the duty to respect the confidentiality of certain commercial information,[146] although protecting the rights and reputation of others (as required by Art. 10(2)) arguably does not equate with protecting commercial interests against well-founded criticism.[147] However, when the interests concerned are not purely commercial and involve a debate of general interest, such as public health, the extent of the margin of appreciation will be reduced.[148] Although artistic expression comes within the scope of Art. 10, on the basis that it affords an opportunity to participate in, and exchange, cultural, political and social information and ideas, such a freedom can only be exercised with due regard to the duties and responsibilities imposed by Art. 10(2).[149]

The English courts emphasised the importance of freedom of expression long before the enactment of the Human Rights Act 1998.[150] In *Reynolds* v. *Times Newspapers Ltd* the House of Lords stressed that freedom of expression is a basic fundamental right,[151] and Lord Steyn went so far as to regard freedom of expression as the rule and the regulation of such expression as the exception requiring justification, underpinned by a pressing social need.[152] Section 12 of the Act was introduced specifically to meet concerns about press freedom[153] and 'applies if a court is considering whether to grant any relief which, if granted, might affect

[145] *Markt Intern and Beermann* v. *Germany* (1990) 12 EHRR 161, 173; *Jacubowski* v. *Germany* (1995) 19 EHRR 64, 77.

[146] *Markt Intern and Beermann* v. *Germany* (1990) 12 EHRR 161, 175 (publication of customer's expressions of dissatisfaction by company not justified by Art. 10).

[147] J. Coppel, *The Human Rights Act 1998: Enforcing the European Convention in the Domestic Courts* (Chichester, 1999), 342.

[148] *Hertel* v. *Switzerland* (1999) 28 EHRR 534, 571 (statements concerning safety of microwave ovens).

[149] *Muller* v. *Switzerland* (1991) 13 EHRR 212, 228 (display of sexually explicit artistic works).

[150] See, e.g., *Attorney-General* v. *Guardian Newspapers (No. 2)* [1990] 1 AC 109, 283 *per* Lord Goff; *Derbyshire County Council* v. *Times Newspapers* [1993] AC 534, 551 *per* Lord Keith; *R* v. *Home Secretary ex parte Simms* [2000] 2 AC 115, 126 *per* Lord Steyn. See also *Imutran Ltd* v. *Uncaged Campaigns Ltd* [2001] 2 All ER 385, 389–90 *per* Morritt VC, and the references cited.

[151] [1999] 3 WLR 1010, 1029.

[152] *Ibid.*, 1030, and see Lord Nichols at 1023; *McCartan Turkington Breen* v. *Times Newspapers Ltd* [2000] 3 WLR 1670, 1686 *per* Lord Steyn.

[153] See *Hansard, Sixth Series*, HC, vol. 315, col. 538, 2 July 1998.

Privacy interests in English law 221

the exercise of the Convention right to freedom of expression'.[154] This has been interpreted as requiring a balance to be struck between conflicting rights, on the merits, without giving additional weight to one right.[155] Regard must be had to the Strasbourg jurisprudence and the ways in which it has 'given particular weight to freedom of expression, while at the same time drawing attention to considerations which may nonetheless justify restricting that right'.[156] This does not require the court to treat freedom of speech as paramount and the requirement in section 12(4) to pay 'particular regard' to freedom of expression 'contemplates specific and separate consideration being given to this factor'.[157] Nor should this requirement be seen as bypassing long-established common law principles, since the Convention has not been incorporated directly into English law; Strasbourg jurisprudence should be used to test whether English law is consistent with the rights guaranteed by the ECHR.[158]

Two provisions are particularly relevant. According to section 12(3), no interlocutory relief which might affect the exercise of the Convention right to freedom of expression under Art. 10 is to be granted to restrain publication, unless the court is satisfied that the applicant is likely to establish that publication should not be allowed. Thus, in *Douglas* v. *Hello!* it was held that the claimants had to show more than the *American Cyanamid*[159] threshold of a serious issue to be tried. The court has to look at the merits of the case and has to be satisfied that the scales are likely to come down in the applicant's favour, which requires the court to consider how each right is to be balanced against the other. This is a matter of balancing one right against the other, on the merits, without giving additional weight to one right.[160] Further, under section 12(4), which clearly applies directly between parties in private litigation,[161] the court has to have particular regard to freedom of expression when granting relief. Where the proceedings relate to material which is claimed, or which appears to the court, to be journalistic, literary or artistic material (or to conduct connected

---

[154] Section 12(1). See, generally, Grosz, Beatson and Duffy, *Human Rights*, 99; Clayton and Tomlinson, *Human Rights*, 1095.
[155] *Douglas* v. *Hello! Ltd* [2001] 2 WLR 992, 1032 *per* Keene LJ.
[156] *Ashdown* v. *Telegraph Group Ltd* [2001] 3 WLR 1368, 1378.
[157] *Imutran Ltd* v. *Uncaged Campaigns Ltd* [2001] 2 All ER 385, 389–90 *per* Morritt VC; *Mills* v. *News Group Newspapers Ltd* [2001] EMLR 957, 970; *Harris* v. *Harris* [2001] 2 FLR 895, 933.
[158] *Branson* v. *Bower (No. 1)* (Queen's Bench Division, 21 November 2000), para. 12 *per* Eady J (affirmed, *Branson* v. *Bower (No. 1)* [2001] EMLR 800 (Court of Appeal)).
[159] *American Cyanamid Co.* v. *Ethicon Ltd* [1975] AC 396.
[160] [2001] 2 WLR 992 *per* Keene LJ, 1032.
[161] *Ibid.*, 992, 1027 *per* Sedley LJ; *Mills* v. *News Group Newspapers Ltd* [2001] EMLR 957, 965.

222   The commercial appropriation of personality

with such material), the court must consider the extent to which the material has, or is about to, become available to the public or whether it is, or would be, in the public interest for the material to be published, and must also have regard to any privacy code.

Relatively little guidance can be found in the recent English case law, although in the early cases the Convention rights have been alluded to while interpreting existing causes of action, without treating them as overriding general principles. Thus, the defences to copyright infringement have been interpreted having regard to the right to freedom of expression and the limits to that right, while stating that it 'should not normally carry with it the right to make free use of another's work'.[162] A handful of cases have required the courts to balance freedom of expression with interests in personal privacy. The early cases have involved applications for injunctions against newspapers, or publishers, rather than advertisers or merchandisers. As such, considerations of freedom of expression have weighed quite heavily against interests in privacy.

In *Douglas* v. *Hello!* reference was made to the Press Complaints Commission's Code of Practice which seeks to protect both the rights of the individual and the public's right to know.[163] According to Brooke LJ, section 12, coupled with the current wording of the relevant privacy code, meant that in any case concerning freedom of expression in a journalistic, literary or artistic context, the court is bound to pay particular regard to any breach of the rules set out in Cl. 3 of the Code, especially where none of the public interest claims set out in the Code is asserted. Thus, a newspaper which flouts the Code's provisions on privacy would be likely, in such circumstances, to have its claim to an entitlement to freedom of expression trumped by Article 10(2) considerations of privacy. According to Brooke LJ, 'unlike the court in *Kaye* v. *Robertson*, Parliament recognised that it had to acknowledge the importance of the requirement in Article 8(1) to respect private life, and it was able to do so untrammelled by any concerns that the law of confidence might not stretch to protect every aspect of private life'.[164] On the facts, section 12 of the 1998 Act and Cl. 3 of the Press Complaints Commission's Code provided the ground rules by which the competing considerations of freedom of expression and privacy could be weighed. In this respect, the first

---

[162] *Ashdown* v. *Telegraph Group Ltd* [2001] 3 WLR 1368, 1382. Cf. *O'Shea* v. *MGN Ltd and Free4internet.net Ltd* [2001] EMLR 943 (strict liability identification rule in defamation has not been extended to cover look-alike photographs on the basis that it would constitute 'an unjustifiable interference with the vital right of freedom of expression...disproportionate to the legitimate aim of protecting the reputations of "look alikes"', contrary to Article 10).

[163] See, generally, 49–50 above.

[164] *Douglas* v. *Hello! Ltd* [2001] 2 WLR 992, 1018.

Privacy interests in English law

two claimants' claim to privacy was rather weak; the wedding was not private in any normal sense, given its nature and scale.[165]

In *Mills* v. *News Group Newspapers*,[166] where a celebrity model sought to prevent publication of the address of her new home, the High Court was influenced by the relative weakness of the breach of confidence claim and the importance of countervailing factors. While the Court must have regard to the importance of freedom of expression, by virtue of section 12(4)(a)(i) where the proceedings relate to inter alia journalistic material, one of the relevant factors is the extent to which 'material has, or is about to, become available to the public', together with any relevant privacy code. The rationale of the Press Complaints Commission's Code of Practice in prohibiting the publication, in newspapers, of a celebrity's address was, according to Collins J, not simply the fact that the address might be protected information, but that celebrities might be at risk of danger to their physical safety, or might otherwise be vulnerable. The evidence of risk to the claimant was very slight and the fact that information relating to her home had already become known to the public, partly through previous publicity in the press and partly as a result of living in a busy and populous town, was a relevant factor 'both in assessing the degree to which publication should be restrained, and the impact of publication on her privacy and security'.[167] This factor distinguished the case from the earlier decision in *Venables* v. *News Group Newspapers*[168] where there was a risk of injury to, or the death of, the persons involved.

The weakness of the breach of confidence claim was also a crucial factor in *B* v. *H Bauer Publishing Ltd*.[169] The High Court struck out a claim relating to an article published by the defendants which identified the claimant as having been acquitted of a charge of rape despite compelling evidence of his guilt. This was in breach of an anonymity order intended to prevent a respondent from being identified in a criminal case where the Attorney-General is appealing on a point of law.[170] There was no evidence which would have placed the defendants under a duty of confidence, since there was nothing inherently confidential about the information concerned and it had not been imparted in circumstances which suggested an obligation of confidence, nor could it be considered to be information of a personal or private nature.[171] A broader argument, based on invasion of privacy, as guaranteed by Art. 8, was regarded as

---

[165] *Ibid.*   [166] [2001] EMLR 957, and see note 61 above.
[167] *Ibid.*, 973.   [168] See note 59 above.   [169] [2002] EMLR 145.
[170] Based on the Criminal Appeal (Reference of Points of Law) Rules 1973 (SI 1973 No. 1114).
[171] *B* v. *H Bauer Publishing Ltd* [2002] EMLR 145, 153.

224 The commercial appropriation of personality

being intimately linked with the law of confidence and, on that basis, was dismissed.[172] A 'judicially imposed law of privacy' to protect the plaintiff's anonymity and prevent further enquiry would be a 'startling restriction' on the defendants' right to freedom of expression which would have to be justified as being necessary in a democratic society by reference to Art. 10(2). Such a shift from the principle of open justice could not begin to pass such a test.[173] Finally, in *Harris* v. *Harris*,[174] injunctions in family proceedings were varied to allow the publication of the father's name and photograph, on the basis that his rights to freedom of expression justified such a publication, when balanced against the children's right to privacy. The defendant had been involved in a long-running and very public family dispute and had been in contempt of court on numerous occasions. Publication of his identity was justified by the public's right to know, underpinned by Arts. 6 and 10 of the ECHR, which were duly balanced against the children's right to privacy and respect for their private and family life, underpinned by Art. 8.[175] Stressing the liberty of the press,[176] the court held that the proper remedy was publicity for the truth. Speech, rather than enforced silence, best served to expose falsehoods and fallacies, through open discussion.[177]

Insights from Canada and Germany

Canada

The Canadian experience offers some instructive insights. As noted above, Canada has rejected a direct horizontal approach in favour of an indirect application of charter values in developing the common law.[178] It has also rejected the American approach of a constitutional rights 'hierarchy'.[179] Privacy and freedom of expression have an equal status and must be balanced accordingly.[180] For example, in *Hill* v. *Church of Scientology*[181] the Supreme Court of Canada rejected a higher standard of proof for defamation actions in cases involving public officials, since freedom of expression had to be balanced with the competing constitutional

---

[172] *Ibid.*, 156. [173] *Ibid.*, 158.
[174] [2001] 2 FLR 895. [175] *Ibid.*, 945.
[176] *Ibid.*, citing *Attorney-General* v. *Guardian Newspapers Ltd* [1987] 1 WLR 1248, 1320 *per* Lord Oliver.
[177] [2001] 2 FLR 895, 945, citing *Whitney* v. *California* (1927) 274 US 357, 377.
[178] See text accompanying note 116 above.
[179] *Dagenais* v. *CBC* [1994] 3 SCR 835, 877, cited by J. D. R. Craig and N. Nolte, 'Privacy and Free Speech in Germany and Canada: Lessons for an English Privacy Tort' [1998] EHRLR 162, 168.
[180] *Ibid.* [181] (1995) 126 DLR 129.

values of reputation and privacy. Generally, the courts will have regard to a number of factors,[182] including: the nature of the information (for example, whether it might be reasonably expected to be essentially personal or intimate or whether it relates to an event or issue of public concern); the motivation of the publisher (for example, whether it is a desire to inform or to make a profit); and the subject's reasonable expectation of privacy, depending on the subject's status and the severity of the defendant's invasion.[183]

The decision of the Canadian Supreme Court in *Aubry* v. *Éditions Vice-Versa Inc.* is of particular interest. It concerned a claim against the defendants for taking and publishing a photograph, without consent, showing the plaintiff, a seventeen-year-old girl, sitting on a step in front of a building in Montreal. The plaintiff relied on section 5 of the *Quebec Charter of Human Rights and Freedoms*,[184] which provides succinctly that '[e]very person has a right to respect for his private life'. The Quebec *Charter*, unlike the Canadian Charter, has horizontal effect, and the rights and freedoms it guarantees may be relied on by parties in private litigation.[185] Although caution should be exercised in drawing direct parallels between such a rights-based charter and the scheme under the Human Rights Act 1998,[186] it offers some interesting insights into the way in which competing interests may be balanced, bearing in mind that it is likely that a right of privacy will be developed by the courts in the wake of the Human Rights Act 1998, as outlined above.

According to the majority, the right to one's own image, which has an extrapatrimonial and a patrimonial aspect, was an element of the right to privacy under section 5 of the Quebec *Charter*. This was consistent with the Supreme Court's previous liberal interpretation of the concept of privacy, which was regarded as a guarantee of a sphere of individual autonomy for all decisions relating to choices of a fundamentally private or inherently personal nature. If the purpose of the right to privacy was to protect such a sphere of personal autonomy, it should include the ability to control the use made of an individual's image, since the right to one's

---

[182] See Craig and Nolte, 'Privacy and Free Speech', 171–2.

[183] See, e.g., *Silber* v. *BCTV* (1986) 69 BCLR 34 (SC) (no invasion of privacy where a defendant film company filmed a struggle with the plaintiff in his factory parking lot in reporting on a labour dispute concerning the plaintiff). Cf. *Valiquette* v. *The Gazette* (1992) 8 CCLT (2d) 302 (Que. SC) (invasion of privacy where newspaper disclosed that a schoolteacher was suffering from AIDS, motivated by commercial interests rather than desire to inform public), and see, further, Craig and Nolte, 'Privacy and Free Speech', where the decisions are discussed.

[184] RSQ c C-12.

[185] *Ibid.*, ss. 9.1 and 49, and see text accompanying note 115 above. See, generally, J. E. C. Brierley and R. A. Macdonald, *Quebec Civil Law* (Toronto, 1993).

[186] *Douglas* v. *Hello! Ltd* [2001] 2 WLR 992, 1013 *per* Brooke LJ.

226   The commercial appropriation of personality

image was based on individual autonomy and a person's right to control his or her personal identity.[187]

As to the balance to be struck between the right of privacy and the right of freedom of expression, guaranteed by section 3 of the Quebec *Charter*, the Court stated that an individual's right to respect for private life would have to be limited in certain circumstances where the public had an interest in knowing about certain traits of the plaintiff's personality. The balancing would depend on the nature of the information and the circumstances of the individual concerned. Certain aspects of the private life of a person engaged in public activity, or those who had achieved some degree of notoriety, could become matters of public interest. This would obviously apply to entertainers, politicians and 'those whose professional success depends on public opinion', and would also extend to previously unknown individuals who find themselves playing a high-profile role in matters 'within the public domain, such as an important trial'. The public interest would also prevail where an individual was photographed where his own unwitting conduct might place him incidentally in a photograph, such as a person in a crowd at a sporting event or in a demonstration, or where a person appears in an incidental manner in a photograph of a public place.[188]

In holding for the plaintiff, the Supreme Court rejected a distinction between 'socially useful information' and information of a primarily commercial nature, derived from the United States case law which only protects the former.[189] A photograph of an individual could be 'socially useful' in that it might illustrate a cultural, artistic or sporting theme, but that would not necessarily make its publication acceptable, the Court held, since it might infringe the right to privacy. An interpretation based on commercial purpose would be inconsistent with section 9.1 of the Quebec *Charter* requiring that regard be had, in exercising an individual's fundamental freedoms and rights, to the democratic values, public order and general well-being of other citizens. On the facts, the artistic expression of the photograph, intended to illustrate contemporary urban life, could not justify the infringement of the plaintiff's privacy it entailed. The public interest in viewing the work and the artist's interest in publishing the work were not absolute; they had to be defined by reference to competing values and, on the facts, did not outweigh the plaintiff's

---

[187] *Aubry* v. *Éditions Vice-Versa Inc.* (1998) 78 CPR (3d) 289, 306, citing *Godbout* v. *Longueuil (City)* (1997) 152 DLR (4th) 577, 632.

[188] (1998) 78 CPR (3d) 289, 308.

[189] *Ibid.*, 309, citing *Estate of Presley* v. *Russen*, 513 F Supp. 1339 (DNJ 1981) and *Current Audio Inc.* v. *RCA Corp.*, 337 NYS 2d 949 (Sup Ct 1972), and see, generally, J. T. McCarthy, *The Rights of Publicity and Privacy*, 2nd edn (New York, 2001), Ch. 8.

right to privacy.[190] The practical difficulties in obtaining the subject's consent could not justify extending a photographer's right at the expense of others.[191] Indeed, Lamer CJ drew a parallel with the obligation of diligence that the news media must meet in gathering information in order to avoid liability for defamation should their comments prove to be inaccurate.[192] A reasonable person should have been more diligent than the defendants had been, and would have taken some steps to obtain the subject's consent to being photographed.[193]

The relevant damage to the plaintiff's interests could be extrapatrimonial or patrimonial and the majority was prepared to accept that 'the commercial or promotional exploitation of an image, whether of a well-known person or a private individual [could] cause the victim material prejudice'.[194] The evidence of damage was rather limited, essentially consisting of the plaintiff's claim that people had laughed at her, although the majority of the Supreme Court was reluctant to interfere with the findings of the trial judge. The damages contemplated by the Court were much more modest than the $2,000 awarded at trial for moral damages, which were not appealed. Lamer CJ, dissenting, argued that evidence that people had laughed at the plaintiff was insufficient and there was no evidence that she had suffered prejudice through a loss of anonymity. While the unconsented dissemination of a person's image might result in damage, this had not been made out on the facts.

The German right of personality: introduction

The German experience is interesting in several ways and merits a brief excursus, from the point of view of possible patterns of development, the problems encountered in reconciling the economic and dignitary aspects of commercial exploitation of personality, and those in balancing competing interests, particularly freedom of expression.[195] Although protection for interests in personality, particularly privacy, has been secured by means of a general personality right, development has often been the result of a piecemeal incremental process, not far removed from the common law model.

While the Roman *actio injuriarum* protected a triad of interests of *corpus*, *dignitas* and *fama*,[196] the second element was conspicuously

---

[190] *Ibid.*, 310.   [191] *Ibid.*, 311.   [192] *Ibid.*   [193] *Ibid.*, 299.

[194] *Ibid.*, 313. Cf. the requirement of damage in the Ontario tort of appropriation of personality (127 above) and the right of publicity in the United States (181 above).

[195] Only a brief sketch can be included here. For a much fuller discussion, see H. Beverley-Smith, A. Ohly and A. Lucas-Schloetter, *Privacy, Property and Personality* (Cambridge, forthcoming, 2003), Ch. 4.

[196] See 141–2 above.

228   The commercial appropriation of personality

absent from the German Civil Code, the BGB, which was drawn up relatively late compared to other European codifications.[197] The provisions on delict were rather narrower than in its European counterparts and, in particular, a result of the predominant legal opinion in late nineteenth-century Germany that damages for non-pecuniary loss should not be recoverable. This reflected a reaction against the *actio injuriarum* which had come to be associated almost exclusively with insults; the award of money damages for such insult was regarded somewhat disfavourably by nineteenth-century legal opinion.[198] This stood in stark contrast to the trend to provide enhanced protection for interests in personality which was evident in the United States during the same period.[199] Although some writers proposed the idea of a general right of personality which embraced 'the social, intellectual and economic activities, opportunities and amenities which combine to form the sum total of [an individual's] experience',[200] this was not included in the BGB.[201] Thus, Art. 823(1) BGB provides that a person who wilfully or negligently injures the life, body, health, freedom, property or other right of another contrary to law is bound to compensate him for any damage arising therefrom. Such a provision did not encompass protection for reputation, since it was traditionally a matter covered by the crime of insult or slander. However, these could also give rise to damages by virtue of §823(2) BGB which provides a private law remedy for the violation of a statutory provision intended to protect the rights of others,[202] such as the offences of libel and slander under §§185–7 of the Criminal Code. Similarly, the notion of '*dignitas*' was excluded from the BGB.

Advocates of enhanced protection for rights of personality sought to base protection on the notion of 'other right' (*ein sonstiges Recht*). However, the view that such words should be construed *eiusdem generis*, by reference to rights in the nature of proprietary rights,[203] prevailed, supported

---

[197] See, generally, C. Von Bar, *The Common European Law of Torts Vol. I* (Oxford, 1998), 20; B. S. Markesinis, *The German Law of Obligations, Vol. II, The Law of Torts: A Comparative Introduction*, 3rd edn (Oxford, 1997), 21; K. Zweigert and H. Kötz, *An Introduction to Comparative Law*, 3rd edn (Oxford, 1998), Ch. 11.

[198] See P. R. Handford, 'Moral Damage in Germany' (1978) 27 ICLQ 849, 855.

[199] See 146–51 above.

[200] See R. Zimmermann, *The Law of Obligations* (Oxford, 1996), 1083, n. 256 and the references cited.

[201] See Handford, 'Moral Damage', 856; Von Bar, *European Law of Torts*, 26.

[202] See, generally, Markesinis, *German Law of Obligations: Torts*, 890–4.

[203] Cf. the early United States case law which sought to deny the existence of a right of privacy on the basis that it was not a right akin to property, in particular, *Roberson v. Rochester Folding Box Co.*, 171 NY 538 (1902) (151–3 above).

Privacy interests in English law

by the fact that specific rights are dealt with elsewhere in the BGB.[204] Thus, in the absence of anything resembling a general right of personality, German courts in the late nineteenth and early twentieth centuries dealt with injuries to interests in personality in an essentially casuistic manner. For example, the publication of photographs of Bismarck on his deathbed was restrained through an order for destruction of the negatives at his relatives' suit, on the basis that there had been a trespass to property in obtaining the photographs.[205]

The public outrage which resulted from the case led to specific provisions being introduced into the Kunsturhebergesetz (KUG) (Artistic Copyright Act) of 1907. Thus, the Kunsturhebergesetz provides that portraits may only be distributed or publicly exhibited with the consent of the portrayed person.[206] Where there is doubt, consent is deemed to have been given if the person portrayed received remuneration. Furthermore, after the death of the portrayed person the consent of his or her relatives (the surviving partner of a marriage, children or parents) is required.[207] Certain exceptions apply to this general rule, whereby portraits may be distributed or publicly displayed without consent in the case of pictures: in the realm of contemporary history; depicting a person incidentally in a landscape or other location; featuring assemblies, processions or other similar events; which have not been produced under a commission but whose distribution or display would be in the higher interests of art. Consent is not, however, effective where distribution and display infringe the legitimate interests of the subject or the next of kin.[208] Protection for other aspects of personality, such as an individual's name, is provided by §12 BGB (the German Civil Code). Thus, if the right to the use of a name by the person entitled to it is challenged by a third party or if the interests of a person entitled to use a name are injured by the unauthorised use of another, the person entitled to use the name has the right to restrain such unauthorised use by another. However, the mere mention of a name does not give rise to liability in the absence of confusion regarding the identity

---

[204] H. C. Gutteridge, 'The Comparative Law of the Right to Privacy I' (1931) 47 LQR 203, 206.

[205] RG 28.12.1899, RGZ 45, 170. See H. Stoll, 'The General Right to Personality in German Law: An Outline of its Development and Present Significance' in Markesinis (ed.) *Protecting Privacy*, 30; Zweigert and Kötz, *An Introduction to Comparative Law*, 688.

[206] See, generally, A. Vahrenwald, 'Photographs and Privacy in Germany' [1994] Ent LR 205; C. Krüger, 'Right of Privacy, Right of Personality and Commercial Advertising' (1982) 13 IIC 183; S. Bergmann, 'Publicity Rights In the United States and Germany: A Comparative Analysis' (1999) 19 LoyLA Ent LJ 479.

[207] KUG 1907, s. 22.   [208] KUG 1907, s. 23.

230   The commercial appropriation of personality

of the person named and the law does not recognise a claim to remain anonymous.

The development of the right of personality

The statutory provisions are considered in detail elsewhere[209] and, for present purposes, the interest lies in the way in which the gaps left by the two specific provisions on the right to one's image and right to one's name have been filled by applying the more general right of personality, which developed largely as a result of judicial initiative and provides an interesting illustration of the influence of constitutional values in creating private law rights. Following the Nazi regime's extreme violation of fundamental human rights, the Basic Law (*Grundgesetz*) or Constitution of Bonn (1949) was adopted to entrench the most basic individual rights. Most relevant, for the present discussion, Art. 1 provides that 'the dignity of man shall be inviolable. To respect it shall be the duty of all state authority', while Art. 2(1) provides that '[e]veryone has the right to the free development of his personality, in so far as he does not violate the rights of others or offend against the constitutional order or the moral code'. Although constitutional provisions do not apply directly in disputes between private individuals, by virtue of the doctrine of 'Drittwirkung' or 'indirect effect' the German courts have been able to interpret the civil law in accordance with the values embodied in the Constitution.[210]

In the first major case, the *Schacht* decision,[211] the defendants were held to have infringed the plaintiff's 'general right of personality' created by Arts. 1 and 2 of the Basic Law. The plaintiff, attorney to prominent financier Hjalmar Schacht, had sent a letter, under instructions, requesting corrections to the defendant's newspaper article critical of Schacht's national socialist past. The letter was published under the heading 'letters from readers', giving the misleading impression that the plaintiff was offering his opinion in his personal capacity rather than under instructions, in particular by omitting passages which made it clear that the plaintiff was seeking a correction under the Press Law. The Court of Appeal, the Oberlandesgericht, rejected the claim on the basis that personality could not be protected independently of copyright in respect of publications of letters, since the law did not provide any positive statutory provisions on

---

[209] See the references cited in note 206 above.
[210] See, generally, B. S. Markesinis and S. Enchelmaier, 'The Applicability of Human Rights as Between Individuals Under German Constitutional Law' in B. S. Markesinis (ed.) *Protecting Privacy*; Markesinis 'Privacy, Freedom of Expression, and Horizontal Effect'. Cf. 214 above.
[211] BGHZ 13, 334 (1954) (translated in Markesinis, *German Law of Obligations: Torts*, 376).

Privacy interests in English law

a general personality right. However, drawing on the Basic Law's recognition of the right of an individual to have his dignity respected and to the free development of his personality, the highest civil appeal court, the Bundesgerischtshof, reasoned that a general personality right must be regarded as a constitutionally guaranteed fundamental right. Since every expression of a definite thought emanated from the author's personality or will, the Court reasoned, only the author was entitled to decide whether and in what form his writing should be communicated to the public.[212] A modified reproduction infringed the personality rights of the author, since such unauthorised alterations could create a false impression in the minds of others. On its face, this is an interest which common law systems would regard as an interest in reputation, protected by the torts of defamation and, in the United States, the false light branch of the privacy tort,[213] although here it was cast in the much broader terms of a general personality right.

As Stoll notes, the Court could have proceeded on a rather narrower basis than the sweeping new personality right, for example by recognising the right to reply under the Press Law as a private law remedy which most Federal States now allow by civil action, whereas at the time it was only enforceable by criminal sanction.[214] Moreover, it was somewhat strange that the publication of a letter which was written by the plaintiff under instructions, on another person's behalf, should be detrimental to the plaintiff's own personality. What is most significant, particularly in view of the foregoing discussion, is that the Bundesgerichtshof drew on constitutional values in recognising a general private law right to personality.[215]

The existence of the general right to personality was affirmed in subsequent cases. For example, in the *Dahlke* case the BGH held that the unconsented publication of the photograph of a well-known actor, Paul Dahlke, in an advertisement for motor scooters infringed his right to personality, although the decision rested primarily on a breach of §22 KUG (Artistic Copyright Act) for which damages were awarded on the basis of the appropriate licence fee, rather than damages for the injury to personality as such.[216] Subsequently, in the Horse Rider case[217] the court

---

[212] Cf. S. Warren and L. Brandeis, 'The Right to Privacy' (1890) 4 HarvLRev 193, 199, and see 146–50 above.
[213] See, further, 261–5 below.
[214] Stoll, 'The General Right to Personality', 33.
[215] See, further, Markesinis, 'Privacy, Freedom of Expression and Horizontal Effect', 49 et seq.; Craig and Nolte, 'Privacy and Free Speech', 172 et seq.
[216] BGHZ 20, 345 (1956); and see Handford, 'Moral Damage', 868. See also BGHZ 15, 249 (1954) (unauthorised publication of Cosima Wagner's private letters, although claim failed on facts).
[217] BGHZ 26, 349; BGH GRUR 1958, 408 (1958) (*Herrenreiter*) (translated in Markesinis, *German Law of Obligations: Torts*, 380).

232   The commercial appropriation of personality

awarded damages for immaterial loss even though such damages were excluded by the Civil Code on the basis that they were not expressly provided for by §§253 and 847. This decision was somewhat more revolutionary than would at first appear to a common lawyer's eyes. The plaintiff, a co-owner of a brewery and an amateur, or gentleman, showjumper, brought an action against the defendants who had used a picture of the plaintiff, obtained through a third party advertising agency, in an advertisement for their pharmaceutical preparation reputed to increase sexual potency. The Bundesgerichtshof rejected the notion of a fictitious licence agreement which the plaintiff might have charged, since there was no real pecuniary loss at all, and since the notion of the fee that a person of the plaintiff's social standing would have demanded was artificial. Similarly, a claim based on unjust enrichment was precluded since, in the absence of pecuniary disadvantage to the plaintiff, there was no pecuniary shift of the kind envisaged by §812 BGB. The award was interpreted as a reflection of the satisfaction due to the plaintiff for the disparagement of his personality, making him the object of ridicule and humiliation, as protected by Arts. 1 and 2 of the Constitution and §22 of the Artistic Copyright Act, rather than economic loss as conventionally understood. The concept of human personality was regarded as one of the basic supra-legal values directly concerned with protecting the inner realm and the self-determination of the individual, infringement of which gave rise to immaterial damage, expressed in a degradation of the personality. Similarly, the protection afforded by §22, although pre-dating the Constitution, was interpreted as resting on the fundamental principle of an individual's freedom in his private life, of which the outward manifestation or appearance formed an essential part. The unauthorised publication of an individual's photograph by a third party thus deprived the individual of his freedom in deciding whether and by what means his interest in his own individual sphere should be surrendered.

Proceeding by analogy, the court extended the provisions of §847 BGB, which provides equitable compensation for non-pecuniary loss in cases of deprivation of liberty or freedom, which was interpreted to cover any attack on the free and undisturbed exercise of the will. The effective legal protection of the personality offered by the Constitution could only be attained by including it within the injuries mentioned in §847 and extending it to the right to use one's own portrait. In this respect, the decision in the previous *Dahlke* case,[218] which held that immaterial damage could not give rise to a claim for money damages in the absence of an express legal provision, was distinguished, since the facts in that case disclosed

[218] BGHZ 20, 345 (1956), 352.

Privacy interests in English law 233

pecuniary damage which could be estimated on the basis of a licence fee.[219]

In 1959 an attempt was made (the Draft Law) to amend the Civil Code, the BGB, to include the right to personality expressly. This attempt failed, partly due to the objections of the press, which viewed such a measure as a restriction on free speech, an argument with an obvious resonance for the debate in the United Kingdom,[220] although in Germany the courts were able to fashion a new law to fill what was deemed to be an obvious legislative gap.[221] This creative approach, which had been subjected to criticism in some quarters, received the approval of the Constitutional Court in the *Soraya* case, concerning a fabricated interview rather than commercial appropriation.[222] Since the legislature had not included such a right in §847 BGB it was legitimate for the courts to develop the law in a creative manner.[223]

Scope of the German right of personality

It was subsequently held that the individual's right to personality (*Personlichkeit*) survived the death of an individual, so that an individual's relatives could prevent the publication of a novel which distorted the real life of an individual.[224] Thus injuries to personality, honour or reputation remain actionable following the subject's death. For example, the descendants of a celebrated scientist expert in the field of fresh cell therapy, Professor Niehans, were able to prevent the defendants from using his name in advertisements for cosmetics, basing their case on an invasion of the general right to personality deriving from Art. 1(1) of the Constitution, which did not end on the death of the individual. The advertisement, it was held, would convey the misleading impression that Professor Niehans had applied his scientific experience in the field of cosmetics,

---

[219] See also BGHZ 35, 363 (1961); BGH GRUR 1961, 105 (1961) (*Ginsengwurzel*) (translated in Markesinis, *German Law of Obligations: Torts*, 386), where the plaintiff professor of international and ecclesiastical law succeeded in an action against the defendant manufacturers of tonic containing ginseng, on the basis that using his purported scientific authority in advertising (in fact his connection with ginseng was extremely tenuous) unlawfully infringed his personality right as guaranteed by §823 I BGB, making him an object of ridicule and lessening his scholarly reputation. The defendant's disregard of the plaintiff's rights of personality in promoting its commercial product justified an award of DM 10,000 satisfaction.

[220] See 238–41 below.

[221] J. A. Lehman, 'The Right to Privacy in Germany' (1968) 1 NYUJl of International Law and Politics 106, cited by Handford, 'Moral Damage', 859; see also Vahrenwald, 'Photographs and Privacy in Germany'.

[222] BverfGE 34, 269 (1973).

[223] See Markesinis, 'Privacy, Freedom of Expression and Horizontal Effect', 56.

[224] BverfGE 30, 173 (1971) (*Mephisto*). See Handford, 'Moral Damage', 866.

234 The commercial appropriation of personality

and that the products benefited from his techniques, thus damaging his reputation.[225] Subsequently, the son of the well-known comedian and author Heinz Erhardt was able to prevent the imitation of his late father's idiosyncratic voice in an advertisement on the basis of his father's personality rights which continued to subsist and had not terminated at his death. The advertisement invoked the living memory of Erhardt's artistic personality and it would not be acceptable, in the Court's view, that such artistic personality could be imitated for commercial ends. This held true in respect of both the dignity of the deceased individual and the economic interests in commercial exploitation enjoyed by the heirs. According to the Court, such protection from unauthorised commercial advertising did not affect the artistic interest of imitators or the legitimate reporting of news by the media.[226]

Although the right to one's image remains rooted in the notion of protection of human dignity, it also protects commercial interests as recently stressed in the *Marlene Dietrich* judgment.[227] The case concerned a claim brought by the heir of the deceased actress against the producers of a musical based on her life who had registered the trade mark 'Marlene' and had subsequently used it in merchandise related to the musical and licensed it to a car manufacturer. The defendant argued that the uses were artistic expressions and should be exempted from liability and that the infringement of post-mortem personality rights did not give rise to compensation since they protected only non-material interests. The Kammergericht (Berlin Court of Appeal) held that the general personality right protected by §823(1) BGB protects not only non-material personality interests, particularly entitlement to worth and respect, but also material or economic interests. Attributes of personality, such as name, likeness or voice, could have a substantial de facto value, often resulting from fame and reputation in the public eye in such fields as sport and the arts. Indeed, in such cases financial detriment would often be the gravamen of the complaint, rather than damage to honour or reputation. The right of personality should, accordingly, protect the right to decide whether and under what conditions an individual might choose to exploit attributes of his personality.[228] This right had passed to the plaintiff as heir to the Dietrich estate, since these interests were descendible, in contrast to the highly personal non-material interests which were bound to

---

[225] BGH 17.05.82 (Case No. I ZR 73/82) (1982) (*Fresh Cell Cosmetics*) (translated in (1986) 17 IIC, 426).

[226] OLG Hamburg 08.05.89 (Case No. 3 W 45/89) (1989) (*Heinz Erhardt*) (translated in (1990) 21 IIC, 881).

[227] BGH 1.12.1999 (1999) (translated in B. S. Markesinis, *Always on the Same Path* (Oxford, 2001), 401).

[228] BGH 1.12.1999 (1999), 408.

Privacy interests in English law

the individual concerned and could not be renounced or sold. To do so would contradict the Basic Law's guarantee of personal dignity.

The question of whether the economic aspects of personality were transferable and descendible had been left open and had not been decided expressly by the Bundesgerichtshof.[229] According to the Kammergericht, a number of factors suggested that economic interests in personality should not be bound to the individual in the same manner as non-economic or dignitary interests, although it only had to consider the question of descendibility rather than assignability. The character of a right could change from being essentially a right of personality to an interest of an economic nature, for example trade mark law was categorised as a personality right, although it became completely detached from its relationship to the business and personality of an individual entrepreneur. Changing technical and economic circumstances had offered new marketing opportunities and well-known personalities contributed to the creation of economic value. Effective post-mortem protection of elements of personality could only be secured by granting descendants enforceable rights to damages, going beyond the non-monetary remedies available to protect pure personality interests. The heirs, according to the court, would have a better claim to the economic worth of their deceased relatives than unconnected third parties,[230] although it is not clear why the public domain should be disregarded. The lack of certainty regarding the duration and extent of such a post-mortem right could not be a valid objection and, in determining the extent of such protection, the court drew an analogy with the ten-year period of protection for non-material interests.[231]

Public and private figures: the balancing exercise

The German courts have considerable experience of balancing interests in personality or privacy with free speech interests. Several factors are

---

[229] Cf. BGH 14.10.86 (Case No. VI ZR 10/86) (1986) (*Nena*) (translated in (1988) 19 IIC, 269) (collecting society with an exclusive contract relating to a singer's image merchandising rights could maintain an action against a third party. An argument that the assignment of the right to the plaintiff's likeness formed part of the general personality right and was not, as such, transferable, was rejected. The Bundesgerichtshof held that the plaintiff was entitled to recover a fee in respect of the exploitation of the singer's image on the basis that the defendant had been unjustly enriched at the plaintiff's expense (which did not depend on a legal assignment of the right to the singer's image), thus the plaintiff collecting society was entitled to the gain which the defendant had made in the form of a fee of DM 5,500).

[230] Markesinis, *Always on the Same Path*, 410–11.

[231] *Ibid.*, 412, referring to KUG 1907 §22(3). See, generally, Vahrenwald, 'Photographs and Privacy in Germany', 207.

236 The commercial appropriation of personality

considered in the weighing exercise, which are considered in detail elsewhere and may only be outlined here. For example, the court will consider whether the publisher's motive is to inform the public or make a profit; the value of the information, for example whether it informs or whether it provides entertainment; the means by which the information was obtained; the extent to which the information is disseminated and its accuracy; and the extent to which the plaintiff seeks to limit the defendant's freedom of expression.[232]

Under the right to one's own image and right to personality, the subject of a photograph is, prima facie, the only person who can decide whether and by what means such a photograph should be published, although the rights are hedged with certain exceptions, most notably in cases concerning what is referred to as 'the sphere of contemporary history'. Thus, monarchs, heads of state and eminent politicians belong to a group regarded as 'absolute contemporary persons' who form a part of contemporary history and the public has a justified interest in the publication of photographs of such persons. Nevertheless, in the *Princess Caroline* case,[233] the Bundesgerichtshof held that there were limits to the extent to which pictures of such persons could be published and, according to §23 II KUG, publication is prohibited where the justified interests of the individual outweigh the other interests at stake. The plaintiff sought to prevent the publication, in Germany, of photographs depicting various aspects of her life in France. The Court held that the plaintiff could claim the right to respect her own sphere of private life, despite the fact that she was a person of contemporary history, since even such persons did not need to tolerate the publication of pictures which depicted central aspects of their private lives.

The right to respect of one's own sphere of private life could be claimed by anyone, including the plaintiff, regardless of the fact that she was a person of contemporary history, if the photographs depicted central aspects of her private life. The Court of Appeal took the view that the public's interest in information ended at the subject's doorstep, and did not include the private sphere of a person's home. Accordingly, since the plaintiff was in a public place, a restaurant, and not in her private sphere, the publication was legitimate. The Bundesgerichtshof, drawing on academic

---

[232] Markesinis, 'Privacy, Freedom of Expression, and Horizontal Effect', 62; Craig and Nolte, 'Privacy and Free Speech', 172–7.

[233] BGH, NJW 1996, 1128 (1995) (translated in Markesinis, *German Law of Obligations: Torts*, 998), and see, generally, B. S. Markesinis and N. Nolte, 'Some Comparative Reflections on the Right of Privacy of Public Figures in Public Places' in Birks (ed.) *Privacy and Loyalty* (Oxford, 1997), 113. For the background to the previous decisions see P. Schlechtriem, 'Some Thoughts on the Decision of the BGH Concerning Princess Caroline of Monaco' in Markesinis (ed.) *Protecting Privacy*, 131.

opinion, rejected such a spatial restriction of the private sphere of life to an individual's domestic environment, taking the view that a person can be in a private area worthy of protection outside the purely domestic environment. Where a person such as the plaintiff had retreated to a place of seclusion (a private part of a garden restaurant), which could be objectively ascertained by third parties, then they could be regarded as being in a private sphere. The taking and subsequent publication of pictures of those who believed themselves to be unobserved and in private constituted an invasion of such a sphere. The greater the interest of the public in being informed, the more the protected interest of the person of contemporary history would have to recede in favour of the public's need for information. Conversely, the need to protect privacy would increase as the value of the information obtained by the public decreased. The photographs published by the defendants contained little of informational as opposed to entertainment or gossip value. Indeed, the defendant's motivation in publishing was primarily economic.[234] However, other photographs, where the plaintiff, although in public, had not retreated into a place secluded from the general public, could not be prevented from being published.

Although the adoption of such a sweeping new right as a right to privacy in a common law environment might no longer be regarded as being 'pregnant with danger',[235] it remains somewhat alien to the English common law model, even in the more hospitable rights-friendly world following the Human Rights Act 1998. Even if the Act proves to be the pretext for judicial development of a right of privacy, such a general right will still be unwieldy. The difficulties in reconciling the economic and dignitary aspects of commercial exploitation of personality, experienced both in Germany and in the United States,[236] will remain. Objections based on the problems of balancing competing interests cannot be sustained given the more explicit weighing of competing rights following the Human Rights Act. There are enduring reasons for severing the problem of appropriation of personality from the general privacy debate. Indeed, judicial recognition of a tort of appropriation of personality entails judicial activism of an interstitial kind and on a much more modest scale and is perfectly in keeping with the common law tradition. Whether such severance is possible remains to be seen. In this respect it is useful to revisit the previous legislative attempts to introduce such a right. The principal arguments and objections will inevitably resurface as a law of privacy (in whatever form) is developed by the courts.

[234] See Craig and Nolte, 'Privacy and Free Speech', 176.
[235] Gutteridge, 'The Comparative Law of the Right to Privacy I', 203, 217.
[236] See 172–4 above.

238   The commercial appropriation of personality

Appropriation of personality and United Kingdom legislative initiatives

In contrast with most other jurisdictions, widespread concern about privacy in English law has been fairly recent.[237] The 1990s, in particular, saw an increased interest in the question of privacy and the accompanying issue of press regulation, prompted by the activities of increasingly intrusive elements in the press. There is an obvious danger that the privacy debate effectively becomes a battle between media interests, particularly the newspaper industry, and the government. As a result, other aspects of the problem are ignored and the debate is reduced to an over-simplistic censorship versus free speech argument. Although these issues are undeniably important, there is clearly rather more to the debate.[238] Governments are, in any case, generally more reluctant to address morally or socially sensitive issues in their legislative programmes.[239]

The problem of privacy is merely one example in the age-old debate concerning the proper respective roles of the judiciary and legislature, where the balance has traditionally been against judicial activism. It has become increasingly clear that the impetus in creating a general tort remedy for invasion of privacy must come from the courts rather than the legislature, although the courts have been criticised for their reluctance to develop new rights, a hesitancy which is seen as a lack of spirit of adventure, progress or innovation on the part of judges and counsel.[240] This stands in marked contrast to the bold judicial initiatives shown in developing the right of privacy in the United States and the general right of personality in Germany. In the era following the Human Rights Act, this issue might seem less relevant, although early indications show that there will be difficulties in developing a general right of privacy and the problems in accommodating commercial exploitation within such a right will remain.

---

[237] The first privacy bill was Lord Mancroft's Privacy Bill 1961. For a review of the background to the current privacy debate see Lord Chancellor's Department, *Infringement of Privacy: A Consultation Paper* (London, July 1993), Ch. 2, and Seipp, 'Right to Privacy', 345–50.

[238] See B. Neill, 'Privacy: A Challenge for the Next Century', in Markesinis (ed.), *Protecting Privacy*, 1, 22. See also E. Barendt, 'Privacy and the Press' in E. Barendt (ed.) *Yearbook of Media and Entertainment Law 1995* (Oxford, 1995), 41, arguing that the Calcutt Committee's terms of reference (see note 2 above) were misconceived and that it is wrong in principle to treat different branches of the media in different ways; the right of privacy should be guaranteed against every potential defendant, and one of the practical effects of focusing on the press has been to make the privacy debate a battle between the political establishment and the newspaper industry.

[239] D. Feldman, 'Privacy-related Rights and Their Social Value' in P. Birks (ed.) *Privacy and Loyalty* (Oxford, 1997), 15, 50.

[240] H. Street, *Freedom, the Individual and the Law*, 5th edn (London, 1984), 264, cited by Wacks, *Personal Information*, 39.

Privacy interests in English law 239

To date, there have been seven attempts to introduce a statutory right of privacy.[241] Although appropriation of name or likeness featured prominently in the early American and German cases, the three principal contemporary concerns in the United Kingdom, when the first privacy bills were introduced, were the threat of governmental intrusion, the activities of the press, and the new challenges posed by new technological means of surveillance and data gathering.[242] The first two bills were limited in scope. Lord Mancroft's Right of Privacy Bill 1961 (withdrawn at Committee stage) applied only to invasions of privacy by the press, television, sound broadcasting and films and related only to the publication of words relating to a person's personal affairs to the extent that such publication was calculated to cause a person distress or embarrassment. Alex Lyon's Right of Privacy Bill 1967 was primarily directed at intrusion and surreptitious surveillance, defining a right of privacy as the 'right of any person to preserve the seclusion of himself, his family, or his property from any other person'.[243] The Bill would have given 'any person who has been subject to any serious and unreasonable infringement of his right of privacy' a cause of action against the offender and sought to establish a general principle allowing the courts to decide whether there had been an infringement of privacy. There was no second reading. Neither Bill encompassed appropriation of personality unless it might have come within a very loose interpretation of personal seclusion in Alex Lyon's Bill.

Following a comprehensive review, in 1970 Justice recommended the introduction of a general statutory right of privacy,[244] rejecting both the alternative options of adjusting existing causes of action (seen as artificial and distorting) and the introduction of piecemeal causes of action

---

[241] See also Photographs and Films (Unauthorised Use) Bill 1994 (34 above) and Data Protection and Privacy Bill 1996 (Harry Cohen) seeking to overhaul the provisions of the Data Protection Act 1984 rather than to introduce a new general tort remedy for invasion of privacy (see now Data Protection Act 1998 (note 31 above and accompanying text)). For fuller discussions of the early privacy bills see W. F. Pratt, *Privacy in Britain* (London, 1979), Chs. 7 and 8 (with interesting contemporary background); Younger Committee, Report on Privacy, Ch. 22. Discussion of subsequent bills and their texts may be found in Lord Chancellor's Department, *Infringement of Privacy Consultation Paper*.

[242] See Pratt, *Privacy in Britain*, Ch. 5. The first of these concerns was partly addressed, at least at an international level, by the Universal Declaration of Human Rights 1948, Art. 12, which, in turn, influenced the European Convention on Human Rights 1950, Art. 8. These two instruments, although not incorporated in UK domestic law, arguably marked the first linking of privacy with the notion of human dignity: see Pratt, *Privacy in Britain*, 87.

[243] Cf. Gavison's three core irreducible elements of secrecy, anonymity and solitude (166–9 above), and Prosser's four torts of intrusion upon seclusion or solitude, disclosure of embarrassing private facts, false light publicity and appropriation (161–4 above).

[244] Justice, *Privacy and the Law*, para. 127.

240   The commercial appropriation of personality

for infringement of privacy (which failed to reflect the Committee's view that one principle should underlie all the different types of case). A draft of the Bill prepared by Justice had already been introduced by Brian Walden and received its second reading shortly after the Justice report was published.[245] Its supporters emphasised the limitations of the piecemeal approach, particularly the difficulty in anticipating every objectionable invasion of privacy, which would be overcome by a general right to privacy,[246] while its opponents stressed the potential threats it might pose to freedom of speech, particularly the activities of the press.[247] The government took the view that more consideration should be given to defining the types of activity which were objectionable,[248] a task entrusted to the Younger Committee after the Walden Bill was withdrawn following its second reading.

The privacy debate lay dormant for the next eighteen years until William Cash's Right of Privacy Bill 1988, which, like the Walden Bill, was virtually identical to the draft Bill proposed by Justice,[249] although there was no second reading. Subsequently, two bills, more limited in scope, aimed at the unauthorised use or disclosure of private information were introduced.[250] Predictably, fears as to the possible effect on press freedom were expressed,[251] while, significantly for the development of a general right, the government took the position that even such narrowly drawn bills was too broad[252] and ultimately sought refuge in the Younger Committee's recommendation against the creation of a general right of privacy. More recently, a piecemeal measure in response to highly publicised cases of taped private conversations, which sought to make it an offence to sell or buy tapes or transcripts of private conversation without the consent of the conversers, failed to gain a second reading.[253]

The seven Private Members' Bills inevitably reflect different conceptions of the proper subject matter and scope of the right of privacy. Only the Bills based on the Justice model (Walden and Cash) included appropriation within the ambit of a right of privacy. In the most recent reports, the Calcutt Committee rather tellingly took the view that a remedy for appropriation of personality did not meet their criteria of pressing

---

[245] Right of Privacy Bill 1970.
[246] *Hansard, Fifth Series*, HC, vol. 794, cols. 868 and 888–9, 23 January 1970.
[247] *Ibid.*, cols. 876–80.   [248] *Ibid.*, col. 943.
[249] The second wave of Privacy Bills are discussed in Lord Chancellor's Department, *Infringement of Privacy Consultation Paper*, Annex D.
[250] Protection of Privacy Bill 1988 (John Browne) (withdrawn before the Report stage); Protection of Privacy Bill 1988 (Lord Stoddart) (identical to John Browne's Bill, although no second reading).
[251] *Hansard, Sixth Series*, HC, vol. 145, col. 1312, 27 January 1989.
[252] *Ibid.*, col. 1340.
[253] Protection of Privacy (No. 2) Bill (Sir Patrick Cormack).

Privacy interests in English law   241

social need,[254] while the Lord Chancellor's Department's Consultation Paper suggested that appropriation should be seen as involving a different, though related, right from privacy, and that a new right should be limited to the protection of privacy.[255] The National Heritage Select Committee also recommended a new statutory tort of invasion of privacy,[256] and although four American privacy statutes were examined, three of which encompassed commercial appropriation of personality,[257] such conduct was excluded from its ambit. However, the proposed new tort would have provided redress in cases involving the obtaining or publication of harmful or embarrassing personal material or photographs, and thus would have remedied certain limited cases of appropriation of personality.[258] The government response, which also took account of the Calcutt Committee's review of press regulation, and the Lord Chancellor's Department's Consultation Paper, was that there was insufficient public consensus on which to base statutory intervention, and that no convincing case for a new tort had been made out. Although it acknowledged that there were shortcomings in the existing system of press self-regulation, the government took the view that the system might be improved and that there was no need to introduce a new statutory civil remedy.[259]

Interests in freedom from mental distress

A further strand of the de facto interests which interplay in cases of appropriation of personality needs to be considered: interests in freedom from mental distress. The concern lies with the infliction of mental distress *simpliciter*, be it labelled 'distress, frustration, anxiety, displeasure,

---

[254] Calcutt Committee, Report on Privacy and Related Matters, para. 12.8. In his subsequent report, Report of Press Self-Regulation, Cm 2135 (1993), Calcutt recommended that further consideration should be given to the introduction of a statutory tort of infringement of privacy.

[255] Lord Chancellor's Department, *Infringement of Privacy Consultation Paper*, para. 5.33. The Department (para. 5.22) proposed a new civil wrong of invasion of privacy, which would include matters appertaining to a person's health, personal communications, and family and personal relationships, and a right to be free from harassment and molestation. Liability would only arise in respect of conduct which would cause substantial distress to a person of ordinary sensibilities, subject to defences such as consent, lawful authority, privilege and public interest.

[256] National Heritage Select Committee, *Fourth Report: Privacy and Media Intrusion* (London, 1993), para. 47.

[257] *Ibid.*, Annex 1.

[258] The proposed new tort was obviously primarily directed at the activities of the media and included: obtaining and/or publishing private information or photographs; publishing inaccurate or misleading personal information; and violating the peace of another by intruding upon him or persistently communicating with him (*ibid.*, para. 47).

[259] Department of National Heritage, *Privacy and Media Intrusion: The Government's Response*, Cm 2918 (1995), para. 4.13.

242   The commercial appropriation of personality

vexation, tension or aggravation',[260] rather than psychiatric damage, involving 'some recognisable psychiatric illness, with or without psychosomatic symptoms',[261] that is, 'some serious mental disturbance outside the range of normal human experience, not merely the ordinary emotions of anxiety, grief or fear'.[262] The basic position in English law can be summarised by Lord Wensleydale's dictum in *Lynch* v. *Knight*: that the law cannot value or provide a remedy for mental pain or anxiety by itself, although where there is damage to a material interest, a jury might take the plaintiff's mental anxiety into account in assessing damages.[263] Damages are frequently awarded for mental distress which is inflicted in the course of the commission of various torts,[264] such as assault,[265] battery,[266] false imprisonment[267] and defamation,[268] since they protect what may be broadly labelled as 'interests in personality'[269] which might

[260] *Watts* v. *Morrow* [1991] 1 WLR 1421, 1445 *per* Bingham LJ (claim for damages for mental distress caused by the physical consequences of a breach of contract). Cf. N. J. Mullany and P. R. Handford, *Tort Liability for Psychiatric Damage* (Sydney, 1993), 26, suggesting that mental distress usually consists of a combination of the following unpleasant emotions: (i) fear or apprehension, (ii) horror, (iii) grief, sorrow and loneliness, (iv) shame, humiliation and embarrassment, (v) anger, annoyance and vexation, (vi) disappointment and frustration and (vii) worry and anxiety.

[261] *McLoughlin* v. *O'Brian* [1983] 1 AC 410, 431 *per* Lord Bridge. The alternative and widely used expression 'nervous shock' has been described as 'misleading and inaccurate': see *Attia* v. *British Gas Plc* [1988] QB 304, 317 *per* Bingham LJ.

[262] *Page* v. *Smith* [1996] AC 155, 166 *per* Lord Keith; *White* v. *Chief Constable of South Yorkshire Police* [1999] 2 AC 455, 500 *per* Lord Hoffman. See, generally, Mullany and Handford, *Psychiatric Damage*.

[263] (1861) 9 HL Cas. 577, 598, 11 ER 854, 863. See also *Alcock* v. *Chief Constable of South Yorkshire Police* [1992] 1 AC 310, 401 *per* Lord Ackner.

[264] See F. A. Trindade, 'The Intentional Infliction of Purely Mental Distress' (1986) 6 OJLS 219, 221; Mullany and Handford, *Psychiatric Damage*, 45 et seq. See also P. Giliker, 'A "New" Head of Damages: Damages for Mental Distress in the English Law of Torts' (2000) 20 LS 19.

[265] See, e.g., *Fogg* v. *McKnight* [1968] NZLR 330, 332 *per* McGregor J; J. G. Fleming, *Introduction to the Law of Torts*, 2nd edn (Oxford, 1985), 48.

[266] *Cole* v. *Turner* (1704) Holt KB 108, 90 ER 958 *per* Holt CJ; *Pursell* v. *Horn* (1838) 8 AD & E, 602, 112 ER 966; *Nash* v. *Sheen* [1953] CLY 3726.

[267] *Meering* v. *Grahame-White Aviation Co. Ltd* (1920) LT 44, 53–4 *per* Atkin LJ, approved obiter by the House of Lords in *Murray* v. *Ministry of Defence* [1988] 1 WLR 692; *Walter* v. *Alltools Ltd* (1944) 61 TLR 39, 40 *per* Lawrence LJ; *Hook* v. *Cunard Steamship Co.* [1953] 1 WLR 682, 686. The fact that false imprisonment affects a person's dignity and reputation as well as his liberty is reflected in the award of general damages, although no breakdown of the awards feature in the cases: see H. McGregor, *McGregor on Damages*, 17th edn (London, 1997), para. 1619.

[268] See *John* v. *MGN* [1996] 3 WLR 593, 608 *per* Bingham MR; *Fielding* v. *Variety Inc.* [1967] 2 QB 841, 855 *per* Salmon LJ, and 851 *per* Denning LJ; *Ley* v. *Hamilton* (1935) 153 LT 384, 386; *McCarey* v. *Associated Newspapers Ltd* [1965] 2 QB 86, 104 *per* Pearson LJ.

[269] See, e.g., the use of the term in the *Restatement, Second, Torts*, Vol. I, Div. I Ch. 2, where under the heading 'Intentional Invasions of Interests in Personality' are: the interest in freedom from harmful bodily contact; the interest in freedom from offensive bodily

Privacy interests in English law

be said to include interests in freedom from mental distress.[270] English law remains reluctant to recognise the infliction of mental distress, without more, as an independent actionable wrong.

The rule in Wilkinson v. Downton *and infliction of mental distress*

At first glance, this line of authority seems quite far removed from the typical problem of appropriation of personality, reflecting the lack of adequate remedies to address the problem directly, and forcing English lawyers to do their best with what are often inappropriate or inadequate tools for the job. However, its relevance will become apparent in discussing: (i) its frequently mooted potential development into a remedy for invasion of privacy and (ii) the residual role that the tort of intentional infliction of mental distress plays in cases of appropriation of personality in the United States and the possible application of English authorities to a similar effect.

In *Wilkinson* v. *Downton*,[271] the plaintiff was told by the defendant, as a practical joke, that her husband's legs had been broken in an accident, causing her to suffer 'a violent shock to her nervous system, producing vomiting and more serious and permanent physical consequences at one time threatening her reason, and entailing weeks of suffering and incapacity to her'.[272] The defendant was held liable on the basis that he had 'wilfully done an act calculated to cause physical harm to the plaintiff – that is to say, to infringe her legal right to safety' and had in fact thereby caused physical harm to her. In Wright J's view, that proposition was sufficient to found a good cause of action, in the absence of justification for the defendant's act and even though no malicious purpose nor any motive of spite could be imputed to the defendant.[273] Since it was difficult to imagine that such a statement could fail to produce such an effect, an intention to produce such an effect was imputed to the defendant.[274]

---

contact; the interest in freedom from apprehension of a harmful or offensive contact; the interest in freedom from confinement; and the interest in freedom from emotional distress.

[270] See, also, *Cornelius* v. *De Taranto* [2001] EMLR 329 (damages for mental distress following breach of contractual obligation of confidence), and see A. Stewart, 'Damages For Mental Distress Following Breach of Confidence: Preventing or Compensating Tears' [2001] EIPR 302.

[271] [1897] 2 QB 57.   [272] *Ibid.*, 58.

[273] *Ibid.*, 59. The decision is a rare example in the law of tort of a new rule being formulated to address a novel factual situation, rather than the gradual expansion or adaptation of existing torts. See also P. R. Handford, '*Wilkinson* v. *Downton* and Acts Calculated to Cause Physical Harm' (1985) 16 UnivWA LRev 31, 37, suggesting that the judgment was inspired by Pollock's general theory that it was tortious to do wilful harm to another without lawful justification or excuse.

[274] *Ibid.*

244   The commercial appropriation of personality

It has at times been suggested that the rule in *Wilkinson* v. *Downton* could be extended to encompass invasions of privacy, while not being of such general application as to be liable to attack as a restriction on the freedom of the press.[275] The main limitation on such a development relates to the nature of the harm suffered, and the fact that, as the courts currently construe the rule, psychiatric harm is required rather than mere emotional distress. As the English authorities currently stand, liability will arise (i) where the defendant's conduct amounts to actual physical or psychiatric damage[276] or where (ii) the court is prepared to accept that there is an obvious risk that the cumulative effect of an existing and continuous course of conduct will result in psychiatric damage (as opposed to mere emotional distress) and may be restrained on a *quia timet* basis.[277] Expanding liability to cover conduct which (iii) results in (serious)[278] mental distress (or the possibility of such a condition) inevitably involves crossing the Rubicon which separates actionable psychiatric damage from mental distress which is not currently actionable in itself. Indeed, covering situation (ii) arguably involves an element of fiction to allow actions for what is arguably mental distress *simpliciter*. It is a moot point whether, for example, the publication of a surreptitiously obtained photograph of a scantily clad person[279] would satisfy a test of serious mental distress. Of course, much will depend on the facts of each particular case, and the test would be much easier to satisfy if, for example, a photograph of a grossly overweight person was used in an advertisement for a slimming product. Ultimately, the move from the rule in *Wilkinson* v. *Downton,* as applied more broadly in *Khorasandjian* v. *Bush,* to a situation where it might provide a remedy

---

[275] See, e.g., B. Neill, 'The Protection of Privacy' (1962) 25 MLR 393, 402; G. Dworkin, 'The Common Law Protection of Privacy' (1967) 2 U Tas LR 418, 443–5; *Tucker* v. *News Media Ownership Ltd* [1986] 2 NZLR 716, 733 *per* McGechan J, but cf. *Bradley* v. *Wingnut Films* [1993] 1 NZLR 415. See also R. Bagshaw, 'Obstacles on the Path to Privacy Torts' in P. Birks (ed.) *Privacy and Loyalty* (Oxford, 1997), 133, 143: 'trespass to the person is ripe for extension to psychological battery'.

[276] *Wilkinson* v. *Downton* [1897] 2 QB 57, 58; *Janvier* v. *Sweeney* [1919] 2 KB 316, 320.

[277] *Khorasandjian* v. *Bush* [1993] QB 727, 736. See also *Bradley* v. *Wingnut Films* [1993] 1 NZLR 415, requiring the plaintiffs to establish something more than a transient reaction, however initially severe (*ibid.*, 421), to establish liability where images of a tombstone, to which the plaintiff had the exclusive right of burial in perpetuity, were featured in a comedy horror film which the plaintiffs found offensive. See, further, J. Bridgeman and M. A. Jones, 'Harassing Conduct and Outrageous Acts: A Cause of Action for Intentionally Inflicted Mental Distress?' (1994) 14 LS 180, 196, and *Burris* v. *Azadani* [1995] 1 WLR 1372, 1377.

[278] American law draws the line here, requiring severe mental distress or conduct which most people would find outrageous: see text accompanying note 291 below.

[279] See R. Wacks, *Privacy and Press Freedom* (London, 1995), 88.

Privacy interests in English law 245

for interests in personal privacy is a considerable one, although such an approach certainly provides some limited protection for privacy-related interests.[280]

The arguments for a tort of intentional infliction of mental distress have been adequately canvassed elsewhere,[281] and only two closely related points need to be made here. First, while there are a number of policy arguments for restricting recovery to cases involving some kind of recognisable psychiatric illness where the defendant's conduct is negligent (e.g., the fear of opening the floodgates to a deluge of fraudulent and exaggerated claims),[282] such objections are somewhat less persuasive in cases involving intentionally inflicted mental distress.[283] Second, recognition of such a cause of action would avoid exaggerated claims of symptoms such as 'sick headaches, nausea, insomnia, etc.' to make out a technical basis of bodily injury upon which to base the parasitic recovery for mental distress.[284] Recovery should arguably be limited to cases of *serious* mental distress, producing a substantial and enduring effect, rather than a mere transient reaction,[285] and while defining such a notion is difficult, distinguishing trifling insults or annoyance from serious wrongs requires nothing more than the application of some common sense to eliminate trivial claims brought by hypersensitive individuals.[286] Indeed, it seems that the fears, in the United States, of a flood of litigation involving trivial or falsified claims have not been well founded.[287]

Intentional infliction of mental distress in the United States

The intentional infliction of mental distress now forms the basis of an independent action in tort in most states, though the law has been slow to recognise that interests in peace of mind are entitled to independent legal protection.[288] For some time, the same objections to development

---

[280] See D. Feldman, 'Secrecy, Dignity, or Autonomy? Views of Privacy as a Civil Liberty' (1994) 47 CLP 41, 49.

[281] See, e.g., Trindade, 'Intentional Infliction'.

[282] See Law Commission Consultation Paper No. 137, 'Liability for Psychiatric Illness' (1995), paras. 4.1–4.13, for a summary of these arguments.

[283] Prosser, 'Intentional Infliction of Mental Suffering: A New Tort' (1939) 37 Mich L Rev 874, 878, and see *Hunter* v. *Canary Wharf Ltd* [1997] 2 WLR 684, 709.

[284] C. Magruder, 'Mental and Emotional Disturbance in the Law of Torts' (1936) 49 HarvLRev 1033, 1059.

[285] *Ibid.*, 229.

[286] Prosser, 'Intentional Infliction of Mental Suffering', 878.

[287] See P. R. Handford, 'Intentional Infliction of Mental Distress – Analysis of the Growth of a Tort' (1979) 8 Anglo-AmLR 1, 11.

[288] See, generally, W. P. Keeton, *Prosser and Keeton on the Law of Torts*, 5th edn (St Paul, 1984), 54–66.

246   The commercial appropriation of personality

in this area that still apply to a large extent in English law carried weight. The injury was long regarded as being too subtle and incapable of proof, and there was a pervasive fear that the recognition of such a new claim might lead to a flood of claims that were at best spurious and at worst fraudulent. However, recovery was not denied in all cases. Although the courts attempted to do justice within the traditional causes of action such as the intentional torts to the person (assault, battery, false imprisonment), trespass to land, nuisance, and the then fledgling tort of invasion of privacy, it became apparent that, in many cases, no such traditional ground could be discovered, and that the intentional infliction of mental disturbance by extreme and outrageous conduct constituted a cause of action of itself, though it is difficult to identify one particular case as the source of the new cause of action.[289]

A cause of action will lie in most states where a defendant engages in extreme and outrageous conduct which intentionally or recklessly causes severe emotional distress to another.[290] Intentional infliction of emotional distress is found where conduct exceeds all bounds usually tolerated by a decent society and causes mental distress of a very serious kind.[291] The courts have been careful to place limits on the recovery for mental distress, and have attempted to balance the liberty of one person to express an unflattering opinion of another, in the interests of free speech, with the interest of another person in not having his feelings wounded.[292] There can be no recovery for mere profanity or abuse or for insults or threats which amount to nothing more than mere annoyance.[293] Thus, there was no liability where the defendants took and circulated photographs depicting their workmate standing next to another employee, clad only in underwear and with his hands over his genitals. The defendants had viewed the photograph as a joke and did not think that it would be hurtful or painful

---

[289] It has been suggested that the first case establishing such independent liability was the Arkansas case of *Wilson* v. *Wilkins* (1930) 25 SW 2d 428: see Mullany and Handford, *Psychiatric Damage*, 297.

[290] *Bradley* v. *Hall* 720 NE 2d 747, 752 (Ind.App., 1999), citing *Restatement, Second, Torts*, §46.

[291] *Restatement, Second, Torts* §46 comment *d*: 'liability has been found only where the conduct has been so outrageous in character, and so extreme in degree, as to go beyond all possible bounds of decency, and to be regarded as atrocious, and utterly intolerable in a civilised community. Generally, the case is one in which the recitation of the facts to an average member of the community would arouse his resentment against the actor and lead him to exclaim "Outrageous!"'.

[292] See Keeton, *Prosser and Keeton on the Law of Torts*, 59.

[293] *Ibid.*, 59–60. Most jurisdictions in the United States have been reluctant to recognise liability for *negligently* inflicted emotional distress (see *Restatement, Second, Torts* §§312–13 and §436A), although some states have permitted actions for the negligent infliction of serious emotional distress without the plaintiff needing to show any resulting physical injury or illness as a result, or damage to property rights (see, generally, Keeton, *Prosser and Keeton on the Law of Torts*, 361–5).

Privacy interests in English law 247

and it could not be said that they intended to harm the plaintiff in any way.[294]

Intentional infliction of mental distress as a residual category

The most immediate application of the rule in *Wilkinson* v. *Downton* lay in the potential development of a new tort of harassment,[295] although this has now been effectively forestalled by the Protection from Harassment Act 1997.[296] It might have some residual effect in cases involving de facto invasions of privacy or appropriation of personality. Consider the facts of *Charleston* v. *News Group Newspapers*[297] where the plaintiff actors' photographs were depicted in a newspaper, superimposed on the bodies of models engaged in pornographic activity, illustrating an article reporting the fact that a computer game featuring the photographs in question was in circulation. The decision of the House of Lords turned on a formal point of libel law: the publication had to be given the natural and ordinary meaning which it would convey to the mind of the ordinary reasonable and fair-minded reader. A claim for libel could not be founded on a headline or photograph in isolation from the accompanying text. The question of whether an article was defamatory had to be answered by reference to the response of the reader to the entire publication and the ordinary reader could not, in the circumstances, have gained the impression that the plaintiffs were engaged in making pornographic films. The appeal turned on these matters alone, and did not concern 'any question of journalistic ethics nor . . . whether the publication of the photographs by itself constituted some novel tort'.[298] To what extent might the facts of such a case disclose a cause of action for intentional infliction of mental distress? Many would regard the conduct of the defendants as being outrageous, although there might be considerable difference of

[294] *Branham* v. *Celadon Trucking Services, Inc.* 744 NE 2d 514, 524 (Ind.App., 2001). See also *Cheatham* v. *Paisano Publications, Inc.*, 891 F Supp. 381 (WD Ky 1995), 387 (claim based on intentional infliction of emotional distress did not satisfy the standard of outrageous conduct causing severe emotional distress (see note 291 above), where photograph of plaintiff's bottom, clad in cut-out jeans, was published in magazines and printed on T-shirts). Cf. *Hustler Magazine Inc.* v. *Falwell* 485 US 46 (1988) (claim for intentional infliction of emotional distress outweighed by Constitutional free speech guarantees (*New York Times Co.* v. *Sullivan* 376 US 254 (1964)) even though defendants' conduct was outrageous).
[295] It was reported that the late Diana, Princess of Wales secured an injunction restraining a photographer from approaching within 300 metres of her, and from communicating with her, harassing her or interfering with her safety, security or well-being: *Independent*, 17 August 1996, p. 5. It is not clear on what basis the injunction was granted.
[296] See, generally, N. Addison and T. Lawson-Cruttenden, *Harassment Law and Practice* (London, 1998).
[297] [1995] 2 WLR 450, noted by P. Prescott, 'Libel and Pornography' (1995) 58 MLR 752.
[298] [1995] 2 WLR 450, 452 *per* Lord Bridge.

248   The commercial appropriation of personality

opinion as to whether such conduct should give rise to tortious liability. As English law currently stands, recovery would only be possible where physical injury or some recognised psychiatric disorder might result. In the United States, recovery might be possible if it could be shown that the plaintiffs had suffered severe emotional distress, in the absence of any countervailing First Amendment considerations, although liability would not extend to mere hurt feelings, embarrassment or humiliation.

Conclusions

It remains to be seen to what extent the traditional incremental or casuistic English approach to protecting interests in personal privacy will be abandoned in favour of a more principled approach. While the principle of privacy has arguably existed in English common law for some time, it has been re-affirmed (if such re-affirmation were necessary) following the incorporation of the European Convention on Human Rights in the Human Rights Act 1998. Although this does not provide for new causes of action based on Convention rights, the principles or values enshrined in the European Convention will have some degree of indirect horizontal effect. The shift to more explicit rights-based reasoning in Convention cases, requiring the courts to start with the general proposition that a right is protected,[299] may well permeate the common law, and reasons of substance may well prove to be more important than the formal reasons which have thus far denied the existence of a right of privacy in English law.[300]

The action for breach of confidence will probably be the area where a new law of privacy is developed. It is likely that, in typically English fashion, the cause of action will be extended to cover interests in privacy, through a generous interpretation of its key requirements. Such a line of development is, of course, some way removed from the problem of appropriation of personality. It may now cover a case where photographs are obtained by surreptitious means. Whether it would also cover the unauthorised use of a photograph, which has been taken initially with the subject's consent, is a different matter. The resulting damage to the individual's economic or dignitary interests would seem to lie outside the realm of breach of confidence. Such a line of development may, in turn, develop into a general right of privacy through gradual expansion. The law of the United States, examined in Chapter 7, offers an obvious model, although such a course of action is not free of difficulties, and resistance to such a general right will no doubt remain.

---

[299] See N. Browne-Wilkinson, 'The Impact on Judicial Reasoning' in B. S. Markesinis (ed.) *The Impact of the Human Rights Bill on English Law* (Oxford, 1998), 21, 22–3.
[300] See, e.g., *Kaye* v. *Robertson*, note 14 above.

9 Interests in reputation

Introduction

Interests in reputation, protected by the tort of defamation, occupy a central position in relation to the problem of appropriation of personality in English law and the systems which follow it, in the sense that recovery for damage to any other interests has traditionally been parasitic upon the recovery for injury to reputation. It is only after a substantive injury to reputation has been established that other interests, such as interests in personal privacy, or interests in freedom from mental distress, can be considered as factors which might be taken into account in assessing the quantum of damages. That is not to say that interests in reputation lie at the heart of the de facto problem of appropriation of personality.[1] Indeed, injuries to what are essentially economic interests, interests in personal privacy, or interests in freedom from mental distress, independent of any interests in reputation, might well be more important in a case of appropriation of personality. Other legal systems have taken a more direct approach. Most notably in the United States, the right of privacy and, subsequently, the right of publicity, have provided the predominant legal responses to appropriation of personality and the tort of defamation has played a relatively limited role,[2] although claims for defamation have occasionally been made to substitute for claims of invasion of privacy[3] or to supplement claims for invasion of privacy where the conduct of the defendant injured both interests in reputation and interests in privacy.[4] However, in English law, unless the unauthorised exploitation injures a plaintiff's reputation, the law generally has

---

[1] See 8–12 above.

[2] See, generally, J. T. McCarthy, *The Rights of Publicity and Privacy*, 2nd edn (New York, 2001), §5.97.

[3] See, e.g., *Sperry Rand Corp.* v. *Hill* 356 F 2d 181 (1966) (privacy claim failed on basis of estoppel).

[4] See, e.g., *Russell* v. *Marboro Books* 183 NYS 2d 8 (1959); *Newcombe* v. *Adolf Coors Co.* 157 F 3d 686 (9th Cir. 1998).

250   The commercial appropriation of personality

not recognised any actionable injury, and has not allowed the plaintiff a remedy.[5]

What emerges from an analysis of the English case law in this area is that the tort of defamation has been doing the work of more than one tort and that, in some cases, the notion of an injury to reputation has been stretched to encompass other interests. In other cases, where actions in defamation have not been successful, plaintiffs have arguably been denied a remedy as a result of the courts' reluctance to consider other possible bases of liability such as invasion of privacy or appropriation of personality. With the foregoing discussion in mind, it is crucial to draw a clear distinction between three separate notions which often converge in cases involving an unauthorised use of a person's name or likeness: defamation, invasion of privacy and appropriation of personality.

The economic and dignitary aspects of reputation

Surprisingly perhaps, there is no significant English legal literature on the meaning of reputation and why it is valued and deemed worthy of a high degree of protection.[6] In this respect it is useful to recall the place of the action for defamation in the general historical scheme of common law actions. Whereas actions for trespass *vi et armis* and actions on the case for negligence, conversion and nuisance protected a plaintiff from interference with his person or property, the action on the case for defamatory words protected a much more subtle interest. The action did not arise as a result of an insult to the plaintiff or for an injury to his feelings in themselves, 'but for the economic or social damage done to the plaintiff through the withdrawal of third parties from some relationship with him'.[7] Since the common law remedy was an action on the case, damage was the gist of the action and damage was construed in a narrow, proprietary sense.[8] Indeed, in Pollock's view, 'the law went wrong from the beginning in making the damage and not the insult as the cause of action'.[9] Consequently, it was necessary that there be publication to

---

[5] Except to the extent that a remedy may be available for breach of confidence, infringement of copyright, malicious falsehood or, more contentiously, passing off.

[6] See E. Barendt, 'What Is the Point of Libel Law?' [1999] CLP 110; E. Barendt, 'Privacy and the Press' in E. Barendt (ed.) *The Yearbook of Media and Entertainment Law 1995* (Oxford, 1995), 29. Cf. R. C. Post, 'The Social Foundations of Defamation Law: Reputation and the Constitution' (1986) 74 CalifLRev 691, 693–719, identifying three distinct concepts of reputation that the common law of defamation has attempted to protect at various times in its history: reputation as property; reputation as honour; and reputation as dignity (cited by Barendt, 'Privacy and the Press', 29).

[7] J. H. Baker, *An Introduction to English Legal History*, 3rd edn (London, 1990), 509.

[8] W. S. Holdsworth, 'Defamation in the Sixteenth and Seventeenth Centuries' (1924) 40 LQR 302, 304.

[9] F. Pollock, *The Law of Torts*, 12th edn (London, 1923), 243.

Interests in reputation

some third party, truth was a defence to the action, and the action died with the person.[10] Such historical roots account for the fundamental difference between an injury to reputation and an invasion of privacy. In modern actions for libel it is not necessary for the plaintiff to prove that the words caused him actual damage, since the law will presume that some general damage has resulted from the wrong,[11] although in cases of slander the plaintiff has to prove special damages, except in the limited cases where slander is actionable *per se*.[12]

Few modern authorities have addressed the question of the precise interest protected by an action in defamation, although it has been noted that 'reputation is an integral and important part of the dignity of the individual' which 'forms the basis of many decisions in a democratic society which are fundamental to its well-being'.[13] Damage to a person's reputation '[c]annot be measured as harm to a tangible thing is measured' and, special damages apart, reputation and money are not commensurables.[14] Moreover, a plaintiff in a defamation action is not compensated for his damaged reputation, but 'gets damages because he was injured in his reputation, that is, simply because he was publicly defamed'. Thus, compensation by damages serves a twofold function: 'as a vindication of the plaintiff to the public and as a consolation to him for a wrong done. Compensation is here a *solatium* rather than a monetary recompense for harm measurable in money.'[15]

Although reputation is often a valuable economic asset, it is difficult to quantify its value in money terms; what is more important is the bare fact that the plaintiff's interests in reputation are violated. Consequently, the aims which underlie the imposition of tortious liability deviate from what is widely, but perhaps erroneously, regarded as the compensatory norm.[16] In a defamation case, a plaintiff might be equally concerned with gaining vindication or satisfaction as with securing compensation for loss of reputation.[17] Moreover, an award of damages functions as solace for injured feelings rather than as compensation for a specific and

[10] See Holdsworth, 'Defamation in the Sixteenth and Seventeenth Centuries', 397.
[11] *Ratcliffe* v. *Evans* [1892] 2 QB 524, 529 *per* Bowen LJ; *Hayward & Co.* v. *Hayward & Sons* (1887) 34 Ch D 198, 207 *per* North J.
[12] See B. Neill and R. Rampton, *Duncan and Neill on Defamation*, 2nd edn (London, 1983), 21.
[13] *Reynolds* v. *Times Newspapers Ltd* [1999] 3 WLR 1010, 1023 *per* Lord Nicholls.
[14] *Uren* v. *John Fairfax & Sons Pty Ltd* (1965–6) 117 CLR 118, 150 (High Ct of Aus.) *per* Windeyer J (the case concerned the availability of punitive damages in defamation, where the High Court of Australia declined to follow the limitations placed by the House of Lords in *Rookes* v. *Barnard* [1964] AC 1129).
[15] (1965–6) 117 CLR 118. Cf. 21–3 above.
[16] Which Windeyer J alluded to: *Uren* v. *John Fairfax & Sons Pty Ltd* (1965–6) 117 CLR 118, 149.
[17] See, e.g., *Khodaparast* v. *Shad* [2000] EMLR 265, 276.

252 The commercial appropriation of personality

readily quantifiable loss. In common with other dignitary interests, such as privacy and freedom from mental distress, when the harm is to a person's interests in personality, the different aims and functions of tort law, such as compensation, punishment, vindication and deterrence, often converge.[18]

The notion of an injury to reputation is flexible, and there is no definitive or consistent definition of a defamatory statement,[19] although Lord Atkin's dictum in *Sim* v. *Stretch*[20] has been widely cited: '[w]ould the words tend to lower the plaintiff in the estimation of right thinking members of society generally?'[21] The absence of a statutory definition of what constitutes a defamatory statement provides an element of flexibility but also inevitably leads to some confusion, which should be borne in mind in approaching the English case law. In some cases it appears that the somewhat flexible notion of an injury to reputation has been stretched to its limits, raising the need to consider other bases of liability. A tripartite division of the authorities is adopted here. The first group of cases may be regarded as the core injury to reputation cases where an injury to reputation can clearly be seen. The second category calls for a differentiation between the notion of injury to reputation and the notion of invasion of privacy, since it is arguable that some of the English cases lie at the limits of what may be regarded as injuries to reputation and show limited judicial recognition of interests in personal privacy. The third category suggests another alternative basis for liability, appropriation of personality, which avoids the problems of a general right to privacy discussed in the previous chapter. Such a division is not an end in itself, but merely an aid to a clearer understanding of the problem and the differentiation of what are substantially different concepts, although it is not without its dangers. Some regard must be given to the social, historical and factual context in which the cases were decided. Inevitably, the decisions reflect the prevailing social conditions, values and prejudices of their times, a factor which should be borne in mind when interpreting the earlier authorities.

---

[18] See Chapter 1 at 21–3.

[19] *Berkoff* v. *Burchill* [1996] 4 All ER 1008, 1011 *per* Neill LJ. See, generally, Neill and Rampton, *Defamation*, Ch. 7, and P. F. Carter-Ruck, *Carter-Ruck on Libel and Slander*, 4th edn (London, 1992), Ch. 4.

[20] (1936) 52 TLR 669.

[21] Alternatively, in *Parmiter* v. *Coupland* (1840) 6 M&W 108, Parke B defined a defamatory statement as a statement which exposes the plaintiff to 'hatred, contempt or ridicule'. In *Youssoupoff* v. *Metro-Goldwyn-Mayer Pictures Ltd* (1934) 50 TLR 581, 584, Scrutton LJ adopted the formulation of Cave J in *Scott* v. *Sampson* (1882) 8 QBD 491, 503, where he referred to a man's 'right to have the estimation in which he stands in the opinion of others unaffected by false statements to his discredit'. The Faulks Committee took the view that this definition was of little value since the word 'discredit' is vague and imprecise: Report of the Committee on Defamation, Cmnd 5909 (1975), paras. 61–2.

Interests in reputation

The core injury to reputation cases

In the well-known case of *Tolley* v. *Fry & Sons Ltd*[22] the defendants, a firm of chocolate manufacturers, issued an advertisement featuring a caricature of the plaintiff, the leading amateur golfer of his time, Cyril Tolley. The advertisement showed the plaintiff playing golf, with a packet of Fry's chocolate protruding from his pocket, accompanied by a caddy depicted comparing the excellence of the plaintiff's drive with the excellence of the defendant's chocolate in a doggerel verse which accompanied the caricature. The plaintiff brought an action for damages for libel, claiming that the advertisement might be understood to mean that he had allowed his portrait to be used for the purposes of advertising the defendants' products in return for payment and consequently might have compromised or 'prostituted' his status as an amateur golfer.[23] The statement in the advertisement was not defamatory prima facie and the plaintiff had to rely on an innuendo which he claimed arose from the statement. At first instance, Acton J held that the statement was capable of bearing a defamatory meaning and left the case to the jury who found for the plaintiff on the facts and awarded substantial damages. The crucial issue on appeal was how that innuendo should be construed. The plaintiff claimed that the defendants had suggested that (i) he had agreed or permitted his portrait to be exhibited in the advertisement; (ii) this agreement was for payment or reward; and (iii) by doing so, he had prostituted his reputation as an amateur golf player; and (iv) he had been guilty of conduct that was unworthy of his status as an amateur golfer.[24] Much turned on the interpretation of the evidence, particularly evidence of the significance that would be placed on a player's amateur status in golf,[25] and in the House of Lords it was held that the statement was not incapable of bearing a defamatory meaning, and there was a case to go to the jury. The finding of the court at first instance was affirmed although a new trial was ordered in respect of the assessment of damages which were found to be excessive.

Due to the particular facts of the case Cyril Tolley was able to prevent the unauthorised appropriation of his image for commercial gain. If the facts had been different, for example if the plaintiff had been a leading professional golfer, no action in defamation would lie.[26] In his dissenting speech in the House of Lords, Lord Blanesburgh noted that

---

[22] [1931] AC 333.   [23] [1930] 1 KB 467, 468.   [24] *Ibid.*, 467, 483.

[25] See [1930] 1 KB 467, 489. Cf. [1931] AC 333, 339.

[26] The distinction between amateur and professional sportsmen has, in any case, often been an extremely fine one. See, e.g., E. Grayson, *Sport and the Law*, 3rd edn (London, 2000), 456, noting that '[i]n 1895 the professional doctor, W. G. Grace, playing cricket as an amateur, surprisingly retained that status with Gloucestershire and England while also retaining £9,073 8s 3d from three separate sources'.

254   The commercial appropriation of personality

if the subject of the advertisement had been a distinguished statesman, a great scientist, scholar or captain of industry, the statement would have remained innocent and it would not have been possible for such people to raise an innuendo which might establish a case in defamation.[27] In His Lordship's view it seemed anomalous that, due to the sole fact that the plaintiff was an amateur golfer, an action in defamation could succeed, whereas in the case of others who were equally well-known and eminent there would be no remedy in defamation. Despite being the highest authority in this area, *Tolley* v. *Fry* is not particularly significant in terms of the legal issues raised.[28] The main issue turned on the proper interpretation of the innuendo, with the Court of Appeal and House of Lords coming to different conclusions based on the evidence before them. The significance of the case, or at least the decision of the House of Lords, lies in what it did not decide and the fact that alternative approaches to the tort of defamation in addressing the problem were not considered.[29] Passages from the judgment of Greer LJ in the Court of Appeal[30] suggested that the Court disapproved of the defendant's conduct, although it was equally clear that the Court was unprepared to go beyond what could be accomplished within the bounds of the action for defamation. Indeed, in a comment on the decision of the Court of Appeal, Winfield suggested an alternative approach based on invasion of privacy.[31] This point is pursued in detail below.

In a series of unreported cases in the 1930s several actions were brought to restrain the unauthorised use of images in newspapers and advertising. For example, in *Honeysett* v. *News Chronicle*[32] a picture of the first plaintiff and a young man other than her husband was used to illustrate an article entitled 'Unchaperoned holidays' (reflecting a change in holiday

---

[27] [1931] AC 333, 347.

[28] See also the earlier case of *Dunlop Rubber Co. Ltd* v. *Dunlop* [1920] 1 IR 280, where the defendants had published advertisements in which the plaintiff inventor's features had been adapted (from a portrait bust which had been supplied by the plaintiff), and placed on the body of a very tall man, dressed in an exaggeratedly foppish manner, wearing a tall white hat, a white waistcoat and carrying a cane and eye glasses. It was not the plaintiff's habit to wear or carry such items, and an injunction was granted on the grounds that the publication was libellous and calculated to expose the plaintiff to ridicule or contempt. *Quaere* whether the result would have been the same if the plaintiff had not been depicted in such a foppish manner?

[29] It seems that counsel for Tolley relied exclusively on a cause of action in defamation and that it had not occurred to them that a remedy might be secured based on a common law right to privacy, a fact recounted by Lord Conesford in the debate on Lord Mancroft's Right of Privacy Bill 1961 (see 239 above): see *Hansard, Fifth Series*, HL, vol. 229, col. 654, 13 March 1961, cited by W. F. Pratt, *Privacy in Britain* (London, 1979), 224, n. 46.

[30] [1930] 1 KB 467, 477–8.   [31] P. H. Winfield, 'Privacy' (1931) 47 LQR 23.

[32] *Times*, 14 May 1935.

arrangements). The defendants had photographed the first plaintiff and a female companion on a cycling holiday, substituting the picture of the companion for a picture of a man who appeared to be leering at the plaintiff across the handle-bar of his bicycle. The plaintiff husband and wife claimed that readers of the article would form the opinion that the first plaintiff was amusing herself by going away on an unchaperoned holiday with a strange man, who was not her husband, and that the publication implied that she was a woman of loose morals and low character, had committed adultery and was not a proper person to be received into decent society; and that the male plaintiff, was unable to exercise any control over his wife, was a complacent husband who deserved no respect or sympathy, and one who, through weakness, failed to uphold the dignity of married life.[33]

The jury found for the plaintiffs and awarded £100 in damages. Significantly, the original, unaltered, photograph of the wife and her companion had been previously published in a newspaper without objection.[34] Evidently the primary objection related to the element of falsity in the advertisement, and the fact that it would damage the wife's reputation in the eyes of others. It is easy to dismiss this case as being very much a product of its time[35] and to view the plaintiffs as hypersensitive individuals, though this would ignore the very particular notions of honour, morality and injury to reputation which prevailed in British society at the time.[36]

---

[33] *Ibid.*   [34] *Ibid.*

[35] See also the earlier case of *Wallis* v. *London Mail Ltd*, *Times*, 20 July 1917, where the defendants had published a photograph of the plaintiff, which had been taken with the plaintiff's consent some years earlier before she had married, wearing Mexican costume, accompanied by a caption describing her as 'The Whitsun Girl'. The plaintiff claimed that the publication suggested that she was not of a staid character and held her up as a girl whom any man could pick up on his Whitsun holidays. Despite the submission of Sir Edward Marshall Hall KC for the defendant that the publication was incapable of bearing a defamatory meaning, the issue was allowed to go to the jury who awarded the plaintiff £110 in damages.

[36] See, also, *Hood* v. *W. H. Smith and Son Ltd*, *Times*, 5 November 1937 (plaintiff professional actress and model awarded £335 damages against the distributors of the *Paris Magazine* for using a photo of her on the cover accompanied by the words 'Dans le numero. Confidences d'une Amoureuse' on the basis that the publication implied that she was a 'loose and abandoned woman who would allow her photo to appear either gratuitously or for reward in a filthy and degrading magazine'); *Griffiths* v. *Bondor Hosiery Co. Ltd*, *Times*, 10, 11 and 12 December 1935 (professional model awarded damages for injury to her professional reputation, after her head and shoulders had been superimposed on another model's body and legs in an advertisement for stockings, on the basis that the publication could be taken to mean that she had consented to being photographed in an indecent manner and had displayed her legs for tantalising appeal, conduct which was inconsistent with, and detrimental to, her standing as a high-class model). Cf. *Wood* v. *Sandow*, *Times*, 30 June 1914, where an action for defamation failed on similar facts.

256   The commercial appropriation of personality

In a much more modern case, *Khodaparast* v. *Shad*, a clear injury to reputation could be seen where the defendant had passed on, to the daughter of an editor of a London-based Iranian newspaper, documents containing pictures of the defendant's former lover, which had been altered to appear as pages from pornographic magazines advertising telephone sex services.[37] While the documents were not, in the event, published in a newspaper, they were distributed in the London Iranian community with the result that the plaintiff lost her position and any prospects of work as a schoolteacher. Although the claim was brought under the tort of malicious falsehood,[38] described as 'a species of defamation',[39] rather than the tort of defamation itself, the interest protected by both torts is an interest in reputation. Accordingly, the plaintiff was awarded £20,000 damages which included an element of aggravated damages for the injury to feelings caused by the defendant's conduct, in addition to the sum awarded for actual pecuniary damage.

Little is served by further illustrations.[40] What is important is that these cases show that the tort of defamation or, exceptionally, the tort of malicious falsehood will provide a remedy where there has been an injury to a person's reputation, which is one of the possible injuries that a plaintiff might suffer in a case of an unauthorised appropriation of personality. As noted above, there is no precise definition of a defamatory statement,

---

[37] [2000] EMLR 265. Cf. *O'Shea* v. *MGN Ltd and Free4internet.net Ltd* [2001] EMLR 943, where a photograph of a model resembling the plaintiff appeared in an advertisement for a pornographic internet site. Morland J held that the strict liability rule whereby reference to the plaintiff may be established if an ordinary sensible reader understands the statement as referring to the plaintiff, regardless of the intention of the publisher (*Hulton* v. *Jones* [1910] AC 20; *Morgan* v. *Odhams Press* [1971] 1WLR 1239), could not cover a look-alike photograph. Such an approach would constitute 'an unjustifiable interference with the vital right of freedom of expression disproportionate to the legitimate aim of protecting the reputations of "look alikes"', contrary to Art. 10 of the European Convention on Human Rights ([2001] EMLR 943, 956).

[38] Cf. *Joyce* v. *Sengupta* [1993] 1 All ER 897.

[39] [2000] EMLR 265, 280 *per* Stuart-Smith LJ.

[40] For similar cases see, e.g., *Stockwell* v. *Kellog Company of Great Britain*, *Times*, 31 July 1973 (plaintiff awarded damages for the publication of a photograph which had been altered to make her look as though she was pregnant when in fact she was not pregnant and was unmarried); *Debenham* v. *Anckorn*, *Times*, 5 March 1921 (the plaintiff awarded £500 damages when the defendants' newspaper published a photograph of the plaintiff 'with her little daughter Peggie', when in fact, the plaintiff was a single woman). See, also, *Garbett* v. *Hazell, Watson & Viney Ltd and Others* [1943] 2 All ER 359, where the plaintiff succeeded in an action for libel, having been pictured in a magazine carrying on his business as an outdoor photographer, showing pictures to two women. On the opposite page was a picture of a naked woman standing in a mountain stream, and the publication represented the plaintiff saying to one of the women, 'of course, for another shilling madam . . . you can have something like this'. The plaintiff gave evidence that the publication had affected his position and pleaded an innuendo meaning that he showed indecent photographs to women, or that he had pornographic pictures in his possession, or that he was guilty of the offence of endeavouring to procure indecent pictures in a public place, or that he attempted to insult females by showing them indecent photographs.

Interests in reputation

a fact which provides a good degree of flexibility for the courts, but inevitably creates some uncertainty. Most of the cases involving appropriation of personality were brought as actions in defamation and it is arguable that in some cases the courts might have given redress for a rather different kind of injury than an injury to a person's reputation *stricto sensu*. Indeed, it would seem that the tort of defamation is doing the work of more than one tort,[41] with two unfortunate consequences.

First, a lack of realism enters the law when the facts of a particular case are stretched as far as possible in order to comply with the requirements of the tort of defamation, which does nothing except exercise the capacity of lawyers to exaggerate claims of injuries to reputation in the pleadings.[42] A second, and graver, consequence is that where the facts of a case do not disclose a cause of action in defamation, or where the courts are not willing to take a liberal approach as to what constitutes an injury to reputation, plaintiffs are denied a remedy which might otherwise be available under a different head of liability. Despite occasional expressions of disapproval of the conduct of the defendants[43] the English courts have been content to rely on the existing causes of action, without considering whether other solutions to the problem might be available. It is to one of these alternative bases of liability, invasion of privacy, that we now turn. Although the suggestion that the courts have been giving limited recognition to interests in personal privacy through flexible interpretation of the requirements of the tort of defamation is not new,[44] it merits a more detailed examination than it has hitherto received.

---

[41] Cf. Barendt, 'Privacy and the Press', 26, making a similar argument in relation to privacy, defamation and the public disclosure of embarrassing private facts.

[42] See, e.g., *Honeysett* v. *News Chronicle*, note 32 above, and *Hood* v. *W. H. Smith*, note 36 above. Of course, exaggerated claims of mental distress might be made under other bases of liability such as invasion of privacy, or appropriation of personality, for the purposes of maximising damages. Cf. *Roberson* v. *Rochester Folding Box Co.*, 171 NY 538 (1902), 151–2 above.

[43] See, e.g., Greer LJ in the Court of Appeal in *Tolley* v. *Fry & Sons Ltd* [1930] 1 KB 467, 477–8; *Dockrell* v. *Dougall* (1899) 15 TLR 333, 334 (CA); *Sim* v. *H. J. Heinz & Co. Ltd* [1959] 1 WLR 313, 317 (action for libel and passing off). See also *Charleston* v. *News Group Newspapers Ltd* [1995] 2 WLR 450, 452 *per* Lord Bridge.

[44] See, e.g., J. G. Fleming, *The Law of Torts*, 9th edn (Sydney, 1998), 669; L. Brittan, 'The Right of Privacy in England and the United States' (1963) 37 Tulane L Rev 235, 258; Barendt, 'Privacy and the Press', 26. In a Ghanaian case, *Anthony* v. *University College of Cape Coast* [1973] 1 GLR 299, it was held that the unauthorised commercial exploitation of a distinctively coiffured woman's photograph on postcards amounted to both libel and invasion of privacy. The decision was reversed on appeal on both grounds, and it was held that the applicable English authorities did not support the existence of a right of privacy: *University College of Cape Coast* v. *Anthony* [1977] 2 GLR 21, 33–6. See also S. K. Date-Bah, 'Defamation, The Right to Privacy and Unauthorised Commercial Use of Photographs: *Kate Anthony* v. *University of Cape Coast Revisited*' (1977) 14 UGhana LJ 101, and S. K. Murumba, *Commercial Exploitation of Personality* (Sydney, 1986), 79, where the foregoing references are cited.

258   The commercial appropriation of personality

Defamation and invasion of privacy

Early flirtations with privacy

Following the decision of the Court of Appeal in *Tolley* v. *Fry*,[45] denying the plaintiff a remedy in defamation, Winfield was the first to advocate invasion of privacy as an alternative basis of liability[46] in English law, which had been almost completely destitute of literature on the subject, even though invasion of privacy was firmly established as a cause of action in many jurisdictions in the United States at the time.[47] Winfield's contemporaries in Commonwealth jurisdictions were developing similar views. In a comment on the decision of the Court of Appeal in *Tolley* v. *Fry*, the *Australian Law Journal* noted that a person might have suffered great annoyance as a result of the unauthorised use of his likeness, and expressed the 'desirability of some remedy, in cases not covered by the law of defamation, against persons or corporations who, without authority, make use of another's name or portrait for advertising purposes'.[48] The note cited an article, which had appeared three years previously in the *Canadian Bar Review*, by J. D. Falconbridge,[49] then Dean of Osgoode Hall Law School, suggesting reform to give greater protection to interests of personality, as distinguished from interests of substance and property, as one of a number of desirable changes in the common law.[50] Among the examples given were cases involving unauthorised appropriation of personality. The law should be amended, Falconbridge concluded, to give a person a right of privacy in his 'face, personal appearance, sayings, acts and personal relations',[51] a change which he saw as just one further phase in the development of what Pound had described as the right of inviolate personality.[52]

Some borderline cases

The cases noted above all involved an injury to reputation, although the flexibility of this notion allowed the courts a great degree of latitude. How much support is there for the contention that some cases brought

---

[45] [1930] 1 KB 467.   [46] 'Privacy' (1931) 47 LQR 23.

[47] See Chapter 7. See also Note (Anon.), 'Is this Libel? More About Privacy' (1894) 7 HarvLRev 492, commenting on *Monson* v. *Tussauds Ltd* [1894] 1 QB 671; and Note (Anon.), 'The Right to Privacy' (1898) 12 HarvLRev 207, commenting on *Dockrell* v. *Dougall* (1897) 78 LT 840. Both notes observed the English courts' reluctance to go beyond the bounds of the tort of defamation.

[48] Note (Anon.), 'The Unauthorised Use of Portraits' (1930) ALJ 359.

[49] 'Desirable Changes in the Common Law' (1927) 5 Can B Rev 581.

[50] *Ibid.*, 602.   [51] *Ibid.*, 605.

[52] *Ibid.*, 605–6, citing R. Pound, 'Interests of Personality' (1914) 28 HarvLRev 343 and 445, on which see 6–7 and 149 above.

Interests in reputation 259

in defamation might be better viewed as cases involving invasions of privacy? There are obvious dangers in attempting to reinterpret such cases. Despite the fact that a plaintiff's reasons for bringing an action in defamation might be highly subjective, for example a highly developed sense of honour or dignity and a correspondingly strong desire for vindication of personal reputation, the standard applied by the law is the objective standard of the right-thinking member of society in general.[53] Although perceptions of an injury to reputation change over time, and it is difficult to place oneself in the shoes of a judge and jury of a different period and social milieu, the project is not totally futile. New causes of action can only develop if previously accepted assumptions are occasionally challenged and other competing categories are considered.

In *Corelli* v. *Wall*,[54] the plaintiff, a well-known author, brought an action in libel to restrain the defendants from publishing postcards depicting imaginary incidents in her life, such as feeding a pair of ponies, toying a pet dog, and presenting a prize cup to the Stratford-on-Avon Boat Club. The plaintiff claimed to have suffered great annoyance as a result of the sale of the postcards, which was exacerbated when the defendants hired men bearing sandwich boards to parade the streets of Stratford to advertise the postcards. Swinfen Eady J stated that a case in libel had not been made out on the facts, although he recognised that the defendants had proceeded with their course of conduct purely for their own profit, without any respect or regard to the feelings of the plaintiff.[55] The plaintiff also claimed that as a private person she was entitled to restrain the publication of a portrait of herself which had been made without her authority and which, although professing to be her portrait, was totally unlike her. It is not clear from the report how vigorously this line of argument was pursued and whether any precedents were cited in support but, in the absence of any authority, Swinfen Eady J understandably refused to grant an interlocutory injunction.[56] This is probably the case where the facts came closest to disclosing a possible cause of action for invasion of privacy.[57]

The rather bizarre case of *Plumb* v. *Jeyes Sanitary Compounds Co. Ltd*[58] shows the courts taking a very liberal view as to what constituted an

---

[53] *Sim* v. *Stretch* (1936) 52 TLR 669.
[54] (1906) 22 TLR 532. See Winfield, 'Privacy', 31.   [55] *Ibid.*   [56] *Ibid.*
[57] See also the earlier case of *Monson* v. *Tussauds Ltd* [1894] 1 QB 671, 678, where Collins J, at first instance, declined to express any opinion on the question of whether a private person could restrain the publication of a portrait or effigy of himself which had been obtained without his authority, although a comment on the case suggested that it might be an 'inarticulate recognition of the tendency to extend the rights of the person to cover the case of unwarranted and unauthorized representations': see Note (Anon.), 'Is this Libel? More About Privacy'.
[58] *Times*, 15 April 1937.

injury to reputation, where a claim based on invasion of privacy might have been more realistic. A news photographer had photographed the plaintiff police constable removing his helmet and wiping his brow. The photograph, accompanied by the caption 'Phew! I am going to get my feet into a Jeyes' Fluid foot bath', later appeared in the defendants' advertisement, without the plaintiff's permission. The plaintiff alleged that 'the publication meant that, by reason of slovenly and uncleanly habits or otherwise, the exudations and/or general condition of his feet was so unpleasant and noisome that a bath or wash would be inadequate and a solution of Jeyes' fluid sanitary compound would be necessary to deodorize or disinfect his feet'.[59] The defamatory elements of the statement were essentially that the constable's feet smelled, and the plaintiff alleged that, as a result of the publication, he had been held up to ridicule and contempt and had been injured in his credit and reputation. The plaintiff also claimed that he might have been injured in his capacity as a public servant (at the time of the action the plaintiff had left the police force and was working as a sorter in the post office) since anyone who sold such a photograph for commercial purposes would be regarded disfavourably, as it was against his rules of employment to do so. The jury was convinced by these arguments and awarded the plaintiff £100 in damages.

Obviously, *Plumb* v. *Jeyes* shows the flexibility of the notion of an injury to reputation and, according to one well-known definition, a statement is defamatory if it exposes a plaintiff to 'hatred, ridicule or contempt'.[60] Indeed, it has long been held that publishing a statement which renders a man ridiculous is actionable, since it cuts him off from society.[61] The line between mockery and defamation is often difficult to draw and, when this is the case, it should be left to the jury to draw such a line.[62] Although it may have been perfectly reasonable for the judge to have allowed the case to go to the jury, it is equally reasonable to argue that there might be some difference in opinion from one jury to another as to whether the statement was in fact defamatory. It is unlikely that a modern jury would reach the same result on similar facts and, although invasion of privacy was not argued, it would seem to be a more realistic basis for liability.

In a New Zealand case, *Kirk* v. *A. H. & A. W. Reed*,[63] the plaintiff brought an action in defamation after the first defendants had published a photograph of the plaintiff dressed in what Wild CJ described as 'Saturday morning clothes'[64] leaning against a rubbish bin in the main street of

---

[59] *Ibid.*
[60] *Parmiter* v. *Coupland* (1840) 6 M&W 105, 108 *per* Parke B.
[61] *Villers* v. *Monsley* (1769) 2 Wils KB 403, 403–4 *per* Gould J.
[62] *Berkoff* v. *Burchill* [1996] 4 All ER 1008, 1011 *per* Millett LJ.
[63] [1968] NZLR 801.   [64] *Ibid.*, 802.

Interests in reputation

a typical New Zealand town holding a flagon of beer. The photograph, which appeared in the defendants' publication *The New Zealanders in Colour*, was accompanied by a caption stating 'Christmas beer: a reveller with his Christmas beer supply waits for the bus at High Street, Lower Hutt'. The plaintiff claimed that the second defendants, who had taken the picture, had held themselves out to be tourists and had asked him to pose for them as 'a typical New Zealander on the booze'. Further, he claimed that he was not told that the pictures were intended for publication and would not have consented to their being taken if he had been so told. The plaintiff succeeded in his action for damages for libel since the publication as a whole could result in the plaintiff being held up to contempt or ridicule. Wild CJ stressed the importance of the fact that the plaintiff was not told that the photograph was intended for publication and sale, since it might have indicated that the plaintiff had adopted something different from his normal attitude or position to satisfy the second defendants' request.[65] Although the plaintiff succeeded in an action for defamation, the facts could also be seen as an example of invasion of privacy, particularly the 'false light' category in Prosser's reductionist scheme.[66]

There is room for legitimate disagreement as to how these cases should be classified, and some of those cases classified here as 'core injury to reputation' cases could alternatively be viewed as cases involving invasion of privacy.[67] What should be clear is that these examples show the limits of the notion of an injury to reputation, and suggest that the gravamen in many of the cases might have been an invasion of the plaintiff's interests in privacy.

Defamation and 'false light' privacy

There is no need to repeat the earlier discussion of the law of privacy in the United States, although one aspect of privacy, dubbed by Prosser as 'false light' invasion of privacy, is noteworthy since, like defamation, it protects interests in personal reputation.[68] In many states, one who gives publicity to a matter concerning another which places the other before the public in a false light, is liable for an invasion of privacy if the false

---

[65] *Ibid.*   [66] See text below.

[67] Cf. Brittan, 'Privacy in England and the United States', 258–9, citing *Honeysett* v. *News Chronicle* (note 32 above) as an example where the existence of a de facto invasion of privacy makes the court sympathetic towards the suggestion that a defamatory imputation is present.

[68] For a detailed account of the development of this branch of privacy law see D. Zimmerman, 'False Light Invasion of Privacy: The Light That Failed' (1989) 64 NYULRev 364.

262   The commercial appropriation of personality

light in which the other was placed would be highly objectionable to a reasonable person and if the defendant acted knowingly or in reckless disregard of the falsity of the publicised matter, and the false light in which the other would be placed.[69] Thus the interest protected by the false light tort of invasion of privacy is an individual's interest in not being made to appear before the public in an objectionable false light or false position. Although in many cases such false publicity might be defamatory, it is not necessary for the plaintiff to be defamed to maintain an action for false light invasion of privacy. It is enough that he is given unreasonable and highly objectionable publicity which places him in a false light in the eyes of the public, due to the attribution of false characteristics, conduct or beliefs.[70]

The false light cases had made 'a rather nebulous appearance' in a line of decisions which included some false attribution to the plaintiff of some opinion or utterance such as a fictitious testimonial used in advertising, or spurious books or articles purporting to be written by the plaintiff.[71] Prosser recognised that there was a danger that this branch of privacy could engulf the tort of defamation, particularly if it resulted in plaintiffs being able to circumvent the safeguards provided by the technical rules of defamation which had been built up by centuries of reasoned decisions.[72] However, Wade[73] was among several who welcomed this prospect if it would result in the effective avoidance of some of the anomalies and absurdities of the law of defamation.[74] Moreover Wade and others[75] viewed the law of privacy as one stage in the development of a larger tort of intentional infliction of mental suffering which would absorb established torts such as assault, defamation and invasion of privacy and join them together with other innominate torts to form a single integrated system of protecting the plaintiff's peace of mind.[76]

---

[69] *Restatement, Second, Torts* (1977) §652 E.   [70] *Ibid.*, comment *b*.

[71] W. Prosser, 'Privacy' (1960) 48 CalifLRev 383, 398. According to Prosser, this form of invasion of privacy made its first appearance in an early English case, *Byron* v. *Johnston* (1816) 2 Mer 29. Although the report does not state the grounds for the decision, it is often treated as a case of passing off (63 and 65 above) and seemed to be a common law precursor to the statutory right against false attribution of authorship (see, now, Copyright Designs and Patents Act 1988, s. 84). However, it requires quite a stretch to treat this case as an example of invasion of privacy.

[72] Prosser, 'Privacy', 401.

[73] J. W. Wade, 'Defamation and the Right of Privacy' (1962) 15 Vand L Rev 1093.

[74] *Ibid.*, 1121. See also *Douglass* v. *Hustler Magazine Inc.* 769 F 2d 1128, 1133 (1985), *per* Posner J, and see L. Blom-Cooper's foreword to A. Westin, *Privacy and Freedom* (London, 1967), x.

[75] Wade, 'Defamation and Privacy', 1125. See esp. note 168 and the references cited therein.

[76] This was not the case, and the privacy tort, which was initially regarded as a somewhat residual tort, became all-engulfing: 161 above.

Interests in reputation 263

Such a prospect did not appeal to the Younger Committee on Privacy[77] which took the view that placing someone in a false light should be regarded as an aspect of defamation rather than privacy.[78] Concerns were expressed about threats to freedom of speech if the safeguards built into the law of defamation were put in jeopardy by the process of subsuming defamation into a wider tort which was implied by the doctrine of false light. In the Committee's view the concepts of defamation and invasion of privacy should be kept distinct from one another.[79] Indeed these reasons underlie the refusal of some United States jurisdictions to recognise the false light branch of the privacy tort.[80] The Faulks Committee on Defamation[81] shared the view that defamation and privacy should remain separate;[82] no definition of a defamatory statement would be improved by the inclusion of the notion of being placed in a false light. However, the Committee noted that when a person is placed in a false light he may be defamed, although, equally, he may be accorded esteem which he does not deserve to enjoy. In this respect, the Committee argued, it is somewhat misleading to regard the placing of someone in a false light as an aspect of defamation.[83]

Applying the 'false light' criterion, many of the cases involving injury to reputation discussed above could be viewed as invasions of privacy. Clearly this would apply to the 'New Zealander on the Booze' in *Kirk* v. *Reed*,[84] thus providing an alternative cause of action to the successful defamation action. Similarly, if the plaintiff in *Plumb* v. *Jeyes Hygiene*[85] could satisfy the requirements of the tort of defamation, it would not be difficult to establish that the publicity which he had received by being depicted in the advertisement as having malodorous feet would be highly objectionable publicity. The plaintiff who had been portrayed as embarking on an unchaperoned holiday in *Honeysett* v. *News Chronicle*[86]

---

[77] Younger Committee, Report of the Committee on Privacy, Cmnd 5012 (1972), paras. 71–2.

[78] *Ibid.*, para 71. [79] *Ibid.*, para 72.

[80] *Lake* v. *Wal-Mart Stores Inc.*, 582 NW 2d 231 (Minn. 1998) (Minnesota); *Cain* v. *Hearst Corp.* 878 SW 2d 577 (Tex. 1994) (Texas); *Renwick* v. *News and Observer Publishing Co.* 312 SE 2d 405 (N.C. 1984) (North Carolina). Cf. D. McLean, 'False Light Privacy' (1997) 19 Comm & L 63.

[81] Faulks Committee, at paras. 67–70. The Porter Committee took the view that invasion of privacy did not properly fall within the scope of the law of defamation and, in any case, was outside the Committee's terms of reference: Report of the Committee on the Law of Defamation, Cmd 7536 (1948), para. 26. The Calcutt Committee also noted the overlap between intrusions of privacy and defamation but stressed the fact that improvements in the law of defamation would not resolve many of the problems of intrusion into privacy since privacy and reputation are distinct interests: Report of the Committee on Privacy and Related Matters, Cm 1102 (1990), paras. 7.1–7.2.

[82] Faulks Committee, para. 68. [83] *Ibid.*, para. 69. [84] Note 63 above.

[85] Note 58 above. [86] Note 32 above.

264   The commercial appropriation of personality

could also claim that her privacy had been invaded by unwanted publicity placing her in a false light in the public eye. Similarly, the plaintiff who had been falsely depicted as an 'amoureuse' in *Hood* v. *W. H. Smith*[87] could bring a claim for false light invasion of privacy.[88]

On balance, the false light privacy claim adds little to the existing law of defamation. All the defamation cases discussed above could be re-categorised as 'false light' cases, providing that the false light in which the plaintiffs were placed would be such that a reasonable person would find it offensive. Obviously, this is only true because, in almost all of the cases discussed above, the plaintiffs succeeded in their actions in defamation.[89] More significant are the borderline cases which might not have been brought since they were unlikely to succeed in defamation, although here we are entering a field of pure speculation. It would seem that all that a false light privacy tort would provide would be a means for the courts to recognise the claims more openly as claims of 'invasion of privacy', rather than stretching the ambit of the tort of defamation by giving a benevolent interpretation to some of the claims. In turn, this would at least save the plaintiffs from exaggerating their claims in the pleadings, for example by arguing that the publications meant that they were 'loose or abandoned' (*Hood*) or unable to 'uphold the dignity of married life' (*Honeysett*), although such exaggerated claims might continue to be made in privacy actions in order to convince the courts that plaintiffs might have suffered mental distress or indignity. Apart from the extra flexibility, which would spare the courts having to construe claims in highly artificial ways (the benefits of which would obviously have to be balanced against the increased confusion and uncertainty accompanying a new alternative basis of liability), it would seem that little would be gained by the recognition of such a cause of action. Moreover, if the interests in question are interests in *reputation*, then protection should be secured through the tort of defamation, rather than through a nebulous and arguably superfluous new category.[90] Indeed, writers who have examined the law of privacy

---

[87] Note 36 above.

[88] Presumably, the same could be said of 'Whitsun Girl' in *Wallis* v. *London Mail Ltd* (note 35 above), the 'pregnant mum' in *Stockwell* v. *Kellog* (note 40 above), the foppish old gentleman inventor in *Dunlop Rubber Co. Ltd* v. *Dunlop* (note 28 above) and the alleged purveyor of indecent photographs in *Garbett* v. *Hazell, Watson & Viney* (note 40 above).

[89] The solitary exception is *Wood* v. *Sandow* (see note 36 above). Cf. *Blennerhasset* v. *Novelty Sales Services Ltd* (1933) 175 LT 392, where the plaintiff failed to show that the statement referred to him. The same principle of identification would doubtless apply in a case of false light invasion of privacy, or indeed any other type of invasion of privacy. In defamation cases, the plaintiff must show that the statement was published 'of and concerning the plaintiff' (*Restatement, Second, Torts* (1977) §564): see, e.g., *Geisler* v. *Petrocelli*, 616 F 2d 636 (2nd Cir. 1980), and, generally, McCarthy, *Rights of Publicity and Privacy*, §3.8.

[90] See Barendt, 'What is the Point of Libel Law?' 125.

Interests in reputation 265

from an English perspective are sceptical about the utility of the false light category.[91]

Cases where there is no element of falsity which would be regarded as placing the plaintiff in false light that would be highly objectionable to a reasonable person deserve closer scrutiny. Recall the facts of *Corelli* v. *Wall*,[92] where the plaintiff author was depicted in imaginary incidents of her life such as feeding a pair of ponies, toying a pet dog, and presenting a prize cup to the Stratford-on-Avon Boat Club. Although the plaintiff may have been depicted in a false light, in the sense that she might never have fed any ponies, petted any dogs or presented any prizes, such a false light would not be highly offensive to most reasonable people. Here, the focus shifts from the notion of an injury to reputation to an injury to a different interest. This may be described as an interest in personal privacy, *simpliciter*, without going further, and without trying to specify a particular sub-category of privacy, although there are problems with this approach since English law, in particular, is reluctant to recognise a legal right in anything so general as 'a right to be left alone'. One of the reasons why the reductionist approach to the law of privacy has proved to be so attractive in the United States is that it allows specific claims for injuries to specific interests to be rationalised and organised within a broader general notion of a right to privacy. Adopting Prosser's quadripartite reductionist analysis requires us to consider the fourth tort, appropriation. Alternatively, if we were to accept a core conception of privacy which excludes commercial exploitation,[93] alternative causes of action, such as passing off, need to be considered to protect commercial interests in personality. Both these positions can be reconciled by formulating a *sui generis* tort of appropriation of personality.

Defamation, privacy and appropriation of personality

The convergence of interests

Cases such as *Corelli* v. *Wall*[94] call for an alternative basis for liability where there is no injury to reputation or any falsity that might bring the

---

[91] See R. Wacks, 'The Poverty of Privacy' (1980) 96 LQR 73, 84; G. Dworkin, 'The Common Law Protection of Privacy' (1967) 2 U Tas LR 418, 426. D. Zimmerman, 'False Light', argues that the false light branch of privacy lacks justification and resulted from the courts' desire to give plaintiffs greater control over unwanted publicity, rather than through principled development, and is often at odds with the constitutional free speech guarantees.

[92] See note 54 above.

[93] See, e.g., R. Gavison, 'Privacy and the Limits of Law' (1980) 89 Yale LJ 421, and see 166–9 above.

[94] (1906) 22 TLR 532.

266 The commercial appropriation of personality

facts of the case within a false light invasion of privacy. Two factors become relevant. First, the status of the plaintiff: in this case, a well-known author. Second, the essence of the complaint. Ostensibly the claim was for injury to reputation, although it was argued in the alternative that the plaintiff was entitled to restrain the publication of a portrait of herself without her authority.[95] We can only speculate as to why the second claim was put forward. To redress an invasion of privacy and protect or maintain the plaintiff's solitude or anonymity? To protect the plaintiff's interest in marketing her own postcards or the value of a licence to a third party to manufacture such cards? To preserve the commercial value of the plaintiff's image from dilution? Or did such a claim express the plaintiff's aversion to any form of merchandising or advertising, motivated by a desire to preserve her artistic integrity? These questions are unanswerable. They merely serve to illustrate the convergence and interplay of a variety of de facto dignitary and economic interests which might motivate a plaintiff to bring a legal action.

Public and private figures

The position of the plaintiff golfer in *Tolley* v. *Fry*[96] seemed somewhat anomalous. He was sufficiently famous for his image to be worth appropriating, although his status as an amateur ensured that, on the facts of the case, his action in defamation succeeded. If he had been a distinguished statesman, a great scientist, scholar or captain of industry, rather than an amateur golfer, the action would have failed since no innuendo could be raised in such a case to establish a cause of action in defamation.[97] As the development of the right of privacy in the United States illustrates, a person's claim for invasion of privacy might be deemed to be inconsistent with that same person's status as a famous person or public figure, particularly if he himself is involved in exploiting his image for his own gain. However, as a matter of principle, a person's name or reputation does not necessarily become public property simply by virtue of the fact that a person has entered a profession or attained a position which subjects that person to public criticism or scrutiny.[98]

The remaining cases involve plaintiffs who were, to a certain degree, public figures, although the distinction between public and private figures is often difficult to draw.[99] In *Clark* v. *Freeman*[100] the plaintiff,

---

[95] *Ibid.* [96] See text accompanying note 22 above.

[97] *Tolley* v. *Fry* [1931] AC 333, 347.

[98] Cf. *Mazatti* v. *Acme Products* [1930] 4 DLR 601, 604 (public or private status of the plaintiff may be a factor in construing a defamatory statement), and see P. Milmo and W. V. H. Rogers, *Gatley on Libel and Slander*, 9th edn (London, 1998), para. 2.5.

[99] Cf. 172–4 above. [100] (1848) 11 Beav 112.

Sir James Clark, the Queen's physician and an expert in the treatment of consumptive diseases, sought to restrain the defendant from selling and advertising pills under the name of 'Sir J. Clarke's Consumption Pills' (*sic*).[101] The plaintiff claimed that the advertisement gave the impression that the pills were prepared or sold either on his behalf or with his sanction, and argued that such a use might result in injury to his professional character and loss of professional income. Indeed, he believed that the use of the medicine could be positively harmful since it contained elements of mercury and antimony.[102] The main reason why an injunction was refused was procedural: at the time, the jurisdiction to grant an injunction was only exercisable by the Court of Chancery, which would only grant an injunction once the case had been put to the jury at common law.[103] Although Lord Langdale MR stated that the publication might be a serious injury to the plaintiff by way of slander, the correct proceeding was at common law and a judge sitting in the Court of Chancery could not decide the matter. If that had been established, and if it was found that an injury had been done to the plaintiff's property or profession, then Lord Langdale MR was prepared to accept that the Court might be prepared to grant an injunction. However, His Lordship went on to note that he did not believe that a physician as eminent as the plaintiff could have been seriously injured in his reputation as a result of the defendant's conduct, noting that '[i]t is one of the taxes to which persons in his station have become subjected, by the very eminence they have acquired in the world. Other persons try to avail themselves of their names and reputations for the purpose of making profit for themselves; that unfortunately continually happens.'[104]

The facts and the outcome of *Dockrell* v. *Dougall*[105] were similar. The plaintiff, Dr Morgan Dockrell, a physician and lecturer at St John's Hospital London, sought an injunction to restrain the defendant from publishing leaflets which suggested that he recommended the defendant's mineral water 'Sallyco'. The plaintiff claimed that the use of his name on the leaflets was detrimental to his standing in his profession since the suggestion that he might be pushing the sale of a particular medicine was contrary to both the rules of his hospital and the general etiquette of his profession. The action failed, not on procedural grounds as in *Clark* v. *Freeman*, but because the jury decided that the publication was incapable of bearing a defamatory meaning, a decision which one commentator has suggested was perverse.[106] The appeal proceeded on the basis that

---

[101] *Ibid.*, 113   [102] *Ibid.*, 115–16.   [103] See 64–5 above.
[104] (1848) 11 Beav 112, 116.   [105] (1899) 15 TLR 333.
[106] D. L. Mathieson, 'Comment on *Sim* v. *H. J. Heinz & Co. Ltd*' (1961) 39 Can B Rev 409, 421.

268   The commercial appropriation of personality

the plaintiff had a property right in his name *per se*, a proposition that was rejected by the Court of Appeal, in the absence of any damage to his property, business or profession.[107] Both these decisions seem somewhat surprising to the modern reader, although it seems that the practice of using the images of celebrities and members of the medical profession in advertisements for patent medicines was common at the time, despite the British Medical Association's protestations.[108] The prevalence of such a practice, and the fact that it might well have reflected very different norms from those prevailing in modern advertising practice, where such conduct is generally disapproved of,[109] might help explain both the jury's finding of fact in *Dockrell* v. *Dougall* and Lord Langdale's indifference to the plaintiff's predicament in *Clark* v. *Freeman*.[110]

Finally, in *Sim* v. *H. J. Heinz & Co. Ltd*[111] the plaintiff, the well-known actor Alastair Sim, sought an interlocutory injunction to restrain the defendants from imitating his distinctive voice in their advertisement. The plaintiff claimed that a number of people had believed that the voice being used was Sim's voice, and were of the opinion that allowing his voice to be used in such a way was beneath the dignity of his standing as an actor.[112] A claim was brought for libel and passing off.[113] It is a well-established rule in libel actions that the jurisdiction to grant an interlocutory injunction should only be exercised in the clearest of cases, where any jury would say that the matter complained of was libellous, and where, if the jury did not so find, its decision would be set aside by the court as unreasonable.[114] Consequently, counsel for the plaintiff abandoned the application for an interlocutory injunction on the grounds of libel.

Invasion of privacy was not pleaded as an alternative cause of action in any of these cases. *Clark* v. *Freeman* obviously predated the development of the law of privacy in the United States, although the decision in *Dockrell* v. *Dougall* attracted some criticism in the United States on the basis that it hindered the development of a law of privacy.[115] In a lengthy comment on the decision in *Sim* v. *Heinz*, Mathieson suggested that, independently of passing off or libel, a court would restrain the use of a person's image without that person's consent where such unauthorised use would result in an injury to reputation, property, business or profession.[116] Mathieson further argued that if such a principle were

---

[107] (1899) 15 TLR 333, 334.
[108] See T. Richards, *The Commodity Culture of Victorian England* (London, 1990), Ch. 4, esp. 191–3.
[109] See 48 above.   [110] See text accompanying note 104 above.
[111] [1959] 1 WLR 313.   [112] *Ibid.*, 314.   [113] See Chapter 4 at 67–8.
[114] [1959] 1 WLR 316, citing *Bonnard* v. *Perryman* [1891] 2 Ch 269.
[115] See Note (Anon.), 'The Right to Privacy' (1898).
[116] Mathieson, 'Comment', 413.

Interests in reputation

accepted, then a right of privacy would in effect exist in English law, encompassing cases of appropriation of personality and Prosser's false light branch of privacy. By 'bold generalization [*sic*] from the cases in which they have granted remedies in the past', the courts could in effect 'remedy *certain* cases of what might be labelled "invasions of privacy"'.[117]

This is generally consistent with the main argument presented here: that if it is deemed to be desirable to protect interests in personality against unauthorised commercial exploitation,[118] then legal protection should take the form of a suitably narrow tort of appropriation of personality. However, any new tort should be, in different ways, both wider and narrower than that envisaged by Mathieson. It is wider to the extent that any new remedy should arguably encompass dignitary interests such as privacy and freedom from mental distress in addition to damage to property in a business or profession. However, it is narrower in that, although it might encompass certain interests in privacy, it would not, and arguably should not, amount to a general right of privacy through expansive interpretation or 'bold generalisation'.

The principal advantage of such a new rule, and the point that is most immediately relevant to the present discussion, is that a tort of appropriation of personality would avoid the introduction of a potentially wide and undesirable general right of privacy and, moreover, would avoid the potential difficulties in having to reconcile a right of privacy with a plaintiff's status as a public figure. This latter problem, already discussed in detail,[119] resulted in separate rights of publicity and privacy in the United States. Such a problem could be avoided by a *sui generis* tort of appropriation of personality. None of the 'famous' plaintiffs in the cases discussed above (*Clark* v. *Freeman*; *Dockrell* v. *Dougall*; *Sim* v. *Heinz*; and possibly *Correlli* v. *Wall*) seemed to be in the business of exploiting their images for commercial gain. Nevertheless, each plaintiff wished to restrain the unauthorised use of attributes of their personalities.

Conclusions

Ultimately, what is left after the trawl through the English authorities is a handful of cases where claims in defamation were unsuccessful and which would be potentially difficult to reconcile, by virtue of the plaintiffs' celebrity, with the notion of invasion of privacy. It is difficult to determine whether the interests of such plaintiffs as Doctors Clark and Dockrell,

---

[117] *Ibid.*, 429 (italics in original).
[118] See Chapter 11 for a discussion of some underlying justifications.
[119] See 172–4 above.

270   The commercial appropriation of personality

Alastair Sim and Ms Correlli are economic or dignitary interests, or proprietary or non-proprietary interests. Indeed, it does not particularly matter, since a *sui generis* new tort, like the notion of an injury to reputation itself, could encompass both aspects. While the introduction of a general right of privacy was attractive to earlier commentators,[120] and is becoming increasingly so following the Human Rights Act 1998, the experience of the development of the rights of privacy and publicity in the United States now suggests otherwise. A suitably narrowly drawn tort of appropriation of personality could then address both the handful of cases noted above, and the cases which fell on the borderline between defamation and the general notion of invasion of privacy discussed above.[121]

[120] See text accompanying notes 46 to 52 above.
[121] See text accompanying notes 53–67 above.

Part IV

Pervasive problems

10 Property in personality

Introduction

The next two chapters consider two pervasive problems: first, what is meant by a property right or intellectual property right in attributes of personality, and, second, whether such a right can be justified. The problem of appropriation of personality lies on the periphery of intellectual property law, and it is unclear whether attributes of personality should be protected alongside the well-accepted forms of intangible property such as patents, copyright, trade marks and goodwill. The English courts have been reluctant, thus far, to address the issue of whether rights of property may exist in an individual's name, voice or likeness except in limited dicta.[1] While the notion of a property right in the underlying goodwill of a business is uncontroversial, the question of whether a person's name or other indicium of his personality may be considered a part of his property in the goodwill of a trade or profession poses greater difficulties. In this respect the Australian courts have been far more willing than their English counterparts to interpret the core elements of the tort of passing off flexibly, thus broadening the notion of property in goodwill.[2]

A more fundamental issue is whether the courts can recognise a right of property which lies beyond the notion of goodwill in a business or profession. In the United States protection was initially secured from another direction, through the right of privacy, which, as originally conceived, protected essentially dignitary interests. However, in cases involving appropriation of personality the right of privacy quickly developed what

---

[1] See *Clark* v. *Freeman* (1848) 11 Beav 112, 117: 'the courts can interfere in cases of mischief being done to property by the fraudulent misuse of the name of another, by which his profits are diminished'; *Dockrell* v. *Dougall* (1899) 15 TLR 333, 334 (no right of property in a name *per se*, although it was left open as to whether a plaintiff might have rights of property in a business or profession); *Sim* v. *Heinz* [1959] 1 WLR 313, 317–19 (question left open as to whether an actor's goodwill or reputation in his performances could be a right of property capable of being invaded by passing off a third party's performance as the plaintiff's performance); *DuBoulay* v. *DuBoulay* (1869) LR 2 PC 430, 441 (no right of property in patronymic name of family to prevent its assumption by another).

[2] See Chapter 4 above.

273

274   The commercial appropriation of personality

were essentially proprietary attributes and eventually evolved into a separate and distinct right of publicity, a right of 'property' which arguably belongs to the genus of unfair competition.[3] In Canada, on the other hand, a *sui generis* common law tort of appropriation of personality has emerged, seemingly as an offshoot of the tort of passing off, and something of a hybrid tort simultaneously displaying characteristics which might place it among the economic torts, dealing with unfair competition, and elements of a dignitary tort, such as invasion of privacy.[4]

The following questions are addressed in this chapter, in increasingly specific order. First, what do we mean when a particular right is referred to as a property right? Second, what do we mean when we refer to intellectual property rights or property in intangibles? Third, are attributes of personality capable of being described as intangible property? Finally, is there any particular significance in the fact that a certain interest is protected as a property right? It is interesting to note the etymology of the word 'property', and the fact that it derives from the Latin *proprius* meaning 'one's own', or 'something private or peculiar to oneself'.[5] In this respect, what could be more 'one's own' or something that is more 'private or peculiar to oneself' than one's name, likeness or voice? It is useful to bear such an attractively simple notion in mind when considering some of the diverse ways in which the concept of property is used and manipulated by lawyers.

Notions of property

For present purposes, three different senses in which the term 'property' is used may be identified: (a) first, and at its broadest, as a category in legal and political philosophy; (b) second, in its normal everyday conception as land or chattels; and (c) third, in a wider or metaphorical sense, embracing intangibles. Of course, the notion of property is often used in different ways and a search for definition must be separated from attempts at justification. The problems lie at two basic levels. In terms of definition, the problem relates to the move from (b) to (c) above, that is, the move from the traditional notions of property, such as land and chattels, to the notion of property in intangibles and, more specifically, property in personality. It is not necessary to enter a 'forbidding jungle of philosophical argument' in elucidating a legal concept. Rather, we must examine the diverse and complex ways in which specific words work in

---

[3] See 171–80 above.   [4] See Chapter 5 above.
[5] C. T. Onions (ed.) *The Oxford Dictionary of English Etymology* (Oxford, 1966); E. Partridge, *Origins* (London, 1958).

Property in personality   275

conjunction with legal rules.[6] There is no need to batter our heads against a single word, and it will not be necessary to dwell over the meaning of 'property' in the abstract.

As to the question of justification, it must be borne in mind that a term which cannot be given a watertight definition in analytic jurisprudence may nevertheless be useful and important in social and political theory. It must not be assumed that the imprecision or indeterminacy which frustrates the legal technician is fatal to the concept in every context in which it is used.[7] Here the problems concern the move from (a) to (c) above, that is, in using the arguments that seek to justify private property in its widest sense (i.e. the institution of property as a whole) to justify rights in intangibles, specifically intangible property rights in attributes of personality. This chapter focuses on the first aspect and seeks out the ways in which the concept of property is used in the particular context of intangible property and property in personality. The next chapter examines some property-based justifications for personality rights in intangibles as part of the wider arguments for and against (property) rights in name, voice and likeness. The approach is multi-jurisdictional, drawing on the different approaches to the problem of appropriation of personality in the four main common law jurisdictions, although, inevitably, the case law from the United States provides the most fruitful comparative source, where the notion of property rights in attributes of personality is well established.

There is, of course, considerable disagreement as to whether any purpose is served by the use of the term 'property' and whether it relates to any coherent concept in legal theory and political theory.[8] It is difficult to reconcile, within one coherent concept of property, on the one hand the traditional notion of property as 'thing' ownership and, on the other hand, the vastly different modern notion of property which covers a wide range of entitlements. Indeed, most forms of wealth in a modern capitalist economy are intangible property in the form of shares, bonds and insurance policies, as well as the commonly recognised forms of intellectual property such as trade marks, copyrights, patents and business goodwill.[9] Consequently, the arguments used to justify simple 'thing' ownership, when

[6] H. L. A. Hart, 'Definition and Theory in Jurisprudence', reprinted in *Essays in Jurisprudence and Philosophy* (Oxford, 1983), 21.
[7] J. Waldron, *The Right to Private Property* (Oxford, 1988), 31.
[8] See, e.g., K. Gray, 'Property in Thin Air' (1991) 50 CLJ 252, 305, arguing that property is a term of limited content and is consistently the subject of naive and unthinking use, comprising, in large part, a category of illusory reference.
[9] T. C. Grey, 'The Disintegration of Property' in J. R. Pennock and J. W. Chapman (eds.) *Property: NOMOS XXII* (New York, 1980), 69, 70. A distinction may be drawn between documentary intangibles and pure intangibles, such as the common forms of intellectual property, which are not represented by documents: see, generally, R. Goode, *Commercial Law*, 2nd edn (London, 1995), 52–5.

276   The commercial appropriation of personality

private property was a clearly comprehended unitary concept, cannot be readily transferred and applied to more modern forms of wealth.[10] The problem is particularly acute when seeking to justify rights of property in new forms of wealth and new interests that are pressing for recognition. The usefulness of applying traditional theories of property to intangible property rights is questionable and, in moving from the traditional core of property law, real property, to its constantly expanding periphery, 'the image of property law as a game played according to known and well tried rules seems less appropriate'.[11] Indeed, '[t]he meaning of the term "property" or the utility of invoking it as a basis of legal intervention and as an organizing concept for legal doctrine may seem increasingly questionable'.[12]

Property in intangibles

Intellectual property as metaphor

Given the multifarious uses of the term 'property' outlined above, it is not surprising that no dicta offering comprehensive definitions of property can be found.[13] A rough benchmark and useful starting point may be found in the standard incidents of ownership: the right to possess, the right to use, the right to manage, the right to the income, the right to the capital, the right to the security, transmissibility, absence of term, the prohibition of harmful use, liability to execution, and residuary character.[14] A moment's reflection reveals the obvious fact that when we move from tangible property, such as land and chattels, and speak of property rights in intangibles,[15] we are concerned with property in a metaphorical sense.[16]

[10] Grey, 'Disintegration of Property', 78. Cf. S. R. Munzer, *A Theory of Property* (Cambridge, 1990), 31–6.

[11] R. Cotterell, 'The Law of Property and Legal Theory' in W. Twining (ed.) *Legal Theory and Common Law* (Oxford, 1986), 81.

[12] *Ibid.*

[13] Cf. *National Provincial Bank* v. *Ainsworth* [1965] AC 1175, 1247–8 *per* Lord Wilberforce: '[b]efore a right or interest can be admitted into the category of property, or a right affecting property, it must be definable, identifiable by third parties, capable in its nature of assumption by third parties, and have some degree of permanence or stability' (deserted wife's interest in the matrimonial home). See, also, *Minister of State for the Army* v. *Dalziel* (1944) 68 CLR 261, 295.

[14] A. M. Honoré, 'Ownership' in A. Guest (ed.) *Oxford Essays in Jurisprudence* (Oxford, 1961), 107.

[15] Here we are concerned with pure intangibles rather than documentary intangibles, on which see, generally, Goode, *Commercial Law*, 53.

[16] In *Victoria Park Racing and Recreation Grounds Co. Ltd* v. *Taylor* (1937) 58 CLR 479, Latham CJ (497) stated, in the context of an alleged property right in a metaphorical sense in a spectacle, that the appropriateness of the metaphor would depend on the existence of the legal principle; the principle itself cannot be based on such a metaphor.

Property in personality 277

Theoretically, however, this is somewhat untidy. A metaphorical use of a term or phrase presumes the existence of an object or action to which the term or phrase is applied, whereas it is unclear whether there is anything in the nature of a paradigmatic notion of property. The object itself is, paradoxically, somewhat amorphous, and can, at best, only be sketched by reference to the collection of incidents noted above.

Leaving this issue aside for the moment, as we must, it is clear from the most cursory examination of the standard incidents in the context of intellectual property that most intellectual property is only property of a curiously limited nature.[17] Most obviously, although copyrights,[18] patents[19] and trade marks[20] are all declared to be personal property, any pure intangible cannot be physically possessed. Although books, patented devices or goods bearing trade marks may be physically possessed, the intellectual property itself remains incorporeal. While an owner of a piece of land or a chattel may choose to use his property himself, license its use by others or simply choose not to use it at all, a registered trade mark is liable to be revoked if it is not used[21] and a patent may be subject to a compulsory licence if it is not worked to the fullest extent practicable.[22] While copyright,[23] patents[24] and trade marks[25] may be assigned or licensed, property in goodwill cannot be assigned in gross, but only with an accompanying transfer of the underlying business.[26] However, unlike most forms of personal property,[27] statutory intellectual property rights are subject to their own formalities which must be complied with: assignments of copyright[28] and trade marks[29] must be in writing and signed by the assignor, while an assignment of a patent must be in writing and signed by both parties.[30] As to duration, despite the fact that a trade mark is initially registered for a period of ten years,[31] registration may potentially be

[17] For brevity, the following observations are limited to the UK system. For comparative references, see M. Lehmann, 'The Theory of Property Rights and the Protection of Intellectual and Industrial Property' (1985) 16 IIC 525, 530 et seq.
[18] Copyright Designs and Patents Act 1988, s. 1(1).
[19] Patents Act 1977, s. 30(1).   [20] Trade Marks Act 1994, s. 22.   [21] *Ibid.*, s. 46.
[22] Patents Act 1977, s. 48. See, generally, S. Thorley *et al.*, *Terrell on the Law of Patents*, 15th edn (London, 2000), Ch. 9.
[23] Copyright Designs and Patents Act 1988, s. 90.
[24] Patents Act 1977, s. 30(1).
[25] Trade Marks Act 1994, ss. 24–6 and ss. 28–31. For an account of the more restrictive position as regards the licensing of marks under the previous trade mark legislation, see T. A. Blanco White and R. Jacob, *Kerly's Law of Trade Marks and Trade Names*, 11th edn (London, 1986), Ch. 13.
[26] See *Star Industrial Co. Ltd* v. *Yap Kwee Kor* [1976] FSR 256, 269.
[27] See, generally, A. P. Bell, *The Modern Law of Personal Property* (London, 1989), Part III; P. S. Atiyah and J. Adams, *The Sale of Goods*, 9th edn (London, 1995), Ch. 4.
[28] Copyright Designs and Patents Act 1988, s. 90.
[29] Trade Marks Act 1994, s. 24(3).   [30] Patents Act 1977, s. 30(6).
[31] Trade Marks Act 1994, s. 42.

278   The commercial appropriation of personality

renewed indefinitely, subject to the requisite formalities[32] and revocation provisions,[33] while at common law the goodwill in a mark or get-up will generally subsist as long as the underlying business continues.[34] On the other hand, although patents and copyright are also personal property and, as such, are transmissible in much the same way as goodwill and registered trade marks, patents and copyright are strictly determinate interests lasting, respectively, for twenty years[35] and the life of the author plus seventy years (in the case of most works of authorship).[36]

Moreover, the specific and detailed rules for patentability, registration of trade marks and qualification for copyright protection, and the detailed rules governing actionable infringements of those rights, are intended to limit the very scope of any property rights and any harmful uses to which such property might be put. Ownership is qualified in the wider public interest, an obvious example being the range of permitted acts allowed in respect of copyright works.[37] We need not go further to appreciate that, in the case of intellectual property, the term 'property' is used in a purely metaphorical way. It cannot be strictly equated with the paradigmatic forms of property such as land or chattels, and certain consequences or incidents such as those discussed above do not automatically follow from designating certain interests as property rights. Two crucial questions need to be considered, concerning the scope and uses of the property metaphor.

The scope of the metaphor: property and value

Anglo-Australian jurisdictions do not protect all intangible elements of value.[38] Exclusive rights to inventions, trade marks, designs, trade names and reputation are protected 'as special heads of protected interests and not under a wide generalization'.[39] The fact that a product has cost money and labour to produce and has a value for which others are willing to pay

---

[32] *Ibid.*, s. 43.   [33] *Ibid.*, s. 46.

[34] See *IRC* v. *Muller & Co.'s Margarine Ltd* [1901] AC 217; see, further, C. Wadlow, *The Law of Passing Off*, 2nd edn (London, 1995), 140–3.

[35] Patents Act 1977, s. 25.

[36] Copyright Designs and Patents Act 1988, s. 12(1) as amended by the Duration of Copyright and Rights in Performances Regulations 1995 SI 1995 No. 3297.

[37] Copyright Designs and Patents Act 1988, ss. 28–76. See, generally, K. Garnett, J. Rayner James and G. Davies, *Copinger and Skone James on Copyright*, 14th edn (London, 1999), Ch. 9.

[38] *Victoria Park Racing and Recreation Grounds Co. Ltd* v. *Taylor* (1937) 58 CLR 479, 508, cited with approval by Deane J in *Moorgate Tobacco Co. Ltd* v. *Philip Morris Ltd (No. 2)* (1984) 54 CLR 414, 444. Cf. D. Libling, 'The Concept of Property: Property in Intangibles' (1978) 94 LQR 103.

[39] See, generally, 29–30 above.

Property in personality 279

does not, in itself, give rise to a property right.[40] Property, 'a creation of law, does not arise from value, although exchangeable as a matter of fact. Many exchangeable values may be destroyed intentionally without compensation.'[41] As Gordon notes, '[i]f a notion that property automatically arises from value motivates the courts, there is so little reason in it that response is difficult'.[42] Indeed, there is no necessary correlation between value and property; there can be both valueless property and propertyless value.[43]

Clearly, a danger lies in deriving the legal status of property exclusively from the fact that a particular thing or intangible has exchangeable value. This problem is more acute in cases involving the kind of circular reasoning identified by Cohen in the trade mark context: an advertiser who, through ingenuity or effort, has induced consumers to identify with a particular mark or sales device has created a thing of value; a thing of value is property; therefore, the advertiser should be entitled to legal protection against those who seek to deprive him of his property.[44] The obvious problem with such reasoning is that it 'purports to base legal protection upon economic value, when, as a matter of actual fact, the economic value of a sales device depends upon the extent to which it is legally protected'.[45] In such cases, Cohen argued, legal reasoning becomes divorced from questions of social fact and ethical value, while economic prejudice masquerades under the cloak of legal logic.[46] Even where the courts purportedly base their property reasoning on extra-legal factors, such as the de facto value of a person's image as an asset, the reasoning is largely based on certain rudimentary and un-challenged assertions.[47]

The uses of the metaphor

Some interests are often labelled and protected as property rights even though they might not possess all the incidents of ownership in the full

---

[40] *International News Service* v. *Associated Press*, 248 US 215 (1918), 250 *per* Brandeis J.

[41] *Ibid.*, 246 *per* Holmes J.

[42] W. J. Gordon, 'On Owning Information: Intellectual Property and the Restitutionary Impulse' (1992) 78 Virg L Rev 149, 178, citing D. Lange, 'Recognizing the Public Domain' (1981) 44 Law Cont Probl 147, 157, who sees the 'value = property' notion as 'a massive exercise in question begging'. See also *WCVB-TV* v. *Boston Athletic Association* 926 F 2d 42, 45 *per* Breyer CJ (1st Cir. 1991): 'the man who clears a swamp, the developer of a neighbourhood, the academic scientist, the school teacher, and millions of others, each day create "value" (over and above what they are paid) that the law permits others to receive without charge'.

[43] F. S. Cohen, 'Dialogue on Private Property' (1954) 9 RutgLRev 357, 363–4.

[44] F. S. Cohen, 'Transcendental Nonsense and the Functional Approach' (1935) 35 Colum L Rev 809, 815.

[45] *Ibid.*   [46] *Ibid.*, 817.   [47] See text below.

280 The commercial appropriation of personality

sense. Indeed, the main forms of statutory intellectual 'property', and the rights protected under the common law tort of passing off, are only 'property' in a limited and metaphorical sense.[48] In some cases the concept of property is stretched to encompass new interests and one of the arguable advantages of treating intangible assets as property in a purely metaphorical sense is that it emphasises the choice involved in deciding whether to protect an intangible asset by classifying it as property.[49] However, in practice this choice will often be exercised conservatively and a plaintiff will face a heavy burden in showing that a new interest can be regarded as property, since the courts often regard traditional legal concepts such as property as fixed and relatively well defined.[50] The English courts generally prefer to adhere to the specific and well-established heads of protected interest rather than to develop new forms of common law intellectual property, and they have been reluctant to protect new interests under a broad notion of injury to property, interference with trade, or unfair competition.[51]

The law relating to confidential information conveniently illustrates the way in which the property metaphor often appears strained, where the courts often describe rights as proprietary in contexts which make it clear the terms 'property' or 'proprietary' are merely labels placed on rights protected in contract and equity;[52] in such cases, property does not confer an exclusionary right against the whole world.[53] Whatever the underlying basis of the action for breach of confidence,[54] there are considerable difficulties in treating the action as a tortious action for infringement of a proprietary interest.[55] Apart from the question of

[48] See text above.

[49] P. Cane, *Tort Law and Economic Interests*, 2nd edn (Oxford, 1996) 59, citing *Ex Parte Island Records* [1978] Ch 122, 137 and 144, where the majority of the Court of Appeal held that the exclusive contracts between performers and recording companies created 'rights in the nature of rights of property' which could be protected by injunction. This approach, described as the 'injury to property argument' (*Rickless v. United Artists Corp.* [1988] QB 40, 53–4 *per* Browne-Wilkinson VC), has since been held to be wrong: *Lonhro Ltd v. Shell Petroleum Co. Ltd (No. 2)* [1982] AC 173, 187.

[50] See D. Lloyd, 'The Recognition of New Rights' [1961] CLP 39, 41–2.

[51] See, generally, Chapter 3.

[52] See *Cadbury Schweppes Inc. v. Fbi Foods Ltd* [2000] FSR 491, 512 (Supreme Court of Canada) (remedies in breach of confidence depend on a case-by-case balancing of equities rather than the property label).

[53] F. Gurry, *Breach of Confidence* (Oxford, 1984), 47.

[54] Various competing bases of liability such as property, contract, bailment, trust, fiduciary relationship, good faith and unjust enrichment have all been suggested at different times: see Law Commission, Report No. 110, 'Breach of Confidence', Cmnd 8388 (London, 1981), para 3.1, citing G. Jones, 'Restitution of Benefits Obtained in Breach of Another's Confidence' (1970) 86 LQR 463.

[55] See *Cadbury Schweppes Inc. v. Fbi Foods Ltd* [2000] FSR 491, 510, and see, generally, R. G. Toulson and C. M. Phipps, *Confidentiality* (London, 1996), 26–31; Gurry, *Breach of Confidence*, 54.

Property in personality 281

authority,[56] there is a degree of conceptual difficulty surrounding a form of property which comes into existence on the transmission of confidential information but ceases to exist on wider publication. Moreover, certain difficulties result from treating confidential information as property, rather than a personal obligation of confidence, in that the position of an innocent third party recipient of confidential information might be affected to his detriment if he is to become liable for the use of the property even though he was unaware of any breach of confidence.[57] It seems, as the Law Commission concluded, that 'the nature of information is such as to place it in a category of its own, distinct from that of property',[58] although its legal status is the subject of extensive and continuing debate.[59] These issues, fully discussed elsewhere, illustrate some of the difficulties that can be encountered in using property as a general organising legal concept, as an independent basis for liability, or as a metaphorical label to describe interests protected by the law of obligations. Used in this latter sense, how have the courts in the United States and Commonwealth jurisdictions applied the concept of property in protecting attributes of personality under various bases of liability?

Property in personality

Proprietary and non-proprietary analyses

In the United States the right of privacy was originally conceived as a right in inviolate personality, independent of any rights of property, and early objections to its existence, based on the fact that equity's jurisdiction lay in protecting rights of property, were swept aside. However, the right of privacy quickly became a means of protecting essentially economic interests which were often described as 'property' or 'proprietary' interests.[60] Prosser down-played the significance of the property label in his influential reformulation of the right of privacy, taking the view that, even if it was not a right of property, it was a right of value which the plaintiff could

---

[56] See, e.g., *Nicrotherm Electrical Co. Ltd* v. *Percy* [1957] RPC 207, 209 *per* Evershed MR; *Frazer* v. *Evans* [1969] 1 QB 349, 361 *per* Denning MR; *Boardman* v. *Phipps* [1966] 2 AC 46, 127–8 *per* Lord Upjohn; and see, generally, Toulson and Phipps, *Confidentiality*, 26–8; Gurry, *Breach of Confidence*, 48–56.

[57] See, generally, Toulson and Phipps, *Confidentiality*, 30–1 and 92–7; Gurry, *Breach of Confidence*, Ch. 8.

[58] Law Commission, Report on Breach of Confidence, para. 2.10. The Commission argued (at para. 6.2) that a new remedy should be in the form of a statutory tort.

[59] See *Cadbury Schweppes Inc.* v. *Fbi Foods Ltd* [2000] FSR 491, 505.

[60] See, e.g., *Edison* v. *Edison Polyform Mfg Co.* 67 A 392 (1907); *Munden* v. *Harris* 134 SW 1076 (1911); and see 156–9 above.

282   The commercial appropriation of personality

exploit by selling licences.[61] In his opinion, evidence of its proprietary nature could be seen from the fact that an exclusive licensee had a 'right of publicity' which entitled him to prevent the use of the name or likeness by a third person.[62] Such an approach underestimated the difference in the doctrinal bases underlying the separate rights of privacy and publicity, and failed to appreciate the desirability of protecting essentially economic and essentially dignitary interests under separate causes of action. How significant was the shift from protecting interests in personality under the rubric of a right of privacy to a new 'property' right of publicity, and how was the concept of property used in the courts' reasoning?

The significance of the property label in American case law

In the landmark case of *Haelan Laboratories Inc.* v. *Topps Chewing Gum Inc.* the new right was baptised under the name of the right of publicity, and labelled a property right,[63] although Frank J placed little emphasis on the property label, taking the view that it merely symbolised the fact that the courts would enforce a claim which had a pecuniary worth.[64] On the other hand, while the Minnesota Court in *Uhlaender* v. *Henricksen* distinguished between a baseball player's right of privacy and his 'proprietary interest in his public personality',[65] it did not feel that it was necessary to give the proprietary right a specific name. An even more open-ended approach could be seen in the decision of the Ninth Circuit Court of Appeals in *Motschenbacher* v. *R. J. Reynolds Tobacco Co.* where the Court held that it would 'afford legal protection to an individual's proprietary interest in his own identity' but felt that it did not need to decide whether it would do so 'under the rubric of "privacy", "property", or "publicity"'.[66]

Curiously, a case concerning the question of whether rice allotments could be classified as property for taxation purposes, rather than the right of publicity itself, provides some of the most perceptive and illuminating dicta on the use of the concept of property in relation to the right of publicity. As was noted in *First Victoria National Bank* v. *United States*[67] any attempt to define 'property' is an elusive task and it is a matter for the courts to 'fill in the definitional vacuum with the substance of the economics of our time'.[68] The right of publicity was cited as an illustration of the fact that the concept of property evolves over time, and that law and custom may create new property rights where none had previously

---

[61] W. L. Prosser, 'Privacy' (1960) 48 CalifLRev 383, 406.
[62] *Ibid.*, 407.   [63] 202 F 2d 866 (2nd Cir. 1953), 868.   [64] *Ibid.*
[65] 316 F Supp. 1277 (1970), 1282–3.   [66] 498 F 2d 821 (9th Cir. 1974), 825–6.
[67] 620 F 2d 1096 (1980) cited in J. T. McCarthy, *The Rights of Publicity and Privacy*, 2nd edn (New York, 2001), §10.8.
[68] 620 F 2d 1096 (1980), 1102.

Property in personality 283

existed. Despite the fact that courts choose to label the right as a 'property' right, this 'expresses a legal conclusion rather than any independent meaning'.[69] Although an interest labelled as a property right normally possesses certain characteristics in that it may be transferred to others, may be bequeathed, or may be liable to be seized to satisfy a judgment, an interest may qualify as property for some purposes even though it lacks some attributes which a property right might usually possess.[70]

The immediate consequence of the shift in the underlying basis of liability from the right of privacy to the right of publicity was that, unlike a right of privacy, which was a purely personal right, a right of publicity could be freely assignable, and thus could give enforceable rights to third party licensees.[71] Later, plaintiffs sought to establish that the right of publicity could be descendible, pressing the 'property' metaphor even further. For the most part, this did not result from the bare fact that the right of publicity was categorised as a property right. However, in some cases the courts did indeed base their decisions on rather dubious reasoning along the lines of the following syllogism: rights of property were descendible; the right of publicity was a property right; therefore, the right of publicity was descendible. For example, in *Factors Etc. Inc.* v. *Pro Arts Inc.*, a case involving a claim relating to Elvis Presley's estate, the Second Circuit Court of Appeals stated that '[t]he identification of this exclusive right belonging to [the plaintiffs] as a transferable property right compels the conclusion that the right survives Presley's death'.[72] The fallacy of such reasoning is quite self-evident in the light of the foregoing discussion. The fact that a right is labelled as a 'property' right does not automatically mean that consequences x, y and z logically follow and that the property right will possess all the standard incidents of full ownership. Indeed, the common forms of intellectual property are only property in a limited and metaphorical sense, and the mere fact that patents, trade marks, copyright and goodwill are labelled as property rights does not in itself determine the scope of those rights.[73]

In other cases such reasoning only partly accounted for the courts' conclusions, while reference was made to independent substantive reasons for allowing descendibility. For example, when the question of the descendibility of Elvis Presley's right of publicity came to be heard in New Jersey,[74] the District Court's decision that the right of publicity should be descendible relied in part on the conclusion that the right of publicity

---

[69] *Ibid.*, 1103.
[70] *Ibid.*, 1103–4. Cf. the full incidents of ownership, in text accompanying note 14 above.
[71] See *Haelan Laboratories Inc.* v. *Topps Chewing Gum Inc.* 202 F 2d 866 (2nd Cir. 1953).
[72] 579 F 2d 215 (2nd Cir. 1978), 221.
[73] See text accompanying notes 14 to 37 above.
[74] *Estate of Presley* v. *Russen*, 513 F Supp. 1339 (1981).

284 The commercial appropriation of personality

was a property right, although reliance was also placed on the substantive reasons for allowing descendibility, such as the desirability of allowing the fruit of an individual's labour to be passed on to his heirs, and the policy of not allowing a windfall for unauthorised merchandisers.[75] On the other hand, some courts, such as the Supreme Court of Georgia in *Martin Luther King Jr Center for Social Change Inc.* v. *American Heritage Products*,[76] avoided basing their reasoning on the property label and focused solely on the substantive reasons such as the need to encourage effort and creativity and the policy of preventing unjust enrichment, while also noting that the trend since the early development of the common law had been to recognise survivability.[77] Such conclusions depend on the validity of the substantive arguments that are used to support the existence of a right of publicity, such as arguments based on fruits of labour, utilitarian arguments based on incentive, and arguments based on preventing or reversing unjust enrichment. These are considered in the next chapter.

The significance of the property label in Commonwealth case law

While the courts in the United States have gone furthest in recognising proprietary rights in attributes of personality, developments in two other jurisdictions may also be noted. In *Krouse* v. *Chrysler Canada Ltd*[78] a *sui generis* tort of appropriation of personality was recognised in Ontario. At first instance, Haines J acknowledged the fact that personalities such as the plaintiff footballer had valuable de facto economic interests in their names and likenesses[79] and then stated that: '[o]ne would think that the wrongful appropriation of that which in the business world has commercial value and is traded daily must *ipso facto* involve a property right which the Courts protect. Property being an open-ended concept to protect the possession and use of that which has measurable commercial value, logic seems to impel such a result.'[80] Although the reasoning in this passage comes close to the over-simplistic 'everything of value must be property' reasoning noted above, it was based on a recognition of the practical reality (though this was essentially an un-challenged assumption) that certain attributes of personality had specific value, and could be justified by two separate lines of authority: the first based on 'the right of an individual to

---

[75] *Ibid.*, 1355. The Court relied on the dissenting opinion of Bird CJ in *Lugosi* v. *Universal Pictures* Cal. 603 P2d 425 (1979), 434 et seq.

[76] 296 SE 2d 697 (1982).

[77] *Ibid.*, 705. Cf. *Memphis Development Foundation* v. *Factors Etc. Inc.* 616 F 2d 956 (1980), 958 *per* Merritt J for strong arguments against the incentive rationale.

[78] (1972) 25 DLR (3d) 49. See, generally, Chapter 5.

[79] (1972) 25 DLR (3d) 58–61.   [80] *Ibid.*, 61–2.

Property in personality

his elements of identity', and the second based on passing off. As such, no abstract analysis of property was necessary.[81] Although the decision was reversed on appeal, both on the facts of the case and specifically on the passing off point, Estey JA affirmed that a tort of appropriation of personality did exist,[82] and the Court of Appeals did not elaborate on, or depart from, Haines J's analysis of the law at first instance.

A similar process of reasoning could be seen in the decision of the Supreme Court of Jamaica in *The Robert Marley Foundation* v. *Dino Michelle Ltd.*[83] The case involved a claim by the plaintiffs who, after a series of transfers, became the successors in title to the right to use or authorise others to use, in Jamaica, the name and image of the reggae singer Bob Marley, who had died in 1981. The claim for an injunction and damages against a T-shirt manufacturer, who had made unauthorised use of Bob Marley's name and image, succeeded on the grounds both of passing off and of appropriation of personality. The latter ground, as previously noted, involved reasoning which was closely analogous to the reasoning of the Ontario Court in *Krouse* and was based on a number of dicta which, in the Jamaican Court's view, supported the concept of a property interest, distinct from a privacy interest, in personality. However, the decision in *The Robert Marley Foundation* went further in that, unlike the Canadian decisions which concerned claims by living plaintiffs, it involved a claim by the successors in title of the deceased celebrity. The conclusion that the successors in title were entitled to sue did not immediately follow from the fact that the right had been labelled a property right. Rather, the Jamaican Court adopted the substantive reasons for descendibility given by the Supreme Court of Georgia in the *Martin Luther King* case,[84] although the Court also relied on the reasons given by the Court of Appeals of Tennessee in *State of Tennessee, Ex. Rel. The Elvis Presley International Memorial Foundation* v. *Crowell*,[85] which based its decision on descendibility partly on the reasoning that, since the right of publicity is treated as a property right during life, it should also be treated as such after death and therefore should be descendible. The nature of the obligation recognised in *The Robert Marley Foundation* is more extensive and goes further than the Canadian tort of appropriation of personality recognised in *Krouse*.[86] Ultimately, what was decided in *The Robert Marley Foundation* case was that the successors in title had a claim

---

[81] *Ibid.*, 62.
[82] *Krouse* v. *Chrysler Canada Ltd* (1973) 40 DLR (3d) 15, 28.
[83] Unreported Suit No. C.L. R115/1992, judgment 12 May 1994. See also B. Hylton and P. Goldson, 'The New Tort of Appropriation of Personality: Protecting Bob Marley's Face' (1996) 55 CLJ 56, and 125 above.
[84] See note 76 above and accompanying text.
[85] 733 SW 2d 89 (1987).   [86] See 124–7 above.

286   The commercial appropriation of personality

against unauthorised merchandisers, and, until the decision, any licences which were granted to use Marley's image rested on a slender legal foundation, since their enforcement obviously depended on the existence of a valid cause of action. Although the plaintiffs' right was labelled as a property right, that fact in itself did not compel the legal conclusions that were reached in the decision.

Conclusions

Property is an expansive concept. Precise definition is impossible, and its uses are varied and ever changing. In moving from the paradigmatic forms of property, such as land or chattels, to consider property in intangibles, notions of property inevitably change to reflect their context. The fact that an intangible interest protected by a particular tort is labelled and protected as property does not compel the conclusion that such property should possess all of the standard proprietary attributes. Accordingly, the courts should be free to fashion a suitable remedy for appropriation of personality which balances the competing interests of the individual in controlling unauthorised commercial exploitation with the wider interests such as avoiding undesirable monopolies and the suppression of freedom of expression. Questions concerning the nature of a remedy for appropriation of personality, such as whether the remedy should be purely personal, or whether it should be assignable and transmissible, can be decided without treating the property label as conclusively determining every issue. The nature and scope of a remedy for appropriation of personality is examined in Part V following a discussion of the fundamental question of whether such a new remedy can be justified on any rational basis. The next chapter considers whether arguments justifying property in the broad sense, as a category in legal and political theory, may be fruitfully used to justify new forms of intangible property such as property in personality, or whether such arguments are attempts to provide a veneer of intellectual respectability for claims which are devoid of substance.

11 Justifying a remedy for appropriation of personality

Introduction

This chapter considers the following five main arguments which might be used to justify a new remedy to prevent unauthorised commercial exploitation of personality: (i) natural rights of property; (ii) utilitarian arguments; (iii) economic efficiency; (iv) preventing or reversing unjust enrichment; and (v) protecting personal dignity. Aspects of the last two have already been encountered in substance, if not in form, in previous chapters,[1] although they require some elaboration here. The arguments depend, of course, on the nature of the remedy for which a justification is sought. The bases of liability examined in the foregoing parts reveal three main possibilities: (i) a personal tort remedy based on infringement of privacy; (ii) a personal tort remedy based on infringement of a 'proprietary' interest in name, voice or likeness (similar to the Ontario tort of appropriation of personality); (iii) a more extensive right of 'property' in the elements of personal identity, which is fully assignable and has a post-mortem duration akin to copyright (similar to the American right of publicity). The fact that a right is labelled as 'property' or 'proprietary' is not inherently significant and does not mean that the right will have all the characteristic incidents of full ownership. Intellectual property is 'property' in a metaphorical and rather limited sense, and even an interest cast as a 'right of property', such as the American right of publicity, is a strictly determinate interest.[2] The mixture of property-based arguments and arguments based on protecting personal dignity inevitably reflect the hybrid nature of the problem of appropriation of personality and both its economic and dignitary aspects.

Many of the arguments discussed here derive from the American cases and literature where there is a solid and indeed overwhelming consensus within the legal community that the right of publicity is desirable.[3]

---

[1] See 180 and 141–4 above.   [2] See Chapter 7.
[3] M. Madow, 'Private Ownership of Public Image: Popular Culture and Publicity Rights' (1993) 81 CalifLRev 125.

287

288   The commercial appropriation of personality

McCarthy, the right of publicity's most prominent proponent, seems to represent the view generally prevailing amongst commentators that the initial phase of questioning the existence and validity of the right of publicity has passed and that most courts can now concern themselves with refining its shape, scope and limits.[4] Those seeking to question the assumptions made by supporters of the right of publicity, who argue that the initial phase of questioning has been concluded too hastily and that no persuasive case has been made in favour of the right, are in a distinct minority.[5] That said, the American Law Institute's Third Restatement of the Law of Unfair Competition concedes that:

The rationales underlying recognition of a right of publicity are generally less compelling than those that justify rights in trademarks or trade secrets. The commercial value of a person's identity often results from success in endeavours such as entertainment or sports that offer their own substantial rewards. Any additional incentive attributed to the right of publicity may have only marginal significance. In other cases the commercial value acquired by a person's identity is largely fortuitous or otherwise unrelated to any investment made by the individual, thus diminishing the weight of the property and unjust enrichment rationales for protection.[6]

There has been relatively little discussion outside the United States of whether a remedy for appropriation of personality would be desirable and whether such economic and dignitary interests deserve to be protected from unauthorised commercial exploitation. Consequently, the debate has not, as yet, been influenced by the pro-protection, proprietarian zeal which characterises much of the American literature, allowing the issues to be considered afresh, from a rather more detached perspective.

Natural rights of property

Introduction

The Lockean labour theory and the Hegelian personality theory are often invoked in discussions of the underlying philosophical justification of

---

[4] J. T. McCarthy, *The Rights of Publicity and Privacy*, 2nd edn (New York, 2001), §1.34.

[5] As Madow, 'Private Ownership of Public Image', 133, notes, some of the criticism levelled at the right of publicity has come from those outside the American legal community who are concerned with its wider impact on culture and society, citing J. Gaines, *Contested Culture: The Image, The Voice and The Law* (London 1992), and R. J. Coombe, 'Objects of Property and Subjects of Politics: Intellectual Property Laws and Democratic Dialogue' (1991) 69 TexLRev 1853. No attempt will be made to encompass the wider cultural aspects here and the discussion is limited to an appraisal of some of the arguments used by the courts and legal commentators. Madow, 'Private Ownership of Public Image', offers a very full and readable account which combines both perspectives.

[6] *Restatement, Third, Unfair Competition* (1995), §46 comment *c*.

Justifying a remedy for appropriation of personality   289

property rights in general[7] and they have a strong intuitive appeal for those who seek philosophical justifications for property rights in intangibles.[8] Here the concern lies with making the move from property in its broadest sense, that is, as a category in legal and political philosophy,[9] to the notion of property in personality, although such a move is not without its dangers. It is not proposed that we should consider these theories in any detail here, though they merit a brief discussion since they are sometimes invoked when new rights of property in intangibles are considered,[10] and, more specifically, have been invoked to justify property in personality.[11]

Arguments for property rights take place at several different levels:[12] (i) at the highest level, a general justification of property rights deals with the widest question of whether there can be a justification of any property rights in any form; (ii) a specific justification considers whether there can be a specific kind of property right such as full ownership, as opposed to a more limited form of (property) right; (iii) a particular justification addresses the question why a particular person should have a particular form of property right in a particular thing or, in the context of our discussion, in a particular intangible. While a debate as to whether the law should recognise or label a new claim as a property right is obviously concerned with the third, particular, level of justification, most attempts to justify private property rights take place in the context of general works of political philosophy, which are primarily concerned with providing a general justification for property rights.[13] There are considerable

---

[7] See, e.g., M. R. Cohen and F. S. Cohen, *Readings in Jurisprudence and Legal Philosophy* (New York, 1951), Ch. 1; R. G. Hammond, *Personal Property*, 2nd edn (Oxford, 1992), Ch. 2; G. W. Paton and D. P. Derham, *A Textbook of Jurisprudence*, 4th edn (Oxford, 1972), Ch. 22.

[8] See, e.g., P. Drahos, *A Philosophy of Intellectual Property* (Aldershot, 1996); J. Hughes, 'The Philosophy of Intellectual Property' (1988) 77 GeoLJ 287; E. C. Hettinger, 'Justifying Intellectual Property' (1989) 18 *Philosophy and Public Affairs* 31; H. Spector, 'An Outline of a Theory Justifying Intellectual and Industrial Property Rights' [1989] EIPR 270. Cf. B. Sherman and L. Bently, *The Making of Modern Intellectual Property Law* (Cambridge, 1999), 210, n. 16.

[9] See 274–6 above.

[10] See, e.g., M. Spence, 'Passing Off and the Misappropriation of Valuable Intangibles' (1996) 112 LQR 472, 491–6.

[11] See T. Frazer, 'Appropriation of Personality – A New Tort?' (1983) 99 LQR 281, 300 et seq.; McCarthy, *Rights of Publicity and Privacy*, §2.1 and the references cited.

[12] See L. C. Becker, *Property Rights: Philosophic Foundations* (London, 1977), 23. The separability of these different levels of justification may, however, be illusory – for example, it is difficult to envisage how a general justification could proceed until some particular or specific elements were introduced: see A. Reeve, *Property* (London, 1986), 29.

[13] See, e.g., J. Locke, *Two Treatises of Government*, ed. P. Laslett, (Student Edition) (Cambridge, 1988); G. W. F. Hegel, *Philosophy of Right*, trans. T. M. Knox (Oxford, 1942); R. Nozick, *Anarchy, State and Utopia* (Oxford, 1974). Cf. S. R. Munzer, *A Theory of Property* (Cambridge, 1990).

290   The commercial appropriation of personality

dangers in trying to seek particular justifications for particular forms of interests by invoking theories which are directed towards a much wider purpose of justifying the institution of private property as a whole. In moving from the general to the particular it must be borne in mind that general justifications of property rights have a very different purpose – that is, the defence of the very existence of the institution of private property in its entirety – from the particular justifications which we are seeking.

Moreover, each argument for property should ideally be understood in its own particular social, historical and intellectual context. Although some will insist on the autonomy of textual study, believing that the classic texts contain timeless wisdoms, or pure ideas which can be considered without their historical baggage, others maintain that ideas constitute a response to immediate circumstances and that we should not simply study the texts themselves but rather the social and intellectual context which explains how those ideas developed.[14] Grave intellectual damage can result from attempts to transplant ideas from their particular historical context and impose them on a modern-day problem; any statement is 'inescapably an embodiment of a particular intention, on a particular occasion, addressed to the solution of a particular problem and thus specific to its situation in a way that it can only be naive to transcend'.[15] Furthermore, the whole project of justification (or even a justification of justifications) is a rather limited and limiting way of understanding arguments about property, particularly when an interpreter or author has a particular scheme of his own to promote. All too often, this results in the context and detail of a particular work being ignored in order to further or legitimate the author's own ends.[16] The labour theory is rarely invoked as a *general* justification for property rights, although there are intricate arguments about the *specific* kinds of property rights that labour can produce.[17] Consequently, it is not surprising that, of the natural rights theories, Locke's labour theory has been invoked most often in the context of intellectual property and in the particular context of rights in personality. As such, it deserves closer scrutiny than Hegel's theory, which is often invoked as a general justification of property rights, but is rarely invoked as a particular justification for property rights in specific interests.

[14] See Q. Skinner, 'Meaning and Understanding in the History of Ideas' (1969) 8 *History and Theory*, 3, 39–40.
[15] *Ibid.*, 50.
[16] See A. Pottage, 'Property: Re-appropriating Hegel' (1990) 53 MLR 259, 270.
[17] See Becker, *Property Rights*, 32.

Justifying a remedy for appropriation of personality 291

Locke's labour theory

Locke's primary aim in the *Two Treatises* lay not so much in providing a general theory of ownership, but in examining the issue of taxation, particularly arbitrary taxation, although it was inevitable that he would have to discuss the nature of property in addressing this issue and the theory of property he propounded was undoubtedly original and important.[18] Locke starts with the idea of the state of nature which exists before any form of government and before any law and, like any natural rights theorist, seeks to show that there is a valid justification for property rights which pre-exist, and are independent of, any form of government or law. The essence of Locke's labour theory of property acquisition is captured in the following well-known passage from Chapter V of the *Second Treatise*:

Though the Earth, and all inferior Creatures be common to all Men, yet every Man has a property in his own Person. This no Body has any Right to but himself. The Labour of his Body, and the Work of his Hands, we may say, are properly his. Whatsoever then he removes out of the State that Nature hath provided, and left it in, he hath mixed his Labour with, and joyned to it something that is his own, and thereby makes it his Property. It being by him removed from the common state Nature placed it in, it hath by this labour something annexed to it, that excludes the common right of other Men. For this Labour being the unquestionable Property of the Labourer, no man but he can have a right to what is once joyned to, at least where there is enough and as good left in common for others. [*sic*][19]

Although the property which Locke sought to justify by natural right was 'an isolated possession of personal origin',[20] in most cases in a modern industrial economy, with its complex interaction of capital and labour, an individual labourer can no longer be seen as 'a miniature god who has a title to his own creation'.[21] Furthermore, it is increasingly difficult for a labourer to place a mark of personal workmanship on any product since it is usually the result of the labour of a multitude of different workers. Moreover, the product's existence almost invariably depends on the availability of substantial capital for development, production, marketing and distribution.

Nevertheless, Locke's theory has a particular attraction for those seeking philosophical justifications for intellectual property, though perhaps

---

[18] See the introduction to Locke, *Two Treatises*, and J. Tully, *An Approach to Political Philosophy: Locke in Contexts* (Cambridge, 1993).
[19] *Two Treatises*, Book II, Ch. V, para. 27.
[20] W. H. Hamilton, 'Property According to Locke' (1932) 41 Yale LJ 864, 878.
[21] *Ibid.*

292   The commercial appropriation of personality

it fits rather better in the case of copyright than patents. A copyright work is more likely to be the result of an individual author's labour than a patent which, in the usual case, will come into being as a result of corporate investment and co-ordinated effort; for every patent secured by a lone inventor, there are probably many more patents which have resulted from the combined efforts of many, backed by substantial collective capital. That said, many works that attract copyright, such as computer programs, are equally the result of combined endeavour and substantial investment, rather than individual effort,[22] and it is obviously dangerous to make broad generalisations.

One of the prime attractions of Locke's theory is that the state of nature can be equated with a sphere of no ownership, or to use a concept familiar to intellectual property lawyers, the public domain, where there are no private property rights to ground exclusive claims to a tangible or intangible element of value. Through an individual's labour, private property rights can be acquired where none had previously existed, and this justifies taking an object (or in this case an intangible) from the common state of nature and into private ownership, as long as the proviso that there be enough material resources left for others is satisfied. Thus, in the case of a patent, an inventor's expenditure of mental or physical labour entitles him to make a claim for the exclusive ownership of particular subject matter, thus taking the invention out of the unowned common, and into private ownership. Similarly, an author is entitled to a property right in the form of a copyright in a particular work, since the expression of an idea embodied in a particular work is the result of the author's mental labour. This labour, which has resulted in an original copyright work coming into being, justifies the existence of private property rights, moving the work from a state of no ownership analogous to Locke's state of nature and into the realm of private ownership.

General problems with Locke's theory

Problems with Locke's theory exist at two main levels: first, internal inconsistency and, secondly, lack of specific applicability. As regards the first point, philosophers have questioned some of the assertions in the passage cited above – particularly whether there is a logical progression between three key propositions: first, that every man has a right to his own person; second, that every man has a right to own the labour of his person; and third, that every man has a right to own that which he

---

[22] See M. Rose, *Authors and Owners* (Cambridge, Mass, 1993), viii: 'most work in the entertainment industry is corporate rather than individual'.

Justifying a remedy for appropriation of personality 293

has mixed his labour with.[23] For example, can a person be said to have property in his own body?[24] Can a person be said to 'own' his labour, bearing in mind that labour, or labouring, is an activity? While activities can be engaged in or performed, can they in any meaningful sense be owned?[25] Moreover, the metaphor of mixing one's labour with an unowned object is ambiguous; since labour is a series of actions, it is arguably incapable of being mixed with an object in a way which might entitle the labourer to a property right.[26] Furthermore, even if we concede that labour can be owned, and also accept the possibility of mixing one's labour with an object or intangible, should mixing one's labour with an unowned object entitle a person to that object? Or rather is it merely a means of losing one's labour?[27] Finally, can a person be said to deserve property rights in the whole object on which he has laboured, or merely the added value that has resulted from the person's labour?[28] Obviously, none of these questions can be satisfactorily answered here, although they show that Locke's theory has its own inherent problems which should ideally be addressed before using it as a framework for justifying intellectual property rights.

Problems of specific applicability

Assuming that the essence of the labour theory of property can withstand scrutiny, to what extent can the key notion of labour provide a particular justification for intangible property and, more specifically, property in personality? For present purposes we must pass over much of what is controversial in applying the Lockean labour theory to intangible property in general[29] and proceed to consider to what extent the labour theory can provide a convincing justification for property rights in attributes of personality such as name, voice and likeness. Some American authorities have sought to justify the right of publicity in Lockean terms, by arguing that it is a natural right to the fruits of one's labours. For example, McCarthy states that 'perceptive legal commentators do not shy away from defending the right to control commercial use of identity as a

---

[23] For a detailed discussion of Locke's theory, see Becker, *Property Rights*, Ch. 4; J. P. Day, 'Locke on Property' (1966) 16 *Philosophical Quarterly* 207; J. Waldron, *The Right to Private Property* (Oxford, 1988), 177–83.

[24] See Day, 'Locke on Property', 215, and Becker, *Property Rights*, 36–41.

[25] See Day, 'Locke on Property', 210. See also A. Carter, *The Philosophical Foundations of Property Rights* (London, 1989), 24–8.

[26] See Waldron, *The Right to Private Property*, 184–91.

[27] See Nozick, *Anarchy, State and Utopia*, 174–5.   [28] *Ibid.*, 175.

[29] For detailed discussions see Hughes, 'The Philosophy of Intellectual Property', 296–329; Drahos, *Philosophy of Intellectual Property*, Ch. 3.

294   The commercial appropriation of personality

self-evident natural right of every person',[30] going on to cite Nimmer's argument that: '[i]t would seem to be a first principle of Anglo-American jurisprudence, an axiom of the most fundamental nature, that every person is entitled to the fruit of his labors unless there are important countervailing public policy considerations'.[31] Similar views have also been expressed in judicial dicta. For example, in *Uhlaender* v. *Henricksen* Judge Neville stated that, at least for celebrities, the right of publicity provides protection by way of a property right for an asset which a person has built up through hard work and effort:

[i]t is this court's view that a celebrity has a legitimate proprietary interest in his public personality. A celebrity must be considered to have invested his years of practice and competition in a public personality which eventually may reach marketable status. That identity, embodied in his name, likeness, statistics and other characteristics is the fruit of his labors and is a type of property.[32]

This reflects the popular view that what a person creates should be his, and while one person may build a home, and another may knit a jumper, another might well create a valuable personality, all of which should be recognised as property.[33] As McCarthy argues, 'there is probably nothing so strongly intuited as the notion that my identity is *mine*'.[34]

Nevertheless, it is submitted that the labour justification for a right of property in a person's name, voice or likeness is unconvincing. It is commonly claimed that a person's fame is the result of that person's labour. For example, it might be argued that recognising a right of property in, let us say, a sportsman's or actor's image is a just reward for the labour (which is naturally his) that he has expended in creating and developing that image. Yet, this ignores the fact that labour is an activity[35] and, moreover, an activity is invariably purposive and directed towards a particular task or goal.[36] When an athlete labours, his labour is directed towards a particular task such as winning a game or race. The reward for that labour might be a financial reward or merely the satisfaction or prestige gained in asserting his superior athletic prowess. That labour *might* result in fame, in addition to success or failure in the primary activity, though fame does not *necessarily* follow and cannot be regarded as a natural consequence.

If such arguments are seriously intended to establish that a property right in a person's image is a natural right, based on that person's labour, then they result from a confusion of the different senses in which the word

---

[30] McCarthy, *Rights of Publicity and Privacy*, §2.2.
[31] M. B. Nimmer, 'The Right of Publicity' (1954) 19 Law ContProbl 203, 216.
[32] 316 F Supp. 1277 (1970), 1282, cited in McCarthy, *Rights of Publicity and Privacy*, §2.5.
[33] *Ibid.*, §2.5.   [34] *Ibid.*
[35] Assuming that an activity can be owned: see note 25 above and the accompanying text.
[36] See W. J. Gordon, 'A Property Right in Self-Expression: Equality and Individualism in the Natural Law of Intellectual Property' (1993) 102 Yale LJ 1533, 1547.

Justifying a remedy for appropriation of personality 295

'labour' is used. In a natural rights labour theory of property acquisition, such as Locke's, a person's entitlement to a property right derives from the fact that a person owns the 'labour of his body or the work of his hands', which, in turn, derives from the argument that a person owns his body. Mixing his work or labour with an unowned object entitles that person to a property right in the thing laboured on (or at least the value added). Many of the problems involved in the indiscriminate use of the labour theory seem to stem from a confusion of the different senses in which the terms 'labour' or 'work' are used.[37] For example, in one sense the word 'work' is used to describe the actual process of labouring. In a second sense, it is used to describe a particular task or tasks, for example 'the twelve labours of Hercules'. In a third sense, 'work' is used to denote a person's achievements, in the case, for example, of a person's 'life's work' or 'life's labour'.[38] Yet, a natural rights theory such as Locke's logically supports a claim only for a property right based on labour in the first two senses of the word noted above. The third alternative interpretation of the notion of work or labour does not derive naturally from a person's ownership of work (that is, the work of his body), which in turn derives from that person's ownership of his body. In most cases, fame – and the opportunities for its exploitation – does not derive directly from the actual process of labouring or from the performance of particular tasks. In the same way that Locke's turf cutter labours to cut turf, a racing driver labours to win a race, a footballer labours to win a game and an actor labours to deliver a particular performance. The labour theory cannot support a claim for a property right in something as general as a person's achievements, fame or 'life's labours'.

Moreover, in seeking to justify the right of publicity by reference to the labour theory, an unwarranted assumption is made that the value (or at least a substantial part of the value) of a person's image derives directly from that person's labour.[39] In Locke's primitive state of nature it could be assumed that labour 'puts the difference of value on every thing', and that an individual's labour could account for ninety-nine hundredths of the value of a thing.[40] Obviously Locke's state of nature is far removed from the modern world, and attempts to draw parallels grossly oversimplify the means by which value is added to goods or things in general and, in particular, the way in which a person's image can become a valuable commodity. It is simply assumed that the commercial value has been

[37] For a detailed discussion in the context of Locke's theory, see Day, 'Locke on Property', 208 et seq.
[38] *Ibid.*, 209 and 220.
[39] See, e.g., Nimmer, 'The Right of Publicity', 216: 'It is also unquestionably true that in most instances a person achieves publicity values of substantial pecuniary worth only after he has expended considerable time, effort, skill and even money.'
[40] Locke, *Two Treatises*, para. 40.

296 The commercial appropriation of personality

created as a direct result of the labour of the famous person in creating a marketable persona. Yet there are powerful counter arguments which go a long way towards rendering such a view untenable. As Coombe argues in the context of the right of publicity in the United States:

Publicity rights are justified on the basis of the celebrity's authorship, but star images must be made, and, like other cultural products, their creation occurs in social contexts and draws upon other resources, institutions, and technologies. Celebrity images are authored by studios, the mass media, public relations agencies, fan clubs, gossip columnists, photographers, hairdressers, body-building coaches, athletic trainers, teachers, screenwriters, ghostwriters, directors, lawyers, and doctors. Even if we only consider the production and dissemination of the star image, and see its value solely as the result of human labor, this value cannot be entirely attributed to the efforts of a single celebrity author. Moreover... the star image is authored by its consumers as well as its producers: the audience makes the celebrity image the unique phenomenon that it is.[41]

It is submitted that the view adopted in the *Restatement of Unfair Competition* is much more intellectually honest and realistic, conceding that the commercial value of a person's identity often results from success in activities which offer their own rewards or is simply a result of fortuity, rather than individual investment or labour.[42] Indeed, the labour theory is a rather weak attempt at justifying property rights in personality.

Hegel's personality theory

It has also been suggested that a right of property in a person's image can be justified by reference to G. W. F. Hegel's personality theory.[43]

---

[41] R. J. Coombe, 'The Celebrity Image and Cultural Identity: Publicity Rights and the Subaltern Politics of Gender' (1992) 14 *Discourse: Berkeley Journal For Theoretical Studies in Media and Culture* 59, 61. For judicial expressions of similar sentiments see *Cardtoons v. Major League Baseball Players* 95 F 3d 959 (10th Cir. 1996), 975; *Memphis Development Foundation v. Factors Etc. Inc.* 616 F 2d 956 (CA Tenn. 1980), 959 (cf. text accompanying note 86 below). See, also, A. Story, 'Owning Diana, from People's Princess to Private Property' [1998] 5 Web JCLI, noting the importance of the social context of the creation of Princess Diana's image; Spence, 'Passing off and Misappropriation', 479–80, citing the difficulty in determining who created the endorsement or recognition value of the Paul Hogan / Mick Dundee character (the subject of litigation in *Pacific Dunlop Ltd v. Hogan* (1989) 87 ALR 14 (see 95–6 above)) which derived in part from the considerable talent of the actor and film makers, but also drew on the tradition of the Australian bushman stereotype which had existed for generations, and relied on the audience's identification and enjoyment of a character coming from such a tradition.

[42] See text accompanying note 6 above. Although the comments were directed at the investment and incentive rationales (on which, see text below), they are equally applicable to the labour rationale.

[43] See Frazer, 'Appropriation of Personality', 301, and S. K. Murumba, *Commercial Exploitation of Personality* (Sydney, 1986), 132. For uses of this argument in the wider context of property rights in intangibles, see Spence, 'Passing off and Misappropriation', 491–6; Hughes, 'The Philosophy of Intellectual Property', 330–50; Drahos, *Philosophy of Intellectual Property*, Ch. 4.

Justifying a remedy for appropriation of personality 297

For present purposes, this can be dealt with very briefly. Although it has obvious superficial attractions it does little to help us in any search for a justification of property rights in name, voice or likeness. As noted above, arguments concerning the justification of property rights take place at several different levels.[44] While the labour theory of property acquisition, at least in its original Lockean form, was propounded in the context of a general theory of government, it is rarely used as a general justification for property rights, but is more often used in discussing the specific kinds of property that labour might justify.[45] In Hegel's personality theory we also see a general justification for property rights, in the context of a much wider intellectual enterprise, though it cannot readily be applied as a specific justification for specific forms of property rights.

The personality justification for property rights derives from Hegel's *Philosophy of Right*.[46] The German word *recht* has a wider meaning than any corresponding English word such as 'right' and embraces not only jurisprudence but also moral philosophy and political theory.[47] Among Hegel's aims are attempts to accommodate both the central concept of the freedom of the will and social and political freedom within one single theory, a rejection of a sharp dichotomy between the individual and the state, an account of the role of the economy in society, and an appreciation of the role of warfare in the life of a state. In common with other natural rights theorists such as Locke, the background of Hegel's argument is the fiction of a state of nature without any form of established society and, above all, without the coercive power of the state.[48]

In his discussion of abstract right, Hegel envisages a situation where an individual's will, a central idea in Hegelian philosophy, is embodied in an external object. In order to achieve this, a central right of a person is the right to property, an absolute right of appropriation with regards to all things.[49] It is clear that Hegel envisaged a wide notion of 'thing' that was not confined to tangible objects. Although the attainments of an artist or scholar could not easily be described as 'things', since they were essentially inward and mental, such attainments, erudition and talents could be expressed and could thus be embodied in something external, tangible and alienable, thereby allowing them to be placed in the category of 'things'.[50] The point of all of this, and the point of property rights in Hegel's scheme, is not to satisfy a person's physical needs, but to develop or fulfil his personhood. Personhood is purely subjective

---

[44] See text accompanying note 12 above.
[45] Becker, *Property Rights*, 32.   [46] Hegel, *Philosophy of Right*.
[47] See, generally, M. Inwood, *A Hegel Dictionary* (Oxford, 1995), 221.
[48] See K. H. Ilting, 'The Structure of Hegel's *Philosophy of Right*' in Z. A. Pelczynski (ed.) *Hegel's Political Philosophy: Problems and Perspectives* (Cambridge, 1971), 91.
[49] Hegel, *Philosophy of Right*, §44.   [50] *Ibid.*, §43.

298   The commercial appropriation of personality

and needs to realise itself in the external world by claiming some portion of the external world as its own. Thus, the making of property claims contributes to the development of the personality since it invites recognition by others, which, in turn, helps to foster a moral and social dimension in the property claimer.[51] A person's conception of himself ceases to be purely subjective and becomes concrete and recognisable to himself and to others in a public and external world.[52] Thus every individual has a right to embody his will in an external object, and a right to whatever he thereby appropriates, although only the possibility of private property is granted to all and it is an entirely open question what, or how much, an individual may possess as his private property.[53]

Inevitably such a brief summary gives only the barest outline of a complex theory. What should be clear, however, is that Hegel's discussion of property rights is part of a very wide intellectual enterprise, and the arguments concerning property seek to explain the very existence of *any form of property rights whatsoever* through their relationship with the development of an individual's personality. Whatever its merits in a larger scheme directed at explaining the relationship between property rights in general and intangible property rights, and their social, political and economic significance,[54] Hegel's theory of property does little to help us in our present enquiry in seeking justifications for a *particular* and novel form of property right in personality.

Summary

Talk of natural rights of property has always had a strong rhetorical appeal which has not been lost on those who seek to justify private property rights in new forms of wealth, or seek to remove what lies in the public domain into the sphere of private ownership. Closer examination, however, reveals the questionable nature of such arguments and a theory of a natural right of property through labour is a somewhat unconvincing rationale for property rights in a person's name, voice or likeness. Similarly, a personality theory of property rights, though intuitively attractive, does little to justify property rights in specific intangibles such as the attributes of an individual's personality. At their best, these arguments challenge us to think more profoundly about the question of whether private property rights in some forms of intangibles can be justified. At their worst,

[51] Drahos, *Philosophy of Intellectual Property*, 77.
[52] Waldron, *The Right to Private Property*, 353.
[53] See Ilting, 'The Structure of Hegel's *Philosophy of Right*', 93.
[54] See Drahos, *Philosophy of Intellectual Property*, Ch. 4, and Hughes, 'The Philosophy of Intellectual Property'.

Justifying a remedy for appropriation of personality 299

and taken at face value, the arguments are deceptive and are seemingly deployed solely to add intellectual lustre and legitimacy to claims which may well be somewhat lacking in substance.[55] Even so, such a conclusion regarding the substance of the claims is rather premature at this stage, without having considered whether other arguments provide more convincing justifications for a remedy for appropriation of personality.

Utilitarian arguments

The rejection of natural rights

In general, arguments in favour of natural rights of property have not fared well, at least in the Anglo-American legal tradition,[56] reflecting the Benthamite view that there was no such thing as natural property which existed before law; property was entirely a creature of the law and if the laws were taken away, then property would also cease to exist.[57] Moreover, from the nineteenth century onwards, 'the notion that the state itself conferred property rights and could perform "adjustments" in the name of the "best interests of all" was taking hold'.[58] It is well established that the traditional categories of intellectual property recognised in Anglo-American law, that is, patents and copyright, are underpinned by utilitarian considerations, which are rather more familiar and require less background than the natural rights theories discussed above. In the United States the utilitarian tradition is embedded in Art. 1, s. 8 of the Constitution, which gives Congress the power 'to promote the progress of science, and useful arts, by securing for limited times to authors and inventors the exclusive right to their writings and discoveries', a tradition which has been stressed in the patent and copyright decisions of the Supreme Court.[59]

In any case, relatively little significance lies in the choice between utilitarian and natural-rights-based arguments. As Baird succinctly puts it:

[55] Cf. *Cardtoons* v. *Major League Baseball Players* 95 F 3d 959, 975 (10th Cir. 1996): 'blind appeals to first principles carry no weight in our balancing analysis'.

[56] See, e.g., F. Machlup and E. Penrose, 'The Patent Controversy in the Nineteenth Century' (1950) 10 *Journal of Economic History*, 11–17. For a distinction between deontological and consequentialist justifications see Spector, 'An Outline of a Theory Justifying Intellectual and Industrial Property Rights'.

[57] J. Bentham, *Principles of the Civil Code*, Chapter VIII, reprinted in C. B. Macpherson (ed.) *Property: Mainstream and Critical Positions* (Oxford, 1978), 51.

[58] Hammond, *Personal Property*, 51.

[59] See, e.g., *Mazer* v. *Stein* 347 US 201 (1954), 219: 'The economic philosophy behind the clause empowering Congress to grant patents and copyrights is the conviction that encouragement of individual effort by personal gain is the best way to advance public welfare through the talents of authors and inventors in "Science and Useful Arts".'

300   The commercial appropriation of personality

[t]he danger lurking in the common law development of intellectual property rights is not...that judges will embrace an unsound natural rights theory of intellectual property, for in practice, relatively little turns on the choice of underlying theory. Rather, the danger is that judges will fail to identify the interests for which protection is being urged and hence fail to discover the intellectual property cases that provide the most useful analogies.[60]

The choice between utilitarian or natural rights theories might, on the other hand, affect our perceptions of the conduct of the defendant and the legitimacy of the plaintiff's claim against him. If we see an author or other right holder as having a natural right to profit from his work, then we will see the infringer as some sort of thief, whereas if we regard the author/right holder as a beneficiary of a statutory monopoly, it may be easier to see the infringer as embodying the values of free enterprise and competition.[61]

Utilitarianism in copyright and patent law

The Anglo-American copyright system is based on utilitarian foundations rather than any notion of natural rights, a fact reflected in the title of the first English copyright statute, the Statute of Anne 1710: 'An Act for the Encouragement of Learning by Vesting the Copies of Printed Books in the Authors or Purchasers of Such Copies'.[62] In England the argument that an author had a natural and perpetual right of property in his work was pressed primarily in the interests of the booksellers, who wished to secure a longer monopoly than the maximum twenty-eight-year period which the 1710 Act allowed.[63] Although initially successful,[64] such an

---

[60] 'Common Law Intellectual Property and the Legacy of *International News Service v. Associated Press*' (1983) 50 U Chi L Rev. 411. As J. Phillips and A. Firth, *Introduction to Intellectual Property* 3rd edn (London, 1995), 24–5 put it, the rotation of the world on its axis does not depend on the outcome of the natural rights versus utility debate.

[61] J. Waldron, 'From Authors to Copiers: Individual Rights and Social Values in Intellectual Property' (1993) 68 Chic-Kent LRev 841, 842.

[62] The Anglo-American systems are often contrasted with the continental systems, with their emphasis on the author's rights as moral rights, or rights of personality. For example, although French law initially reflected the positivist approach under which the author's rights were a creation of the state, the naturalist approach became increasingly influential, according to which a work was seen as being inseparable from its creator and an expression of his personality: see G. Davies, *Copyright and the Public Interest* (Weinheim, 1994), Ch. 6. It is not possible to reduce either the French *droit d'auteur* to principles of property, or the English notion of copyright to ideas of monopoly, and utilitarian and pragmatic considerations have contributed just as much to the shape of the successive French laws as has natural law: see A. Strowel, '*Droit d'Auteur* and Copyright: Between History and Nature' in B. Sherman and A. Strowel (eds.) *Of Authors and Origins* (Oxford, 1994), 239 and 248.

[63] See L. R. Patterson, *Copyright in Historical Perspective* (Vanderbilt, 1968), 147.

[64] *Millar* v. *Taylor* (1769) 4 Burr 2303, 2341 *per* Aston J and 2398 *per* Mansfield LJ.

Justifying a remedy for appropriation of personality 301

approach was subsequently rejected,[65] thus limiting the author's rights to those provided by the Statute of Anne, denying any further claims to perpetual common law copyright. The decision effectively forestalled a host of analogous claims for misappropriation of other forms of intellectual endeavour, since, following *Donaldson* v. *Beckett*, 'new forms of protection had to be secured from the legislature; and even if a lobby succeeded, the most that could be hoped for would be an exclusive right of limited duration'.[66] Moreover, the focus shifted to the impact that the granting of such new property rights would have.[67] The Anglo-American patent system is similarly based on principles of utility rather than natural rights, although there has been no explicit conflict of the kind seen in early copyright law, and from an early time patents were perceived as statutory monopolies of limited duration, granted in order to stimulate innovation and investment, rather than the natural property of the inventor.[68]

Utility, incentive and appropriation of personality

Supporters of the right of publicity in the United States have also invoked the incentive justification for the right of publicity, by analogy with copyright and patent law, often citing the following dictum in the Supreme Court in *Zacchini* v. *Scripps-Howard Broadcasting Co.*:

Of course, Ohio's decision to protect petitioner's right of publicity rests on more than a desire to compensate the performer for the time and effort invested in his act; the protection provides an economic incentive for him to make the investment required to produce a performance of interest to the public. The same consideration underlies the patent and copyright laws long enforced by this Court . . . These perhaps regard the reward to the owner as a secondary consideration but they were intended definitely to grant valuable enforceable rights in order to afford greater encouragement to the production of works of benefit to the public . . . The Constitution does not prevent Ohio from making a similar choice here in deciding to protect the entertainer's incentive in order to encourage the production of this type of work.[69]

---

[65] *Donaldson* v. *Beckett* (1774) 2 Bro PC 129. In the United States, common law copyright was similarly rejected in deference to statutory copyright in *Wheaton* v. *Peters*, 26–33 US 1055 (1834). For a reappraisal of the contribution of natural law theory see A. Yen, 'Restoring the Natural Law: Copyright as Labor and Possession' (1990) 51 Ohio St LJ 517.
[66] W. R. Cornish, *Intellectual Property*, 4th edn (London, 1999), 341–2.
[67] Sherman and Bently, *Making of Modern Intellectual Property Law*, 39.
[68] See, e.g., E. W. Hulme, 'The History of the Patent System Under the Prerogative and at Common Law' (1896) 12 LQR 141, and 'On the History of Patent Law in the Seventeenth and Eighteenth Centuries' (1902) 18 LQR 280; B. W. Bugbee, *Genesis of American Patent and Copyright Law* (Washington, 1967); M. Coulter, *Property In Ideas: The Patent Question in Mid-Victorian Britain* (Kirksville, Mo. 1991), Ch. 1 and the references cited; Cornish, *Intellectual Property*, 110 et seq. and the references cited.
[69] 433 US 562 (1977), 573.

302   The commercial appropriation of personality

It would be tempting to argue that this dictum should be limited to the immediate and rather unusual facts of the case. The plaintiff's claim related to the unauthorised televising of his human cannonball act. Training and equipping oneself to be shot from a cannon involves a direct investment of substantial effort and money which, in turn, directly results in the performance value of the act. As the Tenth Circuit stated in *Cardtoons* v. *Major League Baseball Players*, Zacchini 'complained of the appropriation of the economic value of his *performance*, not the economic value of his *identity*'.[70] However, it is clear that the dictum in *Zacchini* was intended to apply to the underlying rationale for rights of publicity in general, not only the rights of human cannonballs. Moreover, the incentive rationale has been alluded to in other cases involving the more common factual scenario of the unauthorised commercial exploitation of name or likeness in advertising or merchandising.[71] In her influential dissenting judgment in *Lugosi* v. *Universal Pictures*, Bird CJ stated that while those who feel the immediate benefits of the right of publicity are those who have identities which are commercially valuable, the products of their enterprise are beneficial to society generally since '[t]heir performances, inventions and endeavours enrich our society, while their participation in commercial enterprises may communicate valuable information to consumers'.[72] However, if 'performances, inventions and endeavours' are to be encouraged, then they can be properly encouraged and rewarded through the law of copyright, performance rights (in the United Kingdom, they are, in any case, an aspect of copyright)[73] or patents. In jurisdictions where these rights already exist, it is not clear why a right of publicity should be necessary as a further incentive.[74]

[70] 95 F 3d 959, 973 (10th Cir. 1996), *per* Tacha J (italics in original).

[71] See, e.g., *Estate of Presley* v. *Russen*, 513 F Supp. 1339 (1981), 1355, citing with approval the dissenting opinion of Bird CJ in *Lugosi* v. *Universal Pictures* Cal., 603 P2d 425 (1979), 446; *Carson* v. *Here's Johnny Portable Toilets Inc.* 698 F 2d 831 (6th Cir. 1983), 837 (vindication of right of publicity would tend to encourage achievement in comedian Carson's chosen field: *quaere* would that have any effect on his comic skills?).

[72] Cal., 603 P2d 425 (1979), 441.

[73] See Copyright Designs and Patents Act 1988, ss. 180–212, and see, generally, R. Arnold, *Performers' Rights*, 2nd edn (London, 1997). To fulfil its obligations under the TRIPs agreement, the United States now provides protection for musical performances by virtue of the Uruguay Round Agreements Act, 17 USC §1101, which adds a single section to the Copyright Act (as a *sui generis* neighbouring right rather than part of the Act itself): see M. B. Nimmer and D. Nimmer, *Nimmer on Copyright Vol. III* (New York, 2000), §8E; P. E. Geller (ed.), *International Copyright Law and Practice Vol. II* (New York, 1999), §9[1][a]. Previously, protection for live performances had been secured under state law: see *Nimmer on Copyright, Vol. I*, §1.01[B][3][b]; McCarthy, *Rights of Publicity and Privacy*, §8.102 and §11.52.

[74] As to the second point, one may question whether the use of a celebrity image communicates any information to consumers. Celebrity product endorsements and tie-ups often merely serve to increase the saleability of products and the advertisers' revenues.

Justifying a remedy for appropriation of personality 303

To what extent are supporters of an incentive theory willing to press their view and how do they envisage its precise application in the context of the right of publicity? Proponents of the right of publicity seem to argue that the incentive rationale is not limited to an incentive to develop a licensable persona, but extends to include 'socially enriching actions which bring one's identity into the public eye as a necessary consequence of success in one's profession'[75] and, as was noted in *Matthews* v. *Wozencraft*, 'encourages people to develop special skills, which can then be used for commercial advantage'.[76] Thus, the argument runs, without protection, people will be less willing to engage in activities which might bring them fame and consequently result in crass commercial exploitation of their names or images. If legal recognition of a right to control unauthorised commercial exploitation can even slightly induce socially enriching activities, society as a whole is better off. McCarthy concedes that such assertions are incapable of objective proof and that society's gains or losses cannot be quantified, although the incentive effects of copyrights and patents are difficult to separate and evaluate from a multitude of other motivating factors.[77]

This brings us to the core of the issue. To what extent do patents and copyright act as an incentive to invent and write, and to what extent can analogies be drawn with interests in personality? The objectives underlying the modern patent system are often stated as being to 'encourage invention and innovation and the growth of new industries'.[78] However, it is doubtful whether the patent system in fact provides an incentive for

---

Like many trade marks, celebrities merely create (irrational) differentiation between products, allowing manufacturers to add value to what would otherwise be standard products, and achieve consumer brand loyalty which effectively shields them from price competition (see S. J. Hoffman, 'Limitations on the Right of Publicity' (1980) 28 Bull Copyright Soc'y 111, 120; cf. McCarthy, *Rights of Publicity and Privacy*, §2.7, arguing that the removal of a right of publicity would result in more rather than fewer celebrity 'endorsements' and tie-ins). On the other hand, the use of celebrities as animate trade marks provides information to consumers and, in theory, allows the consumer to rely on the trade mark as an indication of consistent quality, which, in turn, requires the producer to maintain that quality in order to maintain the consumer's loyalty. These are, of course, merely two sides to the wider debate on the economic functions of trade marks (see Chapter 3), although the cynical might argue that, rather than being informed, the consumer is indirectly paying the celebrity's fee, through the higher price that the manufacturer can charge as a result of the celebrity's participation.

[75] McCarthy, *Rights of Publicity and Privacy*, §2.6.
[76] 15 F 3d 432 (5th Cir. 1994), 437, cited in McCarthy, *Rights of Publicity and Privacy*, §2.6. Presumably this means personal commercial advantage, which is assumed to be in the greater social interest.
[77] McCarthy, *Rights of Publicity and Privacy*, §2.6.
[78] J. M. Aubrey, 'A Justification of the Patent System' in J. Phillips (ed.) *Patents in Perspective* (Oxford, 1985), 1.

304   The commercial appropriation of personality

an otherwise uninventive person to invent.[79] Some, if not most, people lack the inherent capacity to invent, a deficiency for which no property incentive can compensate. Even one blessed with a capacity to invent, is, in psychological terms, more likely to be motivated by the desire to solve a particular problem, intellectual curiosity, the need to accumulate knowledge, or desire for the esteem of others than by the prospect of securing a patent.[80] However, even if the incentive to invest rationale is dismissed, the patent system can still be justified on the basis that it acts as an incentive for the inventor to disclose his invention[81] and as an incentive for investment, although the effect of each of these incentives might, in turn, be rather weak.[82] Similarly, the incentive effect of copyright may be questioned and it is doubtful whether the prospect of copyright protection plays any part in influencing the decision of an author to write, although, unlike the case of patents, almost every human being has the inherent capability to produce a copyright work, given the low thresholds for protection in terms of originality in common law systems.[83] However, the prospect of securing copyright protection might play a part in encouraging investment which might not otherwise be made, ranging from the substantial investment involved in producing works such as computer programs and sound recordings to more modest investment involved in bringing more personal works of authorship to fruition. Given the vast range of works that copyright protects, it is dangerous to

[79] Phillips and Firth, *Introduction to Intellectual Property*, 108–9. Taking the system as a whole, it has been noted that patents offer 'only a very limited inducement for industrial invention and innovation. Where really big risks which involve large sums of money are concerned, the patent system may well not offer a sufficient inducement for public interest purposes': C. T. Taylor and Z. A. Silberston, *The Economic Impact of the Patent System: A Study of the British Experience* (Cambridge, 1973), 365.

[80] See F. L. Vaughan, *The United States Patent System* (Norman, Okla., 1956), 4–11, noting (at 11) that although monopoly rights for new inventions became well established during Queen Elizabeth's reign, there was no appreciable change in technological ideas or methods: the Industrial Revolution came some 200 years later and not as a result of monopoly grants to inventors; D. Vaver, 'Intellectual Property Today: Of Myths and Paradoxes' (1990) 69 Can Bar Rev 98, 100 (making a similar point). See also P. Meinhardt, *Inventions, Patents and Monopoly* (London, 1946), 5; Phillips and Firth, *Introduction to Intellectual Property Law*, 108–9.

[81] See, e.g., T. S. Eisenschitz, 'The Value of Patent Information', and C. Oppenheim, 'The Information Aspects of Patents' in Phillips (ed.) *Patents in Perspective.* Cf. Vaver, 'Intellectual Property Today', 123, noting how this aim is frustrated by careful drafting disclosing as little information as possible while broadening the scope of the patent as widely as possible.

[82] For a concise appraisal, see Phillips and Firth, *Introduction to Intellectual Property Law*, 110–16.

[83] See, generally, K. Garnett, J. Rayner James and G. Davies, *Copinger and Skone James on Copyright*, 14th edn (London, 1999), 105 et seq. and 184. Cf. *Feist Publications Inc.* v. *Rural Telephone Service Co. Inc.* 499 US 340, and see J. A. L. Sterling, *World Copyright Law* (London, 1998), Ch. 7.

Justifying a remedy for appropriation of personality 305

generalise, and the investment incentive rationale might differ substantially between different types of copyright works, or even between certain specific examples of a particular type of work, for example different classes of books.[84]

Obviously these assumptions cannot be tested without an empirical enquiry into the economic or psychological evidence.[85] Nevertheless, it is submitted that the analogies between interests in personality and the utilitarian underpinnings of copyright and patent law are unconvincing. While most people will lack the inherent capacity to invent and few will be subject to the incentive effects of the patent system, it is arguable that the incentive effect would affect even fewer in the case of personality rights; most people will lack the capacity to become famous or develop 'recognition value' in their names or other attributes of personality, regardless of any incentive that a right of publicity might provide. Furthermore, in the same way that inventors invent as a result of the need to solve an immediate problem rather than as a result of a patent incentive, people usually become famous for reasons which have nothing to do with the incentive effect of a right of publicity or similar right. Indeed, as Merrit J, sitting in the Sixth Circuit Court of Appeals in *Memphis Development Foundation* v. *Factors Etc. Inc.* noted, although fame and stardom may be ends in themselves, they are normally by-products of other activities. The primary motivating factor is 'the desire to contribute to the happiness or improvement of one's fellows and the desire to receive the psychic and financial rewards of achievement' stemming from an individual's need for the respect and goodwill of others and a need for variety and novelty of experience and opportunity for ingenuity and invention. By contrast, '[t]he desire to exploit fame for the commercial advantage of one's heirs is . . . a weak principle of motivation'.[86] The context of the dictum was the question of the descendibility of the right of publicity. Although the decision has not been followed in Tennessee, and despite the fact that descendibility has been recognised in most states, it provides a rare and well-reasoned argument to counter some of the

---

[84] See S. Breyer, 'The Uneasy Case for Copyright: A Study of Copyright in Books, Photocopies and Computer Programs' (1970) 84 HarvLRev 281, 291–321 (varying levels of economic incentive for different types of books).

[85] Cf. Breyer (*ibid.*), arguing that the economic case for copyright in books, when considered as a whole, is weak, resting not so much on proven need, as on uncertainty as to what would happen if protection were removed, citing F. Machlup, 'An Economic Review of the Patent System' (Senate Judiciary Comm., Subcomm. on Patents Trademarks and Copyright, Study No. 15, 85 Cong, 23 Sess (1958): '[n]one of the empirical evidence at our disposal and none of the theoretical arguments presented either confirms or confutes the belief that the patent system has promoted the progress of the technical arts and the productivity of the economy'.

[86] 616 F 2d 956 (1980), 958.

306 The commercial appropriation of personality

exaggerated and desperate attempts that have been made to justify the right of publicity.

Thus, it is submitted, the incentives to create a licensable persona, or engage in 'socially enriching actions',[87] are weak foundations for the incentive justification. Other elements of the incentive justification which might be relevant to patent and copyright law do not apply. Most obviously, unlike patent law, there is nothing akin to the incentive to disclose, by which it is deemed to be in the wider public interest to grant a limited monopoly right to secure the beneficial effects of full disclosure. Equally, it is submitted that, apart from unusual and highly anomalous cases such as human cannonball acts, the need to encourage investment is less acute where personality rights are concerned than is the case with inventions and copyright works. Indeed, while copyright and patent law protect the primary, if not the sole, source of an author's or inventor's income, the right of publicity protects what is at most an incidental activity,[88] although this might be disputed by proponents of the view that celebrity images should be regarded more as a deliberately manufactured product.

Any utilitarian theory involves a balancing of harms and benefits to provide the greatest happiness in the greatest numbers. A balance must be struck between the costs of private property rights in attributes of personality (of whatever extent) and the wider benefits that might be secured for the public by granting such property rights. The crux of the issue is the question of how strictly we wish to apply the utilitarian incentive test to copyright, patents and other interests such as interests in personality. It is one thing to suggest that a system of intellectual property rights serves economic goals and uses the market to achieve a rough compromise between the author's or inventor's claims to rewards and the wider public need, and quite another to suggest that intellectual property rights for creators are *only* justifiable when the public gains something that it otherwise would not have gained.[89] In the latter case we are approaching a position where a kind of 'but for' test is used, where intellectual property rights are only justified to the extent that they directly encourage the creation of new works or inventions.[90]

The strictness of the test that one wishes to adopt inevitably reflects the relative values that one places on the competing interests of private

---

[87] See text accompanying note 75 above.

[88] *Cardtoons* v. *Major League Baseball Players* 95 F 3d 959 (10th Cir. 1996), 973.

[89] See W. J. Gordon, 'An Inquiry Into the Merits of Copyright: The Challenges of Consistency, Consent and Encouragement Theory' (1989) 41 Stanford L Rev 1343, 1438.

[90] *Ibid.*, 1438, citing *Graham* v. *John Deere Co.* 383 US 1 (1985) where the Supreme Court stated that the patent monopoly was an inducement to bring forth new knowledge and weed out those inventions which would not be disclosed or devised but for the inducement of a patent.

Justifying a remedy for appropriation of personality 307

property and the wider public interest. The difficulty in applying, in the case of interests in personality, tests similar to those used in relation to patents and copyright, relates to the central problem of the nebulous nature of the interests that personality rights protect. In the United States the rights of privacy and publicity protect a person against the unauthorised commercial exploitation of his name, voice, likeness or other indicia of identity.[91] Every person possesses these attributes of personality, although some might have a commercial value, others might not. To what is encouragement and incentive being given, which might justify such protection? Performances, inventions and endeavours?[92] The development of a licensable persona? Socially enriching actions? Special skills for commercial advantage?[93] If we adopt a strict 'but for' test, and ask whether such values would be created but for a right of publicity or some such right, then, human cannonballs aside, the case for protection on the basis of utility and incentive is weak. Indeed, there is much to be said for the view, expressed more recently by the Tenth Circuit in *Cardtoons* v. *Major League Baseball Players*, that the incentive effect has been overstated and that most sports and entertainment celebrities with commercially valuable identities are involved in activities which themselves generate significant rewards. The removal of a right of publicity would not impair the celebrity's ability to earn a living from activities such as sport or acting which generated the commercially marketable fame.[94]

Of course, that does not mean to say that property rights in personality cannot be justified, only that the economic incentive rationale is a rather weak attempt at justification, when other arguments might carry greater weight. Ultimately, attempts to draw parallels between the right of publicity and the traditional core areas of intellectual property seem to suffer from a problem of labels. The following logic seems to be at work: the right of publicity is a right to prevent the unauthorised commercial exploitation of purely economic interests in personality; since it deals with economic interests and involves the creation of monopoly rights, then it must be a form of intellectual property; therefore, the standard tests of intellectual property must apply, and the validity of analogies with copyright and patents must be tested. Such an approach is somewhat misguided since, in any case, the area of intellectual property which is most closely analogous with appropriation of personality is the law of

---

[91] See Chapter 7. [92] See text accompanying note 72 above.
[93] See notes 75 to 76 above and accompanying text.
[94] 95 F 3d 959 (10th Cir. 1996), 973. Cf. McCarthy, *Rights of Publicity and Privacy*, §2.6, noting that, while the general incentive effect of copyright and patents is widely accepted, the courts do not apply a strict 'but for' test in determining the economic incentive effect on individual authors and inventors.

308   The commercial appropriation of personality

trade marks and unfair competition (in the generic sense) rather than copyright or patents; attributes of personality are used as trade symbols to boost the saleability of goods or services.[95] It is a commonplace that common law liability serves two predominant purposes: first, preventing the deception of consumers and, second, protecting a trader's goodwill. As to the second purpose, as the common law tort of passing off moves further away from its classical form, where one trader represents his own goods as the goods of another, the origin functions, product differentiation functions and quality guarantee functions become less important.[96] Essentially what is being protected is the advertising function of the mark or get-up and the underlying investment which has resulted in that value. Unless one argues that whatever is of value must necessarily be a form of property which the law protects,[97] justifying any protection must rest on natural right of labour or utilitarian arguments of the kind that we have already examined. As to the first purpose, one might argue that protecting consumers from misrepresentation might be an alternative rationale for a tort of appropriation of personality, although the notion of a misrepresentation leading to customer confusion or deception is largely a fiction[98] which conceals the gravamen of the complaint: the misappropriation of the kind of valuable intangible whose existence we are trying to justify here.

Economic efficiency

More modern forms of utilitarian analysis look to the law and economics school for a justification of property rights in personality. One line of argument invoked in American right of publicity cases holds that allowing property rights in personality leads to more efficient use of a celebrity's persona. According to the standard allocative efficiency argument, generally applied, in a community where there are no private property rights, where, for example, a parcel of land is held in common, with no restrictions on the use of the land, any rational utility-maximising herdsman will allow his cows to graze freely. Since there is no cost per cow, each herdsman will carry on adding cows regardless of the real social cost, leading to over-exploitation of the land, until it becomes worthless. However, if the

---

[95] This of course raises the question of what should and should not be encompassed by the expression 'intellectual property'. Purists might argue that trade marks are not suitable candidates for inclusion, though they are universally treated as aspects of intellectual property. For the historical background see Sherman and Bently, *Making of Modern Intellectual Property Law*, 168–72.

[96] See 36–8 above.

[97] Cf. 278–79, noting the dubiousness of such reasoning.

[98] See 108–10 above.

Justifying a remedy for appropriation of personality

land lies in private ownership, allowing the exclusion of all others except on payment of an appropriate fee, then the private owner will have an incentive to allow the optimal number of cows to graze on the land.[99] This argument has been applied to the right of publicity by Posner who argues that allowing an individual a property right in a photograph used for advertising purposes will ensure that it will be purchased by the advertiser who finds it to be most valuable (apart from cases where the transaction costs are prohibitive, such as a picture of an individual photographed as part of a crowd).[100] Making the photograph the communal property of all advertisers would not achieve this goal since 'the multiple use of the identical photograph to advertise different products would reduce its advertising value, perhaps to zero'.[101]

This approach was adopted, although not in explicit economic terms by Posner in his judicial capacity in *Douglass* v. *Hustler Magazine Inc.* where it was held that the defendant magazine had violated the plaintiff actress's right of publicity. According to Posner J, the plaintiff 'or her agents must have control over the dissemination of her nude photographs if their value is to be maximized . . . an important aspect of the "right of publicity" is being able to control the place as well as time and number of one's public appearances; for example, no celebrity sells his name or likeness for advertising purposes to all comers'.[102] Similarly, in *Matthews* v. *Wozencraft* the Court of Appeals for the Fifth Circuit cited Posner's extra-judicial writings in stating that, without protection, a person's likeness would be commercially exploited 'until the marginal value of its use is zero', drawing an analogy with the social cost of over-use of a highway, where each user does not consider the increased congestion that his use will inflict on others.[103] Thus, according to the Court, '[c]reating artificial scarcity preserves the value to [the individual], to advertisers who contract for the use of his likeness, and in the end to consumers who receive information from the knowledge that he is being paid to endorse the product'.[104]

Clearly, there are weaknesses in this line of argument. On a general level, such a line of reasoning does not so much prove that private property

---

[99] See, e.g., R. A. Posner, *Economic Analysis of Law*, 3rd edn (Boston, 1986), 31; R. Cooter and T. Ulen, *Law and Economics*, 2nd edn (New York, 1997), Ch. 4; H. Demsetz, 'Toward a Theory of Property Rights' (1967) 57(II) AmEconRev 347, 350 et seq.

[100] Cf. Madow, 'Private Ownership of Public Image', 223–4, noting that when transaction costs involving several potential advertisers are taken into account, it becomes an open question as to whether a photograph will ultimately be assigned to the advertiser who finds the photograph most valuable.

[101] R. Posner, 'The Right of Privacy' (1978) 12 GaLRev 393, 411–4.

[102] 769 F 2d 1128 (1985), 1138.   [103] 15 F 3d 432 (5th Cir. 1994), 437–8.

[104] *Ibid.*

310   The commercial appropriation of personality

best promotes the efficient use of scarce resources, as, at most, offer an argument for placing a scarce resource in the control of someone who can charge the full economic price for its use. As such, 'it is not an argument *for* private property so much as an argument *against* common property'. Moreover the argument assumes that other (non-legal) barriers to overuse, such as social disapproval or custom, do not exist, or are ineffective.[105] The English experience suggests that in the absence of property rights in personality, such norms have an important role to play.[106] More specifically, the advertising value of an individual's photograph 'is not founded on competition among bidders for a scarce resource; rather it is founded on the law which artificially creates a scarcity by giving the individual a property right in its use', a very different proposition from that which applies to truly scarce resources such as land.[107] Thus, if celebrity is viewed essentially as a social creation, there will always be a supply of existing and newly created personalities to exploit.[108] Moreover, even in the unlikely scenario of advertisers effectively running out of celebrities to use, this is not analogous to the exhaustion of a finite and non-substitutable resource such as land. Advertisers would simply resort to other techniques in marketing their wares.[109] Thus, it is possible to adopt a rather robust 'so what if they do' response to the argument that celebrity advertising values would be exploited to zero.[110] Ultimately, the matter depends on how broadly or narrowly we view the notion of efficiency. If we are solely concerned with the economic efficiency of celebrity publicity values (a somewhat narrow frame of reference), then the economic arguments may hold good. However, it should be borne in mind that we are not trying to allocate property rights in personality in the most efficient way possible, but, rather, are trying to justify the very existence of such rights in the first place.

In the United States the Tenth Circuit has subsequently stated that while the efficiency argument is persuasive in the context of advertising, where repeated use of an image may diminish its value, it is not so persuasive when applied to non-advertising uses: '[i]t is not clear, for example,

[105] Madow, 'Private Ownership of Public Image', 220, n. 442.
[106] See 48 above.
[107] E. J. Bloustein, 'Privacy is Dear at Any Price: A Response to Professor Posner's Economic Theory' (1978) 12 GaLRev 429, 448, noting also (*ibid.*) that there was little correlation between the commercial value of the 'property' concerned and the awards of general rather than special damages, although the cases cited in support are privacy rather than right of publicity cases. An awareness of the specific economic loss is generally more acute in the latter type of case and, in the absence of such loss, damages tend to be nominal: see 184 above.
[108] See T. Frazer, 'Appropriation of Personality', 303.
[109] *Ibid.*, 304; Madow, 'Private Ownership of Public Image', 225.
[110] *Ibid.*, 224.

Justifying a remedy for appropriation of personality 311

that the frequent appearance of a celebrity's likeness on t-shirts and coffee mugs will reduce its value; indeed, the value of the likeness may increase precisely because "everybody's got one".[111] Thus, as Madow argues, the marketing of a T-shirt bearing a celebrity's image may increase the demand for other merchandise associated with that celebrity and the best means of maximising economic value may be 'to make the merchandise available to any and every one who is willing to pay the marginal cost of its production'.[112] Nevertheless, it is difficult to see how this could not result in the diminution of the value of a celebrity's image since, although repetition might initially increase the value of subsequent repetitions, there comes 'a point of diminishing marginal returns beyond which subsequent displays and performances diminish the value of the asset'.[113]

Preventing or reversing unjust enrichment

In an early right of privacy case in the United States, *Munden* v. *Harris*,[114] where the photograph of a young boy was used in an advertisement for jewellery, the court stated that the plaintiff's right to exploit the peculiarity of his appearance was 'a right which he may wish to exercise for his own profit, and why may he not restrain another who is using it for gain? If there is value in it, sufficient to excite the cupidity of another, why is it not the property of him who gives it the value and from whom the value springs?'[115] In essence, this was giving expression to the intuitive notion that what was worth taking was worth protecting. Kalven later popularised this notion, arguing that the rationale for the appropriation category of the American privacy case law was 'the straightforward one of preventing unjust enrichment by the theft of goodwill'.[116] In his view, no social purpose was served 'by having the defendant get for free some aspect of the plaintiff that would have a market value and for which he would normally have to pay'.[117] Although Kalven conceded that relatively few of the appropriation privacy cases involved the use of names or likenesses

---

[111] *Cardtoons* v. *Major League Baseball Players* 95 F 3d 959 (10th Cir. 1996), 975, citing Madow, 'Private Ownership of Public Image', 222. Cf. R. Kwok, '*Cardtoons* v. *Major League Baseball Players Association*: Fair Use or Foul Play?' (1998) 5 UCLA Ent L Rev 315, 347.
[112] Madow, 'Private Ownership of Public Image', 222.
[113] See M. F. Grady, 'A Positive Economic Theory of the Right of Publicity' (1994) 1 UCLA Ent L Rev 97, 103 and 119–20.
[114] 134 SW 1076 (1911).   [115] *Ibid.*, 1078.
[116] H. Kalven, 'Privacy in Tort Law: Were Warren and Brandeis Wrong?' (1966) 31 Law ContProbl 326, 331. This argument is, of course, somewhat circular, since the defendant would only normally have to pay if the plaintiff had an enforceable right to demand payment, the very matter under enquiry.
[117] *Ibid.*

312   The commercial appropriation of personality

that had true commercial value, and that the true grievance might lie in seeing one's attributes being used by another, he maintained that 'commercial grievance' made sense as a distinct rationale for the tort.[118] The Supreme Court later adopted Kalven's views as one of the justifications for the right of publicity in *Zacchini* v. *Scripps-Howard Broadcasting Co.*, alongside arguments from utility and incentive.[119] Indeed, it seems that the prevention of unjust enrichment is 'probably the most common judicial theory in favor of the right of publicity'.[120]

The expression 'unjust enrichment', which American courts and commentators use interchangeably with expressions such as 'reaping where one has not sown' and 'unfair competition',[121] is somewhat vague. Indeed, the notion that it is unjust to take advantage of another person's skill or labour is unworkable in seeking a concrete legal application. The issue inevitably becomes circular if the notion of an unjust enrichment is based on the taking of another's (property) right, particularly where such a right is based simply on the fact that something has an economic value.[122] As previously noted, the notion of a cause of action for 'unfair competition' has been rejected in Australia on the grounds of 'the scope that it allows, under high-sounding generalizations, for judicial indulgence of idiosyncratic notions of what is fair in the market place'.[123] Nor have the English courts been prepared to embrace a generalised notion of unfair competition based on a principle of unjust enrichment, although it has been argued that a general action for 'malign competition' should be developed, based on 'the unjust enrichment paradigm' and restitutionary principles rather than the traditional property theories based on reward, incentive and goodwill, thus avoiding the circularity which reliance on the traditional theories entails.[124]

Ultimately, for the purposes of justification, the notion of unjust enrichment does not take us very far.[125] Looking to the law of restitution,

---

[118] *Ibid.*, 331, n. 36. R. Wacks adopts Kalven's rationale as a means of excluding appropriation of personality from the notion of privacy: 'The Poverty of Privacy' (1980) 96 LQR 73, 86.

[119] 433 US 562 (1977), 573–6. See also text accompanying note 69 above.

[120] McCarthy, *Rights of Publicity and Privacy*, §2.2, citing Grady, 'A Positive Economic Theory'.

[121] See McCarthy, *Rights of Publicity and Privacy*, §2.2.

[122] See 278–9 above.

[123] *Moorgate Tobacco Co. Ltd* v. *Philip Morris Ltd (No. 2)* (1984) 56 CLR 414, 445–6 *per* Deane J. See, generally, Chapter 3.

[124] See A. Kamperman Sanders, *Unfair Competition Law* (Oxford, 1997), esp. Chs. 2 and 4. See also W. J. Gordon, 'On Owning Information: Intellectual Property and the Restitutionary Impulse' (1992) 78 Virg L Rev 149.

[125] Cf. D. Gibson, 'A Comment on *Athans* v. *Canadian Adventure Camps Ltd*' (1979) 4 CCLT 37, 44.

Justifying a remedy for appropriation of personality 313

where the notion of unjust enrichment is most frequently invoked as a unifying principle, the leading authors concede that it is not possible to identify a precise common formula.[126] Unjust enrichment is, rather, 'an abstract proposition of justice which is "both an aspiration and a standard for judgment"'. In any case, while unjust enrichment at the expense of another (by subtraction or, for present purposes, by wrong) denotes the causative event, restitution is one of the possible remedial responses once a wrong has been established.[127] Such a wrong can consist of theft of goodwill, infringement of privacy, or infringement of a right of 'property' in name, voice and likeness. Thus, the notion of unjust enrichment at the expense of the plaintiff cannot help us to justify the very existence of a tort of appropriation of personality, since it begs the question of what is 'at the expense of the plaintiff', the very question of whether conduct amounting to appropriation of personality can constitute a wrong.

Protecting personal dignity

Finally, a remedy for appropriation of personality might be justified on the rather lofty basis that a remedy would provide protection and respect for personal dignity. The substance of this argument has already been encountered and need only be summarised briefly here. As already noted, although there is no coherent notion of human dignity as a specific legal right or value, the notion of human dignity is alluded to in various international instruments and in constitutionally entrenched rights. The question of whether such values can be taken into account in developing new rights has yet to be fully resolved, at least in the United Kingdom, and various common law and civil law jurisdictions have adopted different positions on a broad spectrum of varying permutations of direct and indirect effect which constitutional values may have.[128] Even at the weaker end of the spectrum, where the notion of human dignity is used as a value to guide constitutional and legal development, the notion of dignity may be somewhat controversial and is certainly an extremely malleable concept.[129] Thus, even if adopted as a guiding principle, the notion

---

[126] R. Goff and G. H. Jones, *The Law of Restitution*, 5th edn (London, 1998), 14–15. Cf. P. Birks, *Introduction to the Law of Restitution* (Oxford, 1985), Ch. 1 esp. 22–5 (arguing that the principle can be no more than a moral aspiration and that its adoption would undo efforts to derive the notion of an 'unjust' enrichment purely from the cases); and see, also, A. Burrows, *The Law of Restitution* (London, 1993), 55.

[127] See Birks, *Introduction to the Law of Restitution*, Ch. 1.

[128] See 214–16 above.

[129] D. Feldman, 'Human Dignity as a Legal Value – Part I' [1999] PL 682, 698.

314   The commercial appropriation of personality

of dignity as a value may be of little assistance, beyond its rhetorical force, in justifying the existence of a concrete legal right.

The dominance of the reductionist approach to invasion of privacy in the United States illustrates the fact that it is difficult to base a legal cause of action on anything as vague as the notion of 'inviolate personality'[130] or human dignity. Indeed, given the hybrid nature of the problem of appropriation of personality and the economic and dignitary interests encompassed, arguments based on protecting personal dignity can only provide a *partial* justification for such a remedy,[131] and obviously do not justify protecting predominantly economic interests in personality. Attempts to deny this, and to argue that all of the disparate claims brought as invasions of privacy, or all of the interests affected by commercial appropriation of personality, cannot be anything other than an injury to human dignity, are doomed to failure.

Conclusions

By its very nature, a hybrid cause of action such as a *sui generis* tort of appropriation of personality invites a number of different possible justifications. The first option noted above, a personal tort remedy based on infringement of privacy, may be justified on the broad basis that it provides protection for personal privacy and dignity against unauthorised commercial exploitation. Few people wish to be treated as commodities, and many would resent being involuntarily enlisted to help further the commercial interests of advertisers and merchandisers. The privacy perspective, viewing appropriation of personality as a dignitary wrong, focuses on the loss of privacy, indignation and distress that may result from such conduct. As such, damages would tend to be modest, intended to soothe injured feelings, rather than compensate for any specific pecuniary loss, apart from exceptional cases where the defendant's conduct might require an award of punitive damages.

When the focus shifts towards the invasion of essentially proprietary interests, a corresponding shift in underlying justification seems to be required. This certainly seems true from the American experience, where the development of an essentially dignitary interest in privacy into an essentially economic interest in publicity has resulted in the invocation of different and more sophisticated justifications. If a person is to enjoy an extensive property right in his personality or image which allows him to prevent unauthorised commercial exploitation by others, and secure

[130] See E. J. Bloustein, 'Privacy as an Aspect of Human Dignity: An Answer to Dean Prosser' (1964) 39 NYULRev 962, 1001, and see 164–6 above.
[131] See, e.g., *Restatement, Third, Unfair Competition* (1995), §46 comment *c*.

substantial profits for himself, then standard arguments justifying property rights should apply. However, as noted above, the standard arguments (to the extent that they can be regarded as paradigm examples),[132] primarily the utilitarian and natural rights of labour arguments, apply rather uneasily in the case of property rights in personality. The degree of labour and level of incentive required to develop commercially valuable attributes in personality are generally much less than in the case of more orthodox intangibles such as patentable inventions, and artistic and literary works. Attempts to draw analogies between economic interests in personality and the interests protected under the core areas of intellectual property law such as copyright and trade marks somehow seem strained.

At the broadest level, claims for property rights in personality are but one manifestation of the proprietarian creed, which some see as increasingly pervasive in intellectual property law, whereby property rights have a moral priority over other rights and interests, and activities that first give rise to economic value also necessarily create property rights. Property rights trump the wider community interests, and everything is capable of private ownership.[133] On the other hand, and equally broadly, the dignitary aspects of appropriation of personality reflect the increased value that modern societies place on personal privacy, sensibilities and autonomy. Ultimately, we are left with a new remedy that is rather difficult to justify on orthodox grounds. Of course, arguments of the kind outlined above rarely play any significant part in the decisions made by courts as to whether to allow claims for the protection of new interests, and such decisions are made without any consideration of extra-legal philosophical, economic or moral arguments. It remains to be seen whether the formal legal authorities provide support for such a tort. Without denying the usefulness of examining the justifications for a new remedy from a more reflective perspective, the final chapter considers possible patterns for development of the formal legal authorities.

---

[132] Cf. Sherman and Bently, *Making of Modern Intellectual Property Law*, 17, arguing that the search for a paradigm of intellectual property may be misguided and that the development of modern intellectual property law was reactive and subject-specific, rather than reliant on general concepts.

[133] Drahos, *Philosophy of Intellectual Property*, 202.

Part V

Conclusions

12 The autonomy of appropriation of personality

Personality as trading symbol and as an aspect of personal dignity

Two broad themes may be identified from the foregoing discussion: personality as trading symbol and personality as an aspect of an individual's dignity. The former results from the attractiveness of using celebrity recognition values to generate sales, while the latter reflects the increasing emphasis which is being placed on the protection of personal dignity from invasion by others. These two basic themes are reflected in the two principal perspectives on the problem of appropriation of personality: the unfair competition perspective and the dignitary torts perspective.

Although we may speak of the use of an individual's personality as a trading symbol, it is difficult to reconcile such use with the traditional categories of intellectual property rights. In particular, it is difficult to square such use with the orthodox functions of trade marks, both registered and un-registered. The use of a celebrity image in relation to goods or services rarely serves as an indication of origin, a means of product differentiation or a guarantee of quality. More often such use serves a pure advertising or merchandising function, which lies somewhat outside the ambit of trade mark protection, as it is currently perceived. Such matters depend, of course, on the facts of each individual case, although there is a substantial practical burden in showing that consumers rely on indicia of identity in advertising as indicators of origin or guarantees of quality. While the scope for securing trade mark registration for attributes of personality is limited, protection at common law is similarly restricted by the three key requirements of goodwill, misrepresentation and damage. It is difficult to accept that the unauthorised use of a plaintiff's image in advertising or merchandising can constitute a misrepresentation which damages, or is likely to damage, the plaintiff's goodwill in relation to some business or profession. On the other hand, if one accepts that attributes of personality have a de facto economic value, and that such value should be protected from unauthorised exploitation, then a more direct and intellectually honest approach would base legal protection on

319

320   The commercial appropriation of personality

the simple taking or misappropriation of such a valuable intangible. Although attributes of personality may be the subject of intangible property rights, and, as such, may be regarded as a form of 'intellectual property', analogies with the well-established core of intellectual property rights are of limited value and the justifications which underlie the core intellectual property rights apply uneasily to attributes of personality.

English law provides extensive protection for personal reputation, although other dignitary interests, such as interests in privacy and interests in freedom from mental distress, have not, traditionally, received substantive protection. An action for defamation compensates a plaintiff for the economic loss which results from being lowered in the estimation of other right-thinking members of society, although an award of damages also serves to compensate and provides satisfaction for injured feelings and affronted dignity. In the early English cases involving the misuse of the names of prominent professionals[1] the notion of personal reputation and trading goodwill were intertwined. Only later did the idea that an individual might suffer damage to predominantly economic interests in goodwill emerge. The English courts have been reluctant to concede that the relevant misrepresentation and damage to such goodwill has been made out, whether it be goodwill in respect of a business or profession, or in a subsidiary business devoted to exploiting attributes of personality.

In stark contrast, the courts in the United States took a much more direct approach. The tort of invasion of privacy proved to be the predominant vehicle for securing redress in cases of unauthorised appropriation of personality. What was originally conceived as an essentially dignitary tort, focusing on damage to personal dignity, became difficult to reconcile with demands for protection of essentially economic interests in the valuable attributes of an individual's personality. Eventually, the right of privacy begat the right of publicity, which focused on the economic loss of the plaintiff's capacity to exploit his recognition value, rather than the injury to personal dignity which underpinned the tort of invasion of privacy.

Appropriation of personality is a hybrid problem which affects both economic and dignitary interests. Although attributes of personality often have a commercial value and are effectively traded as commodities, they cannot be regarded as purely economic interests.[2] Despite the fact that there may be some form of market for these attributes, and despite the fact that the attributes may have some exchange value, they cannot always be objectively valued, and will often have a wholly subjective worth

---

[1] *Clark* v. *Freeman* (1848) 11 Beav 112; *Williams* v. *Hodge* (1887) 4 TLR 175; *Dockrell* v. *Dougall* (1899) 15 TLR 333; *Sim* v. *Heinz & Co. Ltd* [1959] 1 WLR 313.
[2] See 12–20, above.

The autonomy of appropriation of personality 321

for their owner. A person might have an aversion to being associated with a particular product, or, for that matter, with any form of commerce, for purely subjective reasons. When dignitary interests are involved, the concern goes beyond compensation for material loss, and the bare fact of the infringement of a particular interest in personality becomes objectionable in itself. Vindicating personal dignity and securing the satisfaction of a pecuniary award are aims that are equally as important as securing compensation for loss. Dignitary interests such as reputation, and (in countries which provide substantive protection) privacy, are mostly actionable *per se*, since the interests are deemed to be intrinsically worthy of substantive protection without a plaintiff needing to show actual material damage.

The basic propositions

A whole host of legal categories have been manipulated in the case law to provide ad hoc remedies for certain instances of appropriation of personality. Nevertheless, the basic propositions in English law may be stated quite succinctly, although development of individual causes of action is a rather more complex matter and other common law jurisdictions have gone much further, as explored above. It is well established that there is no right of property in a name *per se*.[3] Thus a person cannot have the absolute right to the use of a particular name, and cannot, for example, prevent the assumption of his name by another. This has long been true, whether it be the assumption of a patronymic name of a family by an illegitimate son of a former slave,[4] or, to use a more modern example, whether it concerns the adoption of the name of a famous singer such as Elvis Presley by a fan, for his own use or as a name for his son, dog or goldfish.[5] Similarly, in the absence of copyright no one has a right of property in his appearance and cannot restrain the reproduction or exploitation of photographs in which he appears.[6] Neither has English law been willing to recognise a general right of privacy, which might restrain one person from exploiting another's image without his consent.[7] Similarly there is no general principle preventing the misappropriation of a valuable intangible belonging to another.[8]

[3] *Dockrell* v. *Dougall* (1899) 15 TLR 333, 334 *per* Smith LJ.
[4] *DuBoulay* v. *DuBoulay* (1869) LR 2 PC 430. See also *Cowley* v. *Cowley* [1901] AC 450.
[5] *ELVIS PRESLEY Trade Marks* [1997] RPC 543, 547 *per* Laddie J.
[6] See, e.g., *Merchandising Corporation of America Inc.* v. *Harpbond Ltd* [1983] FSR 32, illustrating the limits of copyright protection for a person's appearance, and see 33–4 above.
[7] See, e.g., *Kaye* v. *Robertson* [1991] FSR 62, and see generally Chapter 8.
[8] See Chapter 2.

322   The commercial appropriation of personality

On the other hand, a person may not make a misrepresentation that his business and another's business or profession are connected, in a way which damages that other person's goodwill in his business or profession.[9] Neither is it possible to make use of another person's name in a way which exposes him to the risk of liability or litigation.[10] Furthermore, an individual may not publish a statement which is likely to damage another's reputation, by lowering him in the estimation of right-thinking members of society generally.[11] Neither may a photograph be published in breach of some relationship of contract or confidence.[12] At the same time, a defendant will be liable for the intentional infliction of physical harm,[13] although it is not clear to what extent liability might extend to the intentional infliction of mental distress, *simpliciter*.[14] Finally, use of a name or image which involves an infringement of a statutory intellectual property right such as copyright or registered trade mark will, in certain limited circumstances, give rise to liability.[15] By adapting some of these basic propositions, a large body of law has developed in the United States, which now requires a two-volume treatise to explain its development, scope and limits.[16] Canada is proceeding more slowly along broadly similar lines, while the Australian and English courts tread rather more warily.

Towards a new remedy

Addressing a hybrid problem in a satisfactorily coherent manner requires a remedy which encompasses both economic and dignitary aspects. A number of different approaches were considered in examining the several interests in the foregoing chapters, and may usefully be summarised. These are particularly relevant for common law systems such as England and Australia which have not gone beyond interpreting the traditional causes of action with varying degrees of flexibility. The first approach does not involve the introduction of any new causes of action, but requires a flexible view of the existing categories. Thus, a remedy will be available for appropriation of personality where the facts disclose a cause of action for defamation, breach of contract or confidence, malicious falsehood, or possibly where a cause of action might lie under the rule in *Wilkinson* v. *Downton*.[17] The cause of action with the greatest potential to remedy

---

[9] See Chapter 4.
[10] *Routh* v. *Webster* (1849) 10 Beav 561, and see Chapter 4.
[11] See Chapter 9.
[12] See *Pollard* v. *Photographic Co.* (1889) 40 ChD 345.
[13] *Wilkinson* v. *Downton* [1897] 2 QB 57.
[14] See 244–5 above.   [15] See Chapter 3 above.
[16] See J. T. McCarthy, *The Rights of Publicity and Privacy*, 2nd edn (New York, 2001).
[17] [1897] 2 QB 57.

The autonomy of appropriation of personality   323

cases of appropriation of personality, and the one that has received most attention from the courts and intellectual property specialists is the tort of passing off, although there are a number of difficulties, which need not be repeated here, in bringing cases of appropriation of personality within the ambit of the tort of passing off. The second approach involves affording greater protection to intangible business values through the development of a general tort of misappropriation of intangibles, something which the courts have resisted in Anglo-Australian jurisdictions and which has been severely limited by the courts in the United States.[18]

The third possible course of development for English law involves the introduction of a general right of privacy, to give greater protection to dignitary interests in personal privacy. Appropriation of personality is but one of a whole host of activities which elicit calls for a general right of privacy.[19] The general right of privacy in the United States provides protection for a disparate range of interests, although the inevitable drawback is a good deal of conceptual uncertainty. It remains to be seen whether the English courts will develop a general right to privacy. Thus far, privacy interests have been protected in piecemeal fashion and problems of definition and conceptual uncertainty have been used as arguments against the introduction of such a right. The Human Rights Act 1998 may provide a pretext, if one were necessary, for such a development, although the principle of privacy has not seriously been in doubt in English law. English law may become more comfortable in dealing with positive declarations of rights, rather than approaching the law in terms of breaches of specific duties, and the explicit balancing of two conflicting rights such as privacy and freedom of expression will become more familiar. Such changes will, however, take time. Gradual expansion of breach of confidence would certainly be in keeping with the traditional English incremental approach.[20] This might develop, through subsequent judicial expansion, into a more general remedy, although the problems of definition and conceptual indeterminacy would remain. There are some indications of a judicial awareness that reconciling privacy with commercial appropriation will not always be easy. It has been noted that there is no 'bright line between the personal and the commercial'.[21] The fact that privacy might be turned to commercial ends in securing the profits from exclusive use of photographs would not preclude protection,[22] although, ironically, the traditional pragmatic approach compelled the English Court of Appeal to impute a profit motive

[18] See Chapter 2 above.   [19] See 160 above.
[20] T. Bingham, 'The Way We Live Now: Human Rights in the New Millennium' [1998] Web JCLI.
[21] *Douglas v. Hello! Ltd* [2001] 2 WLR 992, 1030 *per* Sedley LJ.   [22] *Ibid.*

324   The commercial appropriation of personality

to bring what was essentially a privacy interest within the tort of malicious falsehood.[23]

Looking at the problem as a whole, the introduction of a general tort of misappropriation or a general tort of invasion of privacy may be rejected in favour of a narrowly circumscribed tort of appropriation of personality, which might encompass both economic and dignitary aspects of the problem. Admittedly, such a remedy is rather difficult to justify on coherent theoretical grounds. Arguments which might, at first glance, be of assistance in considering new forms of intellectual property rights, such as those based on natural rights of property, or arguments based on utility and incentive, fit rather uneasily with the problem. This is of limited practical importance, since justificatory arguments based on underlying principle and policy rarely play any explicit role in the courts' reasoning. What is more fruitful, at this point, is to consider the different means by which new common law remedies have developed.

There are several different techniques of common law development.[24] Most commonly, the requirements of individual torts may be stretched, gradually or more forcefully, to deal with new problems. For example, in its original or classic form, the tort of passing off prevented the defendant from passing off his own goods as the plaintiff's goods,[25] although it has subsequently expanded possibly to the limits of coherence. Sometimes a tort is over-stretched, resulting in the creation of a new tort. It is often not clear at any one time whether the courts have stretched an existing cause of action or over-stretched an existing cause of action resulting in the creation of a new tort. The boundary between the tort of passing off and what might be a new and independent tort of unfair competition serves as an example of this process although, in some cases, the boundary might not always be clear.[26] The English courts have been content to stretch the tort of passing off, while consistently denying the existence of a new and separate tort.[27] At other times, the meaning of a traditional concept such as property is manipulated to accommodate new interests. The courts prefer to manipulate existing and well-established legal concepts such as property which can be stretched to encompass new claims and

---

[23] *Kaye* v. *Robertson* [1991] FSR 62, and see 204 above.

[24] See G. Dworkin, 'Intentionally Causing Economic Loss – *Beaudesert Shire Council* v. *Smith* Revisited' (1974) 1 MonashULRev 4, for a valuable summary.

[25] See, e.g., *Reddaway* v. *Banham* (1896) 13 RPC 429.

[26] See, e.g., *Vine Products & Co. Ltd* v. *Mackenzie & Co. Ltd* [1969] RPC 1, 23 and 29. See also G. Dworkin, 'Unfair Competition: Is the Common Law Developing a New Tort?' [1979] EIPR 241.

[27] See, e.g., *Mail Newspapers* v. *Insert Media (No. 2)* [1988] 2 All ER 420, 424; *Harrods Ltd* v. *Schwartz-Sackin & Co. Ltd* [1986] FSR 490, 494; *Hodgkinson & Corby Ltd* v. *Wards Mobility Ltd* [1994] 1 WLR 1564, 1569.

The autonomy of appropriation of personality 325

interests. This often serves to deny any revolutionary novelty; the law has re-examined and redefined one of its basic concepts and has been able to do justice within the bounds of the traditional legal framework.[28] From a plaintiff's perspective, this is problematic in that the courts tend to regard the existing categories, such as property, as fairly well defined and will therefore tend to put a heavy onus on the plaintiff who argues that his cause of action fits into the existing conceptual scheme.[29]

Logical development would be better served if the courts were candidly to devise or recognise new principles that are more fitting to cope with the novel legal problems. It is rare for a new cause of action to emerge from a synthesis of disparate strands of authority into a new rule. Although the process of stretching existing torts is much more in keeping with the law's process of piecemeal development, a broad-brush approach is occasionally adopted. The formulation of the rules in *Rylands* v. *Fletcher*[30] and *Wilkinson* v. *Downton*[31] may serve as examples. Legal development is often based on the 'rationalisation of principles already immanent in the law'.[32] If the courts can be persuaded that they are merely drawing on existing legal principles, their fears of what they might regard as unacceptable judicial legislating may be assuaged. When the existing legal categories prove inadequate, the courts must be persuaded that recognising a new cause of action is the only way of doing justice in a particular case, without doing violence to the conceptual structure of the existing legal categories and without having to resort to elaborate conceptual contortions. Although there are dicta expressing disapproval of the unauthorised commercial exploitation of personality,[33] the English courts have maintained that they are powerless to develop a new remedy.

The question of precedent remains a difficult one. Without repeating the detail of the foregoing discussion, it is useful to recall the means by which new causes of action were formulated in other jurisdictions. For example, the decisions of the Ontario High Court and Court of Appeal in *Krouse* v. *Chrysler Canada Ltd*,[34] owed more to the broad collation of

---

[28] D. Lloyd, 'The Recognition of New Rights' [1961] CLP 39, 41–2, commenting on the decision in *Sim* v. *H. J. Heinz Co. Ltd* [1959] 1 WLR 313.

[29] *Ibid.*, 44–5.

[30] *Rylands* v. *Fletcher* (1866) LR 1 Ex 265, and see J. Wigmore, 'Responsibility for Tortious Acts: Its History' (1894) 7 HarvLRev 441, 454, cited by W. Friedmann, *Law in a Changing Society*, 2nd edn (London, 1972), 47.

[31] [1897] 2 QB 57.

[32] H. W. Wilson, 'Privacy, Confidence and Press Freedom: A Study in Judicial Activism' (1990) 53 MLR 43, 53.

[33] See, e.g., *Dockrell* v. *Dougall* (1899) 15 TLR 333; *Tolley* v. *J. S. Fry & Sons Ltd* [1930] 1 KB 467, 478 *per* Greer LJ; *Sim* v. *H. J. Heinz & Co. Ltd* [1959] 1 WLR 313, 317 *per* McNair J.

[34] (1972) 25 DLR (3d) 49.

326   The commercial appropriation of personality

precedents than to precise inductive logic. Since the authorities relied on were almost exclusively English cases, the decision should provide a model of judicial synthesis which might be adopted by the English courts. However, as noted above, neither the judgment at first instance, nor that on appeal, was a paradigm example of precise inductive reasoning.[35] The decisions illustrate the fact that the recognition of such a new cause of action involves a considerable logical jump from what can be supported by the formal authorities. The reasoning at first instance that the 'wrongful appropriation of that which in the business world has commercial value and is traded daily must *ipso facto* involve a property right which the Courts protect'[36] involves the familiar technique of stretching the notion of property, although there is very little reason in the assertion that economic value necessarily results in a property right.[37] The early English authorities[38] did not provide much of a basis for a new tort while the application of the tort of passing off was extremely generous.[39] Yet, the Court came to the conclusion that either line of cases would allow the plaintiff to succeed.[40] The Ontario Court of Appeal used an even broader brush. Having noted that actions for appropriation of personality had sometimes 'succeeded in contract, sometimes in tort, and sometimes on some vague theory of property law', the Court considered some cases where relief had been secured on the basis of breach of contract or confidence,[41] or on the basis of libel.[42] The development of the right of publicity in the United States was noted, although not in any detail, before the Court concluded from the 'examination of the authorities in the several fields of tort related to the allegations made therein that the common law does contemplate a concept in the law of torts which may be broadly classified as an appropriation of one's personality'.[43]

Relatively little weight was placed on the need for formal authority. What was more important were the underlying reasons of substance, particularly the apparent commercial reality that a person's image had a

---

[35] See 115–21 above.   [36] (1972) 25 DLR (3d) 49, 61–2.   [37] See 279 above.

[38] *Clark* v. *Freeman* (1867) LR 2 Ch App 307, and subsequent cases discussed at 63 above.

[39] (1972) 25 DLR (3d) 49, 62–8.   [40] *Ibid.*, 68.

[41] *Pollard* v. *Photographic Co.* (1889) 40 ChD 345; *Corelli* v. *Wall* (1906) 22 TLR 532 (although the claim was based on libel rather than breach of contract or confidence); *Palmer* v. *National Sporting Club Ltd* (1906) 2 MacG CC 55 (although there was no contractual relationship between the plaintiff and the defendant); *Sports & General Press Agency Ltd* v. *'Our Dogs' Publishing Co. Ltd* [1917] 2 KB 125 (not a case of appropriation of personality, but held that the exclusive right to take photographs, in this case of a dog show, was not a form of property known to law).

[42] *Tolley* v. *J. S. Fry & Sons Ltd* [1931] AC 333; *Clark* v. *Freeman* (1848) 11 Beav 112 (although plaintiff's claim was unsuccessful).

[43] (1973) 40 DLR (3d) 15, 28.

The autonomy of appropriation of personality 327

de facto value and was effectively traded as a commodity. In this respect, the lack of formal authority made the recognition of such a new tort a rather bold move, which is particularly surprising in view of the fact that the Ontario courts are sometimes regarded as being amongst the most conservative of those of the Canadian provinces.[44] The new tort did not develop through a gradual extension of an existing cause of action, such as passing off or libel, until it formed a separate and autonomous cause of action, but rather through one bold judicial stroke at first instance.

It is also worthwhile recalling the fact that the development of the right of privacy in the United States owed more to the invocation of broad principles than to precise inductive logic. The Warren and Brandeis thesis relied on a handful of English authorities concerning common law copyright and breach of confidence to support the broader principle which they discerned, 'the more general right of the individual to be let alone'.[45] Ultimately, this 'brilliant fraud'[46] was accepted and adopted by the courts although its initial rejection by the New York Court of Appeals[47] rested on a detailed and formal interpretation of the relevant authorities which resembled the English style of judicial reasoning. When the right of privacy was subsequently accepted by the Supreme Court of Georgia,[48] much greater emphasis was laid on broad principle than on formal authority.[49] Later, when the right of publicity emerged from the right of privacy, although there was some reliance on other legal doctrines, the reasoning in the first leading case, *Haelan Laboratories*, involved a considerable logical leap. Only a handful of cases were cited in support of the new right, while others were rather cursorily distinguished.

A much looser doctrine of precedent and a number of other factors account for the very different dynamics of legal change in the United States.[50] Nevertheless, English law in this area seems to be somewhat at odds with all of the major common law systems. There is nothing wrong with that in itself, although there has been a distinct lack of critical analysis of the formal legal authorities and policy factors which underpin those decisions. Admittedly, the disparate English cases, often involving interlocutory proceedings, have not provided the ideal fora for such issues to be aired.

---

[44] See, e.g., J. D. Murphy and R. Rueter, *Stare Decisis in Commonwealth Appellate Courts* (Toronto, 1981), 24.

[45] S. Warren and L. Brandeis, 'The Right to Privacy' (1890) 4 HarvLRev 193, 205, and see Chapter 7.

[46] R. Dworkin, *Taking Rights Seriously* (London, 1977), 119.

[47] *Roberson* v. *Rochester Folding Box Co.*, 171 NY 538 (1902).

[48] *Pavesich* v. *New England Life Insurance Co.* 50 SE 68 (1905).

[49] See, generally, Chapter 7.   [50] See 189–98 above.

328   The commercial appropriation of personality

The preponderance of opinion suggests that any initiative in protecting interests in personality which do not fall under the existing heads of liability will be judicial rather than legislative. This would reflect the experience in the United States and in Germany where the courts rather than the legislatures assumed responsibility for developing the law. The Human Rights Act 1998 provides an opportunity to develop English law in a manner which is consistent with the values of the European Convention on Human Rights. The re-affirmation of the social value of privacy should allow the courts to draw on such values in developing the common law. Common law jurisdictions with systems of constitutionally entrenched rights are somewhat more likely to develop the law in a more principled fashion through the 'cross-pollination of the common law by constitutional principles', even though the constitutional principles do not have direct effect.[51] Judicial application of a pre-existing principle is much easier to defend against attack for usurping the role of the legislature than the development of an entirely new right or cause of action.[52] Moreover, the shift to more explicit rights-based reasoning in Convention cases, requiring the courts to start with the general proposition that a right is protected,[53] may well permeate the common law, and reasons of substance may well prove to be more important than the formal reasons which have thus far denied the existence of a right of privacy in English law.[54] Fears that a new remedy may be harmful to freedom of expression will remain, although such fears may be less prominent, given the explicit balancing of the competing rights of private life and freedom of expression which the Human Rights Act 1998 compels.[55]

The open-textured nature of the rights guaranteed by the European Convention may not provide much assistance in addressing the question of the precise form any new development might take. But in determining the precise method by which the protection of privacy may be achieved, and the scope and nature of any new right, the English courts will increasingly need to consider what may be learned from other countries.

---

[51] J. D. R. Craig, 'Invasion of Privacy and Charter Values: The Common Law Tort Awakens' (1997) 42 McGill LJ 355, 373.

[52] Cf. Warren and Brandeis, 'The Right to Privacy', 213, and see 149 above.

[53] See N. Browne-Wilkinson, 'The Impact on Judicial Reasoning' in B. S. Markesinis (ed.) *The Impact of the Human Rights Bill on English Law* (Oxford, 1998), 21, 22–3. Cf. D. W. Leebron, 'The Right to Privacy's Place in the Intellectual History of Tort Law' (1991) 41 Case West Res L Rev, noting that the American tort law of privacy is imbued with rights terminology, a rather unusual feature which extends back to its genesis in the Warren and Brandeis article; few other modern torts are expressed in such rights-based language.

[54] See, e.g., *Kaye v. Robertson*, above.   [55] See 218–24 above.

While commercial appropriation of personality featured prominently in the development of the right of privacy in the United States and the right of personality in Germany, it may easily be severed from the privacy debate. Timely comparisons of the rather haphazard development in other systems may prove to be extremely fruitful if the English courts should embark on developing a new remedy for commercial appropriation of personality.

Bibliography

Abbott, F., Cottier, T., and Gurry, F., *The International Intellectual Property System Commentary and Materials* (The Hague: Kluwer, 1999).

Adams, J., *Character Merchandising* (2nd edn) (London: Butterworths, 1996).

'Is There a Tort of Unfair Competition?' [1985] JBL 26.

'The Liability of a Trade Mark or Name Licensor for the Acts and Defaults of his Licensees' [1981] EIPR 314.

'Unfair Competition: Why a Need is Unmet' [1992] 8 EIPR 259.

Addison, N., and Lawson-Cruttenden, T., *Harassment Law & Practice* (London: Butterworths, 1998).

Advertising Standards Authority, *British Code of Advertising Practice* (10th edn) (London: Advertising Standards Authority, 1999).

Agrawal, J., and Kamakura, W. A., 'The Economic Worth of Celebrity Endorsers: An Event Study Analysis' (1995) 59(3) *Journal of Marketing* 56.

Akazaki, L., 'Source Theory and Guarantee Theory in Anglo-American Trade Mark Policy: A Critical Legal Study' (1990) 72 JSPTO 255.

Annand, R., and Norman, H., *Blackstone's Guide to the Trade Marks Act 1994* (London: Blackstone Press, 1994).

Arden, M., 'The Future of the Law of Privacy' (1998–9) 9 KCLJ 1.

Arnold, M. S., Green, T. A., Scully, S. A., and White, S. D. (eds.), *On the Laws and Customs of England* (Chapel Hill: University of North Carolina Press, 1981).

Arnold, R., *Performers' Rights* (2nd edn) (London: Sweet Maxwell, 1997).

Atiyah, P. S., and Adams, J., *The Sale of Goods* (9th edn) (London, Pitman, 1995).

Atiyah, P. S., and Summers, R. S., *Form and Substance in Anglo-American Law* (Oxford: Oxford University Press, 1987).

Aubrey, J. M., 'A Justification of the Patent System' in J. Phillips (ed.), *Patents in Perspective* (Oxford: ESC Publishing, 1985).

Bagehot, R., *Sales Promotion: A Legal Guide* (London: Sweet & Maxwell, 1993).

Bagshaw, R., 'Obstacles on the Path to Privacy Torts' in P. Birks (ed.), *Privacy and Loyalty* (Oxford: Oxford University Press, 1997).

Baird, D. G., 'Common Law Intellectual Property and the Legacy of *International News Service v. Associated Press*' (1983) 50 U Chi L Rev 411.

Baker, J. H., *An Introduction to English Legal History* (3rd edn) (London: Butterworths, 1990).

Barendt, E. M., *Freedom of Speech* (Oxford: Clarendon Press, 1985).

'Privacy and the Press' in E. M. Barendt (ed.), *Yearbook of Media and Entertainment Law 1995* (Oxford: Clarendon Press, 1995).

'Privacy as a Constitutional Right and Value' in P. Birks (ed.), *Privacy and Loyalty* (Oxford: Oxford University Press, 1997).

'What Is the Point of Libel Law?' [1999] CLP 110.

(ed.), *The Yearbook of Media and Entertainment Law 1995* (Oxford: Clarendon Press, 1995).

Barnett, S. R., 'The Right of Publicity Versus Free Speech in Advertising: Some Counter-Points to Professor McCarthy' (1996) 18 Hastings Comm & Ent LJ 593.

Beatson, J., and Grosz, S., 'Horizontality: A Footnote' (2000) 116 LQR 385.

Becker, L. C., 'Deserving to Own Intellectual Property' (1993) 68 Chi-Kent LRev 609.

Property Rights: Philosophic Foundations (London: Routledge & Kegan Paul, 1977).

Beckerman, J. S., 'Adding Insult to *Iniuria*: Affronts to Honor and the Origins of Trespass' in M. S. Arnold, T. A. Green, S. A. Scully and S. D. White (eds.), *On the Laws and Customs of England* (Chapel Hill: University of North Carolina Press, 1981).

Beddard, R., 'Photographs and the Rights of the Individual' (1995) 58 MLR 771.

Bedingfield, D., 'Privacy or Publicity? The Enduring Confusion Surrounding the American Tort of Invasion of Privacy' (1992) 55 MLR 111.

Beier, F. K., 'The Law of Unfair Competition in the European Community – Its Development and Present Status' [1985] EIPR 284.

Bell, A. P., *The Modern Law of Personal Property* (London: Butterworths, 1989).

Benn, S. I., 'The Protection and Limitation of Privacy' (1978) 52 ALJ 601.

Bergmann, S., 'Publicity Rights In the United States and Germany: A Comparative Analysis' (1999) 19 LoyLA Ent LJ 479.

Berkman, H. I., 'The Right of Publicity – Protection For Public Figures and Celebrities' (1976) 42 Brook L Rev 527.

Beverley-Smith, H., Ohly, A. and Lucas-Schloetter, A., *Privacy, Property and Personality* (Cambridge: Cambridge University Press, forthcoming, 2003).

Bingham, T., 'Should There Be a Law to Protect Rights of Personal Privacy?' [1996] EHRLR 450.

'The Way We Live Now: Human Rights in the New Millennium' [1998] Web JCLI.

Birks, P., 'Civil Wrongs: A New World' in *Butterworth Lectures 1990–91* (London: Butterworths, 1992).

Introduction to the Law of Restitution (Oxford: Clarendon Press, 1985).

'The Academic and the Practitioner' (1998) 18 LS 397.

(ed.), *The Frontiers of Liability* (Oxford: Oxford University Press, 1994).

Wrongs and Remedies in the Twenty-First Century (Oxford: Clarendon Press, 1996).

Blom-Cooper, L., and Pruitt, L. R., 'Privacy Jurisprudence of the Press Complaints Commission' (1994) 23 Anglo-AmLR 133.

332   Bibliography

Bloustein, E. J., 'Privacy as an Aspect of Human Dignity: An Answer to Dean Prosser' (1964) 39 NYULRev 962.

'Privacy is Dear at Any Price: A Response to Professor Posner's Economic Theory' (1978) 12 GaLRev 429.

Bolger, P., 'The Common Law and the Tort of Appropriation of Personality: Part I' (1999) 3 IIPR 16.

Borchard, W., 'The Common Law Right of Publicity is Going Wrong in the US' [1992] Ent LR 208.

Brett, H., 'Unfair Competition – Not Merely an Academic Issue' [1979] EIPR 295.

Breyer, S., 'The Uneasy Case for Copyright: A Study of Copyright in Books, Photocopies and Computer Programs' (1970) 84 HarvLRev 281.

Bridgeman, J., and Jones, M. A., 'Harassing Conduct and Outrageous Acts: A Cause of Action for Intentionally Inflicted Mental Distress?' (1994) 14 LS 180.

Brierley, J. E. C., and Macdonald, R. A., *Quebec Civil Law* (Toronto: Emond Montgomery Publications Ltd, 1993).

Brittan, L., 'The Right of Privacy in England and the United States' (1963) 37 Tulane L Rev 235.

Browne-Wilkinson, N., 'The Impact on Judicial Reasoning' in B. S. Markesinis (ed.), *The Impact of the Human Rights Bill on English Law* (Oxford: Oxford University Press, 1998).

Buchanan, C. L., 'A Comparative Analysis of Name and Likeness Rights in the United States and England' (1988) Golden Gate UL Rev 301.

'The Need For a Right of Publicity' [1988] EIPR 227.

Bugbee, B. W., *Genesis of American Patent and Copyright Law* (Washington: Public Affairs Press, 1967).

Burchell, J., *Principles of Delict* (Cape Town: Juta & Co., 1993).

Burley, S. G., 'Passing Off and Character Merchandising: Should England Lean Towards Australia?' [1991] EIPR 227.

Burns, P., 'The Law of Privacy: The Canadian Experience' (1976) 54 Can B Rev 1.

'Unfair Competition: A Compelling Need Unmet' [1981] EIPR 311.

Burrows, A., 'Reforming Exemplary Damages: Expansion or Abolition?' in P. Birks (ed.), *Wrongs and Remedies in the Twenty-First Century* (Oxford: Clarendon Press, 1996).

Remedies for Torts and Breach of Contract (2nd edn) (London: Butterworths, 1994).

The Law of Restitution (London: Butterworths, 1993).

Buxton, R., 'The Human Rights Act And Private Law' (2000) 116 LQR 48.

Calcutt Committee, Report of Press Self-Regulation, Cm 2135 (London: HMSO, 1993).

Report of the Committee on Privacy and Related Matters, Cm 1102 (London: HMSO, 1990).

Callmann, R., *The Law of Unfair Competition, Trade Marks and Monopolies* (3rd edn) (Mundelein, Ill.: Callaghan & Co., 1967).

Bibliography

Cane, P., 'The Basis of Tortious Liability' in P. Cane and J. Stapleton (eds.), *Essays for Patrick Atiyah* (Oxford: Clarendon Press, 1991).
Tort Law and Economic Interests (2nd edn) (Oxford: Oxford University Press, 1996).
Carter, A., *The Philosophical Foundations of Property Rights* (London: Harvester Wheatsheaf, 1989).
Carter-Ruck, P. F., *Carter-Ruck on Libel and Slander* (4th edn) (London: Butterworths, 1992).
Carty, H., 'Character Merchandising and The Limits of Passing Off' (1993) 13 LS 289.
'Dilution and Passing Off: Cause for Concern' (1996) 112 LQR 632.
'Heads of Damage in Passing Off' [1996] EIPR 487.
'Intentional Violation of Economic Interests: The Limits of Common Law Liability' (1988) 104 LQR 250.
'Passing Off and the Concept of Goodwill' [1995] JBL 139.
'Passing Off at the Crossroads' [1996] EIPR 629.
Chalton, S., Gaskill, S., Walden, I., Grant, G., and Inger, L., *Encyclopaedia of Data Protection* (London: Sweet & Maxwell, 1988–2000).
Chandrani, R., 'Cybersquatting – A New Right to Protect Individual Names In Cyberspace' [2000] Ent LR 171.
'ICANN Now Others Can' [2000] Ent LR 39.
Chong, S., and Maniatis, S. M., 'The Teenage Mutant Hero Turtles Case Zapping English Law on Character Merchandising Past the Embryonic Stage' [1991] EIPR 253.
Chromecek, M., and McCormack, S. C., *World Intellectual Property Guidebook Canada* (New York: Mathew Bender, 1991).
Clayton, R., and Tomlinson H., *The Law of Human Rights* (Oxford: Oxford University Press, 2000).
Cohen, F. S., 'Dialogue on Private Property' (1954) 9 RutgLRev 357.
'Transcendental Nonsense and the Functional Approach' (1935) 35 Colum L Rev 809.
Cohen, M. R., and Cohen, F. S., *Readings in Jurisprudence and Legal Philosophy* (New York: Prentice-Hall, 1951).
Coleman, A., 'The Unauthorised Commercial Exploitation of the Names and Likenesses of Real Persons' [1982] EIPR 189.
Coombe, R. J., 'Objects of Property and Subjects of Politics: Intellectual Property Laws and Democractic Dialogue' (1991) 69 TexLRev 1853.
'The Celebrity Image and Cultural Identity: Publicity Rights and the Subaltern Politics of Gender' (1992) 14 *Discourse: Berkeley Journal for Theoretical Studies in Media and Culture* 59.
Cooter, R., and Ulen, T., *Law and Economics* (2nd edn) (New York: Addison-Wesley, 1997).
Coppel, J., *The Human Rights Act 1998: Enforcing the European Convention in the Domestic Courts* (Chichester: John Wiley & Sons, 1999).
Cornish, W. R., 'Genevan Bootstraps' [1997] EIPR 336.
Intellectual Property (4th edn) (London: Sweet & Maxwell, 1999).
'Unfair Competition? A Progress Report' (1972) 12 JSPTL 126.

334   Bibliography

Cotterell, R., 'The Law of Property and Legal Theory' in W. Twining (ed.), *Legal Theory and Common Law* (Oxford: Basil Blackwell, 1986).

Coulter, M., *Property In Ideas: The Patent Question in Mid-Victorian Britain* (Kirksville, Mo.: The Thomas Jefferson University Press, 1991).

Craig, J. D. R., 'Invasion of Privacy and Charter Values: The Common Law Tort Awakens' (1997) 42 McGill LJ 355.

Craig, J. D. R., and Nolte, N., 'Privacy and Free Speech in Germany and Canada: Lessons for an English Privacy Tort' [1998] EHRLR 162.

Cross, R., and Harris, J. W., *Precedent in English Law* (4th edn) (Oxford: Clarendon Press, 1991).

Crown, G., *Advertising Law and Regulation* (London: Butterworths, 1998).

Curley, D., 'Cybersquatters Evicted: Protecting Names Under the UDRP' [2001] Ent LR 91.

D'Amato, A., 'Comment on Professor Posner's Lecture on Privacy' (1978) 12 GaLRev 497.

Date-Bah, S. K., 'Defamation, The Right to Privacy and Unauthorised Commercial Use of Photographs: *Kate Anthony v. University of Cape Coast Revisited*' (1977) 14 UGhana LJ 101.

Davies, G., *Copyright and the Public Interest* (Weinheim: VCH, 1994).

Day, J. P., 'Locke on Property' (1966) 16 *Philosophical Quarterly* 207.

Demsetz, H., 'Toward a Theory of Property Rights' (1967) 57(II) AmEconRev 347.

Denicola, R. C., 'Institutional Publicity Rights: An Analysis of the Merchandising of Famous Trade Symbols' (1985) 75 TMR 41.

Department of National Heritage, Privacy and Media Intrusion: The Government's Response, Cm 2918 (London: HMSO, 1995).

Department of Trade and Industry, Reform of Trade Marks Law, Cm 1203 (London: HMSO, 1990).

Devlin, P., *Samples of Lawmaking* (Oxford: Oxford University Press, 1962).

  The Judge (Oxford: Oxford University Press, 1981).

Dias, R. W. M. (ed.), *Clerk and Lindsell on Torts* (16th edn) (London: Sweet & Maxwell, 1989).

Dickler, G., 'The Right of Privacy' (1936) 70 USLRev 435.

Drahos, P., *A Philosophy of Intellectual Property* (Aldershot: Dartmouth, 1996).

  'Intellectual Property and Human Rights' [1999] IPQ 349.

  (ed.), *Intellectual Property* (Aldershot: Dartmouth, 1999).

Drechsel, R. E., 'Intentional Infliction of Emotional Distress: New Tort Liability for Mass Media' (1985) Dick LRev 339.

Drysdale, J., and Silverleaf, M., *Passing Off Law and Practice* (2nd edn) (London: Butterworths, 1994).

Duffy, P. J., 'English Law and the European Convention on Human Rights' (1980) 29 ICLQ 585.

Dugdale, A. M. (ed.), *Clerk and Lindsell on Torts* (18th edn) (London: Sweet & Maxwell, 2000).

Duggan, A. J., 'Fairness in Advertising: In Pursuit of the Hidden Persuaders' (1977) 11 MULR 50.

Bibliography

Duxbury, J., *'Ninja Turtles v. Crocodile Dundee'* [1991] EIPR 427.

Dworkin, G., 'Intentionally Causing Economic Loss – *Beaudesert Shire Council v. Smith* Revisited' (1974) 1 MonashULRev 4.

'Privacy and the Law' in J. B. Young (ed.), *Privacy* (Chichester: John Wiley & Sons, 1979).

'Privacy and the Press' (1961) 24 MLR 185.

'The Common Law Protection of Privacy' (1967) 2 U Tas LR 418.

'Unfair Competition: Is the Common Law Developing a New Tort?' [1979] EIPR 241.

Dworkin, R., *Taking Rights Seriously* (London: Duckworth, 1977).

Eady, D., 'Opinion: A Statutory Right to Privacy' [1996] EHRLR 243.

Eisenschitz, T. S., 'The Value of Patent Information' in J. Phillips (ed.), *Patents in Perspective* (Oxford: ESC, 1985).

Elmslie, M., and Lewis, M., 'Passing Off and Image Merchandising in the UK' [1992] EIPR 270.

Epstein, R. A., 'A Taste for Privacy? Evolution and the Emergence of a Naturalistic Ethic' (1980) J Legal Studies 605.

'International News Service v. Associated Press: Custom and Law as Sources of Property Rights in News' (1992) 78 Virg L Rev 85.

'Privacy, Property Rights, and Misrepresentations' (1978) 12 GaLRev 455.

Evans, G. E., 'Comment on the Terms of Reference and Procedure for the Second WIPO International Name Process' [2001] EIPR 61.

Falconbridge, J. D., 'Desirable Changes in the Common Law' (1927) 5 Can B Rev 581.

Faulks, N., Report of the Committee on Defamation, Cmnd 5909 (London: HMSO, 1975).

Fawcett, J. E. S., *The Application of the European Convention on Human Rights* (2nd edn) (Oxford: Clarendon Press, 1987).

Felcher, P. L., and Rubin, E. L., 'Privacy, Publicity, and the Portrayal of Real People by the Media' (1979) 88 Yale LJ 1577.

'The Descendibility of the Right of Publicity: Is There Commercial Life After Death?' (1980) 89 Yale LJ 1125.

Feldman, D., 'Human Dignity as a Legal Value' – Part I [1999] PL 682, Part II [2000] PL 61.

'Privacy-related Rights and Their Social Value' in P. Birks (ed.), *Privacy and Loyalty* (Oxford: Clarendon Press, 1997).

'Secrecy, Dignity, or Autonomy? Views of Privacy as a Civil Liberty' (1994) 47 CLP 41.

'The Developing Scope of Article 8 of the European Convention on Human Rights' [1997] EHRLR 265.

Fenwick, H., and Phillipson, G., 'Confidence and Privacy: A Re-Examination' (1996) 55 CLJ 447.

Fleming, J. G., *Introduction to the Law of Torts* (2nd edn) (Oxford: Oxford University Press, 1985).

The American Tort Process (Oxford: Oxford University Press, 1988).

The Law of Torts (9th edn) (Sydney: The Law Book Co, 1998).

336   Bibliography

Frank, J., *Law and the Modern Mind* (London: Stevens & Sons, 1949).

Frazer, T., 'Appropriation of Personality – A New Tort?' (1983) 99 LQR 281.
'Publicity, Privacy and Personality' [1983] EIPR 139.

Freeman, M. D. A., *Lloyd's Introduction to Jurisprudence* (6th edn) (London: Sweet & Maxwell, 1994).

Freund, P. A., 'Privacy: One Concept or Many?' in J. R. Pennock and J. W. Chapman (eds.), *Nomos XIII Privacy* (New York: Atherton Press, 1971).

Fridman, G. H. L., *Fridman on Torts* (London: Waterlow, 1990).

Fried, C., 'Privacy' (1968) 77 Yale LJ 475.

Friedmann, W., *Law in a Changing Society* (2nd edn) (London: Penguin Books, 1972).

Gaines, J., *Contested Culture: The Image, The Voice and The Law* (London: BFI Publishing, 1992).

Garnett, K., Rayner James, J., and Davies, G., *Copinger and Skone James on Copyright* (14th edn) (London: Sweet & Maxwell, 1999).

Gavison, R., 'Privacy and Its Legal Protection', D.Phil thesis, University of Oxford (1975).
'Privacy and the Limits of Law' (1980) 89 Yale LJ 421.

Geller, P. E. (ed.), *International Copyright Law and Practice* (New York: Mathew Bender, 1999).

Gerety, T., 'Redefining Privacy' (1977) 12 Harv CR-CL Law Rev 233.

Gibson, D., 'A Comment on *Athans v. Canadian Adventure Camps Ltd et al.*' (1979) 4 CCLT 37.
'Common Law Protection of Privacy: What To Do Until the Legislators Arrive' in L. N. Klar (ed.), *Studies in Canadian Tort Law* (Toronto: Butterworths, 1977).
(ed.), *Aspects of Privacy Law* (Toronto: Butterworths, 1980).

Gibson, J. T. R., *Wille's Principles of South African Law* (6th edn) (Cape Town: Juta & Co., 1970).

Giliker, P., 'A "New" Head of Damages: Damages for Mental Distress in the English Law of Torts' (2000) 20 LS 19.

Gitchel, J. M., 'Domain Name Dispute Policy Provides Hope to Parties Confronting Cybersquatters' (2000) JPTOS 611.

Goff, R., and Jones, G. H., *The Law of Restitution* (5th edn) (London: Butterworths, 1998).

Goldstein, P., *Copyright* (Boston: Little, Brown & Co., 1989).

Goode, R., *Commercial Law* (2nd edn) (London: Penguin, 1995).

Goodenough, O. R., 'A Right to Privacy in the United Kingdom: Why not the Courts?' [1993] EIPR 227.
'The Price of Fame: The Development of the Right of Publicity in the United States' [1992] EIPR 55.

Goodhart, A. L., 'The Foundation of Tortious Liability' (1938) 2 MLR 1.

Goodman, E. J., 'A National Identity Crisis: The Need For a Federal Right of Publicity Statute' (1999) 9 DePaul-LCA J Art & Ent L 227.

Gordon, W. J., 'An Inquiry Into the Merits of Copyright: The Challenges of Consistency, Consent and Encouragement Theory' (1989) 41 Stanford L Rev 1343.

Bibliography

'A Property Right in Self-Expression: Equality and Individualism in the Natural Law of Intellectual Property' (1993) 102 Yale LJ 1533.

'On Owning Information: Intellectual Property and the Restitutionary Impulse' (1992) 78 Virg L Rev 149.

Götting, H. P., *Persönlichkeitsrechte als Vermögensrechte* (Tübingen: JCB Mohr (Paul Siebeck), 1995).

Grady, M. F., 'A Positive Economic Theory of the Right of Publicity' (1994) 1 UCLA Ent L Rev 109.

Gray, K., 'Property in Thin Air' (1991) 50 CLJ 252.

Grayson, E., *Sport and the Law* (3rd edn) (London: Butterworths, 2000).

Gregory, C. O., and Kalven, K., *Cases and Materials on Torts* (2nd edn) (Boston: Little, Brown & Co., 1969).

Grey, T. C., 'The Disintegration of Property' in J. R. Pennock and J. W. Chapman (eds.), *Property: Nomos XXII* (New York: New York University Press, 1980).

Grodin, J. R., 'The Right of Publicity: A Doctrinal Innovation' (1953) 62 Yale LJ 1123.

Gross, H., 'The Concept of Privacy' (1967) 42 NYULRev 34.

Gross, L., Katz, J. S., and Ruby, J., *Image Ethics: The Moral Rights of Subjects in Photographs Film and Television* (Oxford: Oxford University Press, 1988).

Grosz, S., Beatson, J., and Duffy, P., *Human Rights: The 1998 Act and the European Convention* (London: Sweet & Maxwell, 2000).

Gurry, F., *Breach of Confidence* (Oxford: Clarendon Press, 1984).

Gutteridge, H. C., 'The Comparative Law of the Right to Privacy I' (1931) 47 LQR 203.

Hadley, H. S., 'The Right to Privacy' (1894) 3 Northwestern U L Rev 1.

Hamilton, M. A., *et al.*, 'Rights of Publicity: An In-Depth Analysis of the New Legislative Proposals to Congress' (1998) 16 Cardozo Arts & Ent LJ 209.

Hamilton, W. H., 'Property According to Locke' (1932) 41 Yale LJ 864.

Hammond, R. G., *Personal Property* (2nd edn) (Oxford: Oxford University Press, 1992).

Handford, P. R., 'Damages for Injured Feelings in Australia' (1982) 5 UNSWLJ 291.

'Intentional Infliction of Mental Distress – Analysis of the Growth of a Tort' (1979) 8 Anglo-AmLR 1.

'Moral Damage in Germany' (1978) 27 ICLQ 849.

'*Wilkinson* v. *Downton* and Acts Calculated to Cause Physical Harm' (1985) 16 UnivWA LRev 31.

Harper, F. W., and James, F., *The Law of Torts* (Boston: Little, Brown & Co., 1956).

Harris, D., 'Can the Law of Torts Fulfil its Aims' (1990–1) 14 NZULR 113.

Remedies in Contract and Tort (London: Weidenfeld & Nicholson, 1988).

Hart, H. L. A., 'Definition and Theory in Jurisprudence' reprinted in *Essays in Jurisprudence and Philosophy* (Oxford: Clarendon Press, 1983).

The Concept of Law (2nd edn) (Oxford: Clarendon Press, 1994).

Hegel, G. W. F., *Philosophy of Right*, trans. T. M. Knox (Oxford: Oxford University Press, 1942).

Henkin, L., 'Privacy and Autonomy' (1974) 74 Colum L Rev 1410.

338 Bibliography

Henning-Bodewig, F., 'Celebrity Endorsement Under German Law' (1991) 11 IIC 194.

Henry, M. (ed.), *International Privacy, Publicity and Personality Laws* (London: Butterworths, 2001).

Hettinger, E. C., 'Justifying Intellectual Property' (1989) 18 *Philosophy and Public Affairs* 31.

Heuston, R. V. F., and Buckley, R. A., *Salmond and Heuston on the Law of Torts* (21st edn) (London: Sweet & Maxwell, 1996).

Heydon, J. D., *Economic Torts* (2nd edn) (London: Sweet & Maxwell, 1978).

Hixson, R. F., *Privacy in a Public Society* (New York: 1987).

Hobbs, G., 'Passing Off and the Licensing of Merchandising Rights' [1980] EIPR 47.

Hoffman, S. J., 'Limitations on the Right of Publicity' (1980) 28 Bull Copyright Soc'y 111.

Holdsworth, W. S., 'Defamation in the Sixteenth and Seventeenth Centuries' (1924) 40 LQR 302.

Holyoak, J., 'United Kingdom Character Rights and Merchandising Rights Today' [1993] JBL 444.

Honoré, A. M., 'Ownership' in A. Guest (ed.), *Oxford Essays in Jurisprudence* (Oxford: Oxford University Press, 1961).

Hoppe, T., 'Profit from Violation of Privacy Through the European Tabloid Press' (1999) 6 MJ 1.

Howell, R. G., 'Character Merchandising: The Marketing Potential Attaching to a Name, Image, Persona or Copyright Work' (1991) 6 IPJ 197.

'Is There an Historical Basis for the Appropriation of Personality Tort?' (1988) 4 IPJ 265.

'Personality Rights: A Canadian Perspective: Some Comparisons With Australia' (1990) 1 IPJ (Australia) 212.

'The Common Law Appropriation of Personality Tort' (1986) 2 IPJ 149.

Hughes, J., 'The Philosophy of Intellectual Property' (1988) 77 GeoLJ 287.

Hughes, R. T., *Hughes on Trade Marks* (Toronto: Butterworths, 1999).

Hulme, E. W., 'On the History of Patent Law in the Seventeenth and Eighteenth Centuries' (1902) 18 LQR 280.

'The History of the Patent System Under the Prerogative and at Common Law' (1896) 12 LQR 141.

Hunt, M., 'The "Horizontal Effect" of the Human Rights Act' [1998] PL 423.

Hylton, B., and Goldson, P., 'The New Tort of Appropriation of Personality: Protecting Bob Marley's Face' (1996) 55 CLJ 56.

Ilting, K. H., 'The Structure of Hegel's *Philosophy of Right*' in Z. A. Pelczynski (ed.), *Hegel's Political Philosophy: Problems and Perspectives* (Cambridge: Cambridge University Press, 1971), 91.

Irvine, J., 'The Appropriation of Personality Tort' in D. Gibson (ed.), *Aspects of Privacy Law* (Toronto: Butterworths, 1980).

Isaac, B., 'Merchandising or Fundraising?: Trade Marks and the Diana, Princess of Wales Memorial Fund' [1998] EIPR 441.

'Personal Names and the UDRP: A Warning to Authors and Celebrities' [2001] Ent LR 43.

Bibliography 339

Isgour, M., and Vinçotte, B., *Le Droit à l'image* (Brussels: Larcier, 1998).

Jacobs, F. G., and White, R. C. A., *The European Convention on Human Rights* (2nd edn) (Oxford: Oxford University Press, 1996).

Jaffey, P., 'Merchandising and the Law of Trade Marks' [1988] IPQ 240.

Jones, G., 'Restitution of Benefits Obtained in Breach of Another's Confidence' (1970) 86 LQR 463.

Jones, S., 'A Child's First Steps: The First Six Months of Operation – The ICANN Dispute Resolution Procedure for Bad Faith Registration of Domain Names' [2001] EIPR 66.

Justice, *Privacy and the Law* (London: Stevens & Sons, 1970).

Kalven, H., 'Privacy in Tort Law: Were Warren and Brandeis Wrong?' (1966) 31 Law ContProbl 326.

Kamperman Sanders, A., *Unfair Competition: A New Approach* (London: The Intellectual Property Institute, 1996).

Unfair Competition Law (Oxford: Clarendon Press, 1997).

Kaplan, B., *An Unhurried View of Copyright* (New York: Columbia University Press, 1967).

Kaufmann, P. J., *Passing Off and Misappropriation* (Weinheim: VCH, 1986).

Keeton, W. P., *Prosser and Keeton on the Law of Torts* (5th edn) (St Paul: West Publishing Co., 1984).

Kelly, J. M., 'The Inner Nature of the Tort Action' (1967) 2 IrJur (NS) 279.

Kendtridge, S., 'Lessons from South Africa' in B. S. Markesinis (ed.), *The Impact of the Human Rights Bill on English Law* (Oxford: Oxford University Press, 1998).

Kitchin, D., Llewelyn, D., Mellor, J., Meade, R., and Moody-Stewart, T., *Kerly's Law of Trade Marks and Trade Names* (13th edn) (London: Sweet & Maxwell, 2001).

Klar, L. N., *Tort Law* (Toronto: Carswell, 1991).

(ed.), *Studies in Canadian Tort Law* (Toronto: Butterworths, 1977).

Klippert, G. B., *Unjust Enrichment* (Toronto: Butterworths, 1983).

Knowlson, J., *Damned to Fame: The Life of Samuel Beckett* (London: Bloomsbury, 1996).

Korn, A. H., 'Character Merchandising' [1981] JBL 432.

Krüger, C., 'Right of Privacy, Right of Personality and Commercial Advertising' (1982) 13 IIC 183.

Kwok, R., '*Cardtoons v. Major League Baseball Players Association*: Fair Use or Foul Play?' (1998) 5 UCLA Ent L Rev 315.

Laddie, M., Prescott, P., and Vitoria, M., *The Modern Law of Copyright and Designs* (3rd edn) (London: Butterworths, 2000).

Lahore, J., *Copyright and Designs* (Sydney: Butterworths, 1996).

Patents, Trade Marks and Related Rights, Vol. I (Sydney: Butterworths, 1996).

'The *Pub Squash* Case: Legal Theft or Free Competition?' [1981] EIPR 54.

Landon, P. A., *Pollock's Law of Torts* (15th edn) (London: Stevens & Sons, 1951).

Lange, D., 'Recognizing the Public Domain' (1981) 44 Law ContProbl 147.

Larremore, W., 'The Law of Privacy' (1912) 12 Colum L Rev 693.

340   Bibliography

Law Commission, Consultation Paper No. 132, 'Aggravated, Exemplary and Restitutionary Damages' (London: HMSO, 1993).

Law Commission, Consultation Paper No. 137, 'Liability for Psychiatric Illness' (London: HMSO, 1995).

Law Commission, Report No. 110, 'Breach of Confidence', Cmnd 8388 (London: HMSO, 1981).

Leebron, D. W., 'The Right to Privacy's Place in the Intellectual History of Tort Law' (1991) 41 Case West Res L Rev 769.

Lehmann, M., 'The Theory of Property Rights and the Protection of Intellectual and Industrial Property' (1985) 16 IIC 525.

Leigh, I., 'Horizontal Rights, The Human Rights Act And Privacy: Lessons From the Commonwealth' (1999) 48 ICLQ 57.

Lester, A., 'English Judges as Lawmakers' [1993] PL 269.
    'Private Lives and Public Figures: Freedom of Political Speech in a Democratic Society' (1999) 4 Comms L 43.

Lester, A., and Oliver, D. (eds.), *Constitutional Law and Human Rights* (London: Butterworths, 1997).

Lester, A., and Pannick, D., 'The Impact of the Human Rights Act on Private Law: The Knight's Move' (2000) 116 LQR 380.
    (eds.), *Human Rights Law and Practice* (London: Butterworths, 1999).

Libling, D., 'The Concept of Property: Property in Intangibles' (1978) 94 LQR 103.

Liddy, J., 'Article 8: The Pace of Change' (2000) 51 NILQ 397.

Linden, A. M., 'Torts Tomorrow – Empowering the Injured' in N. J. Mullany and A. M. Linden (eds.), *Torts Tomorrow: A Tribute to John Fleming* (Sydney: LBC, 1998).

Linden, L. M., *Canadian Tort Law* (4th edn) (Toronto: Butterworths, 1988).

Lloyd, D., 'The Recognition of New Rights' [1961] CLP 39.

Lobbin, S. M., 'The Rights(s) of Publicity in California: Is Three Really Greater Than One?' (1995) 2 UCLA Ent L Rev 157.

Locke, J., *Two Treatises of Government*, ed. P. Laslett (Student Edition) (Cambridge: Cambridge University Press, 1988).

Logeais, E., 'The French Right to One's Image: A Legal Lure?' [1994] Ent LR 163.

Lord Chancellor's Department, *Infringement of Privacy: A Consultation Paper* (London: Lord Chancellor's Department, July 1993).

Loucaides, L. G., 'Personality and Privacy Under the European Convention on Human Rights' (1990) 61 BYBIL 175.

MacCormick, N., 'A Note Upon Privacy' (1973) 89 LQR 23.
    'Privacy: A Problem of Definition?' (1974) 1 JLS 75.

Machlup, F., and Penrose, E., 'The Patent Controversy in the Nineteenth Century' (1950) 10 *Journal of Economic History*, 11.

Macpherson, C. B. (ed.), *Property: Mainstream and Critical Positions* (Oxford: Basil Blackwell, 1978).

Madow, M., 'Private Ownership of Public Image: Popular Culture and Publicity Rights' (1993) 81 CalifLRev 125.

Bibliography 341

Magruder, C., 'Mental and Emotional Disturbance in the Law of Torts' (1936) 49 HarvLRev 1033.

Marconi, J., *Image Marketing* (Chicago: NTC Business Books, 1997).

Markesinis, B. S., *Always on the Same Path* (Oxford: Hart Publishing, 2001).

'Ligitation Mania in England, Germany and the USA: Are We So Very Different?' [1990] CLJ 233.

'Our Patchy Law of Privacy – Time to do Something About It' (1990) 53 MLR 802.

'Privacy, Freedom of Expression, and the Horizontal Effect of the Human Rights Bill: Lessons From Germany' (1999) 115 LQR 47.

'The Calcutt Report Must Not be Forgotten' (1992) 55 MLR 118.

The German Law of Obligations, Vol. II, The Law of Torts: A Comparative Introduction (3rd edn) (Oxford: Clarendon Press, 1997).

'The Right to be Let Alone Versus Freedom of Speech' [1986] PL 67.

(ed.), *Protecting Privacy* (Oxford: Oxford University Press, 1999).

The Gradual Convergence: Foreign Influences and English Law on the Eve of the 21st Century (Oxford: Clarendon Press, 1994).

Markesinis, B. S., and Deakin, S. F., *Tort Law* (4th edn) (Oxford: Clarendon Press, 1999).

Markesinis, B. S., and Enchelmaier, S., 'The Applicability of Human Rights as Between Individuals Under German Constitutional Law' in B. S. Markesinis (ed.), *Protecting Privacy* (Oxford: Oxford University Press, 1999).

Markesinis, B. S., and Nolte, N., 'Some Comparative Reflections on the Right of Privacy of Public Figures in Public Places' in P. Birks (ed.), *Privacy and Loyalty* (Oxford: Clarendon Press, 1997).

Marsh, N. S., 'Hohfeld and Privacy' (1973) 89 LQR 183.

Martino, T., *Trademark Dilution* (Oxford: Oxford University Press, 1996).

Mathieson, D. L., 'Comment on *Sim v. H. J. Heinz & Co. Ltd*' (1969) 39 Can B Rev 409.

McCarthy, J. T., *McCarthy on Trade Marks and Unfair Competition* (4th edn) (St Paul, Minn.: West Publishing, 1999).

'Public Personas and Private Property: The Commercialization of Human Identity' (1989) 79 TMR 681.

The Rights of Publicity and Privacy (2nd edn) (New York: Clark Boardman Callaghan, 2001).

McEvoy, S. A., '*Pirone v. Macmillan Inc.*: Trying to Protect the Name and Likeness of a Deceased Celebrity Under Trade Mark Law and the Right of Publicity' (1997) 19 Comm & L 51.

McGeehan, A. O., 'Trademark Registration of a Celebrity Persona' (1997) 87 TMR 351.

McGregor, H., *McGregor on Damages* (17th edn) (London: Sweet & Maxwell, 1997).

'Restitutionary Damages' in P. Birks (ed.), *Wrongs and Remedies in the Twenty-First Century* (Oxford: Clarendon Press, 1996).

McKerron, R. G., *The Law of Delict* (7th edn) (Cape Town: Juta & Co., 1971).

McLean, D., 'False Light Privacy' (1997) 19 Comm & L 63.

342   Bibliography

McMullan, J., 'Personality Rights in Australia' (1997) 8 AIPJ 86.

McQuoid-Mason, D. J., *The Law of Privacy in South Africa* (Cape Town: Juta & Co. 1978).

Meinhardt, P., *Inventions, Patents and Monopoly* (London: Stevens & Sons, 1946).

Michaels, A., 'Confusion in and About Sections 5(3) and 10(3) of the Trade Marks Act 1994' [2000] EIPR 335.

Milmo, P., and Rogers, W. V. H., *Gatley on Libel and Slander* (9th edn) (London: Sweet & Maxwell, 1998).

Morcom, C., 'Character Merchandising – a Right or a Mere Opportunity?' [1978] EIPR 7.

Morcom, C., Roughton, A., and Graham, J., *The Modern Law of Trade Marks* (London: Butterworths, 1999).

Morison, W. L., 'Unfair Competition and Passing Off – The Flexibility of a Formula' (1956) 2 Sydney L Rev 50.

Mullany, N. J., and Handford, P. R., *Tort Liability for Psychiatric Damage* (Sydney: The Law Book Co., 1993).

Mullany, N. J., and Linden, A. M. (eds.), *Torts Tomorrow: A Tribute to John Fleming* (Sydney: LBC, 1998).

Munro, C., 'Self-Regulation in the Media' [1997] PL 6.

Munzer, S. R., *A Theory of Property* (Cambridge: Cambridge University Press, 1990).

Murphy, J. D., and Rueter, R., *Stare Decisis in Commonwealth Appellate Courts* (Toronto: Butterworths, 1981).

Murumba, S. K., *Commercial Exploitation of Personality* (Sydney: The Law Book Co., 1986).

Naismith, S. H., 'Photographs, Privacy and Freedom of Expression' [1996] EHRLR 150.

National Heritage Select Committee, *Fourth Report: Privacy and Media Intrusion* (London: HMSO, 1993).

Neill, B., 'Privacy: A Challenge for the Next Century' in B. S. Markesinis (ed.), *Protecting Privacy* (Oxford: Oxford University Press, 1999).

'The Protection of Privacy' (1962) 25 MLR 393.

Neill, B., and Rampton, R., *Duncan and Neill on Defamation* (2nd edn) (London: Butterworths, 1983).

Nelson, V., *The Law of Entertainment and Broadcasting* (2nd edn) (London: Sweet & Maxwell, 2000).

Nicholas, B. N., *An Introduction to Roman Law* (Oxford: Clarendon Press, 1962).

Nimmer, M. B., 'The Right of Publicity' (1954) 19 Law ContProbl 203.

Nimmer, M. B., and Nimmer, D., *Nimmer on Copyright Vol. 3* (New York: Mathew Bender & Co., 2000).

Note (Anonymous), 'An Actionable Right of Privacy? *Roberson v. Rochester Folding Box Co.*' (1902) 12 Yale LJ 35.

'Development of the Law of Privacy' (1894) 8 HarvLRev 280.

'Is this Libel? More About Privacy' (1894) 7 HarvLRev 492.

'The Right to Privacy' (1891) 5 HarvLRev 148.

'The Right to Privacy' (1898) 12 HarvLRev 207.

'The Right to Privacy – The Schuyler Injunction' (1895) 9 HarvLRev 354.

'The Unauthorised Use of Portraits' (1930) ALJ 359.

Nozick, R., *Anarchy, State and Utopia* (Oxford: Basil Blackwell, 1974).

Nyman, B., 'Character Merchandising' [1991] EIPR 134.

O'Brien, D., 'The Right of Privacy' (1902) 2 Colum L Rev 437.

Ollier, P. D., and Le Gall, J. P., 'Various Damages' in A. Tunc (ed.), *International Encyclopaedia of Comparative Law, Vol. XI: Torts* (Tübingen: Martinus Nijhoff, 1981).

Olsen, J., and Maniatis, S. (eds.), *Trade Marks: World Law and Practice* (London: FT Law and Tax, 1998).

Onions, C. T. (ed.), *The Oxford Dictionary of English Etymology* (Oxford: Oxford University Press, 1966).

Oppenheim, C., 'The Information Aspects of Patents' in J. Phillips (ed.), *Patents in Perspective* (Oxford: ESC, 1985).

Osborne, D., 'Domain Names, Registration and Dispute Resolution and Recent UK Cases' [1997] EIPR 644.

'Don't Take My Name in Vain! ICANN Dispute Resolution Policy and Names of Individuals' [2000] 5 Comms L 127.

Osborne, D., and Willoughby, T., 'Nominet's New Dispute Resolution Procedure – They CANN Too!' (2001) 6 Comms L 95.

Pannam, C., 'Unauthorised Use of Names or Photographs in Advertisements' (1966) 40 ALJ 4.

Parker, R. B., 'A Definition of Privacy' (1974) 27 RutgLRev 275.

Partridge, E., *Origins* (London: Routledge, 1958).

Pasek, V., 'Performers' Rights in Sport: The Experts Comment' (1990) 9 CW 12.

'Performers' Rights in Sport: Where Does Copyright Stand?' (1990) 8 CW 13.

Paterson, A., *The Law Lords* (London: Macmillan 1982).

Paton, G. W., 'Broadcasting and Privacy' (1938) Can B Rev 425.

Paton, G. W., and Derham, D. P., *A Textbook on Jurisprudence* (4th edn) (Oxford: Clarendon Press, 1972).

Patterson, L. R., *Copyright in Historical Perspective* (Nashville: Vanderbilt University Press, 1968).

Pennock, J. R., and Chapman, J. W. (eds.), *Nomos XIII: Privacy* (New York: Atherton Press, 1971).

Nomos XXII: Property (New York: New York University Press, 1980).

Phillips, J., 'Life After Death' [1998] EIPR 201.

'The Diminishing Domain' [1996] EIPR 429.

(ed.), *Patents in Perspective* (Oxford: ESC, 1985).

Phillips, J., and Coleman, A., 'Passing Off and the Common Field of Activity' (1985) 101 LQR 242.

Phillips, J., and Firth, A., *Introduction to Intellectual Property Law* (3rd edn) (London: Butterworths, 1995).

Phillipson, G., 'The Human Rights Act, "Horizontal Effect" and the Common Law: A Bang or a Whimper?' (1999) 62 MLR 824.

Phillipson, G., and Fenwick, H., 'Breach of Confidence as a Privacy Remedy in the Human Rights Act Era' (2000) 63 MLR 660.

Picard, E., 'The Right to Privacy in French Law' in B. S. Markesinis (ed.), *Protecting Privacy* (Oxford: Oxford University Press, 1999).

Pinckaers, J. C. S., *From Privacy Towards a New Intellectual Property Right in Persona* (The Hague, Kluwer, 1996).

344   Bibliography

Pinker, R., 'Human Rights and Self Regulation of the Press' (1999) 4 Comms L 51.

Pollock, F., *The Law of Torts* (12th edn) (London: Stevens & Son, 1923).

Porter, Report of the Committee on the Law of Defamation, Cmd 7536 (London: HMSO, 1948).

Posner, R. A., *Economic Analysis of Law* (3rd edn) (Boston: Little, Brown & Co., 1986).

Law and Legal Theory in England and America (Oxford: Clarendon Press, 1996).

Overcoming Law (Cambridge, Mass.: Harvard University Press, 1995).

'The Right of Privacy' (1978) 12 GaLRev 393.

Post, R. C., 'Rereading Warren and Brandeis: Privacy, Property and Appropriation' (1991) 41 Case West Res L Rev 647.

'The Social Foundations of Defamation Law: Reputation and the Constitution' (1986) 74 CalifLRev 691.

Pottage, A., 'Property: Re-appropriating Hegel' (1990) 53 MLR 259.

Potvin, L., 'Protection Against the Use of One's Likeness in Quebec Civil Law, Canadian Common Law and Constitutional Law (Part II)' (1997) 11 IPJ 295.

Pound, R., 'Interests of Personality' (1914) 28 HarvLRev 343 and 445.

Jurisprudence (St Paul, Minn.: West Publishing Co., 1959).

Pratt, W. F., *Privacy in Britain* (London: Associated University Presses, 1979).

Prescott, P., '*Kaye v. Robertson*: A Reply' (1991) 54 MLR 451.

'Libel and Pornography' (1995) 58 MLR 752.

Press Complaints Commission, *Code of Practice* (London: Press Complaints Commission, 1999).

Prosser, W. L., 'Intentional Infliction of Mental Suffering: A New Tort' (1939) 37 Mich L Rev 874.

'Privacy' (1960) 48 CalifLRev 383.

Quint, P. E., 'Free Speech and Private Law in German Constitutional Theory' (1989) 48 Mary L Rev 247.

Ramsay, I., *Advertising, Culture and the Law* (London: Sweet & Maxwell, 1996).

Reeve, A., *Property* (London: Macmillan, 1986).

Reichman, J. H., 'Legal Hybrids Between The Patent and Copyright Paradigms' (1994) 94 Colum L Rev 2432.

Reid, Lord, 'The Judge as Lawmaker' (1972) 12 JSPTL 22.

Rein, I. J., Kotler, P., and Stoller, M. R., *High Visibility* (London: Heinemann, 1987).

Richard, H. G., *Canadian Trade Marks Act Annotated* (Toronto: Carswell, 1991–2000).

Richard, H. G., and Carrière, L., *Canadian Copyright Act Annotated* (Scarborough, Ontario: Carswell, 1993).

Richards, T., *The Commodity Culture of Victorian England* (London: Verso, 1990).

Ricketson, S., 'Confidential Information – A New Proprietary Interest?' (1977) 11 MULR 223.

'Reaping Without Sowing: Unfair Competition and Intellectual Property Rights in Anglo-Australian Law' (1984) 7 UNSWLJ (special issue) 1.

Bibliography

Rijkens, R., and Miracle, G. E., *European Regulation of Advertising* (Oxford: North-Holland, 1986).

Robertson, G., and Nicol, A. G. L., *Media Law* (3rd edn) (London: Penguin, 1992).

Robinson, R. S., 'Preemption, The Right of Publicity, and a New Federal Statute' (1998) 16 Cardozo Arts & Ent LJ 183.

Rogers, W. V. H., *Winfield and Jolowicz on Tort* (14th edn) (London: Sweet & Maxwell, 1994).

Rose, M., *Authors and Owners* (Cambridge, Mass.: Harvard University Press, 1993).

Rubenfeld, J., 'The Right of Privacy' (1989) 102 HarvLRev 737.

Rudden, B., 'Torticles' (1991–2) 6/7 *Tulane Civil Law Forum* 105.

Ruijsenaars, H. E., 'Legal Aspects of Merchandising: The AIPPI Resolution' [1996] EIPR 330.

'The WIPO Report on Character Merchandising' (1994) 25 IIC 532.

Schechter, F., 'The Rational Basis of Trademark Protection' (1927) 40 HarvLRev 813.

Schlechtriem, P., 'Some Thoughts on the Decision of the BGH Concerning Princess Caroline of Monaco' in B. S. Markesinis (ed.), *Protecting Privacy* (Oxford: Oxford University Press, 1999).

Seipp, D., 'English Judicial Recognition of a Right to Privacy' (1983) 3 OJLS 325.

Shanahan, D. R., ' "Image Filching" in Australia: The Legal Provenance and Aftermath of the "Crocodile Dundee" Decisions' (1991) 81 TMR 351.

Sherman, B., and Bently, L., *The Making of Modern Intellectual Property Law* (Cambridge: Cambridge University Press, 1999).

Sherman, B., and Kaganas, F., 'The Protection of Personality and Image: An Opportunity Lost' [1991] EIPR 340.

Singer, E. M., 'The Development of the Common Law Tort of Appropriation of Personality in Canada' (1998) 15 CIPR 65.

Singh, R., 'Privacy and the Media: The Impact of the Human Rights Bill' in B. S. Markesinis (ed.), *Protecting Privacy* (Oxford: Oxford University Press, 1999).

Skinner, Q., 'Meaning and Understanding in the History of Ideas' (1969) 8 *History and Theory* 3.

Spector, H., 'An Outline of a Theory Justifying Intellectual and Industrial Property Rights' [1989] EIPR 270.

Spence, M., 'Passing Off and the Misappropriation of Valuable Intangibles' (1996) 112 LQR 472.

Stapleton, J., 'In Restraint of Tort' in P. Birks (ed.), *The Frontiers of Liability* (Oxford: Oxford University Press, 1994).

Steiner, H. J., and Alston, P., *International Human Rights is Context* (2nd edn) (Oxford: Oxford University Press, 2000).

Sterling, J. A. L., *World Copyright Law* (London: Sweet & Maxwell, 1998).

Stewart, A., 'Damages For Mental Distress Following Breach of Confidence: Preventing or Compensating Tears' [2001] EIPR 302.

Stewart, S. M., *International Copyright and Neighbouring Rights* (2nd edn) (London: Butterworths, 1989).

346   Bibliography

Steyn, J., 'Does Legal Formalism Hold Sway in England?' [1996] CLP 43.

Stoll, H., 'The General Right to Personality in German Law: An Outline of its Development and Present Significance' in B. S. Markesinis (ed.), *Protecting Privacy* (Oxford: Oxford University Press, 1999).

Story, A., 'Owning Diana, from People's Princess to Private Property' [1998] 5 Web JCLI.

Strasser, M., 'The Rational Basis of Trademark Protection Revisited: Putting the Dilution Doctrine into Context' (2000) 10 Fordham Intell Prop Media & Ent LJ 375.

Street, T. A., *The Foundations of Legal Liability* (Northport, N.Y.: Edward Thompson Company, 1906).

Strowel, A., '*Droit d'Auteur* and Copyright: Between History and Nature' in B. Sherman and A. Strowel (eds.), *Of Authors and Origins* (Oxford: Clarendon Press, 1994).

Taylor, C. T., and Silberston, Z. A., *The Economic Impact of the Patent System: A Study of the British Experience* (Cambridge: Cambridge University Press, 1973).

Terrell, T. P., and Smith, J. S., 'Publicity, Liberty and Intellectual Property: A Conceptual and Economic Analysis of the Inheritability Issue' (1985) 34 Emory LJ 1.

Terry, A., 'Image Filching and Passing Off in Australia: Misrepresentation or Misappropriation? *Hogan v. Koala Dundee Pty Ltd*' [1990] EIPR 219.

'The Unauthorised Use of Celebrity Photographs in Advertising' (1991) 65 ALJ 587.

'Unfair Competition and the Misappropriation of a Competitor's Trade Values' (1988) 51 MLR 296.

Theedar, S., 'Privacy in Photographic Images' [1999] PLPR 59.

Thorley, S., *et al.*, *Terrell on the Law of Patents* (15th edn) (London: Sweet & Maxwell, 2000).

Thwaite, G. J., and Brehm, W., 'German Privacy and Defamation Law: The Right to Publish in the Shadow of the Right to Human Dignity' [1994] EIPR 336.

Toulson, R. G., and Phipps, C. M., *Confidentiality* (London: Sweet & Maxwell, 1996).

Treece, J. M., 'Commercial Exploitation of Names, Likenesses and Personal Histories' (1973) 51 TexLRev 637.

Trindade, F. A., 'The Intentional Infliction of Purely Mental Distress' (1986) 6 OJLS 219.

Trindade, F. A., and Cane, P., *The Law of Torts in Australia* (2nd edn) (Melbourne: Oxford University Press, 1993).

Tully, J., *An Approach to Political Philosophy: Locke in Contexts* (Cambridge: Cambridge University Press, 1993).

Twining, W. (ed.), *Legal Theory and Common Law* (Oxford: Basil Blackwell, 1986).

Vahrenwald, A., 'Photographs and Privacy in Germany' [1994] Ent LR 205.

Van Caenegem, W., 'Different Approaches to the Protection of Celebrities Against Unauthorised Use of Their Image in Advertising in Australia, the United States and the Federal Republic of Germany' [1990] EIPR 452.

Van Der Kamp, G., 'Protection of Trade Marks: The New Regime – Beyond Origin?' [1998] EIPR 364.

Vaughan, F. L., *The United States Patent System* (Norman, Okla.: University of Oklahoma Press, 1956).

Vaver, D., 'Intellectual Property Today: Of Myths and Paradoxes' (1990) 69 Can B Rev 98.

'What's Mine Is Not Yours: Commercial Appropriation of Personality Under the Privacy Acts of British Columbia, Manitoba and Saskatchewan' (1981) 15 UBCL Rev 241.

Veitch, E., 'Interests in Personality' (1972) 23 NILQ 423.

Von Bar, C., *The Common European Law of Torts Vol. I* (Oxford: Oxford University Press, 1998).

Wacks, R., *Personal Information* (Oxford: Clarendon Press, 1989).

Privacy and Press Freedom (London: Blackstone Press, 1995).

'The Poverty of Privacy' (1980) 96 LQR 73.

The Protection of Privacy (London: Sweet & Maxwell, 1980).

(ed.), *Privacy*, 2 vols. (Aldershot: Dartmouth, 1993).

Wade, J. W., 'Defamation and the Right of Privacy' (1962) 15 Vand L Rev 1093.

Wade, W., Horizons of Horizontality' (2000) 116 LQR 217.

'Human Rights and the Judiciary' [1998] EHRLR 520.

Wadlow, C., *The Law Of Passing Off* (2nd edn) (London: Sweet & Maxwell, 1995).

Waelde, C., 'Commercialising the Personality of the Late Diana, Princess of Wales – Censorship by the Back Door?' in N. Dawson and A. Firth (eds.), *Perspectives on Intellectual Property, Vol. VII: Trade Marks Retrospective* (London: Sweet & Maxwell, 2000), 211.

Waldron, J., 'From Authors to Copiers: Individual Rights and Social Values in Intellectual Property' (1993) 68 Chic-Kent LRev 841.

The Right to Private Property (Oxford: Clarendon Press, 1988).

Walton, F. P., 'The Comparative Law of the Right to Privacy II' (1931) 47 LQR 219.

Warbrick, C., 'The Structure of Article 8' [1998] EHRLR 32.

Warren, S., and Brandeis, L., 'The Right to Privacy' (1890) 4 HarvLRev 193.

Watts, J., *Signatures and Portraits as Trade Marks* (London: Intellectual Property Institute, 1998).

Wee Loon, N. L., 'Emergence of a Right to Privacy from Within the Law of Confidence?' [1996] IPR 307.

Welkowitz, D. S., 'Catching Smoke, Nailing Jell-O To a Wall: The Vanna White Case and the Limits of Celebrity Rights' (1995) 3 J Intell Prop L 67.

Wernick, W., *Promotional Culture* (London: Sage, 1991).

Westin, A., *Privacy and Freedom* (London: Bodley Head, 1967).

White, G. E., *Tort Law in America – An Intellectual History* (Oxford: Oxford University Press, 1980).

White, T. A. Blanco, and Jacob, R., *Kerly's Law of Trade Marks and Trade Names* (12th edn) (London: Sweet & Maxwell, 1986).

Whitford Committee, Report of the Committee to Consider the Law on Copyright and Designs, Cmnd 6732 (London: HMSO, 1977).

348 Bibliography

Wigmore, J., 'Responsibility for Tortious Acts: Its History' (1894) 7 HarvLRev 441.

Williams, G. L., 'The Aims of the Law of Tort' [1951] 4 CLP 137.

'The Foundations of Tortious Liability' [1941] 7 CLJ 111.

Williams, G. L., and Hepple, B. A., *Foundations of the Law of Tort* (2nd edn) (London: Butterworths, 1984).

Wilson, H. W., 'Privacy, Confidence and Press Freedom: A Study in Judicial Activism' (1990) 53 MLR 43.

Winfield, P. H., 'Privacy' (1931) 47 LQR 23.

'The Foundation of Liability in Tort' (1927) 27 Colum L Rev 1.

The Province of the Law of Tort (Cambridge: Cambridge University Press, 1931).

Winner, E. P., 'Right of Identity: Right of Publicity and Protection of a Trademark's "Persona"' (1981) 71 TMR 193.

Wood, J. P., *The Story of Advertising* (New York: The Ronald Press Company, 1958).

World Intellectual Property Organisation, *Model Provisions on Protection Against Unfair Competition* (Geneva: WIPO, 1996).

Protection Against Unfair Competition (Geneva: WIPO, 1994).

'The Recognition of Rights and the Use of Names in the Internet Domain Name System: Interim Report of the Second WIPO Internet Domain Name Process' (Geneva, 12 April 2001).

Yen, A., 'Restoring the Natural Law: Copyright as Labor and Possession' (1990) 51 Ohio St LJ 517.

Young, D., *Passing Off* (3rd edn) (London: Longman, 1994).

Younger Committee, Report of the Committee on Privacy, Cmnd 5012 (London: HMSO, 1972).

Zimmerman, D., 'False Light Invasion of Privacy: The Light That Failed' (1989) 64 NYULRev 364.

'Requiem to a Heavyweight: A Farewell to Warren and Brandeis's Privacy Tort' (1983) 68 Cornell L Rev 291.

Zimmerman, R., *Roman Law, Contemporary Law, European Law* (Oxford: Oxford University Press, 2001).

The Law of Obligations (Oxford: Clarendon Press, 1996).

Zimmermann, R., and Visser, D., *Southern Cross: Civil Law and Common Law in South Africa* (Oxford: Clarendon Press, 1996).

Zweigert, K., and Kötz, H., *An Introduction to Comparative Law* (3rd edn) (Oxford: Clarendon Press, 1998).

Index

Note. To avoid unhelpful duplication of entries no attempt has been made to index under individual countries. Where there is extended discussion of the position in a particular country (eg 'Australia') or pair of countries ('Australia/UK'), this is indicated either as part of the heading or as a sub-heading. As in the text, 'England' is the term usually used rather than 'United Kingdom'. Where the two are used side-by-side, the form 'England/UK' is used in the index.

For references to cases, users should generally consult the Table of Cases. The index includes only landmark cases where they are discussed at some length in relation to a particular concept.

advertising codes, *see* Advertising
  Standards Authority Code of
  Advertising Practice (UK);
  Independent Television Commission
  Code of Advertising Standards and
  Practice (UK); Press Complaints
  Commission Code of Practice (UK)
**Advertising Standards Authority Code
  of Advertising Practice (UK)**, 50–3
  coverage/exceptions, 50
  economic interests, protection of, 52–3
  endorsements, 51–2
  judicial review of decisions, 51
  legal authority, 51
  privacy, right of, 51–3
    infrequency of complaints, 53
  Royal Family, 52
  sanctions, 51
    injunction under Control of
      Misleading Advertisements
      Regulations 1988, 51
  variations between editions of, 52–3
applicable law, ICANN panel, 54
appropriation of personality tort, *see*
  misappropriation of personality
  (Canada); specific remedy for
  commercial appropriation of
  personality
assault and battery, 15

bad/good faith, relevance
  domain name protection, 54, 55–8
  burden of proof, 56
  requirements, 55, 57
  trade marks, 38–9, 41, 43
balance of convenience, 68–9, 88–9
battery, *see* assault and battery
Bill of Rights (South Africa),
  applicability between private
  individuals, 216
breach of confidence (England),
  207–11, 322
  as basis of general right to privacy, 248
  information surreptitiously obtained,
    209
  property right, relevance, 280–1
  requirements
    breach of obligation of confidence,
      208–9, 210–11, 223
    confidential quality, 208
    unauthorised use, 208
business goodwill, *see* goodwill as
  requirement in passing off action
  (Australia/England)

Calcutt Reports
  Press Self-Regulation (1993), 241
  Privacy and Related Matters (1990)
    (England)
    defamation/right of privacy, 263
    definition of privacy, 201 n. 2
    appropriation of personality,
      exclusion, 240–1
    pressing social need test, 240–1

350　Index

character merchandising, 5–6, 73, 76,
81, 83–4, 92–7, 103–4, 108–10; *see
also* misrepresentation requirement in
passing off action (Australia/
England); passing off (Australia/
England)
**Charter of Human Rights and
Freedoms (Quebec)**, 17, 111
applicability between private
individuals, 225
freedom of expression in relation to
other rights, 135, 225–7
image, right to control, 225–7
**Charter of Rights and Freedoms
(Canada)**
applicability between private
individuals, 215–16
relevant factors, 225
freedom of expression in relation to
other rights, 224–6
common field of activity test, 74–8, 82,
85–7, 88, 89, 99, 100–1
Krouse, 118
measure of damages and, 100
compensation, *see* damages
**confusion as requirement in passing
off**, 60, 72, 73–6, 77, 80–4, 91–2,
94–5, 105–7
contingent fee rules, as factor in
development of privacy law, 191
contract, breach (England), 18
copyright; *see also* intellectual property;
patents; performance rights; trade
marks
as economic interest, 19
as property right, 275, 277–8
Locke's labour theory and, 291–2
character merchandising and, 5, 83,
93–4
creative effort, relevance, 5
fictitious characters and, 5, 93–5
natural law theory and, 301 n. 65
performance rights and, 34–5, 302
utilitarian basis, 303–7
copyright (Australia), character
merchandising and, 93–4
copyright (England)
character merchandising and, Whitford
Committee Report on the Law on
Copyright and Designs (1977), 83
common law/statutory right, 147 n. 16,
300–1
Copyright Act 1956, 34
Copyright Designs and Patents Act
1988, 33–4, 205, 302 n. 73

name, 75, 83–4
ownership, 34–5
photography, 34
right of privacy and
common law, 148–9
Human Rights Act 1998, 222
utilitarian basis, Act for the
Encouragement of Learning, etc.,
1710, 300–1
value of process, 32
copyright (Germany)
Kunsturhebergesetz (KUG) (Artistic
Copyright Act) 1907, 229, 231
personality, right of, and, 230–1
copyright (USA)
as property right, 148
common law/statutory right, 301 n. 65
dignitary interests and, 147–9
right of privacy and, 147–9
courts' willingness to develop law
in Australia, 109–10, 113–15
dignitary interests, protection, 15–16
in England, 109–10, 113–15, 191,
194–6, 204, 238, 324–9
in Germany, 7, 22–3, 227–30, 328
in Ontario, 325–7
in USA, 109–10, 119, 155–6, 191,
327–8

**damage, need for in case of
misappropriation of personality
(Canada)**, 127–37
actionability *per se*, 128–31
damage or risk of damage to business or
professional goodwill, 127
presumption of, 127–8
**damage, need for in defamation
actions (England)**, 7, 247–8, 250–1
action on the case as basis, 250–1
difficulty of determining, 251–2
presumption of, 62, 251
sufficiency of intent, 203 n. 19
**damage, need for in passing off action
(Australia/England)**, 60, 64,
66, 71
divergence between Australian and
English jurisprudence, 98
economic interests/reputation
distinguished, 71, 78
McCulloch, 73–5
proof, need for, 98–9
burden, 75, 99
presumption of damage, 62, 88, 98–9
reputation/misrepresentation cases
distinguished, 98–9

Index

351

qualification as
actual or probable damage, 98
damage to business goodwill, 60,
61–2, 63, 64, 66, 71, 97–107
professional, artistic or literary
occupation distinguished,
100–1
dilution, 105–7
common law, 106
confusion, relevance, 105–7
Trade Marks Act 1994, 106
diversion of trade, 98, 99
exposure to liability/litigation, 64, 74,
101–2
Consumer Protection Act 1987,
101
Routh v. *Webster* rule, 63–4, 101
injurious association, 99–101, 102
loss of control of reputation, 102–3
lost licensing opportunity, 79, 88,
103–5
Stringfellow, 103–4
Tot Toys (New Zealand), 104–5
real risk of damage to professional
reputation, 74, 100–1
risk of damage to business, 91–2,
100–1
**damage, need for in privacy actions
(Quebec)**, 227
damages
as factor in development of right of
privacy, 191, 218
dignitary interests, 131
satisfaction/compensation
distinguished, 20, 321
divergency, 10
in England
'Aggravated, Exemplary and
Restitutionary Damages'
(Law Commission) (1993),
21, 22
exemplary, 22
mental distress, 242–3, 245, 247–8
reputation, injury to as primary
factor, 249–50
satisfaction/compensation
distinguished, 21, 251–2, 320
entitlement
emotional distress, 246–7, 248
mental distress, 242–3, 245, 247–8
in France, *faute* as basis for, 7
in Germany
moral, 227–8, 231–3
satisfaction/compensation
distinguished, 22–3, 232

measure
as determinant of general legal right,
189
common field of activity test, 100
difficulty in case of violation of
personality, 6
injury to feelings, 147
mental distress, 242–3
exaggeration, 264
reputation, injury to as primary
factor, 249–50
value of 'property', relevance,
310 n. 107
moral
nineteenth-century Germany, 227–8
unauthorised dissemination of
person's image, 227, 231–3
punitive
defamation (Australia), 251 n. 14
publicity, right of (USA), 185
satisfaction/compensation distinguished,
21–3
defamation (England), 251–2, 320
dignitary interests, 20, 321
Germany, 22
in USA, emotional distress, 246–7, 248
death, relevance, *see* descendibility
defamation, 4, 15
as dignitary tort, 15
as remedy for appropriation of
personality, 4, 23
divergency of damages awards, 10
passing off and, 67, 70, 71
privacy, right of and, 18
defamation (Australia), punitive
damages, 251 n. 14
defamation (England)
as sole remedy for appropriation of
personality, 18, 23, 124, 253–7
damage, need for, 247–8
difficulty of determining, 251–2
presumption of, 251
sufficiency of intent, 203 n. 19
damages, satisfaction/compensation
distinguished, 251–2, 320
definition, absence, 252, 256–7
mental distress, freedom from and,
247–8
privacy, right of and
as alternative remedy, 258–70
Calcutt Report (1990), 263
Porter Report on the Law of
Defamation (1948), 263 n. 81
Younger Report on Privacy (1972),
263

352   Index

defamation (New Zealand), privacy, right of as alternative remedy, 263
defamation (Quebec), diligence, obligation of, 227
defamation (USA)
false light distinguished, 261–2
overlap with passing off, 262
privacy, right of and, 147, 162, 249
unsatisfactory nature of remedy, 262
descendibility, 124–7, 136–7, 150–1, 234–5, 283–4, 285–6
dignitary interests, 4; *see also* dignitary torts; economic interests, interaction with dignitary interests; mental distress, freedom from; privacy, right of; reputation
as basis of appropriation of personality remedy, 313–15, 319–21
constitutional provisions, 17–18, 144
definition/elements, 141
difficulty, 10–11
non-marketability, 10–11
obverse of economic interests, 10
in England, 17–18
limitations of available remedies, 142
Germany, constitutional provisions, 17–18, 230–3
international instruments
European Convention on Human Rights (1950), 17, 144
UN Charter, 17
Universal Declaration of Human Rights (1948), 17
real/fictitious person, 5
subjective nature, 10
inadequacy of monetary compensation, 10
in USA, *see* privacy, right of (USA)
dignitary torts, 15–16; *see also* assault and battery; dignitary interests; mental distress, freedom from; privacy, right of
damages, 131
satisfaction/compensation distinguished, 321
in England
damnum/dedecus, 141
injuria, 141–2
per se actionability of injury to dignitary interests, 22, 321
defamation, 62
in Germany, *injuria*, reaction against, 227–8
injuria, 141–3, 227–8
in Roman law, *injuria*, 141
in South Africa

injuria, 142–3
actio injuriarum, requirements, 142–3
right of privacy and, 143
unfair competition distinguished, 16
diligence, obligation of, 227
dilution doctrine, 27, 105–7
Disputes.org/eResolution. caConsortium, 54
domain name protection
bad faith and, 54, 55–8
burden of proof, 56
requirements, 55, 57
dispute resolution, 53–8
Disputes.org/eResolution. caConsortium, 54
ICANN administrative procedures, 54
applicable law, 54
limited nature of remedies, 54
mandatory, 54–5
precedent, relevance, 54
Nominet UK Ltd, 53–4
Uniform Domain Name Resolution Policy (UDRP), 54–8
WIPO jurisprudence, 54
Barnes, 56–7
Brown, 56
Springsteen, 55–6
Sting, 57
Winterson, 55
intellectual property right, exclusion, 53
passing off remedy, 53, 56–8
private individuals, 58
registration, effect, 56

eavesdropping, 162
economic efficiency as justification for property rights in personality, 308–11
scarce resource argument, 309–10
economic interests; *see also* copyright; endorsement (UK); goodwill as requirement in passing off action (Australia/ England); patents; performance rights; trade marks
Advertising Standards Authority Code of Advertising Practice (UK), 52–3
existing trading or licensing interests, 8–9, 47, 69–71, 158
features
acceptability of monetary compensation as full recompense, 8

Index

marketability of interest, 8
possibility of finite monetary
compensation for invasion, 8
susceptibility to objective evaluation, 8
intangible recognition values, 8, 9–10,
47, 69–71, 131, 158, 319–20
interaction with dignitary interests, 5,
8–12, 16, 20, 21, 23–4, 62
appropriation of personality remedy,
124, 126–7, 270, 287–8, 314–15,
319–21
as underlying divide, 12–13
damnum/dedecus in English law, 141
personality, right of, 234, 237
privacy, right of, 16, 156–9, 218, 237,
265–70, 323–4
reputation, interest in, 11, 21, 62, 67,
126–7, 250–2
latent recognition value, *see* intangible
recognition values *above*
patents as, 19
emotional distress, *see* mental distress,
freedom from
endorsement (UK)
Advertising Standards Authority Code
of Advertising Practice, 51–2
'attention-grabbing devices'
distinguished, 9, 91
examples, 9
Independent Television Commission
Code of Advertising Standards and
Practice, 49
television advertising, 49
uncertainty of definition, 5
endorsement misrepresentation, 72,
84–7, 89–93; *see also*
misrepresentation requirement in
passing off action (Australia/England)
misappropriation of personality
(Canada) and, 131–6
Krouse, 119–21, 134
sponsorship distinguished, 90–1
'tools of the trade', 86–9, 91
**European Convention on Human
Rights (1950)**
appeal, right of as right, 215
applicability in England, 214–24
between private individuals
(horizontal effect), 214–18
courts' obligations, 214 n. 105
ECHR jurisprudence, relevance,
221
Human Rights Act 1998, 214–18,
248, 328–9
Bill of Rights (South Africa)
compared, 216

Charter of Rights and Freedoms
(Canada) compared, 215–16
courts' obligation to develop
common law in accordance
with Convention, 214 n. 105,
216–18, 328–9
failure to incorporate, 215, 221
dignitary interests, 17, 144
freedom of expression in relation to
other rights, 48, 219–20, 328;
see also privacy, right of *below*
commercial information, 219–20
restrictions on, 220
implementation as task of domestic
authorities, 213
margin of appreciation, 213, 219–20
privacy, right of, 211–24
breadth of right, 211–12
freedom of expression and,
219–20
truthful information, 219–20
justified interference, 212–13
police photography, 212–13
States' obligation to protect/provide
remedy, 213–14

fair competition, *see* unfair competition
Faulks Report, defamation and right of
privacy distinguished, 263
false light
defamation and
England, Younger Report on Privacy
(1972), 263
USA, 261–2
usefulness of distinction, 264–5
privacy, right of and
England, 262 n. 71, 263–5
Faulks Report, 263
USA, 161, 162, 180, 239 n. 243
fame, *see* misappropriation of intangibles;
public figure
fictitious characters
copyright law and, 5, 93–5
dignitary interests and, 5
economic interest in, 5
misrepresentation and, 75–6, 92–7
unfair competition and, 5
freedom of expression
as fundamental right (England), 220
European Convention on Human
Rights (1950), 219–20; *see also*
European Convention on Human
Rights (1950)
personality, right of and (Germany),
233, 235–7
pressing social need restriction, 220

354 Index

freedom of expression (*cont.*)
privacy, right of and, 150, 151, 154, 163, 180, 218–27
public interest and
Canada, 135, 226–7
England, 50, 221–2, 224
European Convention on Human Rights (1950), 220
Germany, 236–7
in relation to other rights
Canada, 132–3
appropriation of identity tort, 132–3
privacy, right of, 224–6
privacy, right of (Quebec), 225–7
England 220–4
freedom of the press, 220–1
Human Rights Act 1998, 48, 220–4, 328
privacy, right of and, 218–24
European Convention on Human Rights (1950), 219–20, 221
USA
privacy, right of, 150, 151, 154, 163, 180
publicity, right of, 132–3, 185–7
freedom of the press (England), 220–1

goodwill as requirement in passing off action (Australia/England), 59–110; *see also* damage, need for in passing off action (Australia/England); image/name, voice or likeness
as property right, 61–2, 67–9, 277–8
business requirement, 10, 61–2, 68–9, 74, 91
Canadian/UK law distinguished, 10
existing trading interests, 10, 69–71
intangible recognition value, 69–71
character merchandising and, *see* character merchandising
definition, 61, 114
professional, artistic or literary occupation, 62–71, 320
commercial exploitation of personality, 71, 77, 88, 103–4
damage, need for, 62
difficulty of establishing, 320
Dockrell, 100
early jurisprudence, 63–6
exposure to liability/litigation, relevance, 64, 74, 101–2

modern jurisprudence, 67–9
nom de plume/stage name, 63, 68
Lyngstad, 68
public figures, categorisation, 71
Sim, 67–8, 100
trading interest, need for, 62–71
protected interest, *see* business requirement *above*
reputation and, 61–2, 64, 67, 70
trade marks and, 19, 62 n. 21

harassment as tort (England)
Protection from Harassment Act 1997, 247
Wilkinson v. *Downton* rule, 247
Hegel's personality theory, 296–8
human dignity, *see* dignitary interests; dignitary torts
Human Rights Act 1998 (England)
applicability between private individuals (horizontal effect), 214–18
privacy, right of and, 209–11, 218–24, 238, 248
reluctance to accord general right and, 209–11, 218–24, 238, 248

image/name, voice or likeness. *See also* goodwill as requirement in passing off action (Australia/England); photography; signature
name as trade mark, 45–7, 55–8
portrait as trade mark (England), 43–4, 45–7
property right in, 6–7, 8–10, 95, 156–9, 284–6
appearance, 157–8
appropriation of personality tort (Canada) and, 123–7
Locke's labour theory and, 294–5
name, 7, 62–6, 70, 73–4, 75, 83–4, 93, 156–7, 321; *see also* copyright (England), name; goodwill as requirement in passing off action (Australia/England)
voice, 67–8, 100
right to control
Canada, 135, 225–7
England, 257, 258–60, 321
Germany, 229, 232–7
public figure, 236–7
New Zealand, 260
USA, *see* publicity, right of (USA)
WIPO, 31 n. 24

Index

Independent Television Commission Code of Advertising Standards and Practice (UK), 48–9
content of television programmes distinguished, 48 n. 97
endorsement, 49
privacy, right of, 48–9
injunction as remedy, 63–6, 86–9
balance of convenience, 68–9, 88–9
where damages a satisfactory remedy, 69
injuria, *see* dignitary torts, *injuria*
intellectual property 19, 322; *see also* copyright; goodwill as requirement in passing off action (Australia/England); patents; performance rights; trade marks; World Intellectual Property Organisation (WIPO)
as metaphor, 276–81
usefulness, 279–81, 315
domain name, 53
formalities governing, 277–8
Locke's labour theory and, 291–2
passing off, risk from, 83–4
personality as trading symbol and, 319–20
piecemeal nature, 29, 315
public domain, 292
publicity, right of, 178–9, 180, 187
interests in personality, *see* personality, interests in
internet, *see* domain name protection
Internet Corporation for Assigned Names and Numbers (ICANN), *see* domain name protection

judicial law-making, *see* courts' willingness to develop law

liability, *see* damages
libel, *see* defamation
licensing connection, *see* misrepresentation requirement in passing effaction (Australia/England)
Locke's labour theory, *see under* natural rights of property

malicious falsehood (England)
privacy, right of and, 203–4, 218 n. 134, 323–4
reputation, interests in and, 256
margin of appreciation, privacy, right to, 213

media codes of practice, *see* Advertising Standards Authority Code of Practice (UK); Independent Television Commission Code of Advertising Standards and Practice (UK); Press Complaints Commission Code of Practice (UK)
mental distress, freedom from, 15–16, 22
definition, 12
as dignitary interest, 8, 16
in England, 18–19, 241–5
as independent actionable wrong, 241–3
as interest in personality, 242–3
damage to material interest, need for, 242
damages
as measure of, 242–3
entitlement, 242–3, 245, 247–8
exaggeration, 264
elements constituting, 241–2
intentional infliction as tort, 245, 322
'Liability for Psychiatric Illness' (Law Commission) (1995), 6 n. 13
privacy, right of and, 19, 243–5
psychiatric damage/emotional distress divide, 244–5
Wilkinson v. *Downton*, 243–5
reluctance to recognise liability, 6 n. 13
in USA, 160, 161 n. 102, 162
damages, limitations on, 246
intentional infliction as tort, 7, 18–19, 245–7, 262
'extreme and outrageous conduct which intentionally or recklessly causes severe emotional damage', 246–7, 248
privacy, right of and, 18–19, 160, 161 n. 102, 162
Restatement of Torts, Second (1977), 12 n. 38
misappropriation of intangibles (Australia/England), 14, 29–31, 112–15, 321, 323
trade marks, 37
misappropriation of intangibles (USA), 323
federal statutory intellectual property rights and, 31
International News Service v. *Associated Press*, 28–9, 31, 113, 177, 178–9
publicity, right of, distinguished, 15

356   Index

misappropriation of intangibles (USA) *(cont.)*
Restatement of the Law of Unfair Competition, Third, 31
unfair competition and, 31
misappropriation of intangibles as basis of appropriation of personality remedy, 23, 319–20, 323; *see also* intellectual property; misrepresentation requirement in passing off action (Australia/England); property rights; unfair competition
courts' reluctance to develop new tort, 113–15
difficulty of definition, 114–15
misappropriation of personality (Canada), 115–37
as right of publicity, 136–7
Gould, 125, 126
damage, need for, 127–37
actionability *per se*, 128–31
damage or risk of damage to business or professional goodwill, 127
presumption of, 127–8
descendibility, 124–7, 136–7
Gould, 124–5, 132–4
privacy, right of, distinguished, 125
publicity, right of, distinguished, 125
economic/dignitary interests, coexistence, 124, 126–7
endorsement, 131–6
misrepresentation, relationship, 131–2
identifiability of plaintiff, need for, 135–6
limited nature, 136–7
Ontario, development in, 14, 17, 284–5, 287, 325–7
Athans, 121–2, 123
causes of action approach, rejection, 118, 119
Krouse, 115–22, 134
common field of activity test, 118
endorsement, 120–1, 131–2
passing off, erroneous treatment, 117
privacy, invasion of and, 116
goodwill in business or profession, relevance, 117
protection of property right in exploitation of image/name, voice or likeness, 117–18, 121–2
protection of property right in exploitation of image/name, voice or likeness, 117–18, 123–7

existing trading interests, relevance, 123–4
Horton, 126
misrepresentation requirement in passing off action (Australia/England)
'connection misrepresentation', 72–97
business connection, 72–5, 78, 92, 93–4
endorsement misrepresentation, 72, 84–7, 89–93
Krouse (Ontario), 119–21, 131
'tools of the trade', 86–9, 91
expansive approach, 84–97
licensing connection, 75–82, 87–9, 92–3
strong/weak distinguished, 72, 92–3
sponsorship distinguished, 90–1
definition issues, 72–3
fictitious character, relevance, 75–6, 92–7
jurisprudence (Australia)
10th Cantanae Pty Ltd, 89–91
Henderson, 69, 84–7, 98, 104–5
Honey, 91
Hutchence, 88–9
Koala Dundee, 92–5, 108
Muppets, 79, 87–8
Pacific Dunlop, 95–7
Paracidal, 89
jurisprudence (England)
Erven Warnink, 60–1, 98
Halliwell, 82–3
Lyngstad, 70, 77
McCulloch, 73–5, 82, 100–1, 102
Mirage Studios, 78–80, 82–4
Stringfellow, 78
Tavener Rutledge, 75–6, 82
Wombles, 75
misappropriation distinguished, 108
requirements/elements
common field of activity, 74–8, 82, 85–7, 88, 89, 100–1
confusion or deception, 60, 72, 73–6, 77, 80–4, 91–2, 94–5, 106–7
character merchandising and, *see* character merchandising
common field of activity, relevance, 88, 89
damage, 62, 73–6
public reliance on, presumption of, 79–82, 87–9, 94–7
reputation in name, need for, 73–4

Index

name, *see* domain name protection;
goodwill as requirement in passing
off action (Australia/England);
image/name, voice or likeness;
surname as trade mark (England);
trade marks
natural law
copyright, 301 n. 65
privacy, 154–5
natural rights of property, 288–9
Hegel's personality theory, 296–8
Locke's labour theory, 291–6
applicability to property rights in
attributes of personality, 293–6,
314–15
criticisms, 292–3
intellectual property rights and,
291–2
public domain concept, 292
publicity, right of and, 293–4
relevance to development of
appropriation of personality
remedy, 288–91

**Paris Convention for the Protection of
Industrial Property**, 27, 56
passing off (Australia/England), 4, 30;
see also advertising codes; character
merchandising; copyright; damage,
need for; goodwill in goods, name
or mark as requirement in passing
off action (Australia/England);
misappropriation of intangibles;
misrepresentation requirement in
passing off action (Australia/England);
performance rights; publicity, right of;
trade marks; unfair competition
applicability in appropriation of
personality cases, 13–14, 19–20,
23, 30–1, 59–110, 323, 324
as basis of appropriation of personality
remedy, 72, 87, 308
as interference with property right,
97–8
as remedy for breach of privacy, 203
damage, need for; *see also* advertising
codes; damage, need for;
goodwill as requirement
in passing off action
(Australia/England);
misrepresentation requirement
in passing off action
(Australia/England)
heads of damage, 99–110
presumption of, 98–9

defamation, overlap, 67, 70, 71, 262
definition, 14
as protection of property in
underlying business
goodwill, 97
extension of concept, 59, 67, 72
unfair competition distinguished, 28,
59–60
domain name protection and, 53,
56–8
elements, *see* requirements *below*
expansive approach
Australia, 13–14, 69, 84–97
risk of undermining intellectual
property law, 83–4, 93–4, 109
Whitford Committee Report on the
Law on Copyright and Designs
(1977), 83
extra-legal alternatives, 48–58
injunction as remedy, 86–9
misappropriation of intangibles
distinguished, 112
property right in name, 93–4
requirements, 59, 107–10, 112
common field of activity test, 74–8,
82, 85–7, 88, 89, 99, 100–1
damage to business or goodwill, *see*
damage, need for in passing off
action (Australia/England)
Erven Warnink, 60–1, 98
goodwill, *see also* goodwill as
requirement in passing
off action (Australia/England);
misrepresentation requirement
in passing off action
(Australia/England)
interaction, 71
restrictive model, 107–8
expansive model, 108
trading status, 62–71, 203
statutory alternatives, 32–47
patents; *see also* copyright; intellectual
property; performance rights; trade
marks
as property right, 19, 275, 277–8
Locke's labour theory and, 291–2
trade marks distinguished, 37 n. 34
utilitarian basis, 301, 303–7
performance rights
England
copyright and, 34–5, 302
qualifying rights, 35–6
TRIPs, 302 n. 73
USA, TRIPs obligations,
implementation, 302 n. 73

358 Index

personal dignity, *see* dignitary interests;
economic interests, interaction with
dignitary interests; personality, right
of (*Personlichkeit*) (Germany);
reputation, interests in (England)
personal privacy, *see* privacy, right of
personality, as trading symbol, 12–13,
319–21
personality, interests in, 5–7; *see also*
goodwill as requirement in passing
off action (Australia/England);
image/name, voice or likeness;
mental distress, freedom from;
privacy, right of; reputation,
interests in (England)
as economic asset, 6–7, 69, 87, 117–18,
234–5
commercial exploitation, 71, 77, 88,
103–4, 121–2, 163–4
definition/taxonomy, 6 n. 12
economic/dignitary interests as
underlying divide, 12–13
mental distress, freedom from and, 7,
242–3
reluctance to accord general right
(England), 39–47
Restatement of Torts, Second (1977)
(USA), 7 n. 20, 242 269
statutory intellectual property rights
(England), 32
torts protecting (England), 242–3
**personality, right of (*Personlichkeit*)
(Germany)**, 227–37
appropriation of name or likeness,
229–30
as general right, 231–3
attempt to amend Civil Code, 233
as multiplicity of delicts/crimes
copyright, 230–1
defamation, 228
insult or slander, 228
negligent injury contrary to law, 228
proprietary rights, 228–9
trespass to property, 229
as proprietary right, descendibility,
234–5
assignment, *see* transferability *below*
constitutional provisions on dignity and,
230–3
as fundamental right, 231
damages, moral, 227–8, 231–3
death, relevance, 233–5
dignitas and
actio injuriarum as remedy, 227–8
Civil Code (BGB), 228–9

economic and dignitary interests,
interaction, 234–5
image, right to control and, 234–5
false light compared, 231
freedom of expression and, 233, 235–7
factors for consideration, 235–7
public interest, 236–7
image, right to control and, 234–7
public figure, 236–7
Kunsturhebergesetz (KUG) (Artistic
Copyright Act), 1907, 229, 231–2
piecemeal development, 227–35
reputation compared, 231
transferability, 235
unjust enrichment and, 232
personality merchandising, *see*
character merchandising
photography
ECHR (1950), police photography,
212–13
England
commissioning, relevance, 34
contract/tort law as protection, 34 n.
17
copyright, 34
privacy and, 49–50
public figure, 50
technological advances, relevance, 34
**Porter Report on the Law of
Defamation (1948)**,
defamation/right of privacy, 263
portrait as trade mark (England),
43–4, 45–7
press codes of practice (UK); *see also*
Advertising Standards Authority
Code of Advertising Practice (UK);
Independent Television Commission
Code of Advertising Standards and
Practice (UK); Press Complaints
Commission Code of Practice (UK)
self-regulation of press, 53
Calcutt Report (1993), 241
**Press Complaints Commission Code
of Practice (UK)**, 49–50
privacy and, 49–50, 222–3
risk to complainant, relevance, 223
public interest exception, 49, 50, 222–3
press intrusiveness, right of privacy and,
149, 239, 241
principles as source of law, 169–71
privacy, right of; *see also* personality,
right of (*Personlichkeit*) (Germany)
as principle, 169–71
conceptual uncertainty, 16, 159–61,
171, 198–9

Index

359

defamation and, 18
dignitary interests and, 15–16, 22
economic interests and, 16, 218
European Convention on Human
  Rights (1950) and, *see* European
  Convention on Human Rights
  (1950)
public figure, 11–12, 53
privacy, right of (Canada), 17, 22
reputation and, 225
privacy, right of (England); *see also*
  breach of confidence (England);
  Younger Report on Privacy (1972)
as multiplicity of torts, 201, 202–11; *see
  also* reluctance to accord general
  right *below*
  breach of confidence, *see* breach of
    confidence (England)
  causes of action approach, 239–40,
    248
  defamation, 203, 207; *see also*
    defamation (England), privacy,
    right of and (as alternative
    remedy)
  false light, 207
  malicious falsehood, 203–4, 218 n.
    134
  nuisance, 206
  passing off, 203; *see also* passing off
    (Australia/England)
  trespass to the person, 203
  trespass to property, 203 n. 18, 206
as 'right to be let alone', 265
ASA Code of Advertising Practice, 51–3
conceptual uncertainty, 201
copyright and, *see* copyright (England)
definition
  appropriation of personality, exclusion
    Calcutt Report on Privacy and
      Related Matters (1990), 240–1
    in proposed legislation, 239–41
  Calcutt Report on Privacy and
    Related Matters (1990), 201 n. 2
  pressing social need test, 240–1
  Younger Report on Privacy (1972),
    201 n. 2
differences from US approach, possible
  reasons for, 189–98
  absence of constitutional guarantee of
    rights, 194–6
  academic influence, role, 196–8
  access to courts, limitations, 190–1
  contingent fee rules, 191
  courts' willingness to develop law,
    191, 194–6, 238

precedent, role, 191–4
relative levels of damages, 191
self-regulation, 190
US litigiousness, 190
economic/dignitary interests,
  co-existence, 203–4, 210, 237,
    323–4
freedom of expression and, 218–24
  data protection, 205
  general right, *see* reluctance to accord
    general right *below*
  Human Rights Act 1998, effect,
    209–11, 218–24, 238, 248
  applicability between private
    individuals (horizontal effect),
    214–18
mental distress, freedom from and, 19,
  243–5
press photography, 49–50
public figure, 50, 266–70
  Clark v. *Freeman*, 267–8
  Dockrell v. *Dougall*, 268
  Sim, 268
  Tolley v. *Fry*, 266
public interest exception, 50, 221–2,
  224
reluctance to accord general right, 4,
  15, 160, 171, 189–98, 200–14,
    323–4; *see also* differences from
    US approach, possible reasons for
    above
  attempts to address
    breach of confidence; *see* breach of
      confidence (England)
    Calcutt Report on Press
      Self-Regulation, (1993), 241
    National Heritage Select
      Committee, Fourth Report,
        (1993), 241
    Right of Privacy Consultation Paper,
      241
    statutory, 238–41
  breach of duty approach to law and,
    202, 248, 323, 328
  courts' willingness to develop law
    and, 191, 194–6, 204, 238
  freedom of expression, relevance, 219
  Human Rights Act 1998 and, 225,
    237, 323
  Younger Report on Privacy (1972)
    162 n. 109, 202; *see also*
    differences from US approach,
    possible reasons for *above*;
    Younger Report on Privacy
    (1972)

360 Index

privacy, right of (England) (*cont.*)
self-regulation of press, 53,
190
spatial restriction, 49
statutory provisions / legislative
initiatives
Broadcasting Standards Act 1996,
205–6
concerns to be addressed
data collection, 239
governmental intrusion, 239
press intrusiveness, 239, 241
technological surveillance, 239
Copyright Designs and Patents Act
1988, 205
Data Protection Act 1998, 205, 239
n. 241
Human Rights Act 1998,
effectiveness, 238
Justice recommendations 1970,
239–40
Justice recommendations, Right of
Privacy Bill 1970, 240
omission of appropriation of
personality, 239–41
Right of Privacy Consultation Paper,
241
Photographs and Films
(Unauthorised Use) Bill 1994,
239 n. 241
Protection of Privacy Bill 1988 (John
Browne), 240
Protection of Privacy Bill 1988 (Lord
Stoddart), 240
Right of Privacy Bill 1967 (Alex
Lyon), 239
Right of Privacy Bill 1967 (Lord
Mancroft), 239
Right of Privacy Bill 1988 (William
Cash), 240
Right of Privacy Consultation Paper,
240 n. 249, 241
television advertising, 48–9
privacy, right of (Germany)
freedom of expression and, public
interest, 236–7
public figure, 236–7
spatial restriction, 237
privacy, right of (Ontario), 17,
116 n. 35
privacy, right of (Quebec), 17, *see also*
Charter of Human Rights and
Freedoms (Quebec)
damage, need for in case of, 227
relevant factors
artistic expression, 226–7

commercial appropriation, 226–7
social usefulness, 226–7
privacy, right of (South Africa)
dignitas and, 143
actio injuriarum as remedy, 142–3
privacy, right of (USA), 16, 22, 143–4
as multiplicity of torts, 161–4, 171
appropriation of name or likeness,
161, 162, 163–4, 239 n. 243
false light, 161, 162, 180, 239 n. 243
defamation distinguished, 261–2
intrusion on solitude, 161, 162,
239 n. 243
public disclosure of private facts, 161,
162, 239 n. 243
Restatement of Torts, Second (1977),
164 n. 121, 196
as residual tort, 159–60, 262 n. 76
as 'right to be let alone', 159, 161, 168
as unified legal concept, 164–9
dignitary interest as common thread
164–6, 168, 176; *see also*
economic/dignitary interests,
coexistence *below*
secrecy/anonymity/solitude triad, 167,
239 n. 243
commercial appropriation, relevance,
168–9, 180, 226, 265
common law copyright as basis of
protection, 147–9
right in property/dignitary interests
distinguished 147–9, 273, 282;
see also economic/dignitary
interests, coexistence *below*
common law right, whether, 151–6
courts' willingness to develop law,
relevance, 155–6, 191, 327–8
Pavesich, 154–6, 193
reluctance to allow, 214–15
Roberson, 151–4, 155–6, 192–3
constitutional right to privacy
distinguished, 160–1
contractual remedy, 150–1
defamation and, 147, 162, 249
descendibility, 150–1
eavesdropping, 162
economic/dignitary interests,
coexistence, 147–9, 156–9, 169,
237
existing trading interests/latent
recognition value, 158
proprietary right to name or picture,
16, 156–8, 162, 163–4, 173–4
public figure, 157, 174, 177
freedom of expression and, 150, 151,
154, 163, 180

Index

influence of
Prosser, 196
Warren and Brandeis, 146–50, 196
insult to honour, absence of remedy,
147–8
legislative action, 153
mental distress, freedom from and,
18–19, 160, 161 n. 102, 162, 173
natural law right, 154–5
public figure, 150–1, 157, 176–7,
266
waiver, 172–5
publicity, right of, *see* publicity, right of
(USA)
quantum meruit claim, 174
reputation and, 162
unjust enrichment and, 157 n. 77, 180,
311–12
private individuals, domain name
protection, 58
**professional, artistic or literary
occupation**, *see* goodwill as
requirement in passing off action
(Australia/England),
professional, artistic or literary
occupation; image/name, voice
or likeness
property rights 4; *see also* copyright;
goodwill in goods, name or mark as
requirement in passing off action
(Australia/England); image/name,
voice or likeness; intellectual property;
passing off (Australia/England);
patents; performance rights;
personality, interests in; publicity,
right of (USA); trade marks
appropriation of personality (Canada),
117, 126–7, 285–6
breach of confidence and, 280–1
definition, 274–6
evolution, 283–4
goodwill, 61–2, 67–9, 277–8
intangibles, 273–81
creative effort, relevance, 28–9
documentary intangibles
distinguished, 275 n. 9, 276 n. 15
exchangeable value, relevance, 8,
28–9, 278–9
usefulness of concept, 279–81
labelling as, relevance, 283
name, 7, 62–6, 70, 73–4, 93, 95, 321
property right in exploitation,
117–18, 121–2
natural 288–99; *see also* goodwill as
requirement in passing off
action (Australia/England); natural

rights of property; passing off
(Australia/ England); personality,
interests in
public policy, relevance, 28–9
reputation, 65
public domain, 292
public figure
image/name, voice or likeness, right to
control
Germany, 236–7
USA, 12, 294
privacy, right of
England, 50, 266–70
Germany, 236–7
USA, 150–1, 157, 176–7, 266
economic/dignitary interests,
coexistence, 157, 174, 177
professional, artistic or literary
occupation, classification, 71
public interest
freedom of expression and
England, 50, 221–2, 224
Quebec, 226–7
privacy, right of and
England, 50, 222, 224
Germany, 236–7
public policy, property attribution and,
28–9
publicity, right of (USA); *see also*
privacy, right of
alternatives to, 302
as independent tort, 178–9, 187,
287–8
as intellectual property right, 178–9,
180, 187
as misappropriation of commercial value
of person's identity, 15, 163–4,
175–6, 177–9, 180
acts amounting to appropriation, 182
as proprietary right, 175, 183–4,
281–4
assignability, 183, 283, 285
descendibility, 125, 136–7, 183–4,
283–4
Locke's labour theory, 293–6
Restatement of the Law of Unfair
Competition, Third, 288, 296
Australia/UK distinguished, 121, 179
economic efficiency as justification,
308–11
economic/dignitary interests, overlap,
179, 180, 187–9, 287–8
existing trading interests / latent
recognition value, 181
freedom of expression and, 132–3,
185–7

362 Index

publicity, right of (USA) (*cont.*)
biographical or fictional use of
identity and, 186–7
image/name, voice or likeness, right
to control, 31, 293–4
public figure, 12, 14–15, 294
inter-state differences, 180–1, 184
liability for pecuniary loss/gain, 184–5
measure of damages, 184–5
punitive damages, 185
unjust enrichment, 185, 284
passing off and, 15
privacy, right of and, 15, 16, 31, 144,
159, 166, 171–9, 183–4
continuing overlap, 181
difficulty of reconciling, 172–4
economic/dignitary interests,
relevance, 180, 320
requirements/factors for consideration
falsity or misleading nature, 185–6
identifiability of plaintiff, 182
intent, 182
misrepresentation, 181
trade mark law distinguished, 182
unfair competition and, 15, 177–8, 179
Restatement of the Law of Unfair
Competition, Third, 288, 296
utilitarian basis, 301–3
Zacchini, 179–80, 187

**real/fictitious characters
distinguished**, *see* fictitious
characters
recognition value, 9–10
reparation, duty of, 6 n. 15; *see also*
damages
reputation, interests in (England),
249–70, 322; *see also* defamation;
goodwill as requirement
in passing off action
(Australia/England);
malicious falsehood (England);
misrepresentation requirement in
passing off action (Australia/
England); privacy, right of
appropriation of personality, relevance
to, 249–50, 320
as economic and dignitary interest, 11,
21, 62, 67, 250–2
Canadian practice, 126–7
as property right, 65
as sole dignitary interest protected by
substantive cause of action, 18, 124
damages
as primary element in determining,
249–50

loss of control, 102–3
defamation as remedy, adequacy, 257,
264–5, 320
defamation cases
Corelli v. Wall, 259
Debenham, 256 n. 40
Dunlop, 254 n. 28
Garbett, 256 n. 40
Honeysett, 254–5
invasion of privacy distinguished, 254,
258–61
Khodaparast v. Shad, 256
Kirk v. Reed (New Zealand), 260–1,
263
Plumb v. Jeyes, 259–60
Stockwell, 256 n. 40
Tolley v. Fry, 253–4, 266
definition, absence, 250, 251
goodwill distinguished, 61–2
look alikes, 256
malicious falsehood and, 256
personal/business distinguished, 62
privacy, right to, distinguished, 250–1,
254, 258–61
Royal Family (UK), ASA Code of
Advertising Practice, 52

signature, as trade mark, 43–4, 45–7
'socially useful information', 226–7
**specific remedy for commercial
appropriation of personality**, 30–1,
198–9
in Australia, flexible approach to
existing causes of action and, 30–1,
112–15
bases, 287–315; *see also* economic
efficiency as justification for
property rights in personality;
natural rights of property;
utilitarian arguments as basis for
the development of appropriation of
personality remedy (England/USA)
personal dignity, protection, 313–14,
319–21
privacy, right to, 287
property right in personality, 285–6
appropriateness of arguments
justifying private property,
288–90
economic efficiency as justification,
308–11
in name, voice or likeness, 284–6
natural rights of property, 288–99
in personal identity, 287
publicity, right of and, 282–4, 285
relevance of choice, 299–300

Index

utilitarian arguments, 288–91,
299–308
character merchandising, need to
distinguish, 5–6, 108–10
courts' willingness to develop law and,
324–9
desirability, 6, 23–4, 108–10, 287–8
economic/dignitary interests, inclusion
of both, 270, 287–8, 314
as property right (Jamaica),
descendibility, 125, 285–6
in England, 30–1, 269
absence of remedy, 249–50
Calcutt Report on Privacy and
Related Matters, (1990) 240–1
desirability, 269
flexible approach to existing causes of
action and, 23, 112–15, 322–3,
324–9
potential elements, 269
reluctance to accord general right, 23,
113
statutory provisions / legislative
initiatives and, 239–41
general right of privacy distinguished,
23, 269
in Jamaica, as property right, 285–6
in Ontario, *see* misappropriation of
personality (Canada)
in relation to other rights, 286
sponsorship, endorsement distinguished,
90–1
surname as trade mark (England),
39–43, 45–7; *see also* domain name
protection
evidence of distinctiveness, 42–3

television, *see* Independent Television
Commission Code of Advertising
Standards and Practice (UK)
'tools of the trade', 86–9, 91
tort law; *see also* courts' willingness to
develop law
aims, 21–3
tort law (England)
causes of action approach, 22, 29–30,
32, 109–10, 112–15, 239–40, 248
flexibility as instrument of
development, 322–3, 324–9
trade marks
as economic interest, 19
as intellectual property, 19–20, 275,
277–8, 308 n. 95
character merchandising, 5, 83–4
creative effort, relevance, 19
dilution of value, 27, 105–7

trade marks (England)
100 entry rule, 42
as economic interest, 19, 36–8, 47
bad/good faith, relevance, 38–9,
41, 43
common law protection, 57–8, 319
definition, 39
functions, 36–8, 42
goodwill, 62 n. 21
infringement of registered, 44–7
jurisprudence
ANNE FRANK Trade Mark, 43 n. 72
Diana, Princess of Wales Application, 41
Du Cros (W & G) Ltd, 40–1
ELVIS PRESLEY Trade Marks,
39–41, 44–5
JANE AUSTEN Trade Marks, 41
TARZAN Trade Mark, 40
misappropriation and, 37
patents distinguished, 37 n. 34
portrait, 43–4, 45–7
protection in absence of business or
goodwill, 62 n. 21
registrability, 38–43, 319
courts' cautious approach, 39–47
surname, 39–43
revocation in case of non-use, 43
signature, 43–4, 45–7
[sur]name, 39–43, 45–7
as unregistered trade mark, 55–8
Trade Marks Act, 1994 38–43, 44–7, 62
n. 21
confusion, relevance, 105–6
passing off, effect on, 106
Trade Marks (Amendment) Rules, 1998
45
value of process, 32
trading symbol, personality as, 12–13,
319–21
as intellectual property, 319–20
conceptual difficulties, 319–21
trespass to the person (England), 203
TRIPs, performance rights and, 302 n. 73

UN Charter, dignitary interests, 17
unfair competition, 12–15, 27–137;
see also copyright; goodwill as
requirement in passing off action
(Australia/ England);
misappropriation of intangibles;
passing off (Australia/England);
performance rights; publicity, right of
(USA); trade marks
as generic term for causes of action
protecting against unlawful trading
activities, 13, 19–20, 28, 179

364   Index

unfair competition (*cont.*)
  misappropriation of intangibles, 13
  Moorgate Tobacco, 29–30
  dignitary torts distinguished, 16
  dishonest practices
    confusing/discrediting, 27
    false allegations, 27
    misleading, 27
    Paris Convention for the Protection of
      Industrial Property, 27, 56
  fictitious character, protection, 5
  importance as remedy in appropriation
    of personality cases (Australia/UK),
    179
  licences / 'recognition value' and, 10
  passing off and, 13, 28, 59–60, 177
unfair competition (USA), elements,
  passing off, whether, 177
**Uniform Domain Name Resolution
  Policy (UDRP)**, *see* domain name
  protection
**Universal Declaration of Human
  Rights (1948)**, 17
unjust enrichment
  as basis for appropriation of personality
    remedy, 311–13
  impreciseness of concept, 312–13
  law of restitution and, 312–13
  liability for breach of right of publicity
    and, 185, 284
  right of personality and, 232
  right of privacy and, 157 n. 77, 180,
    311–12

**utilitarian arguments as basis for the
  development of appropriation of
  personality remedy (England/
  USA)**, 288–91, 299–308
  copyright, 300–1, 303–7
  economic efficiency, 308–11
  patents, 301, 303–7
  publicity, right of, 301–3
  US Constitution, 299

voice, *see* image/name, voice or likeness

WIPO, *see* World Intellectual Property
  Organisation (WIPO)
**World Intellectual Property
  Organisation (WIPO)**, *see also* Paris
  Convention for the Protection of
  Industrial Property; TRIPs
  domain name protection 54; *see also*
    domain name protection
  dispute settlement, 55–8
  image/name, voice or likeness, right
    to control, 31 n. 24
wrongs, ways of defining, 5–6
WWW issues, *see* domain name
  protection

Younger Report on Privacy (1972),
  162 n. 109, 202, 208, 239 n. 241
  defamation/right of privacy, 263
  definition of right, 201 n. 2
  false light, 263
  terms of reference, 201 n. 2, 238 n. 238

Cambridge Studies in Intellectual Property

TITLES IN THE SERIES

Brad Sherman and Lionel Bently
The Making of Modern Intellectual Property Law
0 521 56363 1

Irini A. Stamatoudi
Copyright and Multimedia Works
0 521 80819 7

Pascal Kamina
Film Copyright and the European Union
0 521 77053 X

Huw Beverley-Smith
The Commercial Appropriation of Personality
0 521 80014 5

For EU product safety concerns, contact us at Calle de José Abascal, 56–1°, 28003 Madrid, Spain or eugpsr@cambridge.org.

www.ingramcontent.com/pod-product-compliance
Ingram Content Group UK Ltd.
Pitfield, Milton Keynes, MK11 3LW, UK
UKHW011327060825
461487UK00005B/403